Palgrave Studies in Public Debt, Spending, and Revenue

Series Editor
Gerald J. Miller
Arizona State University
Pheonix, AZ, USA

Palgrave Studies in Public Debt, Spending, and Revenue is a broad-ranging and interdisciplinary series dedicated to studying the latest issues, trends, and developments influencing a government's role in its economy. The series of studies covers not only the economy's impact on government size and scope but also the effects of governmental policies on efficient allocation of resources, distribution of income, and macroeconomic stabilization. The series is also dedicated to a fuller understanding of the policies and policy tools through which government leaders develop this role, from fiscal policy to budget and various incentives that provoke particular behaviors. The subjects covered resonate in university economics, public affairs, public policy, public management, and governance schools and departments. This series' primary attention is on North America (especially the United States and Canada) and related comparative policy research. National and sub-national (including state, provincial, regional, metropolitan, and local) topics are included. At the same time, the series tracks comparable developments in China and the European Union. The series focuses on fiscal systems as influenced by the public sector and the economy, in addition to contemporary themes relating to fiscal policy, taxation, public debt, education finance, fiscal federalism, and the effects such policy designs as those found in antipoverty programs, healthcare, agriculture, and defense have on fiscal systems. Books in this series focus on research and compelling professional practices addressing public policy issues that create varying degrees of inevitability in the behavior of individuals, taxpayers, organizations, capital markets, and financial systems.

More information about this series at
http://www.palgrave.com/gp/series/14595

Daniel Williams • Thad Calabrese
Editors

The Palgrave Handbook of Government Budget Forecasting

palgrave
macmillan

Editors
Daniel Williams
Austin W. Marxe School of Public
and International Affairs
Baruch College
New York, NY, USA

Thad Calabrese
Robert F. Wagner Graduate School
of Public Service
New York University
New York, NY, USA

ISSN 2662-5148 ISSN 2662-5156 (electronic)
Palgrave Studies in Public Debt, Spending, and Revenue
ISBN 978-3-030-18194-9 ISBN 978-3-030-18195-6 (eBook)
https://doi.org/10.1007/978-3-030-18195-6

Cover illustration: Carol and Mike Werner / Alamy Stock Photo
Cover design by eStudio Calamar

This Palgrave Macmillan imprint is published by the registered company Springer Nature Switzerland AG.
The registered company address is: Gewerbestrasse 11, 6330 Cham, Switzerland

Contents

1 **Introduction** 1
Daniel Williams and Thad Calabrese

Part I International and National 9

2 **Macroeconomic Theory and Forecasting** 11
Gerald D. Cohen

3 **Evaluating Government Budget Forecasts** 37
Neil R. Ericsson and Andrew B. Martinez

4 **Budget Preparation and Forecasting in the Federal Republic of Germany** 71
Dörte Busch and Wolfgang Strehl

5 **Revenue Forecasting in Low-Income and Developing Countries: Biases and Potential Remedies** 89
Marco Cangiano and Rahul Pathak

6 **The Reliability of Long-Run Budget Projections** 115
Rudolph Penner

7 **CBO Updated Forecasts: Do a Few Months Matter?** 133
James W. Douglas and Ringa Raudla

Part II State and Local 153

8 **State Revenue Forecasting Practices: Accuracy, Transparency, and Political Participation** 155
Emily Franklin, Carolyn Bourdeaux, and Alex Hathaway

9 **Forecasting Post-Crisis Virginia Tax Revenue** 177
Melissa McShea and Joseph Cordes

10 **Bias Associated with Centrally Budgeted Expenditure Forecasts** 201
Thad Calabrese and Daniel Williams

11 **Excessive Revenue Underforecasting: Evidence and Implications from New York City's Property Tax** 217
Geoffrey Propheter

12 **Small Local Government Revenue Forecasting** 241
Vincent Reitano

13 **Current Midyear Municipal Budget Forecast Accuracy** 257
Daniel Williams and Thad Calabrese

Part III Subject Matter Specialties 273

14 **Using Fiscal Indicator Systems to Predict Municipal Bankruptcies** 275
Jonathan B. Justice, Marc Fudge, Helisse Levine, David D. Bird, and Muhammad Naveed Iftikhar

15 **School District Enrollment Projections and Budget Forecasting** 303
Peter Jones, Cole Rakow, and Vincent Reitano

16 **Budget Uncertainty and the Quality of Nonprofit Charter School Enrollment Projections** 325
Todd L. Ely

17 **Forecasting for Prisons and Jails** 345
Bruce D. McDonald III, J. Winn Decker, and Matthew James Hunt

18 **Government and Nonprofit Personnel Forecasting** 361
Vincent Reitano

19 **Forecast Bias and Capital Reserves Accumulation** 377
Vincent Reitano, Peter Jones, Nathan Barrett, and Jacob Fowles

20 **Consensus Forecasting** 397
J. Winn Decker and Bruce D. McDonald III

21 **Ensemble Forecasting** 413
Kenneth A. Kriz

Part IV Conclusion 427

22 **Conclusion** 429
Daniel Williams and Thad Calabrese

Index 437

Notes on Contributors

Nathan Barrett, PhD, is an associate director and senior research fellow at the Education Research Alliance for New Orleans at Tulane University, USA. He researches teacher policies, equity in education, education reform, and student discipline. His recent publications have appeared in *Educational Researcher*, *American Journal of Education*, and *Economics of Education Review*.

David D. Bird, MBA, JD, is a PhD student at the University of Delaware, USA, with expertise in public administration, public finance, public law, public policy, and qualitative and multi-method research.

Carolyn Bourdeaux, PhD, of the Andrew Young School of Policy Studies at Georgia State University, USA, studies state budget, tax, transportation, and environmental policy, as well as land use, economic development, education finance, and administrative reform. Her recent research includes cutback budgeting, tax reform, intergovernmental fiscal relations, and legislative budget processes and decision-making.

Dörte Busch of the Berlin School of Economics and Law's recent work includes evaluation of the law for the promotion and supervision of children in day care and day care of the state of Saxony-Anhalt, and project inventory of the procedural and administrative implementation of the budget for work.

Thad Calabrese, PhD, of the Wagner School at New York University, USA, studies public and nonprofit financial management. His research has appeared in the *Journal of Accounting and Public Policy*, *Public Administration Review*, *Nonprofit and Voluntary Sector Quarterly*, *Public Budgeting and Finance*, *Nonprofit Management & Leadership*, and *National Tax Journal*, among others.

Marco Cangiano, MSc, a former senior staff at the International Monetary Fund (IMF) is a senior research associate with the London-based Overseas Development Institute (ODI) and a senior technical advisor with the Better Than Cash Alliance, consulting for, among others, the IMF, the EC, and the Italian Ministry for the Economy and Finance.

Gerald D. Cohen, PhD, is the former Deputy Assistant Secretary for Macroeconomic Analysis at the U.S. Department of Treasury. He was responsible for monitoring, analyzing, and briefing senior staff on U.S. macroeconomic developments. He is a co-author of *Political Cycles and the Macroeconomy* with Alberto Alesina and Nouriel Roubini.

Joseph Cordes, PhD, is the Associate Director of the School of Public Policy and Public Administration at the George Washington University Regulatory Studies Center. He is the co-editor of *The Encyclopedia of Taxation and Tax Policy*, and co-editor of *Nonprofits and Business*. He has authored or co-authored over 40 scholarly articles and contributed over 20 chapters in edited volumes.

J. Winn Decker, MEd, is a PhD student in Public Administration at North Carolina State University, USA, and has served as an intern for the US Senate Committee on the Budget.

James W. Douglas, PhD, of the Department of Political Science and Public Administration at the University of North Carolina at Charlotte, USA, researches budgeting and forecasting. His recent research has appeared in *Public Organization Review*, *Policy Studies Journal*, *Public Administration Review*, the *Journal of Policy Analysis and Management*, and *Public Budgeting & Finance*.

Todd L. Ely, PhD, of the University of Colorado Denver's School of Public Affairs researches the financing of state and local public services, education finance, and public and nonprofit financial management. He has co-authored *Essentials of Public Service*, an introductory public administration textbook.

Neil R. Ericsson, PhD, is a staff economist in the Division of International Finance, Board of Governors of the Federal Reserve System, Professor of Economics at The George Washington University, and an adjunct professor at the Paul H. Nitze School of Advanced International Studies (SAIS).

Jacob Fowles, PhD, of the University of Kansas School of Public Affairs and Administration, USA, researches secondary and tertiary education finance and policy. His research has appeared in *Public Administration Review*, the

Journal of Policy Analysis and Management, and the *Journal of Higher Education*, among others.

Emily Franklin, MA, is a fiscal analyst with the Carl Vinson Institute of Government and a former public finance fellow at the Center for State and Local Finance and Fiscal Research Center. Her areas of interest include international development and public finance.

Marc Fudge, PhD, of California State University, San Bernardino, USA, researches public budgeting and finance, performance management, and social equity. His recent work has appeared in *Public Financial Management* and the *Journal of Public Budgeting, Accounting and Financial Management.*

Alex Hathaway, DC, MPP, is a research associate with the Center for State and Local Finance and the Fiscal Research Center at Georgia State University, USA. His research interests include healthcare finance, state fiscal practices, higher education policy, and program evaluation.

Matthew James Hunt, MPA, of North Carolina State University, USA, studies public financial management, governmental and nonprofit accounting, public budgeting process, political economy, and revenue forecasting in the public sector.

Muhammad Naveed Iftikhar is a PhD candidate in Urban Affairs and Public Policy at the University of Delaware's Joseph R. Biden, Jr. School of Public Policy & Administration, USA. His research and policy work focuses on public sector governance, entrepreneurship, and cities. He is a co-editor of *Urban Studies and Entrepreneurship (2020).*

Peter Jones, PhD, of the Department of Political Science and Public Administration at the University of Alabama at Birmingham, USA, researches public budgeting and finance, research methods, and education policy financial issues. His research has appeared in *Public Performance & Management Review*, *Metron*, and the *Journal of Education Finance*, among others.

Jonathan B. Justice, PhD, of the University of Delaware's Joseph R. Biden, Jr. School of Public Policy & Administration, USA, researches public budgeting and finance and professional accountability. His recent publications include the *Handbook of Local Government Fiscal Health* and articles in *Public Finance and Management*, *Public Performance and Management Review*, and *Public Integrity.*

Kenneth A. Kriz, PhD, of the University of Illinois at Springfield, USA, researches subnational debt policy and administration, public pension fund management, government financial risk management, economic and revenue forecasting, and behavioral public finance. He has written more than 40 journal articles and book chapters and a textbook on quantitative research methods.

Helisse Levine, PhD, of Long Island University, Brooklyn, USA, researches economic and fiscal constraints on government organizations, social inequities in healthcare and government across race and ethnicity, and public administration pedagogy. Recent publications have appeared in *The American Review of Public Administration* and *Review of Public Personnel Administration.*

Andrew B. Martinez, MPhil, is a D.Phil. student at Oxford University, UK. Recent publications have appeared in *Econometrics, International Journal of Forecasting*, and *Journal of International Commerce and Economics.*

Bruce D. McDonald III, PhD, of the Department of Public Administration, North Carolina State University, USA, is a co-editor of the *Journal of Public Affairs Education* and the *Journal of Public and Nonprofit Affairs.* His research focuses on defense finance and human capital, local government fiscal health, and the history of public administration.

Melissa McShea, PhD, of the Department of Public Management at the John Jay College of Criminal Justice, USA, researches state and local public finance and public policy issues. In addition to working in the private and nonprofit sectors, McShea has served governments at the local, state, and federal levels.

Rahul Pathak, PhD, of the Marxe School of Public and International Affairs at the Baruch College, USA, researches public finance and social policy. His research has appeared in *Public Administration Review*, *Regional Science and Urban Economics*, *State and Local Government Review*, and *State Tax Notes.*

Rudolph Penner, PhD, is retired from the Urban Institute, USA. His previous posts include the Congressional Budget Office, the Office of Management & Budget, and other distinguished appointments. He has received the Peter Rossi Award from the University of Maryland and Association for Public Policy Analysis & Management (APPAM) for his contributions to the theory of program evaluation and the Federal Budgeting Career Legacy Award from George Mason University.

Geoffrey Propheter, PhD, of the School of Public Affairs at the University of Colorado, Denver, USA, researches property tax policy and administration, land and economic development, and sports and urban affairs.

Cole Rakow, PhD, is an economist and revenue forecaster for the New York City Independent Budget Office, USA. His work focuses on the city's business taxes (corporate income tax and unincorporated business tax) and tracking changes in federal and state tax policy that can impact city tax collections.

Ringa Raudla, PhD, of the Ragnar Nurkse Department of Innovation and Governance at Tallinn University of Technology (TalTech), Estonia, researches budgeting, fiscal governance, fiscal policy, and other matters. She has written many articles and is a member of the editorial boards of *Governance*, *Urban Affairs Review*, *Journal of Public Budgeting, Accounting & Financial Management*, and others.

Vincent Reitano, PhD, of the School of Public Affairs and Administration at Western Michigan University, USA, researches public budgeting and finance, public policy, and statistical methodology. His research has appeared in *American Review of Public Administration*, *Contemporary Economic Policy*, and *Public Budgeting & Finance*, among others.

Wolfgang Strehl worked as a guest lecturer at the Berlin School of Economics and Law, Germany, and has worked on business administration and management. His research interests include monetary economics, macroeconomics, economic inequality, the history of economic thought, and economic history. He has written discussion and working papers online at the Berlin School of Economics and Law in Russia and China.

Daniel Williams, PhD, of the Marxe School of Public and International Affairs at Baruch College was previously the budget director for Virginia's Medicaid agency. His recent forecasting publications include *The Status of Budget Forecasting* with Thad Calabrese (*Journal of Public and Nonprofit Affairs*), and *The Rube Goldberg Machine of Budget Implementation* with Joseph Onochie (*Public Budgeting & Finance*).

List of Figures

Fig. 2.1	GDP growth components	14
Fig. 2.2	Contributions to productivity growth	17
Fig. 2.3	Long waves of productivity	22
Fig. 2.4	Ten-year Treasury term premium	29
Fig. 3.1	Government agency forecasts and outcomes (in logs) and forecast errors (in percent, expressed as a fraction) of the federal debt	45
Fig. 3.2	Hedgehog graphs of U.S. government agency forecasts of the federal debt (in logs)	45
Fig. 4.1	The development of Germany's debts	73
Fig. 4.2	The budget of Germany	82
Fig. 4.3	Revenue estimation, Federal Ministry of Finance (11 May 2017)	84
Fig. 5.1	The distribution of study sample across years	100
Fig. 5.2	Mean percentage forecast error (three fiscal years)	101
Fig. 5.3	Mean absolute percent forecast error (three fiscal years)	102
Fig. 5.4	Forecast error and per-capita GDP	103
Fig. 7.1	One-year deficit/surplus projection errors as a percent of GDP	139
Fig. 7.2	Five-year deficit/surplus projection errors as a percent of GDP	139
Fig. 7.3	One-year total revenue projection errors as a percent of GDP	141
Fig. 7.4	One-year individual income tax projection errors as a percent of GDP	141
Fig. 7.5	One-year corporate income tax projection errors as a percent of GDP	142
Fig. 7.6	One-year social insurance tax projection errors as a percent of GDP	142
Fig. 7.7	Five-year total revenue projection errors as a percent of GDP	143
Fig. 7.8	One-year total spending projection errors as a percent of GDP	144
Fig. 7.9	One-year mandatory spending projection errors as a percent of GDP	145

Fig. 7.10 One-year discretionary spending projection errors as a percent of GDP 145
Fig. 7.11 One-year interest projection errors as a percent of GDP 146
Fig. 7.12 Five-year total spending projection errors as a percent of GDP 147
Fig. 9.1 VAR w/exogenous variables (Static) 195
Fig. 9.2 BVAR with exogenous variables 196
Fig. 11.1 Citywide property tax rate, fiscal years 1980–2017 223
Fig. 11.2 OMB's reserve forecast and actuals 228
Fig. 11.3 OMB's reserve forecast and actuals as a percent of yield 229
Fig. 11.4 Comparing forecasted reserve for 2016 to actual reserve 230
Fig. 11.5 Comparing forecasted reserve for 2014, 2015, and 2015 to actual reserve 231
Fig. 11.6 Comparison of property tax revenue forecasts for fiscal year 2016 234
Fig. 15.1 Forecasting accuracy for per-pupil revenues: Error 318
Fig. 15.2 Forecasting accuracy for per-pupil revenues: Percent Error 318
Fig. 19.1 Fiscal slack's relationship with fund balance 385
Fig. 19.2 Marginal impacts of revenue and expenditure biases on capital outlay reserves 389
Fig. 19.3 Marginal impacts of revenue and expenditure biases on building reserves 390
Fig. 21.1 Demonstration of simple average combination method 417
Fig. 21.2 Pseudo-out-of-sample forecast results 424

List of Tables

Table 2.1 How changes in economic assumptions might affect the federal budget (2019–2028) 12
Table 2.2 Five-year forecast errors 30
Table 3.1 Some studies evaluating U.S. federal budget agency forecasts, as characterized by forecaster, forecast horizon, variable forecast, and forecast period 40
Table 3.2 A comparison of root mean squared forecast errors 48
Table 3.3 Forecast-encompassing test statistics 51
Table 3.4 RMSEs of some individual and pooled forecasts 53
Table 3.5 Subsample RMSEs and corresponding Chow statistics 54
Table 3.6 Mincer–Zarnowitz *t*- and *F*-statistics for testing unbiasedness and efficiency 56
Table 3.7 IIS-based estimates of time-varying bias 59
Table 3.8 A summary of tools for forecast evaluation 60
Table 3.9 Estimates of time-varying bias from focused impulse indicator saturation with NBER-based turning-point dummies 62
Table 4.1 Basic structure of the debt brake 77
Table 5.1 Selected studies on revenue forecasting bias at the subnational level in the United States and Europe 94
Table 5.2 Major studies on revenue forecasting bias and its correlates in the EU and OECD countries 96
Table 5.3 Major studies on revenue forecasting bias and its correlates in low-income countries 97
Table 6.1 Errors in current policy projections of the 2018 debt-to-GDP ratio 121
Table 6.2 Average annual values for economic and demographic variables that underlie CBO's extended baseline 126

Table 7.1	CBO forecast error statistics as a percent of GDP (1978–2017)	138
Table 7.2	Difference between CBO's initial and updated forecast errors as a percent of GDP (1978–2017)	148
Table 8.1	Midyear adjustments and MAPE by forecasting type	163
Table 8.2	Reasonable rationales and MAPE by forecasting type	167
Table 9.1	Explanation of levels of data and their descriptive statistics for years 1977–2014	184
Table 9.2	Explanation of data in log differences and descriptive statistics for years 1977–2014	185
Table 9.3	Measures of forecast error	191
Table 10.1	Analysis of central and distributed expenditure budget supluses and deficits	207
Table 10.2	Harrisonburg agencies categorized as distributed	209
Table 10.3	Comparison of surplus between localities	211
Table 11.1	Variance between initial property tax forecast and actual collections	235
Table 13.1	Localities examined	261
Table 13.2	Comparison data for forecast accuracy expectations, MAPE, SMAPE, and percent improved	263
Table 13.3	Analysis of midyear budget forecast improvement	265
Table 13.4	Analysis of errors by year	266
Table 13.5	Evaluation of midyear budget improvement	267
Table 14.1	Three fiscal-indicator systems	288
Table 14.2	California cities in the sample	289
Table 14.3	Index scores for nine California cities using the Michigan system	291
Table 14.4	Index scores for nine California cities using the Crosby and Robbins (2013) system	291
Table 14.5	Index scores for nine California cities using the Ohio Auditor's System (Rescaled)	292
Table 14.6	Component indicators of the Michigan Fiscal Stress Index	296
Table 14.7	Component indicators of the Crosby and Robbins Fiscal Stress Index	297
Table 14.8	Component indicators of the Ohio Auditor of State Index	298
Table 15.1	Forecast accuracy measures for sample of districts	315
Table 15.2	Forecast accuracy measures changes over time for Kentucky school districts	316
Table 16.1	Summary statistics	332
Table 16.2	Missed forecast error model results	339
Table 19.1	Descriptive statistics	386
Table 19.2	Difference of means for explanatory variables, comparing districts that reported a fund balance versus those that did not	387

Table 19.3	Fixed effects regression results without controls	388
Table 19.4	Fixed effects regression results with controls	388
Table 21.1	Variables used in forecasting models	420
Table 21.2	Forecast models estimated	421
Table 21.3	Absolute Percentage Errors (APE) for static 2012 forecast model	422
Table 21.4	Absolute Percentage Errors (APE) for dynamic recursive forecast models	423

1

Introduction

Daniel Williams and Thad Calabrese

Introduction[1]

Sun and Lynch's (2008) *Government Budget Forecasting: Theory and Practice* provided one of the first systematic reviews of government budget forecasting more than a decade ago. More recently, Williams and Calabrese (2016) examined the recent literature on and techniques used in government budget forecasting. We received significant feedback inquiring about an even more thorough treatment of the topic, and the current volume is an outgrowth of these inquiries.

To understand budget forecasting, it is critical to understand what a budget is. While "budget" is a common term used for a variety of purposes, it was introduced into American governmental practice to focus on the planning stage that precedes an appropriation (Cleveland 1913). With this link to

[1] We would like to thank the contributors for their assistance with this introduction.

D. Williams (✉)
Austin W. Marxe School of Public and International Affairs, Baruch College, New York, NY, USA
e-mail: Daniel.Williams@baruch.cuny.edu

T. Calabrese
Robert F. Wagner Graduate School of Public Service, New York University, New York, NY, USA
e-mail: thad.calabrese@nyu.edu

D. Williams, T. Calabrese (eds.), *The Palgrave Handbook of Government Budget Forecasting*, Palgrave Studies in Public Debt, Spending, and Revenue,
https://doi.org/10.1007/978-3-030-18195-6_1

planning, it is clear that forecasting is a critical component of public budgeting. Thus, the current volume is intended as a contribution to the understanding of an essential, yet still understudied, element of public budgeting systems. Further, governments have several budgets, but there are two major types: expense budgets and capital budgets. Expense budgets are for the acquisition of resources that are promptly consumed, usually in the day-to-day operations of the government. Capital budgets are for the acquisition of resources that are retained for long time periods. In both the literature and research, far more is known about expense budget forecasting than capital budgeting, even though capital budgets can be larger than operating budgets. While this collection mostly addresses the first sort, it includes one chapter that brings an aspect of capital budget forecasting into focus.

There are many facets to budget forecasting practice. These can include practices at the international, national, and subnational levels. In the United States, subnational refers to states, cities, counties, and special districts. Similar, but sometimes differently labeled, jurisdictions can be found in other countries. Because public service is also delivered by not-for-profit organizations, we have endeavored to include two chapters on their forecasting. This is a poorly studied domain, with virtually no literature examining how not-for-profit organizations forecast or assessing the quality of their forecasts. Budget forecasting includes the forecasting of revenue and expenditures. For expenditures, the forecast often focuses on factors that lead to or cause public expenditures, such as student enrollment, prison populations, or other similar factors that lead to the need for public funding.

For larger governments, budget forecasting generally reflects economic modelling of the jurisdiction's domestic product. For smaller governments, it may reflect the use of simpler techniques. While there is wide reliance on stochastic modeling, some budget forecasting relies on judgment and some relies on deterministic models. The text includes material across many of these approaches. The chapters included in this volume were peer reviewed by experts on these topics.

This book has four parts. Part I contains chapters related to international and national budget forecasting. These practices have similarities and differences among the countries examined here: the United States, Germany, and a large sample of low-income and developing countries. This section also includes a discussion of macroeconomic modelling for forecasting, which commonly occurs with national forecasts as well as with larger states and potentially some larger local governments.

In Chap. 2, Gerald D. Cohen provides an overview of the economic theory and analysis used by U.S. federal government economists at the CBO and

Troika to derive forecasts for productivity, labor force, inflation, and interest rates. These variables play a key role in the budgeting and policy formation process because exogenous changes in the economic outlook or policies, such as infrastructure or paid family leave that move the needle on these variables, can have significant impact on the budget outlook. Moreover, the interplay between these variables means that forecast errors can cascade.

In Chap. 3, Neil R. Ericsson and Andrew B. Martinez discuss the evaluation of budget forecasts using information from U.S. federal government agencies' forecasts. The authors review the extensive literature on forecast errors and demonstrate the use of various forecast methods with forecasts made by the Congressional Budget Office (CBO), the Office of Management and Budget, and the Analysis of the President's Budget over 30 years. The forecasts of each are examined for bias, efficiency, and other characteristics. They recommend a generalized approach for the study of forecast errors to obtain the best forecast.

In Chap. 4, Dörte Busch and Wolfgang Strehl discuss the legal framework of budgeting in Germany. They discuss the implications of the Maastricht treaty for budgeting and forecasts for budgets. The chapter shows a sharp rise in the debt-to-GDP ratio during the 2008–2012 recession and aftermath and a slow decline thereafter. They describe the links between forecasting and such matters as structural budget balance, the GDP, and the debt break.

In Chap. 5, Marco Cangiano and Rahul Pathak discuss the revenue forecasting landscape in middle and low-income countries with a focus on examining the existence of forecast bias and potential remedies. They construct a dataset of ex-ante revenue forecasts and ex-post realizations for 26 countries using the information from the Public Expenditure and Financial Accountability (PEFA) reports, and find that most of these countries tend to overestimate their revenues. The forecast errors are significantly large and appear to correlate with the measures of income and administrative capacity. They review two institutional innovations for improving the budget process and forecasts: Semi-Autonomous Revenue Authorities (SARAs) and Independent Fiscal Councils, although neither of these institutions has been explicitly tasked with providing independent revenue forecasts that could address the observed bias. Lastly, the chapter highlights the lack of research and data on revenue forecasting in low and middle-income countries and recommends future research.

In Chap. 6, Rudolph Penner examines long-term projections of U.S. federal budget totals. He finds that the predictions are largely driven by a growing elderly population with spending on Social Security, Medicare, and Medicaid growing more rapidly than tax revenues. This is predicted to lead to an explosion in the debt-to-GDP ratio. Recent unusually low interest rates and the dot-com boom of the late 1990s moderated this ratio. However, the Great Recession caused the debt-to-GDP ratio to briefly rise much faster than expected. Despite these surprises the rapid growth of programs serving the elderly has been forecasted fairly accurately. Penner concludes by discussing program designs that adjust to surprises by changing indexing or using trigger mechanisms.

In Chap. 7, James W. Douglas and Ringa Raudla assess the Congressional Budget Office's (CBO) ability to use information effectively to make quality projections by examining whether one-year ahead and five-year cumulative projections updated in the summer are more accurate than its initial winter projections for fiscal years 1978 through 2017. They find that the updated projections are generally more accurate, suggesting that the CBO is effectively using the new information it collects over a short period of time (generally 6–7 months) to improve the quality of its forecasts.

Part II reviews state and local government budget forecasting within the United States. There has been extensive research on these practices extending back at least as far as the 1950s. While it is well known that these governments tend to underforecast their revenue for various reasons, much else remains unknown. This section provides new empirical evidence regarding some of these matters. This part addresses various matters of forecast accuracy, transparency, and bias. It also addresses different types of bias and their likely consequence. Finally, it includes a discussion of the forecasting of especially small—and poorly resourced—local governments.

In Chap. 8, Emily Franklin, Carolyn Bourdeaux, and Alex Hathaway find that significant variation in forecasting practices, particularly consensus forecasting processes, makes it difficult to assess the accuracy and transparency of government revenue forecasting. They look at the diversity of the revenue forecasting processes across the 50 states between FY2015 and FY2017 and assess the extent to which state forecasts have proven to be accurate and transparent. Their results show that these state forecasts were about as accurate as previous research would lead one to expect. More detailed analyses of several states demonstrate that reported revenue forecasts do not always reflect what the state expects to receive in revenue. They conclude that forecasts exist within institutional and political frameworks that can influence the accuracy and transparency of the forecast.

In Chap. 9, Melissa McShea and Joseph Cordes ask whether states can improve the accuracy of revenue forecasts by using more advanced time series and Bayesian vector autoregression (BVAR) forecasting methods. Using state revenue data from Virginia, they first estimate baseline forecasts using autoregression (AR) and vector autoregression (VAR). They then present a theoretical case for estimating a BVAR model, and present and compare forecasts based on AR, VAR, and BVAR. They conclude that there are gains in forecast accuracy in using the BVAR, but that BVAR is not a panacea for forecasting the extremely volatile corporate income tax revenue series.

In Chap. 10, Thad Calabrese and Daniel Williams examine whether the well-established risk-averse behavior associated with revenue underforecasting also extends to overforecasting expenditures. They argue that appropriated funds go to agencies, so overestimated expenditures may generate unintended agency-level discretion rather than buffer against forecast errors. However, when central budget offices, rather than agencies, control expenditure categories, those categories may be overfunded without creating such discretion. They find initial evidence for this sort of behavior, with governments overfunding centralized accounts when they use program budgeting and more general overfunding when line-item control is used.

In Chap. 11, Geoffrey Propheter examines the link between underforecasting and consequential tax increases through the examination of New York City property taxes. This link is labeled fiscal obfuscation, a form of fiscal illusion, because voters cannot easily see the link between underforecasting and tax increases. He argues that underforecasting leads to ratcheting tax revenue because the underforecast suggests a need for additional revenue, and the revenue actually received becomes the basis for planning for the next cycle. He examines whether the tax is excessively and intentionally underforecasted by the mayor's budgeting agency.

In Chap. 12, Vincent Reitano examines the practice of small local government's use of judgment-based forecasting rather than using mathematical modeling. He finds that the literature attributes the use of judgmental forecasts in small local governments to limited resources, which may constrain forecast-related employment and software, and to political official preferences. These factors may lead to large forecast errors and may inhibit the use of long-term forecasts for strategic planning. He recommends empirical research into the relationship between forecast errors and government size and qualitative research into government forecasting practices.

In Chap. 13, Daniel Williams and Thad Calabrese investigate current year budget forecast performance for municipal governments in the United States. They find that there is ample research that examines forecasts beyond the current fiscal year, but little work analyzes forecasts made during the current fiscal year for the remainder of that year. Midyear forecasts are important for governments in maintaining solvency through the budget execution phase and in setting a base for future budgets. Although general forecasting literature suggests that midyear forecasts can reflect substantial improvement, their empirical analysis shows no significant evidence of improvement with municipal governments and finds evidence that expenditure forecasts become worse at shorter time horizons.

Part III focuses attention on forecasting of specific types of data and forecasting with particular methods. While older literature of subnational budget forecasting focuses largely on revenue, this part examines other matters that include the forecast of school enrollment, prison population, municipal bankruptcy, and workforce matters. It tentatively introduces forecasts for nonprofits, which is poorly represented in the literature. It also addresses the use of forecast bias in the building of capital reserves. Finally, it includes material on forecast methods including consensus forecasting and ensemble forecasting.

In Chap. 14, Jonathan B. Justice, Marc Fudge, Helisse Levine, David D. Bird, and Muhammad Naveed Iftikhar examine the forecast accuracy of three procedures for predicting which local governments will experience bankruptcy. They adjust methods focused on Michigan and Ohio to reflect permissible types of revenue in California and then compute the scores for three bankrupt general-purpose local governments and six nonbankrupt matched jurisdictions. This simulation examines which, if any, of these models best transfer from their initial environment to another state and can forecast fiscal distress and bankruptcy. They found that the system developed and currently used by Ohio's Auditor of State performed well. The system developed in 2002 for Michigan's State Treasurer (no longer used) and a system subsequently proposed by academic researchers as a potential improvement to it both performed less well.

In Chap. 15, Peter Jones, Cole Rakow, and Vincent Reitano review the limited literature on school enrollment projections and budgetary forecasts in school districts, and then descriptively analyze forecast errors using a panel of Kentucky school districts from 2001 to 2013. Their results show that forecast errors vary over the business cycle, with revenue underestimations increasing in magnitude during the Great Recession. The chapter concludes that additional research on school district projection and forecast methods is necessary.

In Chap. 16, Todd L. Ely examines the relationship between nonprofit charter school characteristics and the accuracy of enrollment projections, which are the primary driver of organizational revenues and costs. Overall he finds that while the average charter school organization's enrollment projection is quite accurate, there is wide variation in the quality of forecasts. School and organizational factors are especially prominent determinants of projection quality, with larger and older organizations less likely to make and present overly optimistic enrollment projections. Governance structure, including the presence of a charter management organization and different authorizer types, also matter for the quality of projections. He found that charter school forecast of enrollments in subsequent years worsens dramatically.

In Chap. 17, Bruce D. McDonald III, J. Winn Decker, and Matthew James Hunt are concerned with the dramatic increase in prison incarceration in the United States. Relying on the literature on prison forecasting they identify the success and failure of the forecast model and provide a set of best practices for the forecasting of the prison population.

In Chap. 18, Vincent Reitano finds that there is little research into personnel forecasting. Despite the fact that personnel expense is frequently the largest component of governmental expenditures, there are only a few studies that examine government and nonprofit personnel projections. Most available research involves surveys with small samples or are from decades ago. Further, there is almost no insight into the methodologies that are used for personnel projections and forecasts, limiting insight for practitioners looking for evidence-based recommendations. This chapter considers these limitations and makes a variety of recommendations to help pave the way for future research that can build the literature and inform practitioners.

In Chap. 19, Vincent Reitano, Peter Jones, Nathan Barrett, and Jacob Fowles examine the relationship between biased revenue and expenditure forecasts and the use of resultant fiscal slack to build reserve funds. Evidence of the relationship between implicit and explicit fiscal slack is growing but is focused on the general fund. They focus on the unique context of capital funds. With a panel dataset of Kentucky school districts from 2001 to 2013, they estimate two-way, fixed-effects panel models and shows mixed evidence of the implicit-explicit fiscal slack relationship across the type of capital fund. They find small but statistically significant effects of revenue and expenditure forecast bias on building fund fiscal reserves, but not for other capital funds in Kentucky. They recommend further study to investigate the implicit-explicit fiscal slack relationship in school districts and general-purpose local government.

In Chap. 20, J. Winn Decker and Bruce D. McDonald III propose best practices for consensus forecasting in the governmental setting. They find that consensus forecasting involves multiple, potentially competing, parties in reaching an agreed forecast. Consensus estimating seeks to eliminate political fighting and increase transparency and accuracy in the forecasting process. Best practices of consensus forecasting include the involvement of all interested parties (including outside experts), publicizing documents and meetings, codifying the consensus process through legislation or bylaws, and revising the forecast throughout the year. By using these practices, organizations can use a consensus process in which parties feel ownership in the final product, resulting in more political acceptance of the forecast.

In Chap. 21, Kenneth A. Kriz introduces ensemble forecasting. Developed in the late 1960s, this method has become well accepted in the literature on economic forecasting. It involves combining different single forecasts into a combined forecast. He finds that ensemble models have been shown to have better prediction accuracy (lower forecast error variance) than single forecasts in the forecasting of economic and financial variables. He examines this technique using data on sales tax revenue for the city of Chicago from 1982 to 2016 and finds that for five years of pseudo out-of-sample forecasts, ensemble models demonstrated better overall forecast accuracy, while some single forecasts did very well in specific years.

Part IV consists of a single chapter that draws conclusions from these chapters. In Chap. 22, the editors review common themes found, point to some significant differences, and recommend matters for further research.

We thank the authors for all their hard work and contributions to this book. We would also like to thank Tula Weiss, Joseph Johnson, and Arumugam Hemalatha at Palgrave for their help throughout the publication process. We thank Erin Tolman for her assisting with copyediting and indexing, and Amanda Trepel for assistance in gathering hard-to-find budget data for our chapters. Also, Dall Forsythe, Martha Stark, and many of the contributors provided reviews of the chapters; their comments greatly improved the final version. Jonathan Engle connected us with an author, and we appreciate his help. This book in many ways represents a collective effort, and we appreciate all who contributed in some way.

References

Cleveland, F. A. (1913). *How we have been getting along without a budget*. Paper presented at the Proceedings of the American Political Science Association.

Sun, J., & Lynch, T. D. (Eds.). (2008). *Government budget forecasting: Theory and practice*. Boca Raton: CRC Press.

Williams, D., & Calabrese, T. (2016). The status of budget forecasting. *Journal of Public and Nonprofit Affairs, 2*(2), 127–160. https://doi.org/10.20899/jpna.2.2.127-160.

Part I

International and National

2

Macroeconomic Theory and Forecasting

Gerald D. Cohen

Major Points

- Forecasts for productivity, labor force, inflation and interest rates play a key role in the budgeting and policy formation process.
- This chapter describes the economic theory and analysis used by U.S. federal government economists at the Congressional Budget Office (CBO) and Troika to make these forecasts.
- The interplay between these variables means that forecast errors can cascade.

Introduction

Macroeconomic outcomes have a significant impact on short- and long-term budget outcomes. Short-term cyclical variations in economic activity (GDP growth) and unemployment affect automatic stabilizers such as unemployment insurance. In the long term, stronger potential GDP growth improves budget balances as it raises incomes and thus tax revenues and lowers outlays on support programs. This chapter focuses on the economic theory and analysis used by U.S. federal government economists at the Congressional Budget Office (CBO) and in the Executive branch/Administration (also known as the

G. D. Cohen (✉)
Haver Analytics, New York, NY, USA
e-mail: gerald@haver.com

D. Williams, T. Calabrese (eds.), *The Palgrave Handbook of Government Budget Forecasting*, Palgrave Studies in Public Debt, Spending, and Revenue,
https://doi.org/10.1007/978-3-030-18195-6_2

"Troika") to derive forecasts for productivity and labor force growth, inflation and interest rates.[1]

These variables play a key role in the budgeting and policy formation process. That's because exogenous changes in the economic outlook or policies, such as infrastructure or paid family leave that move the needle on these variables, can have significant impact on the budget outlook. The CBO currently estimates that, all else equal, for every one-percentage point higher productivity growth—which as described below flows directly into GDP growth—improves the U.S. budget outlook by a net $2.28 trillion over a ten-year horizon (revenues rise by $3.23 trillion while expenditures increase by $950 billion—see Table 2.1) (Congressional Budget Office 2018).[2] A one-percentage point improvement in labor force growth, the other variable that drives long-term GDP growth, yields a net $1.17 trillion of additional revenue over the next ten years, with a $1.44 trillion increase in receipts slightly offset by $270 billion in additional outlays.

Not surprisingly, higher interest rates raise the cost of government borrowing. Given the $15.50 trillion of debt currently held by the public and baseline budget deficits expected by the CBO, a one-percentage point increase in both short- and long-term interest rates would worsen the budget by an estimated $1.64 trillion in the next ten years as outlays increase by $1.65 trillion and revenues rise by just $10 billion.[3] Somewhat surprising to many, higher

Table 2.1 How changes in economic assumptions might affect the federal budget (2019–2028)

Impact of 1-percentage point increase each year ($ billions)	Change in revenues	Change in outlays	Increase (–) in the deficit relative to CBO baseline
Productivity growth	3230	950	2280
Labor force growth	1440	270	1170
Interest rates	10	1650	–1640
Inflation	2310	3320	–1010

Source: Congressional Budget Office

[1] The Troika consists of members of the Council of Economic Advisors, Office of Management and Budget, and Department of Treasury. The Troika economic forecast is published by the Office of Management and Budget and is used to produce Administration budget forecasts. For a description of the Troika process see Donihue and Kitchen (1999). The CBO procedures are outlined in Arnold (2018).

[2] All of these estimates are based on the assumption of ceteris paribus—holding all else equal. However, they do attempt to incorporate the feedback between variables. For example, that higher potential GDP growth or an increase in inflation will raise interest rates. As a result, unless the shocks are independent, these estimates are not additive.

[3] While total U.S. federal debt is $21.2 trillion, intragovernmental holdings such as the Social Security trust fund total $5.7 trillion.

inflation has a deleterious impact on the budget. While a one-percentage point increase in the rate of inflation raises revenues by $2.31 trillion over ten years, spending is expected to rise by $3.32 trillion, worsening the budget balance by a net $1.01 trillion.

This chapter focuses on these four key variables. It begins by discussing the theoretical underpinnings of potential economic growth. The chapter then delves into the factors that drive labor force and productivity growth as well as the link between short- and long-term GDP forecasts. It then examines the forecasting process for inflation and interest rates. The interplay between forecasts of growth and inflation on interest rates illustrates the endogeneity of these processes and how forecast errors can propagate. As a result, the chapter concludes by discussing forecast errors and the challenges forecasters face of how to respond to these errors.

Potential Economic Growth

Economic activity (GDP) is often measured by summing the variables contributing to aggregate demand—consumption, investment, government spending and the trade balance (exports minus imports). While this tells us how fast the economy is currently growing, these elements don't determine the potential growth rate or how fast an economy can grow without overheating and causing inflation. Potential growth is driven by the aggregate supply or long-term production capacity of the economy. Given the importance of GDP projections on budget outcomes it is not surprising that forecasters spend a significant amount of energy estimating potential growth.[4]

The starting point for most estimates of potential growth comes from the Solow Growth Model (Solow 1956). This model decomposes potential growth into three components: labor, capital and total or multi-factor productivity (TFP or MFP). Labor is defined as the amount of labor hours worked throughout the economy adjusted for changes in the quality of labor that comes from education and training. Capital is the productive services provided to labor by investment in plant and equipment as well as intellectual property: software, research and development, and even long-lived artistic assets such as movies or music. TFP is the residual or growth in output that is not accounted for by the growth in labor hours, labor quality and capital investment.

[4] As described below, estimates of potential have a significant impact on interest rates and even inflation forecasts. Though, as noted above, the CBO's rules of thumb incorporate that feedback.

Most versions of the Solow Growth Model assume a Cobb-Douglas production function, with labor and capital weighted by their share of the production process, which is approximated by their contribution to GDP (see Eq. (2.1) in the Appendix). The Cobb-Douglas production function implies that GDP will grow proportionally to the increase in labor and capital (this is also known as constant returns to scale).

Historically, in the United States these input shares have been equal to roughly two-thirds labor and one-third capital. However, these shares exhibit both cyclical and structural variation, with a notable decrease in the labor share over the last 20 years. As a result, forecasters try to adjust for the cyclicality and incorporate time-varying estimates of these shares. In addition, since the share of labor and capital can vary meaningfully across different sectors of the economy (i.e. the labor share is substantially higher in government), some forecasters, such as the CBO, will estimate potential growth for different sectors, such as nonfarm business, farm, federal and state and local government, household, and nonprofit organizations (Shackleton 2018).

Rearranging the Solow Growth Model produces a somewhat simpler form which can be found in publicly available economic statistics (United States Bureau of Labor Statistics 2019a, 2019c). GDP or potential GDP is the product of two factors: labor hours worked and labor productivity (Eq. (2.4) in the Appendix). Figure 2.1 decomposes U.S. GDP growth into the growth in

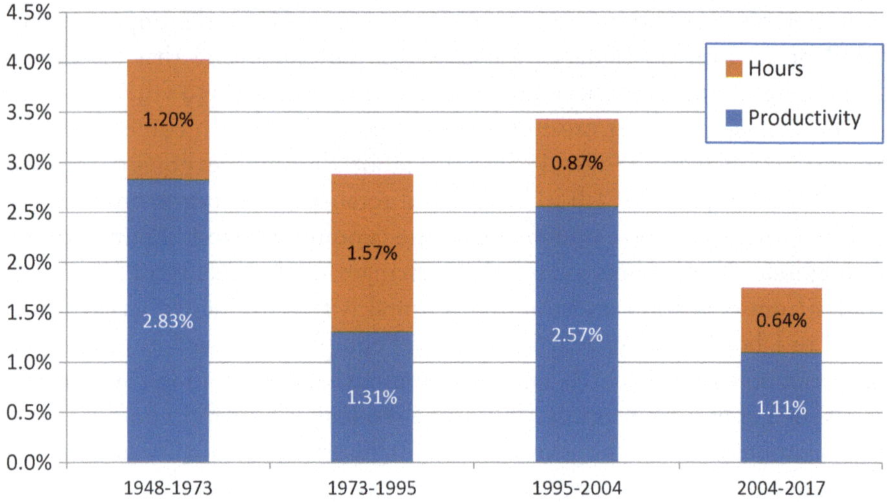

Fig. 2.1 GDP growth components. Source: Bureau of Labor Statistics

hours worked and productivity from 1948 to 2017.[5] This illustrates a number of important issues. First, the significant variation in productivity growth (blue bars) between the different "productivity eras" economists have identified. Second, how much of a role the increase in hours played in maintaining strong GDP growth during the 1970s and 1980s. And finally, the significant slowdown in hours growth the U.S. has experienced since the 1990s (Fig. 2.1).

Total Hours

Digging into each of the factors, labor hours are determined by the product of three variables: total population, the labor force participation rate (LFPR) and average hours worked (Eq. (2.5) in the Appendix). Forecasters use demographics and expected policies to estimate both of these statistics. Population is based on expected birth and death rates as well as immigration. In the United States, population growth has been on a general downtrend since the 1950s, when it grew 1.8% per annum, and is expected to slow further over the next ten years, averaging just 0.7% per year. Furthermore, immigrants are a large and growing share of population growth. Immigration accounted for roughly half of the population growth in recent decades (Mericle 2016). That share is expected to increase given low domestic birth rates. Thus, policies that affect immigration will have a meaningful impact on population growth.

The labor force participation rate reflects a combination of the age, gender, race, marital status and educational composition of the population and the propensity to work of these different cohorts. For example, the participation rate of all 25- to 29-year-olds is 82% in the United States while the participation rate of 65- to 69-year-olds is just 33%. For "prime age" workers, the demographic group of 25- to 54-year-olds who are most likely to work, the participation rate is 89% for men and 75% for women in the United States. Moreover, the participation rate for those 25 years and older with just a high school degree is 58%, while those with a college degree and higher is 74% (United States Bureau of Labor Statistics 2019b).

Adding to the level of complexity, participation rates within demographic groups have not been constant over time either because of changes in behavior or because of policies such as paid family leave which can encourage parents to stay in the workforce. That's one of the reasons why Sweden has a total

[5] When converted into growth rates the product of factors is equal to the sum of the growth rates of those factors. Thus, GDP growth = Hours growth + Productivity growth.

prime age LFPR of 91% vs. 82% in the United States (Organisation of Economic Cooperation and Development 2018).

Taking the product of population and LFPR yields the size of the labor force. Shifting population and LFPR dynamics is one of the reasons why the labor force in the United States grew faster than the overall population in the 1970s and 1980s. Baby boomers moved into the "prime age" and the female participation rate increased substantially during that period.[6] By the mid-2000s both of those trends had reversed—growth in the prime age population slowed meaningfully and participation rates have moved lower.[7]

Forecasters use very detailed data on expected changes in the demographic composition of the population over time and potential changes in participation rates among those cohorts to come up with an estimate of the LFPR for the population as a whole (Aaronson et al. 2014). Predominantly as a result of demographic factors, the labor force is expected to grow more slowly than the population over the next decade. In 2005, 23% of the U.S. population was 55 and over. By 2030 it is expected to be 32% (United States Census Bureau, 2019). When evaluating policy choices, such as paid leave, childcare or skills training, forecasters can look at international comparisons such as the example of Sweden noted above. U.S. prime-age male participation rates are lower and have fallen by more than those of other developed economies (Council of Economic Advisors 2016). Female prime-age participation rates are also lagging behind many countries (Blau and Kahn 2013). This suggests that policies exist that can raise participation rates and offset some of the impact of aging on the labor force.

To round out the calculation of total hours, forecasters need an estimate of average weekly hours (AWH) worked per week or year. AWH can vary substantially over a business cycle; thus, it is important to adjust for that cyclicality. Moreover, hours can differ between industries. However, the dominant force driving AWH has been the structural downtrend in hours since at least the turn of the twentieth century, when the average employee worked over 50 hours per week (United States Census Bureau 1975). That number, which includes both part-time and full-time workers, currently stands at roughly 33 hours per week (Haver Analytics 2019). Thus, forecasters, whether doing an aggregated or disaggregated projections, generally extrapolate the cyclically adjusted trends.

[6] In 1970, the prime-age female participation was 50%, and by 1990, it was 74%. Meanwhile, the prime-age population grew at a 2.0% annual rate in the 1970s and 1980s.

[7] Prime-age LFPR peaked at 84% in the late 1990s. It currently stands at 82%. The decline in participation is striking for U.S. prime-age men. It peaked at 97% roughly 50 years ago and currently stands at 89%. Until the late 1990s this decline was offset by the rise in female participation, but even that peaked in the late-1990s at 77% and has decreased to 75%. Over the last 20 years the prime-age population has grown at just 0.3% annual rate.

Labor Productivity

Labor productivity is determined by growth in three factors scaled to their shares of the production function (Eq. (2.3) in the Appendix): labor quality, which is determined by education, training and experience; capital investment, which provides more structures, equipment and intellectual property for workers to use; and total factor productivity, which captures innovation—both technological and better management of resources—and makes labor and capital more efficient.

Figure 2.2 decomposes productivity growth in the business sector into three components: labor quality (red), capital intensity (green) and total factor productivity (blue).[8] This figure illustrates the drivers of the variation in productivity growth between the different eras noted in Fig. 2.1. In particular, how much of a role TFP plays in overall productivity growth and as the predominant driver of the shift between high and low productivity—swinging by over one-percentage point between the eras. Capital intensity exhibits some of the variation of TFP. Meanwhile, the contribution from labor quality has been relatively stable.

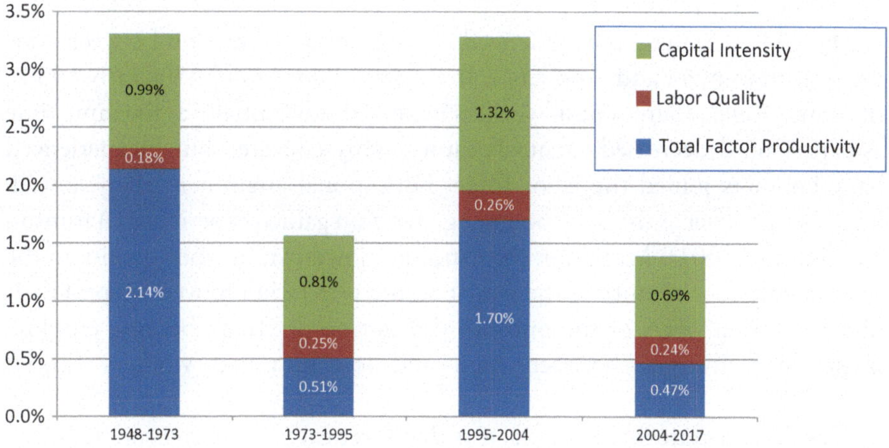

Fig. 2.2 Contributions to productivity growth. Source: Bureau of Labor Statistics

[8] The total size of the bars in Fig.2.2, which is labor productivity in the business sector, is larger than the blue bars in Fig. 2.1, that is, labor productivity for the economy as a whole.

Labor Quality

While we can measure educational attainment, training and experience, which in economic parlance is known as human capital accumulation, it is difficult to assess the impact of those factors on labor quality. Economists use occupations and wages, which are the return to labor, to gauge the impact of those factors on labor quality. For example, wages for computer programmers are generally higher than wages for a fast-food cook. Unfortunately, wages can vary for reasons other than labor quality, such as gender, race, ethnicity or industry. As a result, models of labor quality must control for those factors.

Once those adjustments are made, forecasters assess the human capital of each cohort of the population. This is done by measuring the metrics of educational attainment such as high school and college graduation rates. In many countries, a meaningful driver of the growth in labor quality has been the increase in share of the population with college degrees. The age distribution of the population and participation rates can also drive labor quality. Experience tends to be correlated with age—wages generally rise until workers are in their early 50s—which implies that the productivity or quality of those workers is higher. In other words, workers have gained skills during their tenure in the labor market.

The United States has experienced an interesting interaction between educational attainment and experience. In the late 1960s through the early 1980s, the educational attainment of workers increased substantially at the same time as experienced decreased. That's because highly educated but inexperienced baby boomers joined the labor force. Educational attainment then slowed, but this was offset as the baby boomer generation gained experience (Aaronson and Sullivan 2001). Moreover, the expected slowdown in labor quality in the early twenty-first century as the baby boomer generation moved beyond their highest earning years of the mid-50s did not occur. That's because employment rates diverged between high and low educated workers (Bosler et al. 2016).

This demonstrates the set of factors that forecasters must incorporate when projecting future labor quality. They must forecast future educational attainment and then use their estimates of population growth and the labor force participation rates of various age and educational cohorts to estimate experience.[9] In the United States, the slowdown in improvements in educational attainment combined with demographic trends does not bode well for

[9] Some forecasters, such as the CBO, do not forecast labor quality and just include it in their estimate of TFP.

increases in labor quality. However, one benefit of the Great Recession was that it increased college attendance and graduation rates (Brown and Hoxby 2015). At present, it is not clear if the increase in the share of college educated is a temporary or permanent phenomenon.

Capital Intensity

The second driver of labor productivity is investments in plant, equipment and intellectual property (software, research and development as well as long-lived artistic assets). Economists use historical measures of investment and depreciation to estimate the size of the capital stock (United States Bureau of Economic Analysis 2018). They then measure the contributions of that stock into the production process (this is known as capital intensity, capital deepening or capital services). That's because a $1000 investment in software doesn't immediately yield a $1000 in productivity. Rather the software creates a flow of productive services over its lifetime. Economic theory suggests that the flow of productive services can be measured by its "rental price," which can be measured directly if there is a rental market or indirectly via the cost of the capital good, the cost of financial capital (debt and equity), depreciation, potential capital gains and tax rules (United States Bureau of Labor Statistics 1983, 2007).

Forecasts of capital intensity are based on estimates of investment, depreciation and the factors mentioned above that would impact the rental price, such as interest rates and tax policy. However, the key determinant of capital deepening is investment, thus, it becomes the focus of most forecasts. Estimates of investment are based on the expected labor force (described above) and forecasts of total factor productivity growth (described below), both of which impact returns on investment.[10] As the number of workers increase, businesses would be expected to invest and provide more capital for them to produce goods and services. Furthermore, if TFP is expected to grow, which implies that output is growing faster than the labor force, higher returns to investment should increase capital spending. This is known as an accelerator model in which investment responds to current and future output.[11]

[10] The other factors that determine the rental cost, such as the cost of capital and taxes, are also important drivers of investment, but output dominates. However, these other factors would be incorporated when assessing the impact of changes in tax policy.

[11] Economic theory predicts that companies should put a lot of weight on expected profitability when making investment plans, but the empirical evidence suggests that business investment is correlated more with recent trends rather than future output (Kopp 2018).

The shifting composition of capital spending presents measurement issues of current investment trends and complicates forecasts of future investment. In 1950 structures such as buildings, but also oil and gas drilling rigs, comprised roughly one-third of all nonresidential private sector investment. Now it is less than one-quarter of all investment. Equipment—which includes machinery, transportation and tech hardware—has seen its share fall from almost 60% in 1950 to 45% today, even though investment in tech hardware has grown at an 8% annual rate over the last 50 years (adjusted for inflation and changes in quality, investment in tech hardware has grown at a 12% annual rate).[12] Meanwhile intellectual property comprises roughly one-third of nonresidential private investment up from 8% in 1950 and 13% in 1980 (United States Bureau of Economic Analysis 2019a).

The gap between inflation-and-quality-adjusted and current-dollar spending on tech hardware illustrates a set of issues forecasters face. From 1995 to 2004 the price of computing power fell at an extraordinary 9% annual pace (United States Bureau of Economic Analysis 2019a). This implied that $100 spent on technology in 2004 was equivalent to $235 spent in 1995. Forecasters expected the rate of price decline to continue, spurring productivity growth. Yet despite Moore's law—a doubling of the number of transistors on an integrated circuit every two years—continuing apace, the decline in computing power prices has slowed (Byrne et al. 2018).

Moreover, an increased share of investment is in intangibles, such as software, which are harder to measure in real time and may have longer lags between the investment and the impact on productivity.[13] Still, recent economic research suggests measurement issues do not seem to explain the slowdown in capital spending in the mid-2000s (Syverson 2017). This analysis indicates that while the official statistics tend to understate investment, the degree of understatement has likely *fallen* over time. This implies that while true capital intensity and productivity might be somewhat higher than current estimates, the post-2004 deceleration was even more substantial (Byrne et al. 2016).

Total Factor Productivity

By definition total factor productivity is the residual, or output that cannot be explained from the other factors of production (hours, labor quality and capital intensity). TFP is most commonly thought of as technological innovations that come from research and development, such as hydraulic fracturing

[12] In 1950, tech hardware represented 10% of the private sector's equipment budget; now it is a third.

[13] For an in depth discussion of this topic see Haskel and Westlake (2017).

which allows production of oil from previously un-producible or unprofitable geological resources or the ability of microchip makers to halve the size of transistors every two years (Moore's law).

However, many innovations come from collaboration between colleagues and better management of resources such as redesigning production lines or delivery routes, inventory management or even worker scheduling. Some of these types of improvements come from technological innovation that can be exploited by investment in new equipment or software, such as worker scheduling software. Economists call this "embodied technological progress." This is one of the reasons why there is a correlation between the trends in TFP and capital intensity illustrated in Fig. 2.2.[14]

TFP also includes changes in the utilization rate of capital as well as labor effort, though these tend to be more cyclical phenomena which some economists try to adjust for (Fernald 2014).[15] Moreover, because TFP is a residual, any measurement error in labor quality or capital intensity will carry through to TFP. However, as economists and statisticians improve their measurement of the inputs into the production function, the share of productivity explained by TFP will decline. Still, as Fig. 2.2 illustrates, TFP accounts for over 50% of productivity growth since 1948.

Forecasting TFP—a residual which encompasses innovations—is notoriously difficult. Some economists such as Robert Gordon believe that the U.S. economy experienced a one-time period of tremendous innovations between the late nineteenth and late twentieth centuries such as electrification and indoor plumbing, which are unlikely to be repeated (Gordon 2016). In contrast, his colleague at Northwestern, Joel Mokyr believes the opposite. Innovations of the past build upon each other, enhanced by the emergence of a competitive global marketplace, which will encourage the spread of new technology from its originating locations to other users who do not wish to be left behind (Mokyr 2014).

Not only is technological progress difficult to forecast, but even when innovations are evident, it is difficult to predict when it will have an impact on the economy. Robert Solow, the developer of the Solow Growth Model, famously said in 1987, "*You can see the computer age everywhere but in the productivity statistics*." There is a body of research that suggests that inventions diffuse with an S-curve pattern—a slow ramp-up and then a period of explosive growth

[14] Given the accelerator model for capital spending described above the causality between TFP and capital spending is difficult to ascertain. Expected productivity growth increases investment, which enhances TFP.

[15] For example, during a slowdown, existing plant and equipment are not used to their fullest extent (the capacity utilization rate falls), and though hours may not change, work effort may decline. As a result, TFP growth slows.

and then a plateauing (Griliches 1957). However, the timing and length of the S-curve is hard to forecast. Eight years after Solow's quip, the computer age finally boosted productivity, but the impact seemed to be relatively short lived.

Economists believe the IT-revolution-high-productivity-growth era came to an end in 2004, prior to the Great Recession, with productivity growth averaging just 1.4% per year through 2017 (Fernald and Wang 2015). This slowdown in productivity growth is not limited to the United States, with many countries experiencing downshifts of productivity growth at around the same time (Furman 2015). The post-2004 slowdown in TFP is hard to square with what appears to be continued strong diffusion of technology such as mobile and energy production. However, it may be related to the weak pace of capital deepening, since as noted above, some innovations can only be exploited by investing in new equipment and software.

Given the challenges described above, forecasters tend to take two approaches. Either they assume that TFP will revert to its long-term average. Or, they focus on the different eras of TFP and productivity growth illustrated in Figs. 2.2 and 2.3.

Since at least the late nineteenth century, productivity in the United States has exhibited distinct 10- to 20-year periods of high (roughly 3%) and low

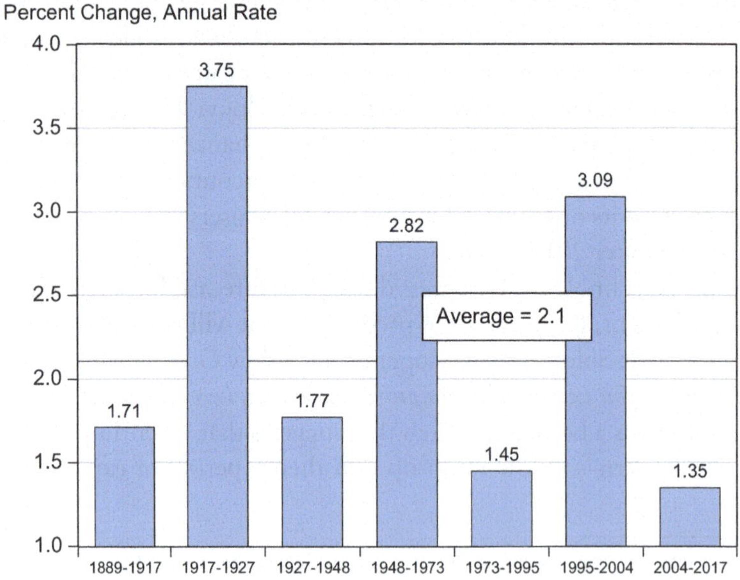

Fig. 2.3 Long waves of productivity. Source: Bureau of Labor Statistics, Kendrick (1961), Author's Calculations

(roughly 1.5%) growth.[16] While it is fairly easy ex post to point to the drivers of the booms—electrification, integration of World War II innovation and the IT revolution—the timing of the turning points and the length of the era have been difficult to predict in anywhere near real time (Cohen 2017b). To deal with this, forecasters such as the CBO project that potential TFP will converge to its weighted average trend over the preceding 25 years, with twice as much weight placed on recent trend rates as on trend rates 25 years in the past (Shackleton 2018).[17]

Productivity, Potential and Short-Run Dynamics

Putting together forecasts of these components: labor quality, capital deepening and total factor productivity, yields an estimate of productivity growth (see Eq. (2.3) in the Appendix). Productivity is the key to improvements in standards of living, and as illustrated above, the most important macroeconomic driver of budget outcomes. Multiplying expected labor force growth—another significant variable in budget forecasts—and expected hours per worker produces labor hours (Eq. (2.5) in the Appendix). GDP is the combination of labor hours and productivity (Eq. (2.4) in the Appendix).

When an economy is operating at full potential, all of the nation's labor and capital are being utilized at their maximum sustainable rates. Forecasters would then expect the economy to grow at its potential growth rate for the remainder of the forecast period. Forecasters are not adept at anticipating turning points in the economy; thus, they generally do not forecast recessions. Rather they use the size of the output gap—the amount of unused capacity or slack—as a guide for their short-term forecast. In other words, estimates of the output gap, which come from potential GDP, act as the link between short- and long-term forecasts.

If there were an output gap, the economy could grow faster than its potential without overheating until the output gap was eliminated. An economy cannot permanently grow above (or below) its potential. If it does, the unemployment rate will fall (rise) and wage and product inflation (disinflation or outright deflation) will occur. Either a policy response or natural forces will

[16] Unfortunately, data is not available to disaggregate productivity growth into its components going back to the late nineteenth century. However, given the correlation between TFP and capital intensity described by both theory and evidence, it would not be surprising if TFP followed the same trend as productivity in the pre-1948 eras.

[17] Pandl and Struyven (2016) describe the short- to medium-term inertia found in TFP growth and estimate potential convergence dynamics.

drive interest rates and the real exchange rate higher (lower), bringing the economy back into equilibrium. Thus, short-term economic forecasts might have the economy growing faster or slower than its potential. However, long-term growth forecasts must be anchored to estimates of potential growth.

Inflation

In the United States and across the globe, there are many different measures of inflation such as the Consumer Price Index (CPI) or the Personal Consumption Expenditures Chain-Price Index (PCE).[18] Some measures, usually referred to as "core" CPI or PCE, exclude food and energy prices. Food and energy prices are omitted because of their volatility and the attenuated impact of economic activity on these prices. As a result, there can be large differences between headline (or overall) and "core" measures of inflation over the course of a few years. However, over the longer term, headline inflation tends to converge to core inflation. Thus, core inflation is a better indicator of future inflation dynamics.

Some price indices such as the PCE deflator use a chain weigh methodology. This technique constantly adjusts for changes in the basket of goods and services resulting from tastes, new technologies, the response to changes prices (switching from meat to chicken if meat prices rise) or the choice of shopping outlets (i.e. department stores vs. e-tailers). The basket of goods and services as well as shopping outlets also change for the CPI, but it does so more slowly because it is based on low-frequency detailed surveys of expenditures. As a result of these and other methodological differences, inflation, as measured by the CPI, has been roughly 0.4 percentage point higher than inflation as measured by the PCE over the last 60 years (United States Bureau of Labor Statistics 2019d; United States Bureau of Economic Analysis 2019b). As Table 2.1 illustrates, a 0.4-percentage point higher inflation raises the deficit by $404 billion over ten years. Thus, forecasters must ascertain which measures of inflation are linked to revenues and outlays—for example, Social Security is linked to headline CPI, while interest rates may be more responsive to the PCE deflator, the Fed's choice of inflation target—and then forecast accordingly.

The overall forecasting methodology is similar across the different inflation measures, with time horizon determining the estimation technique. The key

[18] Another price measure is the GDP deflator, which measures all prices across the economy, not just those experienced by consumers. Since most revenues and expenditures are linked to consumer prices, forecasters focus on these estimates. Not surprisingly, there is a high correlation between the CPI/PCE and GDP deflator.

model for inflation forecasting is the Phillips Curve. The Phillips Curve links changes in core inflation to the measures of slack in the economy, inflation expectations and historical inflation to capture inertia.[19] Short-term forecasts take a somewhat more bottom's up approach to account for significant deviations which can occur to inflation from "special factors." For example, in 2017, core CPI inflation decelerated sharply from 2.1% year-on-year in March to 1.7% year-on-year in June. Much of the slowdown could be explained by a sharp, but temporary decline in the price of wireless phone services after the Bureau of Labor Statistics introduced new methodology for quality adjustment, and wireless service carriers increasingly offered unlimited data packages (Arnold 2018).

In the medium term, the Phillips Curve dominates. If there is an output gap and the economy is operating below its potential, the unemployment rate will be high and there will be downward pressure on wage and price inflation. As the slack diminishes (the output gap closes), the unemployment rate falls and the downward pressure is reduced. If the economy starts operating above potential, then there will be upward pressure on wages and prices. In many models the gap between the unemployment rate and its "natural rate"—the long-run equilibrium unemployment rate—is the preferred measure of slack. Thus, there is an inverse relationship between the unemployment rate (or unemployment gap) and inflation.

Inflation expectations, the second variable in the Phillips Curve, is measured by surveys of inflation, financial-market-based measures, and more recently, central bank inflation targets. Organizations such as the University of Michigan Survey of Consumers measure one-year and five-year inflation expectations monthly (University of Michigan, n.d.). Every quarter, the Philadelphia Fed's Survey of Professional Forecasters asks about inflation expectations over the next ten years (Federal Reserve Bank of Philadelphia, n.d.). Meanwhile, the issuance of U.S. Treasury Inflation Indexed Securities (TIPS) in the late-1990s allowed forecasters to monitor daily U.S. inflation expectations up to 30 years. Finally, central banks have shifted toward setting and announcing a specific inflation target. Forecasters often use a combination of these measures—especially in the medium term—as individual measures can be biased by recent inflation readings, market imperfections or in the case of the central bank questions about its credibility (Detmeister et al. 2016; Bauer and McCarthy 2015).

---

[19] As noted above, food and energy prices are predominantly determined by factors outside this model and are thus forecasted separately—often using financial market forward prices in consultation with field experts.

Over the last several decades in many countries such as the United States central banks' credibility has been very high resulting in an "anchoring" of inflation expectations. Thus medium to long-term inflation expectations have been hovering closely around the central bank inflation target (in the Fed's case, 2% for the PCE). Moreover, inflation expectations are increasingly dominating the inflation propagation process. As a result, the impact of other factors such as slack has diminished. This "flattening" of the Phillips Curve implies that the output or unemployment gap has a smaller impact on inflation than in the past.[20] During the Great Recession, when the unemployment rate jumped to 10%, most forecasters expected inflation to fall with a significant risk of outright deflation (a decline in prices). While the core PCE did slow from 2.2% in 2007 to 1.2% in 2009, inflation rebounded to 1.6% in 2011, even though the unemployment rate was still at 9%.

As noted above, most long-term forecasts have the economy converging to its potential and the unemployment rate settling at its natural rate. At that point, the unemployment gap is equal to zero and inflation equals inflation expectations. Thus, budget forecasters such as the CBO and Troika anticipate long-term inflation (where U.S. inflation will be in ten-year time) of roughly 2% for the PCE, and given the differences described above between PCE and CPI, 2.4% for the CPI (Congressional Budget Office 2019; Office of Management and Budget 2019).

Interest Rates

Interest rates are determined by two factors: expected inflation and the real or inflation-adjusted cost of borrowing. Given the inflation forecasting process discussed above, this section focuses on the determinants of real or inflation-adjusted interest rates. For budgeting purposes, the interest rates that matter most are the rates on government debt. In the case of the U.S. Government, Treasury securities are seen as "risk free" meaning that investors generally believe that United States will not default on its debt. Thus, Treasuries do not include a "risk premium."

U.S. state and local government debt generally include a risk premium as there is some probability of default. Risk premia rise as the probability of default increases. For example, in the fall of 2018 the interest rate on ten-year

[20] While the model described in the text is more complicated than a simple linear regression between two variables, the Phillips Curve is often depicted as a downward sloping line with the unemployment rate or gap on the x-axis and inflation on the y-axis.

State of Illinois debt, which was rated BBB, was 4.19%, while the interest rate on ten-year Maryland debt, an AAA-rated borrower, was 2.53%. At the same time, ten-year Treasuries yielded 3.10%. In the United States, state and local debt has preferential tax treatment, which generally lowers their yield relative to Treasuries.[21]

Since governments issue debt at different maturities (in the United States, typical maturities go from 3 months to 30 years, with the current average maturity of 70 months), forecasters must estimate the cost of borrowing across different maturities. As a starting point forecasters generally begin with an estimate of three-month Treasury bills. The key determinant of three-month Treasuries is the Federal Funds Rate, the overnight interest rate charged by banks on bank reserves.

The Federal Funds Rate is set by the Federal Reserve, and thus, forecasts of three-month Treasuries are guided by the Fed's "reaction function" to economic and financial conditions. Forecasters such as the CBO and Troika use a "Taylor Rule" model described in Eqs. (2.6) and (2.7) in the Appendix. The Taylor Rule relates the federal funds rate to the inflation gap—the difference between inflation and the Federal Reserve's target (currently 2% for the personal consumption expenditure chain price index); output gap—the difference between GDP and potential GDP as a share of potential GDP; neutral real interest rate (described below) and current level of inflation (Taylor 1993).[22]

When inflation is at its target level and there is no output gap, the Fed will set real interest rates equal to their neutral level. In general, if inflation is above (below) its target and/or GDP is above (below) its potential, interest rates will be above (below) neutral. Over the long run, as growth settles at its potential and inflation hits the central bank target, the inflation-adjusted short-term interest rate will converge to its neutral level.

Economic theory says the neutral rate should be determined by factors that drive the return on capital such as labor force and total factor productivity growth. These are buttressed by behaviors that impact savings and investment decisions, as well as the supply and demand for different types of risky assets. Slower labor force growth lowers the return on capital and interest rates as each unit of capital has fewer workers to produce a return. A deceleration in

[21] Given the tax preference of state and local debt at both the federal and state level, some of the difference in state and local government interest rates is the result of variation in state and local tax rates. Since the Illinois and Maryland state income tax rates are similar (4.95% vs. 5.75% for the highest income bracket), most of the deviation in interest rates likely reflects different risk premia.

[22] The weight on output and inflation can vary based on the policy rule. The original Taylor formulation had an equal weight of 0.5. A later formulation by Taylor (1999) had a higher weight of 1.0 on the output gap. Some models also incorporate a level of policy inertia, so that policy reacts more slowly to evolving economic conditions. See Board of Governors of the Federal Reserve System (2018).

TFP means lower productivity for each piece of capital, thus a lower return on capital and interest rates.

Meanwhile, demographic factors such as a rising share of retirees who are drawing down savings implies there is less savings available, which raises interest rates as the competition for investible dollars rises and capital spending decreases. In contrast, if global investors increase their demand for U.S. assets, the supply of investible dollars in the United States rises, increasing investment and lowering neutral interest rates.

During and in the aftermath of the Global Financial Crisis, the supply of "safe" assets declined as investors re-evaluated the riskiness of different assets. As a result, there were fewer remaining truly safe assets, which raised their prices and lowered interest rates.[23] At the same time investors' appetite for risk declined, thus the remaining safe assets such Treasuries and German Government Bunds experienced increased demand, which further lowered their interest rates. Interestingly these factors overwhelmed rising government debt levels, which compete for savings or "crowd out" private investment, and thus are expected to raise neutral interest rates. Unfortunately, the neutral rate is not observed, so policymakers and forecasters often back out the neutral interest rate from the set of economic and financial conditions (Laubach and Williams 2003).[24]

Given the estimate of three-month interest rates described above, forecasters then add a "term premium" to determine longer-term interest rates such as ten-year Treasuries.[25] The term premium is the compensation that bondholders require for the extra risk associated with holding a long-term security instead of investing in a series of shorter-term securities.

Figure 2.4 below depicts an estimate of the term premium. The graph illustrates that the term premium exhibits significant variation over both low and high frequencies. The structural increase from the late-1960s to the early-1980s coincides with the period of rising inflation. The decline that followed occurs as inflation and inflation expectations fell. Interestingly, research suggests that only one-third of the decline in term premia from 1990 to 2004 was the result of falling inflation risk premia (Kim and Wright 2005).

The recent extended period of a negative term premia is notable. This implies that investors see little risk in holding long-term bonds and in fact may prefer them to short-term bonds. That could be because long-term bonds

[23] There is an inverse relationship between the price of a bond and its interest rate.

[24] For examples of Taylor Rules with different neutral interest rates and inertia see Cohen (2017a).

[25] Once the three-month and ten-year reference rates are established, forecasters tend to use a spline methodology to fit intermediate- and long-term rates. See Fisher et al. (1995).

Fig. 2.4 Ten-year Treasury term premium. Source: Adrian et al. (2013)

are currently acting as a hedge against deflation or risks to equity markets. Unfortunately, the size and even sign of the correlation between stocks and bonds can change meaningfully over time making this relationship difficult to forecast.

One important factor driving the decline in term premia has been the expansion of the Federal Reserve's balance sheet through purchases of mostly longer-term securities (Li and Wei 2013). These purchases reduced the amount of long-term Treasury and mortgage-backed securities that the public could hold, putting downward pressure on longer-dated interest rates. A recent study finds that in early 2017 the cumulative effect of the Federal Reserve's Large Scale Asset Purchase and Maturity Extension programs resulted in a reduction in the ten-year Treasury term premium of roughly one-percentage point (Bonis et al. 2017). Given the expected reduction in the Federal Reserve's balance sheet this model suggests that, all else equal, by 2025, the term premium should rise by roughly 0.90 percentage point. Thus the term premium would stand at the levels sustained in the early- to mid-1960s but remain low relative to more recent history.

Given the difficulty of ascribing economic factors to the term premium, forecasters generally use nonstructural statistical models, which tend to have mean reverting properties in the medium-to-long term. They then adjust these estimates for factors such as the expected size of the Federal Reserve's balance and given the recent history of low inflation, the demand for Treasury securities as a possible hedge against a negative inflation shock. As a result, forecasters such as the CBO and Troika expect that while the term premium will rise from its current historically low levels, even in the medium-to-long term, the term premium will remain lower than it was before the late 1990s (Congressional Budget Office 2017a).

Forecast Errors and Adjustments

Forecasting interest rates highlights the interplay between the key variables discussed in this chapter. Forecasts of total factor productivity, labor force growth and inflation directly impact the return on capital. Meanwhile, the interaction between investment decisions which affect capital deepening, and thus overall productivity, and demographic expectations, which are used to inform labor force growth, and thus affect expected savings behavior, also play an important role in estimates of interest rates.

In the short-to-medium term, the size of the output gap is a critical input into the Taylor Rule, which drives forecasts of the inflation-adjusted interest rate. The output gap also impacts inflation, which is also a factor in the Taylor Rule. Thus, a forecast error in productivity or labor force growth cascades through estimates of inflation and interest rates. That is why a one-percentage point shift in productivity growth changes budget outcomes by a net $2.28 trillion over ten years.

Given these magnitudes, it is imperative for forecasters to constantly assess their forecast errors. Table 2.2 below illustrates the CBOs five-year forecast errors for GDP growth, inflation and interest rates in comparison to the Administration (Troika) and Blue Chip Consensus of private sector forecasters (Congressional Budget Office 2017b). From the late- 1970s/early- to mid-1980s to 2011, the CBO and Blue Chip underestimated GDP growth, while

Table 2.2 Five-year forecast errors

Mean (percentage points)	Congressional Budget Office	Administration (Troika)	Blue Chip consensus
Real GDP growth (1979–2011)	0.2	0.4	0.1
CPI inflation (1983–2011)	0.2	0.0	0.4
3-month Treasury bills (1983–2011)	1.2	0.8	1.3
10-year Treasury notes (1984–2011)	0.8	0.3	0.9

Source: Congressional Budget Office

the Administration overestimated growth.[26] Some of these errors reflect the inability to forecast cyclical turning points in the economy as well as the secular shifts in productivity growth discussed above. As a result of these biases the CBO recently changed the way it forecasts productivity growth.

Meanwhile, all forecasters have consistently overestimated interest rates. This persistent upward bias during a period of declining interest rates highlights the dilemma forecasters face. How much of your forecast error do you ascribe to temporary or permanent factors? Are your models correctly incorporating these factors? In hindsight it is easy to differentiate temporary versus permanent shifts. But in real time it is much more difficult. For example, at present, forecasters are asking the following. Is U.S. GDP growth stronger than expected because of the increase in government spending, which temporarily boosts aggregate demand, or is there evidence that the corporate tax cut is permanently boosting capital investment, which will lead to faster long-term potential growth?

Appendix

Solow growth model with Cobb-Douglas production function

$$Y = A \times L^{(1-\alpha)} \times K^{\alpha} \tag{2.1}$$

Where:

Y = Real GDP or potential output
A = Total Factor Productivity
L = Quality adjusted hours of labor
K = Quality adjusted capital intensity
α = Contribution of capital to the production process

$$L = HRS \times LQ \tag{2.2}$$

HRS = Total hours worked by labor in the economy

[26] Some of this difference reflects different baseline assumptions about federal fiscal policy. The CBO assumes no change in policy, while Troika forecasts tend to be "policy forecasts," which incorporate the estimated benefit of Administration-proposed policies into the forecast. Thus, some of the Troika forecast error may be that proposed policies are not enacted and/or that the Administration assumes that those policies will raise growth more than other forecasters. Private sector forecasts incorporate expectations of both, which policies will be enacted and their potential impact.

LQ = Labor quality

Substituting (2.2) into (2.1) and dividing by HRS:

$$Y / HRS = A \times LQ^{(1-\alpha)} \times (K / HRS)^{\alpha} \tag{2.3}$$

Y/HRS = Output per hour = Productivity

Or:

$$Y = HRS \times \text{Productivity} \tag{2.4}$$

Decomposing HRS into its pieces:

$$HRS = POP \times LFPR \times AWH \times 52 \tag{2.5}$$

POP = Population
LFPR = Labor Force Participation Rate
AWH = Average Weekly Hours per worker

Taylor Rule:

$$FF = w_p \times \text{inflation gap} + w_y \times \text{output gap} + r^* + \text{inflation} \tag{2.6}$$

Or

$$FF = w_p \times (p - p^{\text{target}}) + w_y \times ((Y - Y^{\text{potential}}) / Y^{\text{potential}}) + r^* + p. \tag{2.7}$$

Where:

FF = Federal Funds Rate
w_p = weight of Fed reaction function to inflation gap (generally 0.5 or 1)
p = inflation rate
p^{target} = inflation target (currently 2% for personal consumption expenditure inflation rate)
w_p = weight of Fed reaction function to output gap (generally 0.5 or 1)
Y = Real GDP
$Y^{\text{potential}}$ = Potential Real GDP
r^* = the neutral real interest rate

References

Aaronson, D., & Sullivan, D. (2001). Growth in worker quality. *Economic Perspectives-Federal Reserve Bank of Chicago, 25*(4), 53–74.

Aaronson, S., Cajner, T., Fallick, B., Galbis-Reig, F., Smith, C., & Wascher, W. (2014). Labor force participation: Recent developments and future prospects. *Brookings Papers on Economic Activity, 45*(2), 197–275.

Adrian, T., Crump, R. K., & Moench, E. (2013). Pricing the term structure with linear regressions. *Journal of Financial Economics, 110*(1), 110–138.

Arnold, R. (2018). *How CBO produces its 10-year economic forecast.* Congressional Budget Office Working Paper 2018-02. Retrieved from https://www.cbo.gov/system/files/115th-congress-2017-2018/workingpaper/53537-workingpaper.pdf.

Bauer, M. D., & McCarthy, E. (2015). Can we rely on market-based inflation forecasts? *FRBSF Economic Letter, 9*(2015–30).

Blau, F., & Kahn, L. (2013). Female labor supply: Why is the US falling behind? *American Economic Review, 103*(3), 251–256.

Board of Governors of the Federal Reserve System. (2018, March 8). Monetary policy principles and practice. Retrieved from https://www.federalreserve.gov/monetarypolicy/policy-rules-and-how-policymakers-use-them.htm.

Bonis, B., Ihrig, J. E., & Wei, M. (2017). *The effect of the federal reserve's securities holdings on longer-term interest rates.* Washington: Board of Governors of the Federal Reserve System. Retrieved from https://doi.org/10.17016/2380-7172.1977.

Bosler, C., Daly, M. C., Fernald, J. G., & Hobijn, B. (2016). *The outlook for US labor-quality growth.* Federal Reserve Bank of San Francisco Working Paper 2016-14. Retrieved from http://www.frbsf.org/economic-research/publications/working-papers/wp2016-14.pdf.

Brown, J. R., & Hoxby, C. M. (Eds.). (2015). *How the financial crisis and great recession affected higher education.* Chicago and London: The University of Chicago Press.

Byrne, D. M., Fernald, J. G., & Reinsdorf, M. B. (2016). Does the United States have a productivity slowdown or a measurement problem? *Brookings Papers on Economic Activity, 47*(1), 109–182.

Byrne, D. M., Oliner, S. D., & Sichel, D. E. (2018). How fast are semiconductor prices falling? *Review of Income and Wealth, 64*(3), 679–702.

Cohen, G. D. (2017a, May 30). Fed—The art of the juggle. *A Letter from America,* 9–15. Absolute Strategy Research, Retrieved from https://www.absolute-strategy.com/content/1683/ASR%20-%20A%20Letter%20from%20America%20Series.pdf.

Cohen, G. D. (2017b, May 30). What is the potential for potential growth. *A Letter from America,* 2–8. Absolute Strategy Research, Retrieved from https://www.absolute-strategy.com/content/1683/ASR%20-%20A%20Letter%20from%20America%20Series.pdf.

Congressional Budget Office. (2017a). *The budget and economic outlook: 2017 to 2027*. Washington, DC. Retrieved from https://www.cbo.gov/publication/52370.

Congressional Budget Office. (2017b). *CBO's economic forecasting record: 2017 update*. Washington, DC. Retrieved from https://www.cbo.gov/system/files?file=115th-congress-2017-2018/reports/53090-economicforecastaccuracy.pdf.

Congressional Budget Office. (2018). *How changes in economic conditions might affect the federal budget*. Washington, DC. Retrieved from https://www.cbo.gov/system/files?file=2018-06/54052-cbos-rules-thumb.pdf.

Congressional Budget Office. (2019). *Budget and economic data*. Retrieved from https://www.cbo.gov/about/products/budget-economic-data#4.

Council of Economic Advisors. (2016). *The long-term decline in prime-age male labor force participation*. Council of Economic Advisors. Retrieved from https://obamawhitehouse.archives.gov/sites/default/files/page/files/20160620_cea_primeage_male_lfp.pdf.

Detmeister, A., Lebow, D., & Peneva, E. (2016). Inflation perceptions and inflation expectations. *Feds Note*. Retrieved from https://www.federalreserve.gov/econresdata/notes/feds-notes/2016/inflation-perceptions-and-inflation-expectations-20161205.html.

Donihue, M. R., & Kitchen, J. (1999). *The Troika process: Economic models and macroeconomic policy in the USA*. Retrieved from https://www.researchgate.net/profile/John_Kitchen3/publication/43193335_The_Troika_process_Economic_models_and_macroeconomic_policy_in_the_USA/links/0c96052de6dac81059000000.pdf.

Federal Reserve Bank of Philadelphia. (n.d.). *Survey of professional forecasters*. Retrieved from https://www.philadelphiafed.org/research-and-data/real-time-center/survey-of-professional-forecasters.

Fernald, J. G. (2014). *A quarterly, utilization-adjusted series on total factor productivity*. Federal Reserve Bank of San Francisco Working Paper 2012-19. Retrieved from https://www.frbsf.org/economic-research/files/wp12-19bk.pdf.

Fernald, J. G., & Wang, B. (2015). The recent rise and fall of rapid productivity growth. *FRBSF Economic Letter, 9*(2015-04).

Fisher, M., Nychka, D., & Zervos, D. (1995). *Fitting the term structure of interest rates with smoothing splines*. Board of Governors of the Federal Reserve System, Federal Reserve System Working Paper No. 95-1. Retrieved from https://papers.ssrn.com/sol3/papers.cfm?abstract_id=6260.

Furman, J. (2015). *Productivity growth in the advanced economies: The past, the present, and lessons for the future*. Paper presented at the Peterson Institute for International Economics. Retrieved from https://obamawhitehouse.archives.gov/sites/default/files/docs/20150709_productivity_advanced_economies_piie_slides.pdf.

Gordon, R. J. (2016). *The rise and fall of American growth: The US standard of living since the Civil War*. Princeton: Princeton University Press.

Griliches, Z. (1957). Hybrid corn: An exploration in the economics of technological change. *Econometrica, 25*(4), 501–522.

Haskel, J., & Westlake, S. (2017). *Capitalism without capital: The rise of the intangible economy*. Princeton, NJ: Princeton University Press.

Haver Analytics. (2019). *United States Bureau of Labor Statistics*. Unpublished data.

Kendrick, J. W. (1961). *Productivity trends in the United States*. Princeton, NJ: Princeton University Press.

Kim, D. H., & Wright, J. H. (2005). *An arbitrage-free three-factor term structure model and the recent behavior of long-term yields and distant-horizon forward rates*. Finance and Economics Discussion Series (FEDS) Working Paper, No. 2005-33. Retrieved from https://www.federalreserve.gov/pubs/feds/2005/200533/200533pap.pdf.

Kopp, E. (2018). *Determinants of U.S. business investment*. International Monetary Fund Working Paper WP/18/139. Retrieved from https://www.imf.org/en/Publications/WP/Issues/2018/06/15/Determinants-of-U-S-45985.

Laubach, T., & Williams, J. C. (2003). Measuring the natural rate of interest. *Review of Economics and Statistics, 85*(4), 1063–1070.

Li, C., & Wei, M. (2013). Term structure modeling with supply factors and the federal reserve's large-scale asset purchase programs. *International Journal of Central Banking, 9*(1), 3–39.

Mericle, D. (2016, August 17). *US Daily: The immigration slowdown and the U.S. labor market*. Goldman Sachs Research.

Mokyr, J. (2014). The next age of invention: Technology's future is brighter than pessimists allow. *City Journal*, Winter, 14–20. Retrieved from https://www.city-journal.org/html/next-age-invention-13618.html.

Office of Management and Budget. (2019). *Analytical perspectives*. Retrieved from https://www.whitehouse.gov/omb/analytical-perspectives/.

Organisation of Economic Cooperation and Development. (2018). *Employment rate by age group*. Retrieved from https://data.oecd.org/emp/employment-rate-by-age-group.htm#indicator-chart.

Pandl, Z., & Struyven, D. (2016, April 22). US economics analyst: Historical context on the productivity slump. *Goldman Sachs Research: US Economics Analyst*.

Shackleton, R. (2018). *Estimating and projecting potential output using CBO's forecasting growth model*. Congressional Budget Office Working Paper 2018-03. Retrieved from https://www.cbo.gov/system/files/115th-congress-2017-2018/workingpaper/53558-cbosforecastinggrowthmodel-workingpaper.pdf.

Solow, R. M. (1956). A contribution to the theory of economic growth. *The Quarterly Journal of Economics, 70*(1), 65–94.

Syverson, C. (2017). Challenges to mismeasurement explanations for the US productivity slowdown. *Journal of Economic Perspectives, 31*(2), 165–186.

Taylor, J. B. (1993). *Discretion versus policy rules in practice*. Paper presented at the Carnegie-Rochester conference series on public policy.

Taylor, J. B. (1999). A historical analysis of monetary policy rules. In J. B. Taylor (Ed.), *Monetary policy rules* (pp. 319–348). Chicago: University of Chicago Press.

United States Bureau of Economic Analysis. (2018). *Fixed assets*. Retrieved from https://apps.bea.gov/iTable/index_FA.cfm.

United States Bureau of Economic Analysis. (2019a). Retrieved from https://www.bea.gov/data/gdp/gross-domestic-product.

United States Bureau of Economic Analysis. (2019b). Retrieved from https://www.bea.gov/data/personal-consumption-expenditures-price-index.

United States Bureau of Labor Statistics. (1983). Trends in multifactor productivity, 1948–81: Appendix C. *Bulletin* (2178).

United States Bureau of Labor Statistics. (2007). *Technical information about the BLS multifactor productivity measures*. Bureau of Labor Statistics Retrieved from https://www.bls.gov/mfp/mprtech.pdf.

United States Bureau of Labor Statistics. (2019a). *Economic news release*. Retrieved from https://www.bls.gov/news.release/empsit.t18.htm.

United States Bureau of Labor Statistics. (2019b, February 15). *Labor force*. Retrieved from https://www.bls.gov/cps/lfcharacteristics.htm#laborforce.

United States Bureau of Labor Statistics. (2019c). *Labor productivity and costs*. Retrieved from https://www.bls.gov/lpc/.

United States Bureau of Labor Statistics. (2019d). Retrieved from https://www.bls.gov/cpi/.

United States Census Bureau. (1975). *Historical statistics of the United States, colonial times to 1970*. Washington: U.S. Department of Commerce, Bureau of the Census.

United States Census Bureau. (2019). *Population projections*. Retrieved from https://www.census.gov/programs-surveys/popproj.html.

University of Michigan. (n.d.). *Surveys of consumers*. Retrieved from http://www.sca.isr.umich.edu/.

3

Evaluating Government Budget Forecasts

Neil R. Ericsson and Andrew B. Martinez

JEL Classifications H68 • C53

Introduction

Government budgets have attracted considerable attention, especially with federal debt limits, sequestration, and federal government shut-downs in the United States and with continuing discussions about national debt limits in

The first author is a staff economist in the Division of International Finance, Board of Governors of the Federal Reserve System, Washington, DC 20551, USA, a Research Professor of Economics, Department of Economics, The George Washington University, Washington, DC 20052, USA, and an adjunct professor at the Paul H. Nitze School of Advanced International Studies (SAIS), Johns Hopkins University, Washington, DC 20036, USA. The second author is a D.Phil. in the Department of Economics and Institute for New Economic Thinking at the Oxford Martin School, University of Oxford, Oxford, England. The views in this chapter are solely the responsibility of the authors and should not be interpreted as representing the views of the Board of Governors of the Federal Reserve System or of any other person associated with the Federal Reserve System. We are grateful to Jennifer Castle, Mike Clements, David F. Hendry, Jaime Marquez, and Dan Williams for helpful comments and discussions. All numerical results were obtained using PcGive Version 14.1, Autometrics Version 1.5g, and Ox Professional Version 7.10 in 64-bit OxMetrics Version 7.10: see Doornik and Hendry (2013) and Doornik (2009).

N. R. Ericsson (✉)
Division of International Finance, Federal Reserve Board, Washington, DC, USA
e-mail: ericsson@frb.gov; http://www.federalreserve.gov/econres/neil-r-ericsson.htm

A. B. Martinez
University of Oxford, Oxford, England
e-mail: andrew.martinez@economics.ox.ac.uk;
http://sites.google.com/site/andrewmartinezb/

D. Williams, T. Calabrese (eds.), *The Palgrave Handbook of Government Budget Forecasting*, Palgrave Studies in Public Debt, Spending, and Revenue,
https://doi.org/10.1007/978-3-030-18195-6_3

the euro area. Because future outcomes of government revenues and expenditures are unknown, their forecasts may matter in government policy. It is thus of interest to ascertain how good those forecasts are and how they might be improved. Many tools are available for forecast evaluation, including forecast comparisons, tests of predictive failure, and tests of bias and efficiency. The current chapter:

- summarizes the literature on the evaluation of forecasts of the government budget;
- systematically reviews tools for forecast evaluation, empirically illustrating each with different U.S. government agencies' one-year-ahead forecasts of the U.S. gross federal debt over 1984–2018; and
- develops a generic framework for forecast evaluation, drawing on expositions in Clements and Hendry (1998, 1999), Ericsson and Marquez (1998), Martinez (2015), and Ericsson (2017a) *inter alia*.

This chapter is organized as follows. The second section, immediately below, briefly reviews the literature on forecasts of the government budget. The third section describes the data and forecasts used in the empirical illustrations. The fourth section considers various methods for comparing alternative forecasts. The fifth section discusses different approaches to testing for forecast failure, including subsample tests, tests for bias and efficiency, and generalizations thereof. Drawing on these expositions about alternative forecasts and forecast failure, the sixth section proposes a unified approach to forecast evaluation. The seventh section draws out some implications, and the final section concludes. Although this chapter focuses on forecast evaluation *per se*, it is important to highlight that evaluation also provides a promising basis for forecast improvement. Identifying a forecast's weaknesses is key to its improvement. Typically, those weaknesses are not known *ex ante*, so a panoply of evaluation tools is desirable because different evaluation tools have varying power to detect different shortcomings in the forecasts.

Literature Review

A large body of literature evaluates government budget forecasts. The current section focuses on forecasts from U.S. federal budget agencies and includes forecasts of the budget and of other economic variables.

Existing studies can be divided into two types. The first type compares agencies' forecasts by looking at the forecast errors directly or by summarizing the forecasts' properties with statistics such as the root mean squared error (RMSE), mean absolute error (MAE), and mean absolute percent error (MAPE). The second type of study compares different forecasts through regression analysis and regression-based tests. Both types of study can provide valuable information about the forecasts.

Studies of the first type date back to at least Kamlet et al. (1987), who use measures of bias and MAPE to evaluate forecasts of economic variables from their own ARIMA models and from the Congressional Budget Office (CBO), Office of Management and Budget (OMB), and the ASA/NBER survey. McNees (1995) uses MAEs and RMSEs to assess forecasts of economic variables from the Federal Reserve Board (FRB), the CBO, the Council of Economic Advisors (CEA), and several private forecasters. Frendreis and Tatalovich (2000) examine forecast bias in CBO, OMB, and FRB forecasts of economic variables. The CBO also conducts a semi-annual comparison of the bias, MAE, and RMSE for its own economic forecasts and those of the OMB and Blue Chip Consensus; see (e.g.) CBO (2017a). Additionally, CBO (2015b) conducts a similar evaluation of revenue forecasts by the CBO and the OMB.

Studies of the second type use regressions to evaluate and compare the forecasts. For example, Howard (1987) regresses the OMB's forecast errors on the CBO's forecast errors to understand how the two forecasts are related to one another. Belongia (1988) regresses the actual growth rate of economic variables on the growth rates predicted by the CBO, CEA, and private-sector sources in order to assess which forecast outperforms the others. Cohen and Follette (2003) regress the actual budget deficit on forecasts by the OMB, CBO, and FRB in order to determine which forecast contains the most information content. Krause and Douglas (2005) run several forecast-encompassing tests on CBO, OMB, and FRB forecasts of the budget and other economic variables. In a related vein, Corder (2005) uses regression-based tests to evaluate the economic forecasts from the Social Security Administration (SSA), CBO, and OMB; and he examines whether an agency's forecasts could be improved by incorporating information from the other agencies' forecasts.

These various studies provide information on the relative performance of forecasts across different samples, variables, and metrics. Table 3.1 lists a selection of studies that have evaluated the U.S. federal budget agency forecasts.

Table 3.1 Some studies evaluating U.S. federal budget agency forecasts, as characterized by forecaster, forecast horizon, variable forecast, and forecast period

Study	Forecaster			Forecast	Variable forecast					Forecast
	CBO	OMB	Other	horizon	*B*	*Y*	Δp	*U*	*X*	period
CBO (various)	•	•	•	2, 5		•	•		•	Various
Kamlet et al. (1987)	•	•	•	1–6		•	•	•		1962–1985
Howard (1987)	•	•		1		•	•	•	•	1976–1985
Plesko (1988)	•	•		1–5	•	•				1974–1988
Belongia (1988)	•		•	1		•	•	•		1976–1987
Miller (1991)	•			1	•	•				1980–1987
Blackley and DeBoer (1993)		•		1	•	•	•	•	•	1963–1989
Auerbach (1995)		•		1	•					1982–1993
Campbell and Ghysels (1995)		•		1	•					1969–1990
McNees (1995)	•		•	1–4		•	•	•		1962–1994
Auerbach (1999)	•	•	•	1–11	•					1986–1999
Frendreis and Tatalovich (2000)	•	•	•	1		•	•	•		1962–1997
Kliesen and Thornton (2001)	•			1, 5	•					1981–2000
Lipford (2001)	•	•		1–5	•	•	•	•		1980–1999
Penner (2001, 2002)	•			1, 5	•					1980–2000
Kitchen (2003)	•	•		1–5	•					1982–2001
Cohen and Follette (2003)	•	•	•	1	•					1977–2003
Krause and Douglas (2005)	•	•	•	1	•	•	•	•		1976–2001
Corder (2005)	•	•	•	1–5		•	•	•	•	1976–2003
Krause and Douglas (2006)	•	•		1	•					1947–2001
Penner (2008)	•			1, 2, 5	•					1983–2005
Huntley and Miller (2009)	•		•	1–5		•	•	•	•	1993–2003

Kliesen and Thornton (2012)	•		•	1, 5	•					1976–2010
Krol (2014)	•	•	•	2, 5		•				1976–2008
CBO (2015b)	•	•		1–6	•	•				1982–2014
Martinez (2011, 2015)	•	•	•	1, 5	•					1984–2013
Tsuchiya (2016)	•	•	•	1–4		•			•	1984–2012
CBO (2017b)	•	•		1, 6	•				•	1985–2016
Ericsson (2017a)	•	•	•	1	•					1984–2012
Croushore and Van Norden (2017)	•		•	1	•	•		•		1967–2010
Croushore and Van Norden (2018)	•		•	1	•			•		1981–2010

Notes: "CBO (various)" denotes CBO (2002), CBO (2004), CBO (2005), CBO (2006), CBO (2007), CBO (2009), CBO (2010), CBO (2013), CBO (2015a), and CBO (2017a), which examine forecast periods from 1976 through (respectively) 2000, 2003, 2004, 2005, 2006, 2008, 2009, 2010, 2012, and 2014. "Other" forecasters include the FRB, CEA, SSA, APB, SPF, Blue Chip Consensus, the ASA/NBER survey, and various private-sector sources. Forecast horizons are in years. Variables forecast are the budget and related items (*B*), gross domestic product (*Y*), inflation (Δp), unemployment (*U*), and other economic variables (*X*).

Additional studies evaluate budget forecasts other than those by U.S. federal agencies. See in particular Williams and Calabrese (2016) for an extensive and systematic review of the literature, Frankel (2011) for cross-country comparisons, and Feenberg et al. (1989), Gentry (1989), and Sun (2008) on forecasts of U.S. state budgets.

Data

In the sections below, empirical examples illustrate different forecast evaluation methods in order to clarify how those methods are implemented and to highlight their strengths and limitations. The current section describes the forecasts in those examples, which are all of U.S. gross federal debt, and provides a graphical perspective as a prelude to those empirical illustrations.

Data Description

The variable being forecast in the empirical examples is total U.S. gross federal debt outstanding, in billions of dollars, from 1984 through 2018, as measured for fiscal years ending on September 30. The data on total U.S. gross federal debt ("DEBT") are published by the U.S. Department of the Treasury's Financial Management Service in the December issue of the *Treasury Bulletin* and in its *Monthly Treasury Statement.*

For the most part, the forecasts examined are the one-year-ahead forecasts. Those forecasts are denoted by their sources:

- the Congressional Budget Office (CBO), from its *Budget and Economic Outlook*;
- the Office of Management and Budget (OMB), from its *Budget of the United States Government*; and
- the *Analysis of the President's Budget* (APB).

The Congressional Budget Office and the Office of Management and Budget are different agencies within the U.S. federal government. The *Analysis of the President's Budget* is produced by the Congressional Budget Office, but the policy assumptions embedded in the forecasts from the *Analysis of the President's Budget* differ from those in the forecasts from the CBO's *Budget and*

Economic Outlook. Thus, these two forecasts are referred to as the "APB forecast" and the "CBO forecast," respectively, while noting that both are produced by the Congressional Budget Office. For expositional convenience, the three forecasts listed above are referred to as "agency forecasts," although only two agencies are involved. Also, the empirical illustrations below always use logs (rather than levels) of debt and its forecasts.

The three forecasts are released at the beginning of the calendar year—usually about a month apart in January, February, and March—and are of the level of the U.S. federal debt at the end of the (then) current fiscal year and of future fiscal years. Thus, the forecasts are not precisely one year ahead or an integer number of years ahead, but they will be referred to as such for ease of reference. So, the forecast horizon h is denoted $h = 1$ (denoting the end of the current fiscal year) or $h > 1$ (denoting the end of future fiscal years). See Martinez (2015, Fig. 1) for an illustrative timeline, Martinez (2011, Table 2) for specific dates, and Martinez (2015) and Ericsson (2017a) for more detailed descriptions of this measure of debt and of its forecasts.

Importantly, the forecasts are conditioned on different policy assumptions. The CBO forecast assumes that current laws will remain unchanged over the forecast horizon, whereas the OMB and APB forecasts assume that the policy changes proposed in the president's budget will be implemented. From this perspective, the forecasts represent different policy scenarios (or "projections") rather than unconditional forecasts *per se*. That said, it is still of interest to determine how useful these different forecasts are, both relatively and absolutely, and whether any individual forecast subsumes the information in the other forecasts—especially given the prominence that the forecasts play in policy formulation. With that in mind, the agencies' forecasts *are* referred to as "forecasts" below, while recognizing that some of these forecasts may also be usefully viewed as policy scenarios. This broader usage of the term "forecast" is in line with Clements and Hendry (2002, p. 2): "A forecast is any statement about the future." For more information on the forecasts' assumptions, see Martinez (2011).

Discussions of the deficit often overshadow discussions of the federal debt, since the deficit is commonly thought of as equaling the change in debt. Nonetheless, the change in debt differs from the deficit. The latter excludes certain items that are included in the change in debt, such as the Troubled Asset Relief Program (TARP) and changes in cash balances held by the Treasury. The inclusion or exclusion of such items can substantially alter the implied measure of debt; and the CBO and OMB debt forecasts and their relative merits may depend on which measure of debt is used. For example, the difference between the 2009 debt forecasts by the CBO and the OMB was largely due to differences in the agencies' forecasts of the change in financial assets and liabilities in response to the financial crisis. Equally, focusing on the deficit could miss components of debt that are important for policy. Gross federal debt *per se* may be a particularly relevant measure for policy because it is a closer measure of the debt subject to the debt ceiling than is (e.g.) debt held by the public.

Graphical Analysis

Graphs furnish a useful preamble to a more formal statistical comparison and econometric evaluation. To highlight the value of graphical analysis, the current subsection considers the actual debt, its forecasts, and the implied forecast errors in various representations that afford a variety of perspectives on the forecasts themselves. Direct visual comparison of forecasts relative to the outcomes being forecast provides an initial assessment of forecast performance. Figures 3.1 and 3.2 present a smorgasbord of such comparisons.

To start, consider a comparison of forecasts at a *given* horizon with the outcomes being forecast, as in Fig. 3.1 for the one-year-ahead forecasts. Panel A in Fig. 3.1 plots the logs of actual debt and its forecasts, showing just how much debt has grown over the sample period and indicating how the forecasts have performed. Panel B in Fig. 3.1 plots the corresponding forecast errors, where the forecast error is calculated as the log of actual debt minus the log of the forecast. The forecast errors in Panel B are thus in percent of debt, expressed as a fraction. The largest forecast errors were in 1990, 2001, 2002, 2008, 2009, 2011, and 2013. By way of interpretation, in each of these years the United States was entering a recession or expansion (as dated by the National Bureau of Economic Research), or there were major policy changes. For 2008 and 2009, some forecast errors are 4% of debt or more—very large for forecasts of a stock (debt) made within a year of its realization.

Another form of graph—the hedgehog graph—helps ascertain systematic features of the forecasts over *multiple* horizons. There are two types of hedgehog graphs: "takeoff" and "landing." Figure 3.2 presents both types of hedgehog graphs for the log of each agency's forecast, along with the log of actual debt.

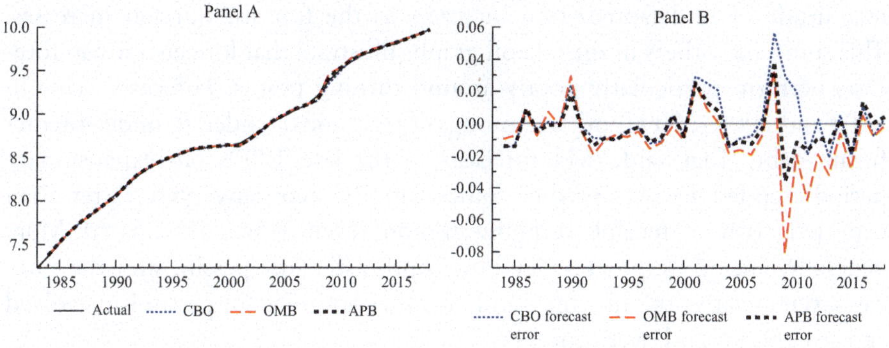

Fig. 3.1 Government agency forecasts and outcomes (in logs) and forecast errors (in percent, expressed as a fraction) of the federal debt

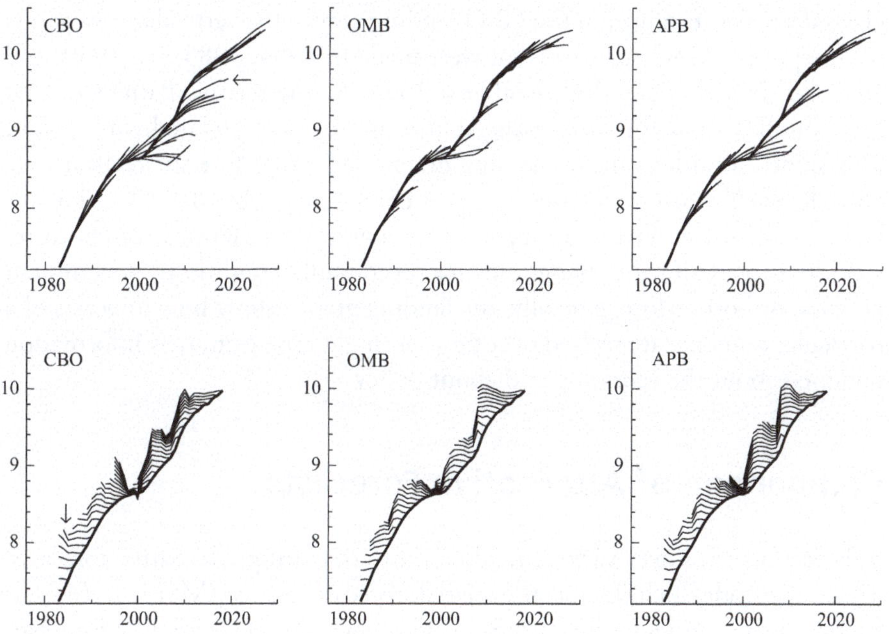

Fig. 3.2 Hedgehog graphs of U.S. government agency forecasts of the federal debt (in logs)

The top row of panels in Fig. 3.2 is hedgehog graphs of takeoff. Each "spine" on a takeoff graph plots a path of forecasts that were made on a given date, across multiple forecast horizons. For instance, in the CBO takeoff graph, the horizontal arrow points to the spine of CBO forecasts that were made in January 2009 for debt at the end of fiscal years 2009, 2010, …, 2018, and 2019. These forecasts substantially under-predict actual debt, and the magnitude of under-prediction increases as the forecast horizon increases. This spine and others in the takeoff graphs illustrate that longer-horizon forecasts perform particularly poorly around turning points. Forecasts made in 2001 and 2008–2009 (both beginnings of recessions) tended to under-predict future debt. That said, debt forecasts in the late 1990s (an expansionary period) tended to over-predict somewhat: the economy grew faster than expected, with tax receipts bringing in more revenue than anticipated. More generally, takeoff graphs portray how "optimistic" or "pessimistic" the forecasts were, relative to outcomes, and how that optimism or pessimism evolved across horizons and over time.

The bottom row of panels in Fig. 3.2 is hedgehog graphs of landing. Each spine on a landing graph plots a sequence of forecasts from the longest horizon to the shortest horizon, where the outcome being forecast occurs on a given date. For instance, in the CBO landing graph, the vertical arrow points to the spine of CBO forecasts that were made in 1984, 1985, …, 1989, and 1990 for debt at the end of fiscal year 1990. As the relative flatness of that spine implies, these forecasts changed little as they were updated year by year. This spine and others in the landing graphs show that forecast revisions are typically small, with many forecast paths being remarkably flat. Occasionally, however, forecasts have large upward or downward revisions, often corresponding to significant changes in macroeconomic conditions, government policies, or both. More generally, the landing graphs show how forecasts of a particular outcome are revised over time, as might arise from new information obtained about the economy and about policy.

Comparison of Alternative Forecasts

This section considers various methods for comparing alternative forecasts. These methods include mean squared forecast errors (MSFEs), forecast encompassing, and (closely related) the pooling and combination of forecasts.

Comparisons of RMSEs

In many frameworks, good forecasts produce small expected losses, while bad forecasts produce large expected losses. One very common loss function is squared error loss, also known as quadratic mean squared error (MSE) loss. The MSE satisfies requirements laid out by Granger (1999) that a loss function (1) has a minimum of zero for a zero forecast error, (2) is greater than zero for nonzero forecast errors, and (3) is non-decreasing as the magnitude of the error increases. Additionally, the MSE is symmetric, and its quadratic nature penalizes larger forecast errors more than proportionately.

In this vein, a forecast can be empirically evaluated by estimating its expected loss with the sample average of the loss. For the MSE, the sample average of the squared forecast errors is:

$$\text{MSE} = \frac{1}{T}\sum_{t=1}^{T}(y_t - \hat{y}_t)^2, \tag{3.1}$$

where y_t is the outcome at time t (i.e., the variable being forecast), $\hat{y}_t$ is a forecast of y_t, and the forecasts are made for T observations (y_t; $t = 1, \ldots, T$).

In practice, the square root of the MSE in Eq. (3.1) is typically reported, rather than the MSE itself, noting that the root mean squared error (RMSE) is the out-of-sample equivalent to the in-sample residual standard error. From the properties of the RMSE, a smaller value indicates a better forecast performance. Hence, it is common to compare forecast performance by comparing the RMSEs across forecasts, with smaller RMSEs indicating better performance. Granger (1989b, pp. 186–187) proposes how to test for statistically significant differences between RMSEs. Diebold and Mariano (1995), and subsequently Giacomini and White (2006), extend and generalize that approach to testing. See Clements and Hendry (1993) on limitations of the RMSE and Diebold (2015) on the use and misuse of the Diebold–Mariano test statistic.

Illustration

Table 3.2 reports the RMSEs for each of the three agencies' one-year-ahead debt forecasts. It also reports the RMSE for forecasts from a simple double-differenced device (DDD), which is a "robust" naive forecast device that is calculated as the previous year's debt plus the change in the previous year's debt; see Hendry (2006). The agency forecasts have smaller RMSEs than the naive forecast. The APB forecast has the smallest (1.39%), followed by the CBO forecast (1.68%) and the OMB forecast (2.17%). Table 3.2 also reports the RMSEs, *relative* to the RMSE of the naive forecast (the DDD forecast). Relative RMSEs are a common way of numerically comparing forecasts to a benchmark forecast.

The penultimate row in Table 3.2 reports Diebold–Mariano test statistics that compare each agency's forecast with the DDD forecast. Associated p-values are in square brackets. The RMSE of each agency's forecast is statistically significantly smaller than the RMSE for the DDD forecast at the 95% level. The final row in Table 3.2 reports the same Diebold–Mariano test statistics but with Andrews's (1991) heteroscedasticity- and autocorrelation-consistent (HAC) correction. The results are similar but at somewhat reduced significance levels.

Table 3.2 A comparison of root mean squared forecast errors

Statistic	CBO	OMB	APB	DDD
RMSE	1.68%	2.17%	1.39%	2.78%
Relative RMSE	0.60	0.78	0.50	1
Diebold–Mariano *t*-statistic	– 2.88** [0.007]	– 2.06* [0.048]	– 3.51** [0.001]	
Diebold–Mariano *t*-statistic (HAC)	– 2.70* [0.011]	– 1.68 [0.101]	– 2.99** [0.005]	

Notes: Asterisks * and ** denote statistical significance at the 5% and 1% levels, respectively, and *p*-values are in square brackets.

Forecast Encompassing

Chong and Hendry (1986) develop the concept of forecast encompassing as an approach for comparing alternative forecasts and determining whether one of them is "sufficient" in a very specific statistical sense. Importantly, having the smallest RMSE is necessary but not sufficient for a given forecast to forecast-encompass other forecasts; see Ericsson (1992). This subsection motivates forecast encompassing through the regression used to test for it. Transformations of and restrictions on that regression provide additional insight on the nature of forecast encompassing; and they also link directly to subsequent sections.

Consider two alternative forecasts $\hat{y}_t$ and $\tilde{y}_t$ of the variable y_t. Chong and Hendry (1986, Eq. (7)) propose running the following "unrestricted" regression with coefficients $\{b_1, b_2\}$ and residual e_t:

$$y_t = b_1 \hat{y}_t + b_2 \tilde{y}_t + e_t, \tag{3.2}$$

and testing $\{b_1 = 1, b_2 = 0\}$. This hypothesis holds when the first forecast $\hat{y}_t$ is an "adequate" forecast for y_t (hence $b_1 = 1$) and, given that first forecast $\hat{y}_t$, the second forecast $\tilde{y}_t$ is redundant (hence $b_2 = 0$).

In that light, Eq. (3.2) has a useful second representation. Subtracting $\hat{y}_t$ from both sides, Eq. (3.2) can be rewritten as:

$$(y_t - \hat{y}_t) = c_1 \hat{y}_t + b_2 \tilde{y}_t + e_t, \tag{3.3}$$

where the dependent variable is the first forecast's forecast error $(y_t - \hat{y}_t)$, and $c_1 = b_1 - 1$. Under the same null hypothesis as before, then $\{c_1 = 0, b_2 = 0\}$: that is, the two forecasts $\hat{y}_t$ and $\tilde{y}_t$ are uninformative in explaining the first forecast's forecast error $(y_t - \hat{y}_t)$.

Chong and Hendry (1986, Eq. (8)) also consider a restricted version of Eq. (3.3) in which $c_1 = 0$ is imposed:

$$\left(y_t - \hat{y}_t\right) = b_2 \tilde{y}_t + e_t \ . \tag{3.4}$$

Equation (3.4) is used to test whether the second forecast $\tilde{y}_t$ is informative about the first forecast's forecast error $\left(y_t - \hat{y}_t\right)$. As Chong and Hendry note, this expresses the regression in a "residual diagnostics" form, with the "residual" being the first forecast's forecast error $\left(y_t - \hat{y}_t\right)$.

Equation (3.2) has a third representation that provides yet additional insight. To obtain that representation, add $+b_2\hat{y}_t - b_2\hat{y}_t$ to the right-hand side of Eq. (3.3). Then, re-arrange terms in that equation to obtain $\hat{y}_t$ (the first forecast) and $\left(\tilde{y}_t - \hat{y}_t\right)$ (the differential of the two forecasts) as regressors:

$$\left(y_t - \hat{y}_t\right) = c_2 \hat{y}_t + b_2\left(\tilde{y}_t - \hat{y}_t\right) + e_t \ , \tag{3.5}$$

where $c_2 = c_1 + b_2 = b_1 + b_2 - 1$. Under the null hypothesis discussed above, then $\{c_2 = 0,\ b_2 = 0\}$: that is, neither the second forecast nor the differential between the two forecasts is informative in explaining the first forecast's forecast error.

In practice, unit homogeneity of the two forecasts with respect to the outcome is sometimes imposed on Eq. (3.5), as would occur if each forecast is cointegrated $(+1 : -1)$ with the outcome; see Ericsson (1993). In Eq. (3.5), that homogeneity restriction corresponds to $c_2 = 0$, resulting in:

$$\left(y_t - \hat{y}_t\right) = b_2\left(\tilde{y}_t - \hat{y}_t\right) + e_t \ . \tag{3.6}$$

Intuitively, Eq. (3.6) examines whether the *additional* information in the second forecast—as captured by the forecast differential $\left(\tilde{y}_t - \hat{y}_t\right)$—can help explain the first forecast's forecast error $\left(y_t - \hat{y}_t\right)$. Put somewhat differently, the forecast differential $\left(\tilde{y}_t - \hat{y}_t\right)$ measures the relevance of information in the second forecast that is not contained in the first forecast. Equivalently, Eq. (3.6) imposes the unit homogeneity restriction $b_1 + b_2 = 1$ on Eq. (3.2). Equation (3.6) also solves a "balance" problem in Eq. (3.4) for integrated-cointegrated forecasts and outcomes; see Ericsson (1992). Equations (3.3) and (3.5) do not impose that homogeneity restriction: they are directly equivalent to Eq. (3.2) but are written in different representations.

To summarize, in each of Eqs. (3.2)–(3.6), the basic question is whether additional information can help explain the first forecast's forecast error or, in essence, help improve the first forecast. These equations can be easily extended in useful directions to include an intercept, to reverse the forecasts' roles, and to compare more than two forecasts; see Ericsson and Marquez (1993), Marquez and Ericsson (1993), and Martinez (2015) *inter alia*. The empirical illustrations below employ these extensions, with three (rather than two) forecasts.

Illustration

To start, consider the "unrestricted" regression (3.2) as applied to actual debt and the three debt forecasts:

$$\underset{}{debt_t} = \underset{(0.032)}{-0.064} - \underset{(0.20)}{0.15} cbo_t - \underset{(0.31)}{1.02} omb_t + \underset{(0.45)}{2.17} apb_t, \qquad (3.7)$$

where estimated coefficients are reported for the intercept and $\{b_{cbo}, b_{omb}, b_{apb}\}$, which generalize $\{b_1, b_2\}$. Lowercase variables denote the logs of uppercase variables, estimated standard errors are in parentheses, and the sample period is 1984–2018.

Building on the discussion of Eq. (3.2), the forecast-encompassing hypothesis $\{b_{cbo} = 1, b_{omb} = 0, b_{apb} = 0\}$ examines whether the CBO forecast is an adequate forecast for actual debt, with the OMB and APB forecasts being redundant, given the CBO forecast. This hypothesis is strongly rejected, with an *F*-statistic of 11.5 and a *p*-value of less than 0.1%. Similar tests can be calculated for the OMB and APB forecasts. As reported in the row for "unrestricted" regressions in Table 3.3, each agency's forecasts could benefit from the other agencies' forecasts: all three statistics for the unrestricted equation reject at standard significance levels.

Next, consider the "residual diagnostic" formulation in Eq. (3.4), with the CBO's forecast error as the dependent variable and the OMB and APB forecasts as regressors:

$$(debt_t - cbo_t) = \underset{(0.044)}{-0.018} - \underset{(0.38)}{0.03} omb_t + \underset{(0.38)}{0.03} apb_t. \qquad (3.8)$$

In Eq. (3.8), the coefficients on *omb* and *apb* are jointly insignificant, with an *F*-statistic of 0.13. However, the implicit unit restriction on *cbo* is strongly rejected, with an *F*-statistic of 34.0, as is apparent from the coefficient on *cbo* in Eq. (3.7). Table 3.3 reports *F*-statistics for the residual diagnostic form for all three forecasts.

Table 3.3 Forecast-encompassing test statistics

Regression type	CBO	OMB	APB
Unrestricted [Eq. (3.2)]	11.5** [0.000] $F(3, 31)$	20.7** [0.000] $F(3, 31)$	4.01* [0.016] $F(3, 31)$
Residual diagnostic [Eq. (3.4)]	0.13 [0.880] $F(2, 32)$	4.60* [0.018] $F(2, 32)$	2.27 [0.119] $F(2, 32)$
Forecast differential [Eq. (3.6)]	13.8** [0.000] $F(2, 32)$	26.5** [0.000] $F(2, 32)$	3.61* [0.039] $F(2, 32)$

Notes: The three entries within a given block of numbers are the value of the *F*-statistic for testing the null hypothesis of forecast encompassing by the forecasting agency listed at the top of the column, the tail probability associated with that value of the test statistic (in square brackets), and the distribution under the null hypothesis, with degrees of freedom in parentheses. Asterisks * and ** denote statistical significance at the 5% and 1% levels, respectively.

Finally, consider the "forecast differential" regression in Eq. (3.6), which imposes $b_{cbo} + b_{omb} + b_{apb} = 1$ on the unrestricted formulation (3.7). With the CBO forecast error as the dependent variable, that forecast-differential regression is:

$$\left(debt_t - cbo_t\right) = \underset{(0.002)}{-\ 0.000} \underset{(0.25)}{-\ 0.61}\left(omb_t - cbo_t\right) + \underset{(0.40)}{1.66}\left(apb_t - cbo_t\right). \quad (3.9)$$

Jointly, the coefficients on both of the forecast differentials ($omb_t - cbo_t$) and ($apb_t - cbo_t$) in Eq. (3.9) are statistically highly significant, with an *F*-statistic of 13.8. The final row in Table 3.3 reports the forecast-differential form of the forecast-encompassing statistic for all three forecasts. For each forecast, its forecast error can be explained in part by the forecast differentials relative to the two other forecasts.

In summary, each agency forecast could be improved by using information in the other two forecasts, as the unrestricted form and forecast-differential form of the forecast-encompassing test statistic indicate. The residual diagnostic form of the forecast-encompassing test appears less informative here, probably because that test imposes an empirically rejectable implicit unit restriction.

Pooling and Combining Forecasts

Bates and Granger (1969) propose combining or "pooling" forecasts to improve forecast accuracy. In essence, forecast combination implies choosing nonzero values for both b_1 and b_2 in Eq. (3.2), which could be advantageous if neither forecast forecast-encompasses the other. Many options have been considered for selecting the weights b_1 and b_2 on the forecasts, including equal weights, regression-based weights, and Bayesian weights. Granger (1989a), Clemen (1989), and Timmermann (2006) review the literature on forecast combinations; Diebold (1989) discusses links and differences between forecast encompassing and forecast combination; Hendry and Clements (2004) consider the possible benefits to pooling the forecasts of differentially misspecified models; and Hansen (2007) examines estimated weights. Forecast combination has potential benefits, and also important caveats, as Hendry and Doornik (2014) discuss.

> ...A combination of forecasts can outperform, on some measures, all the individual forecasts when there are offsetting biases, offsetting breaks, or diversification across relatively uncorrelated forecasts which reduces the variance of the average. Conversely, averaging without any selection for the set of forecasts involved has obvious drawbacks: by way of analogy, with 10 glasses of pure drinking water and one of a virulent poison, it does not seem wise to mix all of these before drinking, rather than select out the glass of poison. (p. 286)

Illustration

The forecast-encompassing equations above can be interpreted as motivation for forecast combination. To illustrate, Table 3.4 augments the RMSEs in Table 3.2 with RMSEs from three pooled forecasts:

- an equally weighted average of the CBO, OMB, and APB forecasts ("Average");
- the regression-based combination of the forecasts from the unrestricted forecast-encompassing regression in Eq. (3.7) (denoted "Reg-Un"); and
- the regression-based combination of the forecasts from the forecast-differential forecast-encompassing regression in Eq. (3.9) (denoted "Reg-FD").

Both of the regression-based forecast combinations have smaller RMSEs than the APB forecast, which itself has the smallest RMSE among the individual agency forecasts. Thus, the APB forecast appears to lack some relevant infor-

Table 3.4 RMSEs of some individual and pooled forecasts

	CBO	OMB	APB	DDD	Average	Reg-Un	Reg-FD
RMSE	1.68%	2.17%	1.39%	2.78%	1.51%	1.15%	1.23%

mation that is available from the other agencies' forecasts. The forecast-encompassing statistics in the final column of Table 3.3 indicate that the CBO and OMB forecasts could improve the APB forecast. The RMSEs in Table 3.4 for the regression-based forecast combinations indicate what that improvement might be. That said, the RMSE for the APB forecast is still smaller than the RMSE for the equally weighted average of the three individual forecasts.

Forecast Failure

This section discusses different approaches to testing for forecast failure, including subsample tests, tests for bias and efficiency, and generalizations thereof. The subsequent section then develops a unified framework that includes these tests and the ones that compare alternative forecasts.

Comparisons Across Subsamples

This subsection examines how forecasts may be evaluated across subsamples, and in particular how such evaluation can help detect predictive failure. In this vein, Chow (1960) proposes comparing the in-sample performance of a given *model* with that same model's out-of-sample performance, utilizing the prediction interval of the (out-of-sample) forecasts. Numerically, Chow's test statistic compares the in-sample estimated residual variance with the out-of-sample mean squared forecast error. Chow's statistic is thus designed to detect a worsening performance of a given model in the out-of-sample period, that is, predictive failure.

Chow distinguishes his statistic from the Fisher (1922) covariance test statistic, which compares the coefficient estimates from one subsample with the coefficient estimates from another subsample. Andrews' (1993) unknown breakpoint test and Bai and Perron's (1998) multiple breakpoint test generalize Fisher's test; see also the discussion below.

As illustrated below, Chow's statistic can also be used for comparing *forecasts* across different subsamples, and not just for comparing model-based in-sample and out-of-sample results. That is, the Chow statistic can compare the performance of a *given* forecast across different subsamples. That contrasts with the Diebold–Mariano and forecast-encompassing statistics, which compare *different* forecasts across the same sample. The Chow statistic thus provides information about the forecasts that is distinct from the information in the Diebold–Mariano and forecast-encompassing statistics; see Ericsson (1992) for further discussion.

Illustration

Table 3.5 reports the RMSEs for the three agencies' forecasts over the subsamples 1984–2000 and 2001–2018, with the RMSEs for the full sample (1984–2018) given as reference. For all agencies, the RMSEs increase markedly from the first subsample to the second. The last row in Table 3.5 reports the Chow statistics for that split of the sample: the increases in RMSEs are statistically highly significant for all three agencies' forecasts.

These Chow statistics quantify what is apparent visually in Panel B of Fig. 3.1: forecast performance worsens substantially after 2000. That worsening could have resulted from any of many potential causes—for instance, greater challenges in forecasting over 2001–2018, which included two major recessions. Chow's (1960) statistic is specific to the particular sample split chosen: discussions below consider how that restriction can be relaxed.

Table 3.5 Subsample RMSEs and corresponding Chow statistics

Statistic	CBO	OMB	APB
RMSE (1984–2018)	1.68%	2.17%	1.39%
RMSE (1984–2000)	0.99%	1.17%	0.95%
RMSE (2001–2018)	2.13%	2.80%	1.71%
Chow statistic	4.63**	5.77**	3.20*
	[0.001]	[0.000]	[0.010]
	$F(18, 17)$	$F(18, 17)$	$F(18, 17)$

Notes: The three entries within a given block of numbers for the Chow statistic are the value of the statistic itself, the tail probability associated with that value of the statistic (in square brackets), and the statistic's distribution under the null hypothesis, with degrees of freedom in parentheses. Asterisks * and ** denote statistical significance at the 5% and 1% levels, respectively.

Tests of Bias and Efficiency

An additional approach for assessing forecast performance is through tests of forecast bias and efficiency. Mincer and Zarnowitz (1969, pp. 8–11) propose testing for forecast bias by regressing the forecast error on an intercept and testing whether the intercept is statistically significant. Continuing in the notation from above, that regression is:

$$(y_t - \hat{y}_t) = b_0 + e_t \ , \tag{3.10}$$

where b_0 is the intercept. A test of $b_0 = 0$ is interpretable as a test that the forecast $\hat{y}_t$ is unbiased for the variable y_t. That is, the forecast error is zero on average. For one-step-ahead forecasts, the error e_t may be serially uncorrelated, in which case a standard t- or F-statistic for $b_0 = 0$ may be appropriate. For multi-step-ahead forecasts, e_t generally will be serially correlated; hence, inference about the intercept may require accounting for that autocorrelation.

Mincer and Zarnowitz (1969, p. 11) also propose how to assess a forecast's efficiency. Their efficiency test uses a slightly more general version of Eq. (3.10) in which the coefficient on the forecast itself is estimated, rather than imposed to be unity:

$$y_t = b_0 + b_1\hat{y}_t + e_t \ , \tag{3.11}$$

where b_1 is the coefficient on $\hat{y}_t$, and $b_1 = 1$ in Eq. (3.10). Mincer and Zarnowitz (1969) interpret a test that $b_1 = 1$ as a test of the efficiency of the forecast $\hat{y}_t$ for the outcome y_t. The joint hypothesis $\{b_0 = 0, b_1 = 1\}$ of unbiasedness and efficiency is also of interest.

Equation (3.11) has a useful alternative representation. Subtracting $\hat{y}_t$ from both sides, Eq. (3.11) can be rewritten in a residual diagnostic form:

$$(y_t - \hat{y}_t) = b_0 + c_1\hat{y}_t + e_t \ , \tag{3.12}$$

where $c_1 = b_1 - 1$, as in Eq. (3.3). The hypothesis $\{b_0 = 0, c_1 = 0\}$ in Eq. (3.12) is equivalent to $\{b_0 = 0, b_1 = 1\}$ in Eq. (3.11). A large literature on forecast efficiency further develops tests of such hypotheses. For example, Patton and Timmermann (2012) extend tests of forecast efficiency to multi-horizon forecasts by examining the forecast revisions across horizons; see also Nordhaus (1987) and Coibion and Gorodnichenko (2015).

Illustration

Using the CBO forecast to illustrate, the regression in Eq. (3.10) is:

$$\left(debt_t - cbo_t\right) = \underset{(0.0029)}{+0.0014}, \tag{3.13}$$

and the regression in Eq. (3.12) is:

$$\left(debt_t - cbo_t\right) = \underset{(0.035)}{-0.014} + \underset{(0.0040)}{0.0018} cbo_t. \tag{3.14}$$

From Eq. (3.13), the CBO forecast has a numerically small bias of +0.14%, and that bias is statistically insignificant, with a p-value of 62.4%. From Eq. (3.14), the estimates of the intercept and the slope coefficient are individually numerically small and statistically insignificant. Jointly, they also appear statistically insignificant, with an F-statistic of 0.22 and a p-value of 80.3%. Table 3.6 reports tests of unbiasedness and efficiency for all three agencies' forecasts. The CBO and APB forecasts appear unbiased and efficient in Mincer and Zarnowitz's sense, whereas the OMB forecasts appear both biased and inefficient.

Table 3.6 Mincer–Zarnowitz t- and F-statistics for testing unbiasedness and efficiency

Null hypothesis	CBO	OMB	APB
Unbiasedness	0.50	-2.47^{*}	-1.38
[Eq. (3.10): $b_0 = 0$]	[0.624]	[0.018]	[0.178]
	$t(34)$	$t(34)$	$t(34)$
Efficiency	0.45	-2.06^{*}	-0.20
[Eq. (3.12): $c_1 = 0$]	[0.655]	[0.047]	[0.845]
	$t(33)$	$t(33)$	$t(33)$
Unbiasedness and efficiency	0.22	5.49^{**}	0.94
[Eq. (3.12): $b_0 = c_1 = 0$]	[0.803]	[0.009]	[0.401]
	$F(2, 33)$	$F(2, 33)$	$F(2, 33)$

Notes: The three entries within a given block of numbers are the value of the test statistic (either t or F) for testing the null hypothesis, the tail probability associated with that value of the test statistic (in square brackets), and the distribution under the null hypothesis, with degrees of freedom in parentheses. Asterisks * and ** denote statistical significance at the 5% and 1% levels, respectively.

General Tests of Forecast Bias

Mincer and Zarnowitz's (1969) test for forecast bias implicitly assumes that the bias b_0 is time-invariant; see Eq. (3.10). In practice, however, the forecast bias may vary over time. If it does, other tests may be more effective than the Mincer–Zarnowitz test at detecting that bias. Moreover, the Mincer–Zarnowitz test may lack power to detect certain forms of time-varying forecast bias, as when a positive forecast bias over part of the sample offsets a negative forecast bias elsewhere in the sample.

By allowing the intercept b_0 in Eq. (3.10) to vary freely over time, a completely general model of time-varying forecast bias may be formulated, as follows:

$$\left(y_t - \hat{y}_t\right) = \sum_{i=1}^{T} d_i I_{i,t} + e_t, \tag{3.15}$$

where $I_{i,t}$ is an impulse dummy equal to unity for $t = i$ and zero otherwise, and d_i is the coefficient on $I_{i,t}$. That is, d_i is the forecast bias in period i. Equation (3.15) can also be written with the intercept b_0 explicit:

$$\left(y_t - \hat{y}_t\right) = b_0 + \sum_{i=1}^{T} a_i I_{i,t} + e_t, \tag{3.16}$$

in which case a_i captures the deviation of the forecast bias in observation i from the average forecast bias b_0. When $a_1 = a_2 = \ldots = a_T = 0$ is imposed, Eq. (3.16) simplifies to Eq. (3.10) for Mincer and Zarnowitz's test.

For unrestricted a_i, Eq. (3.16) is not directly implementable in regression because it has T dummy coefficients for T observations. However, blocks of dummies can be included in regression, and that insight provides the basis for a technique known as impulse indicator saturation (IIS). IIS proceeds in two phases. In the first phase, Eq. (3.16) is estimated for subsets of impulse dummies and, for each subset, significant dummies are retained. In the second phase, Eq. (3.16) is re-estimated with the retained dummies from those subsets, followed by re-selection across those retained dummies. These two phases may be iterated as well. IIS has well-defined statistical properties, including (in the current context) high power to detect time-varying forecast bias.

Hendry (1999) originally proposed IIS as a procedure for testing parameter constancy. As such, IIS is a generic test for an unknown number of breaks, occurring at unknown times anywhere in the sample, with unknown duration, magnitude, and functional form. IIS is a powerful empirical tool for both evaluating and improving existing empirical models. Furthermore, many existing procedures can be interpreted as special cases of IIS in that they represent particular algorithmic implementations of IIS. Special cases include recursive estimation, rolling regression, Chow's (1960) predictive failure statistic, the unknown breakpoint tests by Andrews (1993) and Bai and Perron (1998), tests of extended constancy in Ericsson et al. (1998), tests of nonlinearity, intercept correction (in forecasting), tests of aggregation, and robust estimation.

By testing and selecting over blocks of variables, IIS implements a machine-learning algorithm that solves the problem of having more potential regressors than observations. Notably, that is a problem common to the analysis of big data. Ericsson (2017a, Sect. 4) formalizes how IIS can also be used to test for time-varying forecast bias, as in Eq. (3.16). See also Johansen and Nielsen (2009, 2016), Doornik (2009), Hendry and Doornik (2014), and Ericsson (2017a) *inter alia* for theoretical developments and empirical applications of saturation techniques.

Illustration

Again, using the CBO forecast, IIS applied to Eq. (3.16) obtains:

$$\underset{}{(debt_t - cbo_t)} = \underset{(0.0024)}{-0.0002} + \underset{(0.0144)}{0.0571}\, I_{2008,t}, \tag{3.17}$$

where $I_{2008,t}$ (the impulse indicator for 2008) is retained at a tight (1%) target size or "gauge." Thus, from Eq. (3.17), the CBO forecast appears to have a time-varying bias, with a numerically large and statistically highly significant bias of over 5% in 2008 and a near-zero and statistically insignificant bias for all other years.

Accounting for such time variation can also affect inferences about the average forecast bias, as Table 3.7 highlights. In particular, the average bias for the APB forecast is statistically significant at close to the 1% level when using IIS, but it is statistically insignificant when estimated without IIS in the Mincer–Zarnowitz framework. IIS allows detection of time-varying forecast bias, and it permits more robust and efficient estimation of time-*invariant* bias that may be present.

Table 3.7 IIS-based estimates of time-varying bias

Estimates	CBO	OMB	APB
Estimated coefficients of retained impulse indicators			
$I_{1990,t}$		+ 3.80	
$I_{2001,t}$		+ 3.41	+ 2.95
$I_{2008,t}$	+ 5.71	+ 4.21	+ 4.29
$I_{2009,t}$		− 7.18	− 3.11
$I_{2011,t}$		− 3.87	
IIS estimate of the average bias b_0 [Eq. (3.16)]	− 0.02 (0.24)	− 0.86** (0.18)	− 0.44* (0.17)
Mincer–Zarnowitz estimate of the average bias b_0 [Eq. (3.10)]	0.14 (0.29)	− 0.85* (0.34)	− 0.32 (0.23)

Notes: Estimated biases are reported as percentages. The retained impulse indicators are detected at a 1% target size. Estimated standard errors for the impulse indicators are 1.4, 1.0, and 1.0 for the CBO, OMB, and APB forecasts, respectively. Asterisks * and ** on estimated average biases denote statistical significance at the 5% and 1% levels, respectively. Estimated standard errors are in parentheses.

A Unified Approach

Impulse indicator saturation is not only a valuable tool for forecast evaluation: it also underpins a unified framework for all of the forecast evaluation procedures discussed above. This section sketches that framework.

As a preface, it is useful to note that the saturation approach discussed above applies to linear transformations of the impulse indicators, and not just to the impulse indicators themselves. Examples of such transformations include step functions, broken trends, economic variables, principal components and factors, time-dependent changes in variables' slope coefficients ("multiplicative indicator saturation"), and "designer" breaks. Ericsson (2011) proposes a systematic structure for discussing and developing such extensions.

With this in mind, consider the following equation:

$$(y_t - \hat{y}_t) = b_0 + \sum_{k=1}^{K} a_k x_{kt} + e_t, \tag{3.18}$$

which includes an intercept b_0 and K potential regressors x_{kt} with slope coefficients a_k, and K may be greater than the number of observations T. For suitable choices of b_0, a_k, x_{kt}, and K, Eq. (3.18) can be re-expressed as each of the equations above, which motivate the different forecast evaluation tools. The regressions for the forecast-encompassing, Diebold–Mariano, and efficiency test statistics can be written as Eq. (3.18) because those regressions are all based on the forecasts $\hat{y}_t$ and $\tilde{y}_t$, which can be written as $\sum_{i=1}^{T} \hat{y}_t I_{i,t}$ and $\sum_{i=1}^{T} \tilde{y}_t I_{i,t}$, that is, as linear combinations of impulse indicators. The Chow predictive failure statistic includes impulse indicators for only the out-of-sample period, simply testing their joint significance and not selecting among them; see Salkever (1976). For Mincer and Zarnowitz's test of forecast bias, the regression intercept can be written as $\sum_{i=1}^{T} 1 \cdot I_{i,t}$, which is the sum of the impulse indicators. In this way, the saturation framework provides a basis for interpreting these and many other tests for forecast evaluation.

Table 3.8 summarizes techniques for forecast evaluation, as categorized by the type of evaluation. The first category evaluates forecasts by comparing one forecast with other forecast(s): through graphical analysis, RMSEs, and forecast encompassing. The second category evaluates forecasts by their properties: across subsamples, bias, and efficiency. The third category, as represented by Eq. (3.18), includes generic procedures for evaluating forecasts and subsumes the first two categories.

Equation (3.18) emphasizes that these tools for forecast evaluation are in the spirit of Lagrange-multiplier residual-diagnostic tests; see Engle (1982, 1984). Moreover, regressors from different evaluation procedures can be included together in Eq. (3.18), allowing joint hypotheses to be tested. Also, some regressors may be "forced" to enter Eq. (3.18), as when those regressors are of central importance to the hypotheses being examined; see Martinez (2011), Hendry and Johansen (2015), and Ericsson (2017a) for examples.

Table 3.8 A summary of tools for forecast evaluation

Type of evaluation	Statistical basis	Reference
Alternative forecasts	Graphical analysis	–
	RMSEs	Granger (1989b), Diebold and Mariano (1995)
	Forecast encompassing	Chong and Hendry (1986)
Forecast failure	Graphical analysis	–
	Known subsamples	Fisher (1922)
	Unknown subsamples	Andrews (1993), Bai and Perron (1998)
	Predictive failure	Chow (1960)
	Bias	Mincer and Zarnowitz (1969)
	Efficiency	Mincer and Zarnowitz (1969)
Generic	IIS	Hendry (1999), Johansen and Nielsen (2009)
	Saturation techniques	Ericsson (2011)

Illustration

As the empirical results above with IIS found, turning points in the business cycle may give rise to large errors in forecasts of government debt—and unsurprisingly so because actual outcomes of both expenditures and revenues are liable to be affected when the economy moves from an expansion to a recession or from a recession to an expansion. Following Hendry and Johansen (2015), a natural extension of IIS in this context is to force NBER-based turning-point dummies to enter Eq. (3.16) (and hence Eq. (3.18)), with IIS applied to all remaining observations so as to capture any other important events that might bias the forecasts. That is, Eq. (3.16) becomes:

$$(y_t - \hat{y}_t) = b_0 + \sum_{i \in NBER} a_i I_{i,t} + \sum_{i \notin NBER} a_i I_{i,t} + e_t \,, \tag{3.19}$$

where *NBER* denotes the set of turning-point observations, and selection of impulse indicators is across only the second summation, that is, for $i \notin NBER$. This variation of IIS is thus "focused saturation" in that it focuses attention on certain key regressors (here, the intercept and the turning-point dummies) while still saturating the sample with impulse indicator dummies. Because the focus variables themselves are impulse indicator dummies, saturation does not need to include those particular dummies.

Applying focused saturation at a 1% target size to Eq. (3.19) with the CBO forecast obtains:

$$\left(debt_t - cbo_t\right) = \underset{(0.0017)}{-\ 0.0057} + \underset{(0.0089)}{0.0264}\ I_{2003,t} + \underset{(0.0089)}{0.0256}\ I_{2010,t} + \{NBER\}, \tag{3.20}$$

where $\{NBER\}$ denotes the inclusion of impulse indicators for 1990, 1991, 2001, 2002, 2008, and 2009, that is, the NBER-dated turning points in this sample. Positive biases of about $+2.6\%$ are detected for both 2003 and 2010, and a small statistically significant bias of about -0.6% is present for the sample as a whole.

Table 3.9 summarizes the estimated forecast biases for the three agencies. Turning points typically have numerically large and statistically significant biases, with 2008 and 2009 dominating. Additional time-dependent biases are detected for the CBO and OMB forecasts, but not for the APB forecasts. The IIS estimate of the average bias b_0 indicates relatively small, negative, but highly statistically significant time-invariant biases for all agencies. At a more

Table 3.9 Estimates of time-varying bias from focused impulse indicator saturation with NBER-based turning-point dummies

Estimates	CBO	OMB	APB
Estimated coefficients of NBER-based turning-point dummies			
$I_{1990,t}$	+ 2.95	+ 3.93	+ 2.34
$I_{1991,t}$	+ 0.37	+ 0.46	+ 0.10
$I_{2001,t}$	+ 3.51	+ 3.54	+ 3.09
$I_{2002,t}$	+ 3.10	+ 1.98	+ 1.89
$I_{2008,t}$	+ 6.25	+ 4.34	+ 4.43
$I_{2009,t}$	+ 3.52	− 7.05	− 2.98
Estimated coefficients of retained impulse indicators			
$I_{1986,t}$		+ 1.83	
$I_{1988,t}$		+ 1.72	
$I_{2003,t}$	+ 2.64		
$I_{2010,t}$	+ 2.56		
$I_{2011,t}$		− 3.74	
$I_{2013,t}$		− 2.15	
Focused IIS estimate of the average	-0.57^{**}	-0.99^{**}	-0.57^{**}
bias b_0 [Eq. (3.19)]	(0.17)	(0.16)	(0.16)

Notes: Estimated biases are reported as percentages. Estimated standard errors for impulse indicators are 0.9, 0.8, and 0.8 for the CBO, OMB, and APB forecasts, respectively. The retained impulse indicators are detected at a 1% target size. Asterisks * and ** on estimated average biases denote statistical significance at the 5% and 1% levels, respectively. Estimated standard errors are in parentheses.

general level, Eq. (3.18) and the example in Table 3.9 illustrate the flexibility of the saturation approach—how it can incorporate into the model's structure the economic, institutional, and political insights of the researcher, while allowing for detection of additional phenomena.

Remarks

This section summarizes some implications of forecast evaluation, focusing on policy, predictability, diagnostics, interpretability, and extensions.

First, because forecasts of government budgets play important roles in policy, it is valuable to ascertain how good those forecasts are, and how they might be improved. The procedures discussed above provide a host of tools for evaluating those forecasts and for seeking ways in which to improve them. For the illustration with U.S. gross federal debt, agency forecasts are relatively good during quiescent periods, but they do sometimes deviate significantly from outcomes, particularly at turning points in the business cycle. So, budget forecasts might benefit from improving forecasts of the business cycle itself.

Second, forecast evaluation with Eq. (3.18) emphasizes that evaluation focuses on the possible predictability of forecast errors—specifically, on whether or not the forecast errors have a systematic component. In essence, forecast evaluation with Eq. (3.18) examines whether the forecasts fully utilize the information in the regressors $\{x_{kt}\}$. If the forecasts do not, then improvement in the forecasts may be possible by better utilizing that information. That information may reflect information in another agency's forecasts (as with the Diebold–Mariano and forecast-encompassing statistics) or information specific to subsamples (as with the Chow statistic). Systematic forecast errors need not be persistent, as Granger (1983) highlights in his paper "Forecasting White Noise."

Third, certain challenges arise when interpreting rejection by any diagnostic statistic in forecast evaluation: the diagnostic statistic may have power to detect features other than the ones that it was designed for. Saturation-based tests in particular can detect not only time-varying forecast bias but also other forms of mis-specification, such as outliers due to heteroscedasticity and thick tails. Two items can help resolve this interpretational challenge. The structure of the retained dummies may have implications for their interpretation, as with the pattern of their estimated coefficients over time. And, outside information—such as from economic, institutional, and historical knowledge—can assist in interpreting the results, as with the dates of business-cycle turning points in the empirical illustrations above. While "rejection of the null doesn't imply the alternative," the date-specific nature of saturation procedures can aid in identifying and potentially adjusting for important sources of forecast error. See Ericsson (2017b) for further discussion.

Fourth, from a more constructive perspective, different indicators are adept at characterizing different types of bias: impulse dummies for date-specific anomalies, step dummies for level shifts, and broken trends for evolving developments. Conversely, multiple tools are needed for forecast evaluation because the nature of the forecast errors is not known *ex ante*. Transformations of the variable being forecast may also affect the interpretation of the retained indicators. For instance, an impulse dummy for a growth rate implies a level shift in the (log) level of the variable.

Finally, many extensions are of interest. For instance, Clements and Hendry (1993) analyze system-based multivariate forecasts over multiple horizons, and Hendry and Martinez (2017) further develop that framework. In a policy context, it is often valuable to evaluate the discrepancies between the paths of forecasts and to relate policy decisions to the underlying forecasts; see Martinez (2017) and Castle et al. (2017), respectively.

Conclusions

This chapter describes a spectrum of interrelated new and old techniques for evaluating forecasts in general, and forecasts of the government budget in particular. These tools permit rigorous assessment of forecasts and offer directions for their potential improvement. In so doing, these tools help glean the implications of different forecast errors over time and across forecasting techniques, and they provide a basis for understanding the sources of forecast errors.

References

Andrews, D. W. K. (1991). Heteroskedasticity and autocorrelation consistent covariance matrix estimation. *Econometrica, 59*(3), 817–858.

Andrews, D. W. K. (1993). Tests for parameter instability and structural change with unknown change point. *Econometrica, 61*(4), 821–856.

Auerbach, A. J. (1995). Tax projections and the budget: Lessons from the 1980's. *American Economic Review: Papers and Proceedings, 85*(2), 165–169.

Auerbach, A. J. (1999). On the performance and use of government revenue forecasts. *National Tax Journal, 52*(4), 767–782.

Bai, J., & Perron, P. (1998). Estimating and testing linear models with multiple structural changes. *Econometrica, 66*(1), 47–78.

Bates, J. M., & Granger, C. W. J. (1969). The combination of forecasts. *Operational Research Quarterly, 20*, 451–468.

Belongia, M. T. (1988). Are economic forecasts by government agencies biased? *Federal Reserve Bank of St. Louis Review, 70*(6), 15–23.

Blackley, P. R., & DeBoer, L. (1993). Bias in OMB's economic forecasts and budget proposals. *Public Choice, 76*(3), 215–232.

Campbell, B., & Ghysels, E. (1995). Federal budget projections: A nonparametric assessment of bias and efficiency. *Review of Economics and Statistics, 77*(1), 17–31.

Castle, J. L., Hendry, D. F., & Martinez, A. B. (2017). Evaluating forecasts, narratives and policy using a test of invariance. *Econometrics, 5*(3), 39, 1–27.

CBO. (2002). CBO's economic forecasting record: A supplement to the budget and economic outlook: Fiscal years 2003–2012. Technical Report. Washington, D.C.: Congressional Budget Office.

CBO. (2004). CBO's economic forecasting record: An evaluation of economic forecasts CBO made from January 1976 through January 2002. Technical Report. Washington, D.C.: Congressional Budget Office.

CBO. (2005). CBO's economic forecasting record: An evaluation of economic forecasts CBO made from January 1976 through January 2003. Technical Report. Washington, D.C.: Congressional Budget Office.

CBO. (2006). CBO's economic forecasting record: An evaluation of economic forecasts CBO made from January 1976 through January 2004. Technical Report. Washington, D.C.: Congressional Budget Office.

CBO. (2007). CBO's economic forecasting record: 2007 update. Publication No. 3042, Washington, D.C.: Congressional Budget Office.

CBO. (2009). CBO's economic forecasting record: 2009 update. Publication No. 3255, Washington, D.C.: Congressional Budget Office.

CBO. (2010). CBO's economic forecasting record: 2010 update. Publication No. 4138, Washington, D.C.: Congressional Budget Office.

CBO. (2013). CBO's economic forecasting record: 2013 update. Publication No. 4431, Washington, D.C.: Congressional Budget Office.

CBO. (2015a). CBO's economic forecasting record: 2015 update. Publication No. 49891, Washington, D.C.: Congressional Budget Office.

CBO. (2015b). CBO's revenue forecasting record. Publication No. 50831, Washington, D.C.: Congressional Budget Office.

CBO. (2017a). CBO's economic forecasting record: 2017 update. Publication No. 53090, Washington, D.C.: Congressional Budget Office.

CBO. (2017b). An evaluation of CBO's past outlay projections. Publication No. 53328, Washington, D.C.: Congressional Budget Office.

Chong, Y. Y., & Hendry, D. F. (1986). Econometric evaluation of linear macroeconomic models. *Review of Economic Studies, 53*(4), 671–690.

Chow, G. C. (1960). Tests of equality between sets of coefficients in two linear regressions. *Econometrica, 28*(3), 591–605.

Clemen, R. T. (1989). Combining forecasts: A review and annotated bibliography. *International Journal of Forecasting, 5*(4), 559–583.

Clements, M. P., & Hendry, D. F. (1993). On the limitations of comparing mean square forecast errors. *Journal of Forecasting, 12*(8), 617–637.

Clements, M. P., & Hendry, D. F. (1998). *Forecasting economic time series*. Cambridge: Cambridge University Press.

Clements, M. P., & Hendry, D. F. (1999). *Forecasting non-stationary economic time series*. Cambridge: MIT Press.

Clements, M. P., & Hendry, D. F. (2002). An overview of economic forecasting. In M. P. Clements, & D. F. Hendry (Eds.), *A companion to economic forecasting* (Chapter 1, pp. 1–18). Oxford: Blackwell Publishers.

Cohen, D., & Follette, G. (2003). Forecasting exogenous fiscal variables in the United States. FEDS Working Paper No. 2003–59, Board of Governors of the Federal Reserve System, Washington, D.C.

Coibion, O., & Gorodnichenko, Y. (2015). Information rigidity and the expectations formation process: A simple framework and new facts. *American Economic Review, 105*(8), 2644–2678.

Corder, J. K. (2005). Managing uncertainty: The bias and efficiency of federal macroeconomic forecasts. *Journal of Public Administration Research and Theory, 15*(1), 55–70.

Croushore, D., & Van Norden, S. (2017). Fiscal surprises at the FOMC. CIRANO Working Paper No. 2017S–09, CIRANO, Montreal, Canada.

Croushore, D., & Van Norden, S. (2018). Fiscal forecasts at the FOMC: Evidence from the Greenbooks. *Review of Economics and Statistics, 100*(5), 933–945.

Diebold, F. X. (1989). Forecast combination and encompassing: Reconciling two divergent literatures. *International Journal of Forecasting, 5*(4), 589–592.

Diebold, F. X. (2015). Comparing predictive accuracy, twenty years later: A personal perspective on the use and abuse of Diebold–Mariano tests. *Journal of Business and Economic Statistics, 33*(1), 1–9.

Diebold, F. X., & Mariano, R. S. (1995). Comparing predictive accuracy. *Journal of Business and Economic Statistics, 13*(3), 253–263.

Doornik, J. A. (2009). Autometrics. In J. L. Castle, & N. Shephard (Eds.), *The methodology and practice of econometrics: A festschrift in honour of David F. Hendry* (Chapter 4, pp. 88–121). Oxford: Oxford University Press.

Doornik, J. A., & Hendry, D. F. (2013). *PcGive 14* (3 volumes). London: Timberlake Consultants Press.

Engle, R. F. (1982). A general approach to Lagrange multiplier model diagnostics. *Journal of Econometrics, 20*(1), 83–104.

Engle, R. F. (1984). Wald, likelihood ratio, and Lagrange multiplier tests in econometrics. In Z. Griliches, & M. D. Intriligator (Eds.), *Handbook of econometrics* (Chapter 13, Vol. 2, pp. 775–826). Amsterdam: North-Holland.

Ericsson, N. R. (1992). Parameter constancy, mean square forecast errors, and measuring forecast performance: An exposition, extensions, and illustration. *Journal of Policy Modeling, 14*(4), 465–495.

Ericsson, N. R. (1993). On the limitations of comparing mean square forecast errors: Clarifications and extensions. *Journal of Forecasting, 12*(8), 644–651.

Ericsson, N. R. (2011). Justifying empirical macro-econometric evidence in practice. Invited presentation, online conference *Communications with economists: Current and future trends* commemorating the 25th anniversary of the *Journal of Economic Surveys*.

Ericsson, N. R. (2017a). How biased are U.S. government forecasts of the federal debt? *International Journal of Forecasting, 33*(2), 543–559.

Ericsson, N. R. (2017b). Interpreting estimates of forecast bias. *International Journal of Forecasting, 33*(2), 563–568.

Ericsson, N. R., Hendry, D. F., & Prestwich, K. M. (1998). The demand for broad money in the United Kingdom, 1878–1993. *Scandinavian Journal of Economics, 100*(1), 289–324.

Ericsson, N. R., & Marquez, J. (1993). Encompassing the forecasts of U.S. trade balance models. *Review of Economics and Statistics, 75*(1), 19–31.

Ericsson, N. R., & Marquez, J. (1998). A framework for economic forecasting. *Econometrics Journal, 1*(1), C228–C266.

Feenberg, D. R., Gentry, W., Gilroy, D., & Rosen, H. S. (1989). Testing the rationality of state revenue forecasts. *Review of Economics and Statistics, 71*(2), 300–308.

Fisher, R. A. (1922). The goodness of fit of regression formulae, and the distribution of regression coefficients. *Journal of the Royal Statistical Society, 85*(4), 597–612.

Frankel, J. (2011). Over-optimism in forecasts by official budget agencies and its implications. *Oxford Review of Economic Policy, 27*(4), 536–562.

Frendreis, J., & Tatalovich, R. (2000). Accuracy and bias in macroeconomic forecasting by the administration, the CBO, and the Federal Reserve Board. *Polity, 32*(4), 623–632.

Gentry, W. M. (1989). Do state revenue forecasters utilize available information? *National Tax Journal, 42*(4), 429–439.

Giacomini, R., & White, H. (2006). Tests of conditional predictive ability. *Econometrica, 74*(6), 1545–1578.

Granger, C. W. J. (1983). Forecasting white noise. In A. Zellner (Ed.), *Applied time series analysis of economic data* (pp. 308–314). Washington, D.C.: Bureau of the Census.

Granger, C. W. J. (1989a). Combining forecasts—Twenty years later. *Journal of Forecasting, 8*, 167–173.

Granger, C. W. J. (1989b). *Forecasting in business and economics* (2nd ed.). Boston, MA: Academic Press.

Granger, C. W. J. (1999). Outline of forecast theory using generalized cost functions. *Spanish Economic Review, 1*(2), 161–173.

Hansen, B. E. (2007). Least squares model averaging. *Econometrica, 75*(4), 1175–1189.

Hendry, D. F. (1999). An econometric analysis of US food expenditure, 1931–1989. In J. R. Magnus, & M. S. Morgan (Eds.), *Methodology and tacit knowledge: Two experiments in econometrics* (Chapter 17, pp. 341–361). Chichester: Wiley.

Hendry, D. F. (2006). Robustifying forecasts from equilibrium-correction systems. *Journal of Econometrics, 135*(1–2), 399–426.

Hendry, D. F., & Clements, M. P. (2004). Pooling of forecasts. *Econometrics Journal, 7*(1), 1–31.

Hendry, D. F., & Doornik, J. A. (2014). *Empirical model discovery and theory evaluation: Automatic selection methods in econometrics.* Cambridge, MA: MIT Press.

Hendry, D. F., & Johansen, S. (2015). Model discovery and Trygve Haavelmo's legacy. *Econometric Theory, 31*(1), 93–114.

Hendry, D. F., & Martinez, A. B. (2017). Evaluating multi-step system forecasts with relatively few forecast-error observations. *International Journal of Forecasting, 33*(2), 359–372.

Howard, J. A. (1987). Government economic projections: A comparison between CBO and OMB forecasts. *Public Budgeting and Finance, 7*(3), 14–25.

Huntley, J., & Miller, E. (2009). An evaluation of CBO forecasts. CBO Working Paper Series No. 2009–02, Congressional Budget Office, Washington, D.C.

Johansen, S., & Nielsen, B. (2009). An analysis of the indicator saturation estimator as a robust regression estimator. In J. L. Castle, & N. Shephard (Eds.), *The methodology and practice of econometrics: A Festschrift in honour of David F. Hendry* (Chapter 1, pp. 1–36). Oxford: Oxford University Press.

Johansen, S., & Nielsen, B. (2016). Asymptotic theory of outlier detection algorithms for linear time series regression models. *Scandinavian Journal of Statistics, 43*(2), 321–381.

Kamlet, M. S., Mowery, D. C., & Su, T.-T. (1987). Whom do you trust? An analysis of executive and congressional economic forecasts. *Journal of Policy Analysis and Management, 6*(3), 365–384.

Kitchen, J. (2003). Observed relationships between economic and technical receipts revisions in federal budget projections. *National Tax Journal, 56*(2), 337–353.

Kliesen, K. L., & Thornton, D. L. (2001). The expected federal budget surplus: How much confidence should the public and policymakers place in the projections? *Federal Reserve Bank of St. Louis Review, 83*(2), 11–24.

Kliesen, K. L., & Thornton, D. L. (2012). How good are the government's deficit and debt projections and should we care? *Federal Reserve Bank of St. Louis Review, 94*(1), 21–39.

Krause, G. A., & Douglas, J. W. (2005). Institutional design versus reputational effects on bureaucratic performance: Evidence from US government macroeconomic and fiscal projections. *Journal of Public Administration Research and Theory, 15*(2), 281–306.

Krause, G. A., & Douglas, J. W. (2006). Does agency competition improve the quality of policy analysis? Evidence from OMB and CBO fiscal projections. *Journal of Policy Analysis and Management, 25*(1), 53–74.

Krol, R. (2014). Forecast bias of government agencies. *Cato Journal, 34*(1), 99–112.

Lipford, J. W. (2001). How transparent is the US budget? *The Independent Review, 5*(4), 575–591.

Marquez, J., & Ericsson, N. R. (1993). Evaluating forecasts of the U.S. trade balance. In R. C. Bryant, P. Hooper, & C. L. Mann (Eds.), *Evaluating policy regimes: New research in empirical macroeconomics* (Chapter 14, pp. 671–732). Washington, D.C.: Brookings Institution.

Martinez, A. B. (2011). Comparing government forecasts of the United States' gross federal debt. RPF Working Paper No. 2011–002, Research Program on Forecasting, Center of Economic Research, Department of Economics, The George Washington University, Washington, D.C.

Martinez, A. B. (2015). How good are US government forecasts of the federal debt? *International Journal of Forecasting, 31*(2), 312–324.

Martinez, A. B. (2017). Testing for differences in path forecast accuracy: Forecast-error dynamics matter. Working Paper No. 17–17, Federal Reserve Bank of Cleveland, Cleveland, OH.

McNees, S. K. (1995). An assessment of the 'official' economic forecasts. *New England Economic Review,* 1995(July/August), 13–24.

Miller, S. M. (1991). Forecasting federal budget deficits: How reliable are US Congressional Budget Office projections? *Applied Economics, 23*(12), 1789–1799.

Mincer, J., & Zarnowitz, V. (1969). The evaluation of economic forecasts. In J. Mincer (Ed.), *Economic forecasts and expectations: Analyses of forecasting behavior and performance* (Chapter 1, pp. 3–46). New York: National Bureau of Economic Research.

Nordhaus, W. D. (1987). Forecasting efficiency: Concepts and applications. *Review of Economics and Statistics, 69*(4), 667–674.

Patton, A. J., & Timmermann, A. (2012). Forecast rationality tests based on multi-horizon bounds. *Journal of Business and Economic Statistics, 30*(1), 1–17.

Penner, R. G. (2001). *Errors in budget forecasting.* Washington, D.C.: Urban Institute.

Penner, R. G. (2002). Dealing with uncertain budget forecasts. *Public Budgeting and Finance, 22*(1), 1–18.

Penner, R. G. (2008). Federal revenue forecasting. In J. Sun, & T. D. Lynch (Eds.), *Government budget forecasting: Theory and practice* (Chapter 2, pp. 31–46). Boca Raton, FL: CRC Press.

Plesko, G. A. (1988). The accuracy of government forecasts and budget projections. *National Tax Journal, 41*(4), 483–501.

Salkever, D. S. (1976). The use of dummy variables to compute predictions, prediction errors, and confidence intervals. *Journal of Econometrics, 4*(4), 393–397.

Sun, J. (2008). Forecast evaluation: A case study. In J. Sun, & T. D. Lynch (Eds.), *Government budget forecasting: Theory and practice* (Chapter 10, pp. 223–240). Boca Raton, FL: CRC Press.

Timmermann, A. (2006). Forecast combinations. In G. Elliott, C. W. J. Granger, & A. Timmermann (Eds.) *Handbook of economic forecasting* (Chapter 4, Vol. 1, pp. 135–196). Amsterdam: Elsevier.

Tsuchiya, Y. (2016). Directional analysis of fiscal sustainability: Revisiting Domar's debt sustainability condition. *International Review of Economics and Finance, 41*(January), 189–201.

Williams, D. W., & Calabrese, T. D. (2016). The status of budget forecasting. *Journal of Public and Nonprofit Affairs, 2*(2), 127–160.

4

Budget Preparation and Forecasting in the Federal Republic of Germany

Dörte Busch and Wolfgang Strehl

Major Points

- Germany has long controlled its debt through a rule that excluded consideration of investment debt and permitted both federal and regional governments to take on long-term debt.
- The Maastricht Treaty led to changes in this process.
- Also, the German debt-to-GDP ratio grew to previously unseen levels during the Great Recession.
- New rules, labeled the debt brake, are aimed to control the debt-to-GDP ratio.
- These rules rely heavily on forecasting the debt consequences of the budget process.

Introduction

Among countries in the OECD, Germany is distinctive from most other countries in having a balanced budget amendment in its constitution—the so called schulden bremse, or debt brake. After describing the basic mechanics of the debt brake, we discuss its implications for forecasting public revenues and public expenditures at both the national and state (Länder) levels.

D. Busch (✉) • W. Strehl
Berlin School of Economics and Law, Berlin, Germany
e-mail: doerte.busch@hwr-berlin.de; wolfgang.strehl@hwr-berlin.de

D. Williams, T. Calabrese (eds.), *The Palgrave Handbook of Government Budget Forecasting*, Palgrave Studies in Public Debt, Spending, and Revenue,
https://doi.org/10.1007/978-3-030-18195-6_4

Public budget forecasting is conducted within the framework of a public budget process. As in the United States, where the federal government and the states are each responsible for preparing and financing their own budgets, the German Basic Law (constitution) requires the Bund (Federation) and the States (Länder) to "separately finance the expenditures resulting from the discharge of their respective responsibilities..." As in the United States, the federation and the Länder have independent roles in preparing and implementing their budgets. As such, the budget process landscape is fairly mixed between Länder and the Bund. In some Länder (such as Berlin), the budget is set for two years, while at the federal level, the budget is set for a single year. The single year horizon allows the parliament to discuss and modify budgetary priorities each year.

The German Political Structure

Germany is a federal state consisting of the national government (Federal state) and 16 Länder (states). Two features of the German federal constitution are: (1) language that obliges each of the 16 Länder to be loyal to the Federal Republic, but (2) also obliges each Länder to separately finance its own expenditures.

That means that the Länder enjoy great freedom in planning and financing their own expenditures. However, the requirement of loyalty to the Federation (which itself is embedded within European Union agreement) requires that the Länder consider fiscal impacts and budget decisions outside of or beyond the individual Länder itself.

Federalism Reforms

The current structure of German fiscal institutions reflects the passage of a series of so-called federalism reforms. The Federalism Reform II took effect in 2009. The purpose of these reforms was to establish the legal basis for a new form of cooperation between the federal level and the Länder.

In particular, the Federalism Reform II established what is now known as the schulden bremse (debt brake) for both the federal budget and the budgets of the Länder. Article 115(2) states: "Revenues and expenditures shall in principle be balanced without revenue from credits. This principle shall be satisfied when revenue obtained by the borrowing of funds does not exceed 0.35 percent in relation to the nominal gross domestic product."

The 0.35 percent figure stems from the ESM (European Stability Mechanism that comes from the Maastricht Treaty). Furthermore, Article 115 (2) required: "[D]ebits exceeding the threshold of 1.5 percent in relation to the nominal

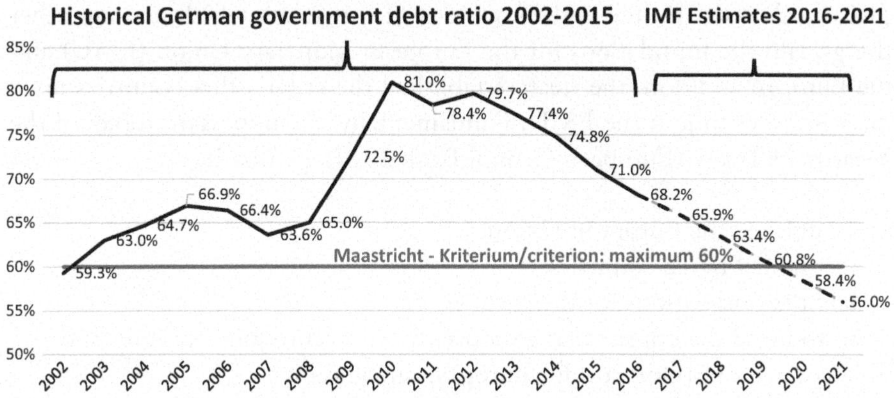

Fig. 4.1 The development of Germany's debts. Source: International Monetary Fund, World Economic Outlook Database, April 2016

gross domestic product are to be reduced in accordance with the economic cycle." This is called "the symmetric approach" because it follows the business cycle. When revenues increase, the government reserves money for the future; when revenues decline, these reserves are consumed. This is consistent with Keynesian deficit spending mechanisms.

As seen in Fig. 4.1, German public debt at all levels of government reached a height that seemed to be previously unthinkable in the mid-2000s. The public debt grew from "approximately 20% of GDP in the 1950s, 1960s and early 1970s to 69.0% in 2009" (Federal Ministry of Finance 2015).[1] This prompted concerns about fiscal stability, leading to the enactment of what amounted to a balanced budget amendment to the German constitution.

The Maastricht Treaty

Germany's membership in the EU has a significant effect on German fiscal policy.[2] EU-wide criteria are embodied in the Maastricht Treaty, signed by members in 1992. Germany and all the other EU members must conduct

[1] The debt-to-GDP ratio was 72.4 percent in 2009 according to the Maastricht definition, which is different from the way in which this ratio is calculated by the German Minister of Finance.

[2] The latest proposal from the president of the European commission would lessen the impact of EU-wide fiscal criteria on the individual members. Instead of the state-by-state threshold described above, the threshold would be EU-wide under this proposal. This would allow individual EU members to have debt greater than the individual amount defined above provided that the threshold was met on an EU-wide basis. Because EU members are independent states, however, the president of the EU commission also called for EU-wide ministers of finance and the economy to ensure that EU-wide targets would still be met.

their fiscal affairs in line with provisions of this treaty which, among other things, laid the foundations for the European Monetary Union (EMU) and the Euro. In addition, the treaty established the criteria that countries must meet in order to join the EMU. Fundamentally, the important topics of the Maastricht Treaty (European Central Bank 2017) are that it

1. established the European Union,
2. was signed by 12 countries,
3. laid the foundations for the euro,
4. introduced the criteria that countries must meet to join the euro, and
5. was a giant leap forward for European integration.

The most important and far-reaching features of the Maastricht criteria are known as the convergence criteria, the criteria that European Union members have to meet for the third stage of the EMU and make the Euro their currency.

Article 121 of the Maastricht Treaty defines the four criteria that finally established the European Community. These four criteria impose control over inflation, public debts, public deficits, exchange rate stability, and the convergence of interest rates:

1. The overall **inflation rate** should be no more than 1.5-percentage points higher than the average of the three best performing (lowest inflation) member states of the EU.
2. **Annual government deficit**: The ratio of the annual government deficit of an EU member to GDP must not be higher than 3 percent at the end of the preceding fiscal year. If a country exceeds that level, it is required to secure a level close to 3 percent. Only exceptional and temporary excesses would be granted for exceptional cases such as with natural disasters.
3. **Government debt**: The ratio of gross government debt to GDP must not exceed 60 percent at the end of the preceding fiscal year.
4. **Exchange Rate**: Applicant countries should have joined the exchange-rate-mechanism (ERM) under the European Money System (EMS) for two consecutive years and should not have any change in its currency during the period.
5. **Long-term interest rate**: The nominal long-term interest rate must not be more than two percentage points higher than it is in the three lowest inflation performing member states of the EU zone.

The reason for these criteria is to maintain price stability within the Eurozone and to make the Euro a "hard" currency.

The entry of Germany into the EU required a rebalancing of the rights and duties of the Länder and the Federal state with regard to service provisions and public financing. This rebalancing occurred in two steps: a series of reforms were enacted in 2006, and, more important for purposes of this essay, a second set of reforms (known as Federal Reforms II) focused on fiscal responsibilities in the German federal republic, which was enacted in 2009.

Federalism Reform I addressed the responsibility for different tasks, while Federalism Reform II addressed the financial linkage between the federal level and the Länder.[3] Federalism Reform II took up the matter of rebalancing the responsibilities between the Länder and the Federal state for the financing of public spending. A rebalancing was necessary because the Maastricht public debt limit criterion was defined with reference to total national and sub-national public debt.

Balanced Budget

The key change associated with Germany's entry to the EU was to limit the structural public debt of Germany to the sum of 0.35 percent of GDP at the federal level plus 0.15 percent at the state level—for a total national debt limit of 0.5 percent of German GDP. Special funds cannot exceed this limitation because all funds (established 2011 and later) are under the debt brake rule.[4]

Golden Rule

One important feature of Reform II was the replacement of the so-called golden rule with the concept of the black null (Schwarze null). The golden rule essentially permitted government borrowing for investment purposes (e.g. infrastructure). In Article 115 of the German constitution prior to Federal Reform II, public debts that were linked to the gross investment of public bodies were "not counted" as debt. In some respects, the "special treatment" of "public investment" spending is similar to the treatment of public debt incurred for the purposes of investment at the state and local level, but not the national level. Virtually, all state and local governments in the United States

[3] It is important to note that the municipalities, although mentioned in Article 28 of the Basic Law, are never counted as being part of the "the state." When Germany's Law speaks about the state, it only refers to the federal level and the Länder, not the municipalities. The Länder are responsible for maintaining responsible budget behavior among their municipalities.

[4] This limitation is fixed differently for each member state of the EU.

are subject to balanced budget rules. These rules, however, apply to the operating budget and not the capital budget, which accounts for public investment spending. There is no capital budget at the U.S. federal level due, in part, to difficulties in defining what consists of capital spending (rather than operating spending) in the national budget. Indeed, difficulty in drawing the line between "investment" and "ordinary" spending is one reason why German public debt increased under the golden rule; and that is one reason why the target of a black zero—in which the entire operating and capital budget is in balance—is carefully defined in the new version of Article 115 of the Basic Law.

Demographic changes that simultaneously increase spending on social security while constraining revenues to finance social security increase upward pressures on the national debt. But public finances can only be sustainable in the long run if the debt-to-GDP ratio is reduced on a long-term basis. The introduction of this principle replaced the "golden rule" policy set out in the old version of Article 115 of the Basic Law. This new budget rule is consistent with basic premise of the European Stability and Growth Pact, according to which EU Member States' budgets should be "close to balance or in surplus" (a medium-term budgetary objective).

The German Debt Brake

German national debt was more than 2 trillion euros as of 30 September 2013. In 2009, as part of Federalism Reform II, the German Bundestag voted to enact a debt brake (schulden bremse)—which is a balanced budget amendment—as part of the German constitution. Initially, there were constitutional concerns about not recognizing the differences between the Federal government and the states. Nevertheless, the German Bundestag and the Bundesrat (the Federal Council of Germany that represents the states, somewhat akin to the U.S. senate) decided to change Article 104 a—Article 115—the German constitutional rules governing public finances with the required majority vote.

The law divided the deficit/surplus into structural and business-cycle components. The business-cycle component is included as an exception to the debt brake rule. Article 143 of the Basic Law regulates the Länder, and does not allow them to run a structural deficit beginning in 2020. The Länder can only borrow for cash management. The federal level is allowed to run an annual deficit, but only 0.35 percent of the GDP. And the federal government is only allowed to issue debt during an economic upswing.

The method for calculating the maximum permissible net borrowing is summarized in Table 4.1, which shows the basic structure of the debt brake of the federal level in Germany. The starting point is the budget—the balance of

Table 4.1 Basic structure of the debt brake

Structural component	Maximal structural net borrowing: 0.35 percent of GDP
Balance of financial transaction	In line with the stability and Growth Pact
Cyclical component	Using EU cyclical adjustment method
(Where appropriate) Obligation to reduce borrowing from control account	Where negative threshold of 1 percent of GDP is exceeded; maximal 0.35 percent of GDP; in economic upswing only
= Maximal permissible net borrowing in general cases	
- Exception for emergency situations (requires parliamentary majority of 50 percent of the members of the Bundestag plus one, together with binding amortization plan)	
- No exceptions for new special funds	

Source: Federal Ministry of Finance (2017, p. 7, Fig. 2)

financial transactions in accordance with the Stability and Growth Pact of the EU (included in the Maastricht Treaty). First, one disaggregates the negative difference in a cyclical (business-cycle dependent) and a structural (business-cycle independent) component. If a 1-percent threshold is exceeded (meaning there is a deficit), the amount is recorded in a control account; a binding amortization plan is then used to repay that money. Therefore, any budget that is not balanced is effectively payed off. Only the federal level can make new debts—normally limited to 0.35% of the nominal GDP (Article 109 Basic Law of Germany). The Länder are not allowed to make new debts. But both can make new debts in case of emergency, such as the 2007 financial crisis or in case of a natural catastrophe, subject to the approval of the Bundestag—the German parliament—with a qualified majority (50% + 1 vote of all MPAs ["chancellor-majority"]).[5]

Nonetheless, the state does have a responsibility to enable long-term growth and sustainable economic development through the public budget. The size of the national public budget has been substantial.[6] But the change in law

[5] The problem is that old special funds can fulfill debit authorizations existing 31 December 2010, but not new ones. (Article 143d Basic Law: "debit authorisations existing on 31 December 2010 for special trusts already established shall remain untouched." Taken from the English translation of the Basic Law). New means all special funds founded when the debt brake came into effect. Old means, for example, the German Railway (Deutsche Bundesbahn [DB]), which used to be a special fund of the federal government but is now a private company. The water works, wastewater works, the transport enterprises, etc. belong to the Laender-level or the municipality-level. The municipalities can organize local services independently (Article 28 (2) Basic Law).

[6] In Germany, the federal level only had spent in 2016 30.4 billion euros for public net investment (Source: Federal Agency for Civic Education (Bundeszentrale für politische Bildung, 2016)). "Die Bruttoinvestitionen des Staates lagen (2015) bei insgesamt 65.9 Mrd. € (5.0% aller öffentlichen Ausgaben)" (English: The gross investment of the state in 2015 was 65.9 billion euros [5 percent of all public expenditures]).

expands attention from the level of public spending to both the level of spending and the size of the budget deficit/surplus. Thus, proposed as well as actual spending needs to be calibrated so as to maintain as much as possible a fiscal balance that is consistent with both the revised version of Article 115 Basic Law and the EU financial rules.

Before the passage of the Federal Reform II, the old Article 115 in the Basic Law allowed the state to follow the "golden rule," in which the state was allowed to borrow annually up to the limit of gross public investment. This constraint, however, proved to be soft mainly because the definition of what constituted public investment was unclear and subject to interpretation. As a result, the states were able to issue a significant amount of debt under the golden rule—an amount that exceeded the Maastricht Criterion. In 2010, the amount of public debt allowed under the Maastricht Criterion was completely overrun by Germany and equaled almost 81 percent of the GDP, as shown in the table above.

Currently, German governments combined are allowed to undertake new debt up to a total of 0.5 percent of the GDP—0.35 percent at the federal level and 0.15 percent by the Länder. The maximum of indebtedness is 60 percent of the GDP. But the German Länder are not allowed to run deficits from 2020 on.

In principle, under the current arrangements, the total budget of the German public sector should be sustainable. However, the state may engage in additional deficit financing in times of economic downturn, with the stipulation that the increased deficit be offset by running budget surpluses in the future following Keynesian principles (Mankiw 2018).

The key issue is that of how to know whether the economy is in a downturn or upturn. In principle, this can be determined by measuring the output gap—the difference between the production potential and the realized GDP. The challenge is that neither the production potential nor the output gap is observable quantities—so that determining whether to aim for a deficit or a surplus is not an exact exercise. One must rely on plausible forecasts from an econometric model. The inputs for such an exercise are based on information provided by the National Accounts of the Federal Statistical Office and, for the estimated years, the current overall economic forecast of the federal government for the short and medium term (Hallerberg 2010; Kastrop et al. 2012).

While the federal level is allowed to run a larger deficit and take on more debt in times of an economic downturn, these borrowings are to be paid back in times of an economic upturn. The funds for this purpose are to be gathered in a control account (cf. Section 7 of the Article 115 Act). The difference between the amount of actual net borrowing and the maximum permitted amount of debts is calculated at the end of each relevant fiscal year.

Control Account

The allowable debt threshold is 1.5 percent of the GDP. If there was any reason to incur more debt, this sum must be paid back over the business cycle. The money must be recorded in the control account and there must be an amortization plan to repay the debt.

This rule does, however, give the state the ability to act in emergency situations. An emergency situation is defined in Article 115 paragraph (2) of the Basic Law; Section 6 of the Article 115 Basic Law. Namely, in case of natural disasters or exceptional circumstances that have an extensive negative impact on the fiscal position of the Federal state, the government is allowed to undertake more debt. This decision, however, must receive the approval of a majority in parliament, and the decision to undertake more debt must be backed by a plan to repay the borrowing.

Federal Fiscal Assistance to the Länder

The provision for federal assistance to the Länder is much narrower than it was before enactment of the debt brake. Article 104b of the Basic Law still states:

1. To the extent that this Basic Law confers on it the power to legislate, the Federation may grant the *Länder* financial assistance for particularly important investments by the *Länder* and municipalities (associations of municipalities) which are necessary to
   (a) avert a disturbance of the overall economic equilibrium,
   (b) equalize differing economic capacities within the federal territory, or
   (c) promote economic growth.

The federation is also permitted to exercise an exemption to the first sentence in the above and provide financial assistance even outside its field of legislative powers in cases of natural disasters or exceptional emergency situations beyond governmental control and substantially harmful to the state's financial capacity.

The version of the Basic Law before Federal Reform 2 promoted the concept of Stability and Growth (StabG), where the state was obliged to achieve four goals[7]: price-level stability, macroeconomic equilibrium, high rate of employment, and balance in foreign trade. But, as can be seen in the footnote in the Basic Law, the provision for StabG was one of the few places that acknowledged that Germany has a market economy. The Basic Law is neutral towards the type of economic system in Germany. The StabG was created in 1967 when Germany faced the first crisis after World War II, but in 2006 it no longer seemed to be adequate for a modern economic system.

Debt Brake

The new Basic Law has been in effect since 2011. Starting in 2020 the Länder will no longer be allowed to run deficits. The federal government is allowed to grant some fiscal assistance to special Länder such as Berlin, Bremen, Saarland, Sachsen-Anhalt, and Schleswig-Holstein in the annual amount of 800 million euros till 2019 (Article 143d (2) Basic Law). In order to ensure that the federal level and the Länder will comply with the debt brake rule and all the other convergence criterions, a stability council was created.

Exceptions

The Länder are not allowed from 2020 onward to borrow funds except for use in cash management (i.e. short-term working capital bonds). One exception is a national catastrophe, which requires increased expenditures,[8] and another is to avoid any disturbance from the economic equilibrium.[9] But if the Länder borrow funds, they must establish an amortization plan. Otherwise, the Stability Council can determine such a repayment plan, and the state who is concerned has no vote in their own case.

---

[7] The federal and state government must comply with the requirements of macroeconomic balance in their economic and fiscal policy measures. The measures must be taken in a way that, within a market economy, they contribute at the same time to the stability of the price level, a high level of employment, and a balance between the external environment and steady adequate economic growth.

[8] For example, the financial crisis that occurred in 2008.

[9] There is a law in effect since 1967 that focuses on four targets (law of stability and promoting economic growth). But nobody really knows what an "economic equilibrium" is.

Stability Council

The Stability Council was founded in 2010, replacing the Financial Planning Council. The Council is meant to represent the interests of the Federation and the Länder. The role of the Stability Council[10] is to monitor the budgets of the federal and state governments and, if necessary, initiate restructuring proceedings. Its main task is to oversee budgetary policy based on information from forecasts and estimates of the German business cycles for both the federal government and the Länder. Members of the Stability Council are all Ministers/Senators of Financial Affairs of the Länder and federal Ministers of Finance and Economics.

Revenue Estimation

If one read German textbooks about Public Finance, one will rarely find much, if any, discussion about the estimates of revenues (Jochimsen and Lehmann 2017).[11] However, achieving budget balance almost inevitably requires estimating the amount of revenue available for public spending.

Figure 4.2[12] shows the budget for Germany in 2018. It shows that spending for the Ministry for Labor and Social affairs accounts for the largest share of public spending—more than one-third of the budget.

Overall, the budget is about 329 billion euros. That is the sum that the advisory board for tax estimation forecasts for tax revenue of the Federal Republic of Germany that will balance the budget based on expected macroeconomic performance of the German economy.

Members of this advisory board are "the Federal Ministry of Finance, which has lead responsibility, other members include the Federal Ministry of Economics and Technology, five economic research institutes, the Federal

[10] Established in 2010 by law (following the Financial Planning Council (Finanzplanungsrat)) concluded in 2009 by the Bundestag and the Bundesrat based on Article 109a Basic Law. According to §51 (1) HGRG (Law on Budgetary Procedures) (*Grundgesetz für die Bundesrepublik Deutschland* 2017; *Section 51—Consultation to coordinate the basic assumptions underlying budgetary and financial planning; observance of budgetary discipline within the framework of European Economic and Monetary Union: Act on the Principles of Federation and Länder Budgetary Law (Budgetary Principles Act)*, 1969), the Stability Council has to debate the macroeconomic and financial framework/basic data by establishing the budgets of the federal and the Länder level. It is founded by law (*Artikel 249 der Verordnung vom 31. August 2015 (BGBl. I S. 1474) geändert worden ist" Stand: Zuletzt geändert durch Art. 249 V v. 31.8.2015 I 1474/Article 249 of the Ordinance of 31 August 2015 (Federal Law Gazette I p. 1474) Status: Last modified by Art. 249 V v. 31.8.2015 I 1474*, 2015).

[11] The German problem is mostly the influence of politicians on these forecasts.

[12] Total budget 2017: 329.1/2018: 343.6 (billion euros) = +4.4 percent.

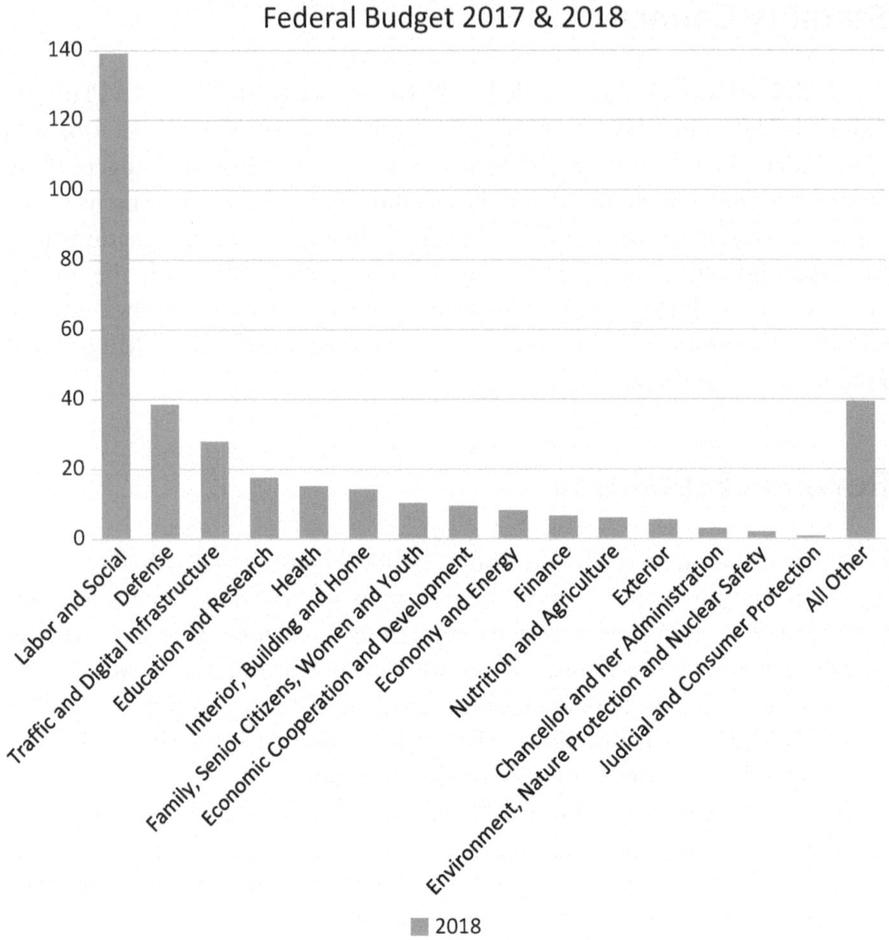

Fig. 4.2 The budget of Germany

Statistical Office, the Bundesbank, the German Council of Economic Experts, the finance ministries of the Länder and the Federation of German Local Authority Associations" (Federal Ministry of Finance 2017). The advisory board meets twice a year in May and in November at different locations in Germany. The advisory board is making tax estimations for both levels: the federal and the Länder. That is why there are taxes that belong to either one of the levels, and there are so-called combined Federal and Länder taxes. That makes it difficult but not impossible for the advisory board to forecast for the Länder.

The Advisory Board was first convened in 1955 to attempt to forecast tax revenues. Individual members are drawn from the Ministry of Finance that has the responsibility for that advisory council, plus additional members from the Ministry of Economic and Technology, Economic Research Institutes (five in number), the Federal Statistical Office, the Federal German Bank, the German Council of Economic Experts[13] (called the "Wise Men"), the Ministries of the Länder, and the Federation of German Local Authority Associations. The Advisory Council is charged with being independent of any political influence and impartial.

Each member of the advisory board comes to each meeting prepared with his or her own proposed estimates using a variety of different methods—as mentioned in Jochimsen and Lehmann (2017) and the methods described there.[14] These estimates are the base of the discussion during the meetings, where each estimate is discussed until a consensus is reached. "Based on the estimates for the individual taxes, the revenue expected to accrue to the German federal government, the Länder, the local authorities and the EU is extrapolated" (Federal Ministry of Finance 2017).

An important part of this process is transparency. After the meetings all the results are required to be aired by German News Corporations. The Federal Ministry of Finance also presents the results in a press release. Finally, a new way to spread this estimation is that all of the results are put online.[15]

The "national" estimates from the advisory council are "regionalized," which refers to the process of dividing the tax estimation to the different Länder in Germany. The process of regionalization is coordinated by the Finance Ministry of Baden-Württemberg with input from the Länder themselves.

Figure 4.3 shows the revenue forecasts. In the columns are shown the tax estimation results for November 2016 and May 2017. The estimation in the spring is dated for the budgetary year and the financial planning period.

In November, the tax revenue forecast is made for the medium term (the actual year and the next four). This estimate includes the final figures for expected tax revenues that are the basis for the next year's budget. The forecast is used as a base for the forthcoming year and the financial planning.

[13] The Sachverständigenrat—expert advisory board—which is popularly referred to as the "five wise men" (even though there is currently one woman on the board) is a long-standing institution, which is based on a law, "Law on the formation of an Expert Council for the Evaluation of macroeconomic development," from 1963.

[14] This chapter principally discusses the forecasting environment and not forecasting methods. According to the Federal Ministry of Finance (2017), "The Working Party bases its estimates on key macroeconomic data supplied by the German federal government and coordinated between the various ministries under the aegis of the Federal Ministry of Economics and Technology."

[15] This process addresses the risk of political bias in forecasting but cannot guarantee the absence of politically motivated bias.

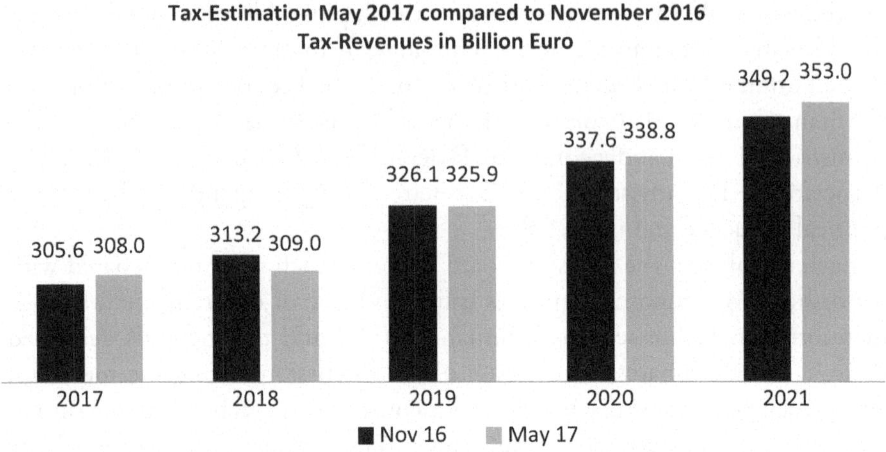

Fig. 4.3 Revenue estimation, Federal Ministry of Finance (11 May 2017)

The Financial Planning

The concept of Financial Planning is defined in one of the most interesting laws in Germany, the Law of Stability and Growth (StabG from 1967), which was enacted at the time of the first crisis of the German economy after World War II and which was inspired by Keynesian Theory. Under the terms of the StabG, German budgetary policy is formulated in a five-year financial plan (§9.1 StabG, §14 StabG) that is based on forecasts of macroeconomic performance.

The procedures for formulating the five-year plan are extensively presented in § 5 (3) HGrG.[16] Both the federal government and the Länder are required to submit the plan along with the accompanying proposed budgets to the Bundestag (parliament). Normally, this plan represents the investments planned by the government.

The medium-term financial planning covers five years. The first year shows the previous year's forecast compared to actual results, the current year's actual results, and the forthcoming three years (all in all—five years). The plan is based on the November tax estimation.

The Financial Plan proposed by the Advisory Board is not politically binding. The actual five-year financial plan is decided by the German parliament (Bundestag), although the plan is provided as information to the parliament.

---

[16] HGrG, Haushaltsgrundsätzegesetz.

Financial Planning at the federal level and the Länder (including the municipalities) must be coordinated. That is the task of the Stability Council. That Council discusses all the Financial Planning taking into account standard macroeconomic theories as interpreted by the national and financial bodies. The deliberations of the Council take into account all financial obligations of the Federal Republic of Germany to the EU. This process is framed by Articles 121, 126, and 136 of the Treaty on the Functioning of the European Union (2012), with respect to the financial discipline and the macroeconomic balance. For Germany, it is also regulated in § 51 (1) HGrG (law on budgetary procedures, where the Financial Planning Council and so the Stability Council are defined).

Budget Planning

The most important role of any budget is to identify the money needed for expenditures for the forthcoming period. For the public sector, the guidelines for preparing the budget are contained in the Federal Budget Code (BHO) in § 2 of the Basic Rules for the Budget (HGrG) and in Article 104–Article 115 of the Basic Law (GG). In principle, the budget should contain the funds needed to provide the public services approved by the legislature, along with an explanation of the need for such public services. Because of the debt-brake rule, the budget must fund public services while also maintaining budget balance.

The process of preparing the budget begins in the spring of the year. The Ministry of Finance sends budget instructions to the different ministries (top down) and waits for their response (bottom up). Each Ministry responds to these instructions with its own proposals that are either approved by the Ministry of Finance or subject to further talks between the relevant ministry and the Ministry of Finance. The final budget is decided upon by the Cabinet and then be subject to intensive debate in the parliament. The final budgetary decision rests with the parliament to decide upon the budget. Debate about the budget is always the starting point for a deep and wide discussion about the policy of the government.

The budget includes all regular revenues and expenditures, the job chart (staff appointments), and all the commitment appropriations. Finally, the budget shows all the policy decisions planned for the forthcoming year. In addition, all of the political jurisdictions (e.g. not just the federal state) have their own budgets, and these are combined to a final sum of total (e.g. national plus sub-national) public revenue and expenditure.[17] The Ministry of Finance must comply with some principles, all written down in the Basic Law of Germany, in the HGrG, and are repeated again in the federal BHO, of how to execute the federal budget. All 16 Länder have equal principles in their LHOs (state budget codes).

The budget only provides for approved public revenues and the expenditures for its period of enactment. Thus, for example, even if a particular subsidy is included in the current budget, there is no implied guarantee that the subsidy will be available in future years. The budget is part of the public law (it must be adopted by law or by statute by the legislative and becomes legally binding as an approved budget, approved by the parliament). But it only gives the government the right to spend money for special purposes if and only if the revenues are included in the budget.

Conclusion

This chapter has summarized the German experience with forecasting and budget balancing. The process has changed significantly over the past decades, due in part to perceived excessive debt levels and also European financial integration. EU requirements lead to a coordination between federal and subnational governments in planning, implementing, and controlling budgets that is unseen in the United States. Given the importance of strict budget balance in Germany now, forecasting is a critical task that will remain central to what German governments are able to undertake and accomplish.

References

Artikel 249 der Verordnung vom 31. August 2015 (BGBl. I S. 1474) geändert worden ist" Stand: Zuletzt geändert durch Art. 249 V v. 31.8.2015 I 1474/Article 249 of the Ordinance of 31 August 2015 (Federal Law Gazette I p. 1474) Status: Last modified by Art. 249 V v. 31.8.2015 I 1474. (2015). Retrieved from https://www.gesetze-im-internet.de/sachvratg/BJNR006850963.html.

Bundesver-fassungsgericht, verdict March 26th 1957—2 BvG 1/55/Federal Constitutional Court, verdict March 26th 1957—2 BvG 1/55, DFR—BVerfGE 6, 309 (Bundesverfassungsgericht/ Federal Constitutional Court 1957).

[17] Although there are 16 Länder and one federal level, all of them are independent in planning their respective budgets. Municipalities are included in this sum as well.

European Central Bank. (2017, February 17). *Five things you need to know about the Maastricht Treaty*. Retrieved from https://www.ecb.europa.eu/explainers/tell-me-more/html/25_years_maastricht.en.html.

Federal Agency for Civic Education (Bundeszentrale für politische Bildung). (2016). *öffentliche Investitionen/Public investment*. Retrieved from http://www.bpb.de/nachschlagen/lexika/lexikon-der-wirtschaft/20247/oeffentliche-investitionen.

Federal Ministry of Finance. (2015). *Germany's federal debt brake*. Berlin: Federal Ministry of Finance. Retrieved from http://www.bundesfinanzministerium.de/Content/EN/Standardartikel/Topics/Fiscal_policy/Articles/2015-12-09-german-federal-debt-brake.pdf?__blob=publicationFile&v=3.

Federal Ministry of Finance. (2017, October 11). *Working party on tax revenue estimates*. Retrieved from https://www.bundesfinanzministerium.de/Content/EN/Standardartikel/Topics/Taxation/Articles/working-party-on-tax-revenue-estimates.html.

Gesetz zur Förderung der Stabilität und des Wachstums der Wirtschaft vom 8. Juni 1967 (BGBl. I S. 582), das zuletzt durch Artikel 267 der Verordnung vom 31. August 2015 (BGBl. I S. 1474) § 1 geändert worden ist. (2015). Retrieved from https://www.gesetze-im-internet.de/stabg/BJNR005820967.html.

Grundgesetz für die Bundesrepublik Deutschland. (2017). Retrieved from http://www.gesetze-im-internet.de/gg/GG.pdf.

Hallerberg, M. (2010). The German debt brake in comparative perspective—When do fiscal rules succeed? In C. Kastrop, G. Meister-Scheufelen, & M. Sudhof (Eds.), *Die neuen Schuldenregeln im Grundgesetz: zur Fortentwicklung der bundesstaatlichen Finanzbeziehungen/The new debt rules in the Basic Law: To develop the federal financial relations* (1. Aufl. ed., pp. 287–303). Berlin: BWV, Berliner Wissenschafts-Verlag.

Jochimsen, B., & Lehmann, R. (2017). On the political economy of national tax revenue forecasts: Evidence from OECD countries. *Public Choice, 170*(3), 211–230. https://doi.org/10.1007/s11127-016-0391-y.

Kastrop, C., Meister-Scheufelen, G., Sudhof, M., & Ebert, W. (2012). Konzept und Herausforderungen der Schuldenbremse/Concept and challenges of the debt brake. *Aus Politik und Zeitgeschichte, 13*, 16–22.

Mankiw, N. G. (2018). *Macroeconomics* (10th ed.). New York, NY: Worth Publishers.

Section 51—Consultation to coordinate the basic assumptions underlying budgetary and financial planning; observance of budgetary discipline within the framework of European Economic and Monetary Union: Act on the Principles of Federation and Länder Budgetary Law (Budgetary Principles Act). (1969). Retrieved from https://www.bundesfinanzministerium.de/Content/EN/Standardartikel/Ministry/Laws/1969-08-19-budgetary-principles-act.pdf.

5

Revenue Forecasting in Low-Income and Developing Countries: Biases and Potential Remedies

Marco Cangiano and Rahul Pathak

Major Points

- This study constructed a new dataset of ex-ante revenue forecasts and ex-post realizations for 26 countries using the information from the Public Expenditure and Financial Accountability (PEFA) reports.
- The study reviews the experience of two institutional innovations for improving the budget process and forecasts:
  - Semi-autonomous revenue authorities (SARAs) and
  - Independent fiscal councils.
- The evidence on the effectiveness of the former in increasing tax-to-GDP ratios remains mixed, whereas the latter is a relatively new institution whose future trajectory is still unknown in most of the low-income countries.

M. Cangiano (✉)
Overseas Development Institute (ODI), London, UK

Better Than Cash Alliance, New York, NY, USA

R. Pathak
Marxe School of Public and International Affairs, Baruch College, New York, NY, USA
e-mail: Rahul.Pathak@baruch.cuny.edu

D. Williams, T. Calabrese (eds.), *The Palgrave Handbook of Government Budget Forecasting*, Palgrave Studies in Public Debt, Spending, and Revenue,
https://doi.org/10.1007/978-3-030-18195-6_5

Introduction

With the 2017 Financing for Development conference, there has been a resurgence of attention on domestic revenue mobilization.[1] This emphasis has been iterated one year later at the first global conference[2] organized by the Platform on Collaboration on Tax (PCT).[3] The objective is to "increase the effectiveness of … tax systems to generate the domestic resources needed to meet the Sustainable Development Goals (SDGs) and promote inclusive economic growth." In spite of these efforts, there has been relatively little attention on revenue forecasting and, in particular, on the upward or downward bias that could be introduced in formulating the annual budgets, medium-term budgetary frameworks, and MTRSs.[4] The scarce literature available has, however, pointed to such bias in low-income countries (Danninger et al. 2005); in the context of the European Excessive Deficit Procedure (Pina and Venes 2011); and among OECD countries (Jochimsen and Lehmann 2017).

Revenue forecasting and its inherent potential bias has become increasingly relevant in the last couple of decades as a systematic increase in spending has not been matched by the capacity to raise taxes (Alesina and Passalacqua 2015). This has led to what the literature has identified as "expenditure drift" or "deficit bias." There have been multiple explanations of such drift or bias, ranging from Wagner's law,[5] to asymmetry of information, common pool resources,[6] and time inconsistency.[7] One of the devices that has been most effectively used

[1] *Financing for Development*, Addis Ababa, July 13–15, 2017. Countries agreed to an array of measures aimed at widening the revenue base, improving tax collection, and combating tax evasion and illicit financial flows.

[2] First Global Conference of the Platform for Collaboration on Tax—Taxation and the Sustainable Development Goals, New York, February 14–16, 2018.

[3] The PCT is a 2016 joint initiative of the International Monetary Fund (IMF), Organization for Economic Co-operation and Development (OECD), United nations, and the World to strengthen collaboration on DRM. The four PCT partners support country efforts through policy dialogue and capacity building. In this context, the PCT has developed the Medium-Term Revenue Strategy (MTRS) as an approach for coordinated and sustained support to comprehensive country-led tax reform.

[4] The concept of the MTRS was introduced in *Enhancing the Effectiveness of External Support in Building Tax Capacity in Developing Countries*, Platform for Collaboration on Tax (IMF, OECD, UN, and WB), July 2016, available at https://www.imf.org/external/np/pp/eng/2016/072016.pdf. A further concept note develops its main components and illustrates the nature of an MTRS document in an appendix. In all this documentation, the need to strengthen revenue forecasting and address potential biases is hardly mentioned.

[5] Named after the German economist Adolph Wagner, the principle states that as nations develop their public sector grow to provide for welfare functions, social activities, and protective actions.

[6] These are resources such as budgets which can be subject to overuse when different groups have conflicting interests, giving rise to what has become known as the "tragedy of the commons," whereby individual pursuing their self-interest behave contrary to the common good (Weingast et al. 1981).

[7] Time inconsistency refers to the changing of decision makers' preferences over time (Kydland and Prescott 1977). The deficit (and debt) bias has also been analyzed and explained in a game theory frame-

to engineer such expenditure drift has been a systematic bias in ex-ante overestimation of revenues. The trick, possibly one of the oldest in the business, works as follows: budgets are in the end an act of parliament providing an authorization to spend (or entering into an obligation or commitment to spend). Such an authority is predicated on an accepted estimate for revenue along, at times, with a legal binding ceiling on borrowing. But whereas the authorization to spend and borrowing ceilings are subject to explicit legislative approval, revenue estimates are typically not. Hence, being overoptimistic (as well as overly pessimistic) on the amount of revenue that will be collected in the upcoming budget year provides more (or less) room for spending. There seems thus to be a political incentive in interfering with the revenue forecasting process in order to manipulate the amount of ex-ante available fiscal space.[8] This is coherent with the long-stated tradition of budgeting as a political game dating back to Wildavsky (1975) and reiterated in more recent times by Schick (2013) and Rubin (2018), among others. One obvious parallel, yet closely related phenomenon is the political manipulation of the forecast of the underlying real economy (e.g., the gross domestic product) on which budget estimates are developed, as discussed in Jonung and Larch (2006). This has reinforced the case for independent fiscal authorities either responsible for a macro-fiscal forecast or tasked with validating governments' forecasts.

The purpose of this chapter is not to review prevailing revenue forecasting practices and processes in low-income countries—Kyobe and Danninger (2005) did that and is a work that begs to be updated—but rather to verify the existence of forecast bias. In so doing, data collection has proved to be a challenge as there is no systematic repository for ex-ante revenue estimates and their ex-post realization. A new data set covering 26 low-income countries is developed by extracting the relevant information from Public Expenditure Financial Accountability (PEFA) reports—not to be confused by PEFA score, as discussed later in this chapter.[9] The presence of bias is simply defined as a systematic discrepancy between ex-ante revenue estimates presented as part of the annual budget documents and their ex-post realization. The chapter takes, therefore, an agnostic view of whether such a bias is due to

work such as the prisoners' dilemma (Hallerberg and von Hagen 1997) or principal-agent relationships (Dixit et al. 1997).

[8] Fiscal space is defined as the "room in a government's budget that allows it to provide resources for a desired purpose without jeopardizing the sustainability of its financial position or the stability of the economy." See Heller (2005).

[9] PEFA is a program that was founded in 2001 as a multi-donor partnership between the European Commission, the IMF, the World Bank, the French Ministry of Foreign and European Affairs, the Norwegian Ministry of Foreign Affairs, the Swiss State Secretariat for Economic Affairs, and the U.K.'s Department for International Development. See www.pefa.org.

political interference,[10] methodological flaws, or other factors. Still, the matter is of the utmost importance as debt ratios appear to be on the rise again in low-income countries that were granted debt relief under the Heavily Indebted Poor Countries (HIPC)[11] initiative.[12] This by itself may trigger an upward bias since donors and international institutions' conditionality may have added pressure on countries to increase their ex-ante DRM efforts so as to increase their tax-to-GDP ratio. The data seems to support the presence of an upward bias whereby ex-post revenue realization seems to fall short of ex-ante revenue estimates. With the caveat that the sample is not particularly large, the issue is then how to address such bias.

The chapter then analyzes two fiscal institutions[13]: semi-autonomous revenue authorities (SARAs) and independent fiscal agencies or councils. While SARAs have been established to enhance revenue collection efficiency so as to contribute to increasing tax-to-GDP ratio, in most cases their mandate did not explicitly task them with revenue forecasting responsibility. However, along with the claimed professionalization and independence of their staff, there was an expectation that the revenue forecast was less prone to biases of various origins. As to fiscal councils, it has been argued for quite some time that the need to provide an independent validation to macroeconomic estimates underlying national budget was an essential feature to ensure fiscal transparency and accountability (IMF 2013). As discussed in the last section of this chapter, whereas the record with SARAs in sub-Saharan Africa in increasing revenue performance has been mixed at best (Dom 2018), there has been a positive influence of fiscal councils on addressing bias in the underlying macroeconomic estimates (Debrun and Jonung 2018; Debrun and Kinda 2014) but so far limited to advanced economies. The chapter concludes pointing to directions for further analysis and better data to ascertain the presence of bias and its determinants in other contexts and ways to address it.

[10] This approach is, thus, different from Danninger et al. (2005) where the focus is on political interference defined as "a significant deviation between the budget forecast and a forecast by technical experts."

[11] Under the HIPC initiative and the related Multilateral Debt Relief Initiative (MDRI), countries eligible for debt relief (decision point) may eventually graduate from the initiative (completion point) so that the debt relief is granted and they can re-access international market for their borrowing. So far, 36 countries (30 of which are in Africa) for a total of US$99 billion worth of debt relief have graduated.

[12] According to a 2018 IMF report, debt burdens and vulnerabilities have risen significantly since 2013 in low-income developing countries (LIDCs) reflecting a mix of factors including exogenous shocks and loose fiscal policies. While the majority of LIDCs remain at low or moderate risk of debt distress, the number of countries at high risk or in debt distress has increased from 13 in 2013 to 24 in January 2018. See IMF 2018, *Macroeconomic Developments and Prospects in Low-Income Developing Countries*.

[13] The word "institution" is here defined, along with Douglas North (1991), as "both informal constraints (sanctions, taboos, customs, traditions, and codes of conduct), and formal rules (constitutions, laws, property rights)."

Previous Research

As is reflected in the other chapters of this book, the study of bias has focused on two broad streams in the revenue forecasting literature. The first theme has focused on technical aspects of bias such as accuracy and rationality of forecasts and the impact of different methodological choices on these outcomes. A substantial portion of this literature developed in the context of subnational governments in the United States and Europe (Table 5.1) (Bretschneider and Schroeder 1985; Feenberg et al. 1989; Gentry 1989; Krol 2013; Mocan and Azad 1995; Williams and Onochie 2014); only a few studies looked at the national governments (Blackley and DeBoer 1993; Kamlet et al. 2018; Krol 2014; McNab et al. 2007). The second stream of literature has examined the political and institutional correlates of observed bias and its implications for the budget process. Again, most of these studies have been carried out in the United States and European subnational context examining the impact of political budget cycles, ideological affiliations, and political fragmentation (Benito et al. 2015; Boukari and Veiga 2018; Boylan 2008; Kauder et al. 2017; Mikesell and Ross 2014; Ríos et al. 2018; Williams 2012).

In spite of the abundance of research on the subject and interest in the topic, there is a striking lack of cross-country comparative work on the determinants and correlates of forecast biases. Furthermore, only a handful of studies pay attention to the forecasting practices and outcomes in the context of the developing economies in the Global South. As noted earlier, the most apparent reason for the lack of this research is inaccessibility of ex-ante and ex-post comparative data that is buried deep in the multi-year budget documents of the respective countries. In recent years, however, there has been some improvement in the availability of data for member countries of the OECD and European Union as the respective secretariats of these organizations have started to compile this information. The information for developing countries remains largely inaccessible since international organizations like the World Bank and International Monetary Fund (IMF) do not collect this information systematically.

Strauch et al. (2004) is one of the early comparative empirical studies that examined the performance and political economy of budgetary forecasts by the EU member states. They use data from 126 stability and convergence programs submitted by the EU members between 1991 and 2002: they find that the forecasts in the member states usually had an optimistic bias and were not rational, that is, they did not use available information efficiently to reduce forecast error. They also find that the form of fiscal governance affected

Table 5.1 Selected studies on revenue forecasting bias at the subnational level in the United States and Europe

Studies	Question	Period	Observations	Methodology	Results
Feenberg et al. (1989)	Do forecasts optimally incorporate all information that is available at the time they are made?	The 1980s	U.S. States (New Jersey, MA, Maryland)	Case study and regressions	Forecasts are not rational, and states tend to underestimate revenues
Mocan and Azad (1995)	The use of different methodologies and their impact on forecast accuracy	1986–1992	U.S. States	Random effects	Quantitative methods improve the accuracy of forecasts
Boukari and Veiga (2018)	Impact of political interference and political cycles	1998–2015 (Portugal) 2004–2015 (France)	French and Portuguese local governments	Fixed effects and GMM on panel data	Biases essentially driven by electoral motivations and by institutional differences across the two countries. Opportunistic forecasting is more prevalent where governments enjoy greater margin of maneuver
Ríos et al. (2018)	Political interference, political cycle on budget forecast	2008–2014	100 largest Spanish municipalities	OLS and 2SLS	Transparency and independent agencies affect both revenue and expenditure forecasts
Benito et al. (2015)	Political cycle effect on budget deviations	2002–2010	2644 Spanish local governments	GMM on panel data	Electoral cycles have a significant impact on revenue forecasts, with incumbent tending to overestimate so as to spend more

forecast biases. Other studies using the European Union data also confirm the existence of optimistic forecasts and political interference (Beetsma et al. 2013; Pina and Venes 2011). An increasing number of studies have focused on the experience of OECD countries and reached similar conclusions (see a summary in Table 5.2). Buettner and Kauder (2010) examine the determinants of revenue forecast accuracy using data from 13 OECD countries during 1996 and 2008. They find that the timing of forecasts and uncertainty in macroeconomic forecasts, mainly, errors in the GDP estimates are an important predictor of revenue forecast error. Next, they construct an index of independence of revenue forecast and find that it also explains the forecast errors significantly. In combination, three factors of macroeconomic uncertainty, timing of projections, and their independence explain 80 percent of differences in forecasting precision. Jochimsen and Lehmann (2017) examine the forecasting bias in a sample of OECD member countries from 1996 to 2012 and mainly focus on the political economy factors. They find a significant impact of partisan politics on the accuracy of tax revenue forecasts. Left wing governments that often tend to pursue more redistributive policies use optimistic projections to enhance their spending potential. Contrary to the findings, some studies that find electoral or political cycles influencing the forecasts (e.g., Pina and Venes 2011) do not find political budget cycles impacting forecast deviations. Furthermore, they find that the increase in political fragmentation leads to pessimistic forecasts, which is contrary to traditional understanding where political fragmentation-induced common pool problems warrant higher spending that could be facilitated by optimistic forecasts. Overall, the research on OECD and EU countries is also far from conclusive, and studies offer a mixed understanding of the directions of bias as the plausible explanation.

Lastly, only a handful of studies that are summarized in Table 5.3 offer some insights into the forecasting process in the low- and middle-income countries. To the best of our knowledge, a set of studies by the IMF staff in the mid-2000s (Danninger 2005; Danninger et al. 2005; Gosolov and King 2002; Kyobe and Danninger 2005) are the only studies that examine the low-income countries in a comparative context. Gosolov and King (2002) use IMF's MONA database to examine the forecast error in IMF's programs for low-income countries from 1993 to 1999 and find significant upward bias in tax revenue forecasts.[14] They also find that the mean absolute percent error in tax

[14] The Monitoring of Fund Arrangements (MONA) database contains comparable information on the economic objectives and outcomes in fund-supported arrangements. It tracks the performance of countries in terms of scheduled purchases and reviews, quantitative and structural conditionality, and macroeconomic indicators. The database is accessible at https://www.imf.org/external/np/pdr/mona/index.aspx.

Table 5.2 Major studies on revenue forecasting bias and its correlates in the EU and OECD countries

Studies	Question	Period	Observations	Methodology	Results
Buettner and Kauder (2010)	Determinants of revenue forecast precision and accuracy	1996–2008	13 OECD countries	Descriptive statistics plus unbalanced panel regression	Revenue accuracy depends on contextual factors such as underlying macro conditions, institutional framework, and independence
Jochimsen and Lehmann (2017)	The impact of politics on tax revenue forecasting outcomes	1996–2012	18 OECD member states	Fixed effects and GMM on panel data	Authors find support for partisan politics impacting revenue forecasts. Left-wing governments seem to produce more optimistic tax revenue forecasts. Contrary to theoretical understanding, more fragmented politics produces more pessimistic tax revenue forecasts. No evidence of political business cycles impacting tax revenue forecasts
Beestma et al. (2013)	Decompose forecast errors between implementation and revisions	1998–2008	14 members of the European Union	Fixed effects and GMM on panel data	Systematic overoptimism between plans, nowcasts, and ex-post realization
Pina and Venes (2011)	Correlation between forecast and economic and institutional factors	1994–2007	15 members of the European Union (EDP reporting data)	Pooled OLS fixed effects	Political cycle influence in terms of opportunistic forecasts
Strauch et al. (2004)	Political and institutional determinants of forecast deviations	1991–2002	15 members of the European Union	OLS	Cyclical position and the form of fiscal governance are important determinants of biases

Table 5.3 Major studies on revenue forecasting bias and its correlates in low-income countries

Studies	Question	Period	Observations	Methodology	Results
Danninger et al. (2005)	Political interference in revenue forecasting	2003 survey	34 countries	Descriptive statistics plus OLS on revenue forecasting efficiency and practices	Transparency and simplicity reduce political interference; formality and autonomous revenue authorities do not seem to have an impact
Kyobe and Danninger (2005)	Institutional framework and practices	2003 survey	34 countries	Descriptive statistics plus OLS on determinants of the revenue forecasting process	High levels of corruption associated with less formal and transparent revenue forecasts
Danninger (2005)	Can overstated revenue forecasts boost unobserved revenue collection?	1998–2002	Case study of Azerbaijan	Descriptive statistics on forecast errors	A biased forecast can be a second-best tool to increase unmonitored revenue collection effort compared to institutional strengthening
Calitz et al. (2016)	Forecasting accuracy of macroeconomic and fiscal aggregates	2002–2011	South Africa	Descriptive and calculation of forecast errors	Substantial forecast errors in some years (overestimation and underestimation prevalent)
Chakraborty and Sinha (2018)	Has the fiscal rule adoption affected forecast errors of the central government?	1991–2017	India	Calculation of errors and partitioning of sources of error	Overestimation of revenue for most of the years. Adoption of fiscal rules reduced errors

revenue forecasts was about 16 percent, significantly higher than the counterparts in the OECD and United States of around 2–3 percent. Kyobe and Danninger (2005) and Danninger et al. (2005) summarize and build on a new database of forecasting practices in 34 low- and middle-income countries based on a survey sent to IMF's fiscal economists in early 2003. They find that most of these countries scored low on the quality of revenue forecasting practices characterized by a lack of formality and transparency and high levels of complexity. For example, they find that the forecasting responsibilities were formally defined only for about a third of their sample. For almost 90 percent of the sample, revenue forecasting was done by just one agency (usually Ministry of Finance), and in only one-third of the countries, any non-government agency participated in the process. The scores on technical aspects of forecasting also revealed a bleak picture, where almost two-thirds of the sample nations forecasted only for one year, 84 percent used basic extrapolation techniques, and only 18 percent undertook any analysis of past development and forecasts. Danninger et al. (2005) also examine the conditions under which the political interference could be minimized and find that transparency and simplicity helped in reducing political interference. However, formality and independent revenue authorities do not seem to have an impact—a point which we elaborate in the later section of this chapter. In addition to these studies, a few studies examine the forecasting performance and practices in selected developing countries. Danninger (2005) uses the case of Azerbaijan to illustrate the theoretical proposition that in the absence of adequate institutional capacities, the overestimation of revenue forecasts may create a nudge to enhance the performance of revenue administration machinery. Some recent studies have also studied the fiscal marksmanship in emerging economies like India and South Africa. Chakraborty and Sinha (2018) use the forecasts, revisions, and actuals in the Indian context to find that overestimation, as well as underestimation of revenue (more instances of overestimation), is observed in fiscal years between 1991 and 2017. They argue that the adoption of fiscal rules regime, that is, Fiscal Responsibility and Budget Management (FRBM) Act has improved the fiscal marksmanship of the national government. Calitz et al. (2016) illustrate a similar overestimation and underestimation bias in South African revenue projections between 2002 and 2011.

Overall, research in the context of low-income countries warrants attention, since strengthening fiscal forecasting in these countries is central to improving public financial management. Also, the natural link between optimistic forecasts and deficit spending becomes a significant issue in the low-income countries since it may lead to unsustainable debt in the absence of adequate tax reform and growth. As more data on revenue projections and realizations are available, researchers may go beyond examining the nature of forecast biases (as attempted in this chapter) and explore the political and institutional correlates of forecast biases. Are the policymakers taking into account all available information to make forecasts, that is, are the forecasts rational? Do political business cycles lead to overestimation of revenues in election years? Is political fragmentation or existence of coalition governments related to overestimation of revenues? No research examines these questions for low- and middle-income countries—something that future studies may focus on.

Data and Findings

As noted in the previous sections, the availability of ex-ante and ex-post data on the performance of the forecasts in developing economies is not easily accessible, since no single agency or international organization (e.g., World Bank and IMF) compiles cross-country budget estimates. For this study, we collected budget forecast estimates and realized revenues for 26 countries based on information available in the Public Expenditure and Financial Accountability (PEFA) reports that are produced by the PEFA Secretariat.

As noted, PEFA was established in 2001 by a group of donor organizations to harmonize the assessments of public financial management practices and fiscal reforms in developing countries. The formal PEFA assessments started in 2005, and since then the assessment framework has undergone substantial changes covering a wide-ranging sample of national and subnational governments. For this study, we selected 26 countries whose PEFA reports were published under the latest 2016 assessment framework.[15] Each PEFA report requires calculation of revenue and expenditure outturns for three fiscal years and report ex-ante and ex-post revenue estimates. Therefore, we obtain a total

[15] Our selection criteria have the following parameters: Status of the report (final), study type (national), assessment framework (2016), and finally we use the reports that are publicly available and have undergone PEFA check. Based on this criterion, we obtained information for 26 countries in October 2018. The sample is substantially representative of the Global South and includes countries from Latin America, West and East Africa, the Middle East, and South and East Asia.

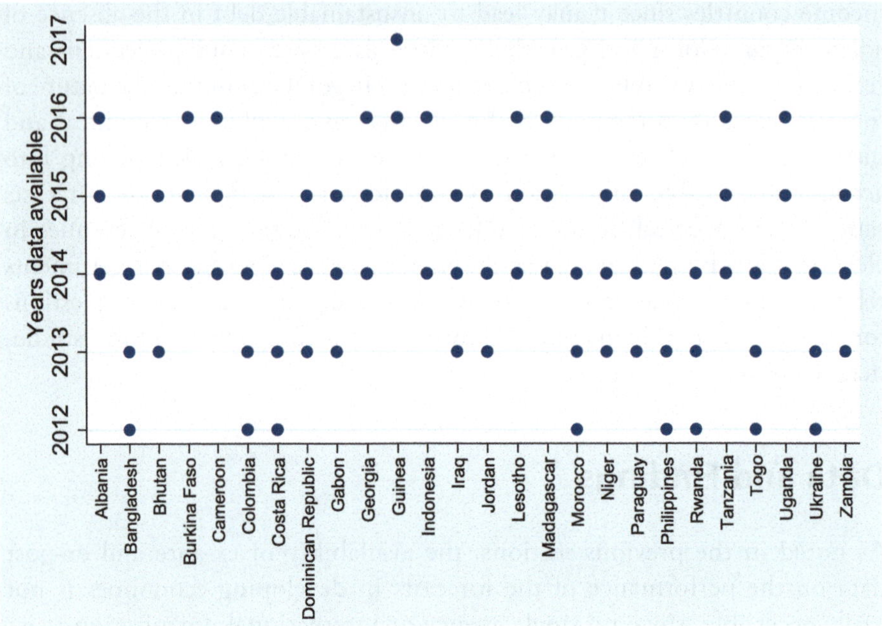

Fig. 5.1 The distribution of study sample across years

of 77 country-years that span FY2012 to FY2017.[16] Figure 5.1 summarizes the countries in the sample and the years represented.

To compare the ex-ante revenue forecasts presented in the annual budget and the ex-post realization of revenue, we calculate two commonly used indicators of forecast errors: mean percent error (MPE) and mean absolute percent error (MAPE), as shown in Eqs. 5.1 and 5.2 below. The parameter $A_{i,\,t}$ represents the revenue realization in the country i during year t, and the parameter $F_{i,\,t}$ represents the corresponding fiscal year's published budget forecasts. MPE measures the size of the forecast errors in percentage terms over the years for which we have the data. However, since MPE includes both the negative and positive errors, it tends to underestimate the overall magnitude of the error. Mean absolute percent errors are based on the absolute (unsigned) value of the error, so it gives a better picture of the overall size of the error in either direction.

[16] Iraq's parliament did not adopt a budget in the FY2014, so the budget information is not available and leads to a corresponding loss of one country year.

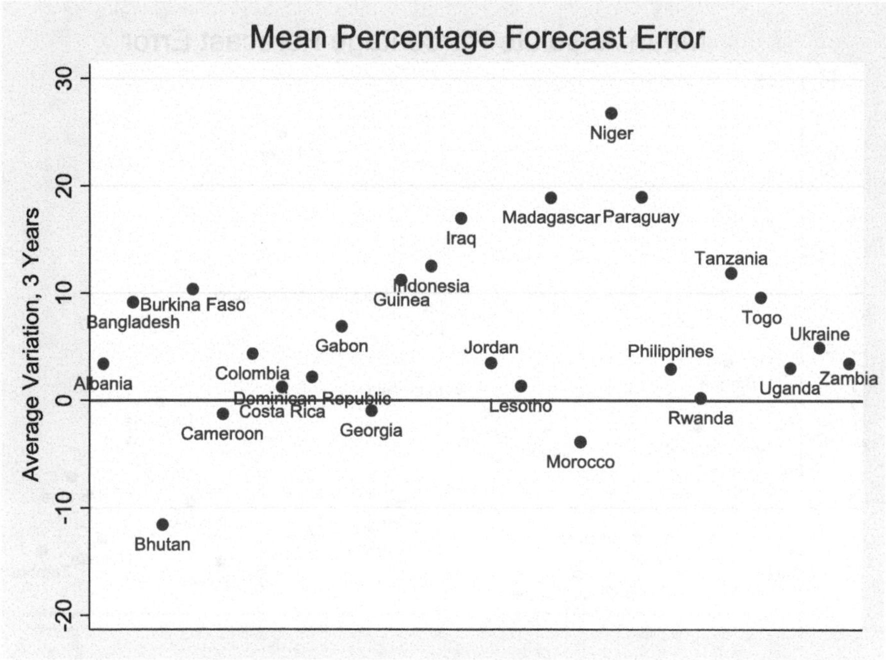

Fig. 5.2 Mean percentage forecast error (three fiscal years)

$$\text{MPE}_{i,t} = \frac{1}{T}\sum_{T=1}^{T} \frac{\left(A_{i,t} - F_{i,t}\right) * 100}{A_{i,t}} \tag{5.1}$$

$$\text{MAPE}_{i,t} = \frac{1}{T}\sum_{T=1}^{T} \frac{|\left(A_{i,t} - F_{i,t}\right)| * 100}{|A_{i,t}|} \tag{5.2}$$

Figure 5.2 summarizes the mean percent errors. In our sample, 85 percent of the countries (22 countries of the total 26) reported an overestimation of revenues. Overall, eight countries in the sample overestimated their revenues by more than 10 percent, and Bhutan was the only country with underestimation of more than 10 percent. This pattern in developing countries seems to be quite different from high-income or advanced economies where underestimation of revenues is relatively more commonplace at not just the subnational but also at the federal level (e.g., see Buettner and Kauder 2010; Williams and Calabrese 2016).

Mean percent error is a good indicator of upward or downward bias in revenue estimates, but the absolute value of forecast errors provide additional insights into the efficacy of the forecasting process. In Fig. 5.3, we plot the

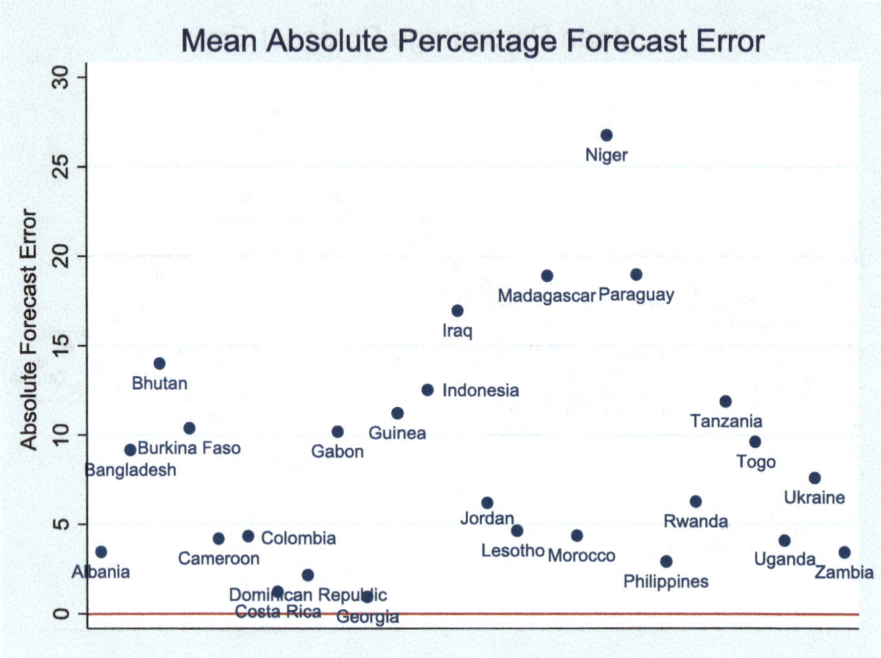

Fig. 5.3 Mean absolute percent forecast error (three fiscal years)

mean absolute percent error for the 26 countries in our sample and find that more than 42 percent of the sample (11 countries) had MAPE of more than 5 percent and the average across all country-years was 8.6 percent, pointing toward the general weakness of revenue forecasting process in these economies. Also, we witness substantial variation within these countries where some Latin American countries have relatively lower forecast errors than African nations with weak state capacities.

To investigate the potential relationship between forecast errors and state capacity, we correlate the absolute forecast errors with the per-capita GDP of the countries in the sample. Arguably, the income or productivity levels of the economy are a good indicator of state and bureaucratic capacity.[17] Figure 5.4 shows the correlation between absolute forecast errors and per-capita GDP for the 26 countries in our sample.[18] As per our expectation, we see a negative relationship between MAPE and per-capita GDP. Within the sample, the

[17] The literature on state capacity finds strong correlation between GDP and various measures of bureaucratic and administrative capacity. However, the direction of the effect is controversial since institutions are often considered endogenous (see, e.g., Hendrix 2010; Cingolani 2013).

[18] We use 2014 values of GDP since that serves as the mid-point of our sample years (FY2012–FY2017).

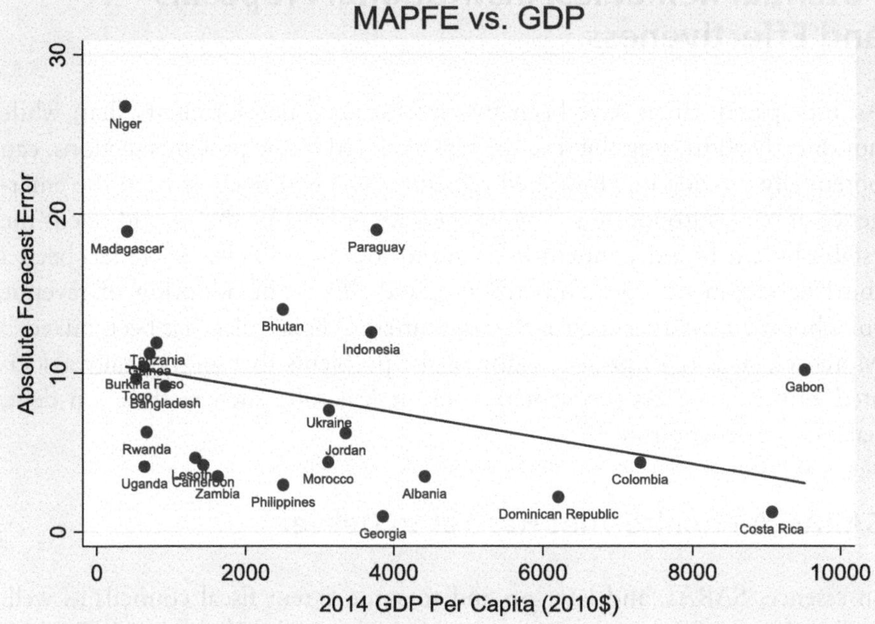

Fig. 5.4 Forecast error and per-capita GDP

relatively more affluent countries like Costa Rica, Colombia, and the Dominican Republic have smaller forecast errors. Similarly, the poorer nations of Africa and Asia like Tanzania, Togo, Burkina Faso, and Bangladesh have significantly higher forecast errors.

Figure 5.4 also highlights interesting contradictions where an upper-middle-income country like Paraguay has substantially higher forecast errors than lower-middle-countries like Cameroon and Zambia.[19] These contradictions require a more in-depth investigation into the specific context of these countries and the generalizable institutional and fiscal factors that govern the political economy of the budget process and revenue forecasting mechanisms.[20]

---

[19] World Bank's Income Classification of Countries, 2018 https://datahelpdesk.worldbank.org/knowledgebase/articles/906519-world-bank-country-and-lending-groups.

[20] Another aspect that deserves more investigation is the presence of a financial arrangement with the IMF. Out of our sample, 14 countries had various financial arrangements with the IMF. The a priori would be that because of the catalytic role of an IMF arrangement and the related conditionality, IFIs and bilateral donors may induce an optimistic bias on macroeconomic and fiscal forecasts. A cursory analysis however does not seem to support the a priori: of the countries showing the largest MAPFE in Fig. 5.4 only two (Madagascar and Niger) had active financial arrangements with the IMF during the observed period.

Potential Remedies: Institutional Proposals and Effectiveness

As anticipated, there have been two institutional developments that, while not directly addressing the revenue bias analyzed in the previous sections, can potentially provide much-desired remedies. The first one has been the emergence of semi-autonomous revenue agencies or SARAs; the second one is the establishment of independent fiscal authorities or councils. There has been a third development worth mentioning, and this is the adoption of revenue rules but their record, much as that of numerical fiscal rules, has been mixed.[21] Moreover, such rules present many of the problems that are typically associated with other—less problematic—numerical rules such as those on debt, balance, or expenditure.[22]

SARAs: A Promise That Has Yet to Deliver

In essence, SARAs, and later on and to some extent fiscal councils as well, emerged as part of a government *agencification* agenda. The rationale for such an agenda was the introduction of private sector modalities (i.e., managerialism) into the civil service, thus making the provision of public goods and services more efficient and effective. What became known as New Public Management was very influential. In a nutshell, an agency is an administrative entity that is formally independent from a ministry or ministerial department. While the political responsibility for setting policy objectives remained at ministerial level, agencies were granted autonomy on how to pursue the stated goals. Their operational autonomy nonetheless continued to be a ministerial responsibility.[23]

---

[21] Based on the IMF Fiscal Rules database https://www.imf.org/external/datamapper/fiscalrules/map/map.htm, as of 2015 only 14 countries had adopted some form of revenue rules, with 8 of them being LDCs under the West Africa Economic and Monetary Union (WAEMU).

[22] As discussed in Schaechter et al. (2012), "revenue rules set ceilings or floors on revenues and are aimed at boosting revenue collection and/or preventing an excessive tax burden (or both). … *but* setting ceilings or floors on revenues can be challenging as revenues maybe have large cyclical component … Exceptions are those rules that restrict the use of windfall revenue for additional spending. Revenue rules alone could *also* result in procyclical fiscal policy, as floors do not generally account for the operation of automatic stabilizers."

[23] Reviewing the rationale as well as the experience of *agencification* is beyond the purpose of this chapter. There is a vast literature that has emerged over the last two decades. A good place to start is Pollitt and Talbot (2003).

Turning to SARAs, these are formally located outside the ministerial structure, are legally independent, and integrate both customs and tax functions.[24] The argument that their political autonomy would lead to an improvement in tax compliance and collection compared to conventional tax administrations was well grounded (Fjeldstad and Moore 2009). Moreover, by transferring tax collection to an independent authority, governments would signal their commitment to a more efficient and fairer collection process compliance (Taliercio 2004). Further, increases in HR, budget, and organizational operational and financial autonomy, most notably the possibility of hiring qualified staff outside the structure of civil service processes and pay scales, would create the managerial flexibility needed to pursue the stated objective—ultimately the increase in the tax-to-GDP ratio and/or minimized compliance costs (Crandall 2010; Kidd and Crandall 2006). The case for tasking SARAs with producing independent revenue forecast was never argued, but as a by-product of their gained autonomy and professionalization, most SARAs in advanced economies substantially enhanced the quality and timeliness of revenue data and methodologies, even if ultimate responsibility for forecasts stayed within the respective ministries of finance or treasuries.

In a recent article, Roel Dom (2018) has reviewed the rationale for and experience of SARAs in 46 sub-Saharan African countries for the period 1980–2015—most of the African countries included in our dataset (all except Morocco and Lesotho) are included in this study. Contrary to earlier studies, his results do not provide any evidence for a systematic relationship between the presence of SARAs and an increase in tax-to-GDP ratios. Dom points to a number of data problems including "situations where countries are coded as having a SARA whereas in reality there is no such institution present." The apparent positive effect of SARAs in previous studies (e.g., von Haldenwang et al. 2014, in comparing Peruvian municipalities with SARAs with those without one) may reflect, on the one hand, a physiological drop in revenue-to-GDP ratios in anticipation of the introduction of a SARA and, on the other, the combination of other reforms and, most of all, political context and commitment (Di John 2010). The revenue increase following the establishment of SARAs also turned out to be not sustainable as argued by Ahlerup et al. (2015) in sub-Saharan Africa. Finally, as in other cases of institutional reforms, SARAs were exported as a "best practice" emerged in advanced economies in different contexts without much needed adaptation to the local con-

[24] Whereas according to Dom (2018) this is a "minimal definition," it allows comparing SARAs' performance with that of conventional tax administrations. Roel also emphasizes that "while they share many elements, there is variation in the nature of SARAs with respect to their competences, organizational set-up, and responsibilities."

text, thus falling in the isomorphic mimicries or capability traps pioneered by Andrews, Pritchett, and Woolcock in a number of papers and articles (Andrews et al. 2013; Pritchett et al. 2010). In other words, SARAs could have benefitted from the problem-driven iterative adaptation (PDIA) approach developed by the same authors (see Andrews et al. 2013, 2017).

Independent Fiscal Authorities

Independent fiscal authorities or councils (hereafter IFCs) are "non-partisan, technical bodies entrusted with a public finance watchdog role" (IMF 2013; Kopits 2013). Their key role is to increase the quality, and at times even quantity, of fiscal information so that legislature and citizens can hold executives accountable for their policy objectives and how these are planned to be achieved. In other words, "instead of tying policymakers' hands, IFCs are expected to raise the reputational and political costs of financially irresponsible choices" (Beetsma et al. 2018). Although IFCs come in many different shapes and forms[25] and fulfill different mandates and functions—see in this regard the IMF Fiscal Councils data set—they have been established across the globe in all sorts of countries—from advanced to LDCs.[26] For the purpose of this chapter, the focus here is on one particular function that most of them have been tasked to pursue, that is, providing "direct inputs to the budget process through the assessment or provision of macroeconomic and budgetary forecasts."[27,28]

[25] According to the IMF Fiscal Council Dataset available at https://www.imf.org/external/np/fad/council/, out of the existing 39 IFCs as of end-2017, about two-thirds are in Europe; only two LDCs—Kenya and Uganda—have established IFCs in the form of Parliamentary Budget Offices, as is the case for South Africa. For a description of the data set, see IMF (2013) and Debrun, X, X. Zhang, and V. Lledó. 2017. "The Fiscal Council Dataset: A Primer to the 2016 Vintage," Background Paper available at http://www.imf.org/external/np/fad/council/.

[26] In 2014, the OECD adopted 22 principles codifying best practices for well-designed IFCs: OECD 2014, *Recommendation of the Council on Principles for Independent Fiscal Institutions*, adopted on February 13, 2014.

[27] Since its first edition issues in 1998, the IMF fiscal transparency code and its subsequent revisions—the most recent of which is dated 2014—have always identified among its principles the need for fiscal information to be externally scrutinized by "a national audit body or an equivalent organization that is independent of the executive." The most recent version states in its pillar 2 Fiscal Forecasting and Budgeting under Budget Credibility that (principle 2.4.1 Independent Evaluation) "the government's economic and fiscal forecasts and performance are subject to independent evaluation." See also the IMF Fiscal Transparency Manual, 2018, pp. 84–88.

[28] Two other key functions—interactions with shareholder and monitoring compliance with fiscal rules where they are in place—while important have a less direct bearing on the scope of this chapter. Of the 39 IFCs describe in the IMF dataset, the most common functions identified are the assessment of government budgetary and fiscal performance in relation to fiscal objectives and strategic priorities (31), forecast assessment (30), monitoring of fiscal rules (28), performing normative analysis or providing recommen-

Beetsma et al. (2018), building on earlier studies, look at the quality of fiscal forecasts by analyzing the IFCs in place as of 2017. The study does not specifically look at revenue estimates but at the underlying real GDP forecast, the primary balance, and the cyclically adjusted primary balance. It does not, thus, disentangle whether a detected bias in the primary balance, for instance, is caused by overly optimistic or pessimistic revenue forecasts. It must be stressed though that since the sample is limited to European countries, all of which have adopted fiscal rules, the result may have its own bias. After controlling for this as well as other factors such as government effectiveness to use the authors' words, "the results provide some suggestive evidence that the presence of fiscal councils seems to eliminate optimistic biases in budgetary forecasts and to improve their accuracy." Of interest is also the authors' observation that tighter fiscal rules tend to be associated with rosier forecasts to create the illusion of strong fiscal performance and ex-ante compliance. The logic of the argument is similar to the risk of creative accounting in response to binding rules (Milesi-Ferretti 2004).

Unfortunately, given that IFCs in LDCs have been in place for too short a period of time, it is too early to say whether the authors' findings could be replicated. Based on the recent fiscal transparency evaluations carried out by the IMF in the case of Kenya and Uganda, it is interesting to note:

> In Kenya, the non-partisan Parliamentary Budget Office (PBO) established in 2007 publishes its separate forecasts in an annual Budget Options document, typically a week after the Treasury's Budget Policy Statement, in which it assesses past fiscal performance and proposes policy options for the annual budget. According to the IMF, "while it does not explicitly evaluate the credibility of the Treasury's forecasts against its own, it does provide a benchmark against which the Treasury's forecasts can be evaluated by parliamentarians and the public. It also provides an explanation of the differences due to differing underlying assumptions. It is worth noting that the PBO has generally been more cautious in its projections of government revenue in the past, which has often proven to be more accurate."[29]
>
> In Uganda, although the Parliamentary Budget Office was established in 2001, it does not perform functions similar to Kenya's IPO. It plays only an ex-post role in scrutinizing budget decisions, limiting its core functions to supporting parliamentarians. As a result, Uganda does not carry out any rec-

dations (27), and assessing long-term sustainability (25). Less common are the costing of policy measures (16) and forecast preparation (17), as reported by Wehner (2018), in Beetsma and Debrun (2018).

[29] Kenya, Fiscal transparency Evaluation, IMF Country Report No. 16/221, June.

oncilation between successive forecast. However, Uganda's revenue estimates for the budget year during the period 2007–2015 were more accurate than Kenya's.[30]

As a way of general caveat, it may be worth to express a few general considerations on the possibility of establishing more IFCs and LDC context. First, the main problem—the existence of systematic bias in revenue forecast—and its consequences have to be clearly identified. Only the magnitude of the bias and its potential repercussions may determine whether it qualifies as a priority or else. Second, capacity and capabilities existing in a given context have to be assessed carefully before establishing new institutions. Many developing countries could certainly benefit from independent scrutiny of their fiscal policy and fiscal forecast, in particular, but may not have access to high-quality local input. Under these circumstances, involving outsiders should be considered when and where it can make a more significant difference than other reforms (Hemming and Joyce 2013). Third, much could be achieved by making those in charge of revenue forecast more accountable by publishing their initial—unconstrained—forecasts along with a technical explanation. Countries have done remarkably well in addressing potential biases by assigning certain functions to independent bodies or panel of experts without necessarily going through the motion of establishing new entities. The example of Chile and the two independent panels setting the long-term price for copper and potential real growth precedes most of the modern IFCs, two-thirds of which were established after 2007. The risk of isomorphic mimicry mentioned above with regards to SARAs is very much valid with IFCs.

Summary and Conclusions

This chapter has discussed revenue forecast biases and some remedial proposals in the context of low- and middle-income countries in the Global South. The analysis of forecast errors for 26 low- and middle-income countries reveals a systemic discrepancy between the ex-ante revenue estimates and their ex-post realizations. From limited years of data that is available, it appears that developing countries tend to have optimistic forecasts and large forecast errors. This finding stands in contrast to relatively more common underestimation of revenues in the OECD countries (see, e.g., discussions in Buettner and Kauder 2010; Williams and Calabrese 2016 and other chapters of this

[30] Uganda, Fiscal transparency Evaluation, IMF Country Report No. 17/130, May.

book). Though the chapter does not analyze the plausible explanations for these differences, the main suspects are differences in institutional capacities of revenue administration, biases introduced by optimistic macroeconomic indicators, and an array of political economy factors. Future studies should explore the precise role of these factors empirically. Both qualitative and quantitative approaches may be useful in highlighting the factors underlying the existence of biases and develop a nuanced understanding of forecasting practices.

The persistence of biases undermines the very credibility of budgets and fuels the expenditure drift experienced by many countries in the last few decades. As low-income countries wish to leverage their capacity to generate revenue domestically in the expectation that aid flows would decline further in the near future, addressing such bias while building capacity and capabilities remains a challenge. The fact that the revenue forecast bias discussed in this chapter remains a relatively under-researched topic vis-à-vis others raises concerns.

Against the above background, the chapter reviews the experience of two institutional innovations that may directly or indirectly help address the revenue forecast bias observed in countries at all levels of development: semi-autonomous revenue authorities (SARAs); and independent fiscal institutions or councils. The evidence on the effectiveness of the former remains mixed, and the latter is a relatively new institution whose future trajectory is still unknown in most of the low-income countries. In parallel, the adoption of numerical fiscal rules (see Lledó et al. 2017) in a large number of middle- and low-income countries has affected the budget process significantly, but its impact on the forecasting is still unclear. These are, however, two potential avenues to address the observed revenue bias: the mandate of SARAs established in a growing number of low-income countries could be expanded so that such institutions could play a more active role in forecasting revenues. The ultimate responsibility should, however, stay with the relevant ministry, subject to external and independent evaluation. In this regards, where capacity exists, independent fiscal institutions could also contribute positively to addressing the issue at hand.

Lastly, the study of forecasting practices and biases in the low- and middle-income countries is severely constrained by the lack of data. Keeping track of revenue estimates, how they feed into the budget process, and their outcomes is not only integral to improving the budget process and financial management but also central to development planning and investments for economic growth. Case studies of individual countries are useful in providing a nuanced understanding of politics and institutional factors that govern the forecasting process, but cross-country empirical studies using panel or time-series approaches are essential to gather generalizable findings that are policy relevant. Therefore, it is imperative that the international organizations that work in this space keep track of this information. PEFA assessments are a step in the right direction, but a more systematic compilation of data is warranted to enable policymakers and researchers to understand the dynamics of revenues and spending. Access to such information will be critical to improving forecasting practices, reduce errors, and promote transparency, accountability, and ultimately credibility of the budget process.

References

Ahlerup, P., Baskaran, T., & Bigsten, A. (2015). Tax innovations and public revenues in sub-Saharan Africa. *Journal of Development Studies, 51*(6), 689–706.

Alesina, A., & Passalacqua, A. (2015). *The political economy of government debt* (Working Paper No. 21821). National Bureau of Economic Research. Retrieved from http://www.nber.org/papers/w21821.

Andrews, M., Pritchett, L., & Woolcock, M. (2013). Escaping capability traps through problem driven iterative adaptation (PDIA). *World Development, 51*, 234–244.

Andrews, M., Pritchett, L., & Woolcock, M. (2017). *Building state capability. Evidence, analysis, action*. Oxford: Oxford University Press.

Beetsma, R., Bluhm, B., Giuliodori, M., & Wierts, P. (2013). From budgetary forecasts to ex post fiscal data: Exploring the evolution of fiscal forecast errors in the European Union. *Contemporary Economic Policy, 31*(4), 795–813.

Beetsma, R., & Debrun, X. (Eds.). (2018). *Independent fiscal councils: Watchdogs or lapdogs?* London: A VoxEU.org Book, CEPR Press.

Beetsma, R., Debrun, X., Fang, X., Kim, Y., Lledó, V., Mbaye, S., et al. (2018). Independent fiscal councils: Recent trends and performance. *European Journal of Political Economy*. Online Only.

Benito, B., Guillamón, M. D., & Bastida, F. (2015). Budget forecast deviations in municipal governments: Determinants and implications. *Australian Accounting Review, 25*(1), 45–70.

Blackley, P. R., & DeBoer, L. (1993). Bias in OMB's economic forecasts and budget proposals. *Public Choice, 76*(3), 215–232.

Boukari, M., & Veiga, F. J. (2018). Disentangling political and institutional determinants of budget forecast errors: A comparative approach. *Journal of Comparative Economics*. https://doi.org/10.1016/j.jce.2018.03.002.

Boylan, R. T. (2008). Political distortions in state forecasts. *Public Choice, 136*(3–4), 411–427.

Bretschneider, S., & Schroeder, L. (1985). Revenue forecasting, budget setting and risk. *Socio-Economic Planning Sciences, 19*(6), 431–439.

Buettner, T., & Kauder, B. (2010). Revenue forecasting practices: Differences across countries and consequences for forecasting performance. *Fiscal Studies, 31*(3), 313–340.

Calitz, E., Siebrits, K., & Stuart, I. (2016). Enhancing the accuracy of fiscal projections in South Africa. *South African Journal of Economic and Management Sciences, 19*(3), 330–343.

Chakraborty, L., & Sinha, D. (2018). Has fiscal rules changed the fiscal behaviour of union government in India? Anatomy of budgetary forecast errors in India. *International Journal of Financial Research, 9*(3), 75–85.

Cingolani, L. (2013). *The state of state capacity: A review of concepts, evidence and measures*. Maastricht Graduate School of Governance. Working Paper 053, United Nations University. Retrieved from https://ideas.repec.org/p/unm/unumer/2013053.html.

Crandall, W. (2010). *Revenue administration: Autonomy in tax administration and the revenue authority model.* Technical Notes and Manuals, Fiscal Affairs Department. International Monetary Fund, Washington, DC. Retrieved from https://www.imf.org/external/pubs/ft/tnm/2010/tnm1012.pdf.

Danninger, S. (2005). *Revenue forecasts as performance targets*. IMF Working Paper 5/14. International Monetary Fund, Washington, DC. Retrieved from https://www.imf.org/en/Publications/WP/Issues/2016/12/31/Revenue-Forecasts-as-Performance-Targets-17924.

Danninger, S., Cangiano, M., & Kyobe, A. (2005). *The political economy of revenue-forecasting experience from low-income countries*. IMF Working Paper 05/2. International Monetary Fund, Washington, DC. Retrieved from https://www.imf.org/en/Publications/WP/Issues/2016/12/31/The-Political-Economy-of-Revenue-Forecasting-Experience-From-Low-Income-Countries-17918.

Debrun, X., & Jonung, L. (2018). Under threat: Rules-based fiscal policy and how to preserve it. *European Journal of Political Economy*. Online Only.

Debrun, X., & Kinda, T. (2014). *Strengthening post-crisis fiscal credibility: Fiscal councils on the rise—A new dataset*. IMF Working Paper.

Di John, J. (2010). The political economy of taxation and resource mobilization in sub-Saharan Africa. In V. Padayachee (Ed.), *The political economy of Africa* (pp. 110–131). London: Routledge.

Dixit, A., Grossman, G., & Helpman, E. (1997). Common agency and coordination: General theory and application to government policy making. *Journal of Political Economy, 105*(4), 752–769. University of Chicago Press.

Dom, R. (2018). Semi-autonomous revenue authorities in sub-Saharan Africa: Silver bullet or white elephant. *Journal of Development Studies*. Online Only.

Feenberg, D. R., Gentry, W., Gilroy, D., & Rosen, H. S. (1989). Testing the rationality of state revenue forecasts. *Review of Economics & Statistics, 71*(2), 300–308.

Fjeldstad, O. H., & Moore, M. (2009). Revenue authorities and public authority in sub-Saharan Africa. *Journal of Modern African Studies, 47*(1), 1–18.

Gentry, W. M. (1989). Do state revenue forecasters utilize available information? *National Tax Journal, 42*(4), 429–439.

Gosolov, M., & King, J. (2002). *Tax revenue forecasts in IMF supported programs* (Working Paper 2/236). International Monetary Fund, Washington, DC.

Hallerberg, M., & von Hagen, J. (1997). *Electoral institutions, cabinet negotiations, and budget deficits in the European Union* (NBER Working Paper No. 6341). National Bureau of Economic Research, Cambridge, MA.

Heller, P. S. (2005). *Understanding fiscal space.* IMF Policy Discussion Paper. International Monetary Fund, Washington, DC. https://doi.org/10.3390/jsan3010064.

Hemming, R., & Joyce, P. (2013). The role of fiscal councils in promoting fiscal responsibility. In M. Cangiano, T. Curristine, & M. Lazare (Eds.), *Public financial management and its emerging architecture.* Washington, DC: International Monetary Fund.

Hendrix, C. S. (2010). Measuring state capacity: Theoretical and empirical implications for the study of civil conflict. *Journal of Peace Research, 47*(3), 273–285.

IMF. (2013). *The functions and impact of fiscal councils.* IMF Policy Paper. International Monetary Fund, Washington, DC.

Jochimsen, B., & Lehmann, R. (2017). On the political economy of national tax revenue forecasts: Evidence from OECD countries. *Public Choice, 170*(3–4), 211–230.

Jonung, L., & Larch, M. (2006). Improving fiscal policy in the EU: The case for independent forecasts. *Economic Policy, 21*(47), 493–534.

Kamlet, M. S., Mowery, D. C., & Su, T.-T. (2018). Whom do you trust? An analysis of executive and congressional economic forecasts. *Journal of Policy Analysis and Management, 6*(3), 365–384.

Kauder, B., Potrafke, N., & Schinke, C. (2017). Manipulating fiscal forecasts: Evidence from the German states. *FinanzArchiv, 73*(2), 213–236.

Kidd, M., & Crandall, W. (2006). *Revenue authorities: Issues and problems in evaluating their success.* Washington, DC: International Monetary Fund.

Kopits, G. (2013). *Restoring public debt sustainability: The role of independent fiscal institutions.* Oxford: Oxford University Press.

Krol, R. (2013). Evaluating state revenue forecasting under a flexible loss function. *International Journal of Forecasting, 29*(2), 282–289.

Krol, R. (2014). Forecast bias of government agencies. *Cato Journal, 34*(1), 99–112.

Kydland, F. E., & Prescott, E. C. (1977). Rules rather than discretion: The inconsistency of optimal plans. *Journal of Political Economy, 85*(3), 473–491.

Kyobe, A., & Danninger, S. (2005). *Revenue forecasting—How is it done? Results from a survey of low-income countries.* IMF Working Paper. International Monetary Fund, Washington, DC.

Lledó, V., Yoon, S., Fang, X., Mbaye, S., & Kim, Y. (2017). *Fiscal rules at a glance*. International Monetary Fund, Washington, DC. Retrieved from http://www.imf.org/external/datamapper/FiscalRules/FiscalRulesataGlance-BackgroundPaper.pdf.

McNab, R. M., Rider, M., & Wall, K. D. (2007). *Are errors in official U.S. Budget receipts forecasts just noise?* Andrew Young School of Policy Studies Research Paper No. 07-22. Georgia State University, Atlanta. https://doi.org/10.2139/ssrn.989050.

Mikesell, J. L., & Ross, J. M. (2014). State revenue forecasts and political acceptance: The value of consensus forecasting in the budget process. *Public Administration Review, 74*(2), 188–203.

Milesi-Ferretti, G. M. (2004). Good, bad or ugly? On the effects of fiscal rules with creative accounting. *Journal of Public Economics, 88*(1–2), 377–394.

Mocan, H. N., & Azad, S. (1995). Accuracy and rationality of state general fund revenue forecasts: Evidence from panel data. *International Journal of Forecasting, 11*(3), 417–427.

North, D. C. (1991). Institutions. *The Journal of Economic Perspectives, 5*(1), 97–112.

Pina, A. M., & Venes, N. M. (2011). The political economy of EDP fiscal forecasts: An empirical assessment. *European Journal of Political Economy, 27*(3), 534–546.

Pollitt, C., & Talbot, C. (2003). *Unbundled government: A critical analysis of the global trend to agencies, quangos and contractualisation*. London: Routledge.

Pritchett, L., Woolcock, M., & Andrews, M. (2010). *Capability traps? The mechanisms of persistent implementation failure*. Washington, DC: Center for Global Development.

Ríos, A. M., Guillamón, M. D., Benito, B., & Bastida, F. (2018). The influence of transparency on budget forecast deviations in municipal governments. *Journal of Forecasting, 37*(4), 457–474.

Rubin, I. (2018). *The politics of public budgeting. Getting and spending, borrowing and balancing* (8th ed.). Los Angeles: SAGE/CQ Press.

Schaechter, A., Kinda, T., Budina, N., & Weber, A. (2012). *Fiscal rules in response to the crisis-toward the "next generation" rules: A new dataset*. IMF Working Paper. Retrieved from http://www.imf.org/external/pubs/ft/wp/2012/wp12187.pdf.

Schick, A. (2013). Reflections on two decades of public financial management reforms. In C. Marco, C. Teresa, & M. Lazare (Eds.), *Public financial management and its emerging architecture*. Washington, DC: IMF.

Strauch, R., Hallerberg, M., & Hagen, J. von (2004). *Budgetary forecasts in Europe-the track record of stability and convergence programmes*. ECB Working Paper Series No. 307. European Central Bank. Retrieved from https://www.ecb.europa.eu/pub/pdf/scpwps/ecbwp307.pdf?8e8cfda0e3b051e91f238b22a3ae3583.

Taliercio, R. R. (2004). Administrative reform as credible commitment: The impact of autonomy on revenue authority performance in Latin America. *World Development, 32*(2), 213–232.

von Haldenwang, C., von Schiller, A., & Garcia, M. (2014). Tax collection in developing countries—New evidence on semi-autonomous revenue agencies (SARAs). *Journal of Development Studies, 50*(4), 541–555.

Wehner, J. (2018). Promoting good practices: The OECD principles and beyond. In R. Beetsma & X. Debrun (Eds.), *Independent fiscal councils: Watchdogs or lapdogs?* (pp. 37–46). London: A VoxEU.org Book, CEPR Press.

Weingast, B. R., Shepsle, K. A., & Johnsen, C. (1981). The political economy of benefits and costs: A neoclassical approach to distributive politics. *Journal of Political Economy, 89*(4), 642.

Wildavsky, A. (1975). *Budgeting: A comparative theory of budgetary processes*. Boston, MA: Little, Brown, and Company.

Williams, D. (2012). The politics of forecast bias: Forecaster effect and other effects in New York City revenue forecasting. *Public Budgeting and Finance, 32*(4), 1–18.

Williams, D., & Calabrese, T. (2016). The status of budget forecasting. *Journal of Public and Nonprofit Affairs, 2*(2), 127–160.

Williams, D., & Onochie, J. (2014). *State revenue forecasting accuracy*. In International Symposium on Forecasting. Rotterdam. Retrieved from https://forecasters.org/wp-content/uploads/gravity_forms/7-2a51b93047891f1ec3608bdbd77ca58d/2014/07/Williams_Daniel__Ononchie_Joseph_ISF2014.pdf.

6

The Reliability of Long-Run Budget Projections

Rudolph Penner

All models are wrong, but some are useful.
—George Box

Major Points

- Long-term U.S. federal budget projections are largely driven by a growing elderly population.
- Spending on Social Security, Medicare, and Medicaid grows more rapidly than tax revenues and ultimately causes an explosion in the debt-to-GDP ratio.
- Two surprises have moderated this growth: unusually low interest rates and a surge in revenues related to the dot-com boom of the late 1990s.
- The Great Recession caused the debt-to-GDP ratio to rise briefly, much faster than expected.
- Despite these surprises, the rapid growth of programs serving the elderly has been forecasted fairly accurately.

R. Penner (✉)
The Urban Institute, Washington, DC, USA

D. Williams, T. Calabrese (eds.), *The Palgrave Handbook of Government Budget Forecasting*, Palgrave Studies in Public Debt, Spending, and Revenue,
https://doi.org/10.1007/978-3-030-18195-6_6

Introduction

Forecasting is a perilous activity. Forecasters often make big mistakes whether they are forecasting the economy, the weather, or the outcome of the World Series. Budget forecasts are no better than any other (Penner 2002), and revenue forecasts are particularly difficult (Auerbach 1999; Congressional Budget Office 2015; Penner 2008). Errors occur even when forecasting with a one-year time horizon. Does that mean that long-run budget forecasts of 30 years or more are totally worthless?

Forecasts do not have to be right—although they sometimes are—to be valuable. It may be difficult to forecast a variable's exact value, but getting information on the direction it is moving can be very useful. Even if the forecaster gets the direction of a particular variable wrong, there may be other components of a forecast that provide valuable information.

Long-run forecasters actually have a few advantages over short-run forecasters. In the short run, the economy is buffeted by the turbulence of business cycles, oil shocks, political upheavals, droughts, etc. Over the longer run, however, more fundamental forces exert themselves and there is some tendency for variables to return to long-run trends. Regression to the mean[1] is the long-run forecaster's best friend and policy makers often react to surprises with policy responses that keep variables within bounds.[2] Unfortunately, the advantages enjoyed by long-run forecasters are not sufficient to make long-run forecasts more accurate than short-run forecasts. They are not. But they are not worthless either.

Long-run budget forecasts produced by different groups may contain significant errors, but they generally reach the same conclusion. Unless they adopt combinations of very optimistic assumptions, they almost always forecast debt-to-GDP ratios that rise indefinitely at an increasing rate. This may be less a testimony to the accuracy of long-run projections than it is to the seriousness of our long-run budget problem. The Office of Management and Budget (OMG) is an exception to the rule. It projects a stable and then declining debt-to-GDP ratio after the last baby boomer has retired. Their results will be discussed in more detail later.

So far, I have used the word "forecasts." Those working on long-run budget issues prefer the word "projections," and the Government Accountability Office (GAO) talks about "scenarios." Whether it is a projection or a scenario,

[1] Defined as the tendency for statistical aberrations to disappear in the long run, for example, abnormally tall fathers are likely to have sons closer to average height.

[2] A strong example of this phenomenon will be discussed later—the remarkable constancy of the revenue-to-GDP ratio.

it purports to show the consequences of a certain combination of economic, demographic, and policy assumptions. The projection will not be very valuable if the many underlying assumptions are not realistic, and any effort to make them realistic involves making a forecast. That diminishes the difference between a projection and a forecast. One difference remains, however. People making projections make them along with a wish that their policy assumptions will not come true because the projections inevitably imply a fiscal disaster. A major reason for making projections is to persuade policy makers to change policies.

Notwithstanding the problems with making long-run projections, there is no shortage of them. They are provided by the Congressional Budget Office (2016) (CBO), the GAO (Irving et al. 2018), and the Office of Management and Budget (United States Office of Management and Budget 2018, Chap. 3). The GAO analysis is now required by the Congress as part of the Consolidated Financial Statement of the United States. The government efforts are complemented by private analyses. For example, Auerbach and Gale (2016) periodically produce long-run budget projections. They focus on estimating a fiscal gap. One variant of the gap is defined as the increase in revenues and/or decrease in noninterest spending as a percent of GDP necessary in each and every year to end up with the same debt-to-GDP ratio after a certain number of years as when the period begins.[3] The Committee for a Responsible Federal Budget also does numerous long-run analyses,[4] and Jeffrey Miron (2016) examines the difference between the present value of noninterest spending and the present value of receipts over the next 75 years. He does this for each year beginning in 1965 and finds a strong upward trend in the gap broken only with the recovery after the Great Recession and the end of the stimulus program.

The different groups making projections often use different methods and assumptions. Most produce more than one path for the budget aggregates, although they typically pay most attention to one path that might be called their base case. All do sensitivity analysis based on varying the value of certain key assumptions, but this is done in very different ways. Often the analysis is for different time periods and that makes comparisons difficult. Policy projections are often based on extending "current law" or "current policy."[5] A major differ-

[3] Steuerle and Quakenbush (2016) argue that aiming for the same debt-to-GDP ratio in some future year is not sufficient because it is unlikely to be sustainable. They feel that policy makers should aim at a lower ratio to provide a cushion. A similar point is made later in this chapter.

[4] See, for example, Committee for a Responsible Federal Budget (2016).

[5] The administration refers to one of its projections as being based on current policy, but the policy assumptions differ little from what CBO calls baseline extended.

ence between these two concepts is that current law often contains temporary provisions that are scheduled to expire, but in fact have been extended year after year. Current policy assumes that many will in fact be extended. However, considerable judgment is required to translate these broad terms into precise policies for the next 30 years, and all of this results in significant differences among various projections. CBO is the only one that investigates the effects of ever-increasing deficits on the future growth of incomes.

CBO's base estimate is called the "extended baseline" and is essentially based on current law. Getting back to the current debt-to-GDP ratio by 2048 implies a relatively small fiscal gap for the 2018–2048 period of 1.9 percent of GDP and a debt-to-GDP ratio in 2048 of 152 percent. Auerbach-Gale project current policy rather than current law, and their projection results in larger medium-term deficits than derived by the CBO. They estimate a fiscal gap of 3.0 percent and a debt-to-GDP ratio of 152 percent that is reached by 2040 compared to CBO's 2048. They do a large number of variants on this base case. The OMB's "current policy"[6] estimates a fiscal gap of 0.7 percent of GDP, and a 2048 debt-to-GDP ratio of less than 94 percent. GAO provides a 75-year fiscal gap estimate of 3.0 percent for an extended baseline case, but no estimate for 30 years. Although the individual estimates vary, the bottom line is almost always the same. The debt-to-GDP ratio is on its way to an explosion.

The similarity in the conclusions of different analyses may not be surprising in that all, but OMB, rely heavily on CBO's baseline demographic and economic assumptions for the first ten years of the projection period. To the extent there are differences, they generally involve the policy assumptions that are emphasized. As just noted, CBO emphasizes results consistent with current law. Auerbach and Gale emphasize current policy and GAO does the same for what they call an alternative path. CBO's time horizon is 30 years while GAO's is 75 years to match the time horizon used by Social Security actuaries. For the period after 2028, GAO often uses economic assumptions that match the values used by CBO for 2028.

OMB's stable debt-to-GDP ratio for what they call current budget policy is primarily the result of their more optimistic productivity and interest rate assumptions. They assume 2 percent annual productivity growth in the long run compared to CBO's 1.5 percent, and they have the interest rate on the ten-year Treasury stabilizing at 3.6 percent in the long run compared to CBO's 4.1 percent. The Administration claims that, if all of the policy changes that

[6] The OMB's definition of "current policy" is close to what others call "current law."

they recommend were adopted, the budget would be balanced by 2039 and the debt-to-GDP ratio would be on a rapidly declining path.

No analyst uses a complicated simultaneous equation model which can be solved to produce a path for the debt-to-GDP ratio. Instead, different components of the overall problem are analyzed using different techniques. For example, demographic analysis provides estimates of the age composition of future populations and is used to estimate how many are eligible for Social Security and Medicare. The number of eligibles who actually apply for the programs is then estimated. The level of Social Security benefits comes from assumptions regarding economic growth, the wage share of GDP, and estimates of the distribution of wages. Assumptions regarding health costs are influenced by historical trends with the experience of recent years given heavier weight. Dozens of specific analyses of this type are pulled together to produce final conclusions.

Looking Backward

The most important single force driving the debt-to-GDP ratio upward in essentially all long-run projections is the rapid growth of the elderly population. It propels the growth of three large spending programs—Social Security, Medicare, and Medicaid—to the point that their spending growth exceeds that of the rest of the budget and the GDP. As more people retire the resulting slowdown in the growth of the labor force also slows economic growth and the growth in revenues. In addition, the projections assume that the resulting increase in debt rapidly increases the interest bill facing the government relative to GDP.

The accuracy of these basic predictions will be examined for the past 20 years. That also happens to be roughly the length of time that CBO has been making long-run projections while GAO has done it for a slightly longer period.

For a time horizon of 20 years the aging of the population is quite predictable, even though there are minor uncertainties surrounding mortality rates and immigration. Health costs are more difficult to forecast. Costs per beneficiary have been growing faster over the long run than GDP per capita. The growth is greater than would be expected looking only at the aging of the population. The growth above that due to aging is known as "excess cost growth." It has slowed unexpectedly in recent years, and it is hard to know how much of the slowdown, if any, will continue. Interest rates are even more uncertain than excess cost growth, thus making the interest bill facing the government especially difficult to project.

Despite being too pessimistic in projecting excess cost growth, those making long-run projections have been basically right that the growth of spending on Social Security, Medicare, and Medicaid would exceed the growth of the rest of spending and the growth of GDP. In 1996, spending on Social Security, Medicare, and Medicaid amounted to about 40 percent of total spending and 8 percent of GDP. By 2018 the importance of the three programs had risen to about half of total spending and 10.3 percent of GDP.[7] The generally correct prediction about the growth of Social Security, Medicare, Medicaid and interest has gone astray in some time periods because of three very big surprises during the past 20 years—two good and one bad. First, contrary to past projections, a precipitous fall in interest rates caused the interest bill facing the government to fall as a percent of GDP from about 3.0 percent in 1996 to 1.6 percent in 2018, despite a very large increase in the debt-to-GDP ratio.[8] Note that the fall in the interest bill relative to GDP offsets approximately 61 percent of the rise in spending on Social Security, Medicare, and Medicaid relative to GDP. The second surprise involved a huge unexpected surge in revenues related to the dot-com boom. As a result, budget surpluses emerged for four years following 1997. The debt-to-GDP ratio fell substantially from 47.0 percent in 1996 to 31.5 percent in 2001 instead of rising as almost all long-run projections had predicted. Third, the Great Recession and the associated stimulus program caused a doubling of the debt-to-GDP ratio from 35.2 percent in 2007 to 73.7 percent in 2014. Only a small part of that increase was the result of the growth of Social Security, Medicare, and Medicaid.

It would be useful to provide a more precise quantitative assessment of the overall accuracy of long-run projections at this point, but that is not possible. The main problem is that none of the prominent long-run projections has come to the end of the time horizon chosen when the projections were first formulated. Indeed, the end points are still far in the distance. Consequently, a projected path for the debt-to-GDP ratio that looks quite accurate up to this point could go badly astray over the next few years. Conversely, a path that now seems far off the mark could become more accurate as time goes by.

Another problem is that most analysts who produce projections provide more than one path and they are often ambiguous as to which path they

[7] 2018 was an unusual year in the spending other than for Social Security, Medicare, and Medicaid grew faster than for those three programs because Congress raised the spending caps that restrained defense and nondefense discretionary spending in earlier years.

[8] While the low interest rate may have been good news for the budget, it reflected bad news regarding economic growth all over the world.

expect to be more accurate. Most often CBO and others project two paths—one assuming current law continues and another assuming current policy where many temporary provisions of current law are extended. For projections made in 2003 and 2005, CBO provided six paths, but very recently they have produced only one path that is based on current law. If we wish to assess the accuracy of the projections up to this point within their time horizons, it is not obvious which path should be examined. Assessing them all would take up a lot of space in this short chapter.

For what it is worth I shall examine the CBO projections for the debt-to-GDP ratio in 2018 that were made in past years. I shall begin the analysis with the projection made in 2009. It was in that year that CBO began producing long-run projections every year and also began producing user-friendly spreadsheets that show the annual projections for the key variables used in the analysis. I shall use their projections based on current policy where available. They generally refer to these as "alternative" projections. As previously noted, only current law projections are available for 2016 and 2017.

A positive sign on the errors indicates that the estimate was too pessimistic; a negative sign indicates overoptimism. Not surprisingly the estimates tend to be quite accurate for projections made closer to 2018. Accidentally, the time period chosen for the table does not contain any projections that are wildly off the mark. That is very unusual. For an example of an estimate with a huge error, one can look back at one of the surprises discussed above. That was the surge in revenues caused by the dot-com boom at the turn of the century. The budget surpluses that resulted provoked discussions of paying off the entire national debt. The projection made in 2000 estimated a significant surplus in 2018 and a negative national debt as it was assumed that the federal government would be investing in nonfederal securities. It was probably the worst error in the history of long-run projections (Table 6.1).

Table 6.1 Errors in current policy projections of the 2018 debt-to-GDP ratio

Year of projection	Estimate minus actual in percentage points
2009	2
2010	3
2011	13
2012	8
2013	4
2014	1
2015	1
2016	1[a]
2017	0[a]

[a]Based on current law projections

Looking Forward

It was earlier said that a wrong projection can have a valuable component. That is true about the projected increases in spending on Social Security,[9] Medicare, and Medicaid, even though projections of the debt-to-GDP ratio have not always been very accurate. As we look forward, the effect of aging on spending will grow over the next 25 years because of the large number of baby boomers that will become beneficiaries of the three programs. The people affected are already with us, and therefore, it is unlikely that projections of the future number of beneficiaries will be very far off. As the three programs grow as a proportion of total spending, it also becomes less probable, although not impossible, that their bad effects on total spending and the deficit will be overwhelmed by good surprises. The fact that two important variables, excess health cost growth and interest rates, are remarkably low relative to levels experienced over past decades would seem to reduce the probability that they could go very much lower. However, we have seen negative interest rates in Europe and Japan and brief periods of health cost growth in the United States falling far below forecasts, so it is true that very surprising good things can happen. But saying that surprising good things can happen is very different from saying that we should count on them.

The analysis will now shift to what those making projections assume about the future of the many variables underlying their analysis. CBO provides considerable detail regarding their assumptions and they will be examined most carefully. Space limitations prevent a detailed examination of all relevant assumptions and only a sampling will be discussed.

Macroeconomic Uncertainty

All major projections show rising deficits and debt through at least the late 2030s. It is important to understand how this affects the macroeconomy and how those effects have secondary feedback effects on the budget. This is no simple task and only CBO attempts it explicitly. CBO assumes that increased deficits increase aggregate demand and GDP growth in the short run, but because this analysis focuses on the long run, the short-run impact of deficits will not be analyzed.

---

[9] All projections assume that scheduled Social Security benefits will be paid trust funds are emptied around 2030. This will require a change in current law.

In the long run, deficits represent a reduction in national saving. This implies increased interest rates and a reduction in investment with a resulting negative effect on economic growth and the growth of wages. These effects are mitigated by borrowing from foreigners. CBO assumes that a $1 increase in federal government borrowing attracts 24 cents in foreign private capital. Although the borrowing from foreigners reduces the fall in wages that would otherwise occur if all borrowing were done within the United States, it does mean that more of Americans' future income must be used to pay interest and dividends abroad, thus reducing American standards of living.

The CBO analysis of the macroeconomic effects of larger deficits assumes that the estimated relationship between deficits and increased foreign capital inflows remains as in past history. That may not be true if a continually rising debt-to-GDP ratio begins to reduce foreign confidence in the United States. If foreigners reduce their investments in the United States or in a worst-case scenario begin to withdraw their capital, it will have negative consequences for economic growth and future government deficits. This may be an area in which CBO is overoptimistic. In addition, our heavy reliance on foreign investors may reduce our flexibility in foreign policy.

Policy Uncertainty

In previous years CBO provided projections based both on their extended baseline and on an alternative fiscal path. Beginning in July 2016 CBO decided that there was not a sufficient difference between the two policy scenarios to warrant doing projections for both, so subsequent reports only include projections based on a continuation of current law. This assumes that certain temporary tax cuts passed in late 2017 will not be extended beyond their current expiration date. In fact, such temporary cuts have been extended routinely in the past, and some that were once temporary, such as the research and experimentation tax credit, have been made permanent. The current law baseline also assumes that the Congress will, through 2021, abide by the caps placed on discretionary spending created in 2011 and reduced in 2013. That will require about a 10 percent cut in appropriations for defense and nondefense appropriations in fiscal 2020. From 2022 through 2025 discretionary spending is assumed to rise with the rate of inflation and after that to remain constant relative to GDP. Subsequent legislation relaxed the caps in 2014, 2015, 2016, and 2017. It is probably reasonable to assume that they will be relaxed further before 2020 and may rise with both inflation and the population during 2021–2025. The extended baseline also assumes that revenues will increase faster than GDP because of real bracket creep. As will be discussed later, the Congress has never allowed that to happen over extended periods.

If the extended baseline assumptions prove accurate, defense spending after 2025 will be at the lowest level relative to GDP since before World War II and nondefense discretionary spending will be 2.6 percent, the lowest level since at least 1962—the first year for which comparable data is available. Over the past 54 years, nondefense discretionary peaked relative to GDP in 1980 when it was 5.2 percent.

It is difficult to believe that the discretionary numbers projected for the next decade will be realized. Could defense sink so low when there are so many threats in the world, especially from China, whose defense budget has been rising at double-digit rates? It is also difficult to be confident about the nondefense numbers given strong calls for additional infrastructure and education spending. Of course, spending in excess of the levels being assumed might be paid for with increased taxes, but Congress is not good at that.

There are other reasons to think that the extended baseline deficits may be exceeded. It is believed by some that remarkably low interest rates make deficits less harmful than they would be otherwise and that we should be more relaxed about borrowing for things like infrastructure investments (Summers 2016).[10] The validity of such beliefs depends on (1) how easy it will be to reverse the extra borrowing if interest rates again rise toward historical norms and (2) on allocating the extra spending efficiently—something that we have not done well in the past.

Revenues

Since World War II revenues have been remarkably constant relative to GDP, almost always varying between 17 and 19 percent. When the ratio went below 17 percent it was usually because of recessions. There were some temporary tax increases in the past 50 years related to war and a very few permanent tax increases. Otherwise, the tax burden was pressured upward by inflation and real growth that pushed income tax payers into higher tax brackets. The effects of inflation were neutralized in the early 1980s when individual income tax brackets, exemptions, and standard deductions were indexed to the CPI. But whatever the cause, every time the total tax burden was pushed above 19 per-

[10] See also Elmendorf and Sheiner (2017).

cent a tax cut followed. That happened after World War II and after the Vietnam War. It happened again after the effects of the high inflation of the late 1970s were countered by the Reagan tax cuts, and yet again with the Bush tax cuts after the turn of the century. Just before the Bush tax cuts, the tax burden had been above 19 percent for three successive years (1998–2000)—the longest period in U.S. history.

In the CBO analysis, the tax burden reaches 19 percent in 2040 and will surpass it later as real bracket creep continues. Given the past aversion to such a high tax burden, it is reasonable to ask whether this is a realistic assumption. On the other hand, the debt will be rising inexorably and that may deter the tax cuts necessary to keep the burden below 19 percent. If tax cuts do occur, the debt-to-GDP ratio will rise above the 152 percent estimated for 2048 in the base case.

Health Costs

There has been a significant slowdown in the rate of excess health cost growth in recent years. For the 38 years between 1975 and 2014, it averaged 1.8 percent per year, but in the last 23 years of the period, from 1990 to 2014, it slowed to 1.2 percent per year. Because the slowdown is not well understood, it is not known if it will be a lasting phenomenon or one that is reversed in the near future. CBO assumptions for the long run are that Medicare excess cost growth rises from 0.7 to 0.9 percent per year over the next ten years. Medicaid excess cost growth starts at 1.4 percent per year as more states cooperate with the Affordable Care Act and then falls to 0.7 percent per year. In the very long run, excess cost growth in both Medicare and Medicaid slowly converges to 1.0 percent, reaching that level in 2046. Excess cost growth and interest rates are the most uncertain variables in long-run projections. They could be much higher or lower than assumed.

Economic and Demographic Assumptions

Table 6.2 provides the value that CBO assumes for important economic and demographic variables. Because of space limitations, I shall briefly discuss only a few assumptions. CBO provides a much more detailed discussion in their 2016 report on the long-term budget outlook.

Table 6.2 Average annual values for economic and demographic variables that underlie CBO's extended baseline

	2016–2026	2026–2040	Overall, 2016–2040
	Economic variables (percent)		
Growth of GDP			
Real GDP	2.1	2.0	2.1
Nominal GDP	4.1	4.1	4.1
Growth of the labor force	0.6	0.3	0.4
Unemployment			
Unemployment rate	4.9	4.9	4.9
Natural rate of unemployment	4.8	4.7	4.7
Growth of average hours worked	−0.1	−0.1	−0.1
Growth of total hours worked	0.5	0.3	0.4
Earnings as a share of compensation	81	81	81
Growth of real earnings per worker	1.2	1.3	1.3
Share of earnings below the taxable maximum	80	77.5	78.4
Growth of capital services	2.4	1.8	2.0
Growth of productivity			
Total factor productivity	1.3	1.3	1.3
Labor productivity	1.6	1.7	1.7
Inflation			
Growth of the CPI-U	2.3	2.4	2.4
Growth of the GDP price index	2.0	2.0	2.0
Interest rates			
Real rates			
On 10-year Treasury notes and the OASDI trust funds	1.6	1.9	1.8
On all federal debt held by the public	0.8	1.6	1.3
Nominal rates			
On 10-year Treasury notes and the OASDI trust funds	3.9	4.4	4.2
On all federal debt held by the public	3.1	4.0	3.6
	Demographic variables		
Growth of the population (percent)	0.8	0.7	0.7
Fertility rate (children per woman)	1.9	1.9	1.9
Immigration Rate (Per 1000 people in the U.S. population)	3.9	3.9	3.9
Life expectancy at birth, end of period (years)	80.6	81.4	80.8
Life expectancy at age 65, end of period (years)	20.2	20.7	20.3

Source: Congressional Budget Office

Immigration

CBO assumes that the rate of legal and illegal immigration per 1000 U.S. residents will mimic that of the past two centuries. They admit that past data is highly variable. There is a wave of anti-immigrant fervor now sweeping Europe and it is clearly also gripping the United States. If immigration falls short of assumed levels, estimates of potential economic growth will also be lowered and the long-run budget outlook will deteriorate.

Inflation

CBO assumes that the inflation rate stays low through 2048 at near the Federal Reserve's target of 2.0 percent. In a separate analysis CBO shows that a rate above that assumed has negative consequences for the budget deficit over the next ten years because it would increase the assumed growth of discretionary spending and the amount that has to be spent on Cost of Living Allowances for indexed entitlement programs. The negative effect is offset as inflation reduces the nominal debt-to-GDP ratio by increasing nominal GDP. If the average maturity of the debt is lengthened, that delays the negative effects of higher inflation by delaying the need for refinancing at higher nominal interest rates. Inflation's beneficial effect on the deficit and the debt would be even greater, if the rate brackets, personal exemptions, and the standard deductions in the personal income tax had not been indexed for inflation in the early 1980s. Analyses of the fall in the national debt from slightly above 100 percent of GDP at the end of World War II to 23 percent in 1974 attribute much of the fall to inflation.

Interest Rates

Interest rates are extraordinarily low compared to past history, and the once unthinkable prospect of negative nominal interest rates has become thinkable because of European and Japanese experience. CBO assumes a steady rise through 2019 but to levels below historical averages. Over the past few years, CBO has continually lowered its interest rate assumptions. If actual interest rates do not increase as much as currently assumed, long-run budget problems will become less dangerous. For example, in an alternative to their base case that adopts CBO assumptions, Auerbach and Gale assume no interest rate increase from current levels. Their estimate of the fiscal gap falls from 3.0

percent of GDP to 1.8 percent. The budget problem is lessened, but it does not go away.

Productivity

CBO assumes that labor productivity will increase at a steady pace of 1.7 percent through 2048. Since 2010 the growth of labor productivity in the business sector has been abysmal. It has varied year to year between 0.1 and 0.7 percent. It is dangerous to place a large weight on recent experience, but five years of very bad experiences tend to make one nervous. If CBO is significantly too optimistic about future productivity growth, it will have significantly underestimated the seriousness of our long-run budget problems.

Sensitivity Analysis

CBO does an elaborate sensitivity analysis, but on only four of the variables included in Table 6.2—labor force participation rates, productivity growth, the interest rate on the government debt, and excess cost growth for spending on Medicare and Medicaid. CBO shows how deviations of the individual variables from assumed values affect the debt-to-GDP ratio projected for 2048. I shall focus on their example where the four variables jointly become more or less optimistic.

To decide on an appropriate range of possible values for the variables going forward, CBO examines their actual values over the past 30 years. CBO's base assumption for the labor force participation rate has it gradually declining from 63 percent in 2015 to 58 percent in the late 2040s. The range of uncertainty is based on different paths that end up in the late 2040s three percentage points higher or lower than 58 percent. The plausible range for the interest rates on the debt and for excess cost growth in Medicare and Medicaid is one percentage point above or below base-case values. The range for productivity growth is 0.5 percentage point above or below. CBO then takes 60 percent of the ranges and asks what happens if labor force participation is on the lower path described above, excess cost growth and interest rates are 0.6 percentage point above the assumed values, and productivity growth is 0.3 percent per year below assumed values. With these most pessimistic values, the debt-to-GDP ratio reaches 247 percent rather than the 152 percent reached in the extended baseline case. With all four variables at the most optimistic end of the range the debt-to-GDP ratio in 2048 is 85 percent.

The range of uncertainty used by CBO for its sensitivity analysis is quite narrow. It would be interesting to see how vulnerable the nation is to more extreme events. CBO could "stress test" their results by assuming another Great Recession and stimulus program or assuming another Iraq War.

Coping with Uncertainty

The previous discussion has identified numerous reasons to be uncertain about the long-run outlook and it merely skimmed the surface, discussing but a small portion of the multitude of assumptions necessary to make a long-run projection. One could think of many budget targets for the next 30 years, but if there is any concern over the possibility of a fiscal crisis, it is important to have a target for the debt-to-GDP ratio. Let us suppose that Congress decides that 60 percent is an appropriate goal for the debt-to-GDP ratio in 2048. That was the frequently-violated upper limit imposed by the Maastricht Treaty for Eurozone countries. Should policy makers design policies that put us on a track for 60 percent given long-run projections or should policy aim at something lower, like 50 or 40 percent, in order to increase the probability that 60 percent or better will be achieved?

A strong case can be made for aiming for something below 60 percent because the risks associated with doing better or worse than expected are not symmetrical.[11] Assume that we are aiming at 60 percent and we do better than expected. There may be a brief period when we have unnecessarily deprived people of benefits and imposed too high a tax burden, but it should be the easiest thing in the world to persuade policy makers to correct by increasing benefits and cutting taxes. Moreover, while we are adjusting, the deficit will be below the expected level and that will be good for the growth of incomes.

Contrast that with a situation in which we are doing worse than expected. It will be excruciatingly difficult to persuade politicians to increase taxes and slow the growth of benefits. The situation may get out of hand and leave us heading for a fiscal crisis. We have seen from recent experience in Europe that fiscal crises are horribly painful as countries respond with abrupt cuts in social benefits and public pensions and taxes are raised quickly and sometimes arbitrarily.

Conservatism in setting goals can be accompanied by conservatism in interpreting deviations from the target path to the goal. Presumably the assumptions underlying the long-run projections will be re-evaluated fre-

[11] For a different approach, see Elmendorf and Sheiner (2017).

quently—perhaps every year. When there is a undesirable deviation from the optimum path, it may be because of a statistical aberration that does not require corrective action or a structural change that does. Often it will be uncertain which it is. A conservative approach would lean in the direction of assuming that it is a structural change that demands attention.

The effects of uncertainty can also be mitigated by carefully designing programs. For example, if programs and taxes are reformed to put us on a path to a 60 percent Debt-to-GDP ratio, triggers can be built into programs, especially those that are growing rapidly, to automatically make them more or less generous or change revenues if there is a deviation from the desired path. For example, the indexing of Social Security can automatically be made less generous with some notice if benefits are growing faster than planned. If benefits later grow more slowly, some or all of the cuts can be restored.[12]

Unfortunately, triggers have often failed because they have been waived by the Congress when they turn out to be too painful. That means that they have to be designed with care. They cannot be too painful, but they must be stringent enough to have a good chance of correcting deviations from the desired spending or revenue path.[13]

A more fundamental approach would initially design programs so that they are easier to reform. Before Social Security's initial benefits were indexed to wages and existing benefits were indexed to the CPI, Social Security's actuary would predict soaring surpluses in future years. The Congress then had the happy task of increasing benefits to absorb the surpluses.[14] Since indexing they face the painful task of limiting benefit growth or increasing revenues, if they wish to make the program sustainable financially.

Conclusions

Long-run budget projections may not be very reliable, but they are valuable. They identify the most predictable force driving us toward a fiscal crisis, that is, the aging of the population. Aging's effect on Social Security, Medicare, Medicaid and the future debt may be offset for limited periods by pleasant

[12] Swedish Social Security triggers take this form. See Kruse and Palmer (2007).

[13] For more detail on the design of triggers, see Penner and Steuerle (2016).

[14] Ironically, indexing was first introduced in the hope that it would save money. It was thought that the Congress could not resist being too generous when it periodically raised benefits. That was because of some very large increases passed in the late 1960s and early 1970s. In retrospect, that appears to have been an unusual time. The Congress had not been nearly as generous earlier in the program's history and has not increased benefits relative to wages since indexing began.

surprises. But negative surprises are just as likely. In the longer run the dire effects of aging might be offset by large efficiencies in the delivery of health care, by robust economic growth, by extraordinarily low interest rates, or by the coincidental movement of a whole array of less important variables in an optimistic direction. But such events would be outside the realm of historical experience. It would be extremely foolish to count on them.

References

Auerbach, A. J. (1999). On the performance and use of government revenue forecasts. *National Tax Journal, 52*(4), 767–782.

Auerbach, A. J., & Gale, W. G. (2016). Once more unto the breach: The deteriorating fiscal outlook. *Tax Notes, 150*(11), 643.

Committee for a Responsible Federal Budget. (2016). *The very, very long-term budget outlook*. Retrieved from http://www.crfb.org/blogs/very-very-long-term-budget-outlook.

Congressional Budget Office. (2015). *CBO's economic forecasting record: 2015 update*. Washington, DC. Retrieved from https://www.cbo.gov/publication/49891.

Congressional Budget Office. (2016). *The 2016 long-term budget outlook*. Washington, DC. Retrieved from https://www.cbo.gov/publication/51580.

Elmendorf, D. W., & Sheiner, L. M. (2017). Federal budget policy with an aging population and persistently low interest rates. *Journal of Economic Perspectives, 31*(3), 175–194.

Irving, S. J., Dacey, R. F., Simpson, D. B., Latimer, J., Morris, K. D., Gebhart, R., et al. (2018). *The nation's fiscal health: Action is needed to address the federal government's fiscal future* (GAO-18-299SP). Washington, DC. Retrieved from http://www.gao.gov/fiscal_outlook/overview; https://www.gao.gov/products/GAO-18-299SP.

Kruse, A., & Palmer, E. (2007). Sweden. In R. G. Penner (Ed.), *International perspectives on social security reform* (pp. 35–54). Washington, DC: Urban Institute Press.

Miron, J. A. (2016). *US fiscal imbalance over time: This time is different*. Retrieved from http://object.cato.org/sites/cato.org/files/pubs/pdf/us-fiscal-imbalance-time_3.pdf.

Penner, R. G. (2002). Dealing with uncertain budget forecasts. *Public Budgeting & Finance, 22*(1), 1–18.

Penner, R. G. (2008). Federal revenue forecasting. In J. Sun & T. D. Lynch (Eds.), *Government budget forecasting: Theory and practice* (Vol. 142, pp. 11–25). Boca Raton, FL: CRC Press, Auerbach Publications, Taylor & Francis Group.

Penner, R. G., & Steuerle, G. (2016). *Options to restore more discretion to the federal budget*. Arlington, VA: Mercatus.

Steuerle, C. E., & Quakenbush, C. (2016). How budget offices should reframe our long-term budget problems. In B. Hoagland & B. Anderson (Eds.), *Fixing fiscal myopia: Why and how we should emphasize the long term in federal budgeting* (pp. 22–42). Washington, DC: The Bipartisan Policy Center.

Summers, L. H. (2016). *A remarkable financial moment*. Retrieved from http://larrysummers.com/2016/07/06/a-remarkable-financial-moment/.

United States Office of Management and Budget. (2018). Analytic perspectives, long-term budget outlook. In *Efficient, effective, accountable: An American budget (budget of the United States government, fiscal year 2019)*. Washington, DC: U.S. Government Publishing Office.

7

CBO Updated Forecasts: Do a Few Months Matter?

James W. Douglas and Ringa Raudla

Major Points

- The Congressional Budget Office (CBO) serves as the forecasting agency for the United States Congress.
- Forecast accuracy is important because the fiscal projections set the parameters for deliberations over taxing and spending policies.
- This study assesses the ability of the CBO to use information effectively to make quality projections.
- It examines whether the CBO's updated one-year ahead and five-year cumulative projections are more accurate than its initial projections for fiscal years 1978 through 2017.
- Updated projections are generally more accurate, suggesting that the CBO is effectively using the new information.

J. W. Douglas (✉)
Department of Political Science and Public Administration, University of North Carolina Charlotte, Charlotte, NC, USA
e-mail: jwdougla@uncc.edu

R. Raudla
Ragnar Nurkse Department of Innovation and Governance,
Tallinn University of Technology (TalTech),
Tallinn, Estonia
e-mail: ringa.raudla@taltech.ee

D. Williams, T. Calabrese (eds.), *The Palgrave Handbook of Government Budget Forecasting*, Palgrave Studies in Public Debt, Spending, and Revenue,
https://doi.org/10.1007/978-3-030-18195-6_7

Introduction

Fiscal forecasts represent policy information that serves a vital role for budgetary planning for governments across the world. Forecast quality, therefore, has received considerable attention by scholars over the years across a variety of settings (e.g. Auerbach 1999; Beetsma et al. 2009; Bretschneider and Gorr 1992; de Deus and de Mendonça 2017; Ericsson 2017; Krause and Douglas 2005, 2013; Pina and Venes 2011; Plesko 1988; Rodgers and Joyce 1996). At the national level in the United States, the Congressional Budget Office (CBO) is the legislative agency responsible for making budget and economic forecasts for Congress every year.[1] Members of Congress rely upon these forecasts to assess the fiscal condition of the government and set the parameters for debates over taxing and spending policies. As a result, it is important that they receive accurate projections of future revenues, expenditures, and deficits/surpluses. The CBO has developed a reputation for producing quality, non-biased information that is trusted by elected officials from both political parties and branches of government (Joyce 2011). Fiscal forecasts, however, are developed under conditions of great uncertainty and, therefore—in the words of former CBO Director Rudolph Penner—"budget forecasts are always wrong" (2002: 1). In fact, Penner admits that the CBO has at times produced projections that proved to be "extremely inaccurate" (1). Furthermore, the longer forecasts are extended into future years, the more inaccurate they tend to be.

Given the important role that fiscal forecasts play in setting policy agendas, it is necessary to assess the ability of the CBO to accurately predict the future. In this chapter, we attempt to do so by examining the differences between the CBO's initial and updated forecasts. Our approach differs from more traditional studies of forecast accuracy and bias where researchers have compared the CBO's forecast outcomes with those of the Office of Management and Budget (OMB) and, in some cases, the Fed or other forecasting entities (e.g. Auerbach 1999; CBO 2017; Ericsson 2017; Krause and Douglas 2005, 2006; Martinez 2015; Plesko 1988). These studies have been useful in showing how different forecasting entities comparatively use information—presuming that

[1] In the international context, establishing independent legislative budget offices is an important trend in the Organisation for Economic Co-operation and Development (OECD) countries, especially in the aftermath of the fiscal crises experienced by many countries (Chohan 2018; Kim 2015; Von Trapp et al. 2016). In existing comparative studies, the CBO is usually ranked first in terms of its independence and analytical capacities (Von Trapp et al. 2016; see also Kim 2015; Wehner 2006). In that light, the CBO can be viewed as the "most likely case" to provide accurate predictions; in other words, if the CBO has problems with accuracy, the other legislative budget offices in the world are likely to face even more severe challenges in forecasting.

superior forecasts are largely due to more complete information and/or better interpretation of the information at hand. In general, these studies have revealed few systematic differences between CBO forecasts and other forecasts, indicating that the various forecasting agencies use and interpret information in similar ways.[2] These studies, however, do not tell us how effectively CBO uses new information to improve its projections. This is important in light of the findings of Federal Reserve Bank of St. Louis economists Kevin L. Kliesen and Daniel L. Thornton (2012). Kliesen and Thornton found that the CBO's deficit projections have been no more accurate than a simple random walk forecast, suggesting that the information used by the CBO and/or its interpretation of that information is not especially useful for predicting the future. By comparing the CBO's initial and updated forecasts, we will be able to make a determination about whether the CBO is using new information to improve its projections. If the updated forecasts prove to be superior to the initial forecasts, that will be a strong indication that the CBO is effectively using information to improve the quality of its forecasts.

This chapter is organized as follows. First, we describe briefly the CBO's forecasting process. Next, we discuss our methodology for assessing the differences between the initial and updated forecasts. We then present our descriptive findings followed by our statistical analysis. Finally, we conclude by summarizing and presenting the implications of our findings.

The Forecasting Process

The CBO's initial forecasts are released in its annual report, *The Budget and Economic Outlook*, generally in January or February. The forecasts are based upon current law (commonly referred to as *baseline projections*), following the assumption that current laws will not change over the forecast period in ways that would affect revenue collections or expenditure totals. The CBO forecasts major revenue sources (individual income taxes, payroll taxes, corporate income taxes, and other) and expenditure categories (mandatory spending, discretionary spending, and net interest) and uses these to produce projections of total revenues, total expenditures, and the deficit/surplus. Projections are made for each of the upcoming ten fiscal years, and cumulative totals are given for both the next five and ten fiscal year periods (e.g. the January 2017

[2] This is not surprising given that economists from the CBO, OMB, and Council of Economic Advisors work together to produce a consensus forecast for the economy and CBO "does not want to deviate far from the consensus" (Penner 2002: 8).

Budget and Economic Outlook provides forecasts for fiscal years 2018 through 2027,[3] as well as cumulative totals for the periods 2018–2022 and 2018–2027). Cumulative totals are useful in that they offer policymakers an indication of the government's long-term fiscal position under current law.

Updated forecasts are released by the CBO in its *Update to the Budget and Economic Outlook* during the summer, usually in August. Revisions to projections are made in response to three types of information: changes in law, changes in the economy, and technical changes[4] (CBO 2017). Whenever the CBO perceives such changes to affect budgetary outcomes, it incorporates them into its updated forecasts. The updated forecasts, therefore, should be based upon superior information to that used when making the initial forecasts. If CBO is properly interpreting this new information, then we should expect the updated forecasts to be more accurate than the initial forecasts. While this may seem obvious, no study has actually tested this assumption in regards to CBO.[5] We do so below.

Methodology

We follow the methodology used by Kliesen and Thornton (2012) when they compared the CBO's one-year-ahead and five-year cumulative initial projections (focusing on the deficit/surplus) to a random walk forecast because they were simply assessing the relative accuracy of the forecasts. We compare the CBO's initial projections with its updated projections by examining the mean errors, mean absolute errors (MAEs), and root mean-squared errors (RMSEs) of the projections—errors are presented as a percentage of nominal gross domestic product (GDP).[6] We test the statistical significance of the difference between the initial and updated forecast errors by regressing the differences (for both the absolute errors and the squared errors, as percentages of GDP)

---

[3] An updated forecast for the current fiscal year (in this example, 2017) is also provided.

[4] Examples of technical changes include "modeling improvements, the incorporation of new demographic information, recent agency actions or judicial decisions, and updated data from federal agencies or other sources" (CBO 2017: 3).

[5] Two studies have assessed updated one-year ahead forecasts in Europe. Carabotta (2014) found that autumn forecasts of Italy's deficit are generally more accurate than the initial spring forecasts, and Pérez (2007) found that updated forecasts of deficits in Eurozone countries tend to outperform initial projections. Both authors attribute the improvements to better information being available at the time of the updated forecasts.

[6] Projection error = e_t = $U(x) = \alpha + \beta x$ with $\beta > 0$; Mean error = $\frac{1}{N}\sum_{i=1}^{N} U(x_i) = \frac{1}{N}\sum_{i=1}^{N}(\alpha + \beta x_i) = \alpha + \frac{1}{N}\beta\sum_{i=1}^{N} x_i$; MAE = $\bar{X}$; RMSE = $\bar{U}(x_i) = \alpha + \beta\bar{X}$

on a constant and testing the hypothesis that the constant term is zero, using robust standard errors. Differences in errors are calculated as the forecast error of the initial forecast minus the forecast error of the updated forecasts (i.e. initial minus update).[7] Thus, positive numbers reflect more accurate updated forecasts and negative numbers signify more accurate initial forecasts. We examine the CBO's one-year-ahead forecasts and five-year cumulative forecasts of total receipts, total outlays, and deficit/surplus. We further assess the one-year-ahead projections for individual income taxes, corporate income taxes, social insurance taxes, mandatory spending, discretionary spending, and net interest. The CBO's first budget forecasts were for fiscal year 1978. We assess forecasts for fiscal years 1978 through 2017. However, the CBO did not report updated forecasts for many categories until later years (e.g. the first updated forecasts for mandatory spending were not reported until fiscal year 1984). As a result, our analysis for these categories begins in the first year in which they are reported in both the initial and updated projections.

It is important to note that we are not trying to identify the sources of error in the CBO's forecasts—that is effectively done elsewhere (e.g. CBO 2017). Rather, we are attempting to ascertain if the CBO is successfully collecting and interpreting new information in order to improve its forecasts, both short and long-term. The CBO claims that its updated forecasts are based upon new information regarding legislative, economic, and technical changes (CBO 2017). We are, therefore, testing whether the CBO adjusts to the new information in a manner that improves its predictions. If it is doing so, then the updated forecasts should be more accurate than the initial forecasts.

Findings

General Descriptives

Table 7.1 presents summary statistics for the CBO's forecast errors. Errors are calculated as the projection minus the actual. Thus, positive numbers signify over-projections (i.e. actual revenues or outlays are **less** than projected; but, actual deficits are **larger** than projected[8]). Conversely, negative numbers signify under-projections (i.e. actual revenues or outlays are **greater** than

[7] The difference in the absolute errors = |initial e_t| − |update e_t|
The difference in the squared errors = (initial e_t)^2 − (update e_t)^2

[8] Deficits are recorded as negative numbers. Thus, if the projected deficit is −\$100 billion and the actual deficit is −\$110 billion, the error would be +\$10 billion (−100 minus −110 = 10).

Table 7.1 CBO forecast error statistics as a percent of GDP (1978–2017)

Series	Beginning year	Mean error		Mean absolute error		Root mean-squared error	
		Initial	Adjusted	Initial	Adjusted	Initial	Adjusted
One-year-ahead forecast errors							
Deficit/surplus	1978	0.67	0.42	1.38	1.09	2.07	1.60
Total receipts	1978	0.48	0.42	1.10	0.80	1.50	1.14
Individual income taxes	1982	0.30	0.24	0.73	0.51	1.01	0.72
Corporate income taxes	1982	0.16	0.13	0.34	0.29	0.45	0.39
Social insurance taxes	1982	0.12	0.10	0.20	0.14	0.27	0.20
Total outlays	1978	−0.16	0.05	0.71	0.57	0.96	0.78
Mandatory	1984	0.47	0.52	0.73	0.73	0.94	0.92
Discretionary	1984	−0.12	0.06	0.30	0.18	0.38	0.24
Net interest	1982	0.06	0.04	0.16	0.10	0.19	0.16
Five-year cumulative forecast errors							
Deficit/surplus	1985	1.27	1.08	2.50	2.15	3.08	2.67
Total receipts	1985	1.05	1.03	1.67	1.62	2.11	2.07
Total outlays	1985	−0.22	−0.03	1.29	1.07	1.46	1.19

projected; but, actual deficits are **smaller** than projected). The mean error column in Table 7.1 shows a general tendency on the part of the CBO to over-project most budget categories. This is particularly true for the deficit/surplus and all revenues. The results for outlays are more mixed, with the initial forecasts under-projecting total and discretionary spending on average. The only category where the updated forecasts show a tendency to under-predict is total outlays for the five-year cumulative projection, but the mean error is quite small (−0.03%). Thus, it appears that the CBO is generally optimistic regarding both expected revenue collections and the size of the deficit, but less so for outlays. Additionally, the updated forecasts produce lower MAEs and RMSEs than the initial forecasts for almost all of the budget categories.

Deficits/Surpluses

The MAE and RMSE are measures of forecast accuracy. Table 7.1 reveals that the errors for the deficit/surplus are rather large for both the one-year ahead and five-year cumulative forecasts. The average deficit for the period 1978–2017 was 3.44% of GDP. This means that the CBO's one-year-ahead MAEs are roughly one-third the size of the average deficit, while the five-year

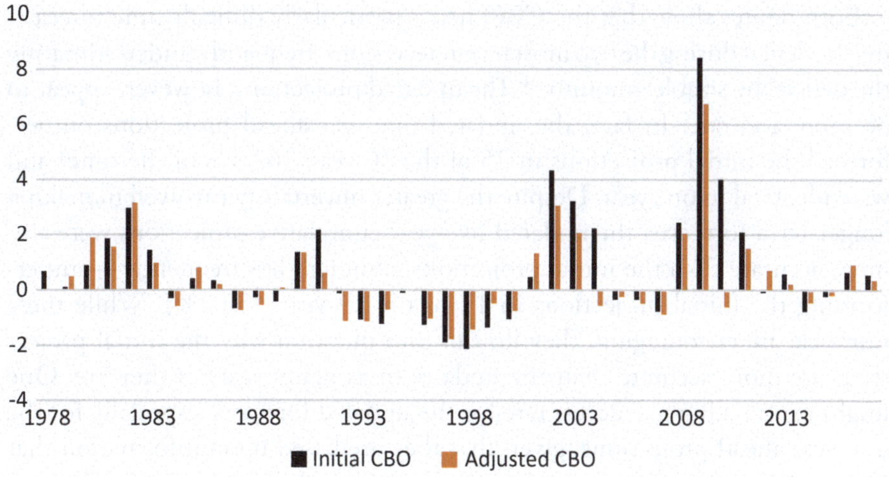

Fig. 7.1 One-year deficit/surplus projection errors as a percent of GDP

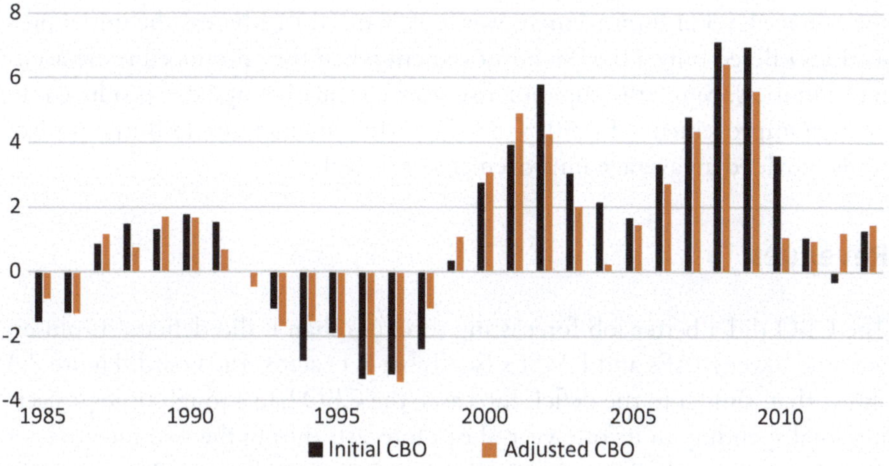

Fig. 7.2 Five-year deficit/surplus projection errors as a percent of GDP

cumulative MAEs are roughly two-thirds the size. The key question, however, is whether the updated forecasts are more accurate than the initial forecasts. The table suggests that this is true, with the updated forecasts producing smaller errors in both the short and long runs. Figures 7.1 and 7.2 illustrate this further. Figure 7.1 shows the CBO's one-year ahead projection errors for the deficit/surplus over the 1978–2017 period, and Fig. 7.2 presents the five-year cumulative projection errors from 1985 to 2013.

Both figures show that the CBO had a particularly difficult time forecasting the deficit during the two most recent recessions, frequently underestimating the deficit[9] by sizable amounts.[10] The updated projections, however, appear to be more accurate. In fact, the updated one-year ahead projections outperformed the initial projections in 25 of the 40 years (62.5% of the time) and were identical in one year. Despite the greater uncertainty involved in making longer-term forecasts, the updated five-year cumulative projections were also more accurate than the initial projections, although less frequently—outperforming the initial projections in 17 of the 29 years (58.2%). While these numbers are encouraging, they do call into question why the initial projections are more accurate than the updates in as many years as they are. One might expect a higher success rate for the updated forecasts, especially for the one-year ahead projections, given that they are based upon information that is several months more up-to-date. Suffice to say that forecasting is always a highly uncertain exercise. It is important to note, however, that in the cases where the updated one-year ahead projections produced superior numbers, the average level of improvement was 0.69% of GDP, whereas the initial projections offered only a 0.41% improvement when they produced more accurate numbers. Similarly, superior five-year cumulative updates produced an average improvement of 0.90% of GDP, while more accurate initial projections provided an average improvement of only 0.43%.

Revenues

The CBO did a better job forecasting revenues than it did deficits/surpluses, yielding lower MAEs and RMSEs (see Table 7.1) across the board. Figure 7.3 shows that, similar to the deficit forecasts, the CBO had a tough time projecting total spending in its one-year-ahead forecasts during the two most recent recessionary periods. However, in the vast majority of years (29 out of 40; 72.5%), the updated forecasts outperformed the initial forecasts, producing an average improvement over the initial forecasts of 0.53% of GDP—whereas in the 11 years where the initial projections were more accurate, the improvement over the updated forecasts was only 0.27% of GDP.

In Figs. 7.4, 7.5, and 7.6, we breakdown the one-year-ahead revenue forecasts by the three largest revenue sources (individual income taxes, corporate income taxes, and social insurance taxes). These figures reveal (as does

[9] Remember that positive errors signify that the deficit was larger than projected.

[10] Recessions, of course, have posed challenges for forecasting accuracy across governments (see, e.g. Mikesell 2018; Reitano 2018).

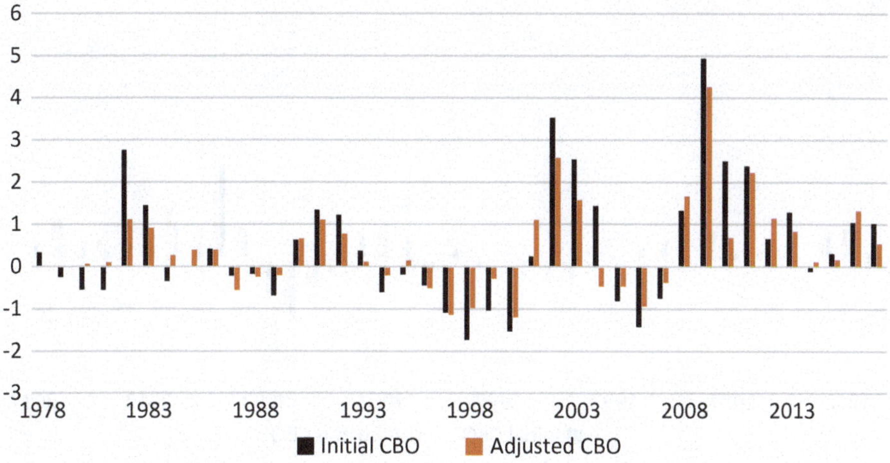

Fig. 7.3 One-year total revenue projection errors as a percent of GDP

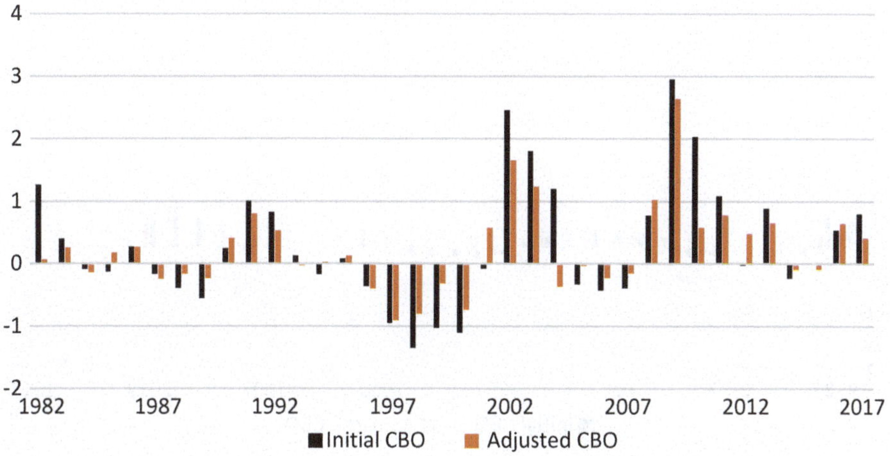

Fig. 7.4 One-year individual income tax projection errors as a percent of GDP

Table 7.1) that the individual income tax is the most difficult of the three to predict. The CBO committed forecast errors for the individual income tax of over 1% of GDP 12 times and 2% of GDP three times between 1982 and 2017, while its errors for the corporate income tax exceeded 1% of GDP only once and its highest errors for the social insurance taxes never reached that threshold. This is not entirely unexpected given that the individual income tax is the federal government's largest revenue source, constituting an average 45.8% of revenues for the period, whereas the corporate income tax and social insurance taxes generated an average of 10.2% and 35.3% of revenues, respec-

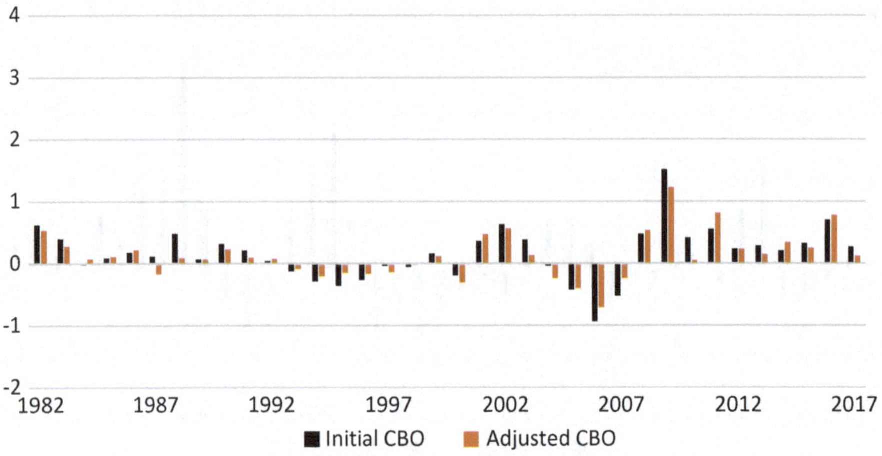

Fig. 7.5 One-year corporate income tax projection errors as a percent of GDP

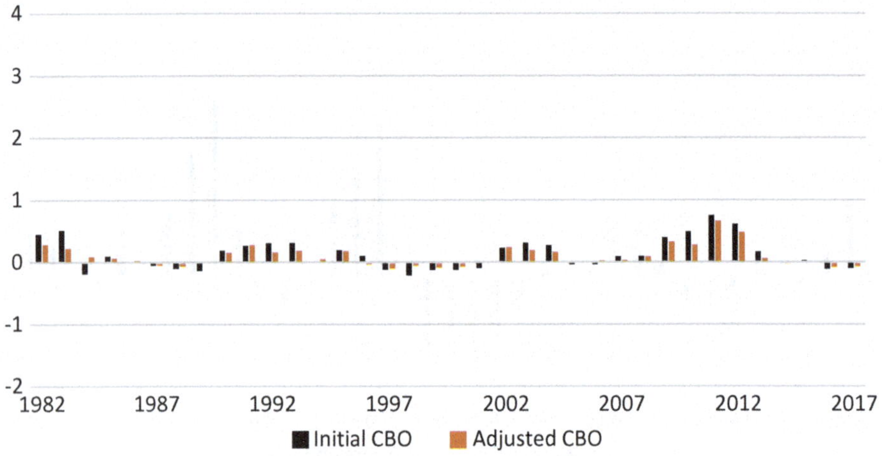

Fig. 7.6 One-year social insurance tax projection errors as a percent of GDP

tively. It is a bit surprising, however, to see such low errors across the time series for the social insurance taxes. After all, these taxes usually produce over one-third of federal receipts. This greater overall forecast accuracy is likely due to the relative stability of employment and wages over the past several decades as well as the facts that the social insurance taxes use single rates that are only applied to wage income, and the tax base cannot be reduced in the same way that the other income taxes can via exemptions, deductions, and credits.

Figures 7.4, 7.5, and 7.6 also show the updated forecasts to be generally more accurate than the initial forecasts for all three revenue sources. For the individual income tax, the updated projections outperformed the initial projections in 24 of the 36 years (66.7% of the time), producing an average improvement of 0.42% of GDP for these years. The updated forecasts performed slightly worse for the corporate income tax, beating the initial forecasts in 21 (58.3%) of the years during this period and improving upon the initial forecasts in these years by an average of 0.15% of GDP. The CBO's ability to improve upon its initial forecasts occurred most often with the social insurance taxes. Between 1982 and 2017, the updated projections were more accurate in 30 of the 36 years (83.3%), and in one of the remaining six years the forecasts were identical. The reduction in error during these years was relatively small, averaging 0.08% of GDP, but this is not surprising given that the average MAE for the initial forecasts was only 0.20% of GDP (see Table 7.1).

Overall, the figures suggest that the CBO is successful at using new information to improve upon its initial one-year-ahead forecasts of revenues. The evidence is less convincing for CBO's longer-term projections. Figure 7.7 provides the five-year cumulative forecast errors for total revenues. The CBO demonstrated a clear tendency to over-project cumulative total revenues, doing so in 22 of the 29 years (75.9%). What is particularly interesting is that the initial projections were superior to the updated projections for 15 of the forecasts (51.8%). This implies that the CBO is not particularly effective at using new information collected in the 6–7 months between its forecasts to improve upon its long-term projections for revenues. It is important to note, however, that when the CBO's updated projections were more accurate, they

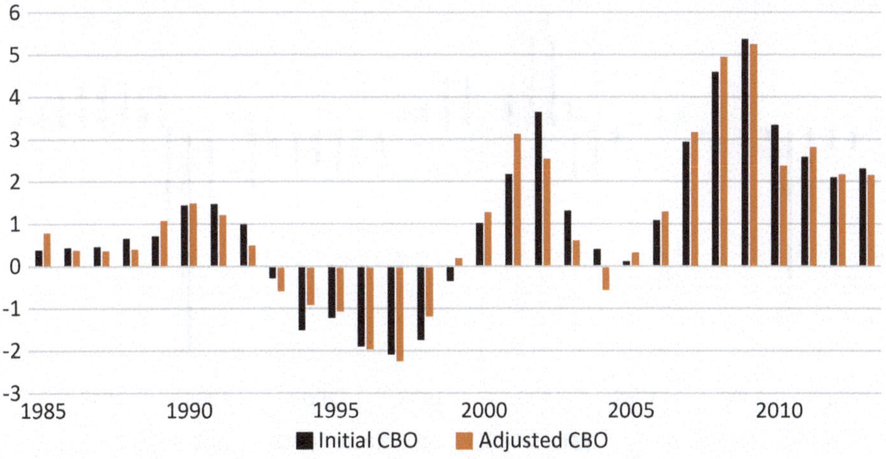

Fig. 7.7 Five-year total revenue projection errors as a percent of GDP

reduced the error by an average of 0.40% of GDP, whereas the superior initial projections produced errors that were only 0.27% of GDP lower than those of the updated projections.

Outlays

The CBO appears to be better at forecasting outlays than either deficits/surpluses or revenues. The MAEs and RMSEs (see Table 7.1) are relatively low for all of the expenditure categories. Figure 7.8 reveals that the CBO had a particularly difficult time projecting total revenues in its one-year-ahead forecasts during the early 1980s, the early 1990s, and the Great Recession. For the most part, the updated forecasts were superior to the initial forecasts, producing more accurate projections in 28 of the 40 years (70.0%), and one year where the projections were identical. In contrast to the deficit/surplus and revenue forecasts, the updated forecasts resulted in smaller relative reductions in projection errors. The average reduction in error was 0.30% of GDP for the 28 years when the updates were more accurate, whereas the reduction was 0.25% of GDP for the 11 years where the initial forecasts were superior.

Figures 7.9, 7.10, and 7.11 display the CBO's one-year-ahead forecast errors for the major expenditure categories of mandatory spending, discretionary spending, and interest on the debt. The figures make clear that the CBO has more difficulty projecting mandatory spending, although its performance regarding this budget category seems to have improved substantially

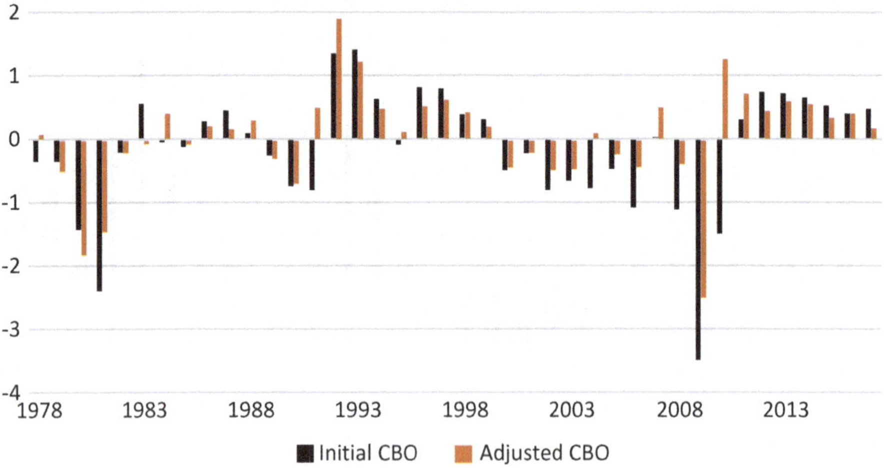

Fig. 7.8 One-year total spending projection errors as a percent of GDP

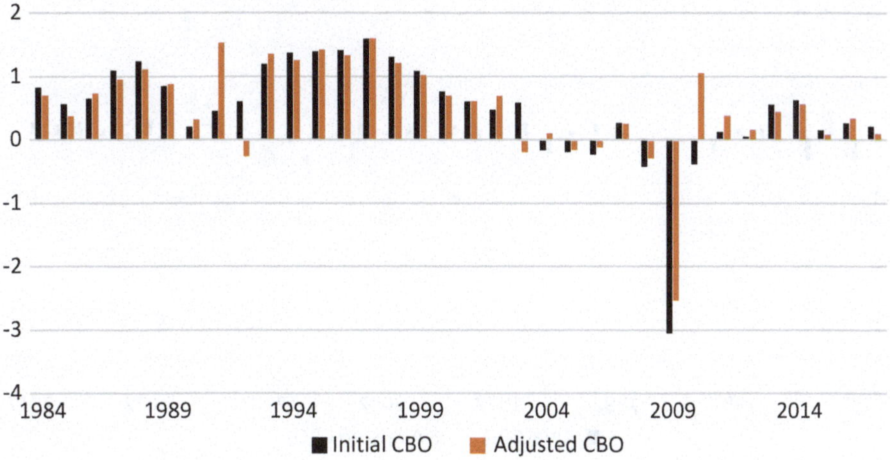

Fig. 7.9 One-year mandatory spending projection errors as a percent of GDP

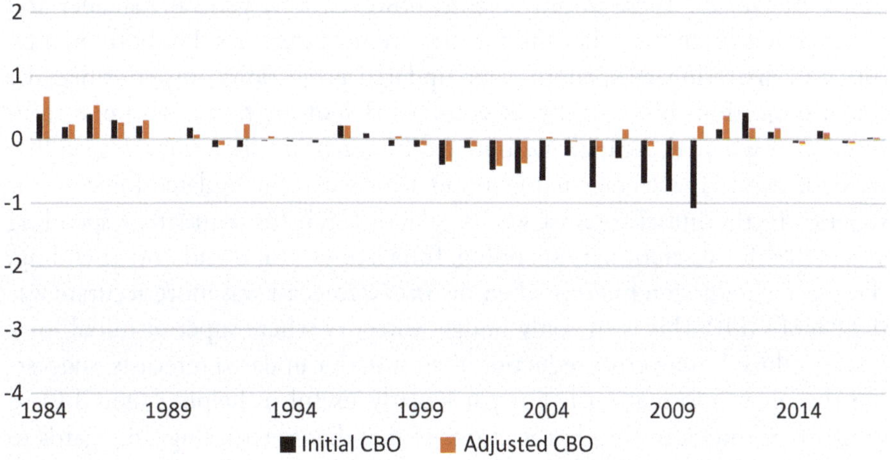

Fig. 7.10 One-year discretionary spending projection errors as a percent of GDP

since the early 2000s, aside from the large errors due to the Great Recession. The CBO has shown a strong bias toward over-projecting mandatory spending, a pattern that does not exist for the other two spending categories. The CBO has reported that mandatory spending is relatively hard to predict because of the uncertainty surrounding the demand for health care services, growth in health care costs, the impacts on Medicaid eligibility resulting from changes in law, and the effects of economic downturns (CBO 2017).

As was true for revenues, Figs. 7.9, 7.10, and 7.11 show the updated forecasts to be generally more accurate than the initial forecasts for all of the

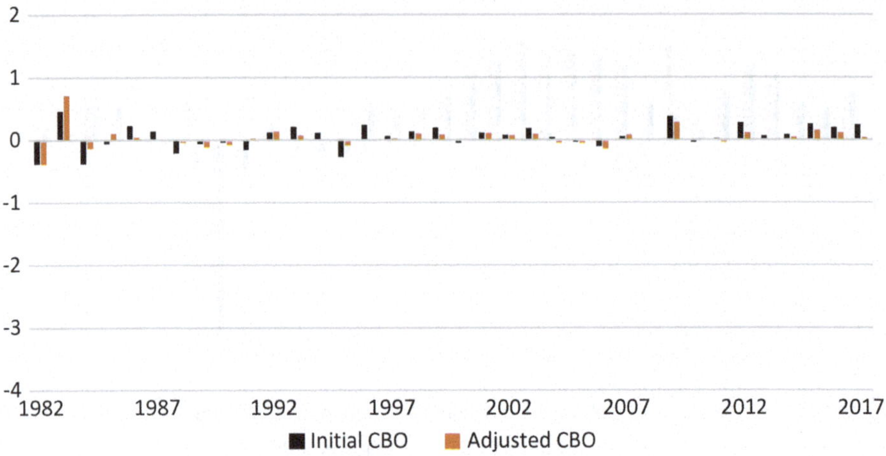

Fig. 7.11 One-year interest projection errors as a percent of GDP

outlay categories. These improvements, however, were generally smaller and occurred less often than they did for the revenue categories. For both mandatory and discretionary spending, the updated projections outperformed the initial projections in 21 of the 34 years (61.8% of the time), with one additional year where the initial and updated forecasts for discretionary spending were identical. The average reduction in error when the updated forecast was superior to the initial forecast was 0.14% of GDP for mandatory spending and 0.20% for discretionary spending. Interestingly, for mandatory spending, the average reduction in error when the *initial* forecast was more accurate was 0.22% of GDP. This is the only budget category where superior initial forecasts produced more error reduction than superior updated forecasts, suggesting that new information is not particularly useful in helping the CBO to improve its one-year-ahead projections of mandatory spending. In regards to interest on the debt, Fig. 7.11 shows that the updated forecasts were more accurate in 24 of the 36 years (66.7%), with three additional years where the initial and updated forecasts were the same. The reduction in error for these 24 years averaged 0.11% of GDP, which is not surprising given that the average MAE for the initial forecasts was only 0.16% of GDP (see Table 7.1) and interest makes up a relatively small portion of the budget.

When we turn to the longer range projections, it appears that the updated forecasts have a tendency to improve upon the initial forecasts. Figure 7.12 provides the errors for the five-year cumulative forecasts. The updated projections were more accurate in 16 of the 29 years (55.2%). When the CBO's updated projections were more accurate, they reduced the error by an average

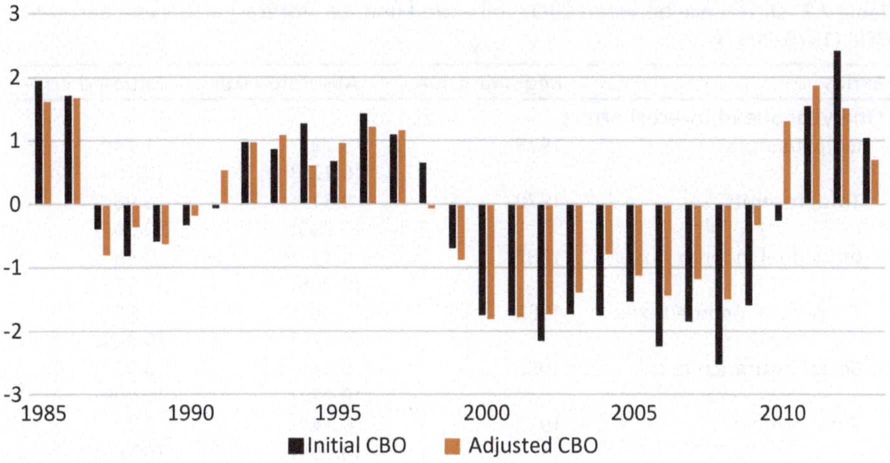

Fig. 7.12 Five-year total spending projection errors as a percent of GDP

of 0.58% of GDP, whereas the superior initial projections produced errors that were only 0.23% of GDP lower than those of the updated projections. Additionally, it appears that the performance of the updated forecasts relative to the initial forecasts has improved in recent years, yielding superior projections in 10 of the last 12 years in the series. These results suggest that, despite the greater uncertainty associated with longer time horizons, the CBO is able to improve its long-term projections with the new information it acquires over the several months between its forecasts.

Regression Analysis

Table 7.2 provides the regression results testing the differences in error (using the absolute error [AE] and the squared error [SE] as a percentage of GDP) between the CBO's initial and updated forecasts. As stated previously, we calculate the differences in error by subtracting the updated projection error from the initial projection error. We then regress the differences on a constant, testing whether the constant is significantly different from zero. We report the coefficient of each constant. Positive values reflect more accurate updated forecasts, and negative values signify more accurate initial forecasts. The results show that the CBO's updated forecasts are systematically more accurate than the initial forecasts for most budget categories. This is true for both short-term and long-term forecasts.

Table 7.2 Difference between CBO's initial and updated forecast errors as a percent of GDP (1978–2017)

Series	Beginning year	Absolute error	Squared error
One-year-ahead forecast errors			
Deficit/surplus	1978	0.29**	1.74**
		[0.129]	[0.784]
Total receipts	1978	0.31****	0.96***
		[0.083]	[0.304]
Individual income taxes	1982	0.23***	0.49***
		[0.068]	[0.155]
Corporate income taxes	1982	0.05**	0.05
		[0.025]	[0.029]
Social insurance taxes	1982	0.06****	0.03****
		[0.012]	[0.009]
Total outlays	1978	0.14***	0.32*
		[0.055]	[0.185]
Mandatory	1984	0.00	0.04
		[0.047]	[0.115]
Discretionary	1984	0.10**	0.09*
		[0.043]	[0.044]
Net interest	1982	0.06****	0.01
		[0.017]	[0.010]
Five-year cumulative forecast errors			
Deficit/surplus	1985	0.35**	2.35**
		[0.161]	[1.000]
Total receipts	1985	0.05	0.18
		[0.082]	[0.400]
Total outlays	1985	0.22**	0.71***
		[0.097]	[0.256]

Robust standard errors are in brackets
**p* = 0.1; ***p* <= 0.05; ****p* <= 0.01; *****p* <= 0.001

The differences in AE and SE for the one-year-ahead projections of the deficit/surplus are both positive and significant. The results for the AE reveal that updated forecasts are on average 0.29% of GDP more accurate than the initial forecasts. Similar results are found for the five-year cumulative projections, with the differences in AE and SE being positive and significant, and the updated forecasts yielding an average improvement of 0.35% of GDP.

The updated one-year-ahead forecasts for total revenues also prove to be more accurate than the initial forecasts by 0.31% of GDP. The same is true for most of the specific revenue sources. The differences in AE and SE are positive and significant for the individual income tax and the social insurance taxes, with an average reduction in error of 0.23% of GDP for the individual income tax and 0.06% of GDP for the social insurance taxes. The results are mixed for the corporate income tax. The difference in AE is positive and significant, but the difference in SE fails to achieve statistical significance. When we move to the longer-term forecasts, we see that the coefficients for the five-year cumulative forecasts are not significantly different from zero, indicating that the updated projections are indistinguishable from the initial projections in terms of their accuracy.

The findings regarding outlays are more mixed. One-year-ahead total outlays are positive and significant, with the updated forecasts improving upon the initial forecasts by 0.14% of GDP. However, the coefficient for SE is only significant at the 0.10 level. The same outcome occurs for discretionary spending (i.e. the AE and SE are both positive and significant, but the latter is only significant at the 0.10 level), while only the AE for net interest achieves statistical significance. In contrast, neither the AE nor SE attain statistical significance for the mandatory spending category, indicating that the CBO is unsuccessful at using new information to improve upon its initial projections for mandatory spending in the short-term. In the longer term, however, the CBO's updates do appear to produce superior predictions—the differences in AE and SE for the five-year cumulative forecasts for total outlays are both positive and significant, with an average reduction in error of 0.22% of GDP.

Conclusion

Fiscal forecasts set the parameters for deliberations over taxing and spending. It is therefore important for elected officials to receive accurate projections of revenues, expenditures, and deficits. Congress relies upon the CBO for fiscal forecasts, but the quality of CBO's projections have been called into question by some scholars (see Kliesen and Thornton 2012; Penner 2002). Thus, it is necessary to assess the ability of the CBO to use information to make quality predictions of the future. We do so by examining whether CBO's updated forecasts produce more accurate predictions than its initial forecasts. We argue that more accurate updated projections demonstrate an ability on the part of the CBO to use new information gathered over a 6–7-month period of time to improve its forecasts. This, in turn, would be an indication that the CBO uses information effectively when it makes its forecasts—that is, we assume that using new information to improve projections is likely only if the CBO generally collects and analyzes information effectively.

Our analysis shows that the CBO's updated forecasts actually do tend to be more accurate than its initial forecasts. We found evidence that the CBO's updated one-year-ahead projections are systematically superior to its initial projections for most of the budget categories we examined. More often than not, the updated projections have proven to be more accurate. This leads us to conclude that the CBO is able to identify, collect, and analyze information that enable it to make better budget forecasts for the upcoming fiscal year. What is particularly interesting is that the CBO also appears to be able to effectively use the new information that it collects over a small time period (generally 6–7 months) to improve the accuracy of its five-year cumulative forecasts for both the deficit/surplus and total outlays. The high degree of uncertainty associated with longer-term forecasts make them especially prone to error, yet these forecasts are a necessary tool for Congress as it grapples with the government's long-term fiscal position. It is therefore encouraging to know that the CBO is able to reduce its projection errors significantly as it receives and processes new information. So, it seems that a few months do indeed matter when making forecasts, even when those forecasts extend beyond the upcoming fiscal year.

This does not mean that there isn't room for improvement. We found little evidence that the CBO's updated forecasts systematically improved upon its initial forecasts for either one-year-ahead mandatory spending or five-year cumulative total receipts. In fact, we found that initial forecasts were more accurate slightly more often for long-term total receipts. Additionally, even for each of the budget categories where the updates clearly outperformed the initial projections overall, there were individual years where the initial projections proved to be superior. This, no doubt, attests to the high degree of uncertainty involved in predicting federal outlays and receipts, but also serves as a signal to the CBO that the new information it uses does not always lead to better results. Fortunately for Congress, in most cases it does.

References

Auerbach, A. J. (1999). On the performance and use of government revenue forecasts. *National Tax Journal, 52*(4), 767–782.

Beetsma, R., Giuliodori, M., & Wierts, P. (2009). Planning to cheat: EU fiscal policy in real time. *Economic Policy, 24*(60), 753–804.

Bretschneider, S. I., & Gorr, W. L. (1992). Economic, organizational, and political influences on biases in forecasting state sales tax receipts. *International Journal of Forecasting, 7*(4), 457–466. https://doi.org/10.1016/0169-2070(92)90029-9.

Carabotta, L. (2014). Which agency and which period is the best? Analyzing national and international fiscal forecasts in Italy. *International Journal of Economic Sciences, 3*(1), 27–46.

Chohan, U. W. (2018). Independent budget offices and the politics–administration dichotomy. *International Journal of Public Administration, 41*(12), 1009–1017.

Congressional Budget Office (CBO). (2017). *An evaluation of CBO's past outlay projections.* Congress of the United States. Washington, DC. Retrieved from https://www.cbo.gov/publication/53328.

de Deus, J. D. B. V., & de Mendonça, H. F. (2017). Fiscal forecasting performance in an emerging economy: An empirical assessment of Brazil. *Economic Systems, 41*(3), 408–419.

Ericsson, N. R. (2017). How biased are US government forecasts of the federal debt? *International Journal of Forecasting, 33*(2), 543–559.

Joyce, P. G. (2011). *The Congressional Budget Office: Honest numbers, power, and policymaking.* Washington, DC: Georgetown University Press.

Kim, C. (2015). A study on compilation and improvement of indices for legislative budgetary institutions. *OECD Journal on Budgeting, 14*(3), 1–29.

Kliesen, K. L., & Thornton, D. L. (2012). How good are the government's deficit and debt projections and should we care? *Federal Reserve Bank of St Louis Review, 94*(1), 21–39.

Krause, G. A., & Douglas, J. W. (2005). Institutional design versus reputational effects on bureaucratic performance: Evidence from US government macroeconomic and fiscal projections. *Journal of Public Administration Research and Theory, 15*(2), 281–306.

Krause, G. A., & Douglas, J. W. (2006). Does agency competition improve the quality of policy analysis? Evidence from OMB and CBO fiscal projections. *Journal of Policy Analysis and Management, 25*(1), 53–74.

Krause, G. A., & Douglas, J. W. (2013). Organizational structure and the optimal design of policymaking panels: Evidence from consensus group commissions' revenue forecasts in the American states. *American Journal of Political Science, 57*(1), 135–149.

Martinez, A. B. (2015). How good are US government forecasts of the federal debt? *International Journal of Forecasting, 31*(2), 312–324.

Mikesell, J. L. (2018). Often wrong, never uncertain: Lessons from 40 years of state revenue forecasting. *Public Administration Review, 78*(5), 795–802.

Penner, R. G. (2002). Dealing with uncertain budget forecasts. *Public Budgeting & Finance, 22*(1), 1–18.

Pérez, J. J. (2007). Leading indicators for euro area government deficits. *International Journal of Forecasting, 23*(2), 259–275.

Pina, Á. M., & Venes, N. M. (2011). The political economy of EDP fiscal forecasts: An empirical assessment. *European Journal of Political Economy, 27*, 534–546. https://doi.org/10.1016/j.ejpoleco.2011.01.005.

Plesko, G. A. (1988). The accuracy of government forecasts and budget projections. *National Tax Journal, 41*(4), 483–501.

Reitano, V. (2018). An open systems model of local government forecasting. *The American Review of Public Administration, 48*(5), 476–489.

Rodgers, R., & Joyce, P. G. (1996). The effect of underforecasting on the accuracy of revenue forecasts by state governments. *Public Administration Review, 56*(1), 48–56.

Von Trapp, L., Lienert, I., & Wehner, J. (2016). Principles for independent fiscal institutions and case studies. *OECD Journal on Budgeting, 15*(2), 9–24.

Wehner, J. (2006). Assessing the power of the purse: An index of legislative budget institutions. *Political Studies, 54*(4), 767–785.

Part II

State and Local

8

State Revenue Forecasting Practices: Accuracy, Transparency, and Political Participation

A Volcker Alliance Project Paper

Emily Franklin, Carolyn Bourdeaux, and Alex Hathaway

Major Points

- Current literature concerning revenue forecast accuracy, transparency, and political participation.
- Assessment of accuracy, transparency, and political participation of revenue forecasts in the 50 states for FY2015 to FY2017.
- Case analyses of several states demonstrate that revenue forecasts exist within institutional and political frameworks that can significantly influence the accuracy and transparency of the publicly reported forecast.
- Conclusions drawn from the Volcker Alliance's *Truth and Integrity in Government Finance* project, 2016–2017

E. Franklin (✉)
Carl Vinson Institute of Government, University of Georgia, Athens, GA, USA
e-mail: emifrank@uga.edu

C. Bourdeaux • A. Hathaway
Andrew Young School of Policy Studies, Georgia State University,
Atlanta, GA, USA

D. Williams, T. Calabrese (eds.), *The Palgrave Handbook of Government Budget Forecasting*, Palgrave Studies in Public Debt, Spending, and Revenue,
https://doi.org/10.1007/978-3-030-18195-6_8

Introduction[1]

The state revenue forecast sets the tone for state budget deliberations. Because most states operate under a balanced budget constraint, the revenue forecast establishes a foundation for fiscal discipline and often sets a cap on state spending. Almost every state has evolved a unique process around revenue estimation, and scholars debate whether certain processes or methodologies are more accurate, more likely to lead to broad political participation, or more likely to provide a firm foundation for fiscal discipline. The academic literature on these processes is vast and by no means conclusive regarding best practices.

This chapter draws on a dataset produced as part of the Volcker Alliance's *Truth and Integrity in Government Finance* project to examine the revenue forecasting processes in all 50 states, as well as accuracy, transparency, and political participation in the development of the revenue estimate. This chapter then draws on several detailed case studies to show how the revenue estimation process is interconnected with other fiscal rules and practices, such as reserve fund practices. An important observation from this analysis is that these fiscal practices can intersect in unexpected ways, sometimes causing the formally published revenue estimate to differ from the actual revenues that state policymakers expect to receive.

Literature Review

Forecasting Processes

One of the most vibrant debates in the literature on state revenue forecasting centers on the forecasting process. Revenue forecasting is roughly divided into three types: executive, separate, and consensus. Executive forecasts are made by the governor and staff without input from the legislature or non-partisan experts. Separate forecasts are formed independently and separately by the executive and legislative branches, while consensus forecasts are jointly produced by the executive and legislative branches (McNichol 2014, 9).

The process most recommended by academics and informed practitioners is a consensus forecast because it is seen as more likely to be accurate, transpar-

[1] Special thanks to the Volcker Alliance for their research support and permission to use their data in this analysis.

ent, and politically acceptable (Mikesell 2008, 427–429; Klay and Vonasek 2008, 379–381; Tebbs 2009, 1–3; Fortuna 2004). According to the National Association of State Budget Officers (NASBO), a consensus revenue forecast is a "revenue projection developed in agreement through an official forecasting group representing both the executive and legislative branches" (National Association of State Budget Officers 2015, 150). However, the three categories of revenue forecasting mask wide variations in structure, particularly around consensus forecasting, which can involve numerous combinations of legislative and executive policymakers. Consensus groups can include legislative and executive staff, elected officials (even those explicitly from opposing political parties), and non-partisan external groups such as academics or businesspersons. A primary interest in the literature is the extent to which these process differences are linked to political participation, accuracy, or transparency in the forecast.

Political Participation

States are divided in the level of political versus professional input into the revenue forecasting process. Similarly, scholars are divided about the appropriate mix. Mikesell and Ross (2014) raise the issue of political contention around the revenue forecast, arguing that key players from both the executive and legislative branches need to be involved in the process to build consensus and reduce conflict over the final estimate (199–200). However, other researchers have used the same logic to call for de-politicizing the revenue forecasting process completely, with the idea that a professional, non-political revenue forecast will be more likely to be accepted by competing political interests (Deschamps 2004, 615; Boylan 2008, 411). There are a number of studies with anecdotal accounts of states adopting consensus forecasts for political reasons to try to reduce conflict (Mikesell and Ross 2014, 199–200; Wong and Ekstrom 2008, 435–438; Alt et al. 2006, 40–42), but an important dimension that deserves more study is who should be at the table in a consensus process. Many states include some form of professional non-political advisor in their revenue forecasting process. As of 2014, at least 36 states include non-governmental experts. Of the 28 states with a consensus forecast, at least 19 states have a consensus forecast with non-governmental experts in their forecasting body (McNichol 2014, 9).

Accuracy

Because revenue collections are affected by state, national, and global economic conditions, they can be difficult to predict. Researchers have looked at which forecasting techniques produce the most accurate results. There is extensive literature showing that combining independent forecasts increases accuracy (Clemen 1989). Updating revenue forecasts as close to the start of the fiscal year as possible has also been shown to increase accuracy (Boyd and Dadayan 2014, 33). Some studies have found that consensus revenue forecasting improves the accuracy of forecasts, though it is not clear why this is the case (Willoughby and Guo 2008, 40; Qiao 2008, 406; Klay and Vonasek 2008, 390). One reason may be that the process often involves a number of experts from different fields who can provide a wealth of economic information and ensure the forecasting method is not unduly influenced by political motives (Randall and Rueben 2017). Crucially, Krause and Douglas (2013) have found that the diversity of a forecasting group only has net benefits when the group is kept small in number. Accuracy may also improve if different preliminary forecasts are combined during the process of forming the official forecast (Qiao 2008, 398). However, Voorhees (2004) found consensus forecasts had less of an effect on accuracy after controlling for the frequency of the state's forecasts, independent expert input, and other factors (668–669). Boyd and Dadayan (2014) agree that consensus forecasting can help insulate the process from undue political influences, but their study did not show that it contributed to the accuracy of the forecast (viii–ix).

The effect of political participation on the accuracy of the revenue forecast is still being debated. Several studies found forecasts became less accurate because of political interference (Krause et al. 2013, 291; Boylan 2008, 411; Buettner and Kauder 2010, 313). Creating politically independent groups with knowledge of the forecasting domain, however, reduced forecasting error (Deschamps 2004, 1). In contrast, Mikesell and Ross (2014) found that the highly politicized Indiana consensus revenue forecast process (which has not only executive and legislative consensus but also Republican and Democratic Party representation) outperformed various simple revenue forecasting processes and had the further benefit of building consensus around the forecast (188–189).

When assessing the accuracy of state forecasts, it is important to note that, according to some studies, states purposely underestimate revenues on a regular basis (Voorhees 2006, 61; Rodgers and Joyce 1996, 48; Rose and Smith 2012, 188; Boyd et al. 2011, 13). Budget-makers have an incentive to underestimate revenues because overestimation can lead to politically unpopular budget cuts or tax increases. Interestingly, for states that created budget stabilization funds (BSFs) with policies governing contributions and withdrawals, Rose and Smith (2012) found that underestimation bias was reduced (188). Their results suggest that BSFs allow policymakers to save surpluses without pressure from taxpayers and special interest groups to spend the surplus funds. Rose and Smith's study also suggests that fiscal institutional factors may affect the accuracy of the revenue forecast.

Transparency

The level of transparency surrounding the estimation process is another relevant aspect of revenue forecasting. The Government Finance Officers Association (GFOA) recommends governments be upfront about their methodological philosophies when they present the forecast's underlying assumptions. Several studies show that many states routinely make forecast underestimations with errors around 2 or 3 percent (Voorhees 2006, 72; Rodgers and Joyce 1996, 48; Boyd and Dadayan 2014, 13). Other studies, however, found little or no evidence of underestimation (Cassidy et al. 1989; Mocan and Azad 1995). However, the authors of this chapter could not locate a study specifically examining which states made forecasting policy—such as whether a state was taking a "conservative approach"—explicit in the budget documents.

GFOA also recommends that governments clearly present underlying assumptions and methodologies in the final budget document (Government Finance Officers Association, 2014, 1). Likewise, the Organisation for Economic Co-operation and Development (OECD) and the International Monetary Fund (IMF) recommend that key economic assumptions be disclosed in budget documents (OECD 2002, 11; IMF 2007, 2.1.4). Such assumptions can include gross domestic product (GDP), growth, employment and unemployment rates, and inflation (OECD, 11). However, McNichol, Lav and Leachman (2015) found that most states do not clearly show how these underlying economic assumptions tie to the revenue forecast and that a few states, such as Alabama and Tennessee, do not publish these assumptions at all (5).

Political and institutional factors can help predict the level of transparency around the revenue forecast. Alt, Lassen, and Rose (2006) provide some anecdotal accounts of states, such as Delaware and Rhode Island, adopting consensus revenue forecasting to increase fiscal transparency (40–41). These efforts were generally adopted during periods of fiscal stress or split governments or after a party turnover in the governor's office. Certain institutional factors can also have an unexpected effect on transparency in the revenue forecasting process. For example, Rose and Smith (2012) found that states with budget stabilization funds (BSFs) were more transparent about the amount of expected surplus in the forecast (188).

This analysis examines three key aspects of revenue forecasting in the 50 U.S. states: the level of accuracy, transparency, and political participation. An interesting question is whether states using consensus forecasts are more likely to publish detailed forecast methodologies and underlying macroeconomic assumptions. While recognizing the endogeneity of a consensus forecast to inter-party political conflict, a further question of interest is whether consensus forecasts are more likely to be accepted as legitimate by policymakers than an executive or separate forecast.

Using data compiled for the *Truth and Integrity in Government Finance* project, this chapter examines state revenue forecasting budget practices and the extent to which state forecasts are accurate and transparent, as well as the political makeup of forecasting groups. The authors then draw on rich contextual detail and case studies to consider how political and institutional factors affect forecast accuracy, transparency, and political participation.

Methods

The Volcker Alliance project assembled a national group of research universities to conduct a survey of the budget and fiscal practices of all 50 states for FY2015, FY2016, and FY2017. Data was gathered by students in public policy, economics, and other programs, assessed as complete by university professors, and then verified by independent reviewers at the Volcker Alliance. The project assessed whether, and to what extent, states face structural deficits. Several questions focused on revenue forecasting processes, multi-year revenue and expenditure forecasts, revenue growth projection rationales, and midyear budget adjustments. The project answered 29 questions in total, but for this chapter, the analysis focuses on the data gathered for the following questions:

1. **Does the state reasonably support revenue growth projections at the time of the initial budget?**
2. **Was there a need for a negative midyear budget adjustment (greater than 1% of the budget)?**

The data were collected for all 50 states and can be combined with NASBO's *Fiscal Survey of the States* data to compare forecasting processes across states and answer basic descriptive questions about political participation in the process as well as the transparency and accuracy of the forecast itself. Additionally, in several states with unexpected variation in the revenue estimate, we called staff and reviewed newspaper articles to better understand how the revenue estimate was developed, constructing more detailed case studies of the process.

For the purposes of the project, the term "budget documents" encompasses the governor's recommended budget, appropriations acts, and supporting documents such as legislative analyses of the budget, presentations, or revenue forecasts, if produced or released in tandem with the budget. "Consensus" revenue forecasts are defined as forecasts with at least executive and legislative participation. "Multi-year," as in "multi-year revenue forecast," refers to a forecast for at least three future fiscal years. Additionally, the analysis draws on more detailed information from the Volcker Alliance data on the shifts in the revenue estimates during budget development, adoption, and implementation.

Results

Political Participation in the Forecasting Processes in the U.S. States

This section discusses different political makeups of the revenue forecasting groups in the states. Twenty-eight states have a consensus forecast, although these processes can vary widely. Nine of the states have an executive process, and 13 have a separate process (one where the legislative branch and executive branch develop independent revenue estimates) (McNichol 2014, 9). As noted earlier, states define "Consensus" in different ways with varying degrees of non-partisan, staff, and elected official participation. Even the executive-dominated processes have different external and staff advisement arrangements. In some states, such as Maryland, only staff are involved in the revenue forecasting process, although the process is still considered consensus because the staff are from the executive branch as well as the legislative research offices and are aware of the policy objectives of their elected officials. Other consensus, staff-driven processes include Florida, Kentucky, North Carolina, and Mississippi. Virginia has an interesting hybrid process with two committees working on the forecast. The first committee is a staff or expert committee, the Joint Advisory Board of Economists (JABE). This committee works on the detailed methodology behind the forecast and produces several options for consideration by the second committee, the Governor's Advisory Council on Revenue Estimates (GACRE). GACRE is chaired by the governor, includes legislative leadership, and ultimately votes on the revenue estimate to use.

Political Acceptance of the Revenue Forecast

Mikesell and Ross (2014) have previously highlighted the importance of acceptance of the forecast by political actors. Their paper includes a case study of Indiana. In the mid-1970s, the governor and Indiana legislators could not agree on a revenue forecast. The governor as well as Democrats and Republicans in the General Assembly ended up using three different forecasts. From this political upheaval, the consensus process Indiana currently employs was born (Mikesell and Ross 2014, 199).

However, a consensus process does not guarantee political acceptance of the forecast. As recently as 2014, the Republican-majority legislature and Democratic Governor in Missouri were unable to come to a consensus on the revenue forecast (Lieb 2014). Missouri has an informal consensus revenue forecasting process in which the Director of Revenue, Commission of Administration, State Treasurer, House and Senate appropriation staff, Division of Budget and Planning, and University of Missouri staff prepare separate forecasts before coming together to decide on a joint forecast (Mikesell and Ross 2014, 191). The governor's estimate was \$8.74 billion (Missouri Office of Administration 2014, 10). The legislature's estimate was about \$15 million lower: \$8.59 billion (Missouri Senate Appropriations Committee, 17). According to the analysis by the *Associated Press*, the different estimates came from different assumptions about the growth of Missouri's economy, but they also stemmed from a disagreement about the interpretation of a Missouri constitutional provision that gives the governor power to cut state spending during a revenue shortfall (Lieb 2014). Article IV §27 of the Missouri Constitution gives the governor the authority to "reduce the expenditures of the state or any of its agencies below their appropriations whenever the actual revenues are less than the revenue estimates upon which the appropriations were based." In the past, Governor Nixon (and other governors) used the power to make cuts to legislative spending priorities even when there was no revenue shortfall. Republican legislators may also have believed a surplus, which would be more likely with a conservative estimate, would lend credibility to a Republican proposal to cut the state income tax (Lieb 2014).

The issues that arose when forming Missouri's FY2015 revenue forecast may have come about because the process is an informal one, and lawmakers are free to use another estimate if they choose. The institutional environment—the governor's ability to cut spending without legislative review—may also have fueled disagreement over the estimate.

Accuracy of the States' Revenue Forecasts

This section discusses the accuracy of revenue forecasts in the states. Table 8.1 groups states by forecasting type (consensus, executive, or separate) and whether or not states made a midyear adjustment greater than 1 percent of the budget in FY2015 and/or FY2016. It also shows the absolute value of the average forecasting error for each group across the time period studied (FY2015–FY2017). University researchers and independent reviewers at the Volcker Alliance determined whether or not a midyear adjustment was made to the budget. Midyear budget adjustments for FY2017 are not included because the fiscal year was ongoing at the time of data collection, resulting in too many missing data points.

The percent error (PE) is the difference between actual general fund collections and the official forecast as a percentage of actual collections. The mean absolute percent error (MAPE) is the absolute value of the mean percent error. The MAPE attempts to capture the magnitude of forecast "misses." The mean percent error (MPE) attempts to capture the forecasting bias of a state or forecasting group. A positive number is an under-forecast, while a negative number is an over-forecast.[2] A table with errors and midyear adjustments by state and year can be found in Appendix 1.[3]

Table 8.1 Midyear adjustments and MAPE by forecasting type

	Did not make a midyear adjustment	Made a midyear adjustment
Consensus	3.2%	3.0%
Executive	3.2%	13.3%
Separate	2.4%	2.5%

[2] Percent Error = $(A_t - F_t) / A_t$

Mean Percent Error = $\Sigma[(A_t - F_t) / A_t]$

Mean Absolute Percent Error = $|\Sigma[(A_t - F_t) / A_t]|$

where A = actual general fund collections, F = official forecast of general fund collections, and t = the fiscal year.

[3] The reader should be wary in comparing errors across states. The portfolio of funds that comprise each state's general fund can be very different. For example, some states have transportation funds separate

Qiao (2008) considered less than 5 percent forecasting error to be a relatively accurate forecast, and a Pew-Rockefeller report on state revenue forecasts generally found that the MAPE was 3.3 percent, while the median was 2.3 percent (403; Boyd and Dadayan 2014, 14). In our data, the MAPE for all the states fell between those two numbers at 4 percent. The MAPE is unsurprising considering FY2015, FY2016, and FY2017 were not particularly volatile years. The median absolute percent error was just above Boyd and Dadayan's at 2.5 percent.

Combining the midyear adjustment and no midyear adjustment groups, the "separate" revenue forecast group had the smallest median absolute error at 2.1 percent, below the median absolute error for all the states of 2.5 percent. At 4 percent, the executive group's median absolute error was well above the median absolute error for all the states. Consensus fell between the other groups at 2.5 percent and was equal to the median absolute error for all the states. Forty-nine percent of consensus states made a midyear adjustment in either FY2015, FY2016, or both, and 46 percent of separate states did so. In contrast, 67 percent of executive states made midyear adjustments to the budget over the study period.

Executive states that made midyear adjustments made large positive errors. The MAPE for the group was 13.3 percent. States in this group included Alaska, Georgia, Oklahoma, and West Virginia. Alaska had errors as large as 50.1 percent, which may have contributed to the large MAPE for the group. Separate and consensus states that made midyear adjustments did not have much worse errors than states in those groups that did not make a midyear adjustment. The separate group, regardless of whether or not the state made a midyear adjustment, had the lowest MAPEs for the time period studied. This analysis suggests a separate process may lead to the most accuracy; however, the state-to-state differences in dependency on volatile revenue sources, for example, mean this analysis is not thorough enough to draw conclusions about the relative accuracy of different forecasting methods.

Furthermore, drawing on more detailed data from various case studies suggests some important considerations when assessing the difference between the forecast and actual revenues. For instance, in the 2015 legislative session, Georgia passed transportation legislation that increased tax and fee revenues

---

from the general fund where they deposit revenues from highway tolls and other transportation-related revenues. Other states put these revenues into the general fund. States can also have different tax structures, which impacts their revenues because different sources of revenue have different levels of volatility. For example, some states do not have income taxes. Finally, the reader should be aware that the general fund forecasts and actual collections are based on NASBO survey numbers, which do not account for post-publication tax base or rate changes, administration collection changes, or changes to the general fund structure.

by $870 million in FY2016; however, the state did not add these new revenues to their budget until the middle of FY2016, which makes the error rate appear to be 6.9 percent (see Appendix 1). Additionally, Georgia adds an increase of 1 percent of net revenue each year to K-12 education funding in the midyear budget out of the revenue shortfall reserve. However, the state consciously pre-funds this by lowballing the revenue estimate in order to force itself to reserve this amount for the upcoming year.[4] Finally, Georgia's governor publicly committed to building a $2 billion reserve fund by the end of his term in 2018 (Salzer 2016). In Georgia, funds are added to the reserve from any year-end general fund surpluses, so the governor intentionally lowballed the revenue estimate to create the surpluses that could be used to build the reserve. None of this is explicit in the budget documents meaning there is no way to know the "true" underlying forecast. While Georgia's forecasting process is not the most transparent, the state's overly conservative revenue estimates do not necessarily reflect poor forecasting capacity, but an intentional effort to significantly underestimate the revenues.

Other states, such as South Carolina, Tennessee, Utah, and Arizona, also appear to substantially underestimate revenues. Like Georgia, South Carolina has designated current-year uses for prior-year reserves, in this case a reserve for capital outlay. In practice, the state uses this capital outlay reserve as a first-resort rainy day fund prior to tapping their revenue shortfall reserve. However, according to a budget official, South Carolina does not make conservative revenue estimates to replenish this fund but to avoid midyear budget cuts and year-end deficits.[5] Similarly, Tennessee does not purposely make conservative revenue estimates, according to a budget official, but the high end of its forecasting group's estimate can generally be achieved with a high degree of certainty.[6]

On the other hand, some states use less conservative approaches to forecasting. Virginia is noteworthy because it missed its revenue forecast substantially (−4.9 percent) in FY2015 (See Appendix 1). The state appears to have intentionally gone into FY2015, the second year in its biennium, knowing that it would overshoot its revenue estimate. According to one account, the state had to formally overshoot its revenue estimate in order to access its reserve funds.[7] Virginia statute stipulates that the state can only access the Revenue Stabilization Fund "if the general fund revenues appropriated exceed the

[4] Interview with Director of Georgia Office of Planning and Budget.

[5] Interview with Executive Budget Office official, South Carolina Department of Administration.

[6] Interview with Director of Tennessee Budget Analyst Agency.

[7] Interview with Staff Director, Virginia House Appropriations Committee.

forecast by more than two percent." Despite passing an adjusted FY2015 budget in June 2014 and making significant provisions for an anticipated shortfall, the legislature did not formally lower the revenue estimate until after an August 2014 revised revenue estimate (which, in turn, was legally triggered by problems with the FY2014 revenue estimate). The legislature then formally inserted the reserves into the revised budget in December 2014.

In detail, Virginia ended the 2014 regular legislative session without a budget due to a budget impasse, which continued into a special session. By May 2014, the state realized it would not meet its forecast for FY2014, which would legally trigger a new forecast on July 1, the first day of the FY2014–2016 biennium. Because the state did not want to use a revised forecast in adopting its new budget, the General Assembly was able to end the impasse, and a budget was adopted based on the old revenue forecast from December 2013. Now the forecast would not be revised until after the start of the new fiscal year, allowing the state to reopen the newly adopted budget and use the Revenue Stabilization Fund. Virginia's constitution does not allow the use of the Revenue Stabilization Fund in building a budget, which is why it was imperative to adopt the new budget using the December 2013 revenue estimate.[8]

Given these variations in managing the revenue estimate, the metric of "forecast error" may be something of a misnomer for many states. Rather than reflecting any lack of internal capacity or methodological problems, forecasting errors at the state level may be more appropriately characterized as a problem of transparency *or* strategies for management of legal and institutional arrangements. Revenue forecasts to some degree have a unique role in the budget process that goes beyond the accuracy around expected revenues. For instance, in Georgia, the balanced budget requirements are tied to the revenue forecast. Since the executive unilaterally sets the forecast, the governor can use it as a policy lever to bound legislative expenditures rather than as a device to communicate anticipated revenues. The same sort of issue is illustrated in the Missouri case mentioned above.

Since many of the states with inaccurate forecasts either face problems like volatile energy prices or have revenue forecasts that do not accurately reflect their revenue expectations, it is difficult to assess the relationship between the forecasting process and outcome. A brief look at the states that appear to produce forecasts intended to accurately reflect expected revenues shows no evidence of any clear linkage between a consensus forecast and accuracy. The most accurate states, such as Vermont, Alabama, and Massachusetts, include

[8] Interview with Budget Director, Virginia House of Delegates.

a mix of forecasting process types. None of the executive forecast states had a MAPE less than 1 percent, but Arkansas's was quite low at 1.2 percent. Obviously, a more sophisticated quantitative analysis is warranted, but as noted above, such an analysis would need to consider actual revenue expectations relative to the reported revenue forecast carefully.

Transparency of States' Revenue Forecasts

Table 8.2 groups states by forecasting type and whether a state had a reasonable rationale for revenue growth projections. The forecasting error is the difference between actual general fund collections and the official forecast as a percentage of actual collections. The mean absolute percent error (MAPE) attempts to capture the magnitude of forecast "misses."

Whether or not a state had a "reasonable rationale" for revenue growth projections was determined by local university research teams. The quality of these answers was then assessed by independent expert reviewers at the Volcker Alliance.

Most states that received a "yes" answer to having a reasonable rationale for revenue growth projections discussed, at a minimum, the general economic assumptions that underpinned their forecast. Some states that received a "no" answer also discussed these trends. Differences in how the question was answered by university researchers who gathered data for the Volcker Alliance project may explain the variance. A table with errors and those states that did not have a reasonable rationale can be found in Appendix 2.

Interestingly, executive states with a reasonable rationale had the largest MAPE (9.1 percent). States in this group included Alaska, Arkansas, Minnesota, North Dakota, Oklahoma, Oregon, Texas, and West Virginia. Perhaps states who know they are going to miss their estimate by a large amount are more likely to provide explanation of their estimate. These states also tended to over-forecast, which may indicate budgetary distress. Executive states without a reasonable rationale included only Georgia. Georgia had the second largest MAPE (5.4 percent) of all the groups, but it was positive, indicating a large under-forecast. Regardless of their forecast-

Table 8.2 Reasonable rationales and MAPE by forecasting type

	State without reasonable rationale	States with reasonable rationale
Consensus	2.9%	3.8%
Executive	5.4%	9.1%
Separate	0.4%	2.8%

ing process, states with reasonable rationales tended to have larger errors. This result is the opposite of the expected result: states that provide poor explanation for their revenue growth projections are expected to be less accurate.

Although best practice suggests that states clearly link macroeconomic assumptions to their revenue forecast calculation, few of the states surveyed did so. Virginia is one state that does make its calculations explicit. The state includes its revenue source calculations in "The Economic Outlook and Revenue Forecast," prepared by the Virginia Department of Taxation for one of its forecasting groups, GACRE (McAuliffe et al. 2016, Appendix C). These calculations illustrate how the estimate for each revenue source was developed. Florida is another good example. Its estimate of revenue from the ad valorem tax is directly linked to new construction and other important variables that affect that the source of revenue. All of these statistics are available online, and it is fairly easy to see how the revenue estimating group arrived at the ad valorem revenue estimate (Florida Revenue Estimating Conference 2017, 1).

While the results of the analysis are interesting from a normative perspective, there is no clear interrelationship between accuracy, consensus forecasts, and transparency around the forecasting methods. Both Florida and Virginia have consensus forecasts. Florida's mean absolute percent error (MAPE) was quite low over the fiscal years studied (0.8 percent); its MAPE was much lower than the MAPE for the consensus group (3.6 percent) and the MAPE for all the states (4 percent). Virginia had a higher MAPE of 2.8 percent, but this was still lower than the rest of the consensus group and total MAPE of all the states. That being said, Virginia did struggle with its forecast during FY2015, significantly downgrading the estimate that ultimately was close to the initial projection prior to the start of the fiscal year. But the state also did a significant—and public—analysis of how the revenue forecast missed and what steps the state would take to avoid such errors going forward (Brown 2014). In contrast, Alabama does not include the macroeconomic assumptions underlying its forecast, but its MAPE of 0.4 percent is lower than that of Florida. See Appendix 1 for all state errors.

Generally, most states regardless of forecasting type seem comfortable providing general economic trends and a forecast that is loosely associated with these trends. However, the rigor around the Virginia and Florida processes is certainly appealing and warrants an expanded analysis of the relationship among rigor, transparency, and accuracy.

Conclusion

The state revenue forecast is an important aspect of the budget-forming process. In a balanced budget environment, the forecast establishes a critical constraint on expenditures. Because forecasts are affected by global, national, and state economic conditions, revenue collections are notoriously difficult to predict. While accuracy is important, so are transparency and political participation. As Mikesell and Ross (2014) commented, revenue "forecast accuracy is irrelevant if the budget process does not respect the forecast as a resource constraint" (188). In other words, a forecasting process that lacks transparency and broad political participation is not likely to be accepted by political stakeholders and can be harmful to the state budget-making process, regardless of the forecast's accuracy.

Using data compiled for the Volcker Alliance's *Truth and Integrity in Government Finance* project, this chapter examined revenue forecasting practices in the U.S. states and found that on average the forecasts were about as accurate as prior research would have led us to anticipate. However, the FY2015, FY2016, and FY2017 budget years were not particularly volatile overall. Additionally, the state case analyses suggest that the forecasts cannot always be taken at face value; the forecasts exist in institutional as well as political frameworks, and for a variety of reasons, the anticipated revenues are not always the same as the formal forecast. This finding will be important when embarking on a larger quantitative analysis assessing forecast accuracy or using forecast accuracy as an independent variable. While certainly not determinative, there was little evidence that consensus forecasts were consistently associated with improved accuracy. In terms of transparency, most states present some generic economic trends, and the forecast is not explicitly connected to these trends. The rigor of the states that clearly explain their models is refreshing, but more research would be required to validate their accuracy.

Appendix 1: General Fund Forecast to Actual Differences and Midyear Adjustments

State by forecasting type	FY2015 percent error	FY2015 midyear adjustment?	FY2016 percent error	FY2016 midyear adjustment?	FY2017 percent error	State mean percent error	State mean absolute percent error (MAPE)
Consensus							
Connecticut	−1.0%	Yes	−2.3%	Yes	0.1%	−1.1%	1.1%
Delaware	0.2%	–	0.2%	–	−2.5%	−0.7%	0.9%
Florida	1.4%	–	−0.6%	–	0.5%	0.4%	0.8%
Hawaii	5.7%	–	4.0%	–	−2.2%	2.5%	4.0%
Indiana	0.3%	–	−1.0%	–	−2.0%	−0.9%	1.1%
Iowa	−0.4%	–	−3.7%	–	−3.5%	−2.6%	2.6%
Kansas	−0.8%	Yes	−8.6%	Yes	−8.6%	−6.0%	6.0%
Kentucky	1.3%	–	2.8%	–	0.0%	1.3%	1.3%
Louisiana	−3.0%	Yes	−8.6%	Yes	0.0%	−3.9%	3.9%
Maine	2.5%	–	1.3%	–	2.3%	2.0%	2.0%
Maryland	−0.4%	Yes	−0.8%	–	−2.5%	−1.2%	1.2%
Massachusetts	0.3%	Yes	−0.4%	–	0.9%	0.3%	0.6%
Michigan	3.7%	Yes	1.3%	–	0.4%	1.8%	1.8%
Mississippi	1.4%	–	0.7%	Yes	3.2%	1.8%	1.8%
Missouri	1.4%	–	1.3%	–	−3.0%	−0.1%	1.9%
Nebraska	2.0%	–	−3.9%	Yes	−3.1%	−1.7%	3.0%
Nevada	−1.7%	Yes	4.9%	–	4.5%	2.6%	3.7%
New Mexico	−0.1%	–	−10.4%	Yes	−7.9%	−6.1%	6.1%
New York	7.3%	–	2.0%	–	−1.5%	2.6%	3.6%
North Carolina	2.1%	–	2.2%	–	−0.3%	1.4%	1.5%
Rhode Island	4.1%	–	3.3%	–	1.2%	2.8%	2.8%
South Carolina	4.3%	–	3.1%	–	0.0%	2.5%	2.5%
Tennessee	4.0%	–	7.0%	–	4.3%	5.1%	5.1%
Utah	7.3%	–	2.4%	–	0.0%	3.2%	3.2%
Vermont	−0.3%	Yes	0.4%	Yes	−0.2%	0.0%	0.3%
Virginia	−4.9%	Yes	0.9%	–	−2.7%	−2.2%	2.8%
Washington	2.7%	–	3.2%	–	2.5%	2.8%	2.8%
Wyoming	−17.0%	–	−77.1%	–	−2.9%	−32.3%	32.3%

Mean	**0.8%**		**−2.7%**		**−0.8%**	**−0.9%**	**3.6%**
Median	**1.3%**		**0.8%**		**−0.1%**	**0.4%**	**2.5%**
Executive							
Alaska	−50.1%	Yes	−43.2%	Yes	13.9%	−26.5%	35.7%
Arkansas	0.2%	–	3.4%	–	0.0%	1.2%	1.2%
Georgia	3.5%	Yes	6.9%	Yes	1.7%	4.0%	4.0%
Minnesota	3.6%	–	1.2%	Yes	−0.8%	1.4%	1.9%
North Dakota	2.1%	–	−31.3%	Yes	−0.5%	−9.9%	11.3%
Oklahoma	−2.0%	Yes	−9.1%	Yes	−5.5%	−5.5%	5.5%
Oregon	2.4%	–	−2.1%	–	0.9%	0.4%	1.8%
Texas	4.9%	–	−5.9%	–	−4.6%	−1.9%	5.1%
West Virginia	−1.4%	Yes	−4.6%	Yes	0.0%	−2.0%	2.0%
Mean	**−4.1%**		**−9.4%**		**0.6%**	**−4.3%**	**7.6%**
Median	**2.1%**		**−4.6%**		**0.0%**	**−1.9%**	**4.0%**
Separate							
Alabama	−0.2%	–	−0.7%	–	0.3%	−0.2%	0.4%
Arizona	2.1%	–	6.7%	–	1.1%	3.3%	3.3%
California	6.0%	–	0.4%	–	−1.3%	1.7%	2.6%
Colorado	2.1%	–	−2.8%	Yes	0.9%	0.0%	1.9%
Idaho	3.2%	–	2.0%	–	1.1%	2.1%	2.1%
Illinois	−0.4%	Yes	–	Yes	−1.6%	−0.7%	0.7%
Montana	2.9%	–	−6.7%	Yes	−5.8%	−3.2%	5.1%
New Hampshire	−2.2%	–	6.4%	–	4.8%	3.0%	4.5%
New Jersey	1.7%	Yes	−2.1%	–	−0.7%	−0.4%	1.5%
Ohio	2.3%	–	−2.6%	–	−2.9%	−1.1%	2.6%
Pennsylvania	5.6%	–	–	Yes	−5.0%	0.2%	3.6%
South Dakota	−0.8%	–	0.3%	–	−1.7%	−0.7%	0.9%
Wisconsin	−1.2%	Yes	−0.7%	–	−1.0%	−1.0%	1.0%
Mean	**1.6%**		**0.0%**		**−0.9%**	**0.2%**	**2.3%**
Median	**2.1%**		**−0.7%**		**−1.0%**	**−0.2%**	**2.1%**
TOTAL							
Mean	**0.1%**		**−3.2%**		**−0.6%**	**−1.2%**	**4.0%**
Median	**1.4%**		**0.2**		**−0.2%**	**0.0%**	**2.5%**

Note: FY2016 has missing values because some states only had proposed forecasts, not enacted

Appendix 2: States Without a Reasonable Rationale and GF Forecast to Actual

State	FY2015 PE	RR?	FY2016 PE	RR?	FY2017 PE	RR?	State PE	State APE
Consensus								
Iowa	−0.4%	No	−3.7%	No	−3.5%	No	−2.6%	2.6%
Kansas	−0.8%	No	−8.6%	No	−8.6%	No	−6.0%	6.0%
Missouri	1.4%	No	1.3%	No	−3.0%	No	−0.1%	1.9%
Virginia	−4.9%	No	0.9%	–	−2.7%	–	−2.2%	2.8%
Executive								
Georgia	3.5%	No	6.9%	No	1.7%	No	4.0%	4.0%
Separate								
Alabama	−0.2%	No	−0.7%	No	0.3%	No	−0.2%	0.4%
Illinois	−0.4%	–	N/A	No	−1.6%	No	−0.7%	0.7%

References

Alt, J. E., Lassen, D. D., & Rose, S. (2006). The causes of fiscal transparency: Evidence from the US states. *IMF Staff Papers, 53*(1), 30–57.

Boyd, D. J., & Dadayan, L. (2014). *State tax revenue forecasting accuracy: Technical report.* Retrieved from http://rockinst.org/wp-content/uploads/2018/02/2014-09-30-Revenue_Forecasting_Accuracy.pdf.

Boyd, D. J., Dadayan, L., & Ward, R. B. (2011). *States' revenue estimating cracks in the crystal ball.* Albany, NY. Retrieved from http://www.rockinst.org/pdf/government_finance/2011-03-01-States_Revenue_Estimating_Report.pdf.

Boylan, R. T. (2008). Political distortions in state forecasts. *Public Choice, 136*, 411–427.

Brown, R. D. (2014). *Governor McAuliffe's proposed amendments to the 2014–2016 budget: Economic outlook & revenue forecast.* Secretary of Finance. Virginia. Retrieved from http://hac.state.va.us/Committee/files/2014/12-17-14/JMC-with-appendix%2012-17-14.pdf.

Buettner, T., & Kauder, B. (2010). Revenue forecasting practices: Differences across countries and consequences for forecasting performance. *Fiscal Studies, 31*, 313–340. https://doi.org/10.1111/j.1475-5890.2010.00117.x.

Cassidy, G., Kamlet, M. S., & Nagin, D. S. (1989). An empirical examination of bias in revenue forecasts by state governments. *International Journal of Forecasting, 5*(3), 321–331.

Clemen, R. T. (1989). Combining forecasts: A review and annotated bibliography. *International Journal of Forecasting, 5*(4), 559–583.

Deschamps, E. (2004). The impact of institutional change on forecast accuracy: A case study of budget forecasting in Washington State. *International Journal of Forecasting, 20*(4), 647–657. https://doi.org/10.1016/j.ijforecast.2003.11.009.

Florida Revenue Estimating Conference. (2017). *Ad valorem assessments conference package.* Retrieved from http://edr.state.fl.us/Content/conferences/advalorem/adval_results.pdf.

Fortuna, D. (2004, July 11). How to fix Albany; real numbers, true accounting. *The New York Times.* Retrieved from http://www.nytimes.com/2004/07/11/opinion/how-to-fix-albany-real-numbers-true-accounting.html?_r=0.

Government Finance Officers Association. (2014). Financial forecasting in the budget preparation process. *Best practice.* Retrieved from http://www.gfoa.org/financial-forecasting-budget-preparation-process.

International Monetary Fund. (2007). Code of good practices on fiscal transparency.

Klay, W. E., & Vonasek, J. A. (2008). Consensus forecasting for budgeting in theory and practice. In J. Sun & T. D. Lynch (Eds.), *Government budget forecasting: Theory and practice* (pp. 379–392). Boca Raton, FL: CRC Press.

Krause, G. A., & Douglas, J. W. (2013). Organizational structure and the optimal design of policymaking panels: Evidence from consensus group commissions' revenue forecasts in the American states. *American Journal of Political Science, 57*(1), 135–149.

Krause, G. A., Lewis, D. E., & Douglas, J. W. (2013). Politics can limit policy opportunism in fiscal institutions: Evidence from official general fund revenue forecasts in the American states. *Journal of Policy Analysis and Management, 32*(2), 271–295.

Lieb, D. A. (2014, January 12). Analysis: Missouri governor, lawmakers disagree over state's budget. *Columbia Missourian.* Retrieved from https://www.columbiamissourian.com/news/state_news/analysis-missouri-governor-lawmakers-disagree-over-state-s-budget/article_95c3a213-0479-5e78-9fc1-e489b404ae4c.html.

McAuliffe, T. R., Brown, R. D., & Burns, C. M. (2016). *The economic outlook and revenue forecast through fiscal year 2020: Governor's confidential working papers.* Retrieved from https://is.gd/c9Mmr6.

McNichol, E. C. (2014). *Improving state revenue forecasting: Best practices for a more trusted and reliable revenue estimate.* Retrieved from Center on Budget and Policy Priorities—CBPP: Washington, DC: https://www.cbpp.org/sites/default/files/atoms/files/8-7-14sfp.pdf.

McNichol, E. C., Lav, I., & Leachman, M. (2015). *Better state budget planning can help build healthier economies.* Retrieved from https://www.cbpp.org/research/state-budget-and-tax/better-state-budget-planning-can-help-build-healthier-economies.

Mikesell, J. L. (2008). State revenue forecasting in the state of Indiana: A consensus system in a politically divided state. In J. Sun & T. D. Lynch (Eds.), *Government budget forecasting: Theory and practice* (pp. 415–429). Boca Raton: CRC Press.

Mikesell, J. L., & Ross, J. M. (2014). State revenue forecasts and political acceptance: The value of consensus forecasting in the budget process. *Public Administration Review, 74*(2), 188–203.

Missouri Office of Administration. (2014). *The Missouri budget fiscal year 2015 Summary.*

Mocan, H. N., & Azad, S. (1995). Accuracy and rationality of state general fund revenue forecasts: Evidence from panel data. *International Journal of Forecasting, 11*(3), 417–427.

National Association of State Budget Officers. (2015). *Budget processes in the states: Spring 2015.* National Association of State Budget Officers: Washington, DC. Retrieved from https://www.nasbo.org/reports-data/budget-processes-in-the-states.

Organisation of Economic Cooperation and Development. (2002). *Best practices for budget transparency.* Retrieved from http://www.oecd.org/governance/budgeting/Best%20Practices%20Budget%20Transparency%20-%20complete%20with%20cover%20page.pdf.

Qiao, Y. (2008). Use of consensus revenue forecasting in US state governments. In J. Sun & T. D. Lynch (Eds.), *Government budget forecasting: Theory and practice* (pp. 393–413). Boca Raton, FL: CRC Press.

Randall, M., & Rueben, K. (2017). *Sustainable budgeting in the states.* Retrieved from http://www.taxpolicycenter.org/sites/default/files/publication/149186/sustainable-budgeting-in-the-states_1.pdf.

Rodgers, R., & Joyce, P. G. (1996). The effect of underforecasting on the accuracy of revenue forecasts by state governments. *Public Administration Review, 56*(1), 48–56.

Rose, S., & Smith, D. L. (2012). Budget slack, institutions, and transparency. *Public Administration Review, 72*(2), 187–195.

Salzer, J. (2016, September 9). Georgia's budget reserves swell to record $2.05 billion. *The Atlanta Journal-Constitution.* Retrieved from http://www.myajc.com/news/state%2D%2Dregional-govt%2D%2Dpolitics/georgia-budget-reserves-swell-record-billion/FOdmIo076opAIjjLd9dk2I/.

Tebbs, J. (2009). *Breaking the stalemate: A proposal for a consensus revenue forecasting process.* Connecticut Voices for Children. Retrieved from http://www.ctvoices.org/sites/default/files/bud09revenueforecasting.pdf.

Voorhees, W. R. (2004). More is better: Consensual forecasting and state revenue forecast error. *International Journal of Public Administration, 27*(8–9), 651–671.

Voorhees, W. R. (2006). Consistent underestimation bias, the asymmetrical loss function, and homogenous sources of bias in state revenue forecasts. *Journal of Public Budgeting, Accounting & Financial Management, 18*(1), 61–76.

Willoughby, K. G., & Guo, H. (2008). The state of the art: Revenue forecasting in US state governments. In J. Sun & T. D. Lynch (Eds.), *Government budget forecast-*

ing: Theory and practice (Vol. 142, pp. 27–42). Boca Raton, FL: CRC Press, Auerbach Publications, Taylor & Francis Group.

Wong, J. D., & Ekstrom, C. D. (2008). Consensus revenue estimating in state government: A case of what works in Kansas. In J. Sun & T. D. Lynch (Eds.), *Government budget forecasting: Theory and practice* (pp. 431–455). Boca Raton, FL: CRC Press.

9

Forecasting Post-Crisis Virginia Tax Revenue

Melissa McShea and Joseph Cordes

Major Points

- In this chapter, we determine the viability of using Bayesian vector autoregression (BVAR) in estimating four major tax revenues for Virginia.
- Although findings are somewhat mixed, it does appear that BVAR models with exogenous variables are the basis of low forecast errors for several of the revenue series.
- There is merit in relying on Bayesian autoregressive models as alternatives to the other models we consider.

M. McShea (✉)
Department of Public Management, John Jay College of Criminal Justice, New York, NY, USA
e-mail: mmcshea@jjay.cuny.edu

J. Cordes
Trachtenberg School of Public Policy and Public Administration, The George Washington University, Washington, DC, USA
e-mail: cordes@gwu.edu

D. Williams, T. Calabrese (eds.), *The Palgrave Handbook of Government Budget Forecasting*, Palgrave Studies in Public Debt, Spending, and Revenue,
https://doi.org/10.1007/978-3-030-18195-6_9

Introduction

Better forecasts allow states to better anticipate revenue declines in advance of a recession. The more advanced warning a state has of revenue shortfalls, presumably the better able it will be to make needed budget adjustments.

The Great Recession, its severity not fully anticipated, resulted in large decreases in state tax revenue nationwide. Consequently, state governments had to make politically painful cuts in state government spending and/or engineer tax increases to fulfill balanced budget requirements written in their state constitutions. For example, Virginia, even though it has been recognized as one of the nation's best managed states, faced stark budgetary choices during this past recession.[1,2]

In the case of Virginia, as in the case of other states, the most significant effects of a recession are experienced on the revenue side of the budget. To explore the consequences of different forecasting approaches, we first use autoregression (AR) and vector autoregression (VAR) methods to forecast revenue collections in Virginia before, during, and after the Great Recession.[3] We then consider the case for using Bayesian statistical inference and estimate Bayesian VAR (BVAR) model. Finally, we present revenue forecasts based on the VAR and the BVAR with the prior knowledge that the BVAR produces better forecasts, as demonstrated by Krol (2010). Although the overall findings are somewhat mixed, it does appear that BVAR models with exogenous variables do result in low forecast errors for many of the revenue series. Hence, there is some policy merit in relying on Bayesian autoregressive models as alternatives to the other models we have considered.

Literature Review

Revenue Forecasting in the United States

Revenue forecasting at the state and local level in the United States ranges in complexity from informal, judgmental approaches that might be found in the budget office of a small locality to formal quantitative forecasts based on statistical models of varying degrees of complexity used in larger cities and state

[1] Virginia is one of Governing Magazine's "Best managed" states, winning awards from professional organizations for the high quality of its financial reporting and maintaining AAA bond rating for two decades (Conant 2010).

[2] For a discussion of the budget preparation process, see Virginia Department of Planning and Budget (2014) and Virginia Senate Committee Staff (2006).

[3] Although there are forecasts from the government of Virginia, we do not analyze and compare them with our model-based forecasts as the data we use are based on different definitions of the various revenue streams.

governments. In any event, forecasting is more art than science as the role of human input and judgment in the form of "consensus forecasting" is valued as it gives a stamp of legitimacy to the widely-perceived notion of a "black box" often seen as characteristic of statistical models. Michigan, for example, has hailed the success of consensus forecasting in light of many non-marginal changes to its tax laws in the early- to mid-1990s (Haas and Knittel 1997).

Despite the wide range of forecasting experience, McNichol (2014) has identified five best practices to implement for generating more reliable forecasts. First, the executive and legislative branches should together issue the revenue estimate. Second, outside experts—such as academics or members of the business community—should be used to help improve forecasts. Third, forecasts and their underlying assumptions should be made publicly available on the Internet. Fourth, meetings of the forecasting council should be open to the public. Finally, estimates should be updated throughout the year.

There is evidence that revenue forecasts became less accurate in the 2000s, especially during the Great Recession. Pew Charitable Trusts (2015) have attributed this problem to a number of factors, including the following: (1) growth of revenue volatility in general, (2) difficulty in estimating corporate income taxes, (3) overall difficulty in estimating revenues during and after recessions but also during expansions, (4) the difficulty of forecasting revenue in smaller states and states where the economy depends largely on a few sectors, (5) an increase in the time elapsed between forecasts and the adoption of the state budget, and (6) slippage in forecast accuracy due to changes in the mix of taxes.

In a piece devoted to post-Great Recession state budgeting, Conant et al. (2012) studied the budgeting situations facing officials from several states, including Virginia. The authors developed a new framework for identifying four basic approaches to pursuing balanced budgets. They classified these approaches along two dimensions. The first dimension is time, where there are short-term and long-term strategies. The second dimension is the structure of the budget, where there is a revenue side and an expenditure side. For each state, they identified primary and secondary approaches to pursuing balanced budgets from FY 2008 to FY 2012, finding continuity in the approaches most states took. As for Virginia, during the Great Recession in FY 2008 and in FY 2009, the primary approach was to pursue long-term expenditure reduction with short-term revenue addition as a secondary tactic. In FY 2010, the primary and secondary approaches remained the same. By FY 2011 and FY 2012, the primary approach shifted to short-term expenditure reduction along with long-term revenue addition as a secondary approach.

In the particular case of Virginia, the Virginia Department of Planning and Budget (2010) groups revenues to be forecast into two silos: the General Fund and the Non-General Fund. The General Fund consists of funds for which the General Assembly has the most discretion to spend and is the focus of this chapter. For the 2008 to 2010 biennium, the General Fund consisted of approximately 41.3 percent of total revenues collected. A total of $29.9 billion was collected for the General Fund. Three revenue types dominate the General Fund. Individual income taxes took up $19.7 billion of the General Fund while corporate income taxes along with sales (and use) taxes consisted of $1.4 billion and $6.1 billion, respectively.

Using VARs and BVARs[4]

Motivation for VAR Modeling

One rationale for using VAR models to forecast revenue rather than a set of single equation ordinary least squares (OLS) models is that the latter fails to capture relationships across equations representing different types of tax revenues, between the endogenous and explanatory variables within each equation, and through time. As an alternative we employ one type of multi-equation model—VAR—that falls into the category of multiple time series models.

There are several approaches to multiple time series models. These models include the autoregressive integrated moving average (ARIMA), error correction model (ECM), and simultaneous or structural equation (SEQ) systems, which are actually special cases of the more general VAR methodology that we focus on in this chapter. Table 1.1 in Brandt and Williams (2007) provides a summary of their properties.

Motivation for Using BVAR Modeling

According to Todd (1984), Bayesian vector autoregression (BVAR) is an improvement over VARs because

> BVAR procedures give modelers more flexibility in expressing the true nature of their beliefs as well as an objective way to combine those beliefs with the historical record. A specific version of the procedures, developed by

[4] Please also see Stock and Watson (2001) for a primer on VAR modeling and Robertson and Tallman (1999) for an overview of VAR forecasting.

> Minnesota researchers, has been used to build models whose unadjusted forecasts seem to be as accurate as the subjectively adjusted forecasts of other common models. The fact that BVAR models forecast well without subjective adjustment also allows them to objectively estimate answers to questions about future events and probabilities that subjectively adjusted models cannot as plausibly address.

Specifying a BVAR model is quite different than frequentist statistical methods that underlie the specification of more traditional econometrics models. The incorporation of one's personal beliefs in a BVAR is perhaps the hallmark of a Bayesian model—and the key strength of BVARs high forecasting accuracy. However, there is a price to be paid for high accuracy: If one truly wants to understand the mechanics of BVAR, a significant amount of time and effort needs to be invested. Fortunately, for forecasting units in state and local governments, commercially available statistical software like EViews can generate BVAR forecasts without deep knowledge of the underpinnings of this model.

Forecasting with VARs and BVARs

What does the prior research say regarding forecasting with VARs and BVARs? Robertson and Tallman (1999) provide a detailed guide to how forecasts can be generated from a VAR model. They find that forecasts arising from transformations from the VAR to the BVAR using the Letterman/Minnesota prior are less accurate than using the Sims and Zha (1998) priors. The authors cover other technical issues that must be addressed for the VAR to be functional. For example, they discuss the use of conditional forecasting to deal with the nature of staggered release of data and the conversion of lower-frequency data to match higher-frequency data.

Carriero, Clark, and Marcellino (2015) "find that very small losses (and sometimes even gains) from the adoption of specification choices make BVAR modeling quick and easy, in particular for point forecasting." This result suggests that BVAR could be a handy tool in a state revenue forecaster's tool box, especially if it means relying on "pre-programmed BVAR tools" in common software such as RATS and EViews.

Carriero, Mumtaz, and Theophilopoulou (2012) find that BVARs can significantly improve upon autoregressive (AR) forecasts, which is a result contrary to most other studies. In forecasting macroeconomic variables such as government revenues, expenditures, and interest payments on outstanding debt for Germany, the United Kingdom, and the United States, the authors demonstrate that BVARs can make much better forecasts than ARs. Furthermore, they find that adopting a large system and allowing for time variation contribute to better forecasts, with the former having a greater influence than the latter.

Building on Krol (2010)

Our essay draws upon Krol (2010). Krol's working paper is the first direct comparison of tax revenue forecasting performance of alternative time series models. He assesses the ability of various time series models to forecast California state tax revenues. The models' forecast accuracy is compared with a benchmark random walk forecast. He uses quarterly data to forecast total tax revenue as well as its three largest components—sales, income, and corporate tax revenue. Krol uses a rolling regression approach for the period 2004 to 2009, making a series of one and four-quarters-ahead forecasts. Using root-mean-squared error to evaluate model forecasts, Krol finds that the BVAR models generally outperformed the VAR and the random walk models. This finding is consistent with previous experience with macroeconomic forecasting, as described by Todd (1984).

The main goal of this essay is to determine the degree to which Krol's result holds up in another U.S. state—Virginia. Some parallels can be drawn between California and Virginia. Although the Commonwealth of Virginia and the state of California adjusted to the Great Recession in different ways, the economies of the two states have important similarities. For example, the high-tech sector plays an important role in the economies of both states as does the defense industry. The bursting of the housing bubble in the 2008–2009 time frame had adverse effects on the real estate markets in both states.

We do not intend to perform a straight replication of Krol (2010). Instead, we expand the scope of his work here. We incorporate most of the exogenous variables he uses in his models in our models.[5] We consider models with and without exogenous variables; Krol adheres to using only models with exogenous variables. We use annual data; Krol uses quarterly data. Krol considers models with levels and first differences; we consider just log first differences. We consider static and dynamic models with up to six-years-ahead forecasts;

[5] Krol uses real defense spending, real crude oil prices, real U.S. personal income, consumer price index, real California housing prices, and real California personal income. We use total vehicle sales, production of defense and space equipment, retail gasoline price, Virginia housing price index, Virginia personal income, and Virginia unemployment rate.

Krol uses dynamic models with four-quarters-ahead forecasts. We consider a gamut of forecast evaluation statistics; Krol hews only to the root-mean-squared error (RMSE) statistic. Krol finds that "BVAR models generally outperformed the VAR and random walk models." Our results indicate that while BVAR with exogenous variables perform well in three out of the four revenue series studied, it is not certain whether BVARs produced better forecasts of corporate income tax revenue: It might be better to stick to using AR models in that case.

Data

In this section, we present the data that are used in this study. The revenues forecasted include total, personal income, corporate income, and state sales tax for Virginia. Annual tax revenue data come from the Governments Division of the U.S. Census Bureau. Other data series include GDP, gas prices, total vehicle sales, housing price index, unemployment rate, and defense industry index. Please also see Tables 9.1 and 9.2, which provide definitions, sources, and selected summary statistics on the data—first, in levels, and then, in log differences. Levels of revenue are relevant for whether the budget has a surplus or deficit. Log differences are considered as well because of the wide disparity between the magnitudes of the levels of revenue data and the independent variables.

The data are collected on a fiscal-year basis.[6] The estimation period for the models runs from fiscal years 1977 to 2008. The forecast period covers fiscal years 2009 to 2014. As in most states, fiscal years in Virginia begin on July 1 and end on June 30.

Models

VAR Model[7]

The standard VAR model is a multivariate autoregressive model where each endogenous variable is regressed on its past values and the past values of the other variables in the system. We use a *reduced-form* version of a VAR which

[6] The data are available from a historical perspective rather than available in real time. This distinction can be extremely important empirically and can alter the rankings of forecast models.

[7] This section draws from Baum (2013), Becketti (2013), Brandt and Williams (2007), Johnston and Dinardo (1997), Lütkepohl (2007), and Parker (2014).

Table 9.1 Explanation of levels of data and their descriptive statistics for years 1977–2014

Variable	Brief description	Mean	SD	Min	Max
Dependent					
TOT	Total taxes in VA[a]	9.982	5.705	2.054	19.2
INC	Individual income tax in VA[a]	5.161	3.334	0.714	10.9
SALES	Total general sales tax in VA[a]	2.037	1.109	0.427	3.708
CORP	Corporate net income tax in VA[a]	0.429	0.228	0.159	0.880
Independent					
CARS	Total U.S. vehicle sales[b]	1233.96	170.044	865.575	1500.65
DEFSPACE	Production of defense & space equipment[c] (index: year 2012 = 100)	85.288	19.582	45.888	115.377
GAS	Motor gasoline regular grade retail price per gallon[d]	1.604	0.880	0.64	3.588
VAHPIS	VA housing price index[e] (index: 1980Q1 = 100)	237.302	122.448	72.465	464.418
VAINC	VA personal income[f]	193.995	116.507	0.374	407.743
VAUR	VA unemployment rate[g]	4.893	1.282	2.417	7.4

Dependent variables and VAINC in billions of nominal dollars. CARS in thousands of units. Seasonally unadjusted

[a]Taken from U.S. Census Bureau, available at https://www.census.gov/govs/statetax/historical_data.html

[b]Originally from Bureau of Economic Analysis, U.S. Department of Commerce. Downloaded from FRED data base, available at https://fred.stlouisfed.org/frd2/series/TOTALNSA

[c]Originally from the Board of Governors of the Federal Reserve System, Downloaded from FRED data base, available at http://research.stlouisfed.org/fred2/series/IPB52300NQ/downloaddata

[d]Taken from Energy Information Administration, U.S. Department of Energy, available at http://www.eia.gov/forecasts/steo/realprices/

[e]Taken from Federal Housing Finance Agency, available at http://www.fhfa.gov/DataTools/Downloads/Documents/HPI/HPI_AT_state.txt

[f]Taken from Bureau of Economic Analysis, U.S. Department of Commerce, available at http://www.bea.gov/regional/downloadzip.cfm

[g]Taken from Bureau of Labor Statistics, U.S. Department of Labor, available at http://data.bls.gov/cgi-bin/surveymost?la

places few restrictions on the data, provides a useful characterization of $\mathbf{y}_t$, and generates joint forecasts of the elements of $\mathbf{y}_t$. Model building in VAR models depends on the selection of the appropriate variables based on theory. Rather than impose structural or dynamic restrictions on the relationships among the four time series, a VAR would have four equations, one for each endogenous variable—total (DLN_TOT), personal income (DLN_INC), corporate income (DLN_CORP), and state sales (DLN_SALES) tax. Exogenous vari-

Table 9.2 Explanation of data in log differences and descriptive statistics for years 1977–2014

Variable	Brief description	Mean	SD	Min	Max
Dependent					
DLN_TOT	Log difference of total taxes in VA[a]	0.060	0.050	−0.098	0.134
DLN_INC	Log difference of individual income tax in VA[a]	0.074	0.066	−0.095	0.203
DLN_SALES	Log difference of total general sales tax in VA[a]	0.057	0.049	−0.057	0.144
DLN_CORP	Log difference of corporate net income tax in VA[a]	0.042	0.172	−0.442	0.362
Independent					
DLN_CARS	Log difference of total vehicle sales in U.S.[b]	0.004	0.095	−0.363	0.211
DLN_DEFSPACE	Log difference of production of defense & space equipment in U.S.[c] (index: year 2012 = 100)	0.021	0.072	−0.140	0.172
DLN_GAS	Log difference of motor gasoline regular grade retail price per gallon in U.S.[d]	0.046	0.133	−0.244	0.417
DLN_VAHPIS	Log difference of VA housing price index[e] (index: 1980Q1 = 100)	0.046	0.052	−0.063	0.172
DLN_VAINC	Log difference of VA personal income[f]	0.065	0.0293	0.005	0.128
DLN_VAUR	Log difference of VA unemployment rate[g]	−0.001	0.179	−0.324	0.512

As the transformed variables are log differences, they are unit-free and are unaffected by the units of the raw variables as presented in Table 9.1.

[a]Taken from U.S. Census Bureau, available at https://www.census.gov/govs/statetax/historical_data.html

[b]Originally from Bureau of Economic Analysis, U.S. Department of Commerce. Downloaded from FRED data base, available at https://fred.stlouisfed.org/frd2/series/TOTALNSA

[c]Originally from the Board of Governors of the Federal Reserve System, Downloaded from FRED data base, available at http://research.stlouisfed.org/fred2/series/IPB52300NQ/downloaddata

[d]Taken from Energy Information Administration, U.S. Department of Energy, available at http://www.eia.gov/forecasts/steo/realprices/

[e]Taken from Federal Housing Finance Agency, available at http://www.fhfa.gov/DataTools/Downloads/Documents/HPI/HPI_AT_state.txt

[f]Taken from Bureau of Economic Analysis, U.S. Department of Commerce, available at http://www.bea.gov/regional/downloadzip.cfm

[g]Taken from Bureau of Labor Statistics, U.S. Department of Labor, available at http://data.bls.gov/cgi-bin/surveymost?la

ables consist of total vehicle sales (DLN_CARS), production of defense and space equipment index (DLN_DEFSPACE), retail gasoline price (DLN_GAS), Virginia housing price index (DLN_VAHPIS), Virginia personal income (DLN_VAINC), and Virginia unemployment rate (DLN_VAUR).

Again, all data series have been log-differenced to achieve stationarity.[8] Due to the limited number of degrees of freedom, we make the simplifying assumption that the other regressors are not endogenous as well. This seems to be a safe assumption to make as Krol (2010) finds that lagged explanatory variables do not help predict tax revenues.

BVAR Model[9]

We motivate estimation by BVAR with some basic observations about the difference between the models we have been considering, which are frequentists, and Bayesian estimation. Research and teaching in statistics have been largely based on the frequentist perspective. According to the frequentist perspective, probability is the result of some limiting relative frequency. So, if we observe enough trials or data we will learn the correct measure of uncertainty. To illustrate, the sample mean will converge to the population mean as sample size grows large. This result is replicable across repeated random samples.

On the other hand, Bayesians believe that assessments of uncertainty are subjective and relative to the conditions under which one would make a bet or have a degree of belief (Brandt 2013). For example, data are observed from a realized sample that is fixed. Parameters are unknown and determined probabilistically.

In the end, the choice between frequentist versus Bayesian methods rests with the preferences of the researcher. Practically speaking, convenience may be the key driver. In some cases, one may find that frequentist methods are easier to apply while in other cases Bayesian methods may be more straightforward. As Kilian and Lütkepohl (2017) stress, although the two "approaches may produce numerically different answers in many cases, their interpretation is fundamentally different, even when the estimates coincide numerically."

[8] Differencing is one of several ways to obtain stationarity. Notably, a cointegrating combination obtains, and the properties of levels forecasts can be improved by taking cointegration into account; see Engle and Yoo (1987). However, further research has shown mixed success when taking cointegration into account. Christoffersen and Diebold (1998) along with Hoffman and Rasche (1996) find mixed results while Shoesmith (1992) as well as Baghestani and McNown (1992) find improved forecasting accuracy. See also Elliott (2006) for further discussion.

[9] See Lütkepohl (2007) and Brandt (2013) for a technical exposition of BVAR models.

Discussion

With the BVAR we combine information about the data and prior information about the regression efficiently through what is called "mixed estimation." We use mixed estimation to provide a tractable estimator for a BVAR model. This is done by formulating our beliefs about the coefficients in the VAR model as stochastic linear restrictions on the coefficients of the reduced form VAR.

When comparing VAR with BVAR estimation, it is must be acknowledged that VAR is a useful tool for theory building and testing dynamic relationships. However, in even a simple VAR model without any exogenous variables the parameter space for k endogenous variables and p lags is $k^2p + k + 0.5^*k(k + 1)$. This number can become quite large and every new variable adds $(k + 1)^*p + 1$ new regression parameters. In addition, one may have expectations or beliefs about many of these parameters, whether they are zero or consistent with low frequency dynamics. There are some aspects of VAR models about which one may have beliefs. Brandt (2013) describes a number of instances where one might want to incorporate prior beliefs so as to transform a VAR into a BVAR: "scale of the covariance matrix, random walk specification of VAR, relative weights of different variables' lags, decay of autoregressive coefficients, variance of the equilibrium level trend (constant term), presence of cointegration in the model, weight of initial conditions or trends." Lastly, model and parameter uncertainty make inferences difficult with VAR.

In sum, one would concur with Karlsson (2013): "[T]he flexibility and ability to fit the data comes from the rich parameterization of VAR models brings with it a risk of overfitting the data, or imprecise inference, and large uncertainty about the future paths projected by the model. This is essentially the frequentist argument for Bayesian VAR models and one reason why Bayesian VAR models forecast better than VARs estimated with frequentist techniques."

Forecasting State Tax Revenues

Motivation

To assess the ability of our model to forecast Virginia state revenues, we compare our VAR forecasting models with actual revenue data from the U.S. Bureau of the Census. Our hypothesis is that our model will overestimate tax revenues in the Great Recession and beyond, but to an unknown extent due to the fact that this particular recession was deeper and more persistent than any other.

We will follow the style of Hendry and Hubrich (2011) who find that the direct forecast of the aggregate, either using only past aggregate or disaggregate information is more accurate than combining disaggregate forecasts. To apply their methodology to this essay, the aggregate is total tax revenue and the disaggregate are the revenue sub-categories. Hence, we forecast total tax revenue based on the components of personal income, sales, and corporate income. This is different from forecasting the components of total revenue separately and aggregating those forecasts.

VAR Forecasting

Under the assumption that the data generating process is unknown, we use estimated VAR coefficients in forecasting. Denoting the optimal h-step forecast by $y_{T+h|T}$, at forecast origin T, an h-step ahead forecast is obtained recursively as

$$\hat{y}_{T+h|T} = \hat{A}_0 + \hat{A}_1 \hat{y}_{T+h-1|T} + \cdots + \hat{A}_p \hat{y}_{T+h-p|T},$$

where $\hat{y}_{T+h|T} = y_{T+j}$ for $j \leq 0$ and the $\hat{A}_i$ s ($i = 1, \ldots, p$) are estimated parameters. The corresponding forecast error is

$$\begin{aligned} y_{T+h} - \hat{y}_{T+h|T} &= \left[y_{T+h} - y_{T+h|T} \right] + \left[y_{T+h|T} - \hat{y}_{T+h|T} \right] \\ &= \sum_{j=0}^{h-1} \Phi_j u_{T+h-j} + \left[y_{T+h|T} - \hat{y}_{T+h|T} \right] \end{aligned}$$

The first term on the right-hand side involves future residuals u_t, with $t > T$ only, whereas the second term is determined by present and past variables if only past variables have been used for estimation. It follows that the two terms are independent if u_t is independent white noise. Furthermore, under standard assumptions, the difference $y_{T+h} - \hat{y}_{T+h|T}$ is small in probability as the sample size used for estimation gets large and the VAR coefficients are estimated more and more precisely.

Turning to forecasting issues, VAR forecasts project forward the past statistical correlations between the variables in the system. The only assumption that they embody is that these correlations will continue to hold in the forecast period. In other words, basic VAR forecasts are unconditional.

According to the discussion by McShea (2011), VAR forecasts have several weaknesses. First, they are likely to perform poorly following structural breaks. Second, including too many lags or too many variables can lead to VAR-derived forecasts performing poorly, even though the model fits the data well in the estimation period. This occurs if the lags of the variables in the system pick up non-systematic relationships between the variables as well as the systematic relationships. So, unless the set of variables and lag lengths is kept small, forecasts derived from VARs are likely to be inaccurate. These weaknesses apply to BVARs, too.

BVAR Forecasting

As noted above we also use a BVAR approach to building model(s) that can explain past Virginia revenues in the spirit of Krol (2010) who studied California state revenues. We make several modifications. In addition to using annual data, we consider additional variants of the models Krol estimated (with and without exogenous variables) and include exogenous variables that Krol had considered but dropped in the final model runs. We assess BVARs accuracy in forecasting the large dip in tax revenue that occurred and compare their performance to VAR models. Krol finds that BVAR models outperform VAR and AR models. Our goal is to determine whether this is also the case with Virginia tax revenues. In particular, we are interested in the accuracy of BVAR in forecasting the large dip in tax revenue that occurred and compare its performance to VAR and AR.

We employ the Letterman/Minnesota framework, which we can write following the *i*th equation,

$$\begin{aligned} y_{it} = c_i + \varphi_{i1}^{(1)} y_{1,t-1} + \cdots + \varphi_{in}^{(1)} y_{1=n,t-1} + \varphi_{i1}^{(2)} y_{1,t-2} + \cdots + \varphi_{in}^{(2)} y_{1=n,t-2} \\ + \varphi_{i1}^{(p)} y_{1,t-p} + \cdots + \varphi_{in}^{(p)} y_{n,t-p} + \varepsilon_{it} \end{aligned}$$

where $\varphi_{i1}^{(1)}$ is considered to be $\varphi_{i1}^{(1)} \sim N\left(1,\ \lambda_1^2\right)$ where λ_1 represents overall tightness of the prior. In addition, there is a dynamic specification and distribution of the prior which can be represented by the hyperparameter

$$\varphi_{ij}^{(s)} \sim N\left(\mu_s, \left\{ \frac{\lambda_1 \text{x}\, \lambda_2 \text{x}\, \hat{\tau}_i}{s^{\lambda_3} \text{x}\, \hat{\tau}_i} \right\} \right)$$

We accept the following default values based on the Minnesota prior set by EViews software. The prior mean, μ_1, is set equal to 0.1. The prior mean is likely to have most or all of its elements set to zero to lessen the risk of overfitting, so we set it close to zero. The overall tightness, λ_1, is set equal to 0.1. This parameter represents overall tightness on the variance (of the first lag) and controls the relative importance of sample and prior information. Small λ_1 means prior information dominates the sample information. The relative cross-variable weight, λ_2, is set equal to 0.99, representing the relative tightness of variance of other variables. Setting λ_2= 0 implies that the VAR is collapsed to a vector of univariate models. The lag decay hyperparameter, λ_3, is set equal to 1 to denote linear decay. Finally, $\frac{\hat{\tau}_i}{\hat{\tau}_j}$ is a correction for the scale of series i compared with series j.

Static Versus Dynamic Forecasting

Forecasts can be classified as static or dynamic. If forecasts are static, the premise is that the world does not change among the historical time periods of the dataset. In other words, since actual values will be missing beyond the last historical time period in the dataset, static forecasts can only forecast one period into the future (assuming only first lags appear in the model); for that reason, they are often called one-step-ahead forecasts, according to Stata (2013). Hence, we will be using the terms "static" and "one-step-ahead" forecasts interchangeably. Dynamic forecasts can be considered a type of multi-step-ahead forecast that is different from a one-step-ahead forecast. Unlike static forecasts, dynamic forecasts do not build upon incremental projections that could enhance its accuracy. Dynamic projections are based only on the data prior to the forecast origin. As a result, this type of forecast may not be as accurate as the one-step-ahead forecasts.

Forecast Evaluation

There are several measures of forecast error we rely on in this study. See Table 9.3. Some of these measures do not distinguish between positive and negative forecast errors; they are used to account for magnitude of error. Other measures maintain the sign and are useful for gauging bias and asymmetries.

One common measure is the root-mean-squared error (RMSE). The RMSE is the square root of the sum of squared forecast errors divided by the number of time periods over which the forecast is generated. A criticism leveled at the

Table 9.3 Measures of forecast error

Root-mean-squared error	$\sqrt{\sum_{t=T+1}^{T+h}\left(\hat{y}_t - y_t\right)^2 / h}$
Mean absolute error	$\sum_{t=T+1}^{T+h} \hat{y}_t - y_t / h$
Mean absolute percent error	$100\sum_{t=T+1}^{T+h}\left\lvert\frac{\hat{y}_t - y_t}{y_t}\right\rvert / h$
Theil inequality coefficient	$\frac{\sqrt{\sum_{t=T+1}^{T+h}\left(\hat{y}_t - y_t\right)^2 / h}}{\sqrt{\sum_{t=T+1}^{T+h}\hat{y}_t^2 / h} + \sqrt{\sum_{t=T+1}^{T+h} y_t^2 / h}}$

RMSE is that it is vulnerable to outlier inflation due to the squaring of the difference between the actual and the forecasted values. If the series being forecast contains outliers, other measures of forecast accuracy that are not so inflatable by the presence of outliers should be used.

An often-used alternative in state revenue forecasting is the absolute value of the error as a percentage of the actual result or absolute percent error. Summary measures of estimating error across years include mean or median of the absolute value of the percent error. We use the mean absolute percent error (MAPE). MAPE is somewhat scale dependent as the measure can easily balloon to 100 percent or more when forecasting very low values or integers according to Yaffee (2010). When using the MAPE, it is important to report it along with the MAE (explained below) to provide a "sense of balance" (Yaffee 2010).

These measures, which treat positive and negative errors the same, may not be appropriate in all situations. To cite a few instances, one must use other measures to examine (1) whether forecasts are biased—if forecasts are more likely to overshoot or undershoot the actual amount of revenues—or (2) whether forecasters think that the costs of overestimates are greater than the costs of underestimates. We refer the reader to the discussion in Boyd and Dadayan (2014) for more details.

In addition to RMSE and MAPE, we use the mean absolute error (MAE) and the Theil inequality coefficient as additional measures of forecast accuracy. All these statistics provide a measure of the deviation of forecasted values from the actual values. If we have a forecast sample such that $j = T + 1, T + 2, \ldots, T + h$, and let the actual and forecasted value in period t be y_t and $\hat{y}_t$, respectively, we can write the forecast evaluation measures as depicted in Table 9.3.

Empirical Results

Modeling

AR Model

The AR model is the first of two baselines against which other statistical models may be compared. This first baseline is an autoregressive process of order one, AR(1), in which revenue at time t is based on actual revenue in time $t-1$ multiplied by a fractional slope plus some random error. Hypothetically, one would like competing models to perform better than either baseline: There would be no point of constructing and implementing these more complicated models if they don't perform better. Looked at from a different perspective, if the AR(1) or the random walk performs better than the model(s) at hand, it could signal that the model(s) may need to be improved upon at the least and perhaps abandoned for another model at the worst.

Random Walk Model

The second baseline is the random walk model—a special case of the AR(1) model—in which the slope parameter is equal to 1. The random walk model is widely used in the field of finance to study movements in stock prices. The random walk forecast in the simplest case that predicts that all future values will equal the last observed value: This is the random walk model *without* drift. Put another way, the future will be the same as today. Because making such a statement requires no statistical training, this model is often referred to as the "naive model." The random walk model *with* drift includes a drift term that represents the average increase from one period to another. In a twist of this model—because we are studying percentage changes in tax revenues—we employ the *geometric* random walk model where the natural logarithm of the revenue series is assumed to follow a random walk with drift. Generally speaking, random walk models serve as a good benchmark against which to judge the performance of more complicated models.

Estimation Results of VAR Models

Because the focus of this chapter is on identifying relationships among the endogenous variables and in determining the suitability of models producing accurate forecasts, our focus is not on discussing regression output of the two

VAR models—with and without exogenous variables. What is relevant to understanding the modeling process is how we determined different lag lengths for the two VAR models. We simply ran diagnostic tests in Stata with and without exogenous variables; these tests indicated that three was the optimal number of lags.

Estimation Results of BVAR Models

The selection of the particular BVAR models also warrants explanation. Using EViews, we ran BVAR models of up to six lags and then used forecast evaluation statistics to find the best performing models. To be more specific, we run a set of models with up to six lags for the following four model classifications: (1) BVAR with exogenous variables for dynamic forecasting, (2) BVAR with exogenous variables for static forecasting, (3) BVAR without exogenous variables for dynamic forecasting, and (4) BVAR without exogenous variables for static forecasting. Within each model classification—for each dependent variable—we determined which lag structure results in the best performing forecast evaluation statistics. We then determined which lag structure produced the greatest number of optimal forecast evaluation statistics; the evidence suggests that one is the optimal number of lags under any of the four model classifications.

Forecasting

This section is motivated by the static and dynamic forecasts performed on the following models: AR, random walk, VAR with and without exogenous variables, and BVAR with and without exogenous variables. We conclude the two sections on static and dynamic forecasts by providing a heuristic view of forecast performance by discussing plots of AR, VAR, and BVAR forecasts.[10]

[10] Empirical results should be sensitive to the choice of model estimation period. Theoretically speaking, earlier years of the model estimation period are less relevant to explaining more recent revenues and hence reduces the accuracy of forecasts. With higher frequency data series, this assertion can be empirically verified. It is also the case that empirical results are sensitive to the choice of forecast period. Forecasts in distant future time periods are less accurate than the time periods closer to the end of the model estimation period.

AR and Random Walk as Baselines

The goal of running the AR model and random walk is to discern whether the substantially more complex models perform any better than forecasts produced by either version of AR. It turns out that the random walk forecasts do poorly across all revenue series, whether static or dynamic; hence, the discussion here focuses on the AR model.

Among static forecasts, DLN_CORP and DLN_SALES are best forecasted by the AR: All four forecast evaluation measures indicate that the AR process predicts DLN_CORP and DLN_SALES the best. This result implies that more complex models cannot handle forecasting DLN_CORP well—the most volatile of the dependent variables. AR forecast performance of DLN_CORP is substantially greater than that of VARs and BVARs as well. Looking at dynamic forecasts, the AR process predicts DLN_CORP the best, also by a wide margin over VARs and BVARs.

To confirm these findings, a visual inspection of the plots of static AR forecasts versus the actuals shows that there is a tendency for forecasts to overshoot the actual numbers. Of the four revenue series, the DLN_CORP forecast appears to be closest to on-target for year 6 of the forecast window, but it misses forecasting the turning points that occur in the actual data. As for the dynamic AR forecasts, there is considerable overshooting of forecasts over the actuals. The dynamic forecasts don't seem to identify the turning points.

Static Forecasts

As for other static forecasts, the AR and VAR with exogenous variables as well as VAR alone score few wins over the two BVAR models. Nonetheless, there are encouraging results in the BVAR models with and without exogenous variables. The BVAR models with exogenous variables forecast DLN_INC and DLN_TOT well in comparison with the other competing models. For DLN_INC, all four forecast evaluation statistics are the lowest for the BVAR with exogenous variables model. For DLN_TOT, the RMSE, MAPE, and Theil inequality coefficient are optimal for the BVAR with exogenous variables. Also, note that there are mixed results for DLN_CORP: RMSE and MAE are optimal for the AR process while MAPE is optimal for VAR with exogenous variables, but Theil inequality coefficient is optimal for the BVAR with exogenous variables.

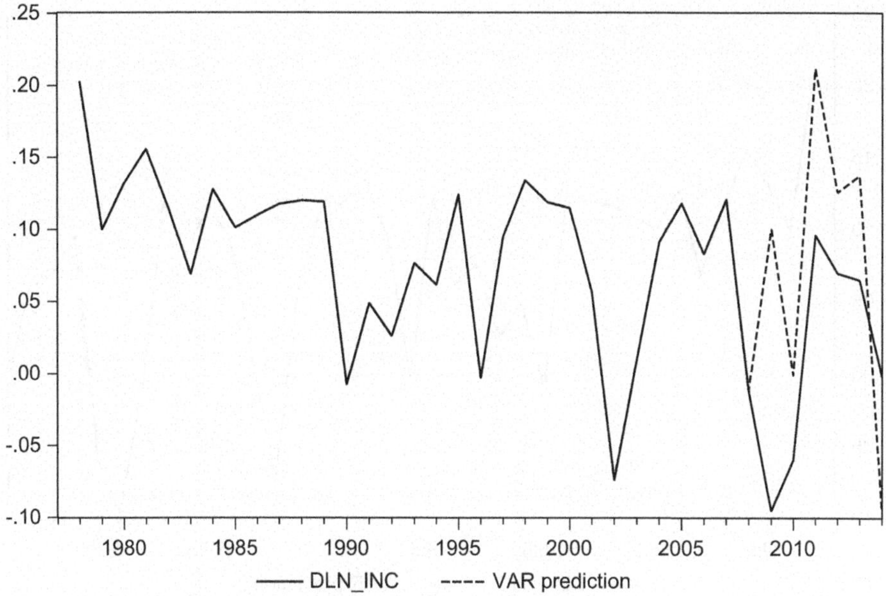

Fig. 9.1 VAR w/exogenous variables (Static)

A visual inspection of plots of forecasted VARs versus actuals with exogenous variables reveals a tendency for forecasts to overshoot and find inflection points that don't exist in the actual data (Fig. 9.1). As for the case of plots of forecasted VARs versus actuals without exogenous variables, forecasts follow actuals better than in actuals with exogenous variables, but there is a tendency for inflection points to be muted for DLN_TOT and DLN_INC. The response of forecasts seems to be delayed for DLN_SALES and DLN_CORP. Plots of forecasted Bayesian VARs versus actuals with exogenous variables indicates that forecasts track actuals quite well (Fig. 9.2). But, there is just a slight tendency to overshoot for three series. The fourth series, DLN_CORP, initially undershoots the actual values in the forecast period; however, by year 6, actual and forecasted values come closer to agreement. The plot without exogenous variables show that forecasts are somewhat less accurate, but forecasts for DLN_CORP undershoots by a less severe amount.

Dynamic Forecasts

Dynamic forecasts clearly favor the BVAR with exogenous variables for the series DLN_INC and DLN_TOT: The four forecast evaluation statistics are among the lowest among the five competing models. This is certainly good

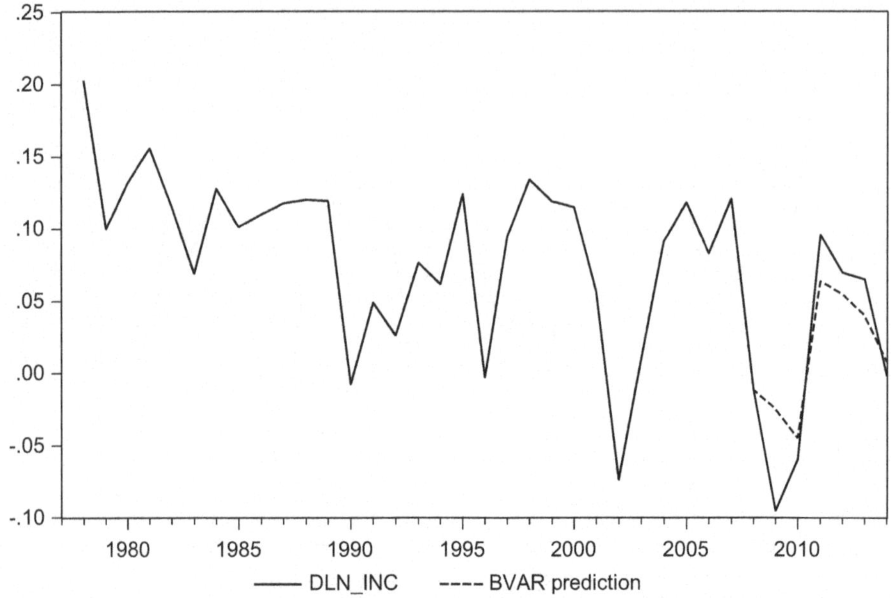

Fig. 9.2 BVAR with exogenous variables

news that the forecasts of two out of four endogenous variables can be best achieved with the BVAR with exogenous variables. However, DLN_CORP, the most volatile of all the series, is best predicted by an AR process according to two out of four forecast evaluation statistics. This finding once again indicates that complicated models do no better than the simpler AR process. A mediating outcome suggests that DLN_SALES performs well using a VAR model on the basis of three out of the four forecast evaluation statistics. And, DLN_SALES performs well under the BVAR according to MAPE.

Beginning with a visual inspection of plots of dynamically forecasted VARs versus actuals with exogenous variables, one sees extensive overshooting of forecasts over actuals and difficulty in sharply identifying turning points. An interesting result is that DLN_TOT is initially severely overforecasted, followed by a series of jagged falls and rises to a forecast above the actual nadir in year 6. Plots of forecasted VARs versus actuals without exogenous variables deliver more bad news: There is a penchant for overshooting and forecasts missing inflection points.

Plots of forecasted Bayesian VARs versus actuals with and without exogenous variables contain some interesting findings. Bayesian VARs with exogenous variables indicate that DLN_TOT comes above the actual values by small amounts. DLN_INC forecasts come below actual values by a little bit. However, DLN_CORP forecasts undershoot by a whole lot, though. Bayesian

VARs without exogenous variables indicate substantial overshooting of DLN_TOT, DLN_INC, and DLN_SALES as well as severe undershooting of DLN_CORP.

Conclusion

In this chapter, we determine the viability of using Bayesian vector autoregression models in estimating total tax revenue along with three major tax revenue categories for the state of Virginia—personal income, sales, and corporate income tax revenues. We use annual data collected by the U.S. Bureau of the Census to mimic what Virginia makes available to the general public in the Governor's annual budget documents. Granted that higher frequency data would have been more desirable for producing more "accurate" forecasts, we still use annual data because policy research is not a theoretical exercise where quarterly data—buried deep in the state government website—would have been used.[11]

Forecasters consider Bayesian VARs useful despite their technical complexities. Bayesian VARs often provide better forecasts than those from an unrestricted OLS estimation of VARs. Bayesian VARs can facilitate a closer relationship between the underlying economics of the forecast problem and the estimation, for example, by imposing economic theory through the prior. It follows that we can select values such that we can control the relative importance of sample and prior information. Lastly, Bayesian forecasts can be thought of as shrinkage methods that reduce the effect of estimation errors.

However, our findings are mixed. Starting with static forecasts, we find that corporate income is best forecasted using an AR process while sales, total, and personal income taxes are best forecasted by the Bayesian VAR models with exogenous variables. Turning to dynamic forecasts, on the one hand, we find that the most volatile tax revenue stream, corporate income, is best forecasted using AR process. In addition, sales tax revenues are best forecasted using VAR models. On the other hand, income and total tax revenues can be best dynamically forecasted using Bayesian vector autoregressions with exogenous variables. In sum, it appears that there is some policy merit in relying on Bayesian vector autoregressions as alternatives to the other models we have compared them to. However, BVARs should not be applied blindly to all series but should be used in concert with other tried-and-true forecasting methods as well.[12]

[11] In fact, publicly available revenue forecasts are made on an annual basis.

[12] According to Elliott and Timmermann (2016), "although the BVAR forecasts generally perform well, no single approach appears to be dominant across variables and forecast horizons, illustrating the need to adopt different approaches to different situations and perhaps also consider forecast combinations."

References

Baghestani, H., & McNown, R. (1992). Forecasting the federal budget with time-series models. *Journal of Forecasting, 11*(2), 127–139.

Baum, C. F. (2013). *VAR, SVAR, and VECM models: Lecture slides for EC 823*. Department of Economics, Boston College (Spring). Retrieved from http://fmwww.bc.edu/EC-C/S2013/823/EC823.S2013.nn10.slides.pdf.

Becketti, S. (2013). *Introduction to time series analysis using Stata*. College Station: Stata Press.

Boyd, D. J., & Dadayan, L. (2014). *State tax revenue forecasting accuracy: Technical report*. Retrieved from http://rockinst.org/wp-content/uploads/2018/02/2014-09-30-Revenue_Forecasting_Accuracy.pdf.

Brandt, P. T. (2013). *Bayesian VAR time series analysis*. Lecture, ICPSR Summer Program Time Series Analysis: Advanced Topics Workshop, Ann Arbor, MI, July 29.

Brandt, P. T., & Williams, J. T. (2007). *Multiple time series models*. Thousand Oaks, CA: Sage Publications.

Carriero, A., Clark, T. E., & Marcellino, M. (2015). Bayesian VARs: Specification choices and forecast accuracy. *Journal of Applied Econometrics, 30*(1), 46–73.

Carriero, A., Mumtaz, H., & Theophilopoulou, A. (2012). *Forecasting fiscal variables using Bayesian VARs with constant and drifting coefficients*. Unpublished (PDF).

Christoffersen, P. F., & Diebold, F. X. (1998). Cointegration and long-horizon forecasting. *Journal of Business & Economic Statistics, 16*(4), 450–456.

Conant, J. K. (2010). Budget deficits in the states: Virginia. *Public Budgeting & Finance, 30*(1), 33–57.

Conant, J. K., Bunch, B., Duncombe, W., Lauth, T. P., Robbins, M., Simonsen, B., et al. (2012). State budgeting in the aftermath of the great recession: A comparative perspective. *Municipal Finance Journal, 33*(2), 1–33.

Elliott, G. (2006). Forecasting with trending data. In G. Elliott, W. J. Granger, & A. Timmermann (Eds.), *Handbook of economic forecasting* (Vol. 1, pp. 555–604). Amsterdam: North Holland.

Elliott, G., & Timmermann, A. (2016). *Economic forecasting*. Princeton, NJ: Princeton University Press.

Engle, R. F., & Yoo, B. S. (1987). Forecasting and testing in co-integrated systems. *Journal of Econometrics, 35*(1), 143–159.

Haas, M. P., & Knittel, M. J. (1997). Revenue forecasting in Michigan. In Proceedings of the Annual Conference on Taxation and Minutes of the Annual Meeting of the National Tax Association (pp. 313–318). Washington, DC: National Tax Association.

Hendry, D. F., & Hubrich, K. (2011). Combining disaggregate forecasts or combining disaggregate information to forecast an aggregate. *Journal of Business & Economic Statistics, 29*(2), 216–227.

Hoffman, D. L., & Rasche, R. H. (1996). Assessing forecast performance in a cointegrated system. *Journal of Applied Econometrics, 11*(5), 495–517.

Johnston, J., & DiNardo, J. (1997). *Econometric methods* (4th ed.). New York: McGraw-Hill.

Karlsson, S. (2013). Forecasting with Bayesian vector autoregression. In G. Elliott & A. Timmermann (Eds.), *Handbook of economic forecasting* (Vol. 2B, 1st ed., pp. 791–897). Amsterdam: Elsevier North-Holland.

Kilian, L., & Lütkepohl, H. (2017). *Structural vector autoregressive analysis.* New York: Cambridge University Press.

Krol, R. (2010). *Forecasting state tax revenue: A Bayesian vector autoregression approach.* Northridge: California State University. Retrieved from http://www.csun.edu/~hcecn001/published/BVAR_Forecast.pdf.

Lütkepohl, H. (2007). *New introduction to multiple time series analysis.* Berlin: Springer.

McNichol, E. C. (2014). *Improving state revenue forecasting: Best practices for a more trusted and reliable revenue estimate.* Center on Budget and Policy Priorities-CBPP, Washington, DC. Retrieved from https://www.cbpp.org/sites/default/files/atoms/files/8-7-14sfp.pdf.

McShea, M. F. (2011). *Forecasting Virginia state revenues: A vector autoregression approach.* Unpublished (PDF).

Parker, J. A. (2014). *Vector autoregression and vector error-correction models.* Unpublished manuscript, Department of Economics, Reed College (Spring). Retrieved from http://academic.reed.edu/economics/parker/s14/312/tschapters/S13_Ch_5.pdf.

Pew Charitable Trusts. (2015). *Managing volatile tax collections in state revenue forecasts.* Washington, DC. Retrieved from http://www.pewtrusts.org/en/research-and-analysis/reports/2015/03/managing-volatile-tax-collections-in-state-revenue-forecasts.

Robertson, J. C., & Tallman, E. W. (1999). Vector autoregressions: Forecasting and reality. *Federal Reserve Bank of Atlanta Economic Review, 84*(1), 4.

Shoesmith, G. L. (1992). Co-integration, error correction and improved medium-term regional VAR forecasting. *Journal of Forecasting, 11*(2), 91–109.

Sims, C. A., & Zha, T. (1998). Bayesian methods for dynamic multivariate models. *International Economic Review, 39*(4), 949–968.

Stata Corporation. (2013). Vector error correction models: Stata Corporation. Retrieved from http://www.stata.com/manuals13/tsvec.pdf.

Stock, J. H., & Watson, M. W. (2001). Vector autoregressions. *Journal of Economic Perspectives, 15*(4), 101–115.

Todd, R. M. (1984). Improving economic forecasting with Bayesian vector autoregression. *Federal Reserve Bank of Minneapolis Quarterly Review*, Fall.

Virginia Department of Planning and Budget. (2010). Frequently asked questions. Retrieved from http://dpb.virginia.gov/budget/faq.cfm.

Virginia Department of Planning and Budget. (2014). *Overview of Virginia's economic and revenue forecasting.* File attachment to e-mail correspondence from John Layman, Chief Economist for State of Virginia.

Virginia Senate Committee Staff. (2006). *Understanding Virginia's budget process.* Richmond. Retrieved from http://sfc.virginia.gov/pdf/understandingvirginiasbudgetprocess.ppt.

Yaffee, R. A. (2010). *Forecast evaluation with Stata.* Paper presented at the United Kingdom Stata Users Group Conference, London School of Hygiene and Tropical Medicine.

10

Bias Associated with Centrally Budgeted Expenditure Forecasts

Thad Calabrese and Daniel Williams

Savings, according to de Blasio, will materialize through several measures including a cap of city health care increases of 3.5% next year and 3% the following year. These savings, said the mayor, are guaranteed and enforceable through arbitration.... "It doesn't seem like a budget-buster," said Howard Cure, director of municipal bond research at Evercore Wealth Management. "It seems like they overbudgeted in health care costs and then made the numbers work and called it savings."

(Burton 2018)

Major Points

- Forecast bias (underforecasting to create a "cushion") is found in revenue forecasts.
- The accepted reasons for revenue forecast bias are: (1) risk aversion and (2) generation of post-budgeting discretion.

T. Calabrese (✉)
Robert F. Wagner Graduate School of Public Service, New York University, New York, NY, USA
e-mail: thad.calabrese@nyu.edu

D. Williams
Austin W. Marxe School of Public and International Affairs, Baruch College, New York, NY, USA
e-mail: Daniel.Williams@baruch.cuny.edu

D. Williams, T. Calabrese (eds.), *The Palgrave Handbook of Government Budget Forecasting*, Palgrave Studies in Public Debt, Spending, and Revenue,
https://doi.org/10.1007/978-3-030-18195-6_10

- Expenditure forecast bias (overforecasting to create a "cushion") might generate unintended agency discretion not controllable by the central government (i.e., the executive branch).
- Limited evidence shows that program budgeting jurisdictions exhibit expenditure bias in centrally controlled accounts.
- Limited evidence suggests that line-item budgeting jurisdictions do not differentiate forecast bias between centrally controlled accounts and accounts distributed to public agencies.

Introduction

There exists a vast body of government budget forecasting literature that shows consistent revenue forecasting bias toward underestimation at the subsovereign level (Bretschneider and Gorr 1992; Bretschneider et al. 1989; Burkhead 1956; Frank 1992, 1993; Frank and McCollough 1992; Frank and Zhao 2009; Kelly 2013; Rodgers and Joyce 1996; Tyer 1993; Williams 2012; Williams and Calabrese 2016). This practice is not necessarily universal, as it is generally not observed in jurisdictions with consistent revenue deficits or with spending financed primarily through debt issuance or transfers. Nevertheless, revenue underestimation can be labeled prudent (Blöndal 2001), conservative (Sun 2008), pessimistic (Penner 2008) or risk adjusted (National Council of State Legislators 2010) because it reduces the risk of not having sufficient resources to fund all the appropriations in a particular fiscal year. Thus, this practice exhibits the use of an asymmetric loss function—a preference for one type of error (in this case, underestimation) over the other (overestimation). Another reason for consistent revenue underestimation is that it reduces the response to political pressure to create or fund additional programs, which would risk increasing taxes in subsequent budget cycles, and, at the same time, discourages tax reduction. It is also thought that the executive prefers to create a surplus which expands both discretion (Levine et al. 1981) and political capital (Crecine 1969).

Revenue, though, is only one-half of the budget equation. Expenditure forecasting should mimic the same risk avoidance through overestimation (Choate and Thompson 1988; Frank 1992; Larkey and Smith 1989; Wildavsky 1986). However, budgeting leads to appropriating, and appropriating authorizes agencies to spend money. Williams and Calabrese (2016) suggest that budgets will not include overestimated expenditures because the resultant appropriation would effectively grant excess discretion to agencies, which central budget authorities try to prevent (Wildavsky 1986; Williams

1997). In other words, overestimating expenditures might lead to spending in excess of revenues. Agencies generally spend more at the end of the fiscal year (Douglas and Franklin 2006; Fichtner and Greene 2014; Hurley et al. 2014; Liebman and Mahoney 2017) to avoid cuts in future forecasted expenditures, and so expenditures are unlikely to be the source of found savings at the end of fiscal years.

Crecine (1969) suggests that a mechanism to both create a surplus and narrow discretion is to appropriate funds in very narrow categories—line item (object of expenditure) appropriations—and prohibit expenditure outside of those categories, that is, to appropriate to line items.[1] This provides very little executive discretion, but may achieve risk avoidance and is consistent with Frank Goodnow's (1913) explanation of legislative budget control.[2] However, for larger jurisdictions, line-item appropriation may not be common in the early twenty-first century.[3] For such jurisdictions, therefore, expenditure overestimation is problematic because appropriating tends to happen at the program level, not at the line-item level; this results in less budgetary control as agencies have more budgetary discretion with programmatic budgeting.

Nevertheless, governments that appropriate to programs or departments (herein, labeled program appropriating) can still overestimate some expenditures—those that are appropriated to centrally controlled accounts; an example of this sort of practice is described in the epigraph of this chapter. This practice allows executive discretion for the chief executive of the jurisdiction while denying it to subordinate agency executives without using the more cumbersome line-item budgeting. Considering this effect, it may provide a strong motivation for central executives to prefer some form of program appropriation. As a companion to program appropriating, expen-

[1] Commonly, this practice is labeled "line-item budgeting"; however, here we explicitly refer to appropriating because budgets can be built using line-item detail, but then appropriated by aggregated programs or departments.

[2] In a variant that allows some central executive discretion while denying it to lower ranking executives, the budget ordinance may appropriate to line items but permit some degree of budget modifications (also known as reprogramming) to the central executive or designee. Regardless of the unit of appropriation, it is likely common, but not universal, that the central executive has some reprogramming authority. This variant would not achieve the Goodnowian legislative budget control.

[3] It is commonly said that line-item budgets are a thing of the past. This view may have its origins with Schick (1966). However, unsystematic observation finds line-item budgeting at the local level among smaller jurisdictions. We have found no authoritative empirical source concerning the distribution of possible units of appropriation across local governments. The most likely sources—GFOA, GASB, ICMA and the Census of Government branch of the U.S. Census—all report that they do not collect these data. While this research has been in progress, we have learned that GFOA has (as of October 2018) a list of 231 localities that report that they use line-item budgeting; however, this matter is further confounded because the term "line-item budgeting" may be used to refer to either the budget presentation or to the appropriation ordinance.

diture overestimation must be allowed only for centrally controlled expenditure categories, so that executives can avoid running out of money at year end while, at the same time, not permitting increased spending at the agency level.

These categories may include such items as pension or health contributions, funds for pay increases, settlements of claims, refunds of disallowed transfer payments (from state or federal grants), debt service, and other costs of the central operation of government.[4] This chapter reports an exploratory study that examines the budget to actual ("BTA") variance of centrally controlled expenditures compared with the variance of those for a distributed expenditures (i.e., not centrally controlled expenditures that are instead appropriated to agencies) in three municipalities: (1) New York City, which both presents its budget and appropriates at an aggregate (program) level; (2) Rocky Mount, North Carolina, which presents its budget at the line-item level, but appropriates at a program level; and Harrisonburg, Virginia, which both presents and appropriates at the line-item level. The expectation is that centrally controlled expenditure BTA variances (New York City) will have larger surpluses/smaller deficits than variances with distributed expenditures, while line-item appropriating jurisdictions (Harrisonburg) will have more similar variances in both categories. It is less clear how the intermediate (Rocky Mount) variances will occur, although the described motivations would suggest results more like program appropriating localities than like line-item appropriating localities. Such a result would provide evidence of previously unexamined risk-averse forecast bias and evidence of concern to suppress agency discretion while simultaneously permitting central executive discretion. As we have found no significant body of literature on this topic, we view this exploratory study as significant.

Methodology

The data for this study come from the New York City Comprehensive Annual Financial Report (CAFR) supplemented with data from the New York City budget documents,[5] Rocky Mount budget documents,[6] and Harrisonburg

[4] Governments may need to be clever about these categories, for example, when negotiating with unions, it may be contrary to the negotiation strategy to overfund pay increases.

[5] The New York City CAFRs are available at https://comptroller.nyc.gov/reports/comprehensive-annual-financial-reports/ and its budget documents are available at https://www1.nyc.gov/site/omb/publications/publications.page.

[6] The Rocky Mount data are available at https://www.rockymountnc.gov/government/city_hall/budget_office/documents/.

budget documents.[7] New York City data are available for the fiscal years 2001–2017. The Rocky Mount data are available for fiscal years 2009–2017. The Harrisonburg data are available for fiscal years 2010–2017.

Based on the identified gaps in the existing public budgeting and forecast literatures, the research hypotheses examined here are as follows:

For jurisdictions that use program budgeting and appropriating:

1. There are small or no positive (surplus) appropriation-to-expenditure variances for distributed accounts (variance type 1).
2. There are positive appropriation-to-expenditure variances in centrally controlled accounts (variance type 2).
3. Variances type 2 are significantly larger positive amounts than variances type 1.

For jurisdictions that use line-item budgeting and appropriating:

4. There will be positive, but relatively small, appropriation-to-expenditure variances for distributed accounts (variance type 1).
5. There will be positive appropriation-to-expenditure variance for centrally controlled accounts (variance type 2).
6. There will be no significant difference in variances between variance type 1 and variance type 2.

Between these two types of localities:

7. Variances type 1 will be larger for line-item appropriating jurisdictions, and both may be positive.
8. Variances type 2 will be larger for program appropriating jurisdictions, albeit both will be positive.
9. The difference between the variances type 1 and variances type 2 will be larger for program budgeting localities.

These hypotheses are indeterminant for localities that budget using line items and appropriate using a program design; however, our preliminary expectation is that the form of the appropriation will be determinative.

[7] The Harrisonburg data are available at https://www.harrisonburgva.gov/budget.

Data Analysis

We classify three categories of centrally budgeted expenditures for New York City. These are pension contributions, miscellaneous, and debt service. These expenditure categories represent amounts that are not distributed to program agencies and are controlled by the mayor. The city budget documents treat these categories as if they are programs separate from the departments to which they provide support. We treat the rest of the city as non-centrally budgeted expenditures. New York City data are found in Section (a) of Table 10.1.

Column 2 of Table 10.1(a) shows the average of the appropriations[8] for these four categories for fiscal years 2001 through 2017. Columns 3 through 5 show the average, minimum, and maximum surplus (the BTA).[9] Column 6 shows the coefficient of variation (CV) for the surplus. Column 7 shows the average surplus divided by the average appropriation displayed as a percentage. To distinguish this from Column 8, this proportion is as follows:

$$\text{PctSurplus} = \frac{\sum_{t=1}^{n} \text{Surplus}_t \,/\, n}{\sum_{t=1}^{n} \text{Appropriation}_t \,/\, n} \tag{10.1}$$

The minimum values for Pension Contribution and Miscellaneous are negative (i.e., they are in deficit when compared with the beginning of year appropriation), which reduces the mean value relative to the standard deviation, resulting in high CVs. The proportionate size of the surplus for Miscellaneous, Debt Service, and Total Central are substantially higher than that of Rest of City. While Rest of City is positive, it is relatively small.

Column 8 of Table 10.1 shows the average of percentage surplus computed yearly. The equation is as follows:

$$PctSurplus = \frac{\sum_{t=1}^{n} Surplus_t \,/\, Appropriation_t}{n} \tag{10.2}$$

---

[8] For New York debt service, the amount shown as appropriation is the appropriated amount plus funds available within the debt service account (primarily the prior year balance). This reflects the city's actual practice as described in Williams and Onochie (2013).

[9] The surplus is calculated as budget minus actual. Where it is negative it is a deficit. For the debt service category, there is a separate debt service account; the surplus for this category is funds available in the debt service account (primarily the carryforward from the prior year) plus the budgeted transfer to this account from the general fund minus the expenditure during the year (thus, it is the carryforward to the next year).

Table 10.1 Analysis of central and distributed expenditure budget supluses and deficits

Surplus (Deficit)	Appropriation ($) Average	Surplus ($) Average	Min	Max	CV	Avg. S/Avg. A (%)	Avg. (S/A) (%)	t	p
(a) New York $n = 17$									
Pension contribution	5,645,561,862	79,591,096	(527,847,920)	720,465,164	3.71	1.41	1.84		
Miscellaneous	1,160,851,526	759,984,113	(863,439,099)	2,706,692,853	1.18	65.47	290.77		
Debt service (acct balance)	4,801,610,195	1,415,797,489	212,470,361	3,142,579,651	0.64	29.49	27.19		
Total central	11,608,023,583	2,255,372,697	440,385,551	4,399,406,690	0.54	19.43	18.67	7.87	<0.001
Rest of the city	48,766,970,692	1,757,871,140	523,420,112	3,230,512,293	0.40	3.60	3.91	11.20	<0.001
Difference of means							14.76	7.87	<0.001
(b) Rocky Mount $n = 9$									
Debt	3,972,709	(9282)	(494,313)	597,658	0.60	−0.23	−0.83		
Benefits, transfers out	10,254,633	(262,938)	(1,288,375)	1,048,524	−2.55	−2.56	−2.75		
Other central	6,156,062	1,436,855	240,490	3,518,890	0.66	23.34	22.47		
Total central	20,383,404	1,164,634	(823,815)	3,672,835	1.24	5.71	5.56	2.20	0.03
Rest of City	46,592,258	1,114,078	(1,351,651)	3,704,211	1.38	2.39	2.35	2.46	0.02
Difference of means							3.21	1.98	0.04
Alternate diff. of means							−1.81	n/a	n/a
(c) Harrisonburg $n = 8$									
Debt	13,178,035	161,635	(561,604)	926,802	2.74	1.23	1.20		
Benefits	7,024,262	487,124	322,413	603,256	0.19	6.93	6.97		
Other central	2,902,143	454,886	208,026	1,082,783	0.61	15.67	15.43		
Total central	23,104,440	1,103,644	315,967	1,932,084	0.488	4.78	5.71	2.77	<0.001
Rest of City	28,719,730	1,198,895	(573,797)	4,232,502	1.28	4.17	4.29	2.18	0.03
Difference of means							0.51	0.24	0.41
Alternate diff. of means							−0.98	n/a	n/a

Columns 9 and 10 show results of *t*-test comparisons for total values. The Rest of City percent surplus is 3.91 percent ($t = 7.87$, $p < 0.001$, $n = 17$). Thus, hypothesis 1—that there is no significant appropriation-to-expenditure variance for distributed accounts—is rejected. The Total Central percent surplus is 18.67 percent ($t = 11.20$, $p < 0.001$, $n = 17$), this result is consistent with the hypothesis 2 that there is a positive appropriation-to-expenditure variance for central accounts. The difference in means of 14.67 percent ($t = 7.87$, $p < 0.001$, $n = 17$, paired *t*-test), this result is consistent with hypothesis 3, that the Central surplus is significantly larger than the Distributed surplus. Consequently, there is strong evidence that New York City (the exemplar program budgeting locality) exhibits a preference for surplus in the centrally controlled accounts. This preference is consistent with the anticipated bias as defined by hypotheses 2 and 3, but not hypothesis 1.

Table 10.1(b) examines the Rocky Mount data. Rocky Mount does not have clearly labeled central accounts, so the accounts have been designated by type of expenditure and functional type of expenditure. Expenditures for the City Clerk, City Manager, Mayor & City Council, Human Resources, Human Relations, Finance, and Central Services are designated as central, except as described below. Expenditures for all other city agencies (Police, Fire, Public Works, Engineering, Parks and Recreation, and Planning and Development) are designated as distributed, except as described next. All salary expenditures, regardless of department, are designated as distributed; and all expenditures for debt, benefits, and "Transfers Out" are designated as central.

As seen in Table 10.1(b), there are negative minimum surplus values (deficits compared with beginning of year appropriation) in all categories except Other Central and the first two categories have negative averages. The Column 7 average (using Eq. 10.1), shows the proportionate surplus ranges from −2.56 percent to 23.34 percent for central expenditures with the Total Central surplus of 5.71 percent. It is 2.39 percent for Rest of City.

The Column 8 (Eq. 10.2) average for Rest of City is 2.35 percent ($t = 2.20$, $p = 0.03$, $n = 9$). For Total Central it is 5.56 percent ($t = 2.46$, $p = 0.02$, $n = 9$). The difference of means 3.21 percent ($t = 3.21$, $p = 0.04$, $n = 9$, paired *t*-test). To examine whether the difference of means comparison is sensitive to the assignment of salary to distributed rather than central, the salary data were reassigned to central and an alternative difference of means test was computed, however the resultant sign was negative.

Because Rocky Mount ambiguously budgets by line item while appropriating by program, it is unclear whether these data should be considered related to hypotheses 1 through 3 or hypotheses 4 through 6. The theoretical assertion, however, is that the form of appropriation is determinative, so these

Table 10.2 Harrisonburg agencies categorized as distributed

• Assessor	• P & R Golf Crse Gds Mgt
• Attorney	• Police Administration
• City Council	• Public Safety Building
• Downtown Parking Maint.	• Purchasing Agent
• Equalization	• Revenue
• Finance	• Treasurer
• Fire Administration	• Zoning Administrator
• Gen. Engineering/Admin.	• Reserve for Contingencies
• Human Resources	• Contributions
• Information Technology	• Debt Service
• Manager	• Independent Auditor
• P & R Administration	

hypotheses are considered. While the *p*-values are much higher than with New York City, the results are similar, that is they reject hypothesis 1 and are consistent with hypotheses 2 and 3.

Table 10.1(c) examines the Harrisonburg data. The Harrisonburg reports show line-item detail in the budget as adopted, which is the format of a line-item appropriating jurisdiction. Except for Debt service, Harrisonburg, like Rocky Mount, does not have clearly labeled central accounts, so central and distributed accounts have been designated in the same manner as with Rocky Mount. Table 10.2 shows the Harrisonburg agencies categorized as Central. All other agencies are labeled Distributed. Functionally, Benefits is labeled Central, while Personal Services (payroll) is Distributed.

There are negative minimum surplus values only for Debt and Rest of City and there are no negative averages. The Column 7 average (using Eq. 10.1) shows the proportionate surplus ranges from −1.23 percent to 15.67 percent for central expenditures with the Total Central surplus of 4.78 percent. It is 4.17 percent for Rest of City.

With Harrisonburg, we consider hypotheses 4 through 6. The Column 8 (Eq. 10.2) average for Rest of City is 4.29 percent ($t = 2.18$, $p = 0.03$, $n = 8$), which is consistent with the hypothesis 4 expectation that there will be a positive, but relatively small, appropriation-to-expenditure variances for distributed accounts. For Total Central it is 5.71 percent ($t = 2.77$, $p < 0.001$, $n = 8$), which is consistent with hypothesis 5 that there will be positive appropriation-to-expenditure variance for centrally controlled accounts. The difference of means 0.51 percent ($t = 0.24$, $p = 0.41$, $n = 8$, paired *t*-test), which is consistent with hypothesis 6, that there will be no significant difference between Distributed and Central accounts. As with Rocky Mount, an alternative difference of means test was computed as a sensitivity analysis, but the resultant sign was negative.

Table 10.3 compares the categorized surpluses by locality to examine hypotheses 7 through 9. Because Rocky Mount has some similarity with line-item appropriating organizations and because of the much higher *p*-values for Rocky Mount than New York, we treat Rocky Mount as a line-item appropriating organization as we consider hypotheses 7 through 9.

Table 10.3(a) compares New York City and Rocky Mount. The first line shows that the percent difference of surplus between New York City and Rocky Mount for Distributed is 1.56. As the sign is opposite, the hypothesized larger variance for line-item budget jurisdictions, hypothesis 7 is rejected. The second line shows that percent Central of surplus between New York City and Rocky Mount for Central is 13.10 ($t = 4.64$, $p < 0.001$). This result is consistent with hypothesis 8, that program budget jurisdictions will have larger appropriation-to-expenditure variances. The bottom line shows that the difference between New York and Rocky Mount with respect to the difference between Central and Distributed is 11.55 percent ($t = 4.66$, $p < 0.001$). This result is consistent with hypothesis 9, that program budgeting localities will have larger differences between the two variances of this sort.

The evaluation of these three hypotheses with respect to the difference between New York City and Rocky Mount treat Rocky Mount as a line-item budgeting locality. However, the true test is with a line-item appropriating locality. Thus, the analysis now turns to Harrisonburg. Table 10.3(b) compares New York City and Harrisonburg. The first line shows that the percent difference of surplus between New York City and Harrisonburg for Distributed is −0.38 ($t = -0.19$, $p = 0.43$). The sign is as expected; however, the *p*-value is not statistically significant, so these results are inconsistent with hypothesis 7. The second line shows that percent Central of surplus between New York City and Harrisonburg for Central is 13.87 ($t = 7.43$, $p < 0.001$). This result is consistent with hypothesis 8, that program budget jurisdictions will have larger appropriation-to-expenditure variances. The bottom line of this subsections shows that the difference between New York and Harrisonburg with respect to the difference between Central and Distributed is 14.25 percent ($t = 5.00$, $p < 0.001$). This result is consistent with hypothesis 9 that program budgeting localities will have larger differences between the two variances of this sort.

Table 10.3(c) compares Rocky Mount and Harrisonburg. Because we are tentatively treating Rocky Mount as more similar to line-item appropriating governments, we are not expecting any of the comparisons to be significant. None of the *t*-values are significant, so the results are consistent with expectations. It is noteworthy, nonetheless, that the actual measured difference for Distributed between Rocky Mount and Harrisonburg is −1.93. This leads to a need for further examination with more data to determine whether the

Table 10.3 Comparison of surplus between localities

	Compare percent surplus by locality							
(a)	NYC	RM	Difference	*t*	*P*	*n*	*df*	Type
Distributed	3.91	2.35	1.56	1.32	0.106	26	12	Unequal variance
Central	18.67	5.56	13.10	4.64	0.000	26	24	Equal variance
Difference in means	14.76	3.21	11.55	4.66	0.000	26	23	Unequal variance
(b)	NYC	Harrisonburg	Difference	*t*	*P*	*n*	*df*	Type
Distributed	3.91	4.29	−0.38	−0.19	0.429	25	8	Unequal variance
Central	18.67	4.80	13.87	7.43	0.000	25	22	Unequal variance
Difference in means	14.76	0.51	14.25	5.00	0.000	25	17	Unequal variance
(c)	RM	Harrisonburg	Difference	*t*	*P*	*n*	*df*	Type
Distributed	2.35	4.29	−1.93	−0.86	0.204	17	11	Unequal variance
Central	5.56	4.80	0.77	0.32	0.378	17	10	Unequal variance
Difference in means	3.21	0.51	2.70	1.01	0.167	17	13	Unequal variance

mixed localities like Rocky Mount are more like line-item appropriating localities, or more like program appropriating localities and to examine all hypotheses, but particularly hypothesis 7 more extensively.

Discussion

There are two principal conceptual hypotheses that are addressed in this chapter. First, we expect that program appropriating local governments use centrally controlled expenditure forecasts to hide surpluses. This assertion leads to the first three operational hypotheses. The examined data are consistent with the second and third hypotheses, but not with the first. The implication of failing to confirm the first hypothesis is that program appropriating governments may risk allowing some discretion to distributed agencies. Further analysis is required. It may be that it is not practical to eliminate all fiscal discretion, or it may be that allowing some discretion is intentional.

Second, we expect that line-item appropriating local governments distribute possible surpluses more widely throughout the budget than do program budgeting local governments. This assertion leads to the next three operational hypotheses. The examined data are consistent with these hypotheses, when the line-item practices are for both budgeting and appropriating. Third, as a consequence of the first two expectations, we expect the forecast practices to differ between program appropriating and line-item appropriating governments. This led to the last three hypotheses. The empirical results are consistent with this expectation.

We examined one municipality that budgets using line-items, but appropriates at the program level. When examining the first three hypotheses, it looks like a program appropriating government, but with a much smaller effect; thus, we do not examine the second three hypotheses. With respect to the third three hypotheses, it looks more like a line-item appropriating government in that it is not distinguishable from the other line-item appropriating government, but can be distinguished from the program appropriating government.

The most interesting findings are that there is evidence that: (1) program appropriating governments exhibit substantial overforecasting of centrally controlled expenditures, which is consistent with the expectation that program budgeting localities can overforecast expenditures so long as they are allocated to central accounts, and (2) line-item appropriating localities tend to overforecast about the same in all categories, relying more on the use of line-item control to prevent excessive discretion among the distributed departments. These findings, while based on limited data, are especially interesting given that the theory about expenditure overforecasting is still relatively underdeveloped (especially compared to revenue underforecasting), and this analysis is among the first to undertake an empirical analysis of the phenomenon. Nevertheless, it should be remembered that this chapter is exploratory. The principal limitation of this analysis is that it uses data from only three jurisdictions, limiting the generalizability of the findings. This approach is reasonable given the limited literature and the lack of other empirical analysis. Because of the limited data and unbalanced length of data series, statistical testing is currently limited to *t*-tests.

Conclusion

The study hypothesizes that program budgeting/appropriating governments use overforecasting of central account expenditures to build a cushion against risk and to generate post-budgeting discretion for central actors. It hypothesizes that line-item budgeting/appropriating governments can achieve these same goals without attributing the overforecasted expenditures to central accounts. The empirical analysis is largely consistent with these expectations. This result provides further insight into the machinations of budget forecasting. The inclusion of a line-item budgeting/program budgeting jurisdiction introduces new complexity that requires further examination. Likewise, this study is limited to three governments and a small number of forecasts; consequently, any results should be viewed as tentative and further study is recommended.

References

Blöndal, J. R. (2001). Budgeting in Canada. *OECD Journal on Budgeting, 1*(2), 39–84.

Bretschneider, S. I., & Gorr, W. L. (1992). Economic, organizational, and political influences on biases in forecasting state sales tax receipts. *International Journal of Forecasting, 7*(4), 457–466. https://doi.org/10.1016/0169-2070(92)90029-9.

Bretschneider, S. I., Gorr, W. L., Grizzle, G. A., & Klay, E. (1989). Political and organizational influences on the accuracy of forecasting state government revenues. *International Journal of Forecasting, 5*(3), 307–319.

Burkhead, J. (1956). *Government budgeting*. New York: Wiley.

Burton, P. (2018, July 3). How De Blasio labor deal invites second-guessing. *The Bond Buyer*, 390, Online.

Choate, G. M., & Thompson, F. (1988). Budget makers as agents: A preliminary investigation of discretionary behavior under state-contingent rewards. *Public Choice, 58*(1), 3–20.

Crecine, J. P. (1969). *Governmental problem-solving; a computer simulation of municipal budgeting*. Chicago: Chicago, Rand McNally.

Douglas, J. W., & Franklin, A. L. (2006). Putting the brakes on the rush to spend down end-of-year balances: Carryover money in Oklahoma state agencies. *Public Budgeting & Finance, 26*(3), 46–64.

Fichtner, J. J., & Greene, R. (2014). *Curbing the surge in year-end federal government spending: Reforming "use It or lose It" rules*. Mercatus Working Paper: Mercatus Center, George Mason University.

Frank, H. A. (1992). Expenditure forecasting. In J. Rabin (Ed.), *Handbook of public budgeting* (pp. 167–209). New York: Dekker.

Frank, H. A. (1993). *Budgetary forecasting in local government: New tools and techniques*. Westport, CT: Quorum Books.

Frank, H. A., & McCollough, J. (1992). Municipal forecasting practice: "Demand" and "supply" side perspectives. *International Journal of Public Administration, 15*(9), 1669–1695.

Frank, H. A., & Zhao, Y. (2009). Determinants of local government revenue forecasting practice: Empirical evidence from Florida. *Journal of Public Budgeting, Accounting & Financial Management, 21*(1), 17–35.

Goodnow, F. J. (1913). The limit of budgetary control. *Proceedings of the American Political Science Association, 9*, 68–77.

Hurley, W. J., Brimberg, J., & Fisher, B. (2014). Use it or lose it: On the incentives to spend annual defence operating budgets. *Defence and Peace Economics, 25*(4), 401–413. https://doi.org/10.1080/10242694.2013.780758.

Kelly, J. M. (2013). Fund balance for budget stabilization: Does the new accounting presentation matter? *Journal of Public Budgeting, Accounting & Financial Management, 25*(4), 719.

Larkey, P. D., & Smith, R. A. (1989). Bias in the formulation of local government budget problems. *Policy Sciences, 22*(2), 123–166.

Levine, C. H., Rubin, I. S., & Wolohojian, G. G. (1981). Resource scarcity and the reform model: The management of retrenchment in Cincinnati and Oakland. *Public Administration Review, 41*(6), 619–628.

Liebman, J. B., & Mahoney, N. (2017). Do expiring budgets lead to wasteful year-end spending? Evidence from federal procurement. *American Economic Review, 107*(11), 3510–3549.

National Council of State Legislators (Ed.). (2010). *Tax policy handbook for state legislators* (3rd ed.). Denver, CO: National Council of State Legislators.

Penner, R. G. (2008). Federal revenue forecasting. In J. Sun & T. D. Lynch (Eds.), *Government budget forecasting: Theory and practice* (Vol. 142, pp. 11–25). Boca Raton, FL: CRC Press, Auerbach Publications, Taylor & Francis Group.

Rodgers, R., & Joyce, P. G. (1996). The effect of underforecasting on the accuracy of revenue forecasts by state governments. *Public Administration Review, 56*(1), 48–56.

Schick, A. (1966). The road to PPB: The stages of budget reform. *Public Administration Review, 26*(4), 243–258. https://doi.org/10.2307/973296.

Sun, J. (2008). Forecast evaluation: A case study. In J. Sun & T. D. Lynch (Eds.), *Government budget forecasting: Theory and practice* (Vol. 142, pp. 223–240). Boca Raton, FL: CRC Press, Auerbach Publications, Taylor & Francis Group.

Tyer, C. B. (1993). Local government reserve funds: Policy alternatives and political strategies. *Public Budgeting & Finance, 13*(2), 75–84.

Wildavsky, A. B. (1986). The poor and certain: Budgeting in American cities. In A. B. Wildavsky (Ed.), *Budgeting: A comparative theory of budgetary processes* (2nd rev. ed., pp. 182–218). New Brunswick, NJ: Transaction Books.

Williams, D. W. (1997, 1998). *Medicaid Forecasting Practices.* Paper presented at the Ninth Federal Forecasters Conference - 1997 Papers and Proceedings, Washington, DC.

Williams, D. W. (2012). The politics of forecast bias: Forecaster effect and other effects in New York City revenue forecasting. *Public Budgeting & Finance, 32*(4), 1–18. https://doi.org/10.1111/j.1540-5850.2012.01021.x.

Williams, D. W., & Calabrese, T. D. (2016). The status of budget forecasting. *Journal of Public and Nonprofit Affairs, 2*(2), 127–160. https://doi.org/10.20899/jpna.2.2.127-160.

Williams, D. W., & Onochie, J. (2013). The Rube Goldberg machine of budget implementation, or is there a structural deficit in the New York City budget? *Public Budgeting & Finance, 33*(4), 1–21. https://doi.org/10.1111/j.1540-5850.2013.12021.x.

11

Excessive Revenue Underforecasting: Evidence and Implications from New York City's Property Tax

Geoffrey Propheter

Major Points

- Scholars have consistently found that governments
  - intentionally underforecast revenue.
  - impound revenue variances into future budget levels, a process known as ratcheting.
- This chapter explores the forecasting dynamics of New York City's property tax.
- It shows that the tax is excessively and intentionally underforecasted by the mayor's budgeting agency.
- It discusses alternatives for overcoming this practice.

Introduction

Governments intentionally and routinely underforecast revenue, with the most common justification being that underforecasting serves as a hedge against unanticipated declines in revenue (Bretschneider and Schroeder 1985; Frank and Wang 1994; Rodgers and Joyce 1996; Williams 2012). An

G. Propheter (✉)
School of Public Affairs, University of Colorado Denver, Denver, CO, USA
e-mail: geoffrey.propheter@ucdenver.edu

D. Williams, T. Calabrese (eds.), *The Palgrave Handbook of Government Budget Forecasting*, Palgrave Studies in Public Debt, Spending, and Revenue,
https://doi.org/10.1007/978-3-030-18195-6_11

underappreciated consequence of underforecasting revenue, and presumably an undesirable consequence from the perspective of taxpayers, is that policymakers build the expenditures in excess of the forecast into next year's forecast, or, in the case of a multi-year financial plan, into any or all future years' forecasts. This phenomenon is known as budget ratcheting and has garnered convincing empirical support (Lee and Plummer 2007; Marlowe 2009). Accept that some degree of underforecasting is prudent, because if revenues exceed forecasts, there is opportunity for benevolent budget-setters to prevent ratcheting by returning the excess to taxpayers. Collections that fall short, however, must be met with spending cuts or tax increases, perhaps a less desirable outcome for politicians and taxpayers alike. Thus, in the absence of omniscience, it is better to underestimate than overestimate (Frank and Zhao 2009; Gianakis and McCue 1999).

However, there is presumably a limit to which underforecasting is prudent. Given a tradeoff exists between the advantages and disadvantages of underforecasting, it stands to reason that there is a point at which underforecasting becomes excessive and undesirable. The existing body of research tells us very little about excessive underforecasting—other than excessive ratcheting as a consequence, which can be deduced. The nature of an empirical analysis of excessive underforecasting may play a role in our limited knowledge. Not only does such an analysis require a definition of "excessive" but also compelling evidence that forecasts far exceed the threshold, whatever that may be, and that they do so consistently. The notion of excessive forecasting is worthy of scholarly attention because its existence would signal the presence of fiscal obfuscation, a concept itself that is underdeveloped. It is most often discussed in the context of fiscal illusion, but the two concepts are distinct. Sanandaji and Wallace (2011, p. 244) describe fiscal obfuscation as lawmakers' "*exploitation* of the public's rational ignorance by hiding information from them" [emphasis added] about the true cost of government. In contrast, fiscal illusion is the "systematic misperception of key fiscal parameters [that] may significantly distort fiscal choices by the electorate" (Oates 1988, p. 65). The key difference between fiscal obfuscation and fiscal illusion is that the former occurs by intentionally concealing government's fiscal standing whereas the latter does not. Fiscal illusion can occur through benevolent lawmaker inattention just as much as it can through taxpayers', but this cannot be true by definition for fiscal obfuscation.[1]

[1] While the public choice literature in particular imparts intentionality on budget-maximizing lawmakers, the existence of fiscal illusion does not imply anything about lawmakers' mental states. Consider that revenue diversification and tax structure complexity can lead to fiscal illusion (Oates 1988), but lawmakers may select more complex tax systems for ostensibly benevolent reasons such as a revenue stabilization

The purpose of this chapter is to offer strong evidence of fiscal obfuscation in the forecasting and budgeting of New York City's property tax. The property tax is an ideal tax to explore because it has received considerable attention from scholars interested in measuring fiscal illusion (Brien 2018; Brien and Sjoquist 2014; Jung 2001; Ross and Yan 2013). It is possible, however, that prior studies identified fiscal obfuscation instead, a possibility that is not testable from the methods and data used. Moreover, by focusing on a single jurisdiction, the black box of local property tax forecasting and budgeting can be unpacked (Williams 2012), allowing an opportunity to more closely scrutinize the processes that serve as evidence of intentionally deceptive lawmaker behavior. Short of lawmakers admitting to excessive underforecasting, which seems unlikely to occur, the evidence offered here is a second-best alternative presented in the hopes of pushing public finance and budgeting scholarship toward a deeper appreciation of the causes and consequences of overly conservative forecasting bias.

In addition, New York City's property tax is an ideal case study for the topic because it has some unique characteristics. A common approach to measuring fiscal illusion is to observe changes in property tax rates, which is possible in most municipalities where the tax rate can float from one year to the next. In New York City, however, while the city charter grants the city council authority to adjust the citywide tax rate to determine the levy, in practice the city council has agreed with the mayor to fix the tax rate at a constant level as a matter of convention. This facilitates budgeting so that negotiations can focus on expenditures rather than revenues. Since policymakers cannot easily adjust the tax rate in order to grow the levy in excess of the median voter's preference, an alternative means of deception is needed. Evidence is provided that policymakers use the property tax forecast to create fiscal obfuscation; via ratcheting the consequence of obfuscation is excessive increases in the levy over the city's financial plan period.

The remainder of the chapter is organized as follows. In the next section the city's property tax system is discussed in greater detail. A focus is on introducing nomenclature, the tax's calculation, and the government-sponsored agencies that produce property tax forecasts. The following section then offers and describes the first piece of evidence of fiscal obfuscation, that the element of the property tax forecast directly in control of policymakers, known as the property tax reserve, is excessively overforecasted by the mayor's budgeting agency, the Office of Management and Budget (OMB), and consistently so. The property tax reserve is all of the revenue the city expects not to collect in a given year, so

strategy, whether that happens in fact or not (Carroll 2009). Where we find fiscal obfuscation we will find fiscal illusion, but where there is illusion there may not be obfuscation.

that by overforecasting these uncollectibles, policymakers in fact underforecast revenue. The next section then offers and describes the second piece of evidence of fiscal obfuscation, that OMB intentionally underforecasts revenue, because its principal (the mayor) has a clear political (budgetary) incentive to underestimate revenue. The city has multiple government-sponsored property tax forecasts, and the other agencies are argued to desire more accurate forecasts than more conservative ones. By comparing the different forecasts of each agency, the political incentives OMB faces can be identified. The chapter closes with a brief recapitulation and suggestions for moving forward. Importantly, none of the evidence that is presented is a smoking gun of fiscal obfuscation. Certainty of fiscal obfuscation would take an incredible act of candor on the part of policymakers. Instead, the evidence of fiscal obfuscation should be evaluated as a whole, in which case while not a smoking gun it is nevertheless compelling.

New York City's Real Property Tax

New York City's property tax system is unique among jurisdictions in the United States in that it contains *all* of the following elements: classified tax rates, classified assessments, assessment caps and growth limits, a (generally) fixed citywide tax rate, and constrained tax base distributions. To fully appreciate the property tax forecast, it is necessary to discuss the mechanics and administration of the property tax in New York City in greater detail.

The city is one of two jurisdictions in New York State (the other being Nassau County) with a classified tax rate and assessment system, of which there are four classes: Class 1 is (generally) 1–3 family homes; Class 2 includes condos, co-operatives, and rental buildings; Class 3 is utilities; and Class 4 is commercial.[2] At present, Class 1 property is assessed at 6.0 percent of fair market value, while all other classes are assessed at 45.0 percent.[3] Fair market value multiplied by the appropriate assessment rate yields what is known as actual assessed value.[4]

[2] Class 1 also includes vacant land adjoining a Class 1 residences, bungalows, residential garages (if separately assessed), and other uncommon real property that ostensible would appear to fit the definition of Class 2 or Class property. For more details, see New York Real Property Tax Law §1802.

[3] New York Property Tax Law §305(2) allows New York City to assess different classes of property at different rates, determinable by local law.

[4] Fair market value for ad valorem purposes is determined through one of the three property valuation approaches: the comparable-sales approach, the income approach, or the cost approach. The comparable-sales approach assigns a value based on recent sales prices of similar properties in the area. It is appropriate when real estate transactions for that particular type of property are abundant. The income approach

Moreover, New York City property owners also enjoy assessment growth limits; though, the mechanics vary by property class. Class 1 properties cannot have their assessed value increased more than 6.0 percent or by 20.0 percent over 5 years. For Class 2 buildings with less than 11 residential units, the annual growth limit is 8.0 percent and the five-year growth limit is 30.0 percent.[5] The assessed value reflecting the growth limits is known as capped assessed value. For Class 2 buildings with 11 or more residential units and for Class 4 properties, there are no growth limits, but instead annual increases in actual assessed value are phased-in over a five-year period. The assessed value after factoring in these limitations is called transitional assessed value. The taxable assessed value, the value of real property for ad valorem purposes, is the lesser of actual assessed value or capped or transitional assessed value, whichever of the latter two are applicable.

Assessment ratios and limits are part of the process to calculate the city's taxable property tax base—the pool of taxable assessed value local lawmakers can tap to finance public goods and services. In many local jurisdictions in the United States, the property tax serves to fill gaps in the upcoming year's budget. Lawmakers determine the upcoming year's spending priorities and the estimated costs, and their staffers estimate the revenue that will be collected from non-property tax sources. The difference between the estimated expenditures and non-property tax revenue is the amount of revenue that needs to be derived from the property tax to balance the budget. Mathematically, the relationship can be expressed generally as:

$$E' = N' + P' \tag{11.1}$$

$$P' = b'r' \tag{11.2}$$

$$E' = N' + b'r' \tag{11.3}$$

and thus

assigns a value according to the amount of net income a property generates. This process can be done using a rate of capitalization (direct capitalization approach) or discounting a stream of estimated net income over time (discounted cash flow approach). The income approach is appropriate when the property generates income but there are relatively few transactions of the property type. The cost approach assigns a value according to how much it would cost to replace (using contemporary building materials) or reproduce (using the original building materials) a property. It is appropriate when there is no income data available, such as brand-new buildings or improvements, or when a property is rare, such as stadiums and arenas. In New York City, generally speaking, Class 1 properties are valued using the comparable-sales approach, and Class 2 and Class 4 on the income approach. Class 3 are generally assessed by the state.

[5] The assessment caps do not apply to increases in assessed value resulting from physical improvements.

$$r' = \left(E' - N'\right) / b' \tag{11.4}$$

where apostrophes denote forecasted values, *E* equals budgeted expenditures, *N* equals non-property tax revenue, and *P* equals property tax revenue. Equation (11.4) indicates that the property tax rate needed to balance the budget will float up and down as budgeted expenses, non-property tax revenue, and the taxable property tax base change. For example, holding the tax base and expenditures constant, a decrease in non-property tax revenues results in an increase in the property tax rate. Holding expenditures and non-property tax revenues constant, increasing the property tax base results in the tax rate decreasing.

In order for lawmakers to set the budget, three of the four parameters of Eq. (11.4) must be known in advance; the fourth will be derivable algebraically as a consequence. Though the parameters vary annually as economic conditions and budgeting decisions change, some states limit how much some parameters can vary through so-called tax and expenditure limitations, the most common of which are limitations on how much the local property tax base or property tax rates can increase each year (National Association of State Budget Officers 2015; Yuan et al. 2009). If a local property tax base increases 5 percent but the property tax rate cannot increase more than 1 percent, budgeted expenditures can only increase 1 percent if non-property tax revenue remains unchanged. Evidence indicates that non-property tax revenue increases in the presence of tax and expenditure limitations (McCubbins and Moule 2010; Jung and Bae 2011), however. This illustrates that by adopting a single limit on any of the inputs, lawmakers can avoid the intent of the limitation (i.e. constraining public spending) by, for instance, increasing user fees. The more parameter constraints introduced, the more difficult it becomes for lawmakers to avoid the intent of TELs.

New York City's property tax operates under two constraints, making the system potentially binding using the terminology in the TEL literature (Joyce and Mullins 1991). The first constraint is the aforementioned assessment growth limits and phase-ins. The second constraint is a (generally) fixed citywide tax rate. It is in general fixed because it is not set in law but instead agreed to by convention between the mayor and city council in order to facilitate budgeting. In the recent past the rate has been set at 12.238 percent. By agreeing to the tax rate in advance, lawmakers effectively agree to a revenue budget, and thus need only negotiate the expenditure budget. Figure 11.1 graphs the citywide tax rate from fiscal year 1980 through 2016. Note that the practice of fixing the citywide rate by convention did not begin until 1994, prior to which the rate floated year-to-year.

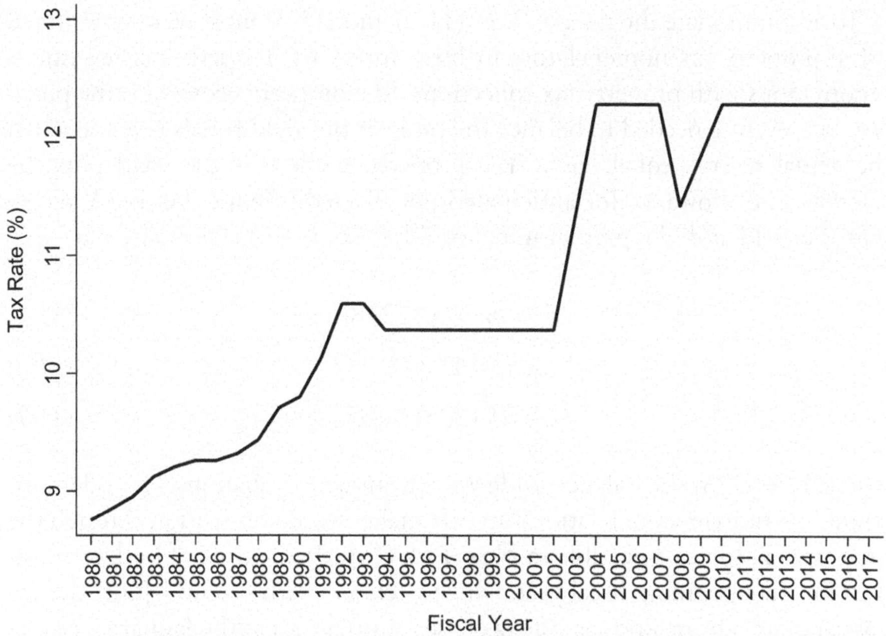

Fig. 11.1 Citywide property tax rate, fiscal years 1980–2017. Source: Annual Property Tax Report, various years, Department of Finance

Equation (11.3) equates the city's budgeted expenditures to the sum of its budgeted non-property tax and property tax revenue; under state law the city is required to forecast and have a balanced budget for the current fiscal year. However, Eq. (11.3) is too general, as it fails to appreciate that tax collections may fall short of expectations for a variety of reasons such as refunds, tax credits, and cancellations, or positive variances can occur in any given year due to overpayments or payments from prior years' outstanding liabilities. With respect to the property tax, these sources of variance are collectively known in New York City as the property tax reserve, also loosely referred to as uncollectibles. While the reserve can in theory take on any positive or negative value after summing the debits and credits, in practice the debits are much greater than the credits. It is therefore appropriate to always think of the reserve as a negative value. As of late the reserve contains about 20 items that affect collections. If the property tax were administered without flaws (necessitating corrections to the tax roll) and taxpayers paid all that was owed on time, there would be no practical reason to forecast and operate a reserve.[6]

[6] An exception to this reasoning could be made for abatements, which in New York City are credits—reductions in tax liability after the class-specific tax rate has been applied to a parcel's taxable assessed

To accommodate the reserve, Eqs. (11.2) and (11.3) must be re-envisioned using property tax nomenclature in New York City. Property tax revenue is synonymous with property tax collections. The property tax yield is the property tax revenue needed to balance the budget; the yield equals revenue when the actual reserve equals zero. The property tax levy is the yield plus the reserve—the allowance for anticipated uncollected revenue. Letting Y represent the yield and U represent uncollectibles, Eq. (11.2) is re-written as:

$$Y' = br = 0.12238\text{b} \tag{11.5}$$

$$L' = Y' + U' \tag{11.6}$$

$$L' = 0.12238b + U' \tag{11.7}$$

where $Y' = E'$ in the balance budget environment. Equation (11.7) demonstrates the fundamental relationship that makes fiscal obfuscation through the property tax forecast possible in New York City. At the time of budget adoption for the upcoming fiscal year, which occurs in early- to mid-June, the tax base and tax rate are known. The tax base is initially set at the January 5 assessment date each year, and then finalized by May 25 after the Department of Finance's internal assessment review board and the Tax Commission address assessment appeals. The citywide rate, as previously noted, tends to be fixed. While lawmakers could agree to change the citywide rate, doing so would be politically costly since the fixed rate is often used by lawmakers to proclaim that property taxes have not been increased. The apostrophes for b and r are dropped to denote the values are known, not forecasted, which is only true for the upcoming fiscal year.[7] The only element not known at budget adoption is the reserve, which is forecasted. Thus, between the start of the current fiscal year in July and the end in June the following calendar year, all variation in the property tax forecast is due to forecasting errors for uncollectibles. Since the levy—the amount property taxpayers are charged—is based upon an assumption about how much revenue will go uncollected, assuming more foregone revenue leads to a higher levy at the start of the fiscal year.

It follows that to maximize collections policymakers must maximize *the forecasted* uncollectibles (i.e. maximize the levy) and minimize *the actual*

value. Abatements are most often awarded as incentives for undertaking property rehabilitations or to otherwise incent other behavior such as installing solar panels. Abatements are financed by all other taxpayers by increasing the levy, but whether abatements should be included in the reserve or not in the first place is controversial.

[7] For all other future years in the forecasting period, b is not known and thus variation in the forecasted levy will be due to variation in both the reserve and tax base.

uncollectibles. The reserve forecast is in lawmakers complete control, and the reserve also has the political benefit of being obscure to the average taxpayer—both in the absolute sense that taxpayers do not know they are taxed based on assumptions about uncollectibles, and in the relative sense that its perceived importance in determining individual tax liabilities may be too small to matter. Therefore, maximizing revenue for the upcoming fiscal year involves setting the reserve forecast at a high enough level that just avoids attracting politically costly attention.

Importantly, good budgeting practices may warrant a level of underestimation of tax collections, which for New York City's property tax for the upcoming fiscal year means forecasting a level of uncollectibles greater than some benchmark. The argument instead is that *excessive* overestimation of the reserve is tantamount to fiscal obfuscation. Lawmakers take advantage of the obfuscation by building the excessive overestimation into the levy, a phenomenon known as ratcheting (Lee and Plummer 2007; Marlowe 2009). If the levy in future years is based upon the levy in the current year, and if the current year's levy is inflated because of excessive underforecasting of revenue (excessive overforecasting of the reserve), then intentionally underestimating revenue pushes spending up faster than what more accurate forecasting would. In New York City where rebudgeting occurs four times each fiscal year and the city budgets over a four-year horizon, excessive underforecasting has a compounding effect.

Excessive as used here means that a reserve forecast over some reasonable threshold is more than what the median voter would support in the absence of fiscal obfuscation. For example, let us assume the benchmark reserve level is $100, meaning that based upon all prior knowledge it is highly unlikely that actual reserves will exceed $100 in the upcoming fiscal year. Further, assume a reasonable forecasting error is 5.0 percent and that at a forecasted reserve of $150 the marginal political cost of the next dollar exceeds its marginal political benefit. At these parameters, the excess levy is $45. That is, the levy is being increased by $45 in excess of a reasonable forecast variance through overestimation of uncollectibles.

This section has thus far discussed features of New York City's property tax system that facilitate fiscal obfuscation. But the key formal difference between fiscal obfuscation and fiscal illusion is lawmaker deception, implied by the term to be intentional behavior resulting in maximizing revenue subject to a political cost-benefit calculus. Evidence of political exploitation of the reserve forecast is possible due to the variety of government-sponsored forecasters in the city, each with different political incentives. Variation in political incentives to forecast excessively identifies the political exploitation implied in fiscal obfuscation.

Three city agencies forecast the property tax.[8] The Office of Management and Budget (OMB) is an executive agency whose head is appointed by and serves at the pleasure of the mayor. OMB generates the budget that serves as the baseline for negotiations with city council during the budget process. The Independent Budget Office (IBO) is a non-partisan agency that provides forecasts, program evaluation, and policy analysis generally at the request of city councilmembers, the media, and community organizations. IBO's director is appointed by a four-member board based upon the recommendation of an advisory board composed of budgeting and finance experts that are not currently public employees with academics at city universities being the notable exception. The Comptroller is the city's accountant and auditor and is popularly elected to a four-year term.

The incentives each agency executive faces presumable vary (Williams 2012). As a mayoral appointee, the director of OMB has an incentive to underestimate revenue, which confers the political advantage of appearing to not be a profligate in the current year while also allowing for overestimation in out-years in the city's multi-year budgeting environment. The director of IBO has no obvious political incentive, nor legislative or executive budgeting authority. As such, IBO forecasts are motivated by accuracy, which follows from the absence of a political incentive to do otherwise and the organizational culture promoted by agency leadership. The Comptroller also does not have legislative or executive budget authority, but the agency's forecast may nonetheless be systematically biased since the position is elected. For example, if the position is a stepping stone for the mayoralty, the Comptroller may find it advantageous to distinguish her revenue forecast from OMB's in some way in order to build political capital.[9] Nevertheless, given that the Comptroller's *raison d' être* is to serve as an impartial auditor, it is safe to assume that the office, like IBO, also forecasts with error minimization as a goal. Whereas conservative forecasting may serve as a hedge against the risk of unanticipated declines in revenue (Rodgers and Joyce 1996), forecasting

[8] The city council's finance division produces a revenue forecast, but for the property tax it largely borrows from OMB. There are some state agencies that produce forecasts of city revenue such as the New York State Comptroller and the Financial Control Board, an oversight committee formed following the city's financial crisis in the 1970s. Since the focus of the article is on local politics, state agencies are ignored.

[9] Williams (2012) characterizes IBO and the Comptroller as revenue finders, and therefore their forecasts underestimate revenue less than OMB's in order to fund expenditures. Since IBO and the Comptroller do not have budgeting authority, it seems remarkable that finding revenue is the correct explanation, particularly in the case of IBO where the agency executive lacks any political incentive to systematically create forecasting bias. It is far more likely that IBO and the Comptroller underestimate less than OMB, because they care about forecasting accurately whereas OMB's incentive is otherwise.

for accuracy puts policymakers in a better position to plan their finances (Beckett-Camarata 2006).[10]

The differences in political incentives presumably yield differences in systematic forecasting bias. In the case of OMB and IBO it seems clear that the former has an incentive to underestimate revenue more than the latter. It is less clear if "the Comptroller will over or underestimate relative to OMB," because the extent of the political incentives is unknown, and likely vary from one Comptroller to the next. Without budgeting authority, though, there seems little reason for the Comptroller to engage in any sort of fiscal obfuscation, particularly in light of its function as a financial monitoring and auditing agency. Only OMB has the strongest political incentive to engage in strategic and excessive underforecasting, and we can use property tax forecasts to demonstrate the merit of this hypothesis.

Evidence the Reserve Is Excessively Overforecasted

The central hypothesis in this chapter is that policymakers intentionally and excessively underforecast property tax revenue as a form of fiscal obfuscation to increase the tax levy. I first present evidence that the property tax reserve is excessively overforecasted. The reserve forecast is the only element of the property tax in control of lawmakers by the time the upcoming fiscal year's budget is adopted. Note that overforecasting the reserve means underforecasting property tax revenue.

Perhaps the most straightforward way to demonstrate the excess is to compare forecasted amounts to actual amounts. Figure 11.2 compares the forecasted and actual reserve levels for each fiscal year from 1996 through 2016 in 2016 dollars. Forecasted amounts change with each financial plan, so the forecasted values presented here are based on the city's adopted budget for each fiscal year. This was chosen because at budget adoption the tax levy is fixed and all variation in collections during the year will be due to changes in the reserve. Over this 21-year period, the cumulative forecasted reserve was $28.7 billion while the cumulative actual reserve was $23.4 billion, a difference of $5.3 billion, or $251 million per year on average. In other words,

[10] Importantly, both forecasting philosophies cannot be pursued jointly as a matter of logic; one cannot both underforecast and minimize forecast error as forecasting goals (Bretschneider et al. 1989). The latter implies an effort to minimize bias while the former implies that bias is desirable to a certain extent for prudent budgeting.

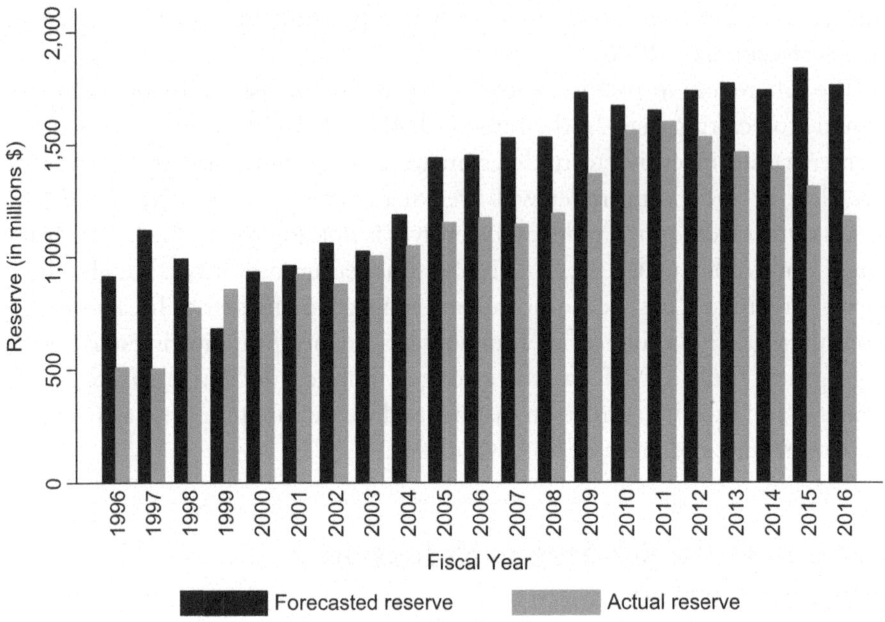

Fig. 11.2 OMB's reserve forecast and actuals

OMB increased the levy by on average $251 million more by overforecasting the size of the reserve.[11]

From Fig. 11.2 we can see that in most years the difference between the forecast and actual reserve is substantial, but Fig. 11.3 offers an alternative perspective that more clearly illustrates forecasts not matching historic patterns. Figure 11.3 maps for each fiscal year at budget adoption OMB's forecast and actual reserve level as a percentage of the yield, recalling that the yield for the current fiscal year is constant. Expressing the reserve as a share of the yield provides a common denominator to make comparisons in percentage terms. On average the actual reserve is 7.5 percent of the yield while the forecasted reserve is on average 9.7 percent of the yield.

[11] OMB forecasts particular items in the reserve separately and the overall reserve forecast equals the sum of the component forecasts. Across reserve components, though, there is great variation in the degree to which OMB overestimates uncollectibles. In recent history, the reserve component that is consistently overestimated the most is property tax refunds. From 2010 through 2016, refunds have been over forecasted by 40 percent compared to actuals on average (the median year was 43.6 percent). Moreover, despite actual refund levels never exceeding 2 percent of the levy from 2002 through 2009, refunds were forecasted to be more than 2 percent of the levy five out of the seven years from 2010 through 2016. Because the overforecast was built into the property tax levy as an uncollectible, if refunds alone were the only component forecasted perfectly and all other forecast variances were unchanged, the annual levy during the seven-year period would have been on average $170 million lesser than what it was in fact.

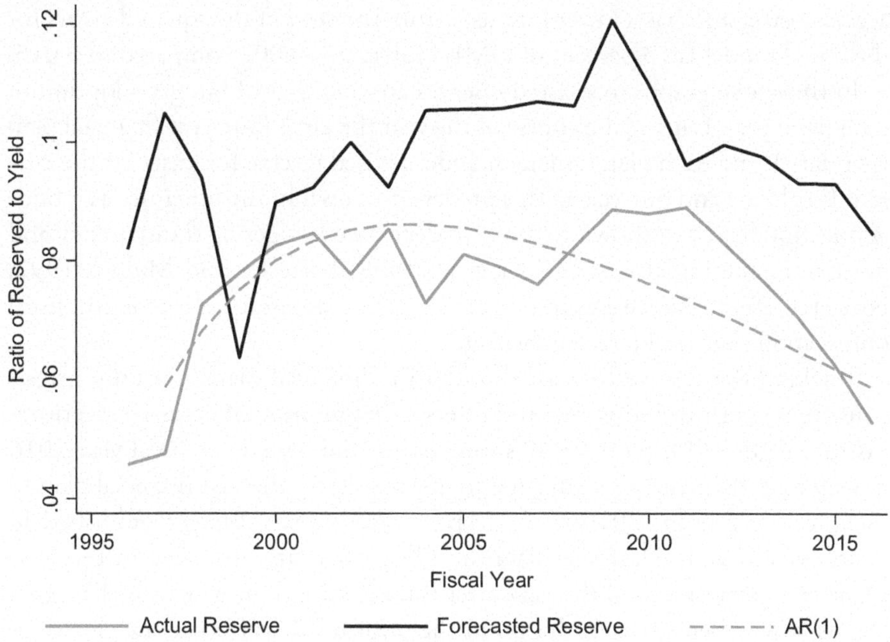

Fig. 11.3 OMB's reserve forecast and actuals as a percent of yield. Note: The forecasted reserve is as of budget adoption in June of each year. Dollars are inflation-adjusted to 2016. Source: City council tax fixing resolution, select years

By overforecasting uncollectibles in excess of average uncollectibles, it increases the levy in excess of the minimum necessary to cover the budget's residual expenditure. Forecasting should be an iterative process where old data are updated and models are re-estimated. Figure 11.3 does not inspire confidence that prior reserve values play a strong role in OMB's reserve forecast. If prior values were incorporated, I suspect the forecast error would not be as substantial so regularly. To illustrate, I constructed an AR(1) model with a drift and deterministic time trend for comparison. I then forecasted each fiscal year based upon known prior year values, essentially running 21 forecasts using the same AR(1) model. The forecasts are mapped in Fig. 11.3 as the dashed line. I selected a forecasting model whose structure is admittedly crude but which could quickly be implemented based upon an introductory knowledge of time series regression techniques on the assumption that analysts conducting such forecasts are constrained by time and resources. I have no doubt that greater consideration would yield a better forecast, though the gains in precision may not outweigh the additional effort. This illustrative attempt has two notable features, both of which should not be surprising: it tracks the actuals better and has a lower forecast error. The sum of the squared errors for the crude model is 13 percent of OMB's forecast—0.002 compared to 0.015.

In the above graphs forecasted reserves are traced as of budget adoption in each fiscal year. During the course of the year the city's four-year financial plan is updated, and each plan update includes revised reserve forecasts for the current fiscal year and out-years. This process is known in the literature as rebudgeting, and has been shown to result in decreased budgeting transparency and positive ratcheting (Bretschneider et al. 1988; Forrester and Mullins 1992; Forrester 1993; Anessi-Pessina et al. 2012), a necessary element for fiscal obfuscation that facilitates ratcheting.

Tracking the reserve forecast through the financial plans not only reveals consistent overforecasting but also offers a first glimpse of excessive overforecasting. Figure 11.4 plots OMB's forecast for the reserve for fiscal year 2016 during each financial plan adjusted to 2016 dollars. The first financial plan to include forecasts for 2016 is the Mayor's Preliminary Budget published in February 2012. The last year data for a fiscal year are produced in the First Quarter Update released the year after budget adoption, which for FY 2016 means November 2016. At this point the prior fiscal year books are closed, so

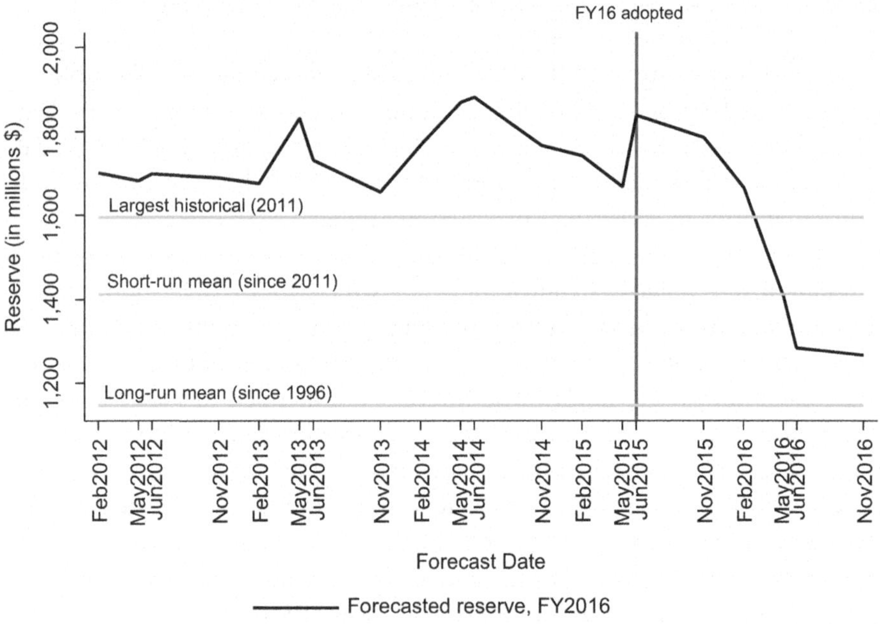

Fig. 11.4 Comparing forecasted reserve for 2016 to actual reserve. Note: Dollars are inflation-adjusted to 2016

to speak. Between these two points, a fiscal year will be forecasted 19 times (excluding November 2016).

Since 1997 in real terms the reserve has never exceeded $1.6 billion, a record established in 2011 (see Fig. 11.1). However, OMB's forecast for the reserve for 2016 consistently assumed a reserve level well in excess of this historic maximum during much of the reserve's forecasted life, as noted in Fig. 11.3. The forecast also consistently exceeded the reserve level average since 2011 and the 21-year average since 1996. Perhaps more interestingly is that over time as we moved closer to 2016 adoption presumably OMB's reserve forecast would approach a short-run or long-run average. Eventually, a sustained decline toward the short-run and long-run averages occurs but it does not start until May 2016, nearly a full year *after* the 2016 fiscal year budget was adopted.

Note further that this forecasting behavior is not unique to 2016. Figure 11.5 graphs the forecasted reserve for each financial plan for fiscal years 2014, 2015, and 2016. In all three instances, the reserve forecast for the current fiscal year does not begin the approach to the short and long-run averages until after the fiscal year's budget is adopted. The decline from adoption through the close of fiscal year books is striking. In real terms, the decline from adoption to close of books is 21.5, 27.7, and 31.9 percent for 2014

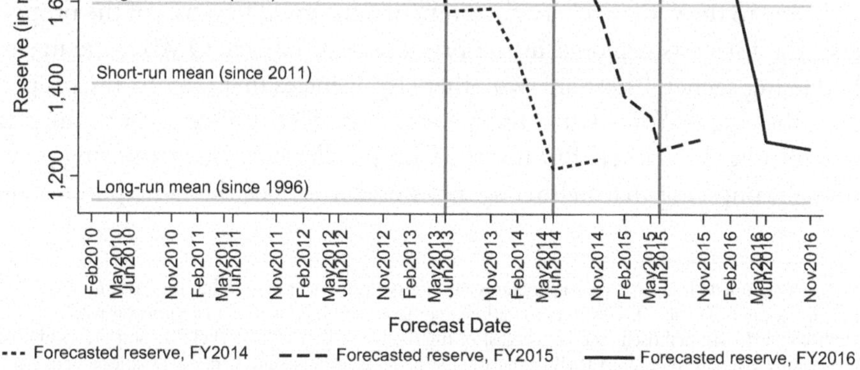

Fig. 11.5 Comparing forecasted reserve for 2014, 2015, and 2015 to actual reserve. Note: Dollars are inflation-adjusted to 2016

through 2016, respectively. These declines are in stark contrast to the reserve forecasts before budget adoption. While the reserve forecast changes from plan to plan, the overall percentage change from initial forecast through adoption is much lower in absolute terms than from adoption to close of books: 6.3, 3.6, and 4.6 percent, respectively. In other words, the reserve forecast is initially set at a level exceeding historic actuals. After the initial forecast, the anticipated reserve swings up and down over the financial plan period, still exceeding historic actuals in each successive forecast, until budget adoption when the forecasted reserve begins a steep descent to long-run and short-run levels.

Evidence the Property Tax Is Excessively Underforecasted on Purpose

The previous section provided evidence that the property tax reserve is excessively overforecasted. The reserve is a prime target for fiscal obfuscation, because it is the only element of the property tax calculus that is in the city council and mayor's control at the time the city budget is adopted. For this behavior to reach the level of fiscal obfuscation, however, the excessive reserve forecast bias must be *intentional*. Evidence of duplicity can be obtained through lawmaker disclosure, which there seems little reason to expect such candor, or through their behavior. The latter route is taken in this section. Because of this, the evidence presented is not a smoking gun of intentionality, but the evidence is nonetheless convincing particularly when coupled with the data presented in the previous section.

Evidence that the property tax forecast is intentionality manipulated is possible due to the variety of city government-sponsored forecasts of the property tax. The forecasts explored in the previous section were OMB's, the mayor's budgeting agency. There are two other city agencies that forecast the property tax: the New York City Independent Budget Office (IBO) and the Comptroller.[12] Neither IBO nor the Comptroller have budget-setting power, though, implying that neither agency's executive face the same political and

[12] The city council's finance division generates a property tax forecast as well, but the vast majority of time the city council accepts OMB's forecast rather than generating its own. An exception was in 1998 and 1999 when the council used its own forecast of the reserve to set the levy. There is good practical reason for the city council to accept OMB's forecast. Doing so facilitates budgeting negotiations between the mayor and council members, allowing them to spend more of the budget season negotiating spending priorities rather than revenue. In addition, the city council benefits from access to more money than less, so it also has little incentive to go with a more accurate forecast.

budgetary incentives as the mayor. The Comptroller is popularly elected, and IBO's executive is appointed by an advisory board. If OMB excessively forecasts, the forecasts made by these other city agencies should be less excessive—that is, more accurate. This section considers these alternative forecasts. Because data on property tax reserve forecasts were not available for all agencies, the discussion in this section focuses on the property tax more generally.

If the mayor's forecasting behavior with respect to the property tax is intentional, then we should observe noticeably different forecasts between OMB, IBO, and the Comptroller. More specifically, we should observe a steeper rate of change in OMB's forecast than in IBO's or the Comptroller's from the first financial plan, when a target year forecast is initially set, to the end of the target year when property tax collections are known. The reason why we should observe this is because in OMB's initial forecast for the target year, forecasted collections are biased downward on purpose based on the theory that the mayor wants to make it appear as though he is fiscally responsible particularly over the financial plan horizon (Williams 2012). Over time the three forecasts will converge toward actuals. At budget adoption the three forecasts should be close and then in the financial plan right before the end of the fiscal year the forecasts should be near identical. Thus, OMB will have purposefully started its forecast at a lower benchmark than IBO and the Comptroller, and since all of the revenue forecasts converge at the end of the target fiscal year, OMB must make larger changes to its forecast on average than the two budget watchdogs.

The evidence bears out these expectations. Figure 11.6 graphs the forecasts made for fiscal year 2016 (the target year) during each forecasting period between February 2012 and November 2016 (the forecast years) by OMB, IBO, and the Comptroller. When the books for 2016 were closed in November 2016, the city had collected $22.974 billion in property tax revenue. In February 2012, the first year 2016 appears in the financial plan, OMB forecasted collections at $20.291 billion while IBO and the Comptroller forecasted $20.944 billion and $20.505 billion, respectively. With each successive forecast approaching the target year, forecasted collections move closer to the actual, but importantly either IBO or the Comptroller forecasted closer to the target than did OMB in every financial plan. Moreover, because IBO and the Comptroller set their baseline at a higher, more accurate level than did OMB, their forecast adjustments are smaller than OMB's. Whereas OMB increased its 2016 projection 13.2 percent from February 2012 to November 2016 in nominal terms, IBO and the Comptroller did so by 9.7 and 12.0 percent, respectively.

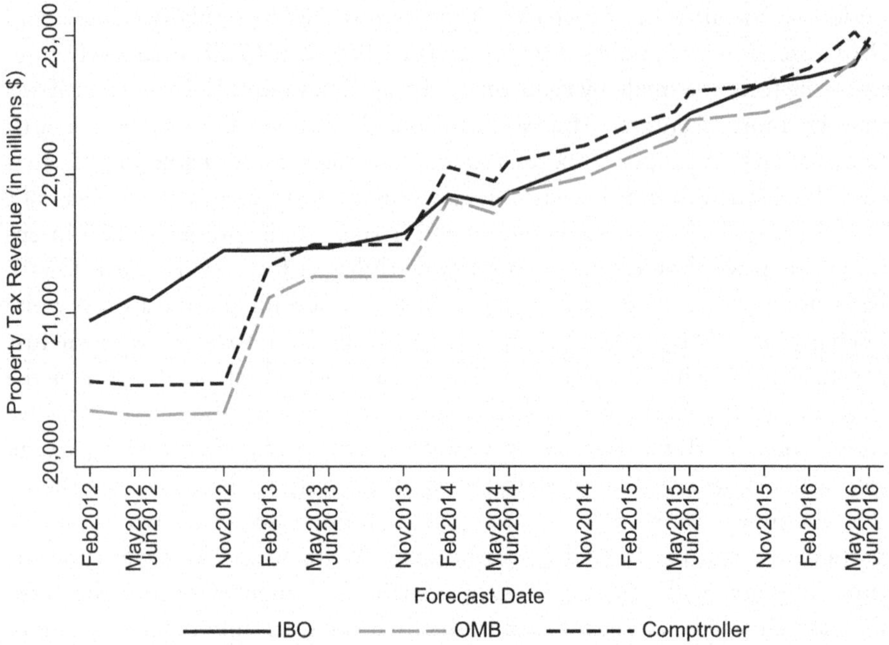

Fig. 11.6 Comparison of property tax revenue forecasts for fiscal year 2016. Note: Dollars are nominal. Source: OMB forecasting documentation, select years; author's research

A limitation of Fig. 11.5 is that it only tracks changes in forecasts for a single target year, fiscal year 2016. My claim is that OMB's behavior is intentional, and were my evidence to begin and end at a single year, my argument could be perceived as a straw man. However, OMB's forecasting behavior is not isolated to 2016 and instead occurs regularly. Table 11.1 details the variance between OMB's, IBO's, and the Comptroller's initial forecast and actual revenue collections for each target fiscal year from 2006 to 2016. When the number is negative, it indicates that an agency underforecasted collections by the noted amount—collections exceeded the initial forecast for the target year made four years prior. When the number is positive, it indicates that collections came under the initial forecast.

In most years, either IBO or the Comptroller forecasted more accurately than OMB. A noteworthy exception is the Great Recession in 2008 and 2009, the occurrence of which revealed an advantage of OMB's property forecasting strategy. OMB had a smaller forecast variance, a result due to their setting the benchmark excessively low four years earlier, and then in the wake of the economic downturn, collections coming in excessively low in fact. This behavior has been observed in other jurisdictions as intentional (Bretschneider and

Table 11.1 Variance between initial property tax forecast and actual collections

Financial plan	Target fiscal year	OMB	IBO	Comptroller
Preliminary Budget, 2002	2006	($2531)	($2659)	($2396)
Preliminary Budget, 2003	2007	($664)	($568)	($537)
Preliminary Budget, 2004	2008	$146	$553	$306
Preliminary Budget, 2005	2009	$184	$855	$339
Preliminary Budget, 2006	2010	($1376)	($197)	($1464)
Preliminary Budget, 2007	2011	$373	$489	($640)
Preliminary Budget, 2008	2012	($1498)	($1458)	($1358)
Preliminary Budget, 2009	2013	($815)	($798)	($671)
Preliminary Budget, 2010	2014	($2320)	($1631)	($2111)
Preliminary Budget, 2011	2015	($2456)	($1753)	($2243)
Preliminary Budget, 2012	2016	($2683)	($2030)	($2469)
Average		($1240)	($836)	($1204)

Note: Dollars are in millions and are not inflation-adjusted. The Preliminary Budget is released at the end of January or beginning of February each year

Schroeder 1985; Reddick 2004; Rodgers and Joyce 1996). Forecasts by IBO and the Comptroller fared comparatively worse off than OMB's because their benchmarks were not set as low. Nonetheless, over this 11-year period, IBO's forecast was more precise than OMB's and the Comptroller's on average; its average variance was $836 million underforecast. OMB and the Comptroller both have average variances of about $1.2 billion.

Figure 11.6 and Table 11.1 are offered as supporting evidence that OMB intentionally biases its forecast downward. Organizationally, OMB's executive and the leaders of the two budget watchdogs face different political incentives, and OMB's persistent underforecasting relative to IBO's and the Comptroller's is consistent with the political narrative of the mayor wanting to appear fiscally conservative. To be sure, there are some methodological differences in how the property tax is forecasted, but for a variety of reasons these differences cannot serve as an alternative explanation for OMB's consistent downward forecast bias. Based on discussion with staff at each agency, the three forecast methodologies are similar in all important respects except one: IBO incorporates an estimate of the pipeline of assessed value waiting to be phased into the tax base into its property tax forecast while the Comptroller and OMB do not.[13] If this mattered as an explanation for the observed pattern of OMB's forecast, it would only explain differences between IBO and OMB; the Comptroller's forecast is nonetheless consistently more accurate than OMB's despite not incorporating the pipeline into its tax base forecast as well. Since

[13] Annual increases in assessed value for Class 2 and Class 4 properties are phased-in over a five-year period, resulting in a pipeline of accumulated value waiting to be added to the tax roll.

there are no other methodological differences substantial enough to explain away the magnitude of the relative variances across agencies, it stands to reason that the observed variances are due to the forecasting assumptions the different agencies make. For OMB, these assumptions lead to overly conservative forecasts, an outcome consistent with the mayor's political incentive to appear frugal and a budgetary incentive to sustain a ratcheting effect over the multi-year financial plan.

Conclusion

Sanandaji and Wallace (2011) have formally defined fiscal obfuscation as "*exploitation* of the public's rational ignorance by hiding information from them" [emphasis added]. Prior to their formalization, obfuscation was typically only discussed as a synonymous term to fiscal illusion, not as a distinct concept. The key difference between garden variety fiscal illusion and fiscal obfuscation is the purposefulness of deceptive budgeting in the latter; the former can arise as an unintended consequence of otherwise benevolent public finance policy, or through general inattention on the part of lawmakers and the median voter alike. Said differently, fiscal obfuscation is malicious, fiscal illusion may not be. Because fiscal obfuscation can lead to fiscal illusion, it is appropriate to consider the former a special case of the latter.

The purpose of this study was to give empirical support to Sanandaji and Wallace's (2011) conception of fiscal obfuscation. The black box of New York City's property tax forecast was unpacked, and evidence offered that lawmakers formulate multi-year budgets based upon OMB forecasts that intentionally, consistently, and excessively underforecast property tax revenue. In a multi-year budgeting environment, purposefully underestimating revenue with strong evidence that actual collections will exceed the forecasts leads to a ratcheting effect whereby variances are impounded into the forecasts over the financial plan (Lee and Plummer 2007; Marlowe 2009). The result of this budgetary decision is a general spending level increase in excess of what would occur in the presence of more accurate revenue forecasting. This study, however, did not measure the extent to which forecast variances are impounded into future revenue forecasts, an unresolved issue left for future work.

Many have observed that lawmakers intentionally underforecast revenues for good budgetary reasons such as hedging against economic downturns (Bretschneider and Schroeder 1985; Rodgers and Joyce 1996; Williams 2012), but the malicious nature of fiscal obfuscation implies that at some point the degree of underforecasting will be excessive. This further implies that while some degree of ratcheting is an unintended consequence, when the downward forecasting bias is excessive, the degree of ratcheting that follows elevates from innocuous to deceptive. Importantly, what counts as excess is a judgment call. In the case of OMB's property tax reserve forecast, evidence was presented that the reserve forecast consistently exceeds historic levels until about six months before the end of the fiscal year when forecasts trend toward the long-run average. In such instances, the appeal is to our intuition that this forecasting behavior reflects excessiveness, yet an alternative could be to look for more objective standards of what is an acceptable forecasting error variance and define excess as anything beyond this value.

Though this study has presented compelling evidence of fiscal obfuscation, it is not a smoking gun. Nonetheless, an important policy question that arises from the possibility of fiscal obfuscation is, "What can be done to combat it?" The political economic explanation for why fiscal obfuscation arises in the first place is due to the ignorance or apathy of the electorate. Presumably better-informed voters would not agree with excessively overforecasting property tax uncollectibles, since the primary consequence of fiscal obfuscation in revenue forecasting is larger public budgets, and thus higher taxes, than what would be obtained with more accurate forecasting. The solution from this perspective, then, is to adopt policies that improve citizens' knowledge about revenue forecasting, and more specifically about when a forecast is reasonably excessive. Implementing this could take a variety of forms, none of which are mutually exclusive. For instance, many states in the United States have so-called truth in taxation laws, and while the specifics of such laws vary, they share in common public disclosure and popular voting requirements for increasing the property tax levy beyond a certain point. However, the empirical evidence on the effectiveness of truth in taxation laws curbing property tax revenue is mixed (Bland and Laosirirat 1997; Cornia et al. 1990; Cornia and Walters 2006). Moreover, for truth in taxation laws to work effectively against excessive revenue overforecasting, alternative forecasts and their underlying rationale must be part of the public disclosure.

An alternative to passing truth in taxation laws is to eliminate the political incentive to overforecast, which most reasonably can be accomplished by placing forecasting responsibility in the hands of a non-partisan and independent public agency. Both attributes are necessary. Non-partisanship can be accomplished by appointing the agency executive and such an appointment should not be directly determined by elected officials with budgeting authority. Thus, appointment by the mayor would not meet this standard but appointment by the comptroller would. The independence of the agency is arguably the more crucial characteristic: its budget should not be subject to political whim. In New York City, IBO fits both of these criteria. (The agency's budget is set at a fixed percentage of OMB's budget, so for the mayor to eliminate the IBO, he must also eliminate OMB.) Obstacles to establishing IBO-type agencies outside of New York City include appropriating funds and overcoming political resistance to formation of a budget watchdog.

While this study represents the first analytic attempt to identify fiscal obfuscation in public budgeting, its case study nature necessarily limits its usefulness in advancing fiscal obfuscation as a theory. In order to build a coherent narrative approaching a full-fledged theory of fiscal obfuscation requires many more observations about government forecasting behavior. Scholars need to unpack the tax administration black box in other jurisdictions to generalize the findings in this study beyond New York City.

References

Anessi-Pessina, E., Sicilia, M., & Steccolini, I. (2012). Budgeting and rebudgeting in local governments: Siamese twins? *Public Administration Review, 72*(6), 875–884. https://doi.org/10.1111/j.1540-6210.2012.02590.x.

Beckett-Camarata, J. (2006). Revenue forecasting accuracy in Ohio local governments. Journal of Public Budgeting, Accounting & Financial Management, 18(1), 77–99.

Bland, R. L., & Laosirirat, P. (1997). Tax limitations to reduce municipal property taxes: Truth in taxation in Texas. *Journal of Urban Affairs, 19*(1), 45–58.

Bretschneider, S. I., & Schroeder, L. (1985). Revenue forecasting, budget setting and risk. *Socio-Economic Planning Sciences, 19*(6), 431–439. https://doi.org/10.1016/0038-0121(85)90017-5.

Bretschneider, S. I., Straussman, J. J., & Mullins, D. (1988). Do revenue forecasts influence budget setting? A small group experiment. *Policy Sciences, 21*(4), 305–325.

Bretschneider, S. I., Gorr, W. L., Grizzle, G. A., & Klay, E. (1989). Political and organizational influences on the accuracy of forecasting state government revenues. *International Journal of Forecasting, 5*(3), 307–319.

Brien, S. T. (2018). Compensating changes to the property tax levy? An empirical test of the residual rule. *Public Finance Review, 46*(6), 949–973.

Brien, S. T., & Sjoquist, D. L. (2014). Do state-funded property tax exemptions actually provide tax relief? Georgia's HTRG program. *Public Finance Review, 42*(5), 608–634.

Carroll, D. A. (2009). Diversifying municipal government revenue structures: Fiscal illusion or instability? Public Budgeting & Finance, 29(1), 27–48.

Cornia, G. C., & Walters, L. C. (2006). Full disclosure: Controlling property tax increases during periods of increasing housing values. *National Tax Journal, 59*(3), 735–749.

Cornia, G. C., Wheeler, G. E., & Smith, S. M. (1990). Effects of truth-in-taxation on property tax revenue in 29 Utah counties. *Public Budgeting and Financial Management, 2*(2), 233–252.

Forrester, J. P. (1993). The rebudgeting process in state government: The case of Missouri. *The American Review of Public Administration, 23*(2), 155–178.

Forrester, J. P., & Mullins, D. R. (1992). Rebudgeting: The serial nature of municipal budgetary processes. *Public Administration Review, 52*(5), 467–473.

Frank, H. A., & Wang, X. (1994). Judgmental vs. time series vs. deterministic models in local revenue forecasting: A Florida case study. *Public Budgeting and Financial Management, 6*(4), 493–517.

Frank, H. A., & Zhao, Y. (2009). Determinants of local government revenue forecasting practice: Empirical evidence from Florida. *Journal of Public Budgeting, Accounting & Financial Management, 21*(1), 17–35.

Gianakis, G. A., & McCue, C. P. (1999). *Local government budgeting: A managerial approach*. Westport, CT: Quorum.

Joyce, P. G., & Mullins, D. R. (1991). The changing fiscal structure of the state and local public sector: The Impact of iax and expenditure limitations. *Public Administration Review, 51*(3), 240–253. https://doi.org/10.2307/976948.

Jung, C. (2001). Does the local-option sales tax provide property tax relief? The Georgia case. *Public Budgeting & Finance, 21*(1), 73–86.

Jung, C., & Bae, S. (2011). Changing revenue and expenditure structure and the reliance on user charges and fees in American counties, 1972–2002. *The American Review of Public Administration, 41*(1), 92–110.

Lee, T. M., & Plummer, E. (2007). Budget adjustments in response to spending variances: Evidence of ratcheting of local government expenditures. *Journal of Management Accounting Research, 19*, 137–167.

Marlowe, J. (2009). Budget variance, slack resources, and municipal expenditures. Retrieved from https://doi.org/10.2139/ssrn.1505646.

McCubbins, M. D., & Moule, E. (2010). Making mountains of debt out of molehills: The pro-cyclical implications of tax and expenditure limitations. *National Tax Journal, 63*(3), 603–622.

National Association of State Budget Officers. (2015). *Budget processes in the states: Spring 2015*. National Association of State Budget Officers: Washington, DC. Retrieved from https://www.nasbo.org/reports-data/budget-processes-in-the-states.

Oates, W. E. (1988). On the nature and measurement of fiscal illusion: A survey. In R. L. Mathews, G. Brennan, B. S. Grewal, & P. D. Groenewegen (Eds.), *Taxation and fiscal federalism: Essays in honour of Russell Mathews*. Sydney; New York: Australian National University Press.

Reddick, C. G. (2004). Assessing local government revenue forecasting techniques. *International Journal of Public Administration, 27*(8/9), 597–613. https://doi.org/10.1081/PAD-120030257.

Rodgers, R., & Joyce, P. G. (1996). The effect of underforecasting on the accuracy of revenue forecasts by state governments. *Public Administration Review, 56*(1), 48–56.
Ross, J. M., & Yan, W. (2013). Fiscal illusion from property reassessment? An empirical test of the residual view. *National Tax Journal, 66*(1), 7–32.
Sanandaji, T., & Wallace, B. (2011). Fiscal illusion and fiscal obfuscation: Tax perception in Sweden. *The Independent Review, 16*(2), 237–246.
Williams, D. W. (2012). The politics of forecast bias: Forecaster effect and other effects in New York City revenue forecasting. *Public Budgeting & Finance, 32*(4), 1–18. https://doi.org/10.1111/j.1540-5850.2012.01021.x.
Yuan, B., Cordes, J., Brunori, D., & Bell, M. E. (2009). Tax and expenditure limitations and local public finances. In N. Y. Augustine, M. E. Bell, D. Brunori, & J. M. Youngman (Eds.), *Erosion of the property tax base: Trends, causes and consequences* (pp. 149–191). Cambridge, MA: Lincoln Institute of Land Policy.

12

Small Local Government Revenue Forecasting

Vincent Reitano

Major Points

- Small local governments frequently use judgmental rather than extrapolation or econometric forecasts.
  - They may have too few resources to hire dedicated forecasters or even acquire forecasting software.
  - Elected officials may prefer judgmental rather than a more rigorous forecasting method.
- Consequently, they may face higher forecast error than larger local governments, and may be less likely to use long-term forecasts for strategic planning.
- Future research is needed to examine forecast errors and obtain insight into the institutional and behavioral reasons why small local governments select particular forecasting methods and practices.

V. Reitano (✉)
School of Public Affairs and Administration, Western Michigan University, Kalamazoo, MI, USA
e-mail: vincent.reitano@wmich.edu

D. Williams, T. Calabrese (eds.), *The Palgrave Handbook of Government Budget Forecasting*, Palgrave Studies in Public Debt, Spending, and Revenue,
https://doi.org/10.1007/978-3-030-18195-6_12

Introduction

Forecasting can help governments to "evaluate current and future fiscal conditions to guide policy and programmatic decisions" (Government Finance Officers Association 2014, 1). At the local level, survey research shows that small governments use judgmental forecasts more often than extrapolation or econometric forecast models used in large governments (Frank and Zhao 2009; Kong 2007). Underlying this tendency are technological constraints and the perceived challenges associated with applying extrapolation and econometric models (Kavanagh and Williams 2016; Reddick 2006). Specifically, small local governments may not have the resources to invest in advanced forecasting software or to hire a forecaster, and decision-makers may not have the technical proficiency to understand econometric forecasts, leading to a decrease in forecast accuracy (Kong 2007; Williams and Kavanagh 2016; Wong 1995). For example, research has shown that small governments face an increase in forecast error, due to the preference of judgmental methods, but evidence is still limited (Kong 2007; Sun 2005). This chapter reviews forecasting practices, and identifies areas for future research in small local governments. The sections of this chapter are outlined here:

- Section "Summary of Literature" presents the research on small government revenue forecasting. The subsections review the literature, small government forecast methods and accuracy, conservative revenue forecasting, and cognitive biases.
- Section "Small Government Forecasting Practices" details small government forecasting practices. The multi-step framework developed in Kavanagh and Williams (2016) is reviewed and considered in context of small local governments.
- Section "Limitations in Literature" lists areas for future research in small government forecasting, including the need for research on forecasting software, empirical studies on forecast accuracy, forecaster perceptions, policies, assessment of best practices, and how forecasting relates to broader question of financial sustainability.
- Section "Conclusion" concludes with a brief summary of the chapter and argues that revenue forecasting is a critical tool in small governments that can help to strategically plan for future uncertainty.

Summary of Literature

Overview

Revenue forecasts play a critical role in the local government budgeting process (Frank and Zhao 2009; Wildavsky 1986). They provide a projection of anticipated revenues and, when combined with expenditure forecasts, can be used for strategic planning and to check for structural balance (Kavanagh 2007; Kavanagh and Williams 2016). At the local level, small governments may lack resources to invest in forecasting, and may also struggle to obtain reliable historical data (Cirincione et al. 1999), which may lead them to use a judgmental approach (Kong 2007; Williams and Kavanagh 2016; Wong 1995). Even if a smaller local government chooses to use an extrapolation or econometric approach, they will likely rely on Microsoft Excel (Kavanagh and Williams 2016). Further, even if more advanced software programs are available, which have preprogrammed advanced forecasting methods, local governments, particularly those that are smaller and with fewer resources, have been hesitant to use them (Frank 1990; Klay 1985; Kong 2007).

Despite the above overview, the literature is still limited on small government forecasting (Kong 2007). Emphasis is often placed on studying forecasting methodology instead of the factors that are associated with forecast accuracy, which can have implications for praxis (Sun 2005). Additionally, research is typically conducted on case studies from a handful of governments or a sample of governments from a single state, which may restrict the generalizability of findings (Frank and Wang 1994; Frank and Zhao 2009). More so, the majority of the literature is from the 1980s and 1990s, and little attention is placed on comparing forecasting practices across different sizes of local governments despite the acknowledged difference in forecasting capacity based on local government size (Kong 2007). In fact, only one paper, Kong (2007), focuses on comparing small versus large county forecasting practices. Given these attributes, the literature is incomplete, and there remains an opportunity for additional research. The subsections which follow detail forecast methods, accuracy, conservative forecasting, and cognitive biases in small local governments.

Small Government Forecast Methods

One of the most consistent findings in the literature is that simple methods in the form of judgmental forecasts are used by local governments (Cirincione et al. 1999; Frank 1990; Frank and McCollough 1992; Gianakis and Frank

1993; Kong 2007). In regard to small governments, forecast methods are examined in early research from Frank (1990) and Gianakis and Frank (1993), and more recent research from Frank et al. (2005), Reddick (2006), Kong (2007), and Frank and Zhao (2009). Discussion of these studies will follow chronologically by their date of publication.

Frank (1990, 52) interviewed 12 Florida cities and found that the use of moving average models rather than more advanced econometric models "might be understandable in smaller cities, where the finance officials interviewed generally were accountants who performed in a 'jack of all trades' role." Frank et al. (2005) conducted a national survey of 800 local governments. The survey data suggests that local governments may try to increase forecast accuracy with different forecast methods. In their regression using the survey data, they consider the logarithm of population size as an independent variable to predict the intention of increased forecast accuracy in relation to Governmental Accounting Standards Board Statement No. 34. In both ordinary least-squares and weighted least-squares models, the latter of which provides a robustness check and adjustment for the sample, the population measure does not significantly predict intention to increase forecast accuracy, challenging their hypothesis that larger relative to smaller local governments would be more inclined to do so.

Reddick (2006) used an International City/County Management Association survey from 1999 that 531 cities with population over 25,000 responded to. Correlation tests show that the smallest size governments in the survey, from 25,000 to 49,000 residents, were statistically more likely to use a judgmental approach. The largest governments, while underrepresented, were more likely to use an econometric approach. Not using advanced quantitative techniques is attributed to the observation that "most of the training comes from workshops or seminars on forecasting" (Reddick 2006, 611). This finding in Reddick (2006) may indicate that small governments train budget and finance professionals rather than hire a dedicated forecaster, which is consistent with Kavanagh and Williams (2016) and Williams and Kavanagh (2016).

Kong (2007, 180) surveyed 42 California counties in 2002 and 2003 (response rate over 70 percent) and demarcated them as either "smallest" or "largest" based on a population classification framework from the California State Board of Equalization. The survey shows that nearly half of large counties use judgmental forecasts, while 60 percent of smaller counties also use this approach. In regard to quantitative techniques, just over a quarter of small governments surveyed use a trend approach, and only one uses an econometric approach, which is less than in large governments surveyed.

In regard to the long term, Kong (2007) finds that most counties do not forecast ten or more years, especially for smaller counties, which are also less likely than larger counties to find long-term forecasts as being relevant to the forecast measure. This is a notable finding, since only Kong (2007) provides survey evidence into the adoption of long-term forecasting for local governments, an area which Wong (1995) lists as limited in terms of usage in local governments and Kavanagh (2007) considers as critical to local government financial management and planning.

Building on Kong (2007), Frank and Zhao (2009) obtained survey data from 113 Florida municipalities but do not differentiate their findings by size of local government, making comparisons between the two papers challenging. Their survey data shows that a majority of local governments use judgmental forecasting, with only one-sixth of respondents using some type of forecasting software. Interestingly, nearly 70 percent of the respondents agreed ("agree," "somewhat agree," or "strongly agree") that judgmental approaches "are more accurate than those derived from mathematical models" (Frank and Zhao 2009, 31), challenging the evidence that quantitative forecasts from extrapolation or econometric models have higher accuracy than judgmental forecasts and should therefore be used at the local level (Kavanagh and Williams 2016). Frank and Zhao (2009) do, however, acknowledge that there are differences between small and large local government forecasting with respect to forecast accuracy, which is discussed in the next section.

Across all of these papers, it becomes clear that there is still a limited understanding of forecast methods in small local governments. One of the chief concerns is that the most recent research is now almost a decade old, in a time when computer information systems capability have increased with respect to historical financial data conversion and storage capacity during financial systems upgrades, potentially addressing the concern over the usability of data in forecasts by Cirincione et al. (1999) and Wong (1995). Another concern is that much of the research above uses either a case study or convenience sample in one state, which may limit the generalizability of findings. Only Frank et al. (2005) conduct a national study, and that paper does not directly examine small local governments, given the use of an ICMA dataset which does not survey local governments with less than 25,000 citizens. Thus, there are notable limitations, which are discussed later in this chapter.

Small Government Forecast Accuracy

In regard to the accuracy of types of forecasts for small local governments, there is limited comparison between judgmental, extrapolation, and econometric forecasts. Instead, emphasis is often placed on comparing the forecast accuracy of extrapolation and econometric forecasts. To an extent, this may stem from the challenges in obtaining forecast data from local governments, particularly those that may use judgmental forecasts which may eschew transparent reporting of assumptions relative to quantitative models that can be replicated (Cirincione et al. 1999; Wong 1995). Only Cirincione et al. (1999) and Kong (2007) compare forecast accuracy between small and large governments. Rubin (1987), Goeminne et al. (2008), and Frank and Zhao (2009) look at government size as a determinant of forecast accuracy.

Cirincione et al. (1999) surveyed all Connecticut local governments but obtained useable monthly data from only six governments for the time period 1990–1996. There are different-sized towns that local governments included in the sample, and forecasts are conducted with different methods from 1 month to 18 months into the future. They conclude that simple models are just as accurate as more advanced models, and that linear models are better than models which include nonlinear quadratic and cubic factors.

Kong (2007) uses historical data to run a simulation of a forecasting competition, effectively testing various methods for forecasting sales tax in counties, to show that econometric forecasts perform better than other quantitative methods, across small and large counties. This simulation contrasts with the survey finding that 60 percent of small counties use a judgmental approach, and for those that do use a quantitative approach, only one applies an econometric method. Survey and interview data allow Kong (2007, 195) to conclude that "this 'now but not later' perception in the use of econometric models can be ascribed to California county forecasters' discomfort and lack of knowledge regarding this sophisticated technique."

In Kong (2007), another finding is that while the average reported county forecast error is lower for smaller counties, the median is higher than larger counties. This finding, however, is potentially due to bias and outliers in the survey data, according to the author.

In regard to the determinants of forecast accuracy, Rubin (1987), Goeminne et al. (2008), and Frank and Zhao (2009) hypothesize and test if population size, a measure for size of government in studies such as Kong (2007), is associated with forecast accuracy. In a study of over 100 Illinois municipalities in 1987, Rubin (1987) does not find a statistically significant association between population and forecast accuracy. Goeminne et al. (2008) study the forecast accuracy of 242 Flemish municipalities. Their dataset is from 1992 to 2002, and they show that population size, which is a proxy for size of government as per studies such as Kong (2007), is not associated with forecast accuracy. In a sample of Florida municipalities, Frank and Zhao (2009) find mixed evidence of the relationship between population and forecast accuracy.

Conservative Revenue Forecasting in Small Local Governments

Conservative revenue forecasting has been documented in local governments (Frank and Zhao 2009; Kong 2007; Rubin 1987). Frank and Zhao (2009) and Rubin (1987) provide empirical evidence in support of revenue forecasting, but do not demarcate their findings by size of government. Only Kong (2007) studies conservative revenue forecasting in small local governments.

Rubin (1987) reviews Illinois Revenue Survey city data and shows that almost half forecast sales tax conservatively and more than three-quarters forecast property tax conservatively. In contrast, almost 60 percent overforecast utilities. Using regression, Rubin (1987, 89) finds that the presence of "revenue problems" and "fiscal stress" is associated with forecast accuracy. Similarly, in Frank and Zhao (2009) data shows that 37 percent of Florida municipalities surveyed have a forecast policy, and of those, the majority under-forecast. However, both Rubin (1987) and Frank and Zhao (2009) does not specifically compare small versus large local governments with respect to conservative revenue forecasting and related revenue forecasting policies.

Kong (2007) uses survey data from California counties to show that smaller local governments have higher tolerances for conservative revenue forecasts than larger local governments on average. However, the median tolerance for conservative revenue forecasts is higher for larger local governments than smaller local governments. Thus, only Kong (2007) systematically tests for the presence of conservative revenue forecasting in small local governments. As noted in earlier sections, there remains limited research on conservative revenue forecasting in small local governments, an area for future study.

Cognitive Biases in Small Local Governments

Underlying the research on small government forecasting detailed in the prior subsection is forecaster cognitive biases. The only study to address this concern at the local level is Bretschneider et al. (1988). Specifically, they hypothesize that a local government forecaster will "correct current revenue forecasts for systematic bias found in past forecasts" and "as an individual's willingness to take risks increases, he or she will generally be more optimistic about actual revenues exceeding predicted revenues" (Bretschneider et al. 1988, 310–311). Under these hypotheses, which are supported with empirical evidence from a quasi-experiment on a medium-sized government, the challenges for small local government forecasting as per Kong (2007) and Frank and Zhao (2009) become evident. Specifically, if local governments are using judgmental forecasts rather than an econometric approach, they cannot make adjustments to a quantitative model.

In regard to decision-maker's perceptions of forecasts, even if a small local government were to use an econometric approach, there are still concerns due to cognitive biases (Bretschneider et al. 1988). As per Frank and Zhao (2009, 31), "mathematically derived forecasts without a downside bias and modeled with transparent assumptions could be viewed as threatening by many local finance officials." Thus, given the challenges of interpreting quantitative data due to cognitive biases, which is widely shown in behavioral research and acknowledged in economic research such as forecasting (see Bretschneider et al. 1988; Hogarth and Soyer 2015), decision-makers in small local governments may not understand how to use a quantitative forecast (Frank and Zhao 2009). Instead, they may challenge or ignore them if they are not clearly presented, unless an approach aimed at informing them, such as the scenario analysis or visualization, is utilized (Kavanagh and Williams 2016). Specifically, scenario analysis can help local governments to show optimistic, pessimistic, and baseline forecasts, while visualization can help to avoid the use of statistical output that may not be accessible (Kavanagh and Williams 2016). Forecasting practices are detailed in the next section.

Small Government Forecasting Practices

Kavanagh and Williams (2016) provide a seven-step framework for local government forecasting in relation to decision-making. The framework does not cater specifically to any size local government, but it does provide a cohesive framework that any local government can use. The seven steps are outlined below, and it is notable that the framework is designed for those with little to no knowledge of advanced forecasting techniques and without forecasting software, thus being relevant to the characteristics of small government forecasters identified in Kong (2007).

The first step involves identifying the problem that can be addressed with forecasting, such as when a local is expecting an acceleration or deceleration of growth, or even political concerns (see Rubin 2015). In the small government context, this should be considered with respect to characteristics such as economies of scale (Shapiro 1963) and if urban or rural, the latter of which carries specific concerns regarding revenue diversification and structural balance over the business cycle (Das et al. 2017). The GFOA Best Practice Financial Forecasting in the Budget Preparation Process (2014) recommends that "fundamental issues" be identified to help shape the forecast and ensure it is relevant to decision-makers (p. 1).

Once the problem(s) are identified, the second step is for the forecaster to collect input information to develop an information set to forecast with, echoing the most recent research on the subject in relation to small local governments from Kong (2007) and Frank and Zhao (2009). Input data can be collected internally from records such as Certified Annual Financial Reports, Excel file, and even records in an enterprise resource planning system. There are differences, however, with respect to where small and large governments may pull data for forecasting. For example, in property tax forecasting, which will often use data in a computer automated mass appraisal system (McCluskey et al. 2013), small and medium-sized governments tend to use lesser known vendors or in-house self-designed systems relative to larger governments at the local level (Reitano 2017). This can potentially influence the availability of input data and even the forecast accuracy, especially if in-house systems cannot directly convert data to newer external systems from vendors or have interfaces to convert to a forecast program, which is a notable concern facing smaller governments (Reitano 2017).

The third step is to analyze the data prior to forecasting, such as with descriptive or trend analysis to identify seasonality. This step is a data analysis exercise, and leads to the fourth step, which is to determine the methodology, whether judgmental, extrapolation, or an econometric approach. Historical data from forecast competitions can be used to determine which methods should be used, and examples in Kavanagh and Williams (2016, 144) clearly show that "[a] single best forecasting technique does not exist for all situations." Specifically, by taking historical data from 10 or 20 years prior, and running a competition to see how different methods perform based on forecast accuracy measures, a forecaster can make an informed decision regarding which method to select (Kavanagh and Williams 2016). The need for different forecast methods is also evident when considering different assumptions and input data available for each revenue source and expenditure being forecasted. For example, forecasting property taxes will require a different set of assumptions, input data, and potentially even a different model relative to forecasting fees or intergovernmental revenue. Assumptions, input data, and modeling strategies would also differ for forecasting other revenue streams outside of property taxes. For example, income and sales tax forecasts will require additional information such as population measures and business statistics. Once the forecast method(s) are determined, step five is to run them.

Step six in Kavanagh and Williams (2016) is to present and adjust the forecast. As per Hogarth and Soyer (2015), presenting complicated information to decision-makers is not an easy task. In the forecasting literature, techniques such as scenario analysis can help to show forecasts in terms of different situations that may result, whether optimistic or pessimistic or even baseline (Kavanagh and Williams 2016). More so, growing evidence that decision-makers use structured analogies to understand forecasts and consider decisions, especially in policy, can be of additional relevance (Green and Armstrong 2007; Savio and Nikolopoulos 2013). Especially for small governments, which use judgmental forecasts more than quantitative forecasts, having a structured analogies approach may help to make forecasts more informed and potentially increase forecast accuracy, although more research is necessary to corroborate this claim at the local level (see Savio and Nikolopoulos 2013). In recent research, Savio and Nikolopoulos (2013) consider structured analogies used in forecasting in relation to the policy process, and develop a framework that can be applied throughout the budgeting process.

The seventh step is about reviewing forecast accuracy. In relation to the literature, Kong (2007) shows that median forecast error is higher in smaller than larger counties, thus indicating the need for measuring and improving forecast accuracy over time, as recommended in Kavanagh and Williams (2016). Thus, the seventh step is consistent with Kong (2007) and the focus of the literature on forecasting accuracy, but Kavanagh and Williams (2016) also provide recommendations regarding the use of the forecast in decision-making. This involves not only looking at accuracy quantitatively but also considering behaviors such as whether decision-makers actively utilize forecasts during the budget process and whether they even contribute to forecasts in regard to developing assumptions and even scenarios relevant to their local community.

Limitations in Literature

While research in the past decade on local government forecasting is limited, there is even less known about small government forecasting practices. Essentially, the only study to systematically consider the differences in forecasting practices between small and large local governments is Kong (2007). Kong (2007) uses data that is more than a decade old and precedes the Great Recession. As researchers and policymakers consider the decade following the start of the Great Recession as brining a "new normal," there remains limited understanding of how forecasting practices may have changed (Ammons et al. 2012; Barrett et al. 2019; Martin et al. 2012). There are six areas that can be advanced in future research.

First, a study of forecast methods and software across multiple states should be conducted. The survey findings from Kong (2007) provide empirical evidence across California counties that judgmental forecasts are used by local governments more than advanced quantitative techniques, especially in smaller-sized governments. As access to new technology has proliferated, and the ability to store historical data has expanded with increases in data storage capacity at a low cost, research should examine whether smaller-sized governments are enabled to use quantitative methods. More so, research should look at not only the use of forecast methods but also the underlying reasons why. As per Frank (1990) and Frank and Zhao (2009), there might be a hesitation due to the technical skillset of forecasters in smaller governments, but this could potentially be addressed with new technology and software.

With respect to technology, greater research emphasis should also be placed on where the budget, finance, and socioeconomic data for forecasts is stored and how it is used. There is anecdotal evidence that Excel is commonly used in local government forecasting relative to other software programs (Kavanagh and Williams 2016). However, whether small and large governments will look to Stata, SAS, or other programs rather than relying on Excel, or have predeveloped modules in their Enterprise Resource Planning (ERP) system which automate the forecasting process, remains largely unknown (Beckett-Camarata 2006; Reddick 2006).

Specifically, local government forecasts may be pulling data to use in their forecasts from their ERP if their system was optimized to do so during requirements specifications (Roque 2010). For example, if a local government has an ERP such as Oracle, SAP, or Infor that stores historical financial data, which is a standard feature, then they can automate forecasts within their ERP budget, finance, business intelligence, or analytics modules (Miranda et al. 2002). However, only Reitano (2017) surveys governments of different sizes and shows that they have different types of ERP systems, but does not provide insight into how that directly relates to forecasting.

Second, research on forecast accuracy in small governments is relegated to a few studies. Expanding the sample of study to a national panel as in Frank et al. (2005) is critical to understanding forecast accuracy and how research findings and recommendations may generalize. Examining forecast accuracy in one state, even if demarcated by government size as in Kong (2007), does not ensure the results generalize beyond that state, as noted by Frank and Zhao (2009). This is particularly relevant due to differences in legal and regulatory requirements that local governments across states may have to follow as well as differences in types of local governments (Kavanagh et al. 2017).

Third, looking at the tendency to forecast conservatively or optimistically is another consideration which should receive greater research, especially across revenue streams, as a follow-up to Rubin (1987) and Kong (2007). More insight should be placed on obtaining historical data for a large sample of local governments and studying how revenue forecasts across property, sales, income, utility, user fee, and other sources may change over time. Additionally, understanding the motivations underlying conservative revenue forecasting, and how it relates to building a cushion into the budget, as per Rodgers and Joyce (1996) and Barrett et al. (2019), is largely unexplored.

Fourth, there is little knowledge of forecast policies and how they relate to the broader portfolio of financial policies a small local government may adopt (Kavanagh 2012). Only Frank and Zhao (2009) survey on the tendency to under-forecast in relation to financial policies, and they acknowledge the results are not definitive. This may involve a systematic survey or review of budget and finance documents and policies of small local governments.

Fifth, there is almost no knowledge of small government long-term forecasting and scenario planning since this was noted by Wong (1995) and subsequently reiterated by Williams and Calabrese (2016) regarding the implications of multi-year forecasting. Kong (2007) provides insight that just over a decade ago a majority of small governments in California do not use it but still consider it as something valuable in the future. Whether this trend holds, particularly as larger local governments have used them to respond to financial crises, is a critical question for smaller governments (Kavanagh and Williams 2016). More so, how forecasts are constructed and presented to stakeholders, such as with scenario planning in Baltimore, is not known in small local governments (Kavanagh and Williams 2016). Specifically, scenarios that are pessimistic, baseline, or optimistic can be constructed to help present forecasts to elected officials and nontechnical stakeholders, so that they can use forecasts to help in decision-making (Kavanagh and Williams 2016). Little is known about scenario planning and the structured analogies approach (Green and Armstrong 2007) in local government forecasting, especially for small governments.

Finally, the question remains of how forecasts play into the broader role of public budgeting and finance (Frank 1992), long-term financial planning (Kavanagh 2007), and financial sustainability (Kavanagh et al. 2017), especially in the years following the Great Recession (Barrett et al. 2019). With consistent evidence that governments of all sizes are forecasting, there remains the question of how forecasts may factor into broader questions regarding fiscal reserves and structural balance (Barrett et al. 2019; Frank and Zhao 2009). Empirical evidence on this question is limited to state and large local governments but not for small local governments (see Rose and Smith 2012; Williams and Onochie 2013).

The Government Finance Officers Association (GFOA) has provided best practices to help guide local governments with respect to forecasting, structural balance, and sustainability, although research has not evaluated their use in practice, with the exception of research on the determinants of adherence to fiscal reserve best practices at the local level (Arapis and Reitano 2018; Arapis et al. 2017). The GFOA Best Practice (2008, 1) on Long-Term Financial Planning states: “financial forecasting is the process of projecting revenues and expenditures over a long-term period, using assumptions about economic conditions, future spending scenarios, and other salient variables.” A systematic study of forecast accuracy examining which factors are associated with increased long-term forecast accuracy would be helpful. More so, it can directly relate to structural balance, which is considered as a measure for financial sustainability in GFOA’s (2012, 1) Best Practice Achieving a Structurally Balanced Budget: “A true structurally balanced budget is one that supports financial sustainability for multiple years into the future.” To date, there is no research linking forecasting practices to structural balance at the local level.

Conclusion

A recent Government Accountability Office (GAO 2016) forecast shows that state and local governments in the aggregate are not projected to have an operating surplus for multiple decades. This report reveals a pressing concern, namely that governments are struggling with financial sustainability. Forecasts are already in widespread use (Frank and Zhao 2009), but how they may or may not help to understand and respond to issues such as structural balance which underlie financial sustainability, is largely unknown, particularly at the local level. To address these broader questions, the literature needs to focus more on surveys and interviews to understand how forecasters, elected officials, and even members of the public may or may not understand forecasts in decision-making (Kavanagh et al. 2017). The literature can also work to develop quasi-experiments with practitioners to try and develop guidance for forecasting in small local governments with respect to methodology and accuracy and the overall context of government financial management. These recommendations can help to reveal how forecasts play a role not only as a technical tool but also as a way to help check if governments can continue public service provision into the future.

References

Ammons, D. N., Smith, K. W., & Stenberg, C. W. (2012). The future of local government: Will current stresses bring major, permanent changes? *State and Local Government Review, 44*(1S), 64S–75S.

Arapis, T., & Reitano, V. (2018). A glimmer of optimism in government savings accumulation? An empirical examination of municipal unassigned fund balance in Florida. *Public Finance Review, 46*(3), 389–420.

Arapis, T., Reitano, V., & Bruck, E. (2017). The fiscal savings behavior of Pennsylvania school districts through the great recession. *Public Budgeting & Finance, 37*(3), 47–70.

Barrett, N., Fowles, J., Jones, P., & Reitano, V. (2019). Forecast bias and fiscal slack accumulation in school districts. *The American Review of Public Administration, 49*(5), 601–613.

Beckett-Camarata, J. (2006). Revenue forecasting accuracy in Ohio local governments. *Journal of Public Budgeting, Accounting & Financial Management, 18*(1), 77–99.

Bretschneider, S. I., Straussman, J. J., & Mullins, D. (1988). Do revenue forecasts influence budget setting? A small group experiment. *Policy Sciences, 21*(4), 305–325.

Cirincione, C., Gurrieri, G. A., & Van De Sande, B. (1999). Municipal government revenue forecasting: Issues of method and data. *Public Budgeting & Finance, 19*(1), 26–46.

Das, B., Leatherman, J., Stallmann, J., Maher, C., Skidmore, M., & Bressers, B. (2017). *Fiscal stress after the great recession: A study of rural counties in the US*. The North Central Regional Center for Rural Development. Retrieved from https://www.researchgate.net/publication/319465413_Fiscal_Stress_after_the_Great_Recession_A_Study_of_Rural_Counties_in_the_US.

Frank, H. A. (1990). Municipal revenue forecasting with time series models: A Florida case study. *The American Review of Public Administration, 20*(1), 45–59.

Frank, H. A. (1992). Public financial management in the 1990s: New directions for research and pedagogy. *The American Review of Public Administration, 22*(3), 189–205.

Frank, H. A., & McCollough, J. (1992). Municipal forecasting practice: "Demand" and "supply" side perspectives. *International Journal of Public Administration, 15*(9), 1669–1695.

Frank, H. A., & Wang, X. (1994). Judgmental vs. time series vs. deterministic models in local revenue forecasting: A Florida case study. *Public Budgeting and Financial Management, 6*(4), 493–517.

Frank, H. A., & Zhao, Y. (2009). Determinants of local government revenue forecasting practice: Empirical evidence from Florida. *Journal of Public Budgeting, Accounting & Financial Management, 21*(1), 17–35.

Frank, H. A., Gianakis, G. A., & McCue, C. P. (2005). Will GASB 34 induce changes in local government forecasting practice? A preliminary investigation. *Journal of Public Budgeting, Accounting & Financial Management, 17*(4), 557–573.

Gianakis, G. A., & Frank, H. A. (1993). Implementing time series forecasting models: Considerations for local governments. *State and Local Government Review, 25*(2), 130–144.

Goeminne, S., Geys, B., & Smolders, C. (2008). Political fragmentation and projected tax revenues: Evidence from Flemish municipalities. *International Tax and Public Finance, 15*(3), 297–315.

Government Accountability Office. (2016). *State and local governments' fiscal outlook: 2016 update*. (GAO-17-213SP). Washington, DC. Retrieved from https://www.gao.gov/assets/690/681506.pdf.

Government Finance Officers Association. (2008). Long-term financial planning. *Best practice*. Retrieved from http://www.gfoa.org/long-term-financial-planning-0.

Government Finance Officers Association. (2012). Achieving a structurally balanced budget. *Best practice*. Retrieved from http://www.gfoa.org/achieving-structurally-balanced-budget.

Government Finance Officers Association. (2014). Financial forecasting in the budget preparation process. *Best practice*. Retrieved from http://www.gfoa.org/financial-forecasting-budget-preparation-process.

Green, K. C., & Armstrong, J. S. (2007). Structured analogies for forecasting. *International Journal of Forecasting, 23*(3), 365–376.

Hogarth, R. M., & Soyer, E. (2015). Using simulated experience to make sense of big data. *MIT Sloan Management Review, 56*(2), 49.

Kavanagh, S. C. (2007). *Financing the future: Long-term financial planning for local government*. Chicago: Government Finance Officers Association.

Kavanagh, S. C. (2012). *Financial policies: Design and implementation*. Chicago, IL: Government Finance Officers Association.

Kavanagh, S. C., & Williams, D. W. (2016). *Informed decision-making through forecasting*. Chicago: Government Finance Officers Association.

Kavanagh, S., Pisano, M., Tang, S. Y., McGrath, M. F., Linkhart, D., Hudson, M., & Colon, E. (2017). *A framework for a financial sustainability Index*. Working Paper: WP17MP1. Lincoln Institute of Land Policy. Retrieved from http://www.gfoa.org/sites/default/files/pisano_wp17mp1_0_0.pdf.

Klay, W. E. (1985). The organizational dimension of budgetary forecasting: Suggestions from revenue forecasting in the states. *International Journal of Public Administration, 7*(3), 241–265.

Kong, D. (2007). Local government revenue forecasting: The California county experience. *Journal of Public Budgeting, Accounting & Financial Management, 19*(2), 178–199.

Martin, L. L., Levey, R., & Cawley, J. (2012). The "new normal" for local government. *State and Local Government Review, 44*(1, suppl), 17S–28S.

McCluskey, W. J., Cornia, G. C., & Walters, L. C. (2013). *A primer on property tax: Administration and policy*. Hoboken, NJ: Wiley.

Miranda, R., Kavanagh, S., & Roque, R. (2002). *Technology needs assessment: Evaluating the business case for ERP and financial management systems*. Chicago: Government Finance Officers Association.

Reddick, C. G. (2006). Assessing local government revenue forecasting techniques. *International Journal of Public Administration, 27*(8/9), 597–613. https://doi.org/10.1081/PAD-120030257.

Reitano, V. (2017). *Investing in collections software to allow for monthly property tax payments*. Working Paper: WP17VR1. Lincoln Institute of Land Policy. Retrieved from https://www.lincolninst.edu/sites/default/files/sources/events/reitano_wp17vr1.pdf.

Rodgers, R., & Joyce, P. G. (1996). The effect of underforecasting on the accuracy of revenue forecasts by state governments. *Public Administration Review, 56*(1), 48–56.

Roque, R. (2010). Optimizing ERP in your organization. *Government Finance Review*, 46–50. Retrieved from www.gfoa.org/sites/default/files/GFR_AUG_10_46.pdf.

Rose, S., & Smith, D. L. (2012). Budget slack, institutions, and transparency. *Public Administration Review, 72*(2), 187–195.

Rubin, I. S. (1987). Estimated and actual urban revenues: Exploring the gap. *Public Budgeting & Finance, 7*(4), 83–94. https://doi.org/10.1111/1540-5850.00766.

Rubin, I. S. (2015). Past and future budget classics: A research agenda. *Public Administration Review, 75*(1), 25–35.

Savio, N. D., & Nikolopoulos, K. (2013). A strategic forecasting framework for governmental decision-making and planning. *International Journal of Forecasting, 29*(2), 311–321.

Shapiro, H. (1963). Economies of scale and local government finance. *Land Economics, 39*(2), 175–186.

Sun, J. (2005). The dynamics of government revenue forecasting from an organizational perspective: A review of the literature. *Journal of Public Budgeting, Accounting & Financial Management, 17*(4), 527.

Wildavsky, A. B. (1986). *Budgeting: A comparative theory of the budgeting process*. Transaction Publishers.

Williams, D. W., & Calabrese, T. D. (2016). The status of budget forecasting. *Journal of Public and Nonprofit Affairs, 2*(2), 127–160. https://doi.org/10.20899/jpna.2.2.127-160.

Williams, D. W., & Kavanagh, S. (2016). Local government revenue forecasting: Competition and comparison. *Journal of Public Budgeting, Accounting & Financial Management, 28*(4), 488–526.

Williams, D. W., & Onochie, J. (2013). The Rube Goldberg machine of budget implementation, or is there a structural deficit in the New York City budget? *Public Budgeting & Finance, 33*(4), 1–21. https://doi.org/10.1111/j.1540-5850.2013.12021.x.

Wong, J. D. (1995). Local government revenue forecasting: Using regression and econometric revenue forecasting in a medium-sized city. *Public Budgeting and Financial Management, 7*, 315–335.

13

Current Midyear Municipal Budget Forecast Accuracy

Daniel Williams and Thad Calabrese

Major Points

- Midyear forecasts (i.e., budget forecasts with shorter than 12-month horizons for the current fiscal year) can reflect substantial improvement.
- The expected improvement results from short time horizons and from the substitution of actual data for forecast for part of the year.
- Nevertheless, empirical evidence shows no statistically significant improvements in revenue forecasts.
- Empirical evidence shows that midyear expenditure forecasts actually worsen compared to the original budget forecasts.

D. Williams (✉)
Austin W. Marxe School of Public and International Affairs, Baruch College, New York, NY, USA
e-mail: Daniel.Williams@baruch.cuny.edu

T. Calabrese
Robert F. Wagner Graduate School of Public Service, New York University, New York, NY, USA
e-mail: thad.calabrese@nyu.edu

D. Williams, T. Calabrese (eds.), *The Palgrave Handbook of Government Budget Forecasting*, Palgrave Studies in Public Debt, Spending, and Revenue,
https://doi.org/10.1007/978-3-030-18195-6_13

Introduction

This chapter examines the accuracy of short-term budget forecasts for both revenues and expenditures. Williams and Calabrese (2016) document three distinct budget periods for which municipalities issue forecasts: the current year (i.e., forecasts about the current fiscal year made in the midyear), the budget year (usually the next fiscal year), and the out years (i.e., the years beyond the budget year). The review shows that there is extensive review of forecast practices for the budget year; additionally, forecast practices for the out years are adequately examined in the literature. However, they cite no sources related to current year (midyear) budget forecast practices. This absence may largely reflect the lack of budget data published on the topic; data for the next fiscal year and the out years are readily available for many jurisdictions but midyear forecasts are not as commonly published or made available in a clear format. This may be because while budget year data are the result of policy choices and political compromise that are important to stakeholders, one of the main purposes of current year budget forecasts is to track budget implementation and to provide meaningful information for the next sequential budget proposal.[1] In other words, the midyear data are most important to public administrators and internal budget analysts, who have access to such data, regardless of whether it is publicly published or not. In this chapter, we situate midyear budget forecasts in the current literature and empirically test the accuracy of municipal midyear forecasts. We find, contrary to what the literature suggests, that midyear forecast accuracy does not improve, and expenditure forecasts actually get worse compared to budget year forecasts. We offer some potential explanations for these findings.

Literature Review

Forecast purposes differ for the three periods (current/midyear, budget year, and out years): for the budget year, the purpose is to determine resource availability and expected program costs. For the out years, the purpose is to address structural balance. For the current year, the purpose is to track performance and address the need for short-term adjustments (Pike and Savage 1998;

[1] Revenue forecasters also look at collections as a preview of economic conditions because these tend to be good coincident indicators of the economy. Expenditure forecasters use current year spending to discern if there are demographic or social condition changes in the jurisdiction, or provide data on signs of unexpected policy outcomes affecting agencies. In both cases, these forecasters are trying to use current year budget forecasts to improve next year's budget.

Williams and Calabrese 2016). Short-term adjustments might be necessary to ensure the government does not overspend in the current year, to ensure compliance with constitutional or statutory balanced budget requirements, or to adjust spending due to previously unknown public concerns. Current midyear forecasts are frequently included in budget year proposals (i.e., modifications to the current year budget are presented in conjunction with financial plans for the next fiscal year).

For a typical budget, the current midyear forecast might be better described as a blended record of actual revenue or expenditure through some point in time with a forecast for the remainder of the year (Isiklar et al. 2006; Lienert 2013; Loungani 2001; Marinheiro 2011; Pardaev 2016; Stekler 1967); however, there is inconsistency in the timing of the midyear point at which the historic data terminates (Marinheiro 2011). For simplicity of expression, we treat this blend of actual and projected data as a forecast.

There are a few studies that have reported current midyear forecast errors with respect to budgetary data. Plesko (1988, pp. 489, 492, Tables 2 and 4) examines forecasts, including current midyear budgets, at the Office of Management and Budget (OMB) and the Congressional Budget Office (CBO) and, for budget forecasts, finds mean absolute percent errors (MAPEs)[2] ranging from 0.85 to 1.59 percent. For other fiscal variables, Plesko (1988, pp. 496, 498, Tables 6 and 8) finds MAPEs ranging from 1.43 to 15.10 percent. Basu et al. (2003) examine the current midyear forecast errors for corporate taxes in the United Kingdom from 1993 through 2003 and find MAPEs under various assumptions ranging from 4.5 to 7.7 percent. Buettner and Kauder (2015, pp. 304, 305, Table 6) examine political forecast bias in Germany. Their primary research objective is not closely related to this study; however, they include a current midyear percent revenue forecast errors for 1971–2013 and report a MAPE of 1.53 percent.[3] De Deus and de Mendonça (2017) examine short-term budget balance and economic growth forecasting, including current midyear forecasting, in Brazil. They find low quality and accuracy; and they find bias in growth forecasts. They report a MAPE of 19.77 percent for current midyear budget balance forecasts and a MAPE of 47.04 percent for GDP growth.

Batchelor (2007, p. 193, Fig. 1) demonstrates that over much of the fiscal year, fiscal forecast errors shrink as the horizon draws nearer. Pardaev (2016) finds that by correcting Uzbekistan state budget forecasts with current (midyear) data, the forecasts can be substantially improved. Pardaev (2016)

[2] The formulas for error measures are provided in Appendix.

[3] Computed by current authors.

examines directly relevant information, to which it would be desirable to compare results; however, the report uses several measures that are dependent on the magnitude of the data. Although Theil's *U* is reported to compare midyear budget accuracy and improvements, this statistic cannot be used comparatively because the report does not adequately define the version of Theil's *U* reported.[4]

Excluded from this literature review are studies of current year or short-term forecasts of economic variables that are not revenues or expenditures, but may influence the budget, budget deficits, and other budget-related or fiscal variables. These excluded studies typically examine national forecast practices and frequently focus on the European Union or its member states. They generally report error measures that are linked to the magnitude of the data; thus, they do not provide meaningful comparative information for this study.[5]

As seen in this literature review, there is no identifiable literature focusing on municipal-level current midyear budget forecast accuracy. The literature that examines federal-level midyear forecasts does tend to find improvements in the accuracy of these forecasts, which is consistent with theoretical expectations. Consequently, this study is a preliminary foray into this topic at the municipal level and will be largely limited to the examination of descriptive statistics.

Methodology

Common measures used in the analysis of forecast accuracy include the root-mean-squared error (RMSE), mean absolute percent error (MAPE), symmetrical mean absolute percent error (SMAPE), and Theil's U_1 or U_2 (Makridakis et al. 1982, 1993; Makridakis and Hibon 2000; Pardaev 2016). Theil's *U* is problematic because there are a plethora of possible definitions. RMSE is inapplicable across multiple series as it is not magnitude independent and, therefore, irrelevant across multiple forecasts. Consequently, the two measures that are considered here are MAPE and SMAPE.

The methodology applied is to examine three forecasts, each from 15 local governments using their budgets published on the internet. The 15 local governments are shown in Table 13.1. The population of these cities ranges from

[4] The *U*-statistic is problematic because there are six or more variations (see Appendix).

[5] Those that specifically report MAPE estimates have been included. Because of the lack of comparability (see Appendix), studies that report Theil's *U* but not MAPE are excluded. No reviewed studies of this sort report symmetrical mean absolute percent errors (SMAPEs).

Table 13.1 Localities examined

• Cary, NC	• Fairfield, CA
• City of Champaign, IL	• Fayetteville, NC
• City of Clarksville, TN	• Palm Bay, FL
• City of Hugo, MN	• Pueblo, CO
• City of Safety Harbor, FL	• Waco, TX
• City of Seagoville, TX	• West Jordan, UT
• Daly City, CA	• Wichita Falls, TX
• Durham, NC	

14,800 to 268,000, with a mean of 113,700. Very large jurisdictions are excluded from this analysis. The sample was randomly drawn from a list of municipalities in the United States with populations under 500,000, and was limited to those cities with publicly available budget data. Localities that do not show a forecast for the current year in the proposed budget or that show the same forecast as that shown in the budget as adopted are discarded.

The three forecasts analyzed are total expenditure, total revenue, and the largest reported revenue category, which is property tax for nine localities, sales tax for five, and "taxes" for one. Five years of data are collected for each locality reflecting fiscal years 2013 through 2017. Two forecasts are collected: the forecast for the upcoming fiscal year as shown in the adopted budget, and the updated forecast for the same year as shown in the next sequential proposed budget. This second forecast is a midyear forecast update and is understood to be a blend of actual revenues or expenditures through part of the year and a forecast for the remainder of the year. The date of the transition from actual to forecast is unknown, so the researchers apply their general knowledge of budget practice to estimate a date as needed below. The estimated point in time is 5.5 months into the fiscal year (5 months for some localities and 6 for others). This estimate assumes that the proposed budget is presented to a legislative body several months before the end of the fiscal year and the forecast must be made earlier than that date to be included in a published budget proposal. Assuming that a legislative session starts in January for a budget fiscal year that starts in July taking up the budget as an early agenda item (a common practice), the forecast must be made in December with data through November (five months of actual data). Some smaller localities may be able to propose the budget nearer to the beginning of the budget year, while other localities may have longer horizons.[6]

[6] "Horizon" refers to the distance from forecast to prediction, so, for monthly forecasts, H3 refers to a forecast for three months into the future.

These two forecasts are compared with the actual revenue and expenditures as reported retrospectively in the third sequential budget cycle proposed budget. Three error values are computed for (1) the forecast used with the adopted budget and (2) the midyear modified forecast, and measure how closely these forecasts were to subsequent actual results. The three error values are MAPE, SMAPE, and Theil's U_2. Equations for these measures are shown in Appendix.

The MAPE, SMAPE, and percent improvement values are compared with benchmark values computed from the M-Competition (Makridakis et al. 1982), M2-Competition (Makridakis et al. 1993), M3-Competition (Makridakis et al. 1982), two studies of judgmental forecasting (Angus-Leppan and Fatseas 1986; Lawrence et al. 1985), and a recent study of tourism forecasting (Athanasopoulos et al. 2011). These studies are not budget forecasts; rather, they are methods studies examining a broad range of forecast methods using a broad range of data series, thus providing a proxy for attainable forecast accuracy. The relevant results from these studies data are shown in Table 13.2. The table shows error measures for horizons ranges of 1–4, 1–6, 1–8, and 1–12, as found in some reports and computed by the current authors from reported data for others. The 1–12 period is a proxy for the forecast of the future budget year; the others are averaged as a proxy for the midyear forecast. They do not show blended forecasts (where actuals are available for part of the year). However, actuals can be expected to be correct, therefore the error is entirely found in the forecast period. Having estimated the actual period as 5.5 periods, the forecast errors are reduced to 6.5/12 (0.5417) of the reported values to approximate the blended forecast errors.

The significance of the percent improvement calculation can be understood from the context of the relative difficulty of the forecast itself. Budgetary expenditures and certain revenues may be less difficult to forecast than the anonymized series forecast in the methods studies. Thus, the MAPE or SMAPE estimates computed from the methods studies for midyear forecasts may underestimate that accuracy that can be achieved with data that are known to budget forecasters and, in the case of the expenditures, may be somewhat controlled by the forecasters or their colleagues. So, the percentage improved from the calculations may set a better benchmark than the MAPE or SMAPE itself.

Table 13.2 demonstrates the calculation of MAPE, SMAPE, blended MAPE, and blended SMAPE, and benchmark percentage improved at midyear based on data reported in six forecast methods studies (Angus-Leppan and Fatseas 1986; Athanasopoulos et al. 2011; Lawrence et al. 1985; Makridakis et al. 1982, 1993; Makridakis and Hibon 2000), which are various reports of either quantitative or qualitative time series forecast methods.

Table 13.2 Comparison data for forecast accuracy expectations, MAPE, SMAPE, and percent improved

Average MAPE or SMAPE		H1–4	H1–6	H1–8	Avg.	Blended	H1–12	Percent improved (%)	Weight (forecasts)
M-Competition	MAPE	14.5	17.2	18.7	16.8	9.1	20.0	54.50	20,994
M2-Competition	MAPE	10.8	13.3	14.2	12.8	6.9	15.2	54.54	828
Tourism	MAPE	19.1	19.6	19.9	19.5	10.6	20.2	47.69	1830
Accounting students	MAPE		20.1		20.1	10.9	25.1	56.47	241
Judgment	MAPE	12.8	14.7	14.9	14.1	7.6	16.1	52.57	212
Weighted avg.								53.99	
M3-Competition	SMAPE	11.5	12.5	12.7	12.3	6.6	13.1	49.33	34,272

Sources:
M-Competition (Makridakis et al. 1982, p. 115, Table 2(a))
M2-Competition (Makridakis et al. 1993, p. 9, Exhibit 3); periods 7, 9, 10, 11 imputed
Tourism (Athanasopoulos et al. 2011, p. 832, Table 4); periods 7, 8, 9, 10, 11 imputed
Judgment (Lawrence et al. 1985, pp. 30–32, Table 1); periods 7, 9, 10, 11 imputed
Accounting students (Angus-Leppan and Fatseas 1986, p. 184, Tables 1, 2, 4); horizons 1–6 and 1–12, other periods and cannot be imputed from the reported data
M3-Competition (Makridakis and Hibon 2000, p. 467, Table 15)
Weights, averages, blended, percent improved, imputed values, and weighted average are computed by the current authors. Weights are computed from reported series, forecasters, repetitions, and other evidence of unique forecasts performed. Imputed values are estimated as linear extrapolations of surrounding values

The table shows forecast horizons for periods 1–4, 1–6, and 1–8 (labeled H1–4, H1–6, and H1–8). The next two columns are labeled Average, which averages the three columns to its left, and Blended, which applies the ratio 0.5417 to approximate the accuracy to expect when 5.5 periods of data are actual rather than forecasted. This value is a proxy for the accuracy (MAPE or SMAPE) that may be found with budget forecasts that are a blend of actuals for the first part of the year and forecasts for the remainder of the year. Thus, the table shows that the estimated blended accuracy (MAPE) for the M-Competition is 9.1 percent. The last two columns are labeled H1–12, which reflects the expected forecast accuracy before the hypothetical budget year begins,[7] and "PCT Imp," which reflects how much better the blended forecast error measure is compared with the forecast before the hypothetical budget year begins, and this last value is the target benchmark for the study. As there are multiple estimates of MAPE, a weighted average is computed based on the number of forecasts contributing the values for each study. The benchmark MAPE is 53.99 percent; however, 45.83 percent of this improvement can be attributed to the blending ratio. The benchmark SMAPE comes from a single study and is 49.33 percent.

Analysis and Results

Table 13.3 shows descriptive results for the 225 forecasts examined. The first quantitative column shows the number of observations. The next two columns show the MAPE values for the adopted and modified (midyear) forecasts. The column labeled "MAPE PCT Improved" shows the value defined by Eq. (13.6) in Appendix. The next three columns show the SMAPE in the same order and the last three columns show Theil's U_2 in the same order.[8] Negative numbers are declines in accuracy. The MAPE and SMAPE percent improved values can be compared with the benchmark values shown in Table 13.2.

The first thing to notice is that whether measured in MAPE, SMAPE, or Theil's U_2, the average forecast accuracy of expenditures declines compared with that at the beginning of the year. All other forecast values (including the average of all values) improve regardless of which measure is used and the relative improvement of MAPE and SMAPE is consistent with the results in Table 13.2—that is, MAPE declines somewhat more than SMAPE. However,

[7] For actual budgets, the horizons may not start at 1, but at some higher numbered period.

[8] The U_2 values are presented, but not compared as discussed in Appendix.

Table 13.3 Analysis of midyear budget forecast improvement

Forecast type	N	MAPE adopted (%)	MAPE modified (%)	MAPE PCT improved (%)	SMAPE adopted (%)	SMAPE modified (%)	SMAPE PCT improved (%)	Theil's U_2 adopted	Theil's U_2 modified	Theil's U_2 PCT improved (%)
All expenditure	75	4.36	4.83	−10.67	4.41	5.07	−15.00	0.7291	0.8449	−15.89
All revenue	75	4.94	3.09	37.55	4.78	3.02	36.96	0.8967	0.7020	21.71
Property tax	45	2.30	1.69	26.76	2.26	1.66	26.44	0.3722	0.3416	8.21
Sales tax	25	3.16	2.22	29.69	3.08	2.20	28.60	0.5841	0.4617	20.95
Taxes	5	2.75	1.52	44.61	2.70	1.51	44.16	0.5956	0.4644	22.03
Grand total	225	3.97	3.26	18.07	3.92	3.30	15.65	0.6945	0.6456	7.04

the amount of improvement (ranging from 26.69 to 44.61 percent for MAPE and 26.44 to 44.16 percent for SMAPE, while averaging much smaller values due to the negative values for expenditures) is substantially lower than the benchmark values of 53.99 and 49.33 percent respectively found in Table 13.2. In fact, these values are smaller than might be expected from simply reducing the error for the midyear historical data to zero. A possible explanation for this is that the midyear forecasts are made earlier in the middle of the budget year than proposed above.

Despite these results that run counter to existing theory, it is also worth noting that these accuracy measures (MAPE and SMAPE) are quite good compared to those reported in the column labeled "Avg." and "H1–12" in Table 13.2. There are several possible reasons for these, ranging from the possibility that the data forecast is less volatile to the possibility that forecaster knowledge of the specific data forecast leads to better forecasts.

Table 13.4 shows the values for MAPE, SMAPE, and percent improved by year for fiscal 2013 through fiscal 2017. The annual MAPE and SMAPE values are relatively small compared with Table 13.2. The values of percent improved range from 6.17 to 25.56 percent (MAPE) and 3.7 0 to 22.56 percent (SMAPE). The accuracy values are quite good compared with Table 13.2, but again, the improvement from before the year begins (Adopted) to midyear (Modified) is smaller than the Table 13.2 benchmarks and below the value that should be expected by simply substituting actual values for forecasts for the first portion of the year.

Table 13.5 reports the results of a regression analysis examining the effects of revenue types on a constructed variable PCTBBR (defined in Eq. (13.7) in Appendix), which reflects the degree to which the midyear budget forecast outperforms the adopted budget forecast while controlling for the locality and fiscal year. Due to the small number of observations the model automatically dropped Sales Tax and "Taxes." As seen in Table 13.5, the coefficients for "Property tax" and "All revenue" are not statistically significant. The "All expenditure" coefficient is significant, but in the opposite direction expected.

Table 13.4 Analysis of errors by year

Fiscal year	N	MAPE adopted	MAPE modified	MAPE PCT improved	SMAPE adopted	SMAPE modified	SMAPE PCT improved
2013	45	2.76	2.59	6.34	2.75	2.63	4.51
2014	45	3.38	2.52	25.30	3.33	2.58	22.65
2015	45	4.58	3.52	23.03	4.43	3.48	21.33
2016	45	4.86	3.62	25.56	4.79	3.71	22.59
2017	45	4.30	4.03	6.17	4.28	4.12	3.70
Grand total	225	3.97	3.26	18.07	3.92	3.30	15.65

Table 13.5 Evaluation of midyear budget improvement

Linear regression, absorbing indicators: Number of obs. = 225				
Dependent variable: PCTBTTR as defined in Eq. (13.7)				
Linear regression, absorbing indicators: Number of obs. = 225				
F(7203)	5.08			
Prob > F	0.0000			
R-squared	0.3249			
Adj R-squared	0.2550			
Root MSE	0.0295			
PCTBTTR	Robust coeff.	Std. err.	*t*	*P* > |*t*|
Property tax	−0.011	0.008	−1.30	0.196
All revenue	0.004	0.007	0.60	0.550
All expenditure	−0.020	0.008	−2.53	0.012
Yr_Dummy2	0.006	0.005	1.22	0.225
Yr_Dummy3	0.008	0.007	1.24	0.217
Yr_Dummy4	0.010	0.006	1.64	0.102
Yr_Dummy5	0.000	0.006	0.06	0.952
_cons	0.009	0.007	1.23	0.221
Locality	Absorbed (15 categories)			

This result is consistent with the descriptive statistics in Table 13.3. Overall, these results show no evidence of improved forecast, and for expenditures, evidence of worsening forecasts at midyear. The model itself explains 25.5 percent of the variation in the data, as the variables of interest explain very little, the control variables, in particular, the locality control variables explain most of the variation.

Discussion

The literature review suggests that midyear forecasts can reflect small improvements in forecast accuracy due to shorter time horizons; larger improvements are also possible as actual values are substituted for forecasted values in the initial periods of the fiscal year. The empirical analysis shows that for the 15 localities studied, there is no evidence of attaining any of these improvements and, in fact, for expenditures, forecast accuracy declines. The current analysis cannot definitively determine why municipalities' midyear forecasts do not improve as theory and other empirical evidence suggests. Further research is needed to answer this question. However, we can speculate. Perhaps budget officers simply add remaining budget allocations to actual spending for the year without updating the underlying forecasts. Perhaps spending is lumpy or seasonal and these fluctuations are not accounted for accurately in midyear budget updates. Or perhaps elected officials make a midyear budget appropriation based on unplanned revenues, and so the expenditure forecast is changed to ensure budget balance. Whatever the reason, the results of this analysis provide some exploratory evidence that current scholarship has overlooked a key component of budget implementation and public administration. The area remains a fruitful avenue for research by scholars and practitioners alike.

Conclusion

This chapter has introduced the study of midyear budget forecast accuracy for municipal governments in the United States. Evidence examined shows that these localities are reasonably accurate at the beginning of the fiscal year, but achieve no significant improvement when producing midyear forecasts and, in fact, become less accurate with midyear expenditure forecasts. These results are puzzling, and run counter to existing theory. Further research should analyze midyear budget forecasts to determine why municipal governments do not improve these forecasts despite having shorter time horizons and more data than before the fiscal year begins. Such research might include comparing different methodologies used in forecasting components of revenue and spending in the current year to determine if simple or complex methods improve current year forecasting more.

Appendix: Equations and Discussion of Theil's *U*

All equations used in this chapter are included in this appendix.

$$\text{APE} = \left| \frac{\text{Actual} - \text{Forecast}}{\text{Actual}} \right| \tag{13.1}$$

$$\text{MAPE} = \frac{\sum \text{APE}}{n} \tag{13.2}$$

$$\text{SAPE} = \left| \frac{\text{Actual} - \text{Forecast}}{(\text{Actual} + \text{Forecast}) / 2} \right| \tag{13.3}$$

$$\text{SMAPE} = \frac{\sum \text{SAPE}}{n} \tag{13.4}$$

$$U_2 = \frac{\left[\sum_{i=1}^{n} (P_i - A_i)^2\right]^{\frac{1}{2}}}{\left[\sum_{i=1}^{n} A_i^2\right]^{\frac{1}{2}}} \tag{13.5}$$

For this Theil's U formula, P = the forecasted change and A = the actual change (Bliemel 1973). For all other equations, the actual and forecast refer to the whole numbers.

$$\text{PCT Improved} = \frac{\text{M Adopted} - \text{M Modified}}{\text{M Adopted}} \tag{13.6}$$

where M refers to an error measure (MAPE, SMAPE or Theil's U_2).

$$\text{PCTBTTR} = \frac{\text{SAPE Adopted} - \text{SAPE Modified}}{\text{SAPE Adopted}} \tag{13.7}$$

Alternate calculations of Theil's U not used:

$$U_1 = \frac{\left[\frac{1}{n}\sum_{i=1}^{n} (P_i - A_i)^2\right]^{\frac{1}{2}}}{\left[\frac{1}{n}\sum_{i=1}^{n} A_i^2\right]^{\frac{1}{2}} + \left[\frac{1}{n}\sum_{i=1}^{n} P_i^2\right]^{\frac{1}{2}}} \tag{13.8}$$

This equation has two variants, where P and A may either refer to the whole numbers (forecast and actual) or the forecasted and actual changes (Bliemel 1973). Zakaria and Ali (2010) offer an apparent clarification of U_1 incorporating the change formulation as:

$$U_3 = \frac{\left[\frac{1}{t}\sum_{i=1}^{t} \left[(P_i - A_{i-1}) = (A_i - A_{i-1})\right]^2\right]^{\frac{1}{2}}}{\left[\frac{1}{t}\sum_{i=1}^{t} (P_i - A_{i-1})^2\right]^{\frac{1}{2}} + \left[\frac{1}{t}\sum_{i=1}^{t} (A_i - A_{i-1})^2\right]^{\frac{1}{2}}} \tag{13.9}$$

It is also possible that U_2 can be calculated in both variants (whole number or change). Bliemel (1973) finds that U_1 fails to effectively distinguish between accurate and inaccurate forecast, but U_2 does. U_1 and U_2 can be confused, as seen with this internet resource[9] that reverses the labels between U_1 and U_2.

Dean (1976) reintroduces the use of mean squared values in the place of squared values for U_2 and gives an alternate equation as[10]:

$$U_2 = \frac{\left[\frac{1}{n}\sum_{i=1}^{n}\left(P_{i+1} - A_i\right)^2\right]^{\frac{1}{2}}}{\left[\frac{1}{n}\sum_{i=1}^{n}A_i^2\right]^{\frac{1}{2}}} \tag{13.10}$$

Carabotta (2014) gives the equation (although labeled "T," it reflects the U statistic development):

$$T = \frac{RMSE_{e_t}}{RMSE_{AR(1)}} \tag{13.11}$$

Next, an internet source[11] uses proportionate values of change and calculates U_2 as[12]:

$$U_2 = \frac{\left[\frac{1}{T}\sum_{i=1}^{T-1}\frac{\left(P_{i+1} - A_{i+1}\right)^2}{A_i}\right]^{\frac{1}{2}}}{\left[\frac{1}{T}\sum_{i=1}^{Tn}\left(\frac{A_{(i+1)} - A_i}{Ai}\right)^2\right]^{\frac{1}{2}}} \tag{13.12}$$

---

[9] https://www.statisticshowto.datasciencecentral.com/u-statistic-theils/. Accessed on 12/30/18.

[10] Some notation has been modified to make the equation more explicit or to be consistent with other equations for Theil's U.

[11] https://www.economicsnetwork.ac.uk/showcase/cook_forecast. Accessed on 12/30/18.

[12] Some notation has been modified to be consistent with other equations for Theil's U.

References

Angus-Leppan, P., & Fatseas, V. (1986). The forecasting accuracy of trainee accountants using judgmental and statistical techniques. *Accounting and Business Research, 16*(63), 179–188.

Athanasopoulos, G., Hyndman, R. J., Song, H., & Wu, D. C. (2011). The tourism forecasting competition. *International Journal of Forecasting, 27*(3), 822–844.

Basu, S., Emmerson, C., & Frayne, C. (2003). *An examination of the IFS corporation tax forecasting record.* The Institute for Fiscal Studies, IFS Working Paper WP 03/21. Retrieved from https://doi.org/10.1920/wp.ifs.2003.0321.

Batchelor, R. (2007). Bias in macroeconomic forecasts. *International Journal of Forecasting, 23*(2), 189–203. https://doi.org/10.1016/j.ijforecast.2007.01.004.

Bliemel, F. (1973). Theil's forecast accuracy coefficient: A clarification. *Journal of Marketing Research, 10*(4), 444–446.

Buettner, T., & Kauder, B. (2015). Political biases despite external expert participation? An empirical analysis of tax revenue forecasts in Germany. *Public Choice, 164*(3–4), 287–307.

Carabotta, L. (2014). Which agency and which period is the best? Analyzing national and international fiscal forecasts in Italy. *International Journal of Economic Sciences, 2014*(1), 27–46.

Dean, A. J. H. (1976). Errors in National Institute forecasts of personal incomes, inflation and employment, 1965–75. *National Institute Economic Review, 78*(1), 48–57.

de Deus, J. D. B. V., & de Mendonça, H. F. (2017). Fiscal forecasting performance in an emerging economy: An empirical assessment of Brazil. *Economic Systems, 41*(3), 408–419.

Isiklar, G., Lahiri, K., & Loungani, P. (2006). How quickly do forecasters incorporate news? Evidence from cross-country surveys. *Journal of Applied Econometrics, 21*(6), 703–725.

Lawrence, M. J., Edmundson, R. H., & O'Connor, M. J. (1985). An examination of the accuracy of judgmental extrapolation of time series. *International Journal of Forecasting, 1*(1), 25–35.

Lienert, I. (2013). The legal framework for public finances and budget systems. In R. Allen, R. Hemming, & B. H. Potter (Eds.), *The international handbook of public financial management* (pp. 63–83). New York: Palgrave Macmillan.

Loungani, P. (2001). How accurate are private sector forecasts? Cross-country evidence from consensus forecasts of output growth. *International Journal of Forecasting, 17*(3), 419–432. https://doi.org/10.1016/S0169-2070(01)00098-X.

Makridakis, S., & Hibon, M. (2000). The M3-competition: Results, conclusions and implications. *International Journal of Forecasting, 16*(4), 451–476.

Makridakis, S., Andersen, A., Carbone, R., Fildes, R., Hibon, M., Lewandowski, R., et al. (1982). The accuracy of extrapolation (time series) methods: Results of a forecasting competition. *Journal of Forecasting, 1*(2), 111.

Makridakis, S., Chatfield, C., Hibon, M., Lawrence, M. J., Mills, T., Ord, K., & Simmons, L. F. (1993). The M2-competition: A real-time judgmentally based forecasting study. *International Journal of Forecasting, 9*(1), 5–22. https://doi.org/10.1016/0169-2070(93)90044-N.

Marinheiro, C. F. (2011). Fiscal sustainability and the accuracy of macroeconomic forecasts: Do supranational forecasts rather than government forecasts make a difference? *International Journal of Sustainable Economy, 3*(2), 185–209.

Pardaev, U. (2016). Analyzes of state budget forecasting errors and issues of forecasting accuracy. *Asian Journal of Management Sciences & Education, 5*, 1.

Pike, T., & Savage, D. (1998). Forecasting the public finances in the Treasury. *Fiscal Studies, 19*(1), 49–62.

Plesko, G. A. (1988). The accuracy of government forecasts and budget projections. *National Tax Journal, 41*(4), 483–501.

Stekler, H. O. (1967). The federal budget as a short-term forecasting tool. *The Journal of Business, 40*(3), 280–285.

Williams, D. W., & Calabrese, T. D. (2016). The status of budget forecasting. *Journal of Public and Nonprofit Affairs, 2*(2), 127–160. https://doi.org/10.20899/jpna.2.2.127-160.

Zakaria, M., & Ali, S. (2010). Fiscal marksmanship in Pakistan. *Lahore Journal of Economics, 15*(2), 113–133.

Part III

Subject Matter Specialties

14

Using Fiscal Indicator Systems to Predict Municipal Bankruptcies

Jonathan B. Justice, Marc Fudge, Helisse Levine, David D. Bird, and Muhammad Naveed Iftikhar

Major Points

- U.S. state governments have developed various methods for predicting fiscal distress and defaults by their local governments.
- A widespread prediction strategy is to compute indexes of fiscal stress based on financial and other indicators.
- This chapter assesses the predictive accuracy of three well-documented and carefully argued indicator systems, to answer two primary questions:
  - Do the indicators all measure the same thing?
  - How effectively do they predict severe fiscal distress and distinguish between cities that did and did not enter bankruptcy?

J. B. Justice (✉) • D. D. Bird • M. N. Iftikhar
Joseph R. Biden, Jr. School of Public Policy & Administration, University of Delaware, Newark, DE, USA
e-mail: justice@udel.edu; dbird@udel.edu; cheema@udel.edu

M. Fudge
California State University San Bernardino, San Bernardino, CA, USA
e-mail: MFudge@csusb.edu

H. Levine
School of Business, Public Administration and Information Sciences, Long Island University-Brooklyn, Brooklyn, NY, USA
e-mail: helisse.levine@liu.edu

D. Williams, T. Calabrese (eds.), *The Palgrave Handbook of Government Budget Forecasting*, Palgrave Studies in Public Debt, Spending, and Revenue,
https://doi.org/10.1007/978-3-030-18195-6_14

- The system developed and currently used by Ohio's Auditor of State performed best among those studied.

Introduction

Being able to forecast and thereby avert or mitigate severe local-government fiscal stress and its consequences is important for state governments and others (Advisory Commission on Intergovernmental Relations 1985; Atwell et al. 2013; Spiotto 2013). In the extreme, bankruptcy, if it occurs, almost certainly means that at least some of a local-government's stakeholders will suffer material losses, and has the potential to require state assistance and create contagion effects that impair bond-market access for the state's other municipalities. Thus, states have material incentives to forecast fiscal distress in time to avert bankruptcy, or at least mitigate its effects.

At the same time, state monitors of local-government finances have to consider the real tradeoffs associated with constraints on data availability, analytic capacity, time, and decision-maker attention when designing and implementing monitoring systems. Accordingly, challenges for monitoring system design include finding a suitable balance of accuracy and parsimony, and avoiding false-negative or false-positive results without imposing insupportable resource demands on a state's fiscal monitors (Justice and Scorsone 2012). There is now available an extensive body of scholarly and practical work on the subject of measuring and forecasting municipal fiscal health, but these efforts have not converged on a single best-practice system of indicators that optimally balances predictive efficacy with parsimony in terms of requirements for data, analytic effort, and demands on decision makers' attention (see, e.g., Bird 2014).

As of 2016, at least 22 states had some type of monitoring program in operation (Pew Charitable Trusts 2016). Those systems vary considerably in their design and operation, with large differences in their data requirements (in both the type and quantity of data), methods of data reduction and computation, decision rules for categorizing degrees of fiscal health and stress, and staffing (Smith et al. 2018). This chapter reports on a test of the forecast accuracy of three carefully thought-out, well-documented, and parsimonious indicator systems, performed by computing indicator scores for a sample of three bankrupt general-purpose local governments and six matched jurisdictions that did not declare bankruptcy, over a ten-year period that included the years leading up to the three bankruptcy proceedings.

The local-government fiscal monitoring system developed in 2002 for the Michigan State Treasurer (Kleine et al. 2002; Kloha et al. 2005a), a proposed improvement to that system (Crosby and Robbins 2013), and the system used by the Ohio Auditor of State as of 2017 (Ohio Auditor of State 2018) all combine a number of fiscal indicators into an additive index of fiscal health. Each system is adaptable for application to local governments in other states, using data from local-governments' comprehensive annual financial reports (CAFRs). For this analysis, the three systems were used to calculate index scores over the period 2004–2013 for three California cities that entered bankruptcy during that period and six comparison cities in California that have not been involved in bankruptcy proceedings, declarations of financial emergency, or neutral mediation under California law governing cities experiencing significant fiscal distress.

The central research question is whether and to what extent each of the monitoring systems generates valid forecasts of municipal fiscal health or distress when applied to the historical data. How effectively does each system indicate or forecast severe fiscal distress, and how effectively does each system distinguish between the cities that are severely distressed (as indicated by bankruptcy filings) and those that were not? Of the three systems, Ohio's performed best: it indicated fiscal stress and forecasted the three bankruptcies reasonably well, and in spite of moderate apparent false positives distinguished fairly well between the bankrupt and non-bankrupt cities. The two Michigan systems were less consistent in forecasting the bankruptcies, and did not distinguish well between the bankrupt cities and the comparison cities.

The following sections of the chapter review the concepts of fiscal health and stress; some practicalities of measuring and forecasting fiscal health, stress, and distress; and the methodology and results of the test of three indicator systems' effectiveness in predicting the bankruptcies of California cities San Bernardino, Stockton, and Vallejo, and distinguishing the bankrupt cities from non-bankrupt comparison cities. A final section offers some conclusions about the use of simple indicator systems of this type to forecast local-government fiscal distress and bankruptcy filings.

Concepts of Fiscal Health and Stress

Like any other effort to measure and forecast some quantity or quality, careful efforts to measure and forecast fiscal health build upon some notion of what fiscal health is, and what its causes, effects, and observable manifestations are. The budgeting and financial management literature abounds with terminology to describe different constructs and dimensions of local-governments' economic, financial, or fiscal condition (Governmental Accounting Standards Board n.d.; Groves et al. 1981), health (Bird 2014; Hendrick 2004), sustainability (Chapman 2008), stress (Rubin 1982), strain (T. N. Clark 1994), pressure (Wolman and Davis 1980), distress (Kloha et al. 2005a), or crisis (Wolff 2004). These variations reflect the complex, multidimensional nature of the relevant construct(s) and the fundamental challenges of defining and measuring any form of generalized "health" or condition (Hendrick 2004; Jacob and Hendrick 2012; Justice and Scorsone 2012).

Fiscal health (or infirmity) itself can generally be understood in terms of fiscal capacities or abilities, and/or the organizational characteristics (financial or otherwise) that are believed to ensure or enhance those capacities. One widely cited approach to construing fiscal health in terms of capacity or ability is the four-dimensional framework associated with the International City/County Management Association's (ICMA) financial trend monitoring system (FTMS, Groves et al. 1981, 2003). The FTMS is grounded upon a framework that understands "financial condition" largely in terms of four capacities or "solvencies," reflecting a fitness-for-purpose view of fiscal health. In descending order of ease of measurement, the solvencies are as follows:

(a) *cash solvency*, the organization's ability to meet its immediate financial obligations;
(b) *budgetary solvency*, the ability to meet financial obligations over a full fiscal year;
(c) *long-term solvency*, the ability to meet financial obligations in future fiscal periods; and
(d) *service-level solvency*, the ability to finance an appropriate level of services (presumably over both the short and long term).[1]

The four-solvencies framework also encompasses the concept of *resiliency*, which makes it possible for organizations to maintain or quickly restore solvency in the face of disruptive events such as natural disasters, economic

[1] Service-level solvency is simultaneously the most significant and the least satisfying of the four dimensions—most significant in that delivering an appropriate level of public services is precisely the *raison d'être* for public organizations in the first place, but least satisfying in that the determination of appropriateness is subject to a vast number of spatially and temporally contingent variables of the organization's political, social, cultural, economic, and institutional context, and hence is virtually impossible to specify with precision even from within a jurisdiction, let alone predict from the outside. In a pluralistic society, it is often the case that unlike Justice Potter Stewart we cannot even say with confidence that we know it when we see it.

contractions, population increases or decreases, and other environmental changes (Groves et al. 2003, p. 2).

Independent work by the Public Sector Accounting Board (PSAB) of the Canadian Institute of Chartered Accountants identified a complementary set of three "elements of financial condition" (Public Sector Accounting Board 2007, pp. 6, 7). *Sustainability* roughly encompasses the four solvencies of the FTMS framework, with the additional stipulation that solvency be attainable "without increasing [an organization's] relative debt or tax burden on the economy within which it operates." *Flexibility* is the ability to incur debt and/or increase its tax share of a local economy in order to meet financial and service obligations. *Vulnerability* is "the degree to which a government is dependent on sources of funding outside its control or influence or is exposed to risks that could impair" its ability to meet its obligations. Like the FTMS framework, the PSAB approach effectively defines fiscal health in terms of the ability to meet financial obligations and deliver appropriate services in the short and long term.

Both the FTMS and the PSAB framework are explicitly framed in open-systems terms, so that a local-government's environmental conditions (legal, political, demographic, economic, natural, etc.) and its internal behavioral choices (political/policy-oriented and managerial) are modeled as both causes and effects of its financial performance in an ongoing environment–behavior–results–environment feedback loop (Groves et al. 2003, Fig. 22; also see Hendrick 2004). Local governments are understood in this approach as both shaping and shaped by their environments, such that a government's management practices and legislative policy choices are presumed to be partially constrained by its socio-economic and political environment. The resulting transformation of inputs through the organization's decisions and activities into organizational outputs yields both immediate financial results (operating surpluses and deficits, accumulated assets and liabilities) and short- and long-term influences on environmental conditions. Those financial results and environmental changes in turn influence the choice set and dispositions that shape further policies and management decisions. This is generally accepted as being the appropriate conceptual approach to modeling fiscal health (see, e.g., Bird 2014; Finkler et al. 2017; Hendrick 2004).

Concepts of fiscal health, or at any rate relative concerns with specific dimensions and subdimensions of it, may vary by stakeholder as well. Residents, taxpayers, and non-profit and for-profit organizations operating within a government's boundaries are of course concerned that the government be able to deliver appropriate quantities and quality of services without demanding insupportable levels of tax and fee revenue. Bondholders, other lenders, vendors, employees, and other creditors are concerned with the government's ability to continue making loan and lease payments, paying for goods and services received, paying current salaries and benefits, and paying promised future benefits such as defined-benefit pensions and post-employment health insurance. State governments are concerned with local-governments' ability to fulfill their service and financial commitments, and with potential indirect effects such as the possibility of "contagion" associated with defaults and bankruptcy. In the case of immediate financial or service failures, other units of government might be expected to pick up the financial and service-delivery pieces. In the case of default or bankruptcy, the concern is that a contagion effect might lead to increased borrowing costs for other local governments as participants in the municipal bond sector develop a generalized concern based on a particular case.

In sum, fiscal health is a multidimensional construct with a set of dimensions that minimally includes long- as well as short-term perspectives; narrowly financial as well as broader service-capacity requirements; environmental and behavioral, as well as financial quantities and qualities; and stakeholder-specific analytic priorities and capabilities.

Forecasting Fiscal Distress in Practice

Many approaches have been proposed and implemented over the years for measuring and forecasting local-governments' fiscal health (Bird 2014; Justice and Scorsone 2012). This is unsurprising in light of the multiple conceptual dimensions involved, and the large number of interested stakeholders, their substantive interests, and considerable variation across stakeholders as to what types of information and analysis can support decisions (Heald 2003; Justice et al. 2015). Familiar systems for measuring local-governments' fiscal health and supported at least some degree of decision-supporting forecasting include:

- The FTMS (Groves et al. 1981, 2003) and other systems developed for expert use by local government managers and other knowledgeable stakeholders (e.g., Brown 1993; Ives 2006; Maher and Nollenberger 2009; Mead 2006; Wang et al. 2007);
- Systems developed by academic experts for use by other academic experts as dependent or independent variables in analyses of the causes and effects of government's financial condition (e.g., Ladd and Yinger 1989);
- The credit ratings produced by such third-party analytic organizations as the nationally recognized statistical rating organizations (NRSOs) Fitch,

Moody's, and Standard & Poor's to provide municipal-bond investors with a simple letter-grade assessment of how likely they are to be repaid; and
- Systems developed by and for state governments, to facilitate state oversight and guide decisions about whether and when to intervene in local governments' financial affairs (Coe 2008; Kloha et al. 2005b; Pew Charitable Trusts 2016).

These approaches vary a great deal in their information and analysis requirements and in the ways they may be used by interested stakeholders. This reflects not necessarily the absolute superiority or deficiency of any specific approach, but rather the need to balance parsimony and conservation of attention with nuanced and predictively valid incorporation of relevant information in ways that are appropriately adapted to information availability, purpose, and audience (Bird 2014; Clark and Chan 1990; Justice and Scorsone 2012).

For instance, bond ratings are produced by teams of professional analysts who acquire and analyze a large amount of information about organizational and environmental characteristics including a government's financial position and results, its policies and management practices, its local economy, and relevant political institutions, as well as characteristics of specific bond issues. This ostensibly complex and sophisticated analysis is then reduced for consumption by bond investors to a basic letter grade, meant to represent the likelihood that a specific financial obligation will be met. The FTMS similarly uses a significant amount of both published and internal information about the government and its environment, but the outputs of the FTMS are a series of trend indicators that do not have a simple, single normative interpretation and are not combined into an index or overall score. The design of each system reflects its intended use. Bond ratings (when calculated and reported in good faith) provide a simple, concise way for investors to know whether experts consider a particular government or bond issue a safe bet. The FTMS generates a more nuanced set of dynamic indicators that managers can use to understand their government's ability to meet all of its financial and service commitments within the constraints of local circumstances, but does not communicate a simple measure of status or rank to attention-constrained or inexpert observers.

Every system in its design and implementation involves some tradeoffs, whether explicit or implicit, between quality or effectiveness (accuracy, predictive validity, reliability, comparability, and timeliness) and feasibility (data availability, computational demands, complexity of interpretation, and suitability to particular audiences). It is often necessary to conserve analytic attention, whether because academic researchers need to build datasets that include summary variables capturing levels of fiscal health, or because state-government oversight requires that a small number of staff hours be used to assess the fiscal health of large numbers of local governments. Accordingly, many fiscal-indicator systems developed for use by academic experts as well as state-government oversight bodies are designed to simplify data gathering, analysis, and interpretation. Such systems frequently use already-available raw data and fairly simple arithmetic to generate a relatively straightforward categorization or numeric index score that facilitates comparison and ranking of many local governments and/or supports simple determinations of whether external intervention is appropriate.

Choices of data inputs, analytic methods, and presentation of results will inevitably reflect explicit and implicit assumptions about both the most important dimensions of fiscal health—often audience-specific—and the measurable indicators and predictors of those dimensions of health. Major dimensions of indicator system design choices include measurement focus and basis of accounting; interpretive approaches, computational requirements, and decision rules; whether information is collected about an organization's environment and behavior as well as its financial quantities; data requirements; and the number and types of comparison used.

Financial Reporting Approaches: Financial Entities and Bases of Accounting

The current generally accepted accounting-principles (GAAP) reporting model for U.S. state and local governments is based on Governmental Accounting Standards Board Statement 34 (GASB-34), which took effect for larger governments beginning in fiscal 2002. In a "sweeping change in government reporting" (Denison et al. 2002, p. 137), GASB-34 requires the reporting of government-wide, accrual-basis, whole-of-government financial information in addition to the presentation of fund-based information that represented the previous reporting approach. In principle, traditional fund accounting is expected to be significantly less comprehensive and informative about fiscal health than the government-wide, full-accrual standard of GASB-34. Among other things, the new statements provided information on long-term governmental liabilities and assets, and changes in net assets. Thus, for example, annual increases in long-term debt, such as the unfunded post-employment obligations that have figured in most municipal bankruptcies, became visible on balance sheets and in income statements. Among indicator systems grounded in the GASB-34 reporting model, some make use of information reported for business-type activities and the entire primary government reported entity (e.g., Mead 2006) while others focus only on governmental activities (e.g., Ohio's monitoring system as applied to city governments [Ohio counties are not required to report on a GAAP basis]).

Still, not all local governments in all states are required to report on a GAAP basis (Mead 2008), and many popular indicators systems either predate the current GAAP (e.g., Brown 1993; Groves et al. 2003; Kloha et al. 2005a) or were developed for use in states that don't consistently require or enforce GAAP reporting by local governments (e.g., Michigan). Assessments that focus on data from a government's general fund have the advantage of using data that are available for virtually any U.S. state or local government, but at the expense of excluding information from other funds (which in some instances may capture a very significant share of a local-government's operating activity) and the long-term asset and liability information that is ignored by the modified-accrual financial reporting used for governmental funds.

Data Reduction and Decision Rules

Some systems, such as the FTMS or the monitoring systems used by North Carolina and Florida, are not designed to generate a single index score or categorical assessment of fiscal health, but instead require case-by-case qualitative assessment and expert evaluation. Other approaches use algorithmic approaches to compute index scores, rankings, or other types of categorization that can be assigned using decision rules that do not require case-by-case judgmental interpretation.

Systems that rely on simple categorizations of individual data points' values and/or basic ratio and index computations are likely to be easier and faster to use by non-specialists than approaches that require more advanced computations and software (such as Hendrick 2004; Ladd and Yinger 1989) or on deep, and often jurisdiction-specific, professional experience and expertise (such as the FTMS). For example, the Michigan system generates an additive index number ranging from 0 to 10, which is then used to categorize a local government as being fiscally healthy (0–4 points), subject to "fiscal watch" (5) or "fiscal warning" (6–7) or experiencing a "fiscal emergency" (8–10) (Kloha et al. 2005a).

Units of Observation

While the open-systems model of local governments is at least implicit in any notion of fiscal health, not all indicator systems attempt to incorporate directly non-financial information about local-government organizations, their environments, or the decisions and behavior of their elected and non-elected officials.

Data Requirements

A closely related dimension is the availability of the data required to compute individual indicators, index scores, rankings, and/or categorizations. Some systems require information that is not typically available externally. The FTMS, for example, requires a significant amount of financial information that is usually available only within the local government. Several state monitoring systems use information that local governments are required to submit to the state, which might or might not also be available in published financial reports and statistical compendia. Systems that use information available from public financial reports and/or published sources of organizational and environmental data (such as the Census Bureau) may be better suited for use by external researchers and monitors.

Types of Comparison

It has been said that, "Almost all of financial analysis involves comparisons of one sort or another. Measures of a government's financial condition are compared with experts' standards, legal ceilings or floors, measures for the same organization at different points in time, and measures for a set of similar organizations" (Berne and Schramm 1986, p. 85). Comparison of an organization's financial information to simple rules of thumb, legal standards, or other fixed benchmarks may require less data than comparisons to larger peer groups. Peer comparisons are often facilitated by the availability of databases compiled by some states, or the financial-indicators databases compiled and distributed by the GFOA, but those databases do always include all of the desired indicators, or all of the peers, or the required entity scope or basis of accounting for every application. Comparisons over time, whether evaluating trends or simply comparing two points in time, similarly require comparable data for all periods being compared.

State Monitoring Approaches

U.S. states' systems for local-government fiscal monitoring and forecasting vary in their conceptual and measurement strategies. Some use information that local governments are required to report to the state, which might or might not be the same as would appear in GAAP-compliant financial reports. The data and computed indicators might measure organizations' finances alone, or might include their environments and behavior as well; might include whole-of-government quantities, governmental funds, or only the general fund; and might or might not include comparisons over time or to peer governments. North Carolina's approach is fairly high-touch in the evaluation stage (as described by Coe 2007) and relies on state examiners' interactions with and expert judgment about local governments, while other states rely on index scores or categorizations to narrow their focus for extensive hands-on staff work to include only governments whose scores indicate impending trouble (Cahill et al. 1994; Kloha et al. 2005b).

The literature abounds in examinations of concepts and measurement challenges (e.g., Hendrick 2004; Jacob and Hendrick 2012; Justice and Scorsone 2012; Stonecash and McAfee 1981; Wang et al. 2007); normative, best-practice advice (e.g., Coe 2008; Pew Charitable Trusts 2016); and how-to advice for designing systems to meet the needs of specific audiences and purposes (e.g., T. N. Clark and Chan 1990; Kloha et al. 2005a), but provides fewer instances of systematic, comparative evaluation of monitoring-and-forecasting systems. Some recent work has examined the power of individual financial indicators to forecast municipal bankruptcies (e.g., Singla et al. 2014; Stone et al. 2015), but there has not been a great deal of comparative evaluation of state indicator systems' predictive efficacy to date.

A Test of Three Systems

For purposes of this preliminary investigation, we evaluated three indicator systems developed for use by state governments—two targeted to Michigan (Crosby and Robbins 2013; Kloha et al. 2005a) and one in use by Ohio (Ohio Auditor of State 2018)—using historical data. All three tested systems use financial statements and other readily available public information to categorize local governments' fiscal health and forecast fiscal distress in order to identify candidates for state intervention. The historical data were drawn from nine California cities' CAFRs for the period 2002–2013, which included a full business cycle and the bankruptcy filings of three of those cities. Two matched non-bankrupt cities were identified for comparison to each bankrupt city.

We began by generating a list of more than 50 systems developed by experts and state government to generate measures of governments' fiscal health for use in a range of scholarly research and public-administration and -policy applications. Although almost certainly incomplete, this list provided a reasonable starting point that allowed us to get a perspective on the range of conceptual approaches used by a variety of analysts and to explore the range of data and computational requirements involved.

We then narrowed the list down in two stages. First, we identified a short list of candidates that met to varying degrees our broad criteria of targeting systems that

- had some history of discussion in the literature,
- were generally appropriate for generating scores or rankings that are easy to interpret,
- used publicly available data and publicly documented procedures to generate results and interpretations,
- had modest computational demands, and
- were designed for or appeared to be readily adaptable to use by state governments for predictive oversight of local governments.

Thus, for instance, the FTMS was excluded both because of its complexity and because it requires information not normally available to people outside the organization of interest. The FTMS also generates outputs that can be complex to interpret. The bond rating agencies' approaches generate a simple letter grade and use information that should in principle be as available to the public as it is to the agencies' analysts, but they do not employ procedures that are well enough documented to be reliably reproduced by others. Hendrick's (2004) approach uses secondary data but imposes significant computational demands (although we included it in our short list because of its high quality and careful documentation, we eliminated it in the second round of narrowing).

In the second stage we chose three systems to test from a short list of 15. Additional criteria we applied to select approaches from the short list included feasibility for our developing research approach. Thus, we eliminated systems that would have required more data or computation than we could reasonably acquire and perform within the resource and time constraints of this exploratory study. The system developed by Wang, Dennis, and Tu (2007) and its modification by Arnett (2011, 2014) as critiqued by Clark (2015) met all of our initial screening criteria, but require standardization across a larger peer group than our nine-city sample provides or our ten-year analysis period allows for (see below for details of our city sample and research design).[2] Various versions of and updates to the Brown Ten-Point Test (Brown 1993, 1996; Maher and Nollenberger 2009; Mead 2006) similarly required peer-group comparisons that we could not feasibly generate for the present project.

[2] We expect to evaluate these two system variants in a future project, however.

Of five state-government systems cited by Coe (2008) as using financial reporting data to generate predictive information, in states identified by Mead (2008) as being in states that require cities to generate financial reports that comply with generally accepted accounting principles (GAAP), three (Florida, Maryland, and North Carolina) are not designed to generate a summary index or categorization, and Pennsylvania uses information that is not available in comprehensive annual financial reports (CAFRs).

The development of the system currently in use in Michigan was extensively documented in the scholarly as well as practitioner-focused literature (Kleine et al. 2002, 2003; Kloha et al. 2005a, 2005b), and has also been the subject of considerable follow-up literature (e.g., Crosby and Robbins 2010, 2013; Plerhoples and Scorsone 2010, 2011). Both the current system, in use for several years, and the modified system proposed by Crosby and Robbins (2010, 2013) were selected for testing. Both systems are straightforward to use to compute an index number for each local government, using publicly available information, and both are designed to generate concise, easily interpreted guidance for decision makers and other stakeholders based on the index score. The system in use by the state of Ohio as of 2017 similarly is well documented (see the numerous documents and media files available at https://www.ohioauditor.gov/FHI/default.html) and uses simple calculations based on publicly available information to compute a series of indicators and compile them into an easily interpreted index score. Although the Ohio system does not produce an index score, it does have a simple set of decision rules for determining whether a local government has an "elevated risk" of fiscal stress based on the values of its 17 indicators.

Table 14.1 summarizes and compares selected characteristics of the three systems. All three emphasize financial indicators, although the Michigan system includes three environmental indicators (changes in population and taxable property value) and the Ohio system one behavioral indicator (failure to comply with the state's budget and financial reporting requirements for local governments). The Michigan system relies on information available in fund-based financial reports, while eight of the ten indicators in the Crosby and Robbins proposal are drawn from the government-wide, accrual-basis statements introduced by GASB-34. Use of government-wide data was a key design feature that Crosby and Robbins (2013) argued should improve accuracy in measuring fiscal health. The Ohio system's 17 indicators draw upon both fund-based and government-wide data. The three environmental indicators in the Michigan system use comparisons over time in real (inflation-adjusted) terms. Eight financial indicators in Ohio's system use short-term current-dollar trends or comparisons over time, and its behavioral indicator

Table 14.1 Three fiscal-indicator systems

	Michigan (Kleine et al. 2002, 2003)	Crosby and Robbins (2010, 2013)	Ohio Auditor of State (2018)
Total number of indicators	9	10	17
Environmental	3	0	0
Behavioral	0	0	1
Financial	6	10	16
Government-wide	0	8	6
Fund-based	6	2	10
Indicators of trends or changes over time	3 Environmental (constant-dollar)	0	8 Financial (current-dollar); 1 Behavioral
Peer-group comparisons	1 Environmental; 3 Financial	2 Financial (implicit)	0

includes a three-year lookback. Crosby and Robbins include no comparisons over time. One of the Michigan environmental and three of the financial indicators are based on peer-group comparisons, as are two of the Crosby and Robbins indicators. More information on each system's design is provided in Appendix.

As a test of the models' forecast accuracy and usefulness, we applied the three selected models to an intentional sample comprising 12 years' (fiscal 2002–2013) data for nine California cities. California is the home state of three general-purpose municipal governments that entered Chap. 9 bankruptcy during or in the aftermath of the 2007–2009 Great Recession, and of 415 non-bankrupt cities from which a matched comparison group could be selected. Vallejo entered bankruptcy in May 2008 (fiscal 2008), Stockton in June 2012 (fiscal 2012), and San Bernardino in August 2012 (fiscal 2013).[3] For each bankrupt city, we selected for comparison two California cities that were similar in population and metropolitan context, but did not encounter fiscal problems that led to bankruptcy or other third-party interventions.[4]

The first step in selecting comparison cities was to select California cities in the population ranges from 50,000 to 150,000 for comparison to Vallejo (pop. 116,508), 150,000 to 250,000 for San Bernardino (pop. 211,076), and

[3] A fourth California municipal bankruptcy filer, Mammoth Lakes, was excluded because of its small size (8286) and because it was dismissed from the bankruptcy process shortly after it was filed.

[4] The neutral evaluation (mediation) process and declaration of a fiscal emergency are the two alternatives available as precursors to Chap. 9 filings under California law (Kuptez 2014). None of the six comparator cities has to date entered bankruptcy, declared a fiscal emergency, or undertaken a neutral evaluation (mediation) process under California AB 506.

Table 14.2 California cities in the sample

City, county	Population in 2010	Land area (sq. mi.)	Fiscal-distress interventions
Vallejo, Solano County	116,508	30.2	Chapter 9: entered May 2008, exited August 2011
Concord, Contra Costa County	122,676	30.6	None
Roseville, Placer County	120,593	36.2	None
Stockton, San Joaquin County	293,515	54.7	Chapter 9: entered June 2012, exited February 2015
Anaheim, Orange County	341,034	49.8	None
Riverside, Riverside County	306,779	81.1	None
San Bernardino, San Bernardino County	211,076	58.8	Chapter 9: entered August 2012, plan filed May 2015
Modesto, Stanislaus County	202,290	36.9	None
Santa Rosa, Sonoma County	168,856	41.3	None

250,000 to 350,000 for Stockton (pop. 293,515). As a way to control for regional- as well state-level features of cities' legal, political, and economic settings that might influence fiscal health, each of the nine cities in the sample is the largest city in its county and the central city of its metropolitan statistical area (MSA), but a satellite city within a larger, multi-MSA combined statistical area (CSA). Screening for population and metropolitan context yielded 13 potential comparison cities for Vallejo, three for San Bernardino, and two for Stockton. Land area was a final criterion to narrow further the comparison groups for San Bernardino and Vallejo. The resulting sample includes Anaheim and Riverside as comparators to Stockton, Modesto and Santa Rosa as comparators to San Bernardino, and Concord and Roseville as comparators to Vallejo. Table 14.2 lists the nine California cities in the full sample.

The period July 2002 through June 2013 captures a full business cycle as well as the bankruptcy entry dates for the cities of Vallejo, Stockton, and San Bernardino. We computed and interpreted fiscal-health indicators and index scores for each city in each fiscal year from 2004 through 2013 (2002 and 2003 data were used to compute indicators that involved over-time comparisons), and compared those assessments to what we know in hindsight to have been the condition of each city at each point in time (on the road to bankruptcy or not, in bankruptcy or not, exiting from bankruptcy or not).

Our methodology for evaluating and comparing indicator systems built on the approach used by Kloha, Kleine, and Weissert (Kloha et al. 2005a) to test their proposal for the Michigan system by using a sample of historical data to evaluate its effectiveness at forecasting fiscal distress. For each of the three systems, we first developed a data-entry template and used it as a guide to gather from each city's published financial statements for fiscal years 2001–2002 through 2012–2013 the data points required to compute indicators and overall city fiscal health scores. The cities in our sample post on their websites CAFRs that cover all those years with few exceptions, and we were able to obtain all the required pages of other CAFRs from the cities by email.

The data input templates and spreadsheet formulas for computing indicator and summary-index scores did require some adaptation to the available data sources and differences in major local-government revenue sources for California cities versus cities in Ohio and Michigan, but none that seriously undermined the basic logics or design assumptions of the three systems. We were able to use available published documentation and author queries to confirm details of each system's core concepts, operational definitions, computational procedures, and peer-group and other comparative benchmarks. Key adaptations included adjusting state-specific benchmarks and computing revenue indicators in ways that recognize the differences between California cities' major revenue sources and those used in Ohio and Michigan.

Once the templates were filled in and the indicators computed, we performed a qualitative assessment of the system's performance by evaluating the indicator scores in light of our historical knowledge of the sample cities' experience or avoidance of severe fiscal distress (as indicated by bankruptcy) and the business cycle over the time period. We reviewed each system's scores for each city over the ten years from 2004 to 2013, in order to evaluate the extent to which each system (1) effectively predicted the impending bankruptcies of Vallejo, Stockton, and San Bernardino, and (2) effectively distinguished between those severely distressed cities' conditions and the conditions of their respective non-bankrupt comparison cities. The next section presents results of that testing.

Results

The three indicator systems exhibit a wide range of forecasting performance in this application, ranging from quite good in the Ohio case to surprisingly poor in the cases of the Michigan and Crosby and Robbins systems. Tables 14.3, 14.4, and 14.5 present summary index scores for ten fiscal years (2004–2013), computed using the Michigan (2002–2005), Crosby and

Table 14.3 Index scores for nine California cities using the Michigan system

	2004	2005	2006	2007	2008	2009	2010	2011	2012	2013
Vallejo (entered bankruptcy May 2008)	5*	0	3	2	4†	5*	4	3	3	2
Concord	1	1	1	1	3	5*	6*	7*	5*	3
Roseville	0	1	4	4	3	3	4	4	6*	6*
Stockton (entered bankruptcy June 2012)	0	0	3	3	1	2	1	2	4†	7*
Anaheim	5*	0	0	2	2	2	1	1	2	3
Riverside	7*	7*	0	0	3	4	4	5*	5*	5*
San Bernardino (entered bankruptcy August 2012)	4	3	3	0	0	7*	6*	6*	6*	7*,†
Modesto	4	5*	4	2	0	0	0	1	1	2
Santa Rosa	0	0	0	0	0	0	0	3	2	1

Note: Interpretations of index point scores are as follows (Kleine et al. 2002):
8–10 points: "Fiscal emergency"
6–7 points: "Fiscal warning"
5 points: "Fiscal watch"
0–4 points: "Fiscally Healthy"

Table 14.4 Index scores for nine California cities using the Crosby and Robbins (2013) system

	2004	2005	2006	2007	2008	2009	2010	2011	2012	2013
Vallejo (entered bankruptcy May 2008)	4	2	4	5*	3†	4	4	2	3	3
Concord	1	1	0	1	1	0	2	2	2	2
Roseville	2	2	2	3	4	2	3	3	3	2
Stockton (entered bankruptcy June 2012)	3	3	1	4	3	4	4	4	6*,†	5*
Anaheim	7*	6*	8*	7*	7*	6*	7*	7*	7*	7*
Riverside	4	4	5*	5*	7*	8*	7	6*	8*	7*
San Bernardino (entered bankruptcy August 2012)	2	3	5*	4	4	4	5*	4	5*	3†
Modesto	2	2	3	3	2	3	3	3	3	4
Santa Rosa	2	2	2	3	4	4	4	3	3	3

Note: Interpretations of index point scores are as follows (Crosby and Robbins 2013):
8–10 points: "Fiscal stress"
5–7 points: "Fiscal watch"
0–4 points: "Neutral"

Table 14.5 Index scores for nine California cities using the Ohio Auditor's System (Rescaled)

	2004	2005	2006	2007	2008	2009	2010	2011	2012	2013
Vallejo (entered bankruptcy May 2008)	6*	3	4	7*	8*,†	7*	6*	4	4	4
Concord	2	0	2	1	2	5*	7*	5*	3	1
Roseville	2	1	1	2	1	4	4	5*	1	5
Stockton (entered bankruptcy June 2012)	4	4	2	5*	6*	8*	8*	9*	6*,†	4
Anaheim	4	4	3	4	4	5	5	6*	3	2
Riverside	4	5*	4	4	4	5*	5*	5*	2	5*
San Bernardino (entered bankruptcy August 2012)	7*	5*	5*	5*	5*	8*	9*	8*	6*	7*,†
Modesto	6*	4	2	6*	4	6*	6*	5*	6*	4
Santa Rosa	3	1	1	2	2	5*	4	2	1	2

Note: Interpretations of index point scores as rescaled here to range from 0 to 10 for ease of comparison are as follows (see Appendix for details of computation and rescaling):
5–10 points: "Higher" fiscal stress or "elevated risk" of fiscal stress

Robbins (2010, 2013), and Ohio (2018, rescaled to a range of 1–10 points for ease of comparison) systems respectively. In each table, the year a city entered bankruptcy is flagged with a dagger (†), and index scores that indicate fiscal "watch," "stress" or an "elevated risk" thereof, "warning," or "emergency" with asterisks (∗).

The original Michigan system (see Table 14.3) appears to do a good job of predicting San Bernardino's bankruptcy, showing "fiscal warning"-level scores beginning in fiscal 2009, a full four years before the bankruptcy filing. At the same time, it distinguishes quite well between San Bernardino and its two comparator cities, Modesto and Santa Rosa, neither of which was flagged as a false positive by the system. On the other hand, this system fails to predict the bankruptcies of Vallejo or Stockton, and in fact indicates fiscal "watch" or "warning" more frequently for their comparison cities, Concord, Roseville, Anaheim, and Riverside. In particular, it generates what can be interpreted as false positives for Concord over 2009–2012, Roseville over 2012–2013, and Riverside in 2004–2005 and 2011–2013. Even more than a failure to distinguish, this appears more like an inversion.

The Crosby and Robbins proposal for an enhanced Michigan system (see Table 14.4) provides little or no warning of the impending bankruptcies of Vallejo, Stockton, or San Bernardino, and generates particularly strong false-positive scores for Anaheim (in contrast to the Michigan system) and Riverside (similarly to the Michigan system). On the other hand, it does differentiate relatively well between Vallejo and San Bernardino and their respective comparison jurisdictions, including Roseville, for which the Michigan system generated a slight false positive. For those six cities, a recalibration of the scoring labels could conceivably yield correct summary evaluations for bankrupts and non-bankrupts, although it might then tip Modesto and Santa Rosa into false-positive territory.

Ohio's system (see Table 14.5) performs fairly well in forecasting bankruptcies. Stockton and San Bernardino are predicted very effectively, but Vallejo less effectively. Index scores for non-bankrupt Roseville, Anaheim, and Santa Rosa very clearly distinguish them from the distressed cities. Index scores for Concord in 2009–2011; Riverside since 2009; and Modesto for 2004, 2007, and 2009–2012, verge on the false positive, but nearly all of those dates correspond to the period of peak impact of the Great Recession on state and local governments' budgets.

Conclusions

Of the three systems tested here, only the Ohio system effectively forecasts the historical bankruptcies of Vallejo, Stockton, and San Bernardino and distinguishes well between the three bankrupts and six comparison cities that did not undergo bankruptcy or other third-party fiscal interventions. Distinguishing characteristics of Ohio's system compared to the Michigan and Crosby and Robbins indexes include its significantly greater number of indicators; its use of both whole-of-government, accrual-based, and governmental-fund, modified-accrual, information; and its extensive use of indicators of short-term trends and changes between reporting periods.

This may to some degree reflect Ohio's somewhat different positioning with respect to the quality-parsimony tradeoff. Certainly that set of indicators was the most laborious of the three to compile, compute, and transform into an index score. But it was not unduly burdensome, and in fact gathering the data by hand from PDF files of CAFRs was the most time-consuming part of the exercise. Electronic reporting, whether by state mandate or by changes in reporting technology such as XBRL implementation, could significantly reduce the data collection effort. In this case, it is possible that less is in fact less, and a less parsimonious approach is required for forecasting, but the performance of the Ohio system suggests that relatively good performance can be achieved with a system that is still very manageable.

There also were differences in the specific correct and incorrect forecasts made by the three systems. This indicates that there are important determinants of bankruptcy that these systems do not capture fully. Some of it may be that entering bankruptcy is the result of political and managerial factors as well as fiscal ones (Singla et al. 2014). (Although it might be tempting therefore to credit the Ohio system's superior performance to its inclusion of a behavioral indicator, that indicator was in fact favorable for every city-year in the sample.) It also seems likely that the systems are not in fact measuring the same thing. Given their parsimony, these systems might even each capture relatively well different facets of the larger complexity of local-government finances without encompassing the whole. Certainly it is not unheard of for organizations to be fiscally healthy in terms of one of the four FTMS solvencies—say, cash solvency—but not in others—say, long-term solvency. Compiling the data for this analysis revealed a surprisingly small overlap in data inputs and indicators across the three systems.

Another surprise was that the Crosby and Robbins system did not perform significantly better than the original Michigan system. Crosby and Robbins (2013) make a good case for the design of their index, particularly its use of information drawn from the government-wide, accrual-based statements. GASB-34 seemed to many observers to promise a major transformation and improvement in the meaningfulness of state and local governments' financial reporting. Our practice of teaching government financial management and analyzing government financial reports suggests strongly that the current reporting model does yield more and better information than its predecessors about governments' financial results and health. Perhaps the government-wide statements, economic resources and full-accrual measurement focus and basis of accounting, and reporting of long-term assets and liabilities required by GASB 34 give us an improved understanding of an organization's financial past and present without necessarily telling us more about its future.

It should also be acknowledged that these monitoring systems—especially the Michigan and Crosby and Robbins indexes—are to some extent simply compilations of financial ratios, and therefore subject to all the limitations of ratio analysis as "an art form rather than a precise science" (Finkler et al. 2017, p. 535). Again, the incorporation of several comparisons over time is a distinctive characteristic of the Ohio approach. Information about trajectories might be more useful for forecasting than static moment-in-time stocks, single-period flows, and ratios. Certainly, that is the logic of the FTMS, and the basis of many parsimonious but effective approaches to forecasting (see Williams and Calabrese 2016, for a review).

Appendix

This appendix provides more information about each monitoring system's specific indicators and index computation.

Table 14.6 lists the indicators used in Michigan's system (as described in Kleine et al. 2002, 2003; Kloha et al. 2005a). All three of the environmental indicators (numbers 1–3) make explicit comparisons over time. The system's six financial indicators (numbers 4–9 in the table) include three (4, 7, and 9) that are peer-referenced, and one of the three constant-dollar interperiod comparisons also uses a peer benchmark (number 3). We calculated those indicators for the California sample by using the sample's mean values as the benchmarks. The index is computed by summing the individual indicator scores. An index score of 8–10 points indicates a "fiscal emergency"; 6 and 7, a "fiscal warning"; 5, a "fiscal watch"; and 0–4, "fiscally healthy" or "neutral."

The system of indicators proposed by Crosby and Robbins (2010, 2013) as an improvement over the Michigan system uses ten indicators to generate an additive index than can range from 0 to 10 points. Table 14.7 lists the indicators. Of the ten indicators, nine draw information from the government-wide statements, and one (number 6) is for the general fund only. None makes comparisons across time. Two (numbers 7 and 8) are implicitly peer referenced (D. Robbins, personal communication) by setting their benchmarks at approximately the means for all Michigan jurisdictions. For the California application we modified the benchmark values to the means for our sample cities: $1071 for number 7, and $1715 for number 8. An index score of 8–10 points indicates "fiscal stress"; 5–7, a "fiscal watch"; and 0–4, "neutral."

Ohio's indicator system, summarized in Table 14.8, includes 16 financial indicators and one behavioral indicator. Of the financial indicators, ten are drawn from funds statements (we used government-wide information as a substitute for two of these, because of data-availability limitations), five from the government-wide statements, and one from the notes (at least it was for our project; Ohio appears to maintain a database of financial information inputted by local governments). Eight of the indicators make interperiod comparisons, of which three assess short-term trends (three fiscal periods). Ohio's indicator system in its native form does not generate an index score. If six indicators are at "critical" values or eight indicators have "cautionary" or "critical" values, the subject local government is judged to have an "elevated risk" of fiscal distress. For purposes of comparing systems, we rescaled the Ohio system to an index score ranging from 0 to 10 points, with five point representing the threshold for "elevated risk."

Table 14.6 Component indicators of the Michigan Fiscal Stress Index

Indicator	Definition	Scoring
1. Population growth	Current-year population—population two years prior	Change < 0 = 1; Change ≥ 0 = 0
2. Real taxable value growth	Current-year real taxable property value—real taxable property value two years prior (using BEA SLG consumption and gross investment price index)	Change < 0 = 1; Change ≥ 0 = 0
3. Large real taxable value decrease	Current-year real taxable property value—real taxable property value two years prior is more than a 4% decrease (approx. one standard deviation below mean for cities and villages)	Change < −0.04 = 1; Change ≥ −0.04 = 0
4. General fund expenditures as a percentage of taxable value	General fund expenditures/taxable property value is > 5% (approx. one standard deviation above mean for cities and villages)	Ratio ≥ 0.05 = 1; Ratio < 0.05 = 0
5. General fund operating deficit	(General fund expenditures-general fund revenue)/general fund revenue for the current year is < −1%	Ratio < −0.01 = 1; Ratio ≥ −0.01 = 0
6. Prior general fund operating deficits	(General fund expenditures-general fund revenue)/general fund revenue for the two prior years	For each year: Ratio < −0.01 = 1; Ratio ≥ −0.01 = 0 (score up to 2 points)
7. Fund balance of the general fund	General fund balance/general fund revenue is < 13% (approx. 1/2 standard deviation below mean for cities and villages)	Ratio < 0.13 = 1; Ratio ≥ 0.13 = 0
8. Fund deficits in current or prior year	Negative fund balance in any major governmental fund for current or prior year	Any value < 0 = 1; All values ≥ 0 = 0
9. General long-term deficit as a percentage of taxable value	General long-term debt/current taxable value for the current year is > 6% (approx. one standard deviation above mean for cities and villages)	Ratio > 0.06 = 1;Ratio ≤ 0.05 = 0

Table 14.7 Component indicators of the Crosby and Robbins Fiscal Stress Index

Indicator	Definition	Scoring
1. Quick ratio, governmental activities (GTA)	GTA cash and investments/GTA current liabilities	Ratio $< 1 = 1$; Ratio $\geq 1 = 0$
2. Quick ratio, business-type activities (BTA)	BTA cash and investments/BTA current activities	Ratio $< 1 = 1$; Ratio $\geq 1 = 0$
3. Revenue-to-expenditure ratio, governmental funds	Governmental funds' total revenues/total expenditures	Ratio $< 0.95 = 1$; Ratio $\geq 0.95 = 0$
4. Revenue-to-expenses ratio, BTA	BTA program and general revenues/total expenses	Ratio $< 0.95 = 1$; Ratio $\geq 0.95 = 0$
5. Intergovernmental revenue dependency, GTA	GTA operating and capital grants/program and general revenues	Ratio $> 0.25 = 1$; Ratio $\leq 0.25 = 0$
6. Unreserved fund balance to expenditures ratio, general fund (GF)	GF unassigned or unreserved fund balance/total expenditures	Ratio $< 0.25 = 1$; Ratio $\geq 0.25 = 0$
7. Long-term debt per capita, GTA	GTA long-term liabilities/population, benchmark $\approx$ peer-group mean	Ratio $> 400 = 1$;Ratio $\leq 400 = 0$
8. Long-term debt per capita, BTA	BTA long-term liabilities/population, benchmark $\approx$ peer-group mean	Ratio $> 600 = 1$;Ratio $\leq 600 = 0$
9. Debt-to-net asset ratio, GTA	GTA long-term liabilities/total net position or assets	Ratio $> 0.25 = 1$;Ratio $\leq 0.25 = 0$
10. Debt-to-net asset ratio, BTA	BTA long-term liabilities/total net position or assets	Ratio $> 0.4 = 1$;Ratio $\leq 0.4 = 0$

Table 14.8 Component indicators of the Ohio Auditor of State Index

Indicator	"Critical" score	"Cautionary" score
1. Unrestricted net assets/position of governmental type activities (GTA)	≤0	One-year decline
2. Unassigned fund balance of the general fund	≤0	One-year decline
3. Change in unrestricted net assets/position for GTA	Negative pattern or rapidly declining three-year trend	Declining three-year trend
4. Change in unassigned fund balance of the GF		
5. GF fund balance/GF revenues	≤4% or rapidly declining trend	≤8% or declining trend
6. Decline in GF property tax revenue	Declining trend	One-year decline
7. Decline in GF income or sales tax revenue		
8. GF [annual surplus]	<0%	≤5%
9. GTA general revenues/net expenses	<100%	Declining trend
10. GF intergovernmental revenues/ total revenues	≥20%	15–20%
11. Accumulated depreciation/total depreciable assets	≥70%	50–70%
12. Governmental funds' DS expend/total revenues	≥15%	12–15%
13. GTA UNA/average daily expenses	≤0 days	<30 days
14. GF unassigned fund balance/ avg. daily expend		
15. GF Cash & Investments/avg. daily expend		
16. GTA Total liabilities/total net assets/position*	Ratio ≥ 70% or TNA < 0	50–70%
17. Budgetary or accounting non-compliance	Three years or more	Current year

References

Advisory Commission on Intergovernmental Relations. (1985). *Bankruptcies, defaults, and other local government financial emergencies* (A-99). Washington, DC.

Arnett, S. (2011). *Fiscal stress in the US states: An analysis of measures and responses.* Ph.D. dissertation, Georgia Institute of Technology, Atlanta, GA. Retrieved from http://hdl.handle.net/1853/42860 Available from Georgia Institute of Technology SMARTech database.

Arnett, S. (2014). *State fiscal condition: Ranking the 50 states*. Retrieved from http://mercatus.org/publication/state-fiscal-condition-ranking-50-states.

Atwell, M. S., Fehr, S., Huh, K., & Russell, A. (2013). *The state role in local government financial distress*. Washington, DC. Retrieved from http://www.pewtrusts.org/en/research-and-analysis/reports/2013/07/23/the-state-role-in-local-government-financial-distress.

Berne, R., & Schramm, R. (1986). *The financial analysis of governments*. Englewood Cliffs, NJ: Prentice-Hall.

Bird, R. M. (2014). Reflections on measuring urban fiscal health. *Municipal Finance Journal, 35*(3), 47–78.

Brown, K. W. (1993). The 10-point test of financial condition: Toward an easy-to-use assessment tool for smaller cities. *Government Finance Review, 9*(6), 21–27.

Brown, K. W. (1996). Trends in key ratios using the GFOA financial indicators databases 1989–1993. *Government Finance Review, 12*(6), 30–34.

Cahill, A. G., James, J. A., Lavigne, J. E., & Stacey, A. (1994). State government responses to municipal fiscal distress: A brave new world for state-local intergovernmental relations. *Public Productivity & Management Review, 17*(3), 253–264.

Chapman, J. I. (2008). State and local fiscal sustainability: The challenges. *Public Administration Review, 68*(s1), S115–S131.

Clark, T. N. (1994, June). Municipal fiscal strain: Indicators and causes. *Government Finance Review, 10*, 27–30.

Clark, B. Y. (2015). Evaluating the validity and reliability of the financial condition index for local governments. *Public Budgeting & Finance, 35*(2), 66–88. https://doi.org/10.1111/pbaf.12063.

Clark, T. N., & Chan, J. L. (1990). Monitoring cities: Building an indicator system for municipal analysis. In T. N. Clark (Ed.), *Monitoring local governments: How personal computers can help systematize municipal fiscal analysis* (pp. 63–161). Dubuque, IA: Kendall/Hunt Publishing Company.

Coe, C. K. (2007). Preventing local government fiscal crises: The North Carolina approach. *Public Budgeting & Finance, 27*(3), 39–49.

Coe, C. K. (2008). Preventing local government fiscal crises: Emerging best practices. *Public Administration Review, 68*(4), 759–767.

Crosby, A., & Robbins, D. (2010, April). *An evaluation of Michigan's fiscal indicator scores*. Paper presented at the Midwest Political Science Association Annual Conference, Chicago.

Crosby, A., & Robbins, D. (2013). Mission impossible: Monitoring municipal fiscal sustainability and stress in Michigan. *Journal of Public Budgeting, Accounting & Financial Management, 25*(3), 522–555.

Denison, D. V., Finkler, S. A., & Mead, D. M. (2002). GASB statement 34: Curriculum and teaching concerns for schools of public policy and management. *Journal of Policy Analysis and Management, 21*(1), 137–144.

Finkler, S. A., Smith, D. L., Calabrese, T. D., & Purtell, R. M. (2017). *Financial management for public, health, and not-for-profit organizations* (5th ed.). Thousand Oaks, CA: CQ Press.

Governmental Accounting Standards Board. (n.d.). Economic condition assessment. Retrieved from http://www.gasb.org/jsp/GASB/Page/GASBSectionPage&cid=1176156742174.

Groves, S. M., Godsey, W. M., & Shulman, M. A. (1981). Financial indicators for local government. *Public Budgeting & Finance, 1*(2), 5–19.

Groves, S. M., Nollenberger, K., & Valente, M. G. (2003). *Evaluating financial condition: A handbook for local government* (4th ed.). Washington, DC: International City/County Management Association.

Heald, D. (2003). Fiscal transparency: Concepts, measurement and UK practice. *Public Administration, 81*(4), 723–759.

Hendrick, R. (2004). Assessing and measuring the fiscal health of local governments: Focus on Chicago suburban municipalities. *Urban Affairs Review, 40*(1), 78–114.

Ives, M. (2006). *Assessing municipal financial condition.* Croton-on-Hudson, NY: Martin Ives and David R. Hancox.

Jacob, B., & Hendrick, R. (2012). Assessing the financial condition of local governments: What is financial condition and how is it measured? In H. Levine, J. B. Justice, & E. A. Scorsone (Eds.), *Handbook of local government fiscal health* (pp. 11–42). Burlington, MA: Jones and Bartlett.

Justice, J. B., & Scorsone, E. A. (2012). Measuring and predicting local government fiscal stress: Theory and practice. In H. Levine, J. B. Justice, & E. A. Scorsone (Eds.), *Handbook of local government fiscal health* (pp. 43–74). Burlington, MA: Jones & Bartlett.

Justice, J. B., McNutt, J. G., & Smith, E. S., Jr. (2015). Understanding and measuring online fiscal transparency. In A. Manohoran (Ed.), *E-government and websites: A public solutions handbook* (pp. 22–46). Armonk, NY: M. E. Sharpe.

Kleine, R., Kloha, P., & Weissert, C. S. (2002). *Fiscal stress indicators: An assessment of current Michigan law and development of a new 'early-warning' scale for Michigan localities.* East Lansing, MI. Retrieved from http://www.michigan.gov/documents/treasury/MSUStudy_238307_7.pdf.

Kleine, R., Kloha, P., & Weissert, C. S. (2003, June). Monitoring local government fiscal health: Michigan's new 10 point scale of fiscal distress. *Government Finance Review, 19*, 18–23.

Kloha, P., Weissert, C. S., & Kleine, R. (2005a). Developing and testing a composite model to predict local fiscal distress. *Public Administration Review, 65*(3), 313–323.

Kloha, P., Weissert, C. S., & Kleine, R. (2005b). Someone to watch over me: State monitoring of local fiscal conditions. *The American Review of Public Administration, 35*(3), 236–255.

Kuptez, D. (2014, October 6). Stockton pension ruling is no surprise. *Los Angeles Daily Journal.*

Ladd, H. F., & Yinger, J. (1989). *America's ailing cities: Fiscal health and the design of urban policy.* Baltimore: Johns Hopkins University Press.

Maher, C. S., & Nollenberger, K. (2009, October). Revisiting Kenneth Brown's '10-point test. *Government Finance Review, 25*, 61–66.

Mead, D. M. (2006). A manageable system of economic condition analysis for governments. In H. A. Frank (Ed.), *Public financial management* (pp. 383–419). Boca Raton: CRC.

Mead, D. M. (2008). *State and local government use of generally accepted accounting principles for general purpose external financial reporting*. Norwalk, CT. Retrieved from http://gasb.org/cs/ContentServer?c=Document_C&pagename=GASB%2FDocument_C%2FGASBDocumentPage&cid=1176156726669.

Ohio Auditor of State. (2018). Financial health indicators. Retrieved from https://www.ohioauditor.gov/FHI/default.html.

Pew Charitable Trusts. (2016). *State strategies to detect local fiscal distress*. Philadelphia, PA. Retrieved from http://www.pewtrusts.org/en/research-and-analysis/reports/2016/09/state-strategies-to-detect-local-fiscal-distress.

Plerhoples, T., & Scorsone, E. (2010). *An assessment of Michigan's local government fiscal indicator system*. Lansing, MI: Michigan State Fiscal Agency.

Plerhoples, T., & Scorsone, E. (2011). *Proposed alterations to the local government fiscal stress indicator system for the State of Michigan*. East Lansing, MI: Michigan State University, Department of Agricultural, Food, and Resource Economics. Retrieved from http://purl.umn.edu/116167.

Public Sector Accounting Board. (2007, September). Statement of principles: Indicators of government financial condition. Retrieved from http://www.psab-ccsp.ca/projects/current-projects/item14558.pdf.

Rubin, I. S. (1982). *Running in the red: The political dynamics of urban fiscal stress*. Albany, NY: State University of New York Press.

Singla, A., Comeaux, J., & Kirschner, C. L. (2014). Blind, broke, and bedlam: Differentiating fiscal stress from bankruptcy in California. *Public Finance and Management, 14*(3), 306–328.

Smith, D. L., Moore, C. K., & Justice, J. B. (2018). *What are states' fiscal monitoring systems monitoring?* Paper presented at the Annual Conference of the American Society for Public Administration, Denver, CO.

Spiotto, J. E. (2013). The role of the state in supervising and assisting municipalities, especially in times of financial distress. *Municipal Finance Journal, 34*(1), 1–32.

Stone, S. B., Singla, A., Comeaux, J., & Kirschner, C. (2015). A comparison of financial indicators: The case of Detroit. *Public Budgeting & Finance, 35*(4), 90–111. https://doi.org/10.1111/pbaf.12079.

Stonecash, J., & McAfee, P. (1981). The ambiguities and limits of fiscal strain indicators. *Policy Studies Journal, 10*(2), 379–395.

Wang, X., Dennis, L. M., & Tu, Y. S. (2007). Measuring financial condition: A study of US states. *Public Budgeting & Finance, 27*(2), 1–21.

Williams, D. W., & Calabrese, T. D. (2016). The status of budget forecasting. *Journal of Public and Nonprofit Affairs, 2*(2), 127–160. https://doi.org/10.20899/jpna.2.2.127-160.

Wolff, G. B. (2004). *Fiscal crises in US cities: Structural and non-structural causes.* Bonn, Germany: Center for European Integration Studies. Retrieved from http://www.zei.de/download/zei_wp/B04-28.pdf.

Wolman, H., & Davis, B. (1980). Local government strategies to cope with fiscal pressure. In C. H. Levine & I. Rubin (Eds.), *Fiscal stress and public policy* (pp. 231–248). Beverly Hills, CA: Sage.

15

School District Enrollment Projections and Budget Forecasting

Peter Jones, Cole Rakow, and Vincent Reitano

Major Points

- Enrollment projections should consider demographic and socio-economic factors, which can then be used to generate forecasts for personnel salary and benefits and other expenditures.
- Revenue forecasts should be conducted for different streams of local, state, and federal revenues and then considered in relation to expenditure forecasts when formulating the budget.
- This chapter reviews analyzes forecast error with a panel of Kentucky school districts from 2001 to 2013.

P. Jones (✉)
Department of Political Science and Public Administration, University of Alabama at Birmingham, Birmingham, AL, USA
e-mail: pajones5@uab.edu

C. Rakow
Economist and Revenue Forecaster, Independent Budget Office, New York, NY, USA
e-mail: ColeR@ibo.nyc.ny.us

V. Reitano
School of Public Affairs and Administration, Western Michigan University, Kalamazoo, MI, USA
e-mail: vincent.reitano@wmich.edu

D. Williams, T. Calabrese (eds.), *The Palgrave Handbook of Government Budget Forecasting*, Palgrave Studies in Public Debt, Spending, and Revenue,
https://doi.org/10.1007/978-3-030-18195-6_15

- Forecast error varies over the business cycle with revenue underestimations increasing in magnitude during the Great Recession.

Introduction

School districts use project enrollment and forecast revenues and expenditures as part of their planning and budgeting processes (Hartman 1988). When tied to demographic and socio-economic measures, enrollment projections help school districts plan for potential long-term changes that may require more or less resources to meet educational demand and the associated need for school facilities (Grip 2009; McKibben 1996, 2006). Then, school districts can use projected student enrollment to help inform revenue and expenditure forecasts and maintain a structural balance to ensure the sustainability of service provision (Government Finance Officers Association [GFOA] 2014, 2017). Despite the critical role that forecasting plays in school districts, the literature primarily focuses on enrollment projections, rather than revenue and expenditures forecasts. Only two studies, Ványolós (2011) and Barrett et al. (2018), focus on revenue and expenditure forecasts in school districts, indicating the need for further research to develop the literature and inform practitioners. The major elements in this chapter are as follows:

- Section "Literature Review" summarizes the literature on school district enrollment projections and forecasting. The subsections review the literature on enrollment projections at different levels of government and revenue and expenditure forecasts in school districts.
- Section "Forecast Accuracy Measures" details forecast accuracy measures, focusing on how to calculate and interpret them in the school district context. It includes an empirical analysis of all Kentucky school district budget forecasts from 2001 to 2014 to show the application and analysis of different forecast accuracy measures.
- Section "The Practice of School District Forecasting" reviews recommendations for the practice of enrollment projections and revenue and expenditure forecasts. Emphasis is placed on how the five-step framework in Hartman (1988) can be used by school districts.
- Section "Limitations in Literature" lists areas for future research in school district enrollment projections and revenue and expenditure forecasting.
- Section "Conclusion" concludes with a brief summary of the chapter and argues that future research should focus on how school districts can use forecasts to address ongoing financial uncertainty.

Literature Review

Overview

The literature on school district forecasting can be segmented by unit of analysis and type of forecast. The unit of analysis is typically the nation, state, or school district, and forecast types include enrollment projections and budget forecasts. One important clarification to make is the difference between the term projection and forecast. As per Smith, Tayman, and Swason (2001, 3), "projections are nonjudgmental, forecasts are explicitly judgmental." For the purpose of this chapter, enrollment is considered in terms of projections while revenue and expenditures are considered in terms of forecasts, which is consistent with the literature (Grip 2009; Hartman 1988).

Enrollment Projections at the National and State Level

In the United States, the National Center for Education Statistics (NCES) produces educational statistics projections at the national level. In the most recent edition of the report, Hussar and Bailey (2018) use exponential smoothing and multiple linear regression to run a variety of projections. Specifically, they employ exponential smoothing for enrollments and graduation rates and multiple linear regression for teacher counts and expenditures. All projections have underlying demographic and economic assumptions. Both single and double exponential smoothing are used for projections depending in part on if the data exhibited a "horizontal pattern" (Hussar and Bailey 2018, 72). More so, smoothing parameters were selected rather than set at a constant, as in previous NCES reports. In regard to the linear regression models, Hussar and Bailey (2018) use different criteria for model selection, such as the r-squared, statistical significance, and whether there were violations of econometric assumptions. Despite careful attention to methodology, Hussar and Bailey (2018, 73) note that: "the equations are intended only to project values for the dependent variables, not to reflect all elements of underlying social, political, and economic structures. Lack of available data precluded the building of large-scale structural models."

Furthermore, other researchers have argued for using alternative methods for enrollment projections. For example, Baker and Richards (1999) test different methods and find that neural networks were better at prediction than regression and other methods when projecting with National Center for

Education Statistics data. In a more recent methodological article, Tang and Yin (2012, 460) show that gray model projections, which provide an alternative systems framework for dealing with information uncertainty relative to regression (see, e.g., Deng 1982, 1989), are "competitive and workable" relative to methods in Hussar and Bailey (2018). Thus, there remains an opportunity for further comparisons of forecasting methods, particularly as new methods emerge from analytics and statistics (Baker and Richards 1999; Tang and Yin 2012).

The problem faced by Hussar and Bailey (2018) for projecting teacher counts and expenditures is less apparent at the state level. At the state level, there are often state forecasting groups with access to detailed state and local data. For example, the Florida Office of Economic and Demographic Research (2018) produces detailed population projections that can help with school enrollment projections. States like New Jersey require that local governments, including school districts, run five-year projections, to ensure that capital assets, namely school buildings, are planned for in the event of upward or downward trends in student enrollment (Grip 2009).

Enrollment Projections in School Districts

Local school district enrollment forecasting can be conducted with a variety of methods (Grip 2009). As per Grip (2009), one approach used in New Jersey school districts is the cohort-survival ratio (CSR) model, since it can be computed relatively easily in a spreadsheet. School districts, like general-purpose governments, do not typically have ready access or the capacity to use advanced forecasting software (Barrett et al. 2018; Frank and Zhao 2009; Kong 2007), reinforcing why New Jersey uses the CSR model. In CSR, population size is a function of existing population, new births, and new entrants via migration. This data can be pulled from census or state data.

Local enrollment projections need not be relegated to CSR. Grip (2009) presents mixed evidence that student race can improve prediction accuracy. Factors such as whether students were born in the United States should also be considered, because: "For instance, the percentage of foreign-born persons may assist school administrators on the need for ESL programs, which is a much more relevant indicator than student race/ethnicity alone" (Grip 2009, 750). Local enrollment projections also need to consider exogenous shocks like policy changes that may affect student entering or leaving the school district (see McKibben 1996).

Revenue and Expenditure Forecasts in School Districts

Local enrollment projections should inform both short-term and long-term planning (Hartman 1988). In the short-term, they should be used to budget for expenditures and to understand how many teachers are necessary for meeting various programmatic needs (e.g., English as a second language programs) (GFOA 2017). In the long-term, as in New Jersey, enrollment projections can help with planning for capital assets, such as new school facilities, that may be contingent on school bond referenda (Grip 2009). These projections can demonstrate to the public the need for capital projects and may influence referenda outcomes.

From a budgeting perspective, both expenditure and revenue forecasts should be disaggregated to the local level to reflect heterogeneity. As per Frank and Wang (1994) and Kavanagh and Williams (2016), it would be of little use to forecast only aggregate revenues or expenditures at the local level. Instead, forecasting specific revenues individually (property, sales, income, utility, user fee, and other revenues) will allow a forecaster to capture variation. Additionally, intergovernmental revenues can be forecasted at the state and federal level. Expenditures should also be disaggregated by program or expenditure object level, depending on how the school district budgets (Hartman 1988).

Though it is clear school districts should forecast expenditures and revenues, researchers have not given the attention this topic deserves. Hulpke et al. (1976) show that California school districts underestimate revenues and overestimate expenditures, and suggest districts strategically forecast to build a budget surplus. Using a panel of New York school districts, Ványolós (2011) explores forecasting in relation to fiscal slack accumulation. Specifically, Ványolós (2011) develops and tests a system of equations to look at the relationship between budgeted (forecasted) and actual amounts revenues and expenditures and fiscal reserves.

In the first equation from Ványolós (2011), the difference between budgeted and actual revenues, plus the difference between budgeted and actual expenditures, plus the appropriated fund balance, is equal to the budgeted fund balance. This equation is subject to the constraint that the unreserved, undesignated portion of the budgeted fund balance, which can be used for any purpose, is less than or equal to 2 percent of the budgeted expenditures. The third equation is an accounting identity of how unassigned fund balance is budgeted. The constraint in the second equation reflects that fund balance accumulation can be subject to state-imposed limitations, in states such as New York (Duncombe and Hou 2014; Ványolós 2011) and Pennsylvania (Arapis et al. 2017), among others.

Using the system of equations, Ványolós (2011) tests a panel regression model of New York school districts. There is statistically significant evidence that school districts overestimate expenditures and underestimate revenues to reach optimal fund balance levels. In fact, the behavior of underforecasting revenues and overestimating expenditures, as per Rodgers and Joyce (1996), can lead school districts in New York to artificially inflate their fund balance beyond state-imposed limits.

In a paper which builds upon Ványolós (2011), Barrett et al. (2018) use a panel of Kentucky school districts to study the relationship between revenue and expenditure forecast bias and the accumulation of unassigned fund balance. In this paper, the authors begin with a descriptive analysis to show that a majority of Kentucky school districts from school years (SY) 2001–2002 to 2013–2014 underestimate revenues and overestimate expenditures. With a panel regression approach, they show that underestimated revenues and overestimated expenditure are associated with building slack into the budget and that this relationship is heterogeneous over the business cycle. These findings are consistent with Ványolós (2011), who looks at compliance with state-imposed fund balance constraints in New York school districts, and those results also reflect findings for general-purpose government forecasting practices from Dougherty et al. (2003), Rose and Smith (2012), and Williams and Onochie (2013).

In regard to the practice of school district revenue and expenditure forecasting, less is known about the perceptions and intent of forecasters, methods and software used, and other considerations commonly considered in research on general-purpose local government forecasting (Kong 2007; Frank and Zhao 2009). As per Ványolós (2011, 170), there is opportunity for research on general-purpose local government forecasting to yield insight for school districts, particularly with respect to revenue and expenditure forecasts, since "the overall structure [of school districts] is very similar to most public organizations' budgeting processes."

While differences exist in the distribution of revenues for general-purpose governments compared to states, in part, due to institutional rules regarding education funding, forecasting for general-purpose and special-purpose governments has similarities because both follow the same general budgeting process (Bartle et al. 2003; Ványolós 2011). For example, forecasting property taxes for general-purpose and special-purpose governments involves consideration of property assessments, local property market, and potential other factors within the boundaries of the government (see McCluskey et al. 2013). As long as the boundaries are correctly drawn and any institutional rules, such as revenue sharing rules across local governments, are considered, then the basic premise of property tax forecasting practices is generally similar irrespective of the type of local government.

There may be some notable differences on the expenditure side. Expenditures for instruction, which are a function of teacher salary and benefits, usually consume a majority of a school district budget (GFOA 2017). Smaller school districts may need to use an Excel file to project individual level employee salary and benefit costs, while larger school districts with an enterprise-resource planning system such as Oracle or SAP can automatically forecast teacher expenditures (see, e.g., Fishbein and Vehaun 2009). Other major expenditures to be projected are for administrators, staff, supplies, and capital infrastructure. As per Hussar and Bailey (2018), capital infrastructure should consider medium- and long-term enrollment projections. Capital infrastructure should be forecasted with a capital improvement plan. Such a plan functions as both a strategic plan to set priorities for capital infrastructure to meet enrollment projections and a financial plan for understanding the cost, financing methods, and effect on the operating budget, among other considerations (Casey and Mucha 2007).

School districts must also consider student transfers to charter schools, if that is applicable to their budgeting. For example, in states such as Pennsylvania, school districts provide funds to charter schools on a per pupil basis, depending on the type of student and the differential costs associated with their accumulation. Evidence is mixed if charter schools have an effect on school district costs, but if charter schools continue to grow, then there may be an effect not only on school district costs but also enrollments, potentially creating fiscal stress over time (Arsen and Ni 2012; Bifulco and Reback 2014; Jones 2018). There may also be a shift in the teacher market, as well, further changing forecasted and actual expenditures for a major aspect of school district budgeting (Welsch 2011). In some states such as Florida, the Department of Education provides forecast estimate worksheets for charter schools to compute, which can help them to understand their funding from school districts.

Forecast Accuracy Measures

Given the inherent uncertainty of trying to predict the future, forecasted revenue will almost certainly diverge from the actual amount of revenue collected. Naturally, a primary objective for forecasting is to generate a forecast that is as accurate as possible and minimizes the challenges that result from dealing with an unanticipated level of revenue. A rigorous forecast procedure will include some attempt to critically analyze the accuracy of previous forecasts, so that valuable adjustments can be made to improve forecasts in the future. Forecast accuracy can be assessed by a variety of methods, all of which are quite straightforward, computationally. Which one is the most appropriate to a school district's purposes depends on the specific goals involved.

Error

Fundamental to all considerations of forecast accuracy is the concept of error. Fortunately, calculating error is extremely intuitive and straightforward. Error is defined as the difference between the actual value of revenue collected (once it is known) and the amount that was originally forecast. The formula for error is provided as follows:

$$e_t = a_t - f_t$$

where e is the error (in a particular time period, t), a is the (*ex post*) actual amount collected, and f is the (*ex ante*) forecast amount. With this basic piece of information, forecast accuracy measures can be constructed to consider the average forecast accuracy over a number of time periods. The most commonly utilized measures are discussed below.

Mean Absolute Error

The most direct and straightforward method of assessing forecast accuracy is to consider the *mean absolute error* (MAE). To calculate MAE, you calculate the amount of error in each forecast for each time period over which you wish to analyze accuracy. These errors are then converted into absolute values and averaged over the number of periods. The formula for MAE is as follows:

$$\text{MAE} = \frac{\sum_{i=1}^{n} |e_i|}{n}$$

where e is the amount of error, as calculated above, for each individual projection, i, over the number of periods observed, n.

Taking the absolute value of the error is necessary, because raw values, which might be positive or negative, depending on if the forecast came in too high or too low in particular periods, could end up cancelling each other out when they are summed as part of the averaging process. Converting all errors to positive values preserves their magnitude and yields an accurate average of the divergence between forecasted and actual amounts.

Mean Squared Error

An alternative measure, building off the basic methodology of mean absolute error, is *mean squared error* (MSE), which instead of taking the absolute value of error in each period, squares it, and calculates the mean value of this squared deviation over the timespan available. The formula for calculating is presented as follows:

$$\text{MSE} = \frac{\sum_{i=1}^{n} e_i^2}{n}$$

The intuition of the squaring process is somewhat akin to its use in ordinary least squares for regression analysis. Squaring the error automatically converts all values to positive (thus making the absolute value step unnecessary) and using squared values will also serve to emphasize larger errors and drive up the value of MSE if such large errors are present. As such, it is a more sensitive and exacting measure of forecast accuracy. It should be noted that the squaring process alters the scale of the data, so the final result is not directly interpretable as an average error or deviation, as with MAE. If you want to take the results of an MSE analysis and obtain a value that is interpretable, you need to take the square root of the result.

Percent Error

Both MAE and MSE will yield results that are particular to the scale of the original data. What qualifies as a particularly large or small average error will depend upon the raw size of the revenue stream being considered. For example, an error of 100,000 dollars for a large school district may not be much of a concern if that district's revenue stream brings in several million dollars, but it would be a very large concern if only a million dollars were collected to begin with. Additionally, if you are working with a revenue stream that is consistently growing or declining over time, the size of the error may naturally be changing as a result, and averaging over all time periods will not take this into effect.

One way to take the analysis of forecast accuracy further, and generate a measure that does take size and scale into account, is to work with percent error. Calculating percent error essentially takes the error, as we have already calculated, and scales it to the magnitude of the data. This is particularly useful if you want to make comparisons of accuracy between different revenue streams. The formula for calculating percent error is as follows:

$$pe_t = \frac{a_t - f_t}{a_t}$$

Mean Percent Error

The most straightforward application of percent error in forecast accuracy analysis is to calculate the average of the percent error for all available time periods, a measure called *mean percent error* (MPE). Doing this is as direct as it sounds, and is similar to the methods discussed above, as you substitute percent errors for raw errors. The formula for MPE is displayed as follows:

$$\text{MPE} = \frac{\sum_{i=1}^{n} pe_i}{n}$$

You may note that this measure of accuracy, unlike MAE or MSE above, preserves the directionality of the percent errors. They are not all made positive through taking the absolute value or square of the raw error. If actual revenue comes in above forecast revenue, the percent error will be positive. If actual revenue comes in below the forecast amount, the percent error will be negative. Since the percent errors are summed as part of the averaging process, positive and negative percent errors can cancel each other out, and result in an MPE with a smaller magnitude than it would otherwise have. However, unlike the other measures, it can be negative, if forecasts are consistently coming in too high. Conceptually, this makes MPE more appropriate to think of as a measure of total forecast accuracy over the period in question—individual years might still diverge by a larger amount.

Mean Absolute Percent Error

To get around the concern of positive and negative percent errors cancelling one another out and potentially improving the forecast accuracy measure, one additional step can be added, which is simply to take the absolute value of the percent error before averaging, which results in the *mean absolute percent error* (MAPE). The formula is as follows:

$$\text{MAPE} = \frac{\sum_{i=1}^{n} |pe_i|}{n}$$

This method will still maintain the natural scaling effect that results from using percent errors as opposed to raw errors, allowing for comparability between different streams. It also ensures that the size of all errors, regardless of direction, are fully considered in the final result.

Forecast Accuracy Measures: Which to Choose?

As noted above, which forecast accuracy measure you might choose depends on how you wish to use it. If you are working with one particular stream of revenue and are discussing accuracy within the context of its magnitude, MAE can be a perfectly acceptable (and straightforward) accuracy measure to select. If you are particularly concerned about instances of larger forecast error and want a measure that punishes large errors more harshly, you might select MSE instead.

If you want to talk about forecast accuracy a bit more generally, and not necessarily within the context of one particular revenue stream and its magnitude, or especially if you want to compare forecast accuracy between different revenue streams of different magnitudes, you will likely want to select a measure that utilizes percent error, such as MPE or MAPE. The MAPE helps alleviate concerns over different directionalities reducing the final measure, and if you are not concerned about directionality at all, it is a good option.

However, there may still be a reason to favor MPE. The directionality issue can become particularly important if the forecasts are generated as part of a process where there may be a fundamental bias in one direction or another, persisting over time. A school district that is trying to expand its expenditures, and that has some freedom in covering budgetary shortfalls (through reserves, debt, or some other mechanism) may be biased toward overestimating its forecasts, taking a particularly optimistic view toward revenue expectations, which allows for inflated expenditure obligations at the time of budgeting. Conversely, a school district that faces stricter constraints—either financially or politically—may be particularly inclined toward underestimating its forecasts, in the effort to avoid problematic shortfalls at all costs. While the latter case is generally viewed as less of an issue (an excess of revenue is easier to deal with than a shortage of revenue), it is also a problem in its own way. Underestimating revenues imposes a constriction on budgeted expenditures. If this is systematic in nature, it represents a failure of the budgeting process to accurately plan for available revenue and spend it accordingly, per the mandate of the institution in question. If you are looking to investigate this sort of systematic forecast bias, a measure that preserves directionality is a useful place to start. In the end, you may choose to calculate multiple or all of the available accuracy measures in order to illustrate different aspects of forecast accuracy, according to their relative strengths.

Analysis of Kentucky School District Revenue Forecast Measures

To demonstrate differences in forecasting accuracy measures, we obtained 2275 annual financial reports from 176 school districts in Kentucky from SY 2001–2002 to 2012–2013.[1] Each school district reported revenue forecasts as well as actual revenues collected for each school year. We transformed actual and forecasted revenues to per-pupil values to control for school district size.

Table 15.1 presents MAE, MSE, MPE, and MAPE for the three smallest, three median, and three largest school districts. The differences between the measures and what they emphasize can be readily observed. MAE shows comparatively little variation across the school districts, ranging from $615 in Fayette County to $2984 in West Point Independent. The variation is much greater when looking at MSE, however, because any individual years with particularly large errors are penalized through the squaring process. In this case the smallest and largest error districts are the same (though that does not have to be the case), yet you can observe that the variation in the measure is *much* greater, ranging from $702,300 in Fayette County to $32,350,910 in West Point Independent. From this observation, it is clear that West Point Independent suffered from particular years of large errors, which are heavily emphasized by the MSE procedure. Recall that MSE totals cannot be

[1] Data were obtained from the Kentucky DoE which maintains a validated longitudinal database.

Table 15.1 Forecast accuracy measures for sample of districts

		MAE	MSE	MPE (%)	MAPE(%)
Smallest districts	Silver Grove Independent	$1722.20	$6,379,144.50	14.50	14.85
	Southgate Independent	$965.32	$3,182,996.80	8.08	9.13
	West Point Independent	$2984.12	$32,350,910.00	16.05	19.36
Median districts	Bardstown Independent	$1048.27	$2,249,198.50	12.10	12.15
	Elizabethtown Independent	$741.93	$1,224,569.80	9.93	9.93
	Union County	$697.14	$875,913.88	7.51	7.51
Largest districts	Boone County	$1489.33	$3,260,440.80	18.30	18.30
	Fayette County	$615.49	$702,300.38	6.42	7.04
	Jefferson County	$2287.76	$13,243,447.00	−5.01	26.20

interpreted as representative deviations, unless you take their square root, in this case $838 and $5688, respectively.

The percent error measures afford greater comparability between districts, but different conclusions. In MPE, the largest positive error belongs to Boone County, while Jefferson County is actually negative. Because MPE preserves directionality, this offers unique information, namely that Jefferson County routinely overestimated its revenues and faced net shortfalls over this period. Looking at MAPE gives a better sense of overall precision, by treating all percentage deviations equally. Here, Fayette County once again performs the best, at 7.04 percent, while Jefferson County has the highest MAPE of 26.20 percent.

Looking at all of these measures together, you can observe some general themes (e.g., Fayette County has low errors across the board) but different conclusions can emerge, depending on what you want to emphasize. With MAE and MSE, both based on the concept of raw errors, West Point Independent has the highest errors in either case. But switching to percent errors, Jefferson County takes the lead, with MPE telling us that it trends toward overestimation, and MAPE revealing that it has the highest errors, in percentage terms. This results from the fact that revenue is much higher in West Point Independent than in Jefferson County, so while the absolute deviations may be larger, they don't represent as much of a scaled difference.

In Table 15.2, we average forecast accuracy measures *within* a particular year *across* school districts; specially, we present the averages of the error, abso-

Table 15.2 Forecast accuracy measures changes over time for Kentucky school districts

	Year	Mean	S.D.	Min	Mdn	Max
Error	2001	$856.56	$917.00	−$1088.69	$540.59	$6796.23
	2002	$780.65	$1277.56	−$1480.62	$308.45	$8774.43
	2003	$770.60	$1122.63	−$248.08	$386.10	$8745.67
	2004	$1310.99	$1871.80	−$1347.82	$594.18	$14,068.82
	2005	$882.18	$1033.17	−$805.77	$558.05	$5595.09
	2006	$1156.74	$1358.90	−$432.10	$689.76	$10,378.23
	2007	$1309.66	$1663.73	−$833.30	$689.85	$9581.25
	2008	$1536.52	$2313.47	−$312.23	$626.96	$18,606.16
	2009	$296.04	$322.88	−$358.45	$219.81	$1395.54
	2010	$336.79	$1062.46	−$9041.96	$353.49	$6067.04
	2011	$406.64	$738.95	−$5247.05	$289.17	$3665.97
	2012	$778.95	$1132.67	−$5570.46	$537.18	$8125.54
	2013	$989.06	$1438.29	−$1371.88	$545.00	$7217.81
Absolute error	2001	$877.69	$896.68	$19.00	$544.17	$6796.23
	2002	$847.59	$1233.92	$0.05	$325.80	$8774.43
	2003	$793.87	$1106.21	$11.05	$386.10	$8745.67
	2004	$1361.11	$1835.47	$5.44	$613.98	$14,068.82
	2005	$907.43	$1010.94	$4.06	$570.26	$5595.09
	2006	$1163.68	$1352.93	$5.51	$689.76	$10,378.23
	2007	$1326.06	$1650.61	$36.91	$689.87	$9581.25
	2008	$1543.73	$2308.64	$7.58	$626.96	$18,606.16
	2009	$317.18	$302.01	$1.23	$235.89	$1395.54
	2010	$550.23	$968.72	$2.23	$377.06	$9041.96
	2011	$509.36	$671.87	$2.16	$296.65	$5247.05
	2012	$862.75	$1069.85	$5.11	$546.33	$8125.54
	2013	$1107.80	$1348.42	$1.05	$560.65	$7217.81
Squared error	2001	$1.60E+06	$4.20E+06	$360.81	$3.00E+05	$4.60E+07
	2002	$2.20E+06	$7.30E+06	$0.00	$1.10E+05	$7.70E+07
	2003	$1.80E+06	$6.70E+06	$122.00	$1.50E+05	$7.60E+07
	2004	$5.20E+06	$1.80E+07	$29.65	$3.80E+05	$2.00E+08
	2005	$1.80E+06	$4.50E+06	$16.50	$3.30E+05	$3.10E+07
	2006	$3.20E+06	$9.50E+06	$30.38	$4.80E+05	$1.10E+08
	2007	$4.50E+06	$1.20E+07	$1362	$4.80E+05	$9.20E+07
	2008	$7.70E+06	$3.10E+07	$57.44	$3.90E+05	$3.50E+08
	2009	$1.90E+05	$3.60E+05	$1.50	$5.58E+04	$1.90E+06
	2010	$1.20E+06	$7.30E+06	4.96	$1.40E+05	$8.20E+07
	2011	$7.10E+05	$2.50E+06	$4.66	$8.80E+04	$2.80E+07
	2012	$1.90E+06	$6.70E+06	$26.14	$3.00E+05	$6.60E+07
	2013	$3.00E+06	$7.60E+06	$1.11	$3.10E+05	$5.20E+07
Percent error	2001	10.97%	9.54%	−15.74%	7.93%	52.53%
	2002	9.33%	12.74%	−22.52%	4.72%	64.35%
	2003	9.58%	12.52%	−2.83%	5.96%	106.07%
	2004	13.80%	14.52%	−20.90%	9.09%	69.35%
	2005	10.89%	10.41%	−11.81%	7.70%	48.33%
	2006	13.13%	11.74%	−6.00%	9.30%	60.78%
	2007	14.32%	13.31%	−8.86%	9.69%	60.88%
	2008	14.88%	14.18%	−4.71%	8.46%	64.73%
	2009	4.04%	4.14%	−3.99%	3.29%	18.41%
	2010	4.36%	12.45%	−118.16%	4.87%	46.20%
	2011	5.38%	8.65%	−59.58%	4.09%	36.40%
	2012	9.83%	11.05%	−66.01%	7.87%	56.47%
	2013	6.40%	8.61%	−7.96%	3.97%	48.09%

(*continued*)

Table 15.2 (continued)

	Year	Mean	S.D.	Min	Mdn	Max
Absolute percent error	2001	11.27%	9.18%	0.30%	8.00%	52.53%
	2002	10.25%	12.00%	0.00%	5.22%	64.35%
	2003	9.90%	12.26%	0.18%	5.96%	106.07%
	2004	14.49%	13.82%	0.08%	9.16%	69.35%
	2005	11.24%	10.02%	0.05%	7.93%	48.33%
	2006	13.22%	11.64%	0.06%	9.30%	60.78%
	2007	14.51%	13.10%	0.54%	9.69%	60.88%
	2008	14.98%	14.08%	0.11%	8.46%	64.73%
	2009	4.33%	3.83%	0.02%	3.42%	18.41%
	2010	7.05%	11.15%	0.03%	5.48%	118.16%
	2011	6.65%	7.72%	0.03%	4.30%	59.58%
	2012	10.86%	10.04%	0.08%	7.92%	66.01%
	2013	7.13%	8.01%	0.01%	4.25%	48.09%

lute error, squared error, percent error, and absolute percent error. These estimates contrast with those presented in Table 15.1 but allow for a comparison of broader trends across the business cycle. On average, a school district underestimated revenue by $878 per-pupil. Underestimations varied across the business cycle and were inflated by a skewed-right distribution, as the median over this time period was $464.

Beginning in SY 2005–2006, average underestimates increased each year to nearly double the sample average in SY 2008–2009. Underestimations dropped following the recession, as the average school district's estimated revenues were only $296 more than actual revenues in SY 2009–2010. This same pattern emerged for the other measures presented in Table 15.1. For example, the average school district's estimated revenues were 6.55 percent less than actual revenues, but this underestimation reached 14.88 percent in SY 2008–2009. Again, MPE dropped to 4.04 percent in SY 2009–2010.

Figures 15.1 and 15.2 show the accuracy measures across the distribution of school districts. Of note, even in years with higher-than-average forecast error, three school districts still overestimated revenues. The number of overestimations rose to 24 and 25 in SY 2009–2010 and SY 2010–2011, respectively. In a sign that Kentucky did not recover from the recession as quickly as other states, 35 school districts overestimated revenues in SY 2013–2014.

The Practice of School District Forecasting

Hartman (1988) creates a five-step framework for practitioners. In the first step, enrollment is projected, to understand the predicted upward or downward trend. There are a variety of considerations for enrollment projections,

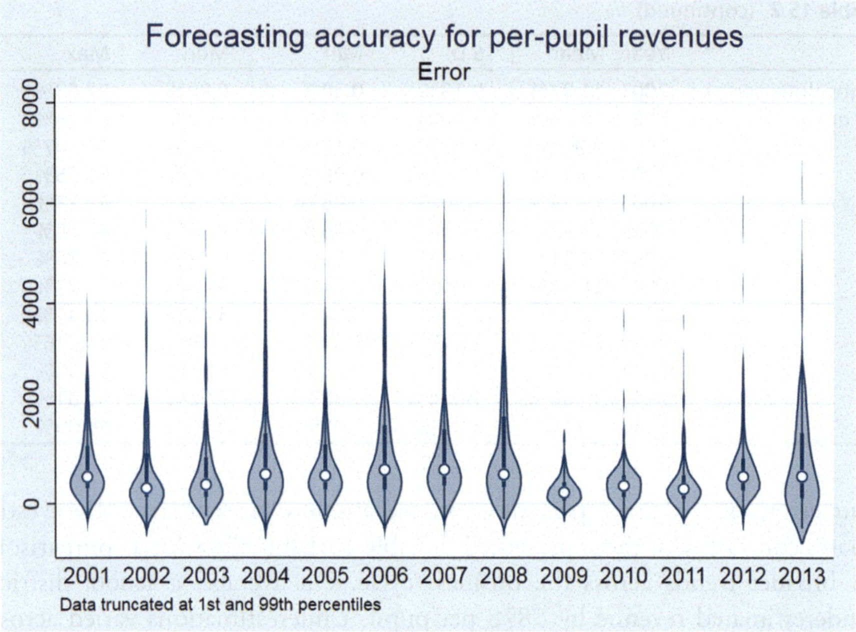

Fig. 15.1 Forecasting accuracy for per-pupil revenues: Error

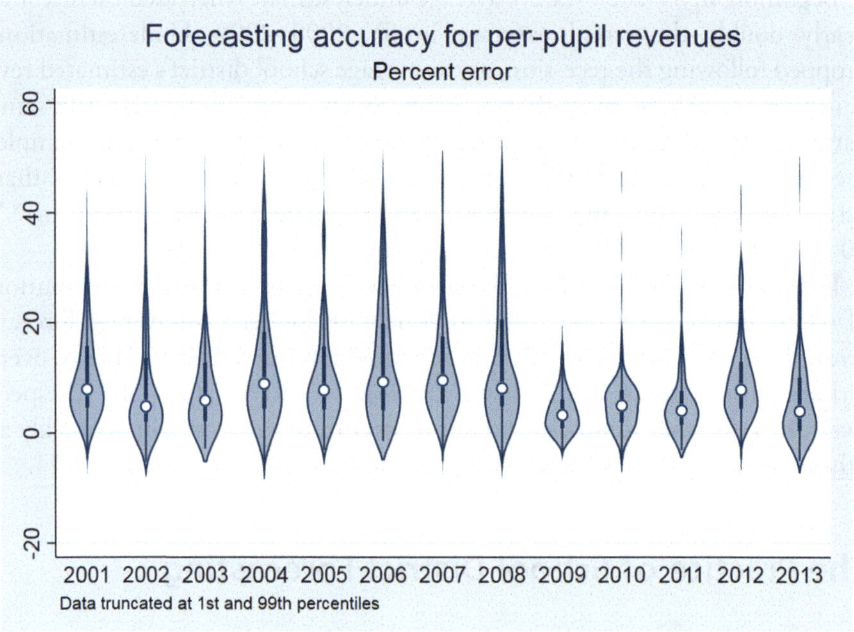

Fig. 15.2 Forecasting accuracy for per-pupil revenues: Percent Error

such as which historical enrollment data to use and what projection methodology is most appropriate. For example, historical enrollment calculated on an average daily membership basis will differ from an average daily attendance or full-time equivalent basis. School districts can determine which is most appropriate depending on whether they are looking for a lower or higher number of historical students to use for projecting into the future, with average daily membership being higher. In regard to methodology, school districts can select a judgmental, regression, or cohort survival approach, the latter of which is detailed in Hartman (1988) and Grip (2009), among others.

The second step is for student enrollment projection to inform personnel budgeting. School district officials can use projections to determine how many teachers, staff, and administrators may need to be added and to take into account issues like retirements and teacher attrition. Hartman (1988) recommends that ratios be considered during this step to understand the student-to-teacher or even student-to-administrator statistics, whether on an aggregate, class, or even programmatic basis (e.g., calculating ratios for special education students to special education teachers). Costs as they relate to new positions, such as salary and benefit as well as training and certifications, need to be carefully considered. This analysis should help with the third step, conducting expenditure forecasts. For example, forecasting teacher expenditures depends on a variety of factors, such as the teaching function (e.g., special education, honors classes), step and grade of their position, education level, and any other factors that could be used to forecast these costs. There are a variety of other personnel (e.g., administration and support staff) and supply costs to be considered.

The fourth step is to run revenue forecasts, which according to Hartman (1988), need to be considered in relation to fund and revenue source. There are a range of funds, from the general to the capital fund. Revenues can be from the local, state, or federal level, and there are multiple revenue sources within each level that need to be forecasted. For example, at the local level, property taxes, any income or sales taxes, fees, and other local revenues need to be individually forecasted (Frank and Wang 1994; Kavanagh and Williams 2016).

Both expenditures and revenues in steps three and four can be forecasted with judgmental, extrapolation, or econometric approaches (Kavanagh and Williams 2016). As discussed below, little is known about school district forecast methods. However, under the assumption that school district forecasting as part of the budgeting process is similar to general-purpose local governments (Ványolós 2011), there might be a proclivity to use simple and judgmental methods rather than more advanced econometric models (see Kong

2007; Frank and Zhao 2009). Hartman (1988) acknowledges this but cautions about the use of simple models with respect to their accuracy and lack of transparency. Irrespective of the method, school districts still need to arrive at a forecast as part of the budgeting process. Specifically, in step five of Hartman (1988), balancing expenditure and revenue forecasts must occur, which is not just a function of the forecasts, but also the normative decisions surrounding resource allocation.

Limitations in Literature

The literature on school district enrollment projections and budget forecasting can be advanced on four fronts. First, while the literature on national-level enrollment projections from NCES is extensive, there is less understanding at the state and local levels. Specifically, much of the literature on school district enrollment projections is relegated to case studies or small samples, such as in Bishop (1979), Grip (2009), McKibben (1996, 2006), and Morrison (1996). These are important and reflect the unique context that each school district conducts its enrollment projections in, but there remains an opportunity to systematically study the accuracy of enrollment projections.

Second, more research needs to be conducted on school district revenue and expenditure forecasts. Two studies on school districts, Ványolós (2011) and Barrett et al. (2018), have shown a relationship between forecasting bias and reserve funds with regression analysis, as well as a proclivity to underestimate revenues and overestimate expenditures in terms of forecasts. These studies, however, are conducted in only two states and cover different business cycles. Further research focusing on forecasting bias and measures of accuracy can advance the literature as well as the practice of budgeting.

Third, in regard to praxis, conducting surveys and interviews can help to understand if best practices around forecasting are being used and what guidance can help guide school district forecasters in the future. Limited research from studies such as Arapis and Reitano (2018) and Arapis et al. (2017) show that there is mixed evidence of adherence to best practices regarding financial management topics at the local level; examples of best practices include the Government Finance Officers Association's (GFOA) guidance on forecasting (GFOA 2014) and school district budgeting (GFOA 2017). Whether or not such guidance is followed is a critical question, as well as how forecasts play into the broader question of school district budgeting. As per Rubin (2015), political conflict needs to be studied further in local budgeting, including in school districts, given resource constraints (Arapis et al. 2017; Dye and Reschovsky 2008).

Conclusion

School districts use enrollment projections and revenue and expenditure forecasts to help plan and budget for providing public education. The literature on enrollment projections is growing. Instead of case studies, there needs to be more systematic research on projection accuracy and for providing technical guidance. The literature on revenue and expenditure forecasts is limited, but the available papers show similarities with research on general-purpose local governments and pave the way for more research (Ványolós 2011). Future research should look not only at forecast methods but also practices to inform practitioners. This can involve mixed-methods research on forecasting such as in Kong (2007), which has both a review of forecast accuracy using quantitative methods as well as a systematic survey and interviews. Thus, there remains significant opportunity for more research on school district forecasting to build the literature and guide practitioners.

References

Arapis, T., & Reitano, V. (2018). A glimmer of optimism in government savings accumulation? An empirical examination of municipal unassigned fund balance in Florida. *Public Finance Review, 46*(3), 389–420.

Arapis, T., Reitano, V., & Bruck, E. (2017). The fiscal savings behavior of Pennsylvania school districts through the great recession. *Public Budgeting & Finance, 37*(3), 47–70.

Arsen, D., & Ni, Y. (2012). The effects of charter school competition on school district resource allocation. *Educational Administration Quarterly, 48*(1), 3–38.

Baker, B. D., & Richards, C. E. (1999). A comparison of conventional linear regression methods and neural networks for forecasting educational spending. *Economics of Education Review, 18*(4), 405–415.

Barrett, N., Fowles, J., Jones, P., & Reitano, V. (2018). Forecast bias and fiscal slack accumulation in school districts. *The American Review of Public Administration*, 1–13.

Bartle, J. R., Ebdon, C., & Krane, D. (2003). Beyond the property tax: Local government revenue diversification. *Journal of Public Budgeting, Accounting & Financial Management, 15*, 622–648.

Bifulco, R., & Reback, R. (2014). Fiscal impacts of charter schools: Lessons from New York. *Education Finance and Policy, 9*(1), 86–107.

Bishop, L. (1979). Dealing with declining school enrollments. *Education and Urban Society, 11*(3), 285–295.

Casey, J. P., & Mucha, M. J. (2007). *Capital project planning and evaluation*. Chicago: Government Finance Officers Association.

Deng, J.-L. (1982). Control problems of grey systems. *Systems & Control Letters, 1*(5), 288–294.

Deng, J.-L. (1989). Introduction to grey systems theory. *The Journal of Grey System, 1*(1), 1–24.

Dougherty, M. J., Klase, K. A., & Song, S. G. (2003). Managerial necessity and the art of creating surpluses: The budget-execution process in West Virginia cities. *Public Administration Review, 63*(4), 484–497.

Duncombe, W., & Hou, Y. (2014). The savings behavior of special purpose governments: A panel study of New York school districts. *Public Budgeting & Finance, 34*(3), 1–23.

Dye, R. F., & Reschovsky, A. (2008). Property tax responses to state aid cuts in the recent fiscal crisis. *Public Budgeting & Finance, 28*(2), 87–111.

Fishbein, J., & Vehaun, D. (2009). Managing the personnel budgeting process. *Government Finance Review*, 67–75. Retrieved from http://www.gfoa.org/sites/default/files/GFR_AUG_09_67.pdf.

Florida Office of Economic and Demographic Research. (2018). *Education estimating conference public schools pre-K - 12 enrollment*. Tallahassee, FL: Florida Office of Economic and Demographic Research. Retrieved from http://edr.state.fl.us/Content/index.cfm.

Frank, H. A., & Wang, X. (1994). Judgmental vs. time series vs. deterministic models in local revenue forecasting: A Florida case study. *Public Budgeting and Financial Management, 6*(4), 493–517.

Frank, H. A., & Zhao, Y. (2009). Determinants of local government revenue forecasting practice: Empirical evidence from Florida. *Journal of Public Budgeting, Accounting & Financial Management, 21*(1), 17–35.

Government Finance Officers Association. (2014). Financial forecasting in the budget preparation process. *Best practice*. Retrieved from http://www.gfoa.org/financial-forecasting-budget-preparation-process.

Government Finance Officers Association. (2017). Best practices in school district budgeting. *Best practice*. Retrieved from http://www.gfoa.org/best-practices-school-district-budgeting.

Grip, R. S. (2009). Does projecting enrollments by race produce more accurate results in New Jersey school districts? *Population Research and Policy Review, 28*(6), 747.

Hartman, W. T. (1988). *School district budgeting*. Lanham: Scarecrow Press.

Hulpke, J. F., Watne, D. A., & Waldo, D. (1976). Budgeting behavior: If, when, and how selected school districts hide money. *Public Administration Review*, 667–674.

Hussar, W. J., & Bailey, T. M. (2018). *Projections of education statistics to 2026.* (NCES 2018-019). National Center for Education Statistics. Retrieved from https://nces.ed.gov/pubsearch/pubsinfo.asp?pubid=2018019.

Jones, P. A. (2018). The influence of charter school competition on public school district revenues across the US. *Journal of Education Finance, 43*(4), 327–359.

Kavanagh, S. C., & Williams, D. W. (2016). *Informed decision-making through forecasting.* Chicago: Government Finance Officers Association.

Kong, D. (2007). Local government revenue forecasting: The California county experience. *Journal of Public Budgeting, Accounting & Financial Management, 19*(2), 178–199.

McCluskey, W. J., Cornia, G. C., & Walters, L. C. (2013). *A primer on property tax: Administration and policy.* Hoboken, NJ: Wiley.

McKibben, J. N. (1996). The impact of policy changes on forecasting for school districts. *Population Research and Policy Review, 15*(5–6), 527–536.

McKibben, J. N. (2006). School district planning and the 2010 decennial census: Data uses and needs. *Journal of Economic and Social Measurement, 31*(3–4), 221–232.

Morrison, P. A. (1996). Forecasting enrollments during court-ordered desegregation. *Population Research and Policy Review, 15*(2), 131–146.

Rodgers, R., & Joyce, P. G. (1996). The effect of underforecasting on the accuracy of revenue forecasts by state governments. *Public Administration Review, 56*(1), 48–56.

Rose, S., & Smith, D. L. (2012). Budget slack, institutions, and transparency. *Public Administration Review, 72*(2), 187–195.

Rubin, I. S. (2015). Past and future budget classics: A research agenda. *Public Administration Review, 75*(1), 25–35.

Smith, S. K., Tayman, J., & Swanson, D. A. (2001). *State and local population projections: Methodology and analysis.* New York: Kluwer Academic/Plenum Publishing Company.

Tang, H.-W. V., & Yin, M.-S. (2012). Forecasting performance of grey prediction for education expenditure and school enrollment. *Economics of Education Review, 31*(4), 452–462.

Ványolós, I. (2011). The impact of state-imposed fund balance limits on school districts: Evidence from New York state. *Journal of Public Budgeting, Accounting & Financial Management, 23*(2), 166–187.

Welsch, D. M. (2011). Charter school competition and its impact on employment spending in Michigan's public schools. *Contemporary Economic Policy, 29*(3), 323–336.

Williams, D. W., & Onochie, J. (2013). The Rube Goldberg machine of budget implementation, or is there a structural deficit in the New York City budget? *Public Budgeting & Finance, 33*(4), 1–21. https://doi.org/10.1111/j.1540-5850.2013.12021.x.

16

Budget Uncertainty and the Quality of Nonprofit Charter School Enrollment Projections

Todd L. Ely

Introduction

This chapter provides the following elements:

- A review of the limited literature on nonprofit forecasting.
- Nonprofit charter school enrollment forecasts are used to assess the accuracy of business planning efforts by nonprofit organizations.
- A look at the uncertainty that pervades charter school operations and nonprofits, generally, and the associated organizational characteristics.
- Consideration of the implications for nonprofits of over- and under-forecasting.
- Raises additional questions, including whether nonprofit forecasting is fundamentally different than making forecasts for other private organizations.

Rarely can outsiders assess the accuracy of forecasting by nonprofit organizations. In the corporate world, executives provide forecasts of financial performance on a quarterly or annual basis, but the required (IRS Form 990) and recommended reporting (audited financial statements) for nonprofit organizations focus on disclosing historical activity rather than on prospective forecasting. The absence of such information keeps researchers from

T. L. Ely (✉)
School of Public Affairs, University of Colorado Denver, Denver, CO, USA
e-mail: todd.ely@ucdenver.edu

D. Williams, T. Calabrese (eds.), *The Palgrave Handbook of Government Budget Forecasting*, Palgrave Studies in Public Debt, Spending, and Revenue,
https://doi.org/10.1007/978-3-030-18195-6_16

understanding the quality of the internal planning process in nonprofits. To begin to fill this gap in analyzing nonprofit forecasting, we examine the relationship between nonprofit charter school characteristics and the accuracy of enrollment forecasting, which is the primary driver of revenues and costs.

This chapter asks how accurate are charter schools' forecasts of student enrollments by comparing past forecasts to actual student numbers in the future. Forecasting error is then explained based on the characteristics of the nonprofit charter schools. Understanding the institutional characteristics correlated with improved forecasts is relevant for predicting which nonprofit organizations are likely to remain financially healthy while providing quality educational services. Specifically, overly optimistic enrollment projections can threaten a charter school's survival.

Overall, we find that while the average charter school organization forecast is quite accurate, there is wide variation in the quality of forecasts. School and organizational factors are especially influential with larger and older organizations less likely to make overly optimistic enrollment forecasts. Governance structure also matters for the accuracy and direction of forecast errors. The ability of charter schools to accurately project enrollments worsens dramatically in the later years of extended forecasts. The paper proceeds with a discussion of charter schools as nonprofits before reviewing the limited literature on nonprofit forecasting. After presenting our data and methodological approach, empirical results are considered along with limitations and conclusions.

Charter Schools as Nonprofit Organizations

Charter schools are publicly funded schools run by private, nonprofit, or for-profit organizations that operate alongside traditional public schools. The overwhelming majority of the charter schools nationwide, more than 85 percent, are nonprofit organizations. As of the 2015–2016 school year, there were 6857 charter schools (increasing from less than 1500 in the year 2000) operating in 41 states and the District of Columbia (Glander 2017). Like the broader nonprofit sector, charter organizations are personnel-intensive, and exhibit great heterogeneity in size and sophistication—from small "mom and pop" operations running a single local charter school to national charter management organizations (CMOs) with a network of related, mission-driven, charter schools. Of the charter schools, nearly three-quarters are stand-alone schools outside of a CMO (Rebarber and Zgainer 2014).

While nonprofit finances are routinely characterized by voluntary contributions from donors, the reality is that the sector generates more revenues from exchange transactions that are generally consistent with organizational mission. In particular, charter school operations depend heavily on government funds paid on a per pupil basis dictated by state education funding systems. This primary funding is supplemented with state and federal grants, extensive fundraising and, in some cases, fee-for-service activities.

Although nonprofits are generally subject to public oversight, charter school regulation by the state and oversight by authorizers is relatively high because of the perceived stakes of the provided service (primary education). A school's charter, or contract to operate, comes with an expiration date at which point the authorizer can renew or revoke the charter. The length of a charter contract varies from 3 to 30 years, with nearly a third of charter school authorizers using a 5-year term (NACSA 2014). Revocations of charters are most commonly associated with missing academic targets, poor financial performance, or a combination of the two. Given the dependence on enrollment-based funding and satisfying authorizer performance requirements, charter schools face the common start-up challenges of most new nonprofits in addition to charter "renewal risk" (Hassel 1999). In fact, roughly 15 percent of charter schools closed between 1992 and 2011, and nearly two-thirds of those closed for financial reasons or mismanagement (Consoletti 2011).

Nonprofit organizations often compete with each other for government contracts, grants, and donor funds. Charter schools face, arguably, even more intense competition for resources in a tightly focused geographic area. Charter schools not only compete with each other, especially where authorization of new charter schools is relatively easy, but also with existing traditional public and private schools, the latter which tend to also be nonprofit organizations. This high degree of competition for financial resources and students makes forecasting especially critical for a charter school's sustainability. The frequent rivalry between charter and traditional public schools is perhaps atypical of the relationship between nonprofits and their public sector partners.

Nonprofit Forecasting and Planning

Budgets are merely plans that indicate what an organization's objectives are, and how it expects to obtain and use resources to achieve these goals. Periodic shortfalls between revenues and expenses might be manageable, but nonprofits in general need to operate with surpluses (i.e., revenues in excess of expenses) to ensure survival, the replacement of assets that wear out, and to maintain purchasing power. Almost all studies of nonprofit finances rely upon historical data based on the Form 990 informational returns filed with the Internal Revenue Service or audited financial statements. In either case, the data are retrospective and do not permit analysis of how well nonprofit organizations manage the basic business process of forecasting revenues and implementing financial plans.

What we do know from the literature does not suggest the sophisticated use of forecasting in nonprofit planning, especially among smaller nonprofits. Frumkin notes that charter school management "consists largely of putting out one fire after another, leaving little time to think more strategically" (2003, 5). Zietlow (1989) studied the financial management practices of 47 religious nonprofit organizations that depend primarily upon voluntary contributions and found that increasingly complex analytical and financial techniques were employed as nonprofits aged, grew larger, and hired managers with finance expertise. In another study, Marwell and Calabrese (2014) find that over 90 percent of child welfare nonprofits in New York State use budget-to-actual variance reports to monitor whether financial projections are being met. These nonprofit organizations tend to be larger, older, and more financially sophisticated than most, which aligns with Zietlow's (1989) findings.

One study surveyed organizations to compare for-profit and nonprofit forecasting behavior and found meaningful similarities and differences (Herbig et al. 1995). Both for-profit and nonprofit organizations reported greater use of qualitative forecasting methods than quantitative approaches, while nonprofits considered their forecasting to be relatively less effective. Nonprofit forecasting was less frequent with longer forecasting cycles than for-profit firms and tended to forecast primarily based on historic trends, surveys of clients, or regression models. Despite greater involvement by the nonprofit organizations' executives in forecasting, the resulting forecasts were deemed less influential in management than in for-profit organizations.

Beyond these studies, there is very little empirical evidence of nonprofit forecasting practices, skill, and accuracy. Nonprofit charter schools provide us a unique opportunity to observe internal forecasts and assess what factors are associated with improved or diminished forecasting capacity. As the first charter school opened in 1992, charter schools also represent (in general) a younger and smaller nonprofit sample compared to prior studies, providing insights on the forecasting capacity of a different and unexamined population.

In the case of charter schools, the key forecast that drives all financial decisions is the expected number of students enrolled. Public school finance formulas across the country are fundamentally tied to the number of students being educated by a district whether measured on a single count date or based on average daily attendance (Ely and Fermanich 2013). The survival of charter schools is therefore dependent on attracting and keeping students. Therefore, the charter school-level planning process necessitates correctly forecasting enrollments.

While revenues are clearly determined in large part by student enrollment, so too are expenses. Common practice, as well as prospective parents, demands particular teacher-student ratios, so student enrollment forecasts require schools to staff accordingly. For a small charter school, adding an additional teacher is a critical organizational decision and one that is difficult to reverse if enrollment and classroom estimates prove overly rosy. This decision is similar to ones facing small, but expanding, nonprofits about adding new staff to help manage such growth. Enrollment forecasts for charter schools are arguably more sensitive than in traditional public schools, since they lack the flexibility of a school district to shift resources in the event of errors in school-level forecasts.

A small number of studies highlight the challenges and uncertainty in charter school forecasting. A study of charter school borrowing collected pro forma financial statement items for 85 charter schools and compared them to the actual outcomes in a single fiscal year (Balboni and Berry 2012). The report finds that the prevalence and size of any errors for each financial measure move in tandem with that of enrollment. Balboni and Berry (2012) report the median difference between forecasted and actual enrollment for their sample of charter schools to be only 0.7 percent; however, the difference between the average enrollment forecast and actual enrollment is a much larger and positive 21.5 percent of actuals (meaning that the average actual enrollment was much higher than forecasted by the schools). Cases where forecasts were greatly overstated (actual enrollment lower than forecasted) were characterized as being small charter schools anticipating growth, while the dramatically understated forecast errors were associated with large CMOs that possibly added new schools into their networks.

At the higher CMO level, a review of charter network growth expectations found that "fewer than half of the 25 CMOs met or were on track to meet their growth targets" (Farrell et al. 2014). Evidence of forecast quality is also found in an assessment of the Next Generation Learning Challenges initiative, which supports technology-supported personalized learning in start-up charter schools (Miller et al. 2014). The study found that across eight newly formed charter schools "many missed projections during their first year of implementation, forcing them to make tough choices about how to spend their resources while balancing their budgets" (Miller et al. 2014, 1). All but one of the charter schools fell short of their projected enrollment. The median enrollment forecast error of 14 percent translated into reduced public support of $135,000 per school (Miller et al. 2014). The authors note the difficulty adjusting labor costs based on revised enrollments and suggest supporting enrollment expectations with adequate recruiting resources, as well as utilizing a flexible budget in case enrollment forecasts prove too optimistic.

Finally, the central role of forecasting student enrollment in charter school operations is apparent from its role in charter school closures. Charter schools are closed far more often for financial troubles (41.7 percent of closures through 2011), most prominently for inadequate enrollment, than for poor academic performance (Consoletti 2011).

Data and Methodological Approach

Data Collection

Nonprofit charter schools do not regularly share enrollment forecasts with external audiences. Enrollment forecasts are not a required component of either IRS Form 990 filings or audited financial statements. Informal annual reports may discuss current charter school growth and plans for new schools, but typically lack detailed enrollment projections. For these reasons, we look to a subset of nonprofit charter schools who disclose forecasted enrollment growth—those borrowing through the municipal bond market—to collect enrollment forecasts.

Enrollment forecasts are included in official statements, which are required by the Municipal Securities Rulemaking Board (MSRB) to describe a public debt issuance, help market and promote the debt sale, and disclose "risks and other material information associated with investment in the securities" (Abola and Spitz 2011, 7–8). We collect official statements for all charter school bond issues from 1998 to 2010 based on a comprehensive national list of activity (see Balboni and 2012). The population of issuances is 483 across 28 states and the District of Columbia. Each official statement, when publicly available through MSRB's EMMA repository, was reviewed and the reported enrollment forecasts were collected for as many years as provided. A single official statement may provide enrollment forecasts for multiple years or no years. Forecasts are most common for the next 1 to 3 years, although 17 percent of the sample represents forecasted enrollments 4 to 6 years away. The unit of analysis for the study is generally the charter school in a specific school year, although in some cases aggregated forecasts for multiple schools require that the CMO is the unit of analysis. The number of enrollment forecast observations in the sample totals 1048 for 287 schools across 23 states.[1] The official statements are only examined through 2010, since the enrollment data

[1] We omit the largest 5 percent of positive and negative forecast errors to lessen mismeasurement concerns. Analysis including the outliers is generally consistent, although the magnitude of statistically significant relationships grows.

necessary to assess forecasts is not broadly available for more current forecasts. High forecast error observations (>10 percent in either direction) were revisited to ensure that the appropriate enrollments are matched with the schools identified in the official statements.

Enrollment forecasts in official statements are classified as forward-looking statements under Section 27A of the Securities Act of 1933 and Section 21E of the Securities Exchange Act of 1934. Although the "completeness and accuracy of the Official Statement" is the responsibility of the issuer, they are typically compiled by legal counsel (disclosure or bond counsel) along with support from "underwriters, financial advisors, feasibility consultants, accountants and attorneys" (Abola and Spitz 2011, 13–14). As all planning is forward-looking, the enrollment forecasts included in official statements are intended to be accurate expectations of the charter school managers.

The debt market enforces discipline on organizations in a number of ways. Primarily, only stronger charter schools even consider issuing public debt versus alternative means of raising capital, such as borrowing from a local financial institution or fundraising and capital campaigns. Since charter schools access the tax-exempt bond market through conduit issuers, the conduit (usually a public authority) must be willing to serve as the intermediary for the school. For details about nonprofit use of conduits and tax-exempt borrowing, see Ely and Calabrese (2017) and Calabrese and Ely (2016), respectively. Even if a charter school works with a conduit to bring a bond issue to market, the ultimate disciplinary force is the interest rate demanded from the market. If the long-term stability of the charter school is perceived as low, then the cost of borrowing will rise. At the extreme, an increase in interest rates will deter the organization from borrowing in the public markets or pursuing the project. The charter schools considered here are expected to be more accurate forecasting future enrollments relative to the average charter school due to greater management capacity. Alternately, charter schools borrowing money may overstate their future enrollments to increase demand for bonds and lower interest costs. Despite these potential biases, the variation in oversight and access to debt across the represented states is substantial.

The enrollment forecast data from official statements are of use to us only when matched with the actual student enrollments experienced by the charter schools in the forecasted years. We use the National Center for Education Statistics (NCES) 12-digit identification number to match the charter school forecasts with descriptive data, including actual enrollments, collected through the NCES Common Core of Data (CCD) program. The matching of bond issues to specific schools is complicated by the fact that many bond issues include multiple schools. In these cases, the official statement may present aggregated enrollment forecasts, typically when the borrower is a CMO with multiple charter schools. For such cases, we aggregate the individual school information from the CCD to match the level of the forecasts.

The CCD provides student demographic information, geographic locale, grades served, and visibility into a school's years of operation. The 2013 National Authorizer-Charter School Catalog from The National Charter School Resource Center is used to identify the type of authorizer for each charter school. Summary statistics are presented in Table 16.1 for the entire sample and by forecast accuracy. The mean forecast error for the sample is 1.6 percent, indicating a slight tendency to plan for larger than realized enrollments.

Table 16.1 Summary statistics

	Full sample			Forecast > 5% over actual	
Variable	*N*	Mean	Std. dev.	*N*	Mean
Forecast error percent	1048	1.64	22.65	361	23.55
Forecast error percent (absolute value)	1048	15.30	16.78	361	23.55
Missed forecast (overforecast of >5%)	1048	0.34	–	361	1.00
School/organizational variables					
Adequate yearly progress (1,0)	734	0.75	–	244	0.75
Size (enrollment)	1048	700.02	595.79	361	579.46
Other grade span (1,0)	1048	0.49	–	361	0.47
High school (1,0)	1048	0.06	–	361	0.07
Middle school (1,0)	1048	0.02	–	361	0.00
Elementary school (1,0)	1048	0.43	–	361	0.45
School age (years)	1048	7.15	3.67	361	6.60
New money (1,0)	1048	0.79	–	361	0.89
Rated (1,0)	1048	0.45	–	361	0.32
Minority student share (fraction)	1048	0.48	0.35	361	0.47
Governance					
CMO (1,0)	1048	0.40	–	361	0.36
Higher education authorizer (1,0)	1048	0.31	–	361	0.44
Independent charter board authorizer (1,0)	1048	0.32	–	361	0.31
Local education agency authorizer (1,0)	1048	0.27	–	361	0.18
Municipality authorizer (1,0)	1048	0.01	–	361	0.01
Nonprofit authorizer (1,0)	1048	0.02	–	361	0.02
State educ. agency authorizer (1,0)	1048	0.07	–	361	0.04
NAPCS state charter law score	1048	140.91	13.86	361	140.29
Environment					
Time-to-forecast (years)	1048	2.15	1.31	361	2.21
Large city (1,0)	1048	0.32	–	361	0.30
Other city (1,0)	1048	0.14	–	361	0.17
Suburb (1,0)	1048	0.31	–	361	0.26
Town (1,0)	1048	0.04	–	361	0.04
Rural (1,0)	1048	0.18	–	361	0.22
County private schools (count)	1048	118.37	156.08	361	93.90

Model and Variables

We model annual enrollment forecast error as a function of organization, governance, and environment characteristics as described in the following:

$$E = f(Q, Z, G, A, P, R, D, M, O, T, S, H, L, C) \qquad (16.1)$$

Where E = Forecast Error, Q = Quality, Z = Size, G = Grade Span, A = Age, P = Growth Plans, R = Risk, D = Student Demographics, M = Charter Management, O = Organization, T = Authorization Type, S = State, H = Time-to-Forecast, L = Locale, and C = Competition.

The analysis uses two primary specifications intended to capture both the magnitude and direction of the forecast errors. Given the stakes involved with failing to meet projected enrollments, we first operationalize the forecast error dependent variable as a dichotomous measure representing a forecasted enrollment that was materially higher than reality (a positive forecast error). We define material as any forecast that was overstated by 5 percent or more. Although there are meaningful, and sometimes problematic, organizational implications for exceeding growth expectations (like stress on facilities and human resources), the primary concern with charter school planning is a shortfall in per pupil revenue. Due to the dichotomous measure of the dependent variable, the model is estimated using probit analysis.

A second operationalization moves beyond the dichotomous representation of forecast error to capture the magnitude of the forecast error as a continuous construct. The dependent variable is the absolute value of the enrollment forecast error in percentage terms. The model is estimated using ordinary least squares (OLS) regression.[2] The continuous dependent variable provides greater visibility into the size of the forecast error as an indication of accurate business planning without judging whether or not the direction of the error is acceptable to the organization. For any specific charter school, forecast error observations are not independent. Last year's forecast is directly related to the following year's enrollment expectations. We address this lack of within-cluster independence using cluster-robust standard errors at the charter school or CMO level.

We include factors expected, based on the literature, to influence the quality of nonprofit forecasting. These variables are divided into three categories: school/organization, governance, and environment. The school, or organization, factors comprised the academic quality, size of the school represented by enrollment, the grades served, the age of the school, the purpose for which the organization is issuing debt, whether a credit rating was

[2] The forecast percent error is calculated for charter school i, in school year t, as: $\frac{\text{predicted}_{it} - \text{actual}_{it}}{\text{actual}_{it}} \times 100$.

received, and the demographic composition of the student body. Governance variables include whether the school is managed by a CMO as part of a charter school network, the type of authorizer, and the charter school's state or the friendliness of a state's laws toward charter schools. Environment factors represent the time-to-forecast, the geographic locale, and competition for students from other nearby schools.

School Variables

School, or organization, level characteristics are expected to be strongly related to management capacity and the ability to accurately forecast future enrollments. Measuring nonprofit service quality is often challenging, but charter school academic performance is regularly assessed within a state accountability framework and in accordance with federal requirements. High-quality educational programs translate into improved recruiting and retention of students and the increased likelihood of charter renewal. Omitting a measure of school quality from our models will likely overstate the role of a school's size and age in business planning since more academically successful schools will be in a position to persist and grow relative to low performers. We use whether a school satisfied adequate yearly progress (AYP) requirements under the No Child Left Behind Act in the prior year as a readily available, but crude, proxy for relative academic quality within a given state. The AYP measure is available starting in the 2003 school year for existing schools, although many states received waivers from its continued use starting in 2012. Although missing data are problematic, we include the charter schools' AYP in an alternative specification as a measure of school quality.

A school's size measured as enrollment, or that of a CMO, is expected to be directly related to improved forecasts. A larger student body is less likely to be proportionately impacted by a small number of student withdrawals or last-minute decisions to attend an alternate school. Scale economies in education also suggest that more resources are available for management functions in schools or networks with larger enrollments. Since public funding is awarded on a per pupil basis, overhead costs can be more widely spread out with more students and organizations are more likely to be able to hire a dedicated position focused on the forecasting and planning functions. The marginal revenue from an additional student added to a school with an empty seat far exceeds the associated marginal costs. This explains the extensive efforts charter schools take to market themselves and recruit students, which often include going door-to-door to increase the school's exposure. The central role of public funding means that the enrollment of a charter school or network is a good proxy for total revenues.

Grade span is represented as a series of dichotomous variables indicating whether elementary, middle, high, or some other combination of those grade levels are served by the school or network. Organizations that serve higher grades or wider grade ranges, like kindergarten through high school, may benefit from less student mobility as older students can travel further distances to and from school even if the family experiences a residential move. Schools covering wide ranges of grades can internally recruit students using lower grades as a pipeline, which reduces uncertainty in the recruitment process.

An organization's age frequently dictates its operational stability. Projecting enrollment becomes easier with experience and a track record, relative to a start-up charter school. The importance of experience also reflects attrition bias, since schools with poor planning and performance do not survive to be more mature charter schools. Frumkin described the developmental stages of charter schools as the "start-up stage," "expansion stage," and "institutionalization stage" (2003, 11). The age of a charter school is determined by the number of years they report activity in the CCD.

The purpose for which the school's borrowing is taking place serves as a proxy for whether the charter school or network has expansion plans or intends on maintaining existing enrollments. The official statements detail the uses of the borrowed funds, but due to the wide range of uses (such as new construction, facility acquisition, renovation, refunding, and combinations of each of these) we control for whether the debt is classified as a new money offering. A new money offering is for capital improvements or acquisitions, rather than the borrower simply lowering the cost of outstanding debt in a manner similar to a mortgage refinancing.

An organization can choose to purchase credit ratings as part of the debt issuance process. The credit rating, which is broadly based on an organization's financial and nonfinancial characteristics (including management and regulatory considerations), reduces information asymmetry by certifying risk levels and credit quality for investors. For our purposes, we control for whether a credit rating was secured for the debt issuance rather than using the actual credit rating. The reported credit rating may obscure the organization's underlying credit quality in the later years we examine or when credit enhancement programs or bond insurance are used. The act of generating a credit rating adds another layer of oversight and scrutiny of the organization's financial condition and forecasts.

The student composition of a charter school or network may matter for the quality of enrollment forecasts if demographic characteristics are associated with varied degrees of student retention and mobility. We use the share of minority students as an indicator of mobility among disadvantaged populations, since data on the number of students that qualify for federal free and reduced lunch programs is more frequently missing for the sample schools.

Governance Variables

The charter school's management, authorizer, and state can also have implications for missing, meeting, or exceeding enrollment forecasts. Charter management organizations (CMOs) operate multiple schools, providing flexibility over time in achieving growth and having additional management resources akin to a school district. Official statements that represent borrowing for multiple-related schools are coded as CMOs. Authorizers are the gatekeepers that control access to charters and are tasked with continuous monitoring, including periodic charter reviews where they can renew or revoke the charter. The variety of authorizer types and the desire to give charter schools multiple authorizing options suggest that each may have meaningful differences in incentives and oversight practices, but the expectations about the effects of different authorizer types on oversight are ambiguous. The different authorizer types are included as a series of dichotomous indicators with independent charter boards, the most common authorizer in our sample, omitted as the reference category.

Charter schools are governed by state law and these laws are often ranked or assessed based on how friendly or supportive they are to charter schools. State-fixed effects are used to control for governance institutions and time-invariant characteristics of each state. Alternately, we use in unreported specifications a score and ranking of state charter school laws based on the 2013 National Alliance for Public Charter Schools (NAPCS) model charter school law (Ziebarth 2014). We present our estimates with state-fixed effects, since they better address concerns over omitted state-level variables and the NAPCS measure does not alter the findings.

Environment Variables

The period for which enrollment is being forecasted, or the forecast horizon, should affect accuracy. The confidence in any forecast decreases as the time-to-forecast grows. With time comes uncertainty, which is the challenge for long-term planning in any organization. A charter school may be confident in its forecasts for the next school year given its current enrollment, number of applications, typical applicant yield, existing competition, and waitlist size. As forecasts move farther into the future, each of these factors may begin to vary in addition to unknown regulatory or policy changes (especially related to charter renewal). We include the years to the enrollment forecast, the forecast year minus the issuance year, as a measure of the planning uncertainty that accrues over time.

Charter schools are generally an urban and suburban education policy reform. Population density matters for the recruiting and availability of students, while there may also be different levels of movement across schools based on available alternatives. We use dichotomous measures of locale type, broadly construed as large city, other city, town, and rural, to control for geography and omit the large city indicator as the reference group. Competition from and proximity to other charter schools, traditional public schools, and private schools may lead to lower or higher than expected enrollments. We include the number of private schools in the charter school's county (aggregated using the Private School Universe Survey from the NCES) as a proxy for the level of competition, as well as opportunity, since private school activity represents families already willing to eschew assigned public schools. We expect more competition to result in increased uncertainty in forecasts.

Results

Missed Forecast Model

We first examine the factors associated with charter school organizations making overly optimistic forecasts, which are considered to be the more damaging type of forecast error (for the probit estimates, see columns 1 and 2 in Table 16.2). Missing enrollment forecasts in this manner limits the organization's ability to benefit from scale economies, reduces public funding levels based on pupil counts, stresses the debt service coverage ratios expected at the time of borrowing, and potentially increases the odds of a charter being revoked. Recall that we define a forecast miss as one that exceeds the actual enrollment by more than 5 percent of the forecast. The probit model correctly classifies 74 percent of the observations. The school and organizational independent variables are the primary influences on missed forecasts.

As anticipated, the size of the organization measured as its enrollment is negatively and statistically significantly associated with the likelihood of overestimating enrollments. An increase in the organization's current enrollment from 700 (the sample mean) to 1300 (a one standard deviation change) decreases the likelihood of materially missing the forecast by 14 percentage points holding all other factors at their means. Relative to charter school organizations that offer a combination of grade levels, middle schools are less prone to overforecasting their enrollment. The magnitude is large with a middle school nearly 28 percentage points less likely to overforecast. Reasons for this relationship may be that middle schools have fewer grades than other grade span types and therefore are less prone to the cumulative effects of student attrition. Alternately, high schools are significantly more likely to overforecast enrollment relative to schools and CMOs offering multiple levels of grades. This may be tied to the fact that some charter high schools stop accepting new students after the sophomore year of high school and are more impacted by attrition or a reflection that stand-alone charter high schools lack the dedicated pipeline of students available to the reference category of organizations that also offer middle school grades.

An organization's age is often equated with increasing stability and more experienced managers. The results here support such a relationship with older schools being statistically significantly less likely to overforecast enrollments. Specifically, a school that is 4 years older, roughly a standard deviation increase from the mean of 7 years, reduces the likelihood of a forecast miss by nearly 5 percentage points from a predicted probability of 0.33–0.28. It is noteworthy that these potentially harmful forecast errors are not significantly different based on the demographics of students being served. Using a reduced sample where AYP information is available, the measure of school quality is not significantly related to a charter school substantially missing its forecast by overforecasting (see column 2 of Table 16.2). This nonfinding potentially reflects the AYP being too blunt a measure to capture the role of quality in attracting and retaining students.

Governance factors, specifically management by a CMO, do not appear to be associated with overly optimistic enrollment forecast misses. The exception is that having a state education agency as authorizer is significantly, both statistically and materially, associated with improved enrollment forecasts relative to independent chartering boards (the reference category). Among environment factors and as expected, the time-to-forecast is positively and significantly related to an increasing likelihood of overforecasting enrollments in the broader sample specification. As forecasts move from the mean of roughly 2 years out to 4 years in the future, the predicted probability of an overforecasting error climbs from 0.32 to 0.38, an increase of 6 percentage points.

Table 16.2 Missed forecast error model results

	Missed forecast model		Absolute percentage error model	
	DV = "1" if forecast was >5% over actual enrollment, "0" otherwise		DV = absolute value of (predicted—actual)/ actual*100	
	(1)	(2)	(3)	(4)
School/organizational variables				
Adequate yearly progress (yes=1, no=0)	–	−0.067	–	−2.354
		(0.163)		(1.946)
Size (enrollment)	−0.066***	−0.061***	−0.265	−0.004*
	(0.021)	(0.022)	(0.218)	(0.002)
High school (1,0)	0.563*	0.593	−2.137	−6.452*
	(0.335)	(0.456)	(3.302)	(3.421)
Middle school (1,0)	−1.461**	−1.407**	−10.770***	−12.144***
	(0.616)	(0.619)	(2.136)	(2.148)
Elementary school (1,0)	−0.033	−0.107	−6.608***	−7.952***
	(0.153)	(0.196)	(1.753)	(1.929)
School age (years)	−0.060**	−0.062**	−0.521**	−0.303
	(0.025)	(0.028)	(0.220)	(0.258)
New money (1,0)	0.143	0.141	2.903	2.905
	(0.241)	(0.250)	(2.207)	(2.401)
Rated (1,0)	−0.007	−0.047	−1.970	−1.848
	(0.191)	(0.224)	(1.969)	(2.019)
Minority student share	0.006	0.072	3.214	3.168
(fraction)	(0.279)	(0.321)	(2.766)	(3.135)
Governance				
CMO (1,0)	−0.131	−0.272	4.199*	4.197*
	(0.228)	(0.266)	(2.157)	(2.367)
Higher education	0.385	1.033	0.697	5.975
authorizer (1,0)	(0.634)	(0.790)	(5.590)	(6.085)
Local educ. agency	0.664	0.678	5.711**	3.865
authorizer (1,0)	(0.421)	(0.534)	(2.574)	(2.657)
Municipality authorizer	−0.122	–	21.499***	21.733***
(1,0)	(0.863)		(6.218)	(6.655)
Nonprofit authorizer	0.262	0.813	18.661**	25.972***
(1,0)	(0.702)	(0.815)	(8.036)	(8.985)
State educ. agency	−0.937*	−4.763***	−1.979	−2.464
authorizer (1,0)	(0.505)	(0.332)	(2.741)	(2.852)
Environment				
Time-to-forecast (years)	0.081*	0.064	2.696***	2.508***
	(0.042)	(0.047)	(0.494)	(0.577)
Other city (1,0)	−0.180	−0.297	−0.131	−0.620
	(0.274)	(0.315)	(2.554)	(2.927)
Suburb (1,0)	−0.136	−0.056	−0.826	−2.523
	(0.238)	(0.260)	(2.387)	(2.487)
Town (1,0)	−0.082	0.311	−7.041*	−7.283
	(0.426)	(0.497)	(3.718)	(4.773)

(continued)

Table 16.2 (continued)

	Missed forecast model		Absolute percentage error model	
	DV = "1" if forecast was >5% over actual enrollment, "0" otherwise		DV = absolute value of (predicted—actual)/ actual*100	
	(1)	(2)	(3)	(4)
Rural (1,0)	0.020	−0.125	−0.120	−0.204
	(0.271)	(0.294)	(2.621)	2.979
County private schools (count)	−0.001	−0.001	−0.002	0.002
	(0.001)	(0.001)	(0.003)	(0.003)
Constant	0.353	−0.131	12.263***	12.715**
	(0.766)	(0.920)	(4.391)	(5.330)
State-fixed effects	Yes	Yes	Yes	Yes
Observations	1048	734	1048	746
Pseudo R-squared/ R-squared	0.1594	0.1711	0.203	0.291
% Correctly predicted/ adjusted R-squared	74.08	75.48	0.235	0.251

Notes: Cluster-robust standard errors (school or CMO level) in parentheses. State-fixed effects unreported

***$p < 0.01$, **$p < 0.05$, *$p < 0.10$

Forecast Absolute Percent Error Model

Switching to a dependent variable that is a more appropriate measure of forecasting error and absent qualitative assessment of the organizational impact (see results in Table 16.2, columns 3 and 4), we see that the size of the organization is not significantly associated with the magnitude of the forecast error (note that the errors are already scaled as percentages). Both middle schools and elementary schools have substantially lower absolute percent errors, suggesting they are generally more accurate in absolute terms than charter schools with nontraditional grade spans. The age of the organization continues to matter for generating more accurate forecasts in the broader sample. Every additional year of being open is associated with a decrease in the absolute percent error of more than half a percentage point. We again use a subsample where AYP information is available and do not find the proxy measure of quality to be significantly related to the absolute value of a charter school's forecasting percent error (see column 4 of Table 16.2). There are minor changes in the statistical significance of other estimated coefficients when including AYP. Further investigation is needed to determine whether these changes are simply an artifact of the smaller sample size.

Governance variables appear to be relevant to the magnitude of forecast errors in a manner not captured in the categorical representation used in the previous analysis. Most notably, being part of a CMO dramatically increases the absolute percent error by over 4 percentage points which is approximately a quarter of the sample mean. This surfaces because CMO error in the sample tends to be through under-forecasting and growing at a faster enrollment rate than originally anticipated. Charter school organizations authorized by local education agencies, municipalities, and nonprofits are all more likely to have substantially larger forecast errors than those chartered by an independent board. It is possible that both local education agency and nonprofit authorizers serve as advocates for their charter schools and their continued growth.

The uncertainty that comes with forecasting farther into the future is also reflected in the absolute percent error results. Every year that passes between when a forecast is made and the enrollments are realized is associated with a 2.7 percentage point increase in error (a 17.6 percent increase from the mean absolute percent error). This means that a forecast made for the upcoming school year is expected to be an average of 10.8 percentage points more accurate than a forecast made for a school year five years from now. By ignoring the direction of the forecast error, we see that charter school organizations in town settings tend to have significantly lower absolute forecast errors (although only at the 10 percent significance level). It is expected that, relative to the dynamic urban environment, there is both less unanticipated competition and growth in potential students in a town environment.

Limitations

The analysis has a number of limitations. As mentioned, the charter school organizations in the sample are more mature than a representative sample. We do believe that this results in conservative findings about the quality and accuracy of forecasting, but it may also bias the relationships presented here. For example, governance may matter more for younger organizations. The sample also suffers from some attrition bias that understates forecast misestimates. Charter schools that have gone out of business, typically due to the revocation of charters, are omitted once they are closed despite the fact that this really represents the largest of possible forecast errors. Of the charter schools with forecasts in our sample, 52 closed either during or following the forecast period.

Conclusions

Charter schools are a growing and policy-relevant segment of the nonprofit sector. Charter schools operate in a competitive environment where recruiting and retaining students is the key to receiving public funds and sustaining operations. Unlike many nonprofits, charter schools both collaborate and compete with their public sector counterparts. We use enrollment forecasts from official statements combined with actual enrollments to consider the factors that contribute to the quality of forecasting. The visibility into operational forecasting is unusual given that most financial reporting for nonprofits is historical.

Overall, we find that while the average charter school organization's enrollment forecast is quite accurate, there is wide variation in the quality of forecasts. Qualitatively, we suggest that overforecasting is more problematic for an organization than inaccurate forecasts that fall below actual enrollments and examine forecast error as both categorical and continuous constructs. School and organizational factors are especially prominent correlates with forecast errors. Larger organizations are less likely to make and present overly optimistic enrollment forecasts. The age of an organization is similarly associated with less problematic forecasting errors. Both organizational size and age may be proxies for management capacity, but age may also indicate that an organization is no longer in the growth phase where uncertainty in forecasting is more prevalent.

Governance structure matters for the accuracy and direction of forecast errors. Although CMOs are not more likely to overestimate enrollments, they do experience larger absolute forecast errors due to faster than anticipated expansion. Authorizers are the gatekeepers to charter school organizations and state education agencies are associated with fewer overly optimistic growth forecasts, while local education agency and nonprofit authorizers are related to higher absolute forecast errors. Our analysis reiterates the uncertainty and challenge of planning for nonprofit organizations, especially when making multi-year plans. The ability to accurately forecast enrollments worsens dramatically as the time to the forecasted period expands.

The implications of these findings for individual nonprofit charter schools, charter school networks, and authorizers include recognizing the common fallibility of forecasts and the potential financial challenges associated with overforecasting enrollments. Networked CMOs have, on average, understated their actual pace of growth to investors and should potentially be less cautious in presenting future enrollments to avoid looking riskier than needed.

Authorizers, on the other hand, should carefully consider their role in guiding charter school growth and expanding oversight to enrollment forecasts used to support borrowing activity. Charter school bond investors and credit rating agencies would be wise to consider organizational characteristics, like size, age, and authorizer, when assessing the likelihood of forecasted enrollments being realized.

This research provides a preliminary look at the uncertainty that pervades charter school operations and nonprofits, more generally, but also raises a number of questions. Primarily, the question remains whether nonprofit forecasting is fundamentally different than for other organizations. Does mission and resource dependency alter the forecasting process relative to for-profit and government organizations? The sector's receipt of potentially volatile donations is potentially a key source of differentiation. Ultimately, small and nascent nonprofits may share more in common with other start-up organizations than their larger and more established nonprofit peers. A key source of differentiation may be the stakes involved, given the public-supporting purposes of nonprofits. In the case of charter schools, an inability to accurately forecast enrollments can lead directly to fiscal deterioration, a loss of charter, and school closure. The burden of such school closures falls primarily on existing students and their families who must cope with the displacement and disruption to their education.

References

Abola, B. D., & Spitz, S. A. (2011). *Disclosure obligations of issuers of municipal securities*. San Francisco, CA: Orrick, Herrington & Sutcliffe LLP.

Balboni, E., & Berry, W. (2012). *Charter school bond issuance: A complete history volume 2*. The Educational Facilities Financing Center of Local Initiatives Support Corporation. Retrieved from http://www.charterlenders.org/wp-content/uploads/2013/09/LISC-Charter-School-Bond-Issuance-September-2012.pdf.

Calabrese, T. D., & Ely, T. L. (2016). Borrowing for the public good: The growing importance of tax-exempt bonds for public charities. *Nonprofit and Voluntary Sector Quarterly, 45*(3), 458–477.

Consoletti, A. (2011). *The state of charter schools: What we know – and what we do not – about performance and accountability*. Washington, DC: The Center for Education Reform (CER).

Ely, T. L., & Calabrese, T. D. (2017). Public borrowing for private organizations: Costs and structure of tax-exempt debt through conduit issuers. *Public Budgeting & Finance, 37*(1), 3–25.

Ely, T. L., & Fermanich, M. L. (2013). Learning to count: School finance formula count methods and attendance-related student outcomes. *Journal of Education Finance, 38*(4), 343–369.

Farrell, C., Nayfack, M. B., Smith, J., & Wohlstetter, P. (2014). One size does not fit all: understanding the variation in charter management scale-up. *Journal of Educational Change, 15*(1), 77–97.

Frumkin, P. (2003). *Creating new schools: The strategic management of charter schools.* The Annie E. Casey Foundation: Baltimore, MD. Retrieved from https://files.eric.ed.gov/fulltext/ED482409.pdf.

Glander, M. (2017). *Selected statistics from the public elementary and secondary education universe: School year 2015–16.* Washington, DC: National Center for Education Statistics. Retrieved from https://nces.ed.gov/pubsearch/pubsinfo.asp?pubid=2018052.

Hassel, B. (1999). *Paying for the charter schoolhouse: Policy options for charter school facilities financing.* St. Paul, MN: Charter Friends National Network. Retrieved from https://files.eric.ed.gov/fulltext/ED460588.pdf.

Herbig, P., Milewicz, J., & Golden, J. E. (1995). Forecasting behavioral differences between for-profit firms and nonprofit organizations. *Journal of Nonprofit & Public Sector Marketing, 3*(1), 3–15.

Marwell, N. P., & Calabrese, T. D. (2014). A deficit model of collaborative governance: government–nonprofit fiscal relations in the provision of child welfare services. *Journal of Public Administration Research and Theory, 25*(4), 1031–1058.

Miller, L., Gross, B., & Lake, R. (2014). *Is personalized learning meeting its productivity promise? Early lessons from pioneering schools.* Retrieved from https://www.crpe.org/publications/personalized-learning-meeting-its-productivity-promise-early-lessons-pioneering-schools.

National Association of Charter School Authorizers (NACSA). (2014). *The state of charter school authorizing 2013.* Chicago. Retrieved from www.qualitycharters.org/wp-content/uploads/2015/08/NACSA_2013-SOCA.pdf.

Rebarber, T., & Zgainer, A. C. (2014). *Survey of America's charter schools 2014.* Washington, DC: The Center for Education Reform (CER). Retrieved from http://edreform.com/wp-content/uploads/2014/02/2014CharterSchoolSurveyFINAL.pdf.

Ziebarth, T. (2014). *Measuring up to the model: A ranking of state charter school laws.* Retrieved from https://files.eric.ed.gov/fulltext/ED568904.pdf.

Zietlow, J. T. (1989). Capital and operating budgeting practices in pure nonprofit organizations. *Financial Accountability & Management, 5*(4), 219–232.

17

Forecasting for Prisons and Jails

Bruce D. McDonald III, J. Winn Decker, and Matthew James Hunt

Major Points

- Although prison forecasts are conducted by every state, no consensus has emerged on how the population is best projected.
- This chapter suggests best practices for the forecasting the prison population:
  - Disaggregate the prison population to separately forecast repeat offenders.
  - Focus on the long term with annual updates.
  - Model the effects of changing policy.
  - Obtain consensus among stakeholders.

Introduction

U.S. prisons have seen a dramatic increase in their criminal population in recent years. In 2017, more than 2.3 million people were incarcerated in the United States (Wagner and Rabuy 2017), an increase of more than 1 million people over the past 20 years and an increase of 2 million since 1980 (U.S. Department of Justice 1999; Wagner and Rabuy 2017). Approximately

B. D. McDonald III (✉) • J. W. Decker • M. J. Hunt
Department of Public Administration, North Carolina State University, Raleigh, NC, USA
e-mail: bmcdona@ncsu.edu; jwdecker@ncsu.edu

D. Williams, T. Calabrese (eds.), *The Palgrave Handbook of Government Budget Forecasting*, Palgrave Studies in Public Debt, Spending, and Revenue,
https://doi.org/10.1007/978-3-030-18195-6_17

1.3 million of the prison population (about 56.7 percent) are incarcerated by states, and another 630,000 (about 27.4 percent) are in local jails (Wagner and Rabuy 2017). This growth in the prison population over the last few decades poses a significant challenge for state policymakers. These challenges include dealing with the overpopulation of facilities, lack of criminal justice workers, and initiatives to try to curb the prison population growth. It also poses a challenge for policymakers in preparing the state's budget.

The growth in the prison population suggests states should plan for their long-term needs during the budget process. The first step in this planning process is the forecasting of future prison populations. These forecasts help states budget for the costs of incarceration and plan for their long-term facility needs. This chapter acts as a primer for prison forecasting with a review of the literature so that those seeking to craft such a forecast can understand the methods and best practices currently in place in the field. As this chapter shows, considerable variation exists within the literature as to the most efficient method of forecasting prison populations. The methods used to forecast the prison population varies from simple trend analysis to more complex statistical modeling and computer simulations. Further complicating the forecast process are the implications that policy changes may have on the population. While many states mandate the forecasting of their prison populations (Wagner and Rabuy 2017), forecasters are challenged in how to best approach the task.

This chapter addresses the challenge of prison forecasting by providing an overview of how the forecasts are conducted. We begin this chapter with a review of the extant literature on prison forecasting, focusing on academic treatments to understanding prison forecasting. Particular attention is paid to the length of time used in each forecasting formula, highlighting the benefits and limitations of both long- and short-term forecasts. The chapter then turns to a discussion on how policies affect the accuracy of a forecast and how to mitigate this variance. The chapter concludes by offering recommendations and insight. These recommendations include having variables for new and repeat offenders, using long-term forecasts revisited on an annual basis, taking into account the changing policy landscape, and including individuals involved in the criminal justice system in forecasting decisions.

Literature Review

To the academic community, forecasts serve as a key way to test scientific theory (Berk 2008). The accuracy of forecasts is important to each study because that accuracy is how theories and assumptions gain credibility.

However, when forecasts fail to come to fruition, model and forecasting teams lose some credibility (Berk 2008). In the context of forecasting prison populations, academics use models to explain criminal behavior and societal impacts on that behavior (see Glaeser et al. 1996; Pratt and Cullen 2000). In practice, forecasts have a different use. They are intended to provide accurate and impartial data of an event or issue that may affect a state or local government's budget.

For governments, forecasting prison populations helps plan the use of resources. When the prison population is projected to increase, for example, a state may have to plan for the construction of a new prison to prevent the overcrowding of its existing facilities. Such endeavors can be slow and expensive, making the planning and accuracy of the states forecast imperative. Unfortunately, in both the academic literature and the practice of states, how forecasters conduct their estimates vary wildly.

Despite this inconsistency of process, however, there are three major themes that run throughout the literature: (a) consideration of the criminal justice system and how its history influences forecasts today, (b) the methodology and methods involved in different forecasts, and (c) the variables and lengths of time used to create forecast predictions. While each of these themes varies depending on state and academic articles, to understand the process of forecasting for prisons, we must compare and contrast how the literature approaches each theme.

The Criminal Justice System

Since 1980, the U.S. prison population has grown from 330,000 people to more than 2.3 million in 2017 (Stephan 1999). During 1980–1990, the population saw a 134 percent increase, and the largest period of growth has occurred over the past 20 years with more than 1 million being added to the population. In the 1980s, it was projected that the population would level off, potentially even declining in some jurisdictions (Rich and Barnett 1985); however, the data continue to show growth in the prison population across the United States. The hypothesis of leveling off was based on a 1984 report from the Federal Bureau of Investigation that stated the number of serious crimes reported to law enforcement authorities decreased for the second year in a row. Moreover, the federal government's census report on prisons noted the rate of increase in the prison population was beginning to slow (Rich and Barnett 1985). It was hoped that the aging of the baby boomer population, along with the tougher sentencing policies intended to deter crime, and the incapacitation effects of higher incarceration rates would lead to a reduction in crime rates and that the reduction would help solve problems related to the overcrowding of prisons. Unfortunately, these assumptions did not hold. As the U.S. population continued to increase, the economy faltered, and policies were instituted that imprison nonviolent offenders more frequently than before (Martinez 2009; Porter et al. 2016).

The growth in the prison population has continued to put a strain on state budgets and facilities, forcing more money to be allocated to corrections each year (Kyckelhahn 2014). As a result, states have looked for a way to be more prepared for changes in their prison populations. This has led to the rise of states' mandating that forecasts be conducted as an important component of administrative planning. With some predictability of their future prison needs, the states believed that they could more readily prepare budgets and facilities to accommodate the rising population (McDonald and Elwaer 2015).

Measures and Methodologies

The methodologies used to produce prison population projections have not changed significantly in recent decades. In 1984, the U.S. General Accounting Office conducted a survey of the methodologies states employed to conduct prison population forecasting (U.S. General Accounting Office 1984). The methods ranged from simple linear extrapolation to relatively complex computer simulation models. While little research has been conducted on how to forecast for prison needs, what literature there is continues to show that the primary methods used to forecast the population include moving averages, exponential smoothing, simulations, and ad hoc regressions. These different types of forecasting methods may produce useful results, yet different methods can be used in different approaches based on their desired level of accuracy and application and whether a short-term or a long-term forecast is preferred. The methods used are reviewed below, as well as measures involved in the population forecast.

In their study of the adult prison population in New South Wales, Wan et al. (2013) developed a method for a forecasting module using arrest and sentencing data. Using monthly offender data from the period 1998–2013, they estimated the monthly prisoner population using an autoregressive integrated moving average (ARIMA) approach. In forecasting terms, an ARIMA model is a generalized version of an autoregressive moving average model that fits time series data to forecast a future point when the data will show evidence of a nonstationary condition. In an ARIMA model, the societal effects on criminal behavior are ignored. In lieu of outside influences, the approach seeks to understand future populations by capturing past trends in the data (For more information on ARIMA models, see Tsay 2010).

To determine the efficiency of the ARIMA estimates, Wan et al. (2013) compared the forecasts to the observed prison population from January 2011 to March 2013 and found the ARIMA approach produced a fairly reliable prediction of prison population trends over a three-year time horizon. While they did find that an ARIMA provides an accurate forecast in retrospective testing, they noted that it should not be used as the sole basis for projecting prison populations. Rather, future projections should also be based on advice from correctional administrators, police prosecutors, and legal policy analysts about the likely effects of any proposed change to policing, bail or sentencing policies.

Donnelly and Wan (2016) took a comparative approach to understand and determine the most efficient method of forecasting adult inmate populations. Using the same data as Wan et al. (2013), Donnelly and Wan re-estimated the prison population using the ARIMA approach and forecasted the population using a Holt-Winters' additive exponential smoothing method to evaluate the accuracy of that approach. In forecasting terms, the Holt-Winters additive exponential smoothing method, also known as *triple exponential smoothing*, seeks to capture the repetitive trends that appear seasonally in data. Just as with the ARIMA model, the Holt-Winters method ignores societal effects by capturing past trends in the data to project future populations (see Tsay 2010).

To test the efficiency of the two approaches in forecasting the adult prison population, Donnelly and Wan (2016) applied both an ARIMA and the Holt-Winters additive method on short-term forecasts of 1–3 months and long-term forecasts of 6–12 months. These forecasts were then compared to the actual monthly number of prisoners using mean absolute error, root mean squared error, and mean absolute percent error to assess accuracy. Although both approaches gave similar measures of accuracy when applied to short-term prison forecasting, they also concluded that their accuracy diminished as the time period being forecasted was extended. Overall, the ARIMA was more accurate than the Holt-Winters additive when forecasting for the long-term, as supported by smaller forecasting errors.

Rich and Barnett's (1985) study on U.S. prison capacity used a computer simulation approach to project the male prison population. Using population projections from the Census Bureau through 2020, they created a forecast by imposing the imprisonment policies of select states and controlling for key theories of criminal behavior. The result was a forecast for the total prison population through 2020, as well as forecasts for the eight states whose imprisonment policies were used: Arizona, California, Florida, Illinois, Massachusetts, North Carolina, Pennsylvania, and Utah.

The simulation approach used by Rich and Barnett (1985) was built around the assumption that changes in the prisoner population were primarily a function of changes in the population of chronic offenders. According to this assumption, chronic offenders are in one of three statuses: active (i.e., on the street committing crimes), in prison, or retired (i.e., on the street but having abandoned criminal activity for good). From this perspective, the forecast requires simulating (a) the number of chronic offenders at each age at that time and (b) the age-dependent proportions of such offenders who are in prison, rather than active or retired. Once the number of prisoners at each age is determined, summing across the ages yields the forecast. Although the approach may be straightforward, its validity is questionable as it is vulnerable to many uncertainties, such as changes in prison policies, changes in legislation from the states, and changes in population growth.

Martinez (2009) sought to move beyond the mathematical approaches common in the literature and create a dynamic understanding of prison forecasting that can be used to explore the impact of potential policy solutions, such as a change in the parole revocation policy. Martinez accomplished this by developing a systems-based model that identifies the initial inputs into the system and the probability of the offender advancing to the next decision point. It is a combination of a flow model and a dynamic model. To capture the flow of prisoners, Martinez used populations at risk of arrest for serious offenses, probation, and parole revocations to estimate intakes. To this is applied to a dynamic model that accounts for the laws governing releases, parole approval rates, and survival rates to estimate releases. The result is a reflection of the entire criminal justice system rather than just a model of prison populations. In other words, it starts with the population of the state and takes into account arrests, convictions, and incarceration probabilities as well as the failure probabilities of probationers and parolees and the probability of being released early on parole.

The system produced by Martinez (2009) allows for the analysis of policy solutions that can be easily understood by policymakers. Its utility, however, extends beyond simple policy analysis. By including inputs such as the policies that drive the criminal justice system, demographic considerations, the crime rate, and projections for probation or parole revocation, it is of utility for the forecaster in projecting total prison admissions and new felony probation placements. To demonstrate this utility, Martinez estimated the model using data from the state of Texas, though he was quick to note that the approach could be replicated in any other state by adjusting the dynamic portion of the model. Unfortunately, this also implies that the utility may be minimized due to the complexity of estimating the system model.

The above examples from the literature show how difficult it is to create an accurate model for both short- and long-term projections. The variance in their accuracy reflects why states have not come to a consensus on how to forecast their prison populations. Thus, wide variations in the approaches exist across states. Oregon, for example, relies upon a number of variables to derive a monthly forecast over a ten-year period (Office of Economic Analysis 2017). The variables used include the number of inmates and of offenders on probation or parole and their economic growth into the projection. In contrast, South Dakota incorporates a qualitative perspective into their forecast (South Dakota Corrections Commission 2016). The South Dakota Corrections Commission meets onsite at prisons across the state, attends parole hearings, and takes tours of correction facilities (South Dakota Corrections Commission 2016). The goal is to connect a story and understanding to the importance of the forecast to the individuals it affects. Texas chooses yet another path by requiring a biennial forecast (Legislative Budget Board 2015). The state enhanced its forecasting program by conducting focus groups and interviews with practitioners and officials across the criminal system. Additionally, it includes demographic and correctional data to produce a statistical simulation model of the future prison populations.

We could continue this discussion for all 50 states because each state forecasts their prison populations slightly differently. This chapter does not try to coalesce around one model, but instead tries to highlight various variables and timelines used to create more accurate prison population forecasts.

The Length of Time

One of the most common differences across all prison population forecasts is the length of time projected. Some states choose to forecast the prison population on a monthly or annual basis (Berk 2008; Fineran and Barry 2017; Mullis et al. 2016; Office of Policy Management 2017). These short-term forecasts allow policymakers to revisit the estimates more frequently and thus quickly adjust for changes based on economic, policy, or other environmental conditions. Unfortunately, these short-term forecasts make it difficult to plan for the more distant future. Other states forecast their populations on five- or ten-year periods and use these forecasts for long-term planning (Berk 2008; Justice Center 2017). These forecasts allow for states to adjust plans and policies based on a long-term outlook. However, these long-term forecasts are more susceptible to error and environmental changes that can render the forecast obsolete. This subsection discusses the differences in short-term and long-term prison forecasts to provide context for their policy implications.

Short-Term Forecasts

Short-term forecasts project one year into the future or less. Many states use short-term forecasts to forecast the immediate needs of prison services, including the housing of prison populations. Considerable variation exists across states in terms of the time frame in which they are forecasting; however, short-term forecasts are more common in states that budget annually than in those with a biennial budget. Since 1940, there has been a dramatic shift by state governments to annual budgeting, as state budgets have grown larger and more complex (Snell 2011). As federal grant matching programs and local government authority have grown over the past few decades, along with state revenues that are made from sales and personal income taxes, state budgets have become more volatile (Gamage 2010). As a result, states are increasingly revisiting their budgets each year to ensure accuracy (Snell 2011).

The forecasting of U.S. prison populations has followed a similar pattern. While forecasting prison populations were used in the 1940s, the volatility of the prison population has become more pronounced over the last few decades (Berk 2008; Blumstein and Beck 1999; Donnelly and Wan 2016). With the exponential growth in prison population over the last few decades, state budgets are increasingly being dedicated to public safety, furthering the need for a precise prison population forecast (Berk 2008). Several environmental factors such as unemployment rates, public crises like the opioid epidemic, and politics influence prison populations. As a result, some states have chosen to focus on short-term forecasts to ensure accuracy and account for various environmental changes each year.

Looking at the experiences of the states, Colorado has included a prison population forecast as one of the four annual forecasts used in creating its budget (Mullis et al. 2016). Alongside using the assessed value of taxable property, enrollment in primary and secondary schools, and the state's previously budgeted expenditures compared to its actual ones, Colorado believes that understanding the anticipated adult prison and parole population is necessary for adequate budget planning as public safety accounts for a large portion of the state's budget. A second example of a state conducting short-term forecasts of its prison population is Connecticut. Using an analysis of general prison population trends, an input-output model to track operational flows and rate of change, and assessment of proposed legislative and policy changes,

Connecticut's Criminal Justice Policy and Planning Division (CJPPD) produces a prison population forecast that is used by the state legislature to determine the CJPPD' s budget. The annual forecast is codified in state law, furthering the state's reliance on an accurate prison population forecast each year (Office of Policy Management 2017). The final example of a short-term forecast comes from New Mexico, whose Sentencing Commission (NMSC 2015) is tasked with producing the forecast based on historical data. The forecast uses a variety of factors to produce the estimates, including arrest rates, criminal cases in district court, conviction rates, diversion programs, and parole readiness. As with the states discussed above, these annual projections are used by New Mexico in the planning of its state budget.

The benefit of states' approaching the forecasting of prison populations from a short-term perspective is shown in how the states are using the information. In the short term, the forecast can assist states in planning the budgets of the agency that oversees correctional facilities. In the budgeting process, it helps to determine the cost to house, feed, guard, and provide medical care to the inmate populations. Given the cost of managing correctional facilities in relation to the overall state budget and the established legal requirements on the condition and quality of care that inmates must be provided, short-term forecasts provide the necessary guidance for states to allocate their resources. While a long-term forecast could provide states with information that could be used in a similar manner, short-term forecasts have two distinct advantages. First, the research on prison forecasting has shown that short-term forecasts have higher accuracy than their long-term counterparts. The improved accuracy helps states avoid overfunding while avoiding a shortfall that could arise if they are underfunded. Second, by focusing on the short-term, forecasters are better able to adjust for changes in the law that may influence the prison population. The ability to make adjustments when needed also feeds back into the overall accuracy of the forecast and the advantages that a more accurate forecast brings.

Long-Term Forecasts

Long-term forecasts project more than one year into the future. While there is no specific length of time at which long-term forecasts must look, the typical long-term forecast of the prison population projects 5–10 years out (Swanson et al. 2010). A long-term approach to the forecast makes it possible for states to plan for the future of public safety. This includes the determination of whether the construction of a new prison is needed and whether existing prisons can be closed. Further, states tend to align their prison population forecasting practices with their state budget forecasts. That is, states that prepare long-term budget forecasts are more likely to also prepare long-term forecasts of the prison population (Pew Charitable Trusts 2017).

Examples of states that prepare long-term forecasts include North Carolina and Oregon. In North Carolina, the Sentencing and Policy Advisory Commission (NCSPAC) is tasked by general statute to develop and maintain a computerized simulation model that can be used to prepare ten-year prison population forecasts (NCSPAC 2018). The forecast is prepared in two parts: prison population projections for new populations and for current resident prison populations. These projections are prepared on an annual basis in conjunction with the state's Department of Public Safety and are used by the General Assembly to determine long-term resource needs, such as additional correctional officers and the costs of medical care for inmates when preparing the budget. Oregon also uses a long-term forecast projected on a semi-annual basis. The state's Office of Economic Analysis (OEA) projects the offender population that is to be supervised by the Oregon Department of Corrections. Again state statute requires this long-term forecast using the current number of inmates, felons, parolees, and those serving less than 12 months in county jails. The forecast is mandated to estimate monthly populations over a ten-year period and is published on April 1 and October 1 of each year (Office of Economic Analysis 2017). The use of the forecasts is for budgeting by the state and for the analysis of policy (Office of Economic Analysis 2017).

By starting with a long-term forecast, states are able to plan outside of the current fiscal year (Williams and Calabrese 2016). From breaking ground until the prison is ready for new inmates, a prison can take years to construct. When the political debate and considerations about financing the construction are included, a new prison can take at least a decade to be completed. By thinking long term, public managers can see changes in demand and appropriately plan for those changes, whereas short-term forecasts provide little to no warning of changes and leave managers little time to respond to shifts in the population.

Changes in the economic, demographic, social environments, as well as the law, however, make it nearly impossible to accurately predict the prison population in the long-term. Forecasting prison populations for 5–10 years does not mean that a state does not revisit its forecast until that time period is over. As seen in the cases of both North Carolina and Oregon, states that produce long-term forecasts may still require the occasional review and update of the projections. By requiring the periodic review of the prison population projections, managers are able to maintain the benefits of a long-term forecast while capturing the accuracy that a short-term perspective provides.

How Policies Affect Forecasts

The policies that states pass have direct impacts on prison populations. The primary factors driving prison population growth, such as enforcement policies, sentencing procedures, and parole are policy based (Joyce 1992). When changes in a policy occur, regardless of how minor, they will likely affect prison population rates to some degree. For instance, a cut to a state's after-school funding can lead to higher crime rates and an increase in the prison population due to the association between after-school programming and crime in poor and disadvantaged communities (Christle et al. 2005). A policy that has had the most impact is determinate sentencing (Joyce 1992), which eliminated the discretion of judges by standardizing mandatory sentencing and parole dates. When a state has adopted a policy of determinate sentencing, it has resulted in an increased prison population, as well as an increase in the average sentencing time (Marvell and Moody 1996). From the perspective of prison forecasting, this policy has resulted in the U.S. prison population's rising higher than previously projected, resulting in problems in the housing issues for the prisoners, shortages of guards, and budgetary shortfalls. As a result, forecasters have had to take into account the presence of determinate sentencing when producing future forecasts.

While determinate sentencing continues to have an impact today, other policies may also influence the size of a prison population, including education, economic, and medical coverage policies. These policy impacts may vary by state and be seen at the national level. These changing policies add variance and error to forecasting models. As a result, prison population forecasts must take into account these policy changes in their projections and estimates. It is impossible to take into account all the possible impacts of a new policy, and some such impacts may not even be seen until much further down the road. Thus, the forecaster must acknowledge this unpredictable future both in the forecast itself and when presenting it to those for whom it was prepared.

Recommendations and Insight

There is no standardized approach to forecast prison populations. While some states have similar forecasting models that rely on statistical data and quantitative approaches, other states include qualitative methodologies and expert opinions in the determination of their projections. A forecast should adapt to the needs, desires, and environment in which the forecast will be used (McDonald 2015). Through the research four key insights have emerged as recommendations for consideration when designing a prison population forecast.

First, Martinez (2009) showed that the criminal justice system acts as a cycle that retains many of the people who enter into it. Both new and repeat offenders affect the prison population. Once new offenders are in the criminal justice system, they may stay in the system, which further increases the population. It is because of this cycle of new and repeat offenders that both populations need to be included in the model. It is not enough to just include the current prison population because this does not tell the entire story of the population. Instead, by including a measure for both, a forecast can more accurately account for that criminal justice system cycle.

Second, a review of the length of forecasts lends credence to using a long-term forecast that is revisited annually. While a short-term forecast may be more relatable for states that address their budget on an annual basis, long-term forecasts appear to be more effective in proper planning for population growth (Swanson et al. 2010). Long-term forecasts may make emerging patterns or problems more apparent on the front end, allowing time for any necessary adjustments, but these long-term forecasts are not foolproof, and they should be revisited for constant updates and adjustments to the changing environment.

Third, changing state and federal policies should be accounted for in both the modeling and interpretation of a prison population forecast. Policies have both direct and indirect effects on the accuracy of a forecast (Joyce 1992). Despite best efforts, it may not be possible to account for all new policies and their future impacts; however, they should at least be taken into account in the discussions around a population forecast. These policies should also be revisited in the following years, as data start to provide a better glimpse of a new policy's continuing effect.

Finally, the most comprehensive and efficient prison population forecasts are those involving multiple stakeholders inside and outside of government (Klay and Vonasek 2008; Mikesell and Ross 2014). When lawmakers and the governors' staff are the only ones involved in the prison population-forecasting conversation, a wide range of knowledge and expertise is left out. Involving corrections officers and professionals in the field and community can add clarity and information to the model. These stakeholders outside the government understand firsthand how new policies are affecting them, and thus they can add this perspective to the model. However, forecasting is a difficult job, and this makes it important to include government officials who understand the forecasting project and its relation to the budget. When those both inside and outside the government can work to create the forecast, there is more trust in the application for the results.

Conclusions

Forecasting the U.S. prison population is critical when it comes to informed decision-making in the planning and budgeting of the U.S. public safety system. With limited financial resources, producing accurate and reliable forecasts is crucial to state governments. There are many models and methodological approaches that can be used to forecast prison population, and it is the responsibility of the forecasters to choose the approach that produces the most reliable and accurate results for their situation.

In reviewing the extant literature on prison forecasting, four recommendations emerged as best practice. As previously discussed, these include: (a) incorporating data for both new and repeat offenders into the forecast as a means in improving accuracy, (b) long-term forecasts revisited annually to be more effective in recognizing patterns and adjusting to changes in the environment, (c) changes to the policy environment to be factored into the forecast, and (d) incorporating individuals with different backgrounds and knowledge in the forecasting committee to enhance the forecast and minimize errors and biases. Ultimately, a forecast is an educated guess of the future value of a variable of interest. While it is the responsibility of the forecaster to reduce the error in their estimates and produce the most efficient projection possible, the forecast will inevitably be wrong. Nonetheless, projecting prison admissions and correctional populations serve as a planning guide for policymakers and practitioners to decide where limited resources should go.

References

Berk, R. (2008). Forecasting methods in crime and justice. *Annual Review of Law and Social Science, 4*(1), 219–238. https://doi.org/10.1146/annurev.lawsocsci.3.081806.112812.

Blumstein, A., & Beck, A. J. (1999). Population growth in US prisons, 1980–1996. *Crime and Justice, 26*, 17–61. https://doi.org/10.1086/449294.

Christle, C. A., Jolivette, K., & Nelson, C. M. (2005). Breaking the school to prison pipeline: Identifying school risk and protective factors for youth delinquency. *Exceptionality, 13*(2), 69–88.

Donnelly, N., & Wan, W.-Y. (2016). Adult prison population size in New South Wales: Comparative forecasts. *BOCSAR NSW Crime and Justice Bulletin, 199*, 1–8.

Fineran, S., & Barry, T. (2017). *Iowa prison population forecast FY 2017–FY 2027*. Retrieved from http://www.jrsa.org/pubs/sac-digest/vol-27/ia-prison-forecast.pdf.

Gamage, D. (2010). Preventing state budget crises: Managing the fiscal volatility problem. *California Law Review, 98*(3), 749–812.

Glaeser, E. L., Sacerdote, B., & Scheinkman, J. A. (1996). Crime and social interactions. *The Quarterly Journal of Economics, 111*(2), 507–548.

Joyce, N. M. (1992). A view of the future: The effect of policy on prison population growth. *Crime & Delinquency, 38*(3), 357–368. https://doi.org/10.1177/0011128792038003005.

Justice Center. (2017). Appendix D. North Dakota justice reinvestment policy framework. *Justice reinvestment in North Dakota: Policy framework*. Washington, DC: Council of State Governments.

Klay, W. E., & Vonasek, J. A. (2008). Consensus forecasting for budgeting in theory and practice. In J. Sun & T. D. Lynch (Eds.), *Government budget forecasting: Theory and practice* (pp. 379–392). Boca Raton, FL: CRC Press.

Kyckelhahn, T. (2014). *State corrections expenditures, FY 1982–2010*. Washington, DC: US Department of Justice. Retrieved from https://www.bjs.gov/content/pub/pdf/scefy8210.pdf.

Legislative Budget Board. (2015). *Adult and juvenile correction population projection*. The State of Texas. Retrieved from https://is.gd/a6hbnb.

Martinez, P. E. (2009). Projecting felony intakes to the justice system. *The Prison Journal, 89*(4), 383–400. https://doi.org/10.1177/0032885509349558.

Marvell, T. B., & Moody, C. E. (1996). Determinate sentencing and abolishing parole: The long-term impacts on prisons and crime. *Criminology, 34*(1), 107–128. https://doi.org/10.1111/j.1745-9125.1996.tb01197.x.

McDonald, B. D. (2015). A "dirty" approach to efficient revenue forecasting. *Journal of Public and Nonprofit Affairs, 1*(1), 3–17.

McDonald, B. D., & Elwaer, J. (2015). *Forecasting the prison population*. Paper presented at the Annual Midwest Public Affairs Conference, Milwaukee, WI.

Mikesell, J. L., & Ross, J. M. (2014). State revenue forecasts and political acceptance: The value of consensus forecasting in the budget process. *Public Administration Review, 74*(2), 188–203.

Mullis, N., Carey, M., Silbaugh, L., Pino, L., Sobetski, G., Watkins, K., & Grunlien, D. (2016). *Focus Colorado: Economic and revenue forecast*. Colorado Legislative Council Staff Economic Section. Retrieved from https://leg.colorado.gov/sites/default/files/december2016forecast.pdf.

New Mexico Sentencing Commission. (2015). *New Mexico prison population forecast: FY2016–FY2025*. New Mexico Sentencing Commission. Retrieved from https://nmsc.unm.edu/reports/2015/new-mexico-prison-population-forecast-fy-2016-fy2025.pdf.

North Carolina Sentencing and Policy Advisory Commission. (2018). *Prison population projections: Fiscal year 2018 to fiscal year 2027*. Retrieved from https://www.nccourts.gov/assets/documents/publications/2018-popproj_0.pdf.

Office of Economic Analysis. (2017). Corrections population forecast. Retrieved from http://www.oregon.gov/das/OEA/Pages/forecastcorrections.aspx.

Office of Policy Management. (2017). *Prison population projection*. The Connecticut Statistical Analysis Center. Retrieved from http://www.ct.gov/opm/lib/opm/PRISON_POP_PROJECTION_February_2017_final.pdf.

Pew Charitable Trusts. (2017). Public safety, public spending: Forecasting America's prison population 2007–2011. *Federal Sentencing Reporter, 19*(4), 234–252.

Porter, L. C., Bushway, S. D., Tsao, H. S., & Smith, H. L. (2016). How the US prison boom has changed the age distribution of the prison population. *Criminology, 54*(1), 30–55.

Pratt, T. C., & Cullen, F. T. (2000). The empirical status of Gottfredson and Hirschi's general theory of crime: A meta-analysis. *Criminology, 38*(3), 931–964.

Rich, T. F., & Barnett, A. I. (1985). Model-based US prison population projections. *Public Administration Review, 45*, 780–789. https://doi.org/10.2307/3135036.

Snell, R. K. (2011). *State experiences with annual and biennial budgeting*. Washington, DC. Retrieved from http://www.ncsl.org/documents/fiscal/BiennialBudgeting_May2011.pdf.

South Dakota Corrections Commission. (2016, May 18). *Corrections commission minutes*. Retrieved from https://doc.sd.gov/documents/CorrectionsCommissionMinutesMay182016FINAL.pdf.

Stephan, J. J. (1999). *State prison expenditures' 1996*. Washington, DC: Bureau of Justice Statistics. Retrieved from https://www.bjs.gov/content/pub/pdf/spe96.pdf.

Swanson, D. A., Schlottmann, A., & Schmidt, B. (2010). Forecasting the population of census tracts by age and sex: An example of the Hamilton–Perry method in action. *Population Research and Policy Review, 29*(1), 47–63. https://doi.org/10.1007/s11113-009-9144-7.

Tsay, R. S. (2010). *Analysis of financial time series* (3rd ed.). Cambridge, MA: Wiley.

United States General Accounting Office. (1984). *Federal, District of Columbia, and states future prison and correctional institution populations and capacities (GAO/GGD-84-56)*. Washington, DC: United States General Accounting Office.

Wagner, P., & Rabuy, B. (2017). *Mass incarceration: The whole pie 2017*. Northampton, MA. Retrieved from https://www.prisonpolicy.org/reports/pie2017.html.

Wan, W.-Y., Moffatt, S., Xie, Z., Corben, S., & Weatherburn, D. (2013). Forecasting prison populations using sentencing and arrest data. *BOCSAR NSW Crime and Justice Bulletin, 174*, 1–12.

Williams, D. W., & Calabrese, T. D. (2016). The status of budget forecasting. *Journal of Public and Nonprofit Affairs, 2*(2), 127–160. https://doi.org/10.20899/jpna.2.2.127-160.

18

Government and Nonprofit Personnel Forecasting

Vincent Reitano

Major Points

- Accurate personnel expenditure forecasts are also critical to helping an organization budget for short- and long-term costs associated with personnel compensation.
- Despite this essential function of government and nonprofit strategic human resource management (SHRM), there has been little reported research. Many rely on surveys with small samples or are from decades ago.
- There is almost no insight into the methodologies that are used for personnel projections and forecasts.
- This chapter recommends substantial empirical research to determine the effectiveness of personnel-related forecast practices.

Introduction

Governments and nonprofits concentrate their expenditures in human capital to help achieve their mission (Fishbein and Vehaun 2009). These expenditures are relegated to personnel who receive a salary and benefits in exchange for a

V. Reitano (✉)
School of Public Affairs and Administration, Western Michigan University, Kalamazoo, MI, USA
e-mail: vincent.reitano@wmich.edu

D. Williams, T. Calabrese (eds.), *The Palgrave Handbook of Government Budget Forecasting*, Palgrave Studies in Public Debt, Spending, and Revenue,
https://doi.org/10.1007/978-3-030-18195-6_18

fixed or variable amount of work. In the aggregate, salary and benefits account for about 15 percent of state government and 41 percent of local government expenditures (McNichol 2012), respectively, while school districts spend close to 80 percent of their budget on personnel (National Center for Education Statistics 2018). Nonprofits can also contribute a sizeable portion of their budget to human capital, but such expenditures will vary, because nonprofits can range from a large hospital to an organization run by a single volunteer.

Given the need for human capital to help organizations achieve their mission, researchers and practitioners have developed tools and recommendations regarding personnel forecasting (Fishbein and Vehaun 2009). These tools include projections of the supply and demand of current and future personnel as well as expenditure forecasts for personnel salary and benefits (Armstrong and Taylor 2014; Hartman 1998). Specifically, organizations can use personnel data to conduct an internal needs assessment for employees with particular skills, if those employees are available in the labor force to meet organizational needs, and then the cost to hire employees including salary and benefits among others (Armstrong and Taylor 2014; Chen et al. 2015). Thus, while personnel forecasting is typically associated with workforce planning (WP) and strategic human resource management (SHRM), it also plays a role in budget forecasting for all levels of government and nonprofit organizations (Melchor 2013).

This chapter provides an overview of the literature on government and nonprofit personnel forecasting. Section "Practice of Personnel Forecasting," details the process of personnel forecasting as it relates to strategic human resource management (SHRM), as both provide a framework and guidelines for how to link personnel forecasts to budget forecasts and the mission of a government or nonprofit. Thus, this chapter will not only review the research and practice of personnel forecasting, but also demonstrate how it plays a critical role in the current and future operations of public and nonprofit organizations. The chapter is structured as follows:

- Section "Summary of the Literature" presents a detailed review of research on government, school district, and nonprofit employee projections and expenditure forecast. It shows how the literature is limited and tends to focus on the broader question of workforce management relative to personnel forecasting practices and methods.
- Section "Practice of Personnel Forecasting" details the process of personnel forecasting as it relates to strategic human resource management. It also details the need to consider assumptions, methodology with and without an enterprise resource planning (ERP), and how to present results to decision-makers.

- Section "Limitations" details the gaps in the literature and the need for more insight into praxis, based on the prior two sections. It shows how there are notable limitations in research on personnel forecasting methods and few case studies to guide practitioners.
- Section "Conclusion" provides a brief summary of the chapter and lists future areas of research on personnel forecasting.

Summary of the Literature

Context of Personnel Forecasting

A report by the Organization for Economic Cooperation and Development argues that "the capability to forecast capability requirements is not always highly developed in all public organisations" (Melchor 2013, 17). Essentially, public organizations may not have the available resources to devote to projecting the supply and demand of public and nonprofit personnel and the associated short- and long-term expenditures for salaries and benefits. Additionally, even if they have the resources to do so, there may be debate about which methods and metrics to pick for personnel forecasts (Anderson 2004) as well as political concerns from elected officials or board members, particularly in smaller organizations where leadership may be more centralized (Choudhury 2007).

Many of these concerns highlight the broad challenges that government and nonprofit forecasters face. Irrespective of the type of forecast, whether for personnel or the budget, there may be both technical and political challenges mitigating their use for strategic planning purposes. For example, survey research has shown that local governments vary in their use of forecast methods and technology, with size and resource capacity being factors that help determine whether or not a judgmental rather than an extrapolation or econometric approach is utilized (e.g., Frank and Zhao 2009; Kong 2007; Reddick 2006). Using a judgmental forecast rather than an extrapolation or econometric approach, whether for budget or personnel forecasting, can potentially lead to low accuracy, but may appease the agendas of executives or elected officials if the forecast is biased toward their interests (Choudhury 2007; Frank and Zhao 2009).

Despite the aforementioned challenges, both budget and personnel forecasts play a critical role in governments and nonprofits and are closely interrelated. Since the size of personnel expenditures is notable for all levels of government and some nonprofits, they must be appropriately budgeted for as well. Accurately projecting personnel in the short- and long-term as part of workforce planning will ensure that the organization has personnel to meet its mission, and will also inform budget forecasts regarding personnel expenditures (Hartman 1998). Utilizing both will ensure the government or nonprofit is engaged in strategic planning to achieve its mission (Armstrong and Taylor 2014; Fishbein and Vehaun 2009; Kavanagh and Williams 2016).

Specifically, Melchor (2013, 29) states that "workforce planning is linked to the strategic planning of organisations, including business forecasting and planning, budgeting, accountability … and strategic human resource management." This is evident since workforce planning, which contains personnel forecasting, can help a government or nonprofit to understand its current and future need for personnel to achieve its mission. Further, Jacobson (2010, 354) argues that: "Identifying a funding source for a position is not enough. Workforce planning enables local governments to determine their need for human resources to meet their objectives, and the availability of those resource." As a result, despite the aforementioned technical and political challenges related to personnel forecasting, it can play a critical role in governments and nonprofits.

Government Personnel Forecasting

Much of the insight on government personnel forecasting is relegated to conceptual discussion in textbooks (e.g., Armstrong and Taylor 2014), while detailed case studies and research using survey methods or quantitative measures of personnel forecast accuracy is limited. Despite its limited scope, the literature still provides insight into personnel forecast practices across small and large local governments, with size being defined in terms of population, as well as across general purpose and special purpose governments. The research on state and national government personnel forecasting is more applied in nature and focused on guidelines rather than rigorous review of personnel forecast accuracy or surveys of forecasters.

As noted by Choudhury (2007, 265), "human resource management at the federal, state, or large urban levels often are not a good fit for smaller jurisdictions," including research and practices on personnel forecasting. This observation from Choudhury (2007) is consistent with budget forecasting research, which also control for size of government or even show differences in methodology and accuracy across size of government (Kong 2007). Thus, research should demarcate between size and type of government when examining personnel forecasting. This subsection details personnel forecasting research on small and large local governments, then school districts, and finally state and federal governments.

In an early study, Nielsen and Young (1973) use hypothetical public sector data to show step by step how a Markov chain approach can be used to forecast personnel. A later paper from Schroeder (1980) also uses a Markov approach to test a model of personnel forecasting. Schroeder (1980) begins with the assumption that total labor cost for a government is a function of salary and benefits summed across all personnel on a step and grade system. The model also adjusts for inflation and accommodates for the possibility of personnel moving up the step and grade system, new personnel hires, and retirements. Given the model, a Markov approach is used to forecast police personnel expenditures in Syracuse, NY based on data from 1976 to 1977. An annual forecast is provided up to 1982 but there is no comparison of the forecast with the actual expenditure value, thus providing no insight into the accuracy of the forecasts.

In a more recent study of small local government workforce planning, Choudhury (2007) obtained survey data and conducted interviews of 40 local governments in Ohio with a population less than 25,000. According to the survey, while three quarters of respondents did not have an issue with employee turnover, they deem "it important to keep track of their current staffing situation," potentially indicating the need for a system to measure and project employee demand and supply (Choudhury 2007, 274). Follow-up interviews in the study, however, show that small local governments may not be using technological advances, which are available, from an Excel or Access spreadsheet to more advanced enterprise resource planning (ERP) systems modules focused on personnel, since "tracking the current workforce is informal" (Choudhury 2007, 274). The survey and interview results also implied that small local governments are using contextual information regarding the workforce of nearby local governments to gauge workforce trends (Choudhury 2007).

The above findings from Choudhury (2007) appear to be consistent with research on small local government budget forecasting. Tracking information at the individual employee level, potentially due to low staff levels, and using contextual information, potentially to provide a judgmental rather than an extrapolation or econometric forecast, are all broadly similar to budget forecasting in small local governments (Kong 2007). Choudhury (2007, 278) concludes that "elected officials tend to be interested in satisfying their immediate needs; therefore, staffing innovations such as WFP [Workforce Planning] are often ignored." Essentially, given that personnel forecasts in terms of supply and demand are an essential part of workforce planning in the short and long term, it appears the small local governments studied by Choudhury (2007) prefer a judgmental approach.

The conclusion from Choudhury (2007, 278) indicates that workforce planning may not be technically or politically feasible in small local governments in the "immediate" or short term, let alone the long term, the latter of which is critical to personnel forecasting. This could potentially be due to a lack of technology or knowledge around extrapolation or econometric personnel forecasts and political resistance. Interestingly, in a survey of Florida local government, Frank and Zhao (2009, 31) reach a similar conclusion regarding budget forecasting: "mathematically derived forecasts without a downside bias and modeled with transparent assumptions could be viewed as threatening by many local finance officials." Essentially, elected officials and administrators in small local governments may not be open to using technical methods to forecast especially if they deviate from normative behaviors like implicit forecast bias (Barrett et al. 2019; Bretschneider et al. 1988; Reitano 2018).

The conclusions from both Choudhury (2007) and Frank and Zhao (2009) demonstrate that a perceived lack of control over econometric forecasts by elected officials, whether in the budget or personnel forecast, may make them unfeasible in small or politically contentious local governments. Both studies also do not indicate that small local governments are considering workforce planning , let alone budget forecasting, in the long term. These findings indicating a lack of long-term forecasting in local government are consistent with Wong (1995) and echoed by Kong (2007).

The use of ERPs for workforce planning tools such as forecasting may also be less than expected in medium sized and large local governments. Jacobson (2010) obtains survey data from 30 municipalities in North Carolina with a population greater than 15,000. A little over half of respondents indicated planning for short-term staffing, just under 40 percent for long-term staffing, two-thirds for retirement planning, and only 7 percent for a gap analysis (between supply and demand of personnel). The seemingly low use of planning potentially via personnel projections and expenditure forecasts can be explained in part by additional survey results indicating that 60 percent of respondents have "insufficient human resources to manage the program" followed by other factors including senior management and elected officials (Jacobson 2010, 370). Thus, the findings are broadly similar to research on budget forecasting and from Choudhury (2007), potentially indicating that a lack of resources to conduct personnel forecasting (as part of workforce planning) and different stakeholders being resistant to formally projecting and planning for personnel changes.

In a similar paper, Goodman et al. (2015) surveyed the largest local governments in the US and obtained survey data from 184 of them, specifically from human resource directors. Over 60 percent as either important or very important on a question regarding "Mastering [Human Resource Management] HRM software" (Goodman et al. 2015, 143). Despite the majority response, a quarter had a neutral response, and the remaining clearly did not appear to consider HRM software important; this is problematic since the HRM software module, which is typically part of an ERP system, is critical to tracking the hundreds or even thousands of personnel in a large local government and then using that data to forecast personnel needs into the future. Many of these systems allow for either manual or automated projections or forecasts, but such capabilities may not be used for personnel forecasting, despite evidence from Reitano (2017) showing widespread adoption of ERPs at the local level. Clearly, there are trends across the literature on local government regarding the lack of technical sophistication around workforce planning functions, including personnel forecasting (Choudhury 2007; Melchor 2013).

Across Choudhury (2007), Jacobson (2010), and Goodman et al. (2015), survey data is used to infer about the prevalence of personnel forecasting. However, as discussed later in the chapter, there is no research on the accuracy of personnel projections. Essentially, even if a government is using some type of quantitative methodology in an Excel or Access file or an ERP to run personnel projections and personnel expenditure forecasts, that does not mean they are accurate; forecasts that have low accuracy could potentially mislead decision-makers for hiring and even budget forecasting and planning. Jacobson (2010, 368–369) refer to this concern and lists multiple questions to address such as: "Have our projections been on target" and "What is the budgeting impact of the planning process, and what resources are available?" Similar conclusions are also reached in Pynes (2004) as well as from surveys on local governments in North Carolina and Colorado regarding their human resource management through the Great Recession from Jacobson and Sowa (2016).

The latter discussion focuses on general purpose local governments, but does not address special purpose governments such as school districts, which devote about 80 percent of their budget to personnel salary and benefit expenditures (National Center for Education Statistics 2018). Hartman (1998) considers school district personnel forecasting as the second of five steps in a school budget. The first step is student enrollment projections with some type of regression analysis, which must inform school personnel projections since there must be some type of relationship between the two; for example, a school would not project the need for 10 new teachers if the projected student enrollment was flat and there were no impending teacher retirements or policy changes, given the invariance between student to teacher ratios. The second step is to conduct the personnel forecast, which involves projecting particular instructional, administrative, and non-instructional personnel positions for individual schools, then the district, and then the cost of salaries and fringe benefits based on each position.

The process developed in Hartman (1998) is primarily practice based, although case studies are presented to show how to estimate student projections, personnel projections, and even expenditure estimates for different categories. The research on school district personnel forecasts is largely nonexistent, with research focusing instead on student enrollment projections, a related area of research with its own developed literature. Lee and Plummer (2007) provide the only study that examines instructional expenditure forecasts, which are closely related to personnel forecasts, since instruction is a function of teaching staff. Related studies such as Hulpke et al. (1976), Ványolós (2011), and Barrett et al. (2019) examine school district forecasts for expenditures but not specifically instruction or personnel projections. Thus, only Lee and Plummer (2007) are reviewed below, but provide a foundation for future studies.

Lee and Plummer (2007, 139) test the concept of budget ratcheting to operating and instructional expenditures (which are primarily composed of personnel expenditures), which is described as: "government budgets increase more in response to overspending than they decrease in response to underspending." Examining the difference between budgeted and actual expenditures can be of a short- or long-term nature, and described as follows: "The variance could be transitory…or it could be permanent (e.g., the student's families have permanently relocated)" (Lee and Plummer 2007, 145). In this case, both enrollment projections and staff projections would need to be revised in response to an exogenous shock, and correspondingly the personnel expenditure needs to be revised, to reflect the influx of new students and need for a larger budget. To test this hypothesis, Lee and Plummer (2007) use a panel data set of Texas school districts from 1995 to 2002 to show evidence of ratcheting in operating expenditures, which are primarily composed of personnel costs.

Given the dearth of research on both general purpose and special purpose local governments, it is challenging to reach definitive conclusions regarding their personnel forecasting practices. In a review of personnel forecasting practices and metrics based on case studies, Anderson (2004, 370) argues that "looking at the workforce data using a broad-spectrum approach has not received universal acceptance," potentially indicating that use of aggregate data from the Bureau of Labor Statistics to conduct personnel projections and forecasts may not provide an optimal information set for a government to make workforce decisions. Thus, as in budget forecasting, personnel forecasters may not be using a full information set and instead relying on contextual information for a judgmental forecast. This can compound the chance of an inaccurate or indefensible forecast.

Nonprofit Personnel Forecasts

Personnel forecast methods and practices may differ across governments and nonprofits based on their characteristics. In government, personnel can potentially be employed under a collective bargaining agreement, which would clearly need to be a factor when projecting employee need and cost to hire and fill vacant positions. More so, governments have a tax base, and even the smallest local government will have at least one and likely a handful of salaried employees. In comparison, nonprofits may or may not have a collective bargaining agreement, may not have a steady revenue stream, and may not even have a single salaried employee.

From a statistical perspective, nonprofits are skewed in terms of their finances, and that directly influences personnel forecasting practices. Only 10 percent of nonprofits having revenue greater than $500,000 and only 10 percent have 87 percent of all nonprofit assets (Guidestar 2015). Given these statistics, it can be inferred that many nonprofits likely have only a few employees or volunteers, and the need for some type of personnel forecasting methodology is likely limited if not unnecessary.

For example, consider a hypothetical nonprofit which has two part-time employees and has revenue of $300,000; it is probable that if one of the employees leaves, they are going to tell the other employee in advance of leaving to help with succession planning and would have a large impact if not, whereas in a large nonprofit, one part-time employee leaving would likely have little to no immediate effect. However, the opportunity to manage personnel and forecast need is critical, since decision-makers likely cannot see all personnel changes across their organization and need to be informed with data. As a result, the primary concern is how the few nonprofits that have more than half-a-million dollars in revenues can accurately forecast personnel. It is probable that these larger nonprofits with a few hundred or even thousand employees likely use an ERP system which has automated functions for tracking and forecasting personnel across their function, step and grade, and other relevant factors.

Research on nonprofit human resource management is limited and does not directly address questions of personnel forecasting. A search of Google

Scholar for terms such as "nonprofit personnel forecasts" and "nonprofit employee projections" among others revealed no articles of interest. A more systematic review in Scopus for terms such as "nonprofit" and "forecasts" and then filtering for "personnel" yielded around –100 results, and none of the identified journal articles were related to the topic of interest. Individual journals focusing on nonprofits were also searched by similar keywords and no articles were found.

While the nonprofit literature may not be directly studying personnel forecasting, which is considered as a limitation and discussed later on in the chapter, there is a literature on healthcare personnel forecasting. Just over half of all hospitals are non-profits, a fifth are government operated, and the rest for profit or from other categories (American Hospital Association 2018). Irrespective of the type of hospital, as with a government or nonprofit, all hospitals have not only specialized medical staff such as doctors and nurses but administrative and non-administrative staff as well. Thus, the proliferation of research on hospital personnel forecasting may have relevance to other nonprofits and governments as well. That literature is practice based and will therefore be discussed in the section which follows.

Implications for Practice

Personnel forecasting plays a critical role in workforce planning and more broadly strategic human resources management. According to Armstrong and Taylor (2014, 216), manpower planning, which was the antecedent of workforce planning, as considered earlier in Nielsen and Young (1973) and Schroeder (1980), faced the following issue: "It was the failure in many organizations to produce accurate forecasts and therefore prepare meaningful plans that led to its decline if not fall." Although there could be a range of reasons why this was the case, it could be that methodological innovations such as Markov chain-based methods were being applied with little concern for evaluating their accuracy. For example, both Nielsen and Young (1973) and Schroeder (1980) do not discuss potential forecast accuracy measures nor other methods such as ordinary least-squares regression. Despite these early limitations, both WP and SHRM should incorporate forecasting.

Armstrong and Taylor (2014) recommend that a "forecast of future activity levels" inform the personnel supply and demand forecasts. Armstrong and Taylor (2014, 219–220) define each as follows: "Demand forecasting is the process of estimating the future numbers of people required and the likely skills and competences they will need" and "Supply forecasting measures the number of people likely to be available from within and outside the organization." Additionally, Armstrong and Taylor (2014) recommend using scenarios to consider different possibilities which is also considered by Schroeder (1980) and even for budget forecasting (Kavanagh and Williams 2016). Scenarios around various issues pertinent to governments and nonprofits such as revenue fluctuations, business cycle changes, policy and legal changes, and even collective bargaining must be considered (e.g., Armstrong and Taylor 2014; Kavanagh and Williams 2016). Creating optimistic, pessimistic, and baseline scenarios would help to ensure that an organization is prepared for all types of contingencies, ranging from a drop in personnel leaving for different industries or an opportunity to hire more personnel due to increasing funding or demand (Kavanagh and Williams 2016).

There is little consideration given to the assumptions and methodology of personnel forecasting. Assumptions will likely vary due to contextual differences across organization type and size, and that may help to determine which methodological approach is utilized. The literature has provided different perspectives on the interplay of assumptions and methodology depending on the context. At the local level, Hartman (1998) recommends that a regression-based approach be utilized when projecting personnel and their expenditures. Once the quantitatively derived forecast is reached, which should account for differences across personnel classifications (e.g., step and grade, seniority, collective bargaining), it should then inform the development of the budget for expenditures (Chen et al. 2015).

Additionally, in a study of hospital personnel forecasting, there are different approaches regarding assumptions and methodology, depending on the forecaster: "The first of these approaches assumes that activity rates per person will continue and is highly conservative … The second approach usually extrapolates from activity trends over the last 10 to 15 years. The final method uses activity above recent trends" (Maynard 2006, 324). Thus, the input data for a demand forecast in relation to personnel depends on assumptions regarding how past data informs the forecasts. Demographic factors should also be considered (Maynard 2006). In regard to supply, looking at data and trends in the production of doctors is critical (Maynard 2006). Collectively, supply and demand can help to identify if a gap exists in the future regarding demand for services provided by public and nonprofit personnel and how many of these types of personnel are available.

Forecasting methodology can also depend on the technological capacity of an organization. In small local governments or nonprofits, a simple Excel spreadsheet can help to track employees, how close they are to retirement, and all salary and benefits to sum up to total expenditures. A simple forecast could assume a constant or variable growth rate in salary and/or benefits and also factor in new hires and retirements. An approach to considering open positions and whether to leave those open or not should also be incorporated. With these inputs, simple projections could be created and used for planning purposes including for budgeting. Chen et al. (2015) provide detailed insight into potential equations and how they can be simulated and then run in Excel to calculate payroll salaries and benefits over pay periods. They provide examples to show that "one of the most complicated issues in simulating the payroll is dividing pay periods between those before a step increase and those after" (Chen et al. 2015, 6).

In larger organizations, such as major cities, state and national governments, and large nonprofits like hospitals, a human resources module in an ERP would likely be necessary. It would contain all of the aforementioned personnel information and be automatically updated over time, as well as provide a projection of employees based on historical attrition as well as costs. Parameters can be set in an ERP and assumptions clearly defined using conditional logic regarding cost of living adjustments, collective bargaining, required benefit contributions for pensions, and other post-employment benefits, among other factors, to simulate payroll costs (Chen et al. 2015).

The ERP could then create an automated report on a daily, weekly, monthly, quarterly, or annual basis monitoring trends in personnel and forecasting future needs. In an optimized system, these personnel forecast from an HR module would ideally link directly into a budget module, as well, to inform budget forecasts and long-term planning (Miranda et al. 2002; Roque 2010). Thus, an ERP can automate much of personnel forecasting if it is optimized across modules and if users are trained in how to leverage it for evidence-based decision-making (Miranda et al. 2002; Roque 2010).

Limitations

As discussed throughout this chapter, there are a number of limitations regarding personnel forecasting research. This chapter identifies five key areas that would benefit from further research. First, there is very limited literature on personnel forecast practices and methods, with some of the most technical research from decades ago, thereby potentially limiting its generalizability (Nielsen and Young 1973; Schroeder 1980). Systematic surveys and interviews could help to ascertain the prevalence of and methodology used for personnel projections and personnel expenditure forecasts. There is some insight into this topic at the local level, from studies such as Choudhury

(2007), Goodman et al. (2015), and Jacobson (2010), but less so in higher levels of government, and no research in nonprofits outside of healthcare according to a systematic review.

Second, there are no studies that evaluate the use of personnel forecasting in a government or nonprofit organization. For example, Schroeder (1980) uses a Markov chain approach with data from the City of Syracuse, New York, but does not compare the forecast to the actual values. Similarly, Hartman (1998) recommends the use of regression for personnel forecasts but does not fully discuss its accuracy and how it relates to other potential methods, whether more or less complex. Without actual data to test accuracy, it is impossible to know which forecast methods to recommend to practitioners. Obtaining such data might be challenging and require close collaboration with individual governments or nonprofits, since it is not likely to be published in an aggregate format annually like financial data.

Third, following from the prior limitation, research on personnel forecasting is largely detached from praxis. Textbooks such as Armstrong and Taylor (2014) provide a critical foundation for understanding how personnel forecasts play into workforce planning and strategic human resource management. However, specific case studies are rare, and even the literature has focused on surveys and interviews rather than a few in-depth case studies that students and practitioners can benefit from. Obtaining data, interviewing multiple stakeholders and even elected officials, and tracking an organization over time with respect to personnel forecasting would be critical to developing useful case studies.

Fourth, there needs to be greater consideration of how personnel and budget forecasts interact. As noted earlier in this chapter, personnel make up a large portion of government expenditures, especially at the local level. Accurately predicting current and future personnel supply and demand, especially in areas which require technical or advanced training, could help to ensure continued operational efficiency of an organization and help inform budget forecasts. More so, examining how the two may interact during downturns could be critical, since decreased revenues may translate into decreased personnel to cut expenditures (Arapis et al. 2017; Berne and Stiefel 1993). Thus, the linkages between personnel forecasting, budget forecasting, and strategic planning have yet to be systematically examined in the literature.

Fifth, given the linkage between personnel and budget forecasting, more insight into the technology used to conduct each would be helpful. Budget forecasting research has generally shown a proclivity of local governments to use a judgmental approach and shy away from extrapolation or econometric approaches (e.g., Frank and Zhao 2009; Kavanagh and Williams 2016);

however, as technology has proliferated, understanding if human resource, budget, and finance departments are using Excel, Access, or ERP modules to forecast is largely unknown. Additionally, understanding how well these tools help with forecast accuracy and planning would be useful, as well.

Conclusion

This chapter has reviewed the literature on personnel forecasting. There is some research on local government personnel forecasting practices and methods, but less on higher levels of government and nonprofits. Textbooks and articles provide some insight into praxis, but largely at a conceptual level, rather than providing recommended practices for methodology. A range of questions remain unanswered, but still, there is broad acknowledgement that personnel forecasting can play a critical role in government and nonprofit strategic planning.

References

American Hospital Association. (2018). Fast facts on US hospitals. Retrieved from https://www.aha.org/statistics/2018-01-09-fast-facts-us-hospitals-2018.

Anderson, M. W. (2004). The metrics of workforce planning. *Public Personnel Management, 33*(4), 363–378.

Arapis, T., Reitano, V., & Bruck, E. (2017). The fiscal savings behavior of Pennsylvania school districts through the great recession. *Public Budgeting & Finance, 37*(3), 47–70.

Armstrong, M., & Taylor, S. (2014). *Armstrong's handbook of human resource management practice* (13th ed.). Philadelphia, PA: Kogan Page Ltd.

Barrett, N., Fowles, J., Jones, P., & Reitano, V. (2019). Forecast bias and fiscal slack accumulation. *The American Review of Public Administration, 49*(5), 601–613.

Berne, R., & Stiefel, L. (1993). Cutback budgeting: The long-term consequences. *Journal of Policy Analysis and Management, 12*(4), 664–684.

Bretschneider, S. I., Straussman, J. J., & Mullins, D. (1988). Do revenue forecasts influence budget setting? A small group experiment. *Policy Sciences, 21*(4), 305–325.

Chen, G. G., Weikart, L. A., & Williams, D. W. (2015). Calculating payroll. In *Budget tools: Financial methods in the public sector* (2nd ed., pp. Online). Los Angeles: SAGE.

Choudhury, E. H. (2007). Workforce planning in small local governments. *Review of Public Personnel Administration, 27*(3), 264–280.

Fishbein, J., & Vehaun, D. (2009). Managing the personnel budgeting process. *Government Finance Review*, 67–75. Retrieved from http://www.gfoa.org/sites/default/files/GFR_AUG_09_67.pdf.

Frank, H. A., & Zhao, Y. (2009). Determinants of local government revenue forecasting practice: Empirical evidence from Florida. *Journal of Public Budgeting, Accounting & Financial Management, 21*(1), 17–35.

Goodman, D., French, P. E., & Battaglio, R. P., Jr. (2015). Determinants of local government workforce planning. *The American Review of Public Administration, 45*(2), 135–152.

Guidestar. (2015). *Nine things you might not know about non-profits*. Williamsburg, VA: Guidestar.

Hartman, W. T. (1998). *School district budgeting*. Lanham: Scarecrow Press.

Hulpke, J. F., Watne, D. A., & Waldo, D. (1976). Budgeting behavior: If, when, and how selected school districts hide money. *Public Administration Review, 36*, 667–674.

Jacobson, W. S. (2010). Preparing for tomorrow: A case study of workforce planning in North Carolina municipal governments. *Public Personnel Management, 39*(4), 353–377.

Jacobson, W. S., & Sowa, J. E. (2016). Municipal human resource management: Challenges and innovative practices in turbulent times. *State and Local Government Review, 48*(2), 121–131.

Kavanagh, S. C., & Williams, D. W. (2016). *Informed decision-making through forecasting: A practitioner's gide to government revenue analysis*. Chicago: Government Finance Officers Association.

Kong, D. (2007). Local government revenue forecasting: The California county experience. *Journal of Public Budgeting, Accounting & Financial Management, 19*(2), 178–199.

Lee, T. M., & Plummer, E. (2007). Budget adjustments in response to spending variances: Evidence of ratcheting of local government expenditures. *Journal of Management Accounting Research, 19*, 137–167.

Maynard, A. (2006). Medical workforce planning: Some forecasting challenges. *Australian Economic Review, 39*(3), 323–329.

McNichol, E. (2012). Some basic facts on state and local government workers. Retrieved from https://www.cbpp.org/sites/default/files/atoms/files/2-24-11sfp.pdf.

Melchor, O. H. (2013). The government workforce of the future: Innovation in strategic workforce planning in OECD countries. *OECD Working Papers on Public Governance* (21), https://doi.org/10.1787/5k487727gwvb-en.

Miranda, R., Kavanagh, S., & Roque, R. (2002). *Technology needs assessment: Evaluating the business case for ERP and financial management systems*. Chicago: Government Finance Officers Association.

National Center for Education Statistics. (2018). *Public school expenditures*. Washington, DC. Retrieved from https://nces.ed.gov/programs/coe/indicator_cmb.asp.

Nielsen, G. L., & Young, A. R. (1973). Manpower planning: A Markov chain application. *Public Personnel Management, 2*(2), 133–144.
Pynes, J. E. (2004). The implementation of workforce and succession planning in the public sector. *Public Personnel Management, 33*(4), 389–404.
Reddick, C. G. (2006). Assessing local government revenue forecasting techniques. *International Journal of Public Administration 27*(8–9), 597–614.
Reitano, V. (2017). *Investing in collections software to allow for monthly property tax payments.* Working Paper: WP17VR1. Lincoln Institute of Land Policy. Retrieved from https://www.lincolninst.edu/sites/default/files/sources/events/reitano_wp17vr1.pdf.
Reitano, V. (2018). An open systems model of local government forecasting. *The American Review of Public Administration, 48*(5), 476–489.
Roque, R. (2010). Optimizing ERP in your organization. *Government Finance Review,* 46–50. Retrieved from www.gfoa.org/sites/default/files/GFR_AUG_10_46.pdf.
Schroeder, L. (1980). Probabilistic projections of public employment and expenditures. *Public Finance Quarterly, 8*(3), 259–276.
Ványolós, I. (2011). The impact of state-imposed fund balance limits on school districts: Evidence from New York state. *Journal of Public Budgeting, Accounting & Financial Management, 23*(2), 166–187.
Wong, J. D. (1995). Local government revenue forecasting: Using regression and econometric revenue forecasting in a medium-sized city. *Journal of Public Budgeting and Financial Management, 7*, 315–335.

19

Forecast Bias and Capital Reserves Accumulation

Vincent Reitano, Peter Jones, Nathan Barrett, and Jacob Fowles

Major Points

- This study examines implicit fiscal slack used as reserve funds in the context of capital funds.
- It shows mixed evidence of the implicit-explicit fiscal slack relationship across the type of capital funds for Kentucky school districts from 2001 to 2013.
- There are statistically significant effects of revenue and expenditure forecast bias on building fund fiscal reserves, but not for other capital funds.

V. Reitano (✉)
School of Public Affairs and Administration, Western Michigan University, Kalamazoo, MI, USA
e-mail: vincent.reitano@wmich.edu

P. Jones
Department of Political Science and Public Administration, University of Alabama Birmingham, Birmingham, AL, USA
e-mail: pajones5@uab.edu

N. Barrett
Tulane University, New Orleans, LA, USA
e-mail: nbarret@tulane.edu

J. Fowles
School of Public Affairs and Administration, University of Kansas, Lawrence, KS, USA
e-mail: jacob.fowles@ku.edu

D. Williams, T. Calabrese (eds.), *The Palgrave Handbook of Government Budget Forecasting*, Palgrave Studies in Public Debt, Spending, and Revenue,
https://doi.org/10.1007/978-3-030-18195-6_19

Introduction

Local governments strategically accumulate different types of fiscal slack across various funds to foster budgetary flexibility (Arapis and Reitano 2018; Barrett et al. 2019). As defined in Barrett et al. (2019), implicit fiscal slack is generated through biased revenue and expenditure forecasts, while explicit fiscal slack is accumulated in fiscal reserves. Specifically, under-forecasting revenues and over-forecasting expenditures is a common practice that can build explicit fiscal slack into fiscal reserves like the unassigned fund balance (Barrett et al. 2019). The literature, however, has yet to study the implicit-explicit fiscal slack relationship outside of the general fund, such as in a capital project fund.

Fiscal slack can be used for a variety of purposes (Bourgeois 1981; Cyert and March 1963). Governments can use reserves held in the unassigned fund balance to cover recurring expenditures like employee salaries and benefits, but prudent financial management recommends that they be used for non-recurring expenditures that may unexpectedly arise (Arapis et al. 2017; Kavanagh 2007, 2011). Capital reserves are related to the cost of infrastructure such as buildings, roads, and fleets of police cars and school buses (Casey and Mucha 2007; Government Finance Officers Association [GFOA] 2013). Specifically, capital reserves can be used to mitigate contingencies in long-term projects planned for in a capital improvement plan, such as when an infrastructure project has unanticipated costs (GFOA 2013). Some states define capital reserves and provide policy guidance for local governments and school districts (Kentucky Legislative Research Commission 2010; Office of the New York State Comptroller 2010).

Given the critical nature of capital reserves (GFOA 2013; Office of the New York State Comptroller 2010; Kentucky Legislative Research Commission 2010), research on their determinant factors, specifically focusing on implicit slack from forecast bias, will build the literature and inform practitioners. This chapter builds on research from Barrett et al. (2019) regarding the use of forecast bias in the budget process. The major elements in this chapter are detailed by section as follows:

- Section "Summary of Literature" details the literature on implicit and explicit fiscal slack. Implicit slack, generated through biased revenue and expenditure forecasts, is considered in context of the local government forecasting literature. Explicit slack, in relation to capital reserves, is also briefly reviewed. Testable hypotheses are presented.

- Section "Research Methodology" details the econometric identification strategy to test the hypotheses as well as the Kentucky school district data and variable specification.
- Section "Findings" details the evidence, which supports an indirect relationship between revenue forecast bias and capital reserves, and a direct relationship between expenditure forecast bias and capital reserves from a panel dataset of Kentucky school districts from school years 2001–2002 to 2013–2014. These findings build on research from Hulpke et al. (1976), Ványolós (2011), and Barrett et al. (2019).
- Section "Limitations in Literature" details areas for future research, focusing on triangulation of forecast bias research with a mixed methods approach, cognitive biases and risk tolerance, best practices evaluation, and the need for more research to inform practitioners.
- Section "Conclusion and Future Research" considers the implications of the findings for praxis and areas for future research regarding implicit and explicit fiscal slack as well as school district forecasting.

Summary of Literature

Forecast Bias and Fiscal Slack

Slack resources can help to absorb shocks to the organization (Thompson 1967). Given the possibility of absorbing shocks, stakeholders within an organization may vie for the use of slack resources so that their interests are not constrained in the event of a shock such as a recession (Arapis et al. 2017; Bourgeois 1981; Cyert and March 1963). In state and local government budgeting, the literature has recognized two types of slack. Implicit fiscal slack is generated through biased revenue and expenditure forecasts, and explicit fiscal slack is held in fiscal reserves like the unassigned fund balance (Barrett et al. 2019).

A growing literature has provided evidence of implicit slack as measured by forecast bias. Studies on general-purpose government forecast bias will be reviewed first, followed by research on special-purpose governments.

In a study of general-purpose governments, Rubin (1987) uses a survey of 133 small- and medium-sized Illinois cities to show that almost half underestimate sales tax, more than three quarters underestimate property tax replacement, and just over half underestimate fees from motor vehicle taxes. Additionally, Larkey and Smith (1989) provide evidence of under-forecasting revenues and over-forecasting expenditures but only for three local governments. In particular, Larkey and Smith (1989) show forecast bias in the City of Pittsburgh from 1941 to 1983, the Pittsburgh School District from 1946 to 1983, and City of San Diego from 1950 to 1982.

More recent research on general-purpose local government forecast bias echoes Rubin (1987) and Larkey and Smith (1989). In a study of Danish municipalities from 1991 to 2003, Serritzlew (2005) shows consistent evidence of actual exceeded budgeted total expenditures with some variation for particular expenditures. In a survey of 45 California counties from 2002 to 2003, Kong (2007, 190) finds "conservative behavior among government revenue forecasters in the presence of uncertainty." Similar, Frank and Zhao (2009) survey a sample of 113 Florida municipal finance directors and shows that a majority will under-forecast revenues.

The literature on forecast bias has similar findings across general-purpose and special-purpose governments. In the school district context, Hulpke et al. (1976), Ványolós (2011), and Barrett et al. (2019) show evidence of under-forecasted revenues and over-forecasted expenditures. Hulpke et al. (1976) provide evidence that from 1964–1965 to 1973–1974, 24 San Francisco Bay area school districts over-forecasted expenditures more than under-forecasting them in both the operating fund and the capital fund. In a study of New York school districts from 1997 to 2004, Ványolós (2011) finds that 75 percent will overestimate expenditures. Similarly, Barrett et al. (2019) show that 2080 out of 2275 budgets under-forecast revenues and 1871 out of 2275 budgets over-forecast expenditures in Kentucky school districts.

Implicit fiscal slack from forecast bias can be used to accumulate explicit fiscal slack at the local level as shown by Barrett et al. (2019). Explicit fiscal slack can be accumulated in the unassigned fund balance and used on a discretionary basis, such as mitigating a financial contingency (Arapis et al. 2017; Arapis and Reitano 2018). As per GASB Statement No. 54, the unassigned portion of fund balance is defined as: "unassigned fund balance is the residual classification for the general fund. This classification represents fund balance that has not been assigned to other funds and that has not been restricted, committed, or assigned to specific purposes within the general fund" (GASB 2009, 7). In practice, this definition means that the unassigned fund balance can be used on a discretionary basis (Arapis et al. 2017). Further, the GFOA (2015) has recognized that the unassigned portion of fund balance is critical to maintaining fiscal resiliency and sustainability.

The literature on the determinants of explicit fiscal slack generally does not consider fiscal slack's relationship to implicit fiscal slack at the local level. It is still important to review, however, as it provides evidence that implicit fiscal slack is just one of many strategies governments can use to accumulate explicit fiscal slack in the form of reserves. As early as Vasche and Williams (1987) and Wolkoff (1987), researchers have recognized the need for some type of slack fund at the local level for absorbing or stabilizing financial uncertainty. With the advent of research from Hendrick (2004, 2006), a variety of studies have emerged analyzing both the determinants and uses of fiscal slack at the local level, considering factors such as revenue and expenditures as well as local socioeconomic and demographic characteristics (Arapis and Reitano 2018; Arapis et al. 2017; Barrett et al. 2019; Duncombe and Hou 2014; Marlowe 2005; Stewart et al. 2013; Ványolós 2011; Wang and Hou 2012).

The literature has examined the relationship between implicit and explicit fiscal slack at the state and local levels. At the state level, Rose and Smith (2012) provide empirical evidence that budget stabilization funds and forecast bias are inversely related. At the local level, Hulpke, Watne, and Waldo (1976, 672) show that school districts strategically under-forecast revenues and over-forecast expenditures and interpret it as providing some evidence, while not causal, that school districts "hide money." Further, Ványolós (2011) provides evidence of under-forecasted revenues and over-forecasted expenditures and shows these forms of slack help school districts meet or exceed state-imposed rules regarding the accumulation fiscal reserves in New York school districts. In a more recent paper, Williams and Onochie (2013, 4) show that New York City will re-budget to hide a "surreptitious" budget stabilization fund. Thus, these papers provide a foundation for further investigating the different types of slack generated through forecast bias at the state and local levels.

Building on the work of Hulpke et al. (1976), Rose and Smith (2012), and Williams and Onochie (2013), Barrett et al. (2019) develop and test theory around implicit and explicit fiscal slack. Specifically, they hypothesize that under-forecasting revenues and over-forecasting expenditures, both forms of implicit fiscal slack, will be associated with higher explicit fiscal slack, measured by increases in unassigned fund balance. Further, the authors hypothesize that the implicit-explicit fiscal slack relationship will be heterogeneous over the business cycle. Evidence in support of all three hypotheses is supported with a panel dataset of school districts, although the focus is on the general fund, particularly unassigned fund balance. Specifically, they find the effect size of the revenue and expenditure bias coefficients fluctuate each year and increase during and after the Great Recession, reflecting strategic budgeting in response to uncertainty (Arapis et al. 2017).

This chapter takes the hypotheses developed in Barrett et al. (2019) and extends them to capital reserves. The use of capital reserves can help governments to address contingencies in their capital projects, such as if a project goes over budget or if an asset such as a building needs unexpected maintenance (GFOA 2013; Office of the New York State Comptroller 2010). As per the GFOA Best Practice (2013, 1) Capital Planning Policies: "to create a sustainable capital plan, the finance officer and other participants in the capital planning process need to consider all capital needs as a whole, assess fiscal capacity, plan for debt issuance, and understand impact on reserves" and it later recommends "a procedure for accumulating necessary capital reserves for both new and replacement purchases." While it is evident capital reserves play a role at the local level throughout the capital budgeting process, they have yet to be studied in the literature.

Following Barrett et al. (2019), we hypothesize that governments will under-forecast revenues and over-forecast expenditures, both forms of implicit fiscal slack, which will lead to accumulating explicit fiscal slack in capital reserves. As per Rodgers and Joyce (1996, 55), this form of forecasting is strategic and should be referred to as "cushioning" rather than as "biased" since it is a common practice (also see Bart 1989). Specifically, Rodgers and Joyce (1996) note that "costs associated with underestimating revenues are considerably less than the costs associated with overestimating revenues" (p. 49). These forecasting practices can help to build explicit slack into the budget at the local level, as evidenced in Hulpke et al. (1976), Williams and Onochie (2013), and Barrett et al. (2019). Thus, the first two hypotheses test the implicit-explicit slack relationship in relation to capital reserves, which build on the literature:

H1 Governments will bias revenue forecasts, a form of implicit slack, to build explicit fiscal slack into the capital budget in the form of capital reserves.

H2 Governments will bias expenditure forecasts, a form of implicit slack, to build explicit slack into the capital budget in the form of capital reserves.

The above hypotheses can be tested with state or local government data, and for this chapter, we employ data from special-purpose local governments, specifically school districts in Kentucky, to test each hypothesis. As discussed in the next two sections of this chapter, evidence supporting or challenging these hypotheses is needed in other contexts, as well, to understand how widespread the forecast bias fiscal slack relationship is across different types of governments as recommended by Barrett et al. (2019).

Research Methodology

Econometric Identification Strategy

To test the two hypotheses developed in the prior section, we estimate multiple two-way fixed effects panel data models. A two-way fixed effects strategy eliminates unobserved time-variant and invariant factors, which may confound the estimates. The functional form is as follows:

$$Y_{it} = \beta_0 + B_1 Z_{1it} + B_2 Z_{2it} + a_i + b_t + \epsilon_{it} \tag{19.1}$$

where i indexes individual districts and t years; the outcome of interest, explicit fiscal slack, is measured in Y_{it} by three different fund reserves for capital outlay, building and construction; Z_1 includes the implicit fiscal slack measures for revenue and expenditure forecast bias; and Z_2 consists of school district characteristics as control factors. As mentioned already, we include two-way fixed effects, specifically school district unit and yearly time effects, which are noted as a and b, to eliminate unobserved factors that may bias the estimates; finally, ε represents the idiosyncratic error. Finally, we address the presence of heteroscedasticity in Eq. (19.1) by including robust standard errors clustered on the district unit level.

Data and Variable Specification

The functional form of Eq. (19.1) can be estimated with data from any local government to test the two hypotheses developed in this book chapter. This provides a framework for future studies using different datasets, but for the purpose of this chapter, we use a panel dataset of all Kentucky school districts ($n = 176$) from school years 2001–2002 to 2013–2014. We estimate Eq. (19.1) three times with the three dependent variables in vector Y_{it} to reflect that Kentucky school districts can accumulate capital reserves for the capital outlay fund (310), building fund (320), and construction fund (360).

According to the Kentucky Legislative Research Commission (2010, 4), the capital outlay fund (310) "is used primarily to pay for debt service; however, recent changes to statutes and budget language have opened this fund to pay for insurance, maintenance, and operating expenses," while the building fund (320) "is used to pay debt service and can be used for major renovation or new construction of school buildings." Further, the Kentucky Legislative Research Commission (2010, 4) defines the construction fund (360) as: "After a project has KDE approval, funds are transferred to this account from capital outlay, building fund, general fund, or bond proceeds. This is a multiyear fund and is set up like the special revenue fund." Analyzing reserves for 310, and especially 320 more closely, follows the definition of a capital reserve from GFOA (2013) while 360 is more unique to school district construction in Kentucky.

Consistent with Barrett et al. (2019), we include forecast bias measures for revenue and expenditures. Both bias measures were calculated as the difference between predicted revenues/expenditures and actual revenues/expenditures. A negative revenue bias would indicate that a school district underestimated revenues, meaning that district had more revenues than anticipated. Likewise, a positive expenditure bias occurred when a school district overestimated expenditures, meaning the district did not have to spend as much as anticipated.

In line with hypotheses 1 and 2, implicit fiscal slack, as measured by underestimating revenues and overestimating expenditures, should be positively related to changes in fund balances; in short, both result in additional funds that may be used to build explicit slack. Empirically, however, the interpretation of coefficients will not be as straightforward. Underestimating revenues means revenue bias is negative, and as revenue bias increases, the underestimation approaches zero and becomes an overestimation. As such, as revenue bias increases, the school district will have fewer resources to increase explicit fiscal slack, reflecting a negative (indirect) relationship between revenue bias and explicit fiscal slack.

The opposite is true for expenditure bias since overestimating expenditures yields additional funds to build fund balances. For expenditure bias, a positive (direct) relationship exists with the fund balances of interest. We provide Fig. 19.1 as a graphic representation of the opposite relationships regarding the relationship between explicit fiscal slack (fund balance) and implicit fiscal slack from revenue and expenditure forecast bias.

In addition to the main explanatory variables of implicit fiscal slack, we include control factors to capture variation across school districts, which is consistent with research on school district financial management such as Arapis et al. (2017), Duncombe and Hou (2014), and Ványolós (2011). Specifically, we include changes in total revenue and expenditures, total enrollment, percent of minority students, percent of students eligible for free- or reduced-priced lunch, and the district unemployment rate. These factors help to control for variation in revenue accumulation and expenditure allocation across districts, student characteristics, and local economic factors such as the unemployment rate (Arapis et al. 2017). Consider, for example, that the

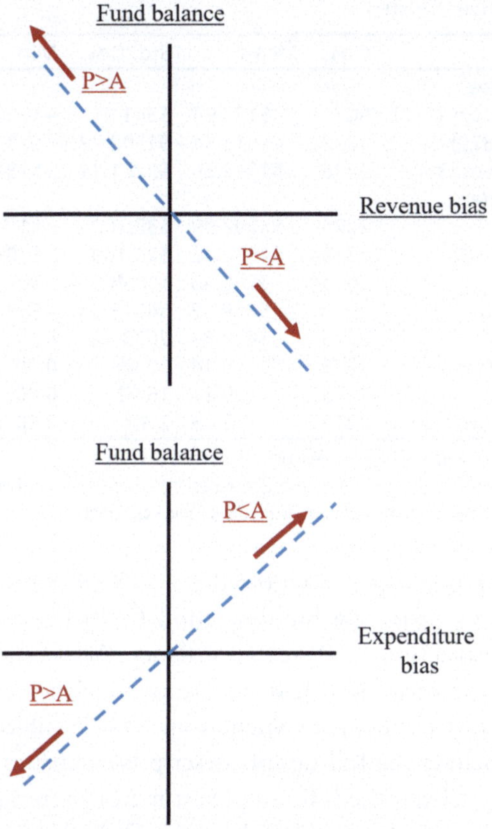

Fig. 19.1 Fiscal slack's relationship with fund balance

composition of student characteristics and their educational needs, such as requiring disability services or a free or reduced-price lunch, can influence budgetary decisions of a school district; further, local economic factors can control for variation in available revenues and expenditures needs across districts that contribute to the budgetary environment school districts operate within (Barrett et al. 2019).

Table 19.1 presents descriptive statistics for the variables included in Eq. (19.1). Of note, 153 unique school districts reported a non-zero balance in their capital outlay (310) fund reserves across the panel, which yielded 907 district-years of capital fund balances. For the building fund (320) reserves, 172 unique school districts report a non-zero balance for a total of 1232 district-years in our sample, and 174 unique school districts reported a non-zero balance for the construction fund (360) reserves across 1446 district-years.

Table 19.1 Descriptive statistics

Variable	Obs	Mean	Std. Dev.	Min	Max
Dependent variables					
Capital outlay reserves (310)	907	−$153.96	$341.91	−$2965.08	$2380.92
Building reserves (320)	1232	−$516.84	$1302.77	−$23,200	$3419.18
Construction reserves (360)	1446	−$1342.66	$9221.11	−$137,000	$36,300
Explanatory variables					
Revenue bias	2275	−$3202.99	$33,700	−$1,120,000	$659,000
Expenditure bias	2275	−$1062.42	$24,100	−$309,000	$623,000
Total revenue Δ	2099	$669.48	$10,400	−$99,000	$123,000
Total expenditure Δ	2099	$469.97	$4573.53	−$84,700	$91,800
Total enrollment	2275	3619.83	7673.82	82	100,316
Minority students (%)	2275	9.14	10.99	0.00	64.11
FRL (%)	2275	59.21	16.99	0.00	99.48
District unemployment rate	2275	7.83	2.49	3.50	19.60

Dollar amounts reported as 1000s. Adjusted for inflation
2001 was our base year; for that year, we are missing observations for "Total revenue Δ" and "Total expenditure Δ" for each of our 176 school districts

On average, a school district reported a −$153,958 capital outlay (310) reserves balance, a −$516,844 building fund (320) reserves balance, and a −$1,342,664 construction (360) reserve balance. Across the three funds, the construction fund reserve (360) had the greatest variance among school districts, and school districts held anywhere from −$137 million to $36 million. For brevity, we include the full-sample descriptive statistics for other covariates, and as we note later, the full-sample estimates are not substantively different across most controls variables. Approximately 91 percent of all school districts budgets had underestimated revenues, and the average underestimation across all districts for all years was 10.4 percent of the actual operating budget. Around 82 percent of all budgets overestimated expenditures with an average overestimation across all districts for all years equal to 9.7 percent of the actual operating budget.

When combining forecasted revenues and expenditures, there is evidence that school districts overwhelmingly predicted yearly budget deficits. Over 88 percent of all forecasted budgets predicted a deficit with an average deficit of over 10 percent of the actual operating budget. For brevity, we include the full-sample descriptive statistics for other covariates, and as we note in the next paragraph, the full-sample estimates are not substantively different across most controls variables, which is shown via *t*-test results.

We are cognizant of potential selection bias in our sample, so Table 19.2 presents *t*-test results from differences of means for each of our explanatory variable. The estimates reported represent the difference between those districts that reported a non-zero reserve balance and those that did not. The

Table 19.2 Difference of means for explanatory variables, comparing districts that reported a fund balance versus those that did not

	Variable	Difference	*t*-statistic
Capital Outlay Reserves (310)	Revenue bias	\$34,157	−0.02
	Expenditure bias	−\$1,046,183	1.01
	Total revenue Δ	\$471,446	−1.01
	Total expenditure Δ	\$418,795.2[a]	−2.04
	Total enrollment	243.1	−0.74
	Minority students (%)	0.29	−0.62
	FRL (%)	−2.986[b]	−4.12
	District unemployment rate	0.422[b]	−3.97
Building Reserves (320)	Revenue bias	\$1,834,819	−1.29
	Expenditure bias	\$1,067,337	−1.05
	Total revenue Δ	\$310,046	−0.68
	Total expenditure Δ	\$725,128.1[b]	−3.64
	Total enrollment	319.2	−0.99
	Minority students (%)	0.504	−1.09
	FRL (%)	−1.682[a]	−2.35
	District unemployment rate	0.991[b]	−9.63
Construction Reserves (360)	Revenue bias	\$2,821,386	−1.92
	Expenditure bias	\$547,967	−0.52
	Total revenue Δ	\$288,495	−0.62
	Total expenditure Δ	\$472,202.3[a]	−2.29
	Total enrollment	−1132.5[b]	−3.4
	Minority students (%)	2.128[b]	−4.47
	FRL (%)	−0.444	−0.6
	District unemployment rate	0.916[b]	−8.56

[a]$p < 0.05$; [b]$p < 0.001$

district's unemployment rate is the only variable consistently different across the funds, with districts reporting a non-zero balance having a higher unemployment rate, as reported in Table 19.2.

Findings

Regression Estimates

Tables 19.3 and 19.4 present results from the estimation of Eq. (19.1) across the three dependent variables—capital reserves for capital outlay (310), building (320), and construction (360). Results are inconsistent across fund balances. Table 19.3 provides a baseline specification without controls but interpretation is focused on Table 19.4, which includes estimates of Eq. (19.1). For example, capital outlay (310) reserves were positively related to revenue bias and negatively related to expenditure bias (both were statistically significant at the 0.05 level). Specifically, a \$1 increase in revenue bias was

Table 19.3 Fixed effects regression results without controls

Variables	Capital reserves (Rob. St. Error)	Debt service (Rob. St. Error)	Construction (Rob. St. Error)
Revenue bias	0.0004	−0.0059[b]	0.0239
	(0.000)	(0.001)	(0.018)
Expenditure bias	0.0006	−0.0012	−0.0329[a]
	(0.001)	(0.001)	(0.016)
Constant	−152,349.5034[b]	−542,705.4264[b]	−1,283,147[b]
	(708.719)	(3059.694)	(56,753.069)
Observations	907	1232	1446
R-squared	0.015	0.053	0.014
Number of districts	157	172	174

[a]$p < 0.05$; [b]$p < 0.1$

Table 19.4 Fixed effects regression results with controls

Variables	Capital outlay reserves 310 (Rob. St. Error)	Building reserves 320 (Rob. St. Error)	Construction reserves 360 (Rob. St. Error)
Revenue bias	0.0019[b]	−0.0051[a]	0.0054
	(0.001)	(0.003)	(0.006)
Expenditure bias	−0.0022[b]	0.0044[c]	0.0224
	(0.001)	(0.002)	(0.017)
Total revenue Δ	0.0074[c]	0.0028	−0.2436[c]
	(0.002)	(0.020)	(0.052)
Total expenditure Δ	−0.0077	0.0083	0.2359[a]
	(0.010)	(0.023)	(0.133)
Total enrollment	−4.7581	−727.6496	−6058.6707[a]
	(94.201)	(591.235)	(3579.750)
Percent minority students	−2903.3755	27,959.2862	117,744.4742
	(5662.051)	(23,970.988)	(189,024.407)
Percent FRL	−1429.7926	−6024.1760[a]	27,195.1511
	(1043.764)	(3439.198)	(23,718.640)
District unemployment rate	−6583.0542	44,614.8316	71,658.9953
	(8435.125)	(33,335.575)	(175,510.986)
Year 2003	5653.6197	−80,244.0482	−732182.6206
	(43,916.310)	(86,257.476)	(608,665.176)
Year 2004	64,302.2856	−96,642.1758	−1.9580e+06[b]
	(39,404.809)	(120,132.405)	(806,490.293)
Year 2005	71,733.1467	−306,810.1725	−297,511.8357
	(56,685.850)	(236,926.566)	(847,015.913)
Year 2006	71,268.4687[a]	52,994.0462	−563155.1132
	(42,459.102)	(154,464.616)	(919,829.664)
Year 2007	29,944.3391	−78,482.1174	−546912.6777
	(43,700.834)	(177,166.371)	(899,183.139)
Year 2008	87,084.7652[b]	−59,612.6102	−940933.5239
	(41,798.383)	(177,036.200)	(890,999.528)
Year 2009	76,837.0405	−539249.6664[b]	−841170.8146
	(63,846.762)	(252,967.902)	(1382341.668)

(continued)

Table 19.4 (continued)

	Capital outlay reserves 310	Building reserves 320	Construction reserves 360
Variables	(Rob. St. Error)	(Rob. St. Error)	(Rob. St. Error)
Year 2010	125,296.9638[b]	−133534.0647	67,755.0305
	(63,105.811)	(227,052.599)	(1197513.612)
Year 2011	185,999.5406[b]	−78,834.1425	454,734.3458
	(88,332.807)	(213,114.737)	(1254995.290)
Constant	−22,762.7093	1910484.1685	2.0558e+07[a]
	(356,795.462)	(1902687.185)	(12396155.490)
Observations	812	1098	1310
R-squared	0.092	0.113	0.257
Number of districts	153	172	174

[a] $p < 0.1$; [b] $p < 0.05$; [c] $p < 0.01$

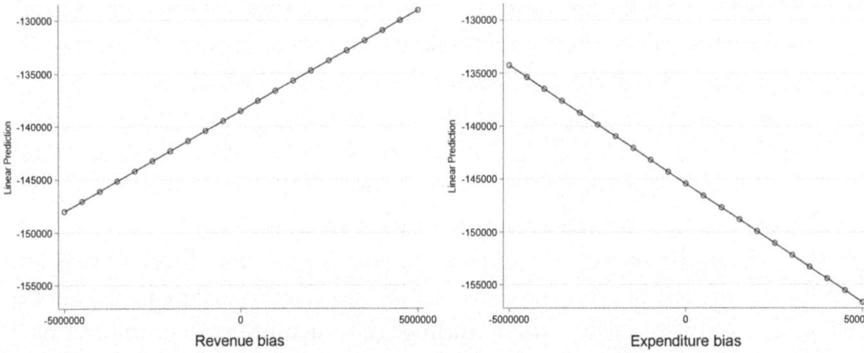

Fig. 19.2 Marginal impacts of revenue and expenditure biases on capital outlay reserves

associated with a $0.0019 increase in the capital reserves, and a $1 increase in expenditure bias was associated with a $0.0022 decrease in capital reserves. These results are opposite of the relationships predicted by hypotheses 1 and 2 and represented in Fig. 19.1.

Considering the capital outlay (310) reserves estimation, the coefficients for our main explanatory variables suggest additional funds that result from underestimating revenues or overestimating expenditures were associated with decreases in capital outlay reserves. Visually, Fig. 19.2 depicts both relationships and shows the opposite relationship predicted in Fig. 19.1.

Conversely, results for the building fund (320) reserves provide evidence for hypotheses 1 and 2. In particular, conservative revenue forecasting, or underestimating revenues, is negatively associated with the building fund reserves and conservative expenditure forecasting, or overestimating expenditures, is positively associated with the building fund reserves. A $1 increase in revenue bias was significantly associated with a $0.0051 decrease in the

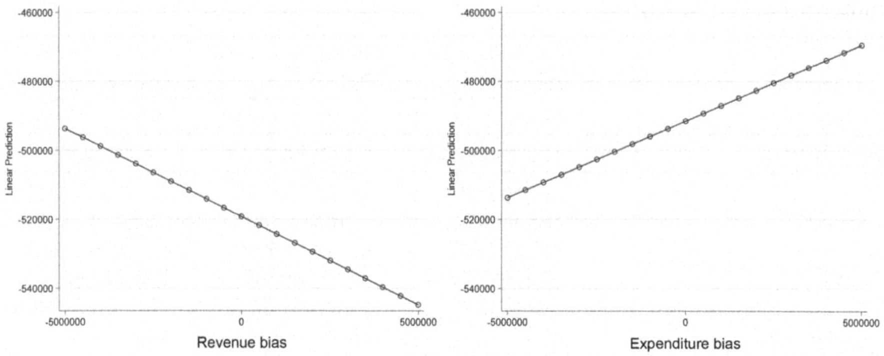

Fig. 19.3 Marginal impacts of revenue and expenditure biases on building reserves

building fund reserves, and a $1 increase in expenditure bias was positively associated with the building fund reserves. Both of these coefficients reflect a relationship between implicit and explicit fiscal slack. Again, we display the marginal impacts for both coefficients in Fig. 19.3, which align with the directional expectations laid out in Fig. 19.1. Since 320 can be used for building fund debt service as well as "major renovation or new construction of school buildings," this particular reserve closely follows the GFOA (2013) Best Practice for how to define and use capital reserves.

It should also be noted that the coefficients for revenue forecast bias and expenditure forecast bias for the construction fund reserves equation were not statistically significant. Thus, these findings do not support hypothesis 1 or 2.

Substantively, the results may be marginal in their practical relevance, given the size of the funds. If one converts the effect sizes into the standard deviation sizes reported in Table 19.1 (i.e. $1 multiplied by the standard deviation of revenue bias), then a one-standard-deviation increase in revenue bias was significantly associated with a $64,030 increase in capital outlay reserves and a $74,140 decrease in the building fund reserves. Doing the same for expenditure bias, a one-standard-deviation increase was significantly associated with a $122,910 decrease in capital outlay reserves and a $106,040 increase in the building fund reserves.

Across the three model estimates, the results from using building fund (320) reserves as a dependent variable provide evidence of the implicit-explicit fiscal slack relationship for accumulating capital reserves for capital projects as anticipated in hypothesis 1 and 2 and depicted in Fig. 19.1. In contrast, 310 and 360 are defined more broadly, which may potentially explain why coefficients challenge or do not support the two hypotheses; in particular, 310 can be used for operating expenses and 360 is specific to Kentucky school district transfers. One may question why 310 can be used for operating expenditures, given it is defined as a capital outlay fund; the answer is as follows: "changes to statutes and budget language have opened this fund [310] to pay for insurance, maintenance, and operating expenses" (Kentucky Legislative Research Commission 2010, 4) during the Great Recession to allow for more budget flexibility given resource constraints. Thus, the mixed evidence in support of the two hypotheses may be due to the context of Kentucky school districts.

However, in school districts in other states, results may differ and adhere to the hypotheses. If there is less budgetary flexibility than in Kentucky, in terms of having less ability to freely transfer between funds as a tool to help alleviate fiscal stress, then school districts in other states may operate differently. Future papers should carefully review the state or local government chart of accounts and any fund transfer rules; this will ensure that future papers carefully consider the unique institutional context that may shape budgetary flexibility and decisions regarding the implicit-explicit fiscal slack relationship.

Limitations in Literature

The literature on the relationship between forecast bias and fiscal slack accumulation has several limitations. In general-purpose local governments, Williams and Onochie (2013) show re-budgeting is used to generate a budget stabilization fund while Dougherty et al. (2003) detail this as a strategy for accumulating slack; however, both papers have small samples, which may restrict the generalizability of findings, reflecting the need for further studies. There is also research on this topic in special-purpose governments that is growing. Hulpke et al. (1976) show the relationship between under-forecasted revenues and over-forecasted expenditures in relation to surplus accumulation in California school districts. Ványolós (2011) studies the relationship between forecast bias and adherence to state-imposed fund balance limits in New York school districts, while Barrett et al. (2019) show forecast bias is associated with slack accumulation. Even with these studies, the literature is still limited, and can be advanced on five fronts.

First, to triangulate the findings from econometric modeling, researchers can survey and interview state and local government budgeters and decision-makers. Understanding who is biasing forecasts (e.g. budget analyst or manager, finance manager, or other administrators) and the reasoning behind the decision in relation to financial management is critical (Barrett et al. 2019). Research can take the form of surveys or interviews and even quasi-experiments as in Bretschneider et al. (1988). These can help to understand cognitive biases and provide insight into the behavioral aspects of state and local government forecasting, and even risk tolerance, which are largely unexplored at the local level (Barrett et al. 2019).

As argued by Miller (2012, 52–53), "common to all whose task is forecasting is uncertainty and ambiguity," and understanding how these factors play into forecasts at the local level is critical. Analysis of forecasts with quantitative methods is helpful and important, but largely looks at forecasts as "computational exercises," which potentially obviates questions that can only be explored with surveys and interviews regarding the "inherent bias…towards high numbers, in someone's political interest, or toward low ones" (Miller 2012, 54–55). In a sense, surveys and interviews of forecasters such as in Kong (2007) and Frank and Zhao (2009) not only help to triangulate findings from quantitative research on forecasting but also look to the organizational and political dimensions of forecasting in the budget process (Sun 2005).

Second, research can continue to examine how specific revenue and expenditure forecasts may help to build slack. Examining total revenues forecast bias and total expenditure forecast bias does not reflect the different revenue sources and expenditures. For example, forecasts of property tax revenue may be biased differently than forecasts of sales or income taxes, as shown in Rubin (1987) and Kong (2007), but how these different revenue forecast biases relate to accumulation of reserves is unknown. Further, how intergovernmental revenue transfers play into the implicit-explicit fiscal slack relationship also requires further research, particularly for the school district context, given the use of state aid formulas for allocation.

Third, research should look at differences in forecast bias and fiscal slack across government types and characteristics. Studying how differences across regions, sizes, or even resource capacity may play a role in the forecast-slack relationship is not fully explored. Barrett et al. (2019) call for more research on this topic, and it can play a critical role in helping to inform practitioners across the variety of governments and contexts they operate within.

Fourth, research can look beyond state and local governments in the United States. As noted in Williams and Calabrese (2016), conservative and liberal revenue forecasts have different meanings to the US federal government and the European Union. Whether or not these differences hold at the subnational level in countries outside the United States, and biased forecasts can build fiscal slack, is also largely unexplored. Studies from Goeminne et al. (2008) and Serritzlew (2005) show that European countries do bias forecasts, but again, the implications for financial management in other countries and regions are still unexplored. Thus, further research on forecasting in a comparative context can help to reveal similarities and differences in financial management.

Fifth, more research needs to be conducted on best practices in the implicit-explicit fiscal slack relationship. The GFOA Best Practice (2013) Capital Planning Policies recognizes the need for governments to accumulate capital reserves, but gives little insight into how to accumulate them. This chapter shows that implicit slack from forecast bias can help to accumulate building fund (320) reserves. Research should test if these findings hold for other governments, and then use them to provide further insight into GFOA's Best Practices regarding capital budgeting and infrastructure financial management.

Overall, each limitation presents an opportunity for further research on forecast bias and how it relates more broadly to budgeting and financial management in and outside the general fund. Future research can help to build the literature and also inform practitioners given the accumulating evidence that governments bias revenue and expenditure forecasts.

Conclusion and Future Research

This chapter builds the literature on forecast bias and more broadly fiscal slack on three fronts. First, it develops and tests the relationship between forecast bias and capital reserves, building on research from Barrett et al. (2019). Second, the use of school district dataset addresses the limited research on school district financial management, noted as a concern in Duncombe and Hou (2014) and Arapis et al. (2017). Third, the chapter provides a framework which can be used in future research on forecast bias and more broadly fiscal slack.

In regard to praxis, this chapter provides insight how practitioners can strategically build slack into the budget, emphasizing the recommendation that strategic forecasting as part of implicit slack should be called "cushioning" rather than being biased (Barrett et al. 2019; Rodgers and Joyce 1996, 55). It also demonstrates that school districts are attempting to build capital reserves with implicit slack, providing some evidence in support of the GFOA Best Practice (2013, 1) Capital Planning Policies which recommends "a procedure for accumulating necessary capital reserves for both new and replacement purchases." More research is needed to validate if the implicit-explicit slack relationship holds for capital reserves in other governments. Thus, there remains a notable opportunity for future research on forecast bias.

References

Arapis, T., & Reitano, V. (2018). A glimmer of optimism in government savings accumulation? An empirical examination of municipal unassigned fund balance in Florida. *Public Finance Review, 46*(3), 389–420. https://doi.org/10.1177/1091142116643386.

Arapis, T., Reitano, V., & Bruck, E. (2017). The fiscal savings behavior of Pennsylvania school districts through the great recession. *Public Budgeting & Finance, 37*(3), 47–70.

Barrett, N., Fowles, J., Jones, P., & Reitano, V. (2019). Forecast Bias and Fiscal Slack Accumulation in School Districts. *American Review of Public Administration,* 49(5), 601–613.

Bart, C. (1989). Budgeting gamesmanship. *The Academy of Management Executive, 2*, 285–294.

Bourgeois, L. J., III. (1981). On the measurement of organizational slack. *Academy of Management Review, 6*(1), 29–39.

Bretschneider, S. I., Straussman, J. J., & Mullins, D. (1988). Do revenue forecasts influence budget setting? A small group experiment. *Policy Sciences, 21*(4), 305–325.

Casey, J. P., & Mucha, M. J. (2007). *Capital project planning and evaluation.* Chicago: Government Finance Officers Association.

Cyert, R. M., & March, J. G. (1963). *A behavioral theory of the firm.* Englewood Cliffs, NJ: Prentice-Hall.

Dougherty, M. J., Klase, K. A., & Song, S. G. (2003). Managerial necessity and the art of creating surpluses: The budget-execution process in West Virginia cities. *Public Administration Review, 63*(4), 484–497.

Duncombe, W., & Hou, Y. (2014). The savings behavior of special purpose governments: A panel study of New York school districts. *Public Budgeting & Finance, 34*(3), 1–23.

Frank, H. A., & Zhao, Y. (2009). Determinants of local government revenue forecasting practice: Empirical evidence from Florida. *Journal of Public Budgeting, Accounting & Financial Management, 21*(1), 17–35.

Goeminne, S., Geys, B., & Smolders, C. (2008). Political fragmentation and projected tax revenues: Evidence from Flemish municipalities. *International Tax and Public Finance, 15*(3), 297–315.

Governmental Accounting Standards Board. (2009). Statement No. 54 of the Governmental Accounting Standards Board: Fund balance reporting and governmental fund type definitions. Norwalk, CT: GASB.

Government Finance Officers Association. (2013). Capital planning policies. *Best practice.* Retrieved from http://www.gfoa.org/capital-planning-policies.

Government Finance Officers Association. (2015). Fund balance guidelines for the general fund. *Best practice.* Retrieved from http://www.gfoa.org/fund-balance-guidelines-general-fund.

Hendrick, R. (2004). Assessing and measuring the fiscal heath of local governments: Focus on Chicago suburban municipalities. *Urban Affairs Review, 40*(1), 78–114.
Hendrick, R. (2006). The role of slack in local government finances. *Public Budgeting & Finance, 26*(1), 14–46.
Hulpke, J. F., Watne, D. A., & Waldo, D. (1976). Budgeting behavior: If, when, and how selected school districts hide money. *Public Administration Review, 36*(6), 667–674.
Kavanagh, S. C. (2007). *Financing the future: Long-term financial planning for local government.* Chicago: Government Finance Officers Association.
Kavanagh, S. C. (2011). *An elected official's guide to fiscal first aid.* Chicago: Government Finance Officers Association.
Kentucky Legislative Research Commission. (2010). *School districts' fund balance study.* Retrieved from http://www.lrc.ky.gov/lrcpubs/rr376.pdf.
Kong, D. (2007). Local government revenue forecasting: The California county experience. *Journal of Public Budgeting, Accounting & Financial Management, 19*(2), 178–199.
Larkey, P. D., & Smith, R. A. (1989). Bias in the formulation of local government budget problems. *Policy Sciences, 22*(2), 123–166.
Marlowe, J. (2005). Fiscal slack and counter-cyclical expenditure stabilization: A first look at the local level. *Public Budgeting & Finance, 25*(3), 48–72.
Miller, G. (2012). *Government budgeting and financial management in practice: Logics to make sense of ambiguity.* Boca Raton: CRC Press.
Office of the New York State Comptroller. (2010). *Local government management guide: Reserve funds.* Albany, NY. Retrieved from https://osc.state.ny.us/localgov/pubs/lgmg/reservefunds.pdf.
Rodgers, R., & Joyce, P. G. (1996). The effect of underforecasting on the accuracy of revenue forecasts by state governments. *Public Administration Review, 56*(1), 48–56.
Rose, S., & Smith, D. L. (2012). Budget slack, institutions, and transparency. *Public Administration Review, 72*(2), 187–195.
Rubin, I. S. (1987). Estimated and actual urban revenues: Exploring the gap. *Public Budgeting & Finance, 7*(4), 83–94. https://doi.org/10.1111/1540-5850.00766.
Serritzlew, S. (2005). Breaking budgets: An empirical examination of Danish municipalities. *Financial Accountability & Management, 21*(4), 413–435.
Stewart, L. M., Phillips, J. N., & Modlin, S. (2013). An evaluation of the connection between economic volatility and governmental savings levels for Illinois, North Carolina, and Mississippi Counties. *Public Finance and Management, 13*(4), 361–382.
Sun, J. (2005). The dynamics of government revenue forecasting from an organizational perspective: A review of the literature. *Journal of Public Budgeting, Accounting & Financial Management, 17*(4), 527.
Thompson, J. D. (1967). *Organizations in action; social science bases of administrative theory.* New York: McGraw-Hill.

Ványolós, I. (2011). The impact of state-imposed fund balance limits on school districts: Evidence from New York state. *Journal of Public Budgeting, Accounting & Financial Management, 23*(2), 166–187.

Vasche, J. D., & Williams, B. (1987). Optimal government budgeting contingency reserve funds. *Public Budgeting & Finance, 7*(1), 66–82.

Wang, W., & Hou, Y. (2012). Do local governments save and spend across budget cycles? Evidence from North Carolina. *The American Review of Public Administration, 42*(2), 152–169.

Williams, D. W., & Calabrese, T. D. (2016). The status of budget forecasting. *Journal of Public and Nonprofit Affairs, 2*(2), 127–160. https://doi.org/10.20899/jpna.2.2.127-160.

Williams, D. W., & Onochie, J. (2013). The Rube Goldberg machine of budget implementation, or is there a structural deficit in the New York City budget? *Public Budgeting & Finance, 33*(4), 1–21. https://doi.org/10.1111/j.1540-5850.2013.12021.x.

Wolkoff, M. (1987). An evaluation of municipal rainy day funds. *Public Budgeting & Finance, 7*(2), 52–63.

20

Consensus Forecasting

J. Winn Decker and Bruce D. McDonald III

Major Points

- Consensus forecasting involves multiple parties who agree on a forecast that is used in policy discussions.
- This forecast method seeks to eliminate political fighting and increase transparency and accuracy in the forecasting process.
- Best practices are
  - the inclusion of all relevant parties,
  - publicizing documents and meetings,
  - codifying the consensus process through legislation or bylaws, and
  - revising the forecast throughout the year.

J. W. Decker (✉) • B. D. McDonald III
Department of Public Administration, North Carolina State University, Raleigh, NC, USA
e-mail: jwdecker@ncsu.edu; bmcdona@ncsu.edu

D. Williams, T. Calabrese (eds.), *The Palgrave Handbook of Government Budget Forecasting*, Palgrave Studies in Public Debt, Spending, and Revenue,
https://doi.org/10.1007/978-3-030-18195-6_20

Introduction

Organizations set budgets to plan and ensure that all programs have the appropriate funds to operate throughout the fiscal year. Forecasting is an essential part of the budgeting process, as forecasts anticipate the revenues and expenditures that an organization will have (Denison and Kim 2018; McDonald 2015; Williams and Calabrese 2016). Good forecasts create budgets that are more accurate by assisting in the decision-making of policies and programs for upcoming fiscal years (Bretschneider et al. 1989). As the political system in the United States has become more polarized, budget forecasts have been caught in the cross-fire (Leslie 2016). Budget discussions have moved away from programs and policy and devolved to partisan arguments about whether the underlying forecast has a partisan lean. Evidence of this politicization can be seen in the legislative responses to forecasts that come out of the Congressional Budget Office. Accuracy and trust in the forecast have also diminished, as the correct numbers may not be the ones that win the political arguments (Mikesell and Ross 2014). As such, governments have looked for better ways to estimate their budget forecasts, preferably ways that can resolve issues of politicization. Consensus forecasting is such a means (Klay and Vonasek 2008; Mikesell 2008).

Consensus forecasting is a technique that develops the forecast for a variable of interests, such as governmental revenue or expenditures, which incorporates input from multiples sources and parties (Klay and Vonasek 2008; National Association of State Budget Officers [NASBO] 2008). When undertaking a consensus forecast, input is sought from experts who have a stake in the variable being forecasted. The experts involved in the consensus process may come from the legislative branch of the government or from executive agencies, but they may also come from universities and private firms. Experts offer new insights, and adding these different perspectives highlights issues or policy impacts that may not be previously seen (McNichol 2014). An example of this can be seen in the Florida Demographic Estimating Conference. In establishing a forecast of Florida's population and demographics, the conference considers the opinions of demographers, medical practitioners, and various state agencies when conducting a consensus-reached forecast (Office of Economic and Demographic Research [OEDR] 2018). While the level of influence of the participatory experts on the forecast may vary, the success of the forecast hinges on the acceptance of a consensus by all parties involved.

The process of undertaking a consensus forecast is more time and resource consuming than traditional forecasting approaches; however, using information from multiple people and sources allows a more robust perspective to be developed. By creating a joint product, all those involved are more likely to use the product in future policy discussions (Mikesell 2008; Mikesell and Ross 2014). This agreement allows the same set of numbers in all budget preparation and reduces debate over the merits of competing forecasts (McNichol 2014).

This chapter intends to provide the reader with a primer on consensus forecasting. This is accomplished by providing a discussion of the process' theoretical underpinnings. Next, we explore the application of the process as it is currently used. In the following sections, we provide guidance to those looking to implement a consensus approach as part of their own forecasting process. This guidance comes in the form of a discussion of the strengths and weaknesses of the consensus process, along with best practices for its adoption. The chapter will conclude by discussing the need for additional research into the process of consensus forecasting.

Theory of Consensus Forecasting

The process of forecasting involves an individual using data and inference to project the future value of a variable of interest (McDonald 2013, 2015; Williams and Calabrese 2016). Although advanced statistical methodologies and the involvement of experts in the forecasting process gives the appearance of accuracy, forecasts are, at best, an educated guess. Inherently, these educated guesses will be wrong. The goal in forecasting is not to develop a perfect estimate for the variable of interest, but rather to develop an efficient estimate of that variable which contains as little error as possible. The adage in forecasting is that if you want to forecast accurately, you can overcome the error by forecasting frequently. Steps can be taken to reduce the error of a forecast, but the inherent inaccuracy of the process opens the door for debate over the validity of the estimate. Such a debate may lead to a revised and improved forecasting process, but it is may also lead to distrust in the process and a discounting of the results.

In addition to the inherent problem of error in a forecast, there are also concerns regarding which statistical methodology is most appropriate to estimate the variable and the expertise, skill, and independence of the forecaster conducting the estimate. In an era of heightening politicization, these issues raise concern on the legitimacy of a forecast (Mikesell 2008). They are not, however, insurmountable. The literature on organizational behavior (see Scott 2008) and group learning (see O'Donnell 2006) has pointed toward the use of groups as a means of addressing differences of opinion. This perspective can also be seen within the direct democracy literature from public administration

(Gabrini 2010). While individuals are not always rational, self-focused beings, rational choice theory permeates decisions economists make (Levin and Milgrom 2004). In reality, individuals are bounded rationally in their actions, making the best decisions based on the limited information available (Simon 1956). When an individual is conducting a forecast, they should choose the best statistical approach available, given the data, and make the assumptions that coincide with the chosen approach. When decisions are made for the group, they are done so by having navigated the desires of each member to reach that agreement. The outcome may not be the ideal or preferred outcome for each member individually, but as a collective, it is the optimal choice.

In practice, the group dynamic forces the individual to consider ideas beyond his or her own. When only one individual is involved in the forecasting process, there is no debate or discussion on how the process should be carried out. In the group dynamic, however, choices must be explained and opponents won over. As people are added to a group, they bring their own perspectives and understanding. With a larger group, it becomes more likely that members will disagree, forcing a true discussion on how the forecast should be conducted. However, a larger group may also allow groupthink to spread through the group, resulting in irrational decisions (Sunstein and Hastie 2015). This makes it important to allow dissenting viewpoints and a critical evaluation of alternatives available. Brooks (2006) looks to combat this idea of groupthink, going further than assuming that a disagreement will take place when a group decision is being made, and suggesting that it is the responsibility of those in government to challenge the information being disseminated as a means of achieving the best outcome (Sunstein and Hastie 2015). The intent of the consensus forecasting process is to utilize this discussion to improve the outcome of the forecast. The forecast is only complete when all members of the group reach an agreement to which they are willing to adhere.

What should be gathered from this discussion is that a consensus process is more of a mediation approach to establishing a forecast than a statistical technique. Significant variation can exist in how the consensus process is established between forecasting groups; however, in each instance, the group is responsible for debating the use of statistical approaches to budget forecasting addressed elsewhere in this book. The group must then reach a consensus on what statistical process and data will be used to estimate the budget variable of interest. In accordance to the theory of consensus forecasting, the outcome produced by the group will be an estimate that derives not on the benefit of an individual forecaster, but on the betterment of the public that the organization serves.

Consensus Forecasting in Practice

Despite the fact that consensus forecasting seeks to produce a more accurate and usable forecast, its adoption as a forecasting strategy has been slow. One of the most prolific uses of consensus forecasting, though, is in state governments. Even across states, the consensus forecasting model varies vastly. Florida was the first state to use consensus forecasting when it held its first consensus revenue forecasting conference in 1970 (OEDR 2018). The consensus process started when a senior officer in the executive branch observed the political arguments and fighting that happened with the current system, so he invited members from both chambers of congress and staff members from revenue committees to join the governor's budget director to create one comprehensive forecast (Klay and Vonasek 2008). This process was originally informal and limited to the forecast of the General Revenue Fund only. In 1980, though, lawmakers formalized the process when they created the Division of Economic and Demographic Research. Through this process, a memorandum of agreement among the parties was achieved, and in 1985, the process was formalized through legal statute (OEDR 2018). Florida's multi-stage process begins with the adoption of a national economic forecast based in part on information from a private forecasting firm, followed by the development of a Florida-specific economic forecast. This process determines the baseline forecasts, and subsequent meetings adjust this baseline to account for any new changes or information. The consensus process has been met with enough success that the state has expanded its use beyond forecasting general revenue, and now uses it for forecasting a number of variables, including demographics, education demand, crime, insurance needs, and retirement (OEDR 2018).

The idea of consensus forecasting soon spread to other states, as three states (i.e., Kansas, New Mexico, and North Carolina), in addition to Florida, began using consensus forecasting in the 1970s (Qiao 2008). As states saw the success of the process, seven more states implemented consensus forecasting in the 1980s: Indiana, Iowa, Louisiana, Mississippi, Nebraska, Washington, and Wyoming. The biggest growth of the consensus process was seen in the 1990s when nine additional states started using the process: Kentucky, Maine, Maryland, Michigan, Missouri, New York, Rhode Island, South Carolina, and Vermont (Qiao 2008; NASBO 2015). Currently, 28 states utilize some form of a consensus process for producing their forecasts.

Some states require the use of a consensus forecast through either state statutes or constitutional amendments (Huaman and McLean n.d.). For example, Iowa created the Revenue Estimating Conference as a way to arrive at a consensus projection of general fund revenue that can be used by both the governor and legislature for their budgeting process (Iowa 2018). The committee consists of a governor appointee, the director of the Legislative Services Agency, and a third person agreed upon by the other two members. They meet at least three times a year to establish a general funded revenue estimate. This estimate is then legally binding to be used in all budgeting processes in the state (Iowa Department of Management 2018).

In another example, The Vermont Emergency Board (E-Board) is composed of the governor and the chairpersons of the four legislative committees dealing with appropriations or the budget (Vermont Agency of Administration 2018). Moreover, two state economists, one appointed by the governor and one by the legislature, are also involved and provide joint recommendations for the board. Working together, this board adopts revenue forecasts in January and July of each year for the general fund, transportation fund, and education fund. This report is then used by the legislature and executive branch in their budget preparations.

Other states have established more informal revenue forecasting groups to determine their operating budget; however, they are not legally binding. For example, North Carolina has used an informal consensus process since 1975. The North Carolina constitution requires that the governor's recommended budget include anticipated revenues for the fiscal period. As a result, the North Carolina Office of State Budget and Management (NCOSBM), which is under the purview of the Governor, works with the Fiscal Research Division of the General Assembly to produce a forecast for the state (NCOSBM 2018). However, the consensus forecast is not legally binding; if no consensus can be reached between the two, then the legislature creates their own forecast to be used (NCOSBM 2018). This is especially prevalent when the Governor and Legislative majority are from opposing parties (Doran 2018).

Maryland is another state that does not legally bind the use of the consensus forecast in budget preparations (Qiao 2008). Maryland law does stipulate the people who are to be involved in their consensus process: the Chief executive and his staff, the deputy comptroller, Office of the Treasurer staff, Department of Budget and Management staff, Department of Transportation staff, and the Office of Policy Analysis staff (Md. Code §6-105. 2013). This group meets and reviews revenue estimates on a monthly basis to ensure the most accurate forecast possible. This process involves many different stakeholders, and as a result produces a forecast that most parties feel comfortable using in their policy development.

Strengths and Weaknesses of Consensus Forecasting

Just as with all forecasting techniques, there are several strengths and weaknesses of consensus forecasting that potential adopters of the process should be aware of. The strength of the consensus process is a result of all parties working together for a common output. This collaboration should result in greater accuracy, increased transparency, and political acceptance of the forecast if proper parameters are set up to ensure groupthink does not take precedent and all agree to use the forecast (Klay and Vonasek 2008; Sunstein and Hastie 2015). However, the demand of collaboration may also lead to the downfall of a consensus process. As new statistical methods and group administration techniques are published, the frameworks set for consensus forecasting groups need to be re-evaluated to incorporate advancements in budgeting. Ultimately, the advantages and drawbacks of the consensus technique depend on how the process is developed.

Strengths of the Consensus Process

Although there are a number of benefits that a government might experience by using a consensus approach in their forecasting, there are two key strengths in using a consensus forecast. These are improved accuracy and increased transparency. As noted previously in this chapter and elsewhere in the book, forecasts are, at best, an educated guess from those doing the estimating. A forecaster may take steps to reduce the statistical error of their forecast, but it is not possible to remove the error altogether. The group nature of a consensus forecast requires that the decisions made by a forecaster be reconsidered, with only the most prominent of the decisions emerging to be used in the final product.

The benefit of a consensus process at improving the accuracy of a forecast can be observed throughout the literature. Abolafia's (2004) discussion of forecasting at the Federal Reserve, for example, shows how a consensus process requires forecasters to incorporate viewpoints outside their own. Through group discussion, the model and statistical techniques used to reach the forecast can be refined and improved to achieve a better, more accurate outcome. Qiao (2008) shows the same effect in state budgeting. States that use the consensus forecast are more likely to make errors of less than 5 percent compared to states that do not use consensus forecasting. Lastly, Mikesell and

Ross (2014) find that use of a state revenue forecasting committee adds value to the technical accuracy by informing more nuanced portions of the forecasting process. Using a consensus decreases the amount of bias that appears in a forecast, thus allowing it to use the most accurate information.

The second strength of a consensus process is its transparency. Forecasts are often viewed as a black box where information goes in and only the forecaster understands how the estimates emerge (see McDonald 2013, 2015). The more people involved in the forecasting process, the more transparent that process becomes (Mikesell 2008; Wong and Ekstrom 2008). Statistical techniques and assumptions must be presented and debated by the group as a means of reaching their outcome. Not only does this ensure that the consensus group understands how the forecast emerged, but also the laws establishing consensus processes frequently require that a report be produced and made public explaining how the consensus was reached.

Weaknesses of the Consensus Process

Accuracy and transparency are important in any forecasting process, but that is not to say that a consensus process does not have its weaknesses as well. The most prominent of these weaknesses is the lack of accountability and the potential for satisficing. When the consensus group is expanded to include those outside of the legislature and governor's office, this allows an individual to be involved in the forecasting process that was not elected by his or her constituents. Depending on the consensus process, positions on the forecasting committee are reserved for academics and people in the private industry that have expertise in budgeting and the economy (Qiao 2008). While this addition of knowledge from outside the public sector helps increase accuracy and transparency, the legislator or governor usually appoints these people. These committee members are not accountable to the public because they are not elected. As such, it may be difficult to hold the consensus group accountable for their final product.

There is also the potential that the quality of the output can be diminished through satisficing. As discussed in the section on the theory underlying the consensus process, the literature on organizational behavior and group learning argue that groups can be used to address differences of opinion (O'Donnell 2006; Scott 2008). Through collaboration, the group can consider all aspects of the issue and reach an outcome that captures the best ideas. There is also, however, that in the group setting, members pursue a satisficed solution rather than the best outcome. Simon's (1947, 1956) model of satisficing suggests that when group dynamics become challenging, the group is more likely to look for the first reasonable solution rather than the optimal outcome. When we consider the political dynamics that establish the consensus process of a government and the political environment in which the outcome will be used, there is the potential that the group dynamic may be hostile (Klay and Vonasek 2008). If this happens, then we should expect the forecasts that the group produces to be subpar. We also expect that the perceived legitimacy of the consensus process would require that the subpar forecast be used in the government's decision-making.

Best Practices in Consensus Forecasting

While consensus forecasting can be successfully used to develop a forecast when considerable disagreement of political discord exists, there is no set formula on how to develop the process. The details of the process, such as who is involved, the frequency of the meetings, and how a consensus will be reached, must be adapted to create a process that best fits the circumstances. There are, however, best practices when implementing a consensus requirement into the forecasting process. Each consensus process should meet five best practices to ensure a reliable and transparent forecast. These five best practices are: involving members of both political parties; including experts that are not elected officials; ensuring transparency through the openness of the process; defining the consensus process in law or organization bylaws; and revising the forecast throughout the year.

Involve Members of Both Political Parties

Consensus forecasting seeks to bring the forecasting process out from behind closed doors and involve multiple people in the process. By involving both political parties in the process, the goal is to lessen the political tension as all groups have a stake in the forecast (McNichol 2014). Research shows that involving people in a deliberative process gives them a sense of ownership in the outcomes (Anderson 1999). If those involved take ownership of their product, then there is a greater likelihood of positive discourse. Nearly all states that have implemented a consensus process require forecasting committee members appointed by both the legislature and governors branch to ensure representation from multiple branches of government (Mikesell and Ross 2014). Being inclusive across party lines increases the likelihood that the forecasted variable will be used in the government's decision-making process (Klay and Vonasek 2008). If representatives of a party are left out of the process, it may undermine the trust in the forecast as a starting point for negotiation (McNichol 2014). However, when all parties are involved, they can be more confident in the final product because they had a representative in the room during the forecasting process.

Include Experts That Are Not Elected Officials

Forecasts reached through a consensus often involve elected officials in the process; however, outside experts, such as individuals from academia and private businesses, as well as economic and budgeting experts from governmental agencies, can bring a much-needed perspective to the process. How outside experts are involved in the consensus process varies greatly, but their inclusion widens the knowledge and experience within the forecasting body (McNichol 2014). Their inclusion also increases transparency and non-partisanship as forecasts generated by outside sources may be estimated without political pressure (Kavanagh and Iglehart 2012). As such, they can hold any elected officials that are involved in the consensus process accountable by ensuring that the outcome is not influenced by a political agenda and that only the most probable forecast is implemented. Further, politicians are more likely to accept the forecast if politically neutral experts are engaged in the process (McNichol 2014).

Ensure Transparency Through Openness of the Process

A criticism of forecasting is that users of the data that emerges from the forecast must blindly put their trust in the output without understanding both the statistical methods used by the forecaster and the assumptions that they made (Klay and Vonasek 2008). The criticism is diminished by the addition of a group to the forecasting process, but it is not eliminated. The direct democracy literature from public administration argues that an informed public is not only an engaged public, but they are a public more accepting of the decisions that the government makes (see Gabrini 2010). Applying this to consensus forecasting, the criticism can be eradicated. Openness in the consensus process improves the trust that the public has in the outcome of the forecast by allowing them to participate. In turn, the participation provides communication between elected officials and the public and connects a personal story to the decisions that officials are making (Franklin and Ebdon 2015). Transparency and openness in the process can be obtained through simple steps, such as announcing the dates of meetings, publishing minutes and reports from meetings, and allowing public comment.

Define the Consensus Process in Law or Organization Bylaws

For a consensus process to work and for its outcome to be trusted, it must have legitimacy. This is obtained by formalizing the process (Tebbs 2009). While 28 states use the consensus forecasting process for revenue predictions, only 17 of those require it by law (Klay and Vonasek 2008). The other 11 states have informal agreements to use consensus forecasting; however, these agreements may be broken at any time. The opportunity to break from the consensus process removes the pressure to pursue a forecast that meets the common good and incentivizes disengagement to pursue a forecast that maximizes the preferences of the individual. Formalization codifies the process by defining its parameters, such as when the process will take place, who is involved, and how decisions are made. Most importantly, the results and product of the forecasting committee should also be legally binding. A legal binding to a forecast generated through a consensus process helps promote healthy debate on substantive policies rather than the merits of the forecast (Qiao 2008).

Revisit the Forecast Throughout the Year

The final best practice for consensus forecasting involves revisiting the forecast throughout the year. Reviewing the forecast to allow for adjustments to economic circumstances or change in policy can improve their accuracy (McNichol 2014). Revising forecasting improves the accuracy of the forecast because adjustments can change in the environment (Deschamps 2004). There is, however, no standardized timetable for revisions to the forecast. While revising estimates multiple times of the year increases accuracy, revisiting the forecast too frequently can actually increase error (Mocan and Azad 1995). Ultimately, each organization must decide how frequently their forecasting committee should convene, and this should be decided as part of the forecasting process that is codified into law.

Opportunities for Further Research

While consensus forecasting has been a focus of recent academic work, there is still much room to explore the impacts of implementing this process at the state government level. For one, consensus forecasting has continued to grow in acceptance and diffused to a majority of states. One place of future research is to explore the state environments that are conducive to implementing a consensus forecasting process. These factors could be structural, such as the way a state government is designed, or environmental, like patterns of gridlock and inaccurate forecasts. By better understanding the factors that support state adoption of consensus forecasting, it is possible to understand why some states did not adopt and if their adoption is likely in the future.

Along with understanding state characteristics that allow for the adoption of consensus forecasting, more research needs to be done on consensus forecasting outside state budgets—as consensus has grown as a technique for forecasting, non-profits and private organizations alike (Fink et al. 1984). Yet, research on organizational use of consensus forecasting is lacking. Future studies should look at how consensus forecasting varies between government entities and non-profit/private organizations. Lessons learned from the non-profit and private sectors may help further improve public sector forecasting.

Further, consensus forecasting needs to be evaluated for accuracy during times of fluctuations in the economy. Other factors outside of the forecast affect its accuracy. One such is fluctuations in the economy. Previous literature has shown that the stability of the economy has a statistically significant impact on the accuracy of a revenue forecast (Wallack 2005). While some states adopted consensus forecasting in the 1970s, it was not until the 1990s that the majority of states started using the consensus process. As such, data on the accuracy during times of economic instability has been lacking. Now that there have been economic cycle swings, there should be more data available about accuracy of these consensus forecasts during this instability. This information would be useful in supporting the use and expansion of consensus forecasting if it is seen to be more accurate during economic instability than traditional revenue forecasting tools.

Finally, research should be done on visibility of consensus forecasting for residents. The majority of literature has focused on the consensus process itself, but the citizens and those affected by the budget have largely been ignored. Two of the main tenets of consensus forecasting are reducing political arguing and increasing transparency. Those heavily involved in the political process may see these two outcomes. However, the everyday citizen fails to notice these outcomes. By gaining public acceptance of the consensus process, a state may be more likely to codify consensus forecasting into their budget requirements each year and have a better understanding of how to improve public access to the forecasting process.

Conclusion

This chapter provides an overview of the revenue forecasting process and argues that consensus forecasting has become the premier forecasting method. The implementation of this process varies by organization, as some require it by law and bound their public officials to use the forecast results; whereas, other states use a more informal process that is agreed upon each year. No matter how an organization implements the consensus process, it is done so to increase accuracy and transparency, reduce partisan fighting, and involve more individuals in the process. The goal is to create an agreed-upon forecast by all parties that can be used to model future estimates.

The best practices for consensus forecasting includes the involvement of all parties (including outside experts), publicizing documents and meetings, codifying the consensus process through legislation or bylaws, and revising the forecast throughout the year. These best practices increase transparency and accuracy in the process, which leads to political acceptance of the final forecast. Critics of the consensus process argue that it allows individuals who were not elected to have an influence on policy and that consensus is an impossible threshold to reach. However, these fears are mitigated by having a clearly defined process that balances public input, expert opinions, and the minority viewpoints.

It is important to note that consensus forecasting will never solve all the problems involved in revenue forecasting. Economic instability, human error, and political bias may all affect the accuracy and usability of the forecast. Further, the consensus process is time- consuming. Getting everyone in the room to agree on everything takes time, patience, and discussion. Differences in political philosophies of those in the room, and political parties in general may also complicate the consensus process. If people enter the room with non-starters for negotiation, a stalemate will ensue. Individuals involved must be willing to leave political agendas at the door and instead work for the best of all people in their state and a final product in which they can be proud to take ownership. Those not directly involved in the forecasting process must trust those they appointed to the forecasting committee to articulate their stance on issues, while also accepting the final product.

All of these issues highlighted above are just some of the challenges faced during a consensus revenue forecasting process. Still, the merits of consensus forecasting outweigh the possible roadblocks. If an organization is willing to commit the time and resources to the forecasting process, then consensus forecasting can serve as a way to eliminate political strife and increase the accuracy of the forecast. Consensus forecasting has seen success at the state budgeting level and looks poised to be the main forecasting process for years to come. Additional research is needed to truly understand the impact of consensus revenue forecasting, on both non-profit and private organizations and the citizens of the state. Even when the consensus process fails, forecasters can learn from their mistakes and improve the process next time. Consensus forecasting brings more people, more information, and more perspectives to the table, which enriches democracy and the voices that have been left out of the budget conversation for so long.

References

Abolafia, M. Y. (2004). Framing moves: Interpretive politics at the Federal Reserve. *Journal of Public Administration Research and Theory, 14*(3), 349–370.

Anderson, G. L. (1999). The politics of participatory reforms in education. *Theory Into Practice, 38*(4), 191–195.

Bretschneider, S. I., Gorr, W. L., Grizzle, G. A., & Klay, E. (1989). Political and organizational influences on the accuracy of forecasting state government revenues. *International Journal of Forecasting, 5*(3), 307–319.

Brooks, M. (2006). *World War Z: An oral history of the zombie war* (1st ed.). New York: Crown.

Denison, D. V., & Kim, S. (2018). Linking practice and classroom: Nonprofit financial management curricula in MPA and MPP programs. *Journal of Public Affairs Education*, 1–18.

Deschamps, E. (2004). The impact of institutional change on forecast accuracy: A case study of budget forecasting in Washington State. *International Journal of Forecasting, 20*(4), 647–657. https://doi.org/10.1016/j.ijforecast.2003.11.009.

Doran, W. (2018, June 13). Legislators override Roy Cooper's veto to pass their $23.9 billion budget. *The News & Observer*, p. Online. Retrieved from https://www.newsobserver.com/news/politics-government/article212974664.html.

Fink, A., Kosecoff, J., Chassin, M., & Brook, R. H. (1984). Consensus methods: Characteristics and guidelines for use. *American Journal of Public Health, 74*(9), 979–983.

Franklin, A. L., & Ebdon, C. (2015). Democracy, public participation, and budgeting: Mutually exclusive or just exhausting? In R. C. Box (Ed.), *Democracy and public administration* (pp. 96–118). New York: Routledge.

Gabrini, C. J. (2010). Do institutions matter? The influence of institutions of direct democracy on local government spending. *State and Local Government Review, 42*(3), 210–225.

Huaman, J., & McLean, C. (n.d.). North Carolina state budget. *North Carolina State Government Publications Collection*. Retrieved from http://ncgovdocs.org/guides/budget.htm.

Iowa Department of Management. (2018). Revenue estimating conference projections. Retrieved from https://dom.iowa.gov/rec-projections.

Kavanagh, S. C., & Iglehart, C. (2012). Structuring the revenue forecasting process. *Government Finance Review, 28*(5), 8–16.

Klay, W. E., & Vonasek, J. A. (2008). Consensus forecasting for budgeting in theory and practice. In J. Sun & T. D. Lynch (Eds.), *Government budget forecasting: Theory and practice* (pp. 379–392). Boca Raton, FL: CRC Press.

Leslie, L. (2016, July 1). Budget, corrections head to governor *WARL.com*. Retrieved from https://www.wral.com/budget-corrections-head-to-governor/15821529/.

Levin, J., & Milgrom, P. (2004). *Introduction to choice theory*. Stanford.edu. Retrieved from http://web.stanford.edu/~jdlevin/Econ%20202/Choice%20Theory.pdf.

McDonald, B. D. (2013). An introduction to dirty forecasting. *Government Finance Review, 29*(5), 57–60. Retrieved from https://www.gfoa.org/sites/default/files/GFR_OCT_13_60.pdf.

McDonald, B. D. (2015). A "dirty" approach to efficient revenue forecasting. *Journal of Public and Nonprofit Affairs, 1*(1), 3–17.

McNichol, E. C. (2014). *Improving state revenue forecasting: Best practices for a more trusted and reliable revenue estimate*. Center on Budget and Policy Priorities-CBPP: Washington, DC. Retrieved from https://www.cbpp.org/sites/default/files/atoms/files/8-7-14sfp.pdf.

Md. Code §6-105. (2013). In *State Finance and Procurement: Consensus revenue monitoring and forecasting group*.

Mikesell, J. L. (2008). State revenue forecasting in the state of Indiana: A consensus system in a politically divided state. In J. Sun & T. D. Lynch (Eds.), *Government budget forecasting: Theory and practice* (pp. 415–429). Boca Raton: CRC Press.

Mikesell, J. L., & Ross, J. M. (2014). State revenue forecasts and political acceptance: The value of consensus forecasting in the budget process. *Public Administration Review, 74*(2), 188–203.

Mocan, H. N., & Azad, S. (1995). Accuracy and rationality of state general fund revenue forecasts: Evidence from panel data. *International Journal of Forecasting, 11*(3), 417–427.

National Association of State Budget Officers. (2015). *Budget processes in the states: Spring 2015*. Washington, DC: National Association of State Budget Officers. Retrieved from https://www.nasbo.org/reports-data/budget-processes-in-the-states.

North Carolina Office of State Budget and Management. (2018). Revenue forecasting. Retrieved from https://www.osbm.nc.gov/budget/revenue-forecasting.

O'Donnell, A. M. (2006). The role of peers and group learning. In P. A. Alexander & P. H. Winne (Eds.), *Handbook of educational psychology* (pp. 781–802). Mahwah, NJ: Lawrence Erlbaum Associates Publishers.

Office of Economic & Demographic Research. (2018). Consensus estimating conferences. Retrieved from http://edr.state.fl.us/Content/conferences/index.cfm.

Qiao, Y. (2008). Use of consensus revenue forecasting in US state governments. In J. Sun & T. D. Lynch (Eds.), *Government budget forecasting: Theory and practice* (pp. 393–413). Boca Raton, FL: CRC Press.

Scott, W. R. (2008). *Institutions and organizations: Ideas and interests* (3rd ed.). Los Angeles: Sage Publications.

Simon, H. A. (1947). *Administrative behavior.* New York: Macmillan Co.

Simon, H. A. (1956). Rational choice and the structure of the environment. *Psychological Review, 63*(2), 129.

Sunstein, C. R., & Hastie, R. (2015). *Wiser: Getting beyond groupthink to make groups smarter.* Boston, MA: Harvard Business Review Press.

Tebbs, J. (2009). *Breaking the stalemate: A proposal for a consensus revenue forecasting process.* Connecticut Voices for Children. Retrieved from http://www.ctvoices.org/sites/default/files/bud09revenueforecasting.pdf.

Vermont Agency of Administration. (2018). *Provisional consensus revenue forecast for the general fund, transportation fund, and education fund [partial].* Vermont: Vermont Agency of Administration. Retrieved from http://aoa.vermont.gov/revenue/emergency-board.

Wallack, J. S. (2005). *Politics, institutions, and data quality: The highs and lows of revenue estimating.* In Mimeo, UC San Diego.

Williams, D. W., & Calabrese, T. D. (2016). The status of budget forecasting. *Journal of Public and Nonprofit Affairs, 2*(2), 127–160. https://doi.org/10.20899/jpna.2.2.127-160.

Wong, J. D., & Ekstrom, C. D. (2008). Consensus revenue estimating in state government: A case of what works in Kansas. In J. Sun & T. D. Lynch (Eds.), *Government budget forecasting: Theory and practice* (pp. 431–455). Boca Raton, FL: CRC Press.

21

Ensemble Forecasting

Kenneth A. Kriz

Major Points

- Developed in the late 1960s, ensemble forecasting has become well accepted in the literature on economic forecasting.
- Forecasts made from different models are combined into an aggregate forecast.
- Ensemble models have lower forecast errors.
- In this study, for five years of pseudo-out-of-sample forecasts, ensemble models demonstrated better overall forecast accuracy, while some single forecasts did very well in specific years.

Introduction

The literature on revenue forecasting has covered several important topics, such as the institutional structure of forecasting, the application of broad classes of models, and the outcomes from existing forecasts (typically assessing the biases inherent in the forecasts). However, scant attention has been paid to a topic which is almost universally accepted in economic forecasting—ensemble models. Ensemble models combine the information from many

K. A. Kriz (✉)
University of Illinois at Springfield, Springfield, IL, USA
e-mail: kkriz4@uis.edu

D. Williams, T. Calabrese (eds.), *The Palgrave Handbook of Government Budget Forecasting*, Palgrave Studies in Public Debt, Spending, and Revenue,
https://doi.org/10.1007/978-3-030-18195-6_21

individual forecasts to form point estimates or probability estimates of variables of interest. The term ensemble is only sometimes applied within economic forecasting. The term is borrowed from meteorological forecasts, where the term is ubiquitous.[1] In the economic forecasting literature, ensemble forecasting is usually called forecast combinations.

In a sense, all forecasting involves the aggregation of information from current and past situations in order to make a forecast of the future. At times, the decision about whether to seek or incorporate new information into a forecast model is trivial. Consider a person trying to make a forecast of rain for that afternoon. Although one could seek out a forecast from a weather forecaster, she might find it easier and less expensive to simply look at the sky to make a rough forecast of weather conditions. However, if she were trying to forecast the weather during a period of marked variations in the weather or come up with a forecast for the afternoon five days into the future, she might be better served to consult a forecast. Further, when the consequences of an incorrect forecast are dire, she might be well advised to seek a professional forecast. A further question is when someone should seek out multiple forecasts to try to resolve uncertainty regarding the probability of rain.

In a less trivial sense (though he too uses rain examples), Morris (1974) sketches out a theory of when professional expert judgment should be sought, and how the judgment of each succeeding expert should be weighed by a decision-maker. The formulation is Bayesian, with prior probabilities being updated as a function of the perceived accuracy of each expert, the strength of the prior probabilities, and the fundamental uncertainty of the variable of interest.

Ensemble or combination forecasting is derived from similar theories. These questions are asked by ensemble forecasting: (1) Given an existing forecast, can we add additional forecasts in a way that reduces forecast error? and (2) By how much should our forecast values or densities change given the new information? In this chapter, we will examine the theory of ensemble forecasting and chart its development in the academic literature. Then we develop an extended example of combination forecasting, using four of the major techniques found in the economic forecasting literature and assess the results. We find overall support for the notion that ensemble forecast models have overall better forecast accuracy than single forecast models. We conclude with a practical discussion of implementation considerations of ensemble models.

[1] Although many sources cite the field of meteorology as coming up with the specific term, the theory and logic around combining forecasts seems to have developed in parallel in meteorological and economic/financial forecasting.

Theory and Literature

Ensemble forecasting developed during the late 1960s during the heart of the "Bayesian revival" in statistics and econometrics. From the 1960s to the 1970s, the previously dormant study of decision-making using Bayesian techniques grew in its use (McGrayne 2011). Despite attacks from frequentist statisticians, Bayesian techniques were demonstrated to be tremendously useful in situations with sparse data and/or significant uncertainties like searching for lost airplanes and submarines. Econometrics also was being rethought along Bayesian terms (see, e.g., Zellner 1971). Ensemble forecasting grew out of the new awareness of Bayesian techniques, essentially asking whether our existing forecasts of an event or value of a variable could be better forecast by adding additional forecast values.

There are two related questions that have been asked in the academic literature on ensemble forecast methods: (1) whether combining single forecasts into an *ensemble of multiple forecasts* will produce gains in terms of lower forecast error variances; and (2) how individual forecasts should be combined to produce the ensemble? The theoretical basis for ensemble models was first set forth by Bates and Granger (1969). They examined both of these questions, setting forth our way of thinking about the problem of combining forecasts. The first question can be framed formally as: Given two unbiased forecasts of a variable f_1 and f_2, can we construct a combined forecast C at time T through weighting (using the variable k to denote the weight given to f_1):

$$C_T = k_T f_{1,T} + (1 - k_T) f_{2,T} \tag{21.1}$$

such that the combined forecast variance $CT_{A,B}$ would be smaller than the individual variances $Ci_A(k)$ and $Cm_A(k)$. They demonstrate that theoretically for situations where the forecasts have zero correlation, the forecast errors should be minimized when the weight k is inversely proportional to the relative forecast error variance of f_1[2]:

$$k_T^{BG} = \frac{\sigma_2^2}{\left(\sigma_1^2 + \sigma_2^2\right)} \tag{21.2}$$

[2] The superscript BG refers to the Bates-Granger weighting method. As we will be evaluating many individual and combination forecasts we will refer to them by initials.

Therefore, as the relative error of forecast Model 2 rises relative to Model 1, the weight given to Model 1 rises and the weight given to Model 2 falls. They examine various weighting schemes that incorporate more empirical information, including ones that take into account the covariance between errors and ones that give more weight to more recent observations. Using international airline passenger data, they show that each of the weighting methods produced lower forecast error variances than the individual forecasts (they used an exponential smoothing method and a Box-Jenkins adaptive forecast error method as their two component forecasts).

The paper by Bates and Granger spurred much more research into optimal forecast combination techniques, the second research question. Over the 50 years since that article appeared, over 100 academic papers have been published on the topic, with dozens of proposed weighting schemes (though Bates and Granger only looked at the two-forecast case, it was later shown that the methods could easily be extended to multiple forecasts, see Timmermann [2006] for a mathematical treatment). In this chapter, we will review the most "popular" of the methods, as judged by the number of publications on the topic and their inclusion into a list in a recent influential article (Hsiao and Wan 2014).

The most straightforward of the weighting methods is to take a simple average of forecasts (see, e.g., Clemen 1989). For N forecasts, $f_1, f_2 \ldots f_N$, find the weight by calculating the simple average:

$$k_T^{SA} = {}^{1}\!/_{N} \tag{21.3}$$

The simple average weighting method has been shown to produce gains in forecast accuracy in situations where forecasts are not highly correlated and are not unbiased.

The concept of ensemble forecasts using simple averages is demonstrated in Fig. 21.1. The actual values of a series (denoted by the line with diamond-shaped markers) follows a certain but unknown data-generating process. Two candidate forecast models (Model 1 values denoted by a line with X markers and Model 2 denoted by a line with square markers) are estimated. Model 1 consistently overestimates the actual value until 2013, then underestimates it after. Model 2 predicts well in the early portion of the data and overestimates after that. A simple average of the two forecasts produces a combination forecast (the line with triangle markers) that is closer on average to the actual values.

A second set of weighting methods was proposed by Granger and Ramanathan (1984). They noted that forecasts themselves were a form of

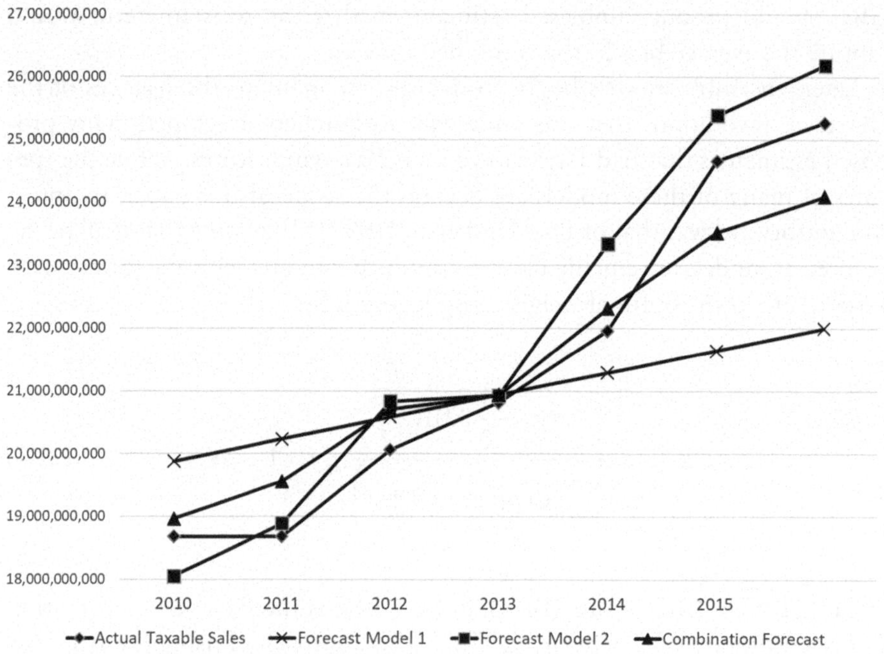

Fig. 21.1 Demonstration of simple average combination method

information that could be treated as such for the purposes of determining proper weights. Further, they challenged the notion that the weights needed to add to one, which had been assumed by Bates and Granger and most of the work that had followed. They proposed that the coefficients from a constrained or unconstrained regression of the actual values on the forecasts would yield a combined forecast with lower forecast errors. Specifically, they proposed three regression variants to produce the optimal weights:

$$y_T = k_i^{\mathrm{GRA}} f_{i,T} + u_t \tag{21.4}$$

$$y_T = k_i^{\mathrm{GRB}} f_{i,T} + u_t, st \sum_{i=1}^{N} k_i = 1 \tag{21.5}$$

$$y_T = \alpha + k_i^{\mathrm{GRC}} f_{i,T} + u_t \tag{21.6}$$

Model GRA (Granger and Ramanathan Model A) is an unconstrained regression of the actual values on the forecasts without a constant term. Model GRB adds the constraint that the weights should sum to 1. Model GRC adds a constant term but removes the constraint. They point out that in the presence of biased forecasts, GRA and GRB could produce biased estimates, but

GRC should produce unbiased estimates in that the constant term would capture the average bias in the combined forecast.

Later, ensemble models began to incorporate many of the features of the "Bayesian revolution" that was underway. Researchers developed many proposed estimators that had Bayesian or semi-Bayesian features. While the specifics of many of these models are beyond the scope of this paper, the most straightforward was that of Buckland et al. (1997). They note that if all of the *N* forecast models are equally likely to produce forecasts with the lowest error variance, then the optimal weights can be found by:

$$k_i^{\mathrm{BMA}} = \frac{\exp\left(-\frac{1}{2}\Delta \mathrm{BIC}_i\right)}{\sum_j^N \exp\left(-\frac{1}{2}\Delta \mathrm{BIC}_j\right)}, i, j = 1\ldots, N \tag{21.7}$$

where $\Delta\mathrm{BIC}_i = \mathrm{BIC}_i - \min_j(\mathrm{BIC}_j)$ and the BIC is the Bayesian Information Criterion proposed by Schwarz (1978).[3] This approach of using the BIC that developed out of this line of research has been termed Bayesian model averaging (BMA).

To summarize, the literature on ensemble models started out with simple weighting schemes and has developed ever more increasing sophistication. The focus has remained the same, to find the optimal forecast weights such that the combined forecast produces the lowest prediction error. Next, we turn to an example of using the various methods of combining forecasts on an actual forecasting problem using sales tax data from a U.S. city.

Data and Forecasting Models

To examine the effectiveness of ensemble forecasts, we gathered data on sales tax revenues for the city of Chicago, Illinois. The city receives sales tax revenues through two separate taxes. The oldest of these is the Retailers' Occupation Tax (ROT), first enacted in 1969. This tax is collected by the state, which remits a portion to local governments. As the state sets the rate and base of this tax, controlling for factors outside of the control of the city would be very difficult in a historical sense. Instead, we focus on the Home Rule Retailers' Occupation Tax (HRROT), enacted in 1981. The HRROT requires retailers

[3] The logic of these type of models is that the weight reflects the posterior probability that the *i*th forecast model has the lowest error variance among all *N* models.

operating in the city to remit an amount equal to their taxable sales times the applicable rate of the tax. The HRROT is the single largest own-revenue source for the city. When combined with the Illinois state transfer of a portion of the state ROT (the city receives 1 percent from the combined state rate of 6.25 percent), sales taxes accounted for 19 percent of city Corporate Fund (General Fund) revenues in 2016 (Chicago Office of the City Clerk 2016). The HRROT rate has changed once during the time that the tax has been in force, in 2005 (from 1 percent to 1.25 percent—The Civic Federation 2018). We adjust for this rate change through normalizing across the rate, essentially creating a measure of the taxable retail sales base: $y_t = {HRROT_t}/{r_t}$, where *HRROT* is the amount of revenue from the tax in year *t* and *r* is the applicable rate for that year.

Our models described below are univariate, bivariate, and multivariate. There are numerous predictor variables that can be used in a bivariate or multivariate modeling environment to aid forecasts. These include the Chicago-Naperville-Elgin MSA population and personal income, state and national personal income, and national gross domestic product.[4] We also include an index measure of the Midwest Economy developed by the Chicago Federal Reserve Bank (Brave and Lu 2010). Table 21.1 describes the variables and their sources.

The data covers the period 1982–2016. We divide the data into an in-sample period of 1982–2011 used for model development and a pseudo-out-of-sample period of 2012–2016 used to evaluate model accuracy. The five-year out-of-sample window was chosen since many revenue forecasts extend for a maximum of five years, recognizing the possibility of structural breaks in out-years.

Our forecast models include two univariate models, a model with two autoregressive terms (AR2—the number of autoregressive terms was chosen using the autocorrelation function and Box-Ljung Q portmanteau statistic) and an exponentially weighted moving average model (EWMA). To this, we add three bivariate models, consisting of a simple time trend (TIME), a bivariate regression of tax base on MSA population (POPN), a bivariate regression on MSA personal income (PERSINC). Finally, we estimate three multivariate models, including a multiple regression on MSA population and personal

[4] We include national- and state-level variables due to a paper by Chudik et al. (2017) who show that economic activity at lower levels of population aggregation (state and local levels) are often influenced by higher-level economic conditions. State gross domestic product data is also available, but it starts in 1997, providing too few in-sample observations for model development.

Table 21.1 Variables used in forecasting models

Variable	Source
Home Rule Retailers' Occupation Tax	City of Chicago, Annual Appropriation Ordinances
MSA Population	US Bureau of Economic Analysis, Table CA1 Personal Income Summary: Personal Income, Population, Per Capita Personal Income
MSA Personal Income	US Bureau of Economic Analysis, Table CA1 Personal Income Summary: Personal Income, Population, Per Capita Personal Income (thousands of current dollars)
State Personal Income	US Bureau of Economic Analysis, Table SA1 Personal Income Summary: Personal Income, Population, Per Capita Personal Income (thousands of current dollars)
US Personal Income	US Bureau of Economic Analysis, National Income and Product Accounts, Table 2.1 (millions of current dollars)
State GDP	US Bureau of Economic Analysis, Gross domestic product (GDP) by state (millions of current dollars)
US GDP	US Bureau of Economic Analysis, Gross domestic product (GDP) by state (millions of current dollars)
MEI_Overall	Midwest Economy Index—Overall, Chicago Federal Reserve Bank

income (POPNPERSINC), a fourth-order vector autoregressive model with tax base, population and personal income as endogenous variables and state and national personal income as exogenous variables (VAR1), and a fourth-order vector autoregressive model with tax base, population and personal income as endogenous variables and the Midwest Economy Index as an exogenous variable (VAR2).[5] In all, there are eight models that form the basis of our analysis. Table 21.2 recaps the models.

In terms of weighting methods, we analyze a simple averaging method (SA from Eq. (21.3)), the Bates-Granger weighting method (BG, Eq. (21.2)), all three variants of the Granger-Ramanathan regression-based weighting method (GRA-GRC, Eqs. 21.4, 21.5, and 21.6), and the BMA method (BMA, Eq. (21.7)).

Practically, we constructed the ensemble forecasts within a Microsoft Excel spreadsheet using forecasts generated by STATA. Calculating the simple average of the forecasts should not need further explanation. To calculate BG weights, we found the error variance for the in-sample period, inverted, and then divided by the sum of all of the models' inverted error variances. To calculate GR methods A through C, we ran regressions in STATA of the actual in-sample values on the forecast values for each of the single forecasts. We

[5] We also estimated a VAR with the same variables as VAR1 except for national GDP instead of national personal income as an exogenous variable. The results were nearly identical to VAR1.

Table 21.2 Forecast models estimated

Model	Methodology	Predictor variables
AR2	ARIMA (2,0,0)	None
EMA	Exponentially Weighted Moving Average	None
TIME	Linear Regression	Year
PERSINC	Linear Regression	MSA Personal Income
POPN	Linear Regression	MSA Population
POPNPERSINC	Linear Regression	MSA Personal Income, MSA Population
VAR1	Vector Autoregression	MSA Personal Income, MSA Population (Endogenous); State Personal Income, U.S. Personal Income (Exogenous)
VAR2	Vector Autoregression	MSA Personal Income, MSA Population (Endogenous); Midwest Economy Index (Exogenous)

then eliminated forecasts with negative coefficients (as they infer a negative weight) in an iterative fashion until only positive coefficients remained. Finally to calculate the BMA weights, we took the difference in the BIC in each of the models from the minimum BIC among models, creating the ΔBIC measure. Then we applied Eq. (21.7) by taking −1/2 times the ΔBIC for each model, calculating the exponential of that value, then divided by the sum of the measures for all of the forecast models.[6]

Results for Single Models and Ensemble Models

Table 21.3 lists the results of our analysis for each of the single forecasts (the top half of the table) and for ensemble models using various weighting methods (bottom half). These results are for the pseudo-out-of-sample observations (2012–16). We use the mean absolute percent error (MAPE) as the measure of goodness of fit.[7] In the top half of the table, highlighted cells indicate the lowest MAPE among single forecast models. In the bottom half, highlighted cells indicate ensemble models with lower MAPE than the best-performing single model.

[6] The Excel file and STATA results are available on request.

[7] We also calculated the mean square prediction error (MPSE) for the models. There were no qualitative differences in the results except that the simple average weighting method no longer was better than the best single model. Full results including weights and procedures available from the author.

Table 21.3 Absolute Percentage Errors (APE) for static 2012 forecast model

Model	2012	2013	2014	2015	2016	Average
AR2	2.60%	0.58%	3.05%	12.25%	12.95%	6.29%
EMA	7.80%	3.73%	5.89%	11.51%	***2.40%***	6.27%
TIME	***2.54%***	***0.01%***	***1.51%***	9.57%	10.66%	4.86%
PERSINC	4.11%	2.85%	1.53%	12.72%	14.28%	7.10%
POPN	3.47%	6.50%	10.85%	20.07%	21.34%	12.44%
POPNPERSINC	9.77%	10.12%	5.75%	7.13%	8.95%	8.34%
VAR1	4.77%	1.49%	7.46%	***3.63%***	4.28%	***4.33%***
VAR2	4.23%	4.68%	5.80%	9.93%	6.86%	6.30%
SA	***0.63%***	0.95%	***0.95%***	7.24%	6.06%	***3.17%***
BG	***1.65%***	0.38%	***0.97%***	4.48%	3.49%	***2.19%***
GRA	***1.95%***	0.02%	2.63%	***1.40%***	***0.42%***	***1.28%***
GRB	***1.85%***	1.81%	2.00%	3.99%	***0.89%***	***2.11%***
GRC	***1.50%***	0.44%	2.01%	***2.08%***	***0.28%***	***1.26%***
BMA	4.39%	1.20%	6.70%	***2.84%***	3.44%	***3.71%***

T = 2012–2016
Note: The lowest APE for each individual model for each year 2012–2016 (top half of the table) is indicated by the highlighted, bolded, and italicized cell. For the ensemble models (bottom half), each model with a lower APE than the lowest individual model is indicated with the same formatting. For example, the lowest APE for an individual model for 2012 is the time trend (TIME). All of the ensemble models with the exception of the BMA Model had lower APEs for that year

The single model with the lowest MAPE over the entire period (average column) was the fourth-order vector autoregression with state and national personal income (VAR1). Only two of the models (TIME and VAR1) had average errors less than 5 percent of the observed value, commonly thought of as a metric for a model with sufficient prediction accuracy. Turning to the ensemble models, all of the weighting methods produced lower overall MAPEs than the best single model.

Examining the results year by year (fitting recursive models where each model is re-estimated for each year—Table 21.4), some interesting patterns emerge.[8] Using this basis of analysis, ensemble models have lower APEs in only two of the years (2012 and 2014), However, three of the ensemble models have a lower MAPE than the best individual model and another model (simple averaging) has about the same MAPE.

[8] Thanks to Dr. John Mikesell, who commented on a presentation of an earlier draft at the 2018 ABFM Conference, for the suggestion to use this method of comparison.

Table 21.4 Absolute Percentage Errors (APE) for dynamic recursive forecast models

Model	2012	2013	2014	2015	2016	Average
AR2	2.60%	3.48%	5.40%	10.73%	0.31%	***4.50%***
EMA	7.80%	3.63%	5.21%	10.96%	2.40%	6.00%
TIME	***2.54%***	***0.25%***	3.40%	12.20%	11.51%	5.98%
PERSINC	4.11%	0.63%	4.60%	11.30%	8.77%	5.88%
POPN	3.47%	6.01%	9.85%	19.10%	20.40%	11.76%
POPNPERSINC	9.77%	4.88%	***1.66%***	***7.18%***	1.86%	5.07%
VAR1	4.77%	4.13%	2.16%	8.15%	6.22%	5.09%
VAR2	4.23%	6.23%	2.64%	11.29%	***0.24%***	4.93%
SA	***0.63%***	0.37%	3.83%	11.37%	6.46%	4.53%
BG	***1.65%***	2.78%	***1.43%***	9.96%	5.40%	***4.24%***
GRA	***1.95%***	3.46%	2.06%	8.22%	6.08%	***4.35%***
GRB	***1.85%***	4.03%	2.05%	8.23%	6.25%	***4.48%***
GRC	***1.50%***	5.98%	2.70%	11.28%	6.25%	5.54%
BMA	4.29%	4.14%	2.14%	8.16%	6.18%	4.98%

T = 2012–2016

This characteristic of "averaging" is shown in Fig. 21.2, which presents the results of the models for the last year of the model period and the entire forecast period. The solid line with no marker indicates the actual value of the sales tax base over time. The candidate models are AR2 (box marker) as it had the lowest MAPE of any single forecast, TIME (circle marker) as it had good early forecast period performance, POPNPERSINC with its good performance during the middle time period (diamond marker) and BG (dashed line with no marker) with the lowest overall MAPE.

The figure shows the strong early performance by TIME, with a nearly perfect fit in 2013. However, the actual tax base series has stronger growth in out-years than predicted by the time trend. The POPNPERSINC model fits fairly well in the middle forecast period, after having over-forecast in the early period. However, it overestimates the actual growth in tax base in 2015–2016. The AR2 model under-forecasts dramatically in 2012–2014, with dramatically improving performance in 2015–2016. The ensemble method (BG) does well over time, smoothing out the overestimation and underestimation biases of other models. In only two years, 2012 and 2014 is it a contender for the best model, but in other years it is not the worst performing model. It is, as the method suggests, a moderating type of forecast model.

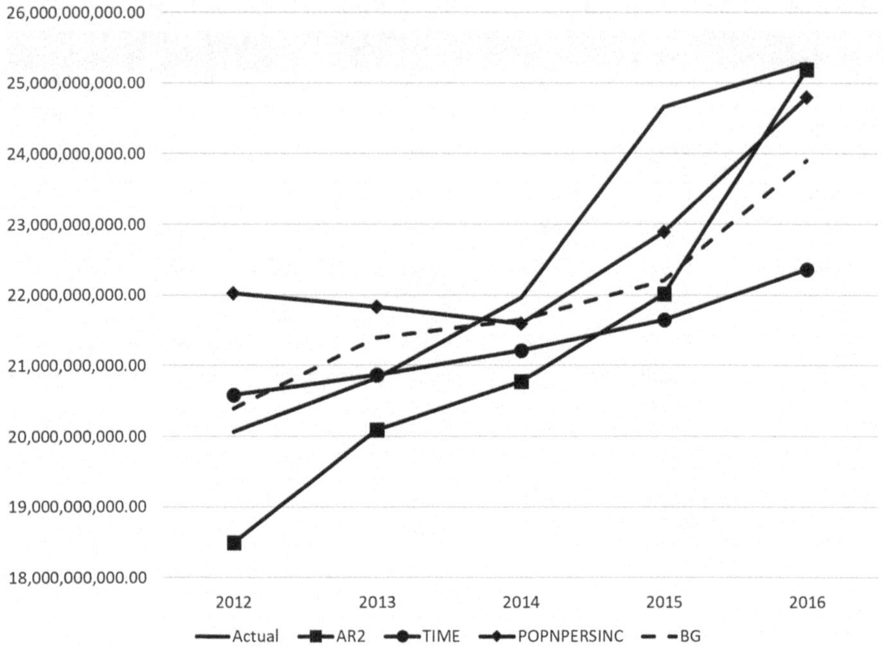

Fig. 21.2 Pseudo-out-of-sample forecast results

Conclusion and Implementation Considerations

This pattern of results provides strong evidence for the usefulness of ensemble models. *If* in 2011 someone would know ex ante that time trend would perform well until 2013 and then the multivariate regression on population and personal income would perform better, a forecasting strategy would emerge. But we only detect this ex post. Ensembles provide a way to incorporate information from all or at least many of the forecast models. What results is similar to a portfolio in investing. Portfolios reduce risk by diversifying across investment assets. Ensembles reduce risk of a single model developing problems over time by incorporating information from many models. As Hsiao and Wan (2014, p. 294) put it,

> *The main arguments favoring combining forecasts are: (i) The true data generating process is unknown. Even the most complicated model is likely to be misspecified and can, at best, provide a reasonable "local" approximation. It is highly unlikely that a single model will dominate uniformly over time. (ii) The best model may change over time in a way that can be difficult to track on the basis of past forecasting performance. Combining forecasts across different models may be viewed as a way to make*

the forecast more robust against misspecification biases and measurement errors in the data set. (iii) It is possible that diversification gains from combining across a set of forecasting models will dominate the strategy of only using a single forecasting models.

There are some considerations that must be understood when implementing ensemble models. First, the more bias there is in individual forecasts, the less gain will be made through combination forecasting. The theoretical basis for averaging assumes that forecasts are unbiased. Second, gains from combining forecasts are greater the lower the correlation between forecasts. In our results, this is demonstrated in the results from 2015 and 2016. All of the individual models under-forecast revenue base growth. Therefore, the ensemble models do not produce a gain in forecast accuracy. Once again, the portfolio analogy seems pertinent. The less that asset returns are correlated, the more a portfolio will "smooth" returns over time. Similarly, the less that forecasts are correlated, the more that results will reflect different sources of information, reducing error.

In this chapter, we have been introduced to the concept of forecast ensembles, combinations of forecasts to produce a model with better prediction accuracy. There is still much work to be done in this area, both in terms of developing new weighting methods and assessing relative performance.

References

Bates, J. M., & Granger, C. W. J. (1969). The combination of forecasts. *Journal of the Operational Research Society, 20*(4), 451–468.

Brave, S., & Lu, C. (2010). A snapshot of the Midwest economy: Past and present. *Chicago Fed Letter, 280*, 1–4.

Buckland, S. T., Burnham, K. P., & Augustin, N. H. (1997). Model selection: An integral part of inference. *Biometrics, 53*, 603–618.

Chicago Office of the City Clerk. 2016. *Annual Appropriation Ordinance for Year 2016 and Associated Year 2015 Supplmental Appropriation* . Chicago, IL: Office of the City Clerk.

Chudik, A., Koech, J., & Wynne, M. (2017). Global and national shocks explain a large share of state job growth. *Economic Letter, 12*(10), 1–4.

Clemen, R. T. (1989). Combining forecasts: A review and annotated bibliography. *International Journal of Forecasting, 5*(4), 559–583.

Granger, C. W. J., & Ramanathan, R. (1984). Improved methods of combining forecasts. *Journal of Forecasting, 3*(2), 197–204.

Hsiao, C., & Wan, S. K. (2014). Is there an optimal forecast combination? *Journal of Econometrics, 178*(P2), 294–309.

McGrayne, S. B. (2011). *The theory that would not die: How Bayes' rule cracked the enigma code, hunted down Russian submarines, & emerged triumphant from two centuries of controversy*. New Haven, CT: Yale University Press.

Morris, P. A. (1974). Decision analysis expert use. *Management Science, 20*(9), 1233–1241.

Schwarz, G. (1978). Estimating the dimension of a model. *Annals of Statistics, 6*(2), 461–464.

The Civic Federation. (2018). *Selected consumer taxes in the city of Chicago – 2018*. Chicago, IL. Retrieved from https://civicfed.org/sites/default/files/civic-federation-2018-consumer-taxes-in-chicago.pdf.

Timmermann, A. (2006). Forecast combinations. In G. Elliott, C. W. J. Granger, & A. Timmermann (Eds.), *Handbook of economic forecasting* (Vol. 1, pp. 135–196). Amsterdam; Boston: Elsevier North-Holland.

Zellner, A. (1971). *An introduction to Bayesian inference in econometrics*. New York: Wiley.

Part IV

Conclusion

22

Conclusion

Daniel Williams and Thad Calabrese

These chapters have reviewed budget forecasting across a broad range of governmental entities and focused on a wide array of topics. Further, several chapters examined forecasting in not-for-profit organizations because of their increasing role in the delivery of public services. In Part 1 there were six chapters focused on national-level budgeting. As Cohen reviewed in Chap. 2, national-level budgeting generally focuses on economic analysis of the economy as a whole. The budget is driven by factors that are mostly outside the government's control, demographics, economic productivity, and other factors. Ericcson and Martinez discuss the analysis of forecast bias, efficiency, and other characteristics demonstrating the analysis with three important U.S. federal forecasts and recommending a generalized method of error evaluation.

Busch and Strehl detailed that Germany tries to control this reliance on debt through legal devices and institutions, which, among other things, regulate the production of budgetary forecasts. The budget is a balance between revenue and expenditures and, as Cangiano and Pathak showed, may reflect a

D. Williams (✉)
Austin W. Marxe School of Public and International Affairs, Baruch College, New York, NY, USA
e-mail: Daniel.Williams@baruch.cuny.edu

T. Calabrese
Robert F. Wagner Graduate School of Public Service, New York University, New York, NY, USA
e-mail: thad.calabrese@nyu.edu

D. Williams, T. Calabrese (eds.), *The Palgrave Handbook of Government Budget Forecasting*, Palgrave Studies in Public Debt, Spending, and Revenue,
https://doi.org/10.1007/978-3-030-18195-6_22

preference to shift some operating costs to debt. Forecasting is linked to this preference for debt because nations use optimistic forecasts—that is, overestimation of revenue and underestimation of expenses—as a cover during the budget-making process. This national-level preference for debt is widespread.

Turning specifically to the United States, Penner discussed the long-run budget prospects of the United States, and expects a growing debt-to-GDP ratio, possibly reflecting some of the same motivations as found among low-income countries. Douglas and Raudla finished this section with an optimistic finding that the Congressional Budget Office improves its forecasts when new information becomes available.

In Part 2, there were six chapters on state and local practices. While Franklin, Bourdeaux, and Hathaway found that state revenue forecasts are fairly accurate, they reported that states do not always report forecasts that reflect their true revenue expectations. McShea and Cordes recommended that Virginia can improve its forecast accuracy by using Bayesian vector autoregression techniques. Turning to local government, Calabrese and Williams found that governments may report risk-averse expenditure forecasts when they can allocate overestimation to accounts that do not incidentally provide discretion to non-central agencies. Continuing the theme of forecast bias, Propheter found that New York City property tax is excessively and intentionally underforecasted. When looking at very small local governments, Reitano found substantial reliance on judgmental forecasting, which may lead to excessive forecast errors. In examining very short forecast horizons, Williams and Calabrese found no evidence that local governments' mid-year forecasts improve over those made before the year begins; this result is contrary to expectations from the forecasting literature.

In Part 3, there were eight chapters focused on specific types of forecasts or on forecast methods. Justice, Fudge, Levine, Bird, and Iftikhar examined the forecast accuracy of three models for predicting fiscal distress and bankruptcy and found that the Ohio model is most effective. In two chapters on school-related forecasts, Jones, Rakow, and Reitano reported large variation in forecast accuracy among Kentucky school districts, and Ely similarly finds wide variation in the quality of charter school forecasts. McDonald, Decker, and Hunt recommend best practices in forecasts of prison population. Reitano examined what is known about forecasting of personnel and found there has been little research into this topic. While there has been little examination of capital budget forecasting in recent years, Reitano, Jones, Barrett, and Fowles connect the use of revenue forecast bias with the building of reserves for capital expenditures.

Turning to methods, Decker and McDonald described consensus forecasting practices focusing on their use to achieve agreement among various interested parties. Focusing on a more quantitative approach, Kriz discussed the use of ensemble forecasting (also known as forecast averaging in the literature) as a way to achieve improved forecast accuracy.

While there is a wide array of forecast methods used in governmental forecasting, these chapters do not provide substantial reason to believe that government budget forecasting research involves a substantial effort to develop new or additional methods themselves, with the limited exception of national-level macroeconomic methods. Some methods are adopted from other environments (e.g., ensemble forecasting), while others that are possibly innovative do not reflect empirical validation (e.g., personnel-related forecasting). Even the recommendations for Bayesian vector autoregression and ensemble forecasting reflect the adoption of well-established techniques to the governmental domain rather than native development of these as new techniques.

Themes and Differences

We do find a few common themes among these chapters. There is frequent reference to politically motivated forecast bias. What is less clear is whether the bias is in the forecast assumptions, the forecast parameters, or the forecast report. It is also not clear whether the forecasters themselves produce biased forecasts or that they are constrained to report biased forecasters by others within their organizations. Another common theme is that demographic factors are important to forecasts, because these lead directly to expenditures. These may be population and employment factors for the entire jurisdiction, or they may be specific demographics related to users of government services, such as school children, prisoners, or retirees.

There are some interesting differences that can be found. Some forms of forecasting are extraordinarily sophisticated. These include the forecasts of national economies and the use of such techniques as Bayesian vector autoregression. Others, such as ensemble forecasting or consensus forecasting, are moderately sophisticated. Yet others, such as judgmental forecasting (in some contexts) and deterministic models used in some personnel forecasting can be quite simple. In general, the moderately and highly sophisticated approaches have better support from empirical research.

Another interesting difference is that some biases are pessimistic while others are optimistic. Optimistic biases generally allow governments to spend more than their revenue would otherwise provide. This may reflect moral hazard, as an anticipation of rescue by an external entity; alternately, it may reflect an implicit belief that the government can manage more debt than it is prepared to openly discuss. In these chapters, optimistic bias has been found among some national governments. Pessimistic bias can reflect risk aversion or it can reflect an intent to generate slack. Slack can be used for various purposes such as redirecting funds to a different purpose or generating discretion. This bias dominates at the subnational level in the United States, and likely reflects the fear of running out of funds during a fiscal year. One chapter also suggests that pessimistic bias can serve as a cover for ratcheting up taxes.

Recommendations for Further Research

Many of the contributors have suggested a need for future research, and we echo this call. Focusing on the national and international level, Cohen's Chap. 2 provides an overview of macroeconomic forecasting and suggests problems that remain, particularly with the overestimation of future interest rates. This problem suggests room for a better understanding of the practices that lead to this overestimation. Ericcson and Martinez's Chap. 3 provides deep insight into forecast errors and recommend particular approaches to the analysis of these errors. While Busch and Strehl do not make specific recommendations, Chap. 4 suggests a need for examining the effectiveness of using forecasts to control excessive debt. In Chap. 5, Cangiano and Pathak recommend better data collection among low- and middle-income countries to allow cross-country empirical studies using panel or time-series approaches. In Chap. 6, Penner describes uncertainty in long-run forecasts. While he makes no specific suggestions for further research, the chapter shows a need for better methods to provide boundaries of uncertainty that may help avoid excessive confidence in forecast projections. In Chap. 7, Douglas and Raudla generally find that CBO's update forecasts outperform their initial forecasts for some categories but fail to systematically improve for mandatory expenditures or five-year cumulative revenue, which suggests that further research could result in improved forecasting within these categories.

Turning to state budget forecasting, in Chap. 8, Franklin, Bourdeaux, and Hathaway raise questions of accuracy both for consensus forecasting and for forecast models. They suggest more research into the models. McShea and Cordes do not make explicit recommendations in Chap. 9, but they demonstrate a need to further understand the statistical properties of data that distinguish between likely AR, VAR, and BVAR model effectiveness.

With local government forecast practice, Calabrese and Williams label their findings in Chap. 10 as tentative and suggest additional examination of expenditure forecasting with respect to central or distributed control over ultimate expenditures. Propheter's examination of fiscal obfuscation likewise requires further study to validate and develop the insights found in Chap. 11. Having found little forecast improvement as the fiscal year progresses in Chap. 13, Williams and Calabrese recommend expanding research into this practice to determine whether the result hold with more data. They also suggest research into why forecasts do not improve, and examine the benefit of various methods for short-term forecasting.

Reitano makes a number of recommendations in Chap. 12. With respect to small governments, he recommends examining whether they can use quantitative methods, and determining the reasons for their choices of forecast methods. He recommends research into the management of forecast-related data, suggesting a need to improve data management. He recommends the use of a large panel to understand small government forecast accuracy. He raises issues of forecast bias related to types of revenue, financial policies, long-term forecasting, and financial sustainability as these issues relate to small governments; and he proposes empirically examining GFOA's related best practices.

With respect to more focal topics, Justice et al. have found in Chap. 14 that a less sophisticated indicator system provides the best result in forecasting fiscal distress. This leads to several potential avenues of researchers. Would the results hold up in other states? Would they hold up if the data for a large number of jurisdictions were computed and with the researchers not knowing in advance which localities might become bankrupt? Would the results be improved if the scoring techniques across several methods were first normalized and then averaged? In Chap. 15, Jones, Rakow, and Reitano recommend future research in school enrollment forecasting examine both methods shown in forecasting literature and those observed in actual practice. With nonprofit charter schools, Ely, in Chap. 16, raises issues of the relationship between donations and revenue volatility. McDonald, Decker, and Hunt describe a wide array of prison population forecast approaches in Chap. 17, which suggests the possibility of research into the comparative effectiveness of these methods.

In Chap. 18, Reitano recommends modernizing the research into personnel forecast as most technical research into this topic is dated. He suggests broad surveys of governments and nonprofits to determine what methods are currently in use. He recommends examining of personnel forecasting effectiveness. He recommends qualitative research into the link between forecasting and workforce planning. There is a recommendation to study the link between personnel forecasting and budget forecasting, and strategic planning. And, there is a recommendation to determine how technology is used in personnel forecasting. In Chap. 19, Reitano et al. address topics of the link of forecasting and capital reserves and make a variety of recommendations that can be summarized as examining when, how, and by whom bias arises within the forecast environment, and the direction of the bias.

Turning to forecast methods, in Chap. 20, Decker and McDonald recommend research comparing consensus forecasting conducted by governments compared with that conducted by nonprofits. They also recommend examination of the decision to adopt consensus forecasting, its relationship to forecasting accuracy, its use in times of volatility, and its relationship to budget transparency and public acceptance of budgetary decisions. In Chap. 21, Kriz recommends continued technical development of ensemble forecast focusing on forecast averaging weights.

More collectively we find other potential avenues for research both with what is included and what is missing in this volume. With what is included, we recommend deep analysis of the motivations behind forecast bias. Commonly it is thought that pessimistic forecasts are a hedge against uncertainty by risk-averse budgeteers. However, another potential motivation is the creation of slack, which Reitano suggests is intended to fund capital expenditures; but older literature suggests such slack is for post-budgeting decision-making (Levine et al. 1981). It can serve as a method of discouraging policy innovation and, therefore avoiding implicit pressure for tax increases, but Propheter has suggested the opposite, that by predicting nonexistent shortfalls, it leads to incremental increases in taxes.

Also, within this volume we have found a variety of discussions of expenditure-related forecasting. These often refer to forecast practices that are not well documented in the budget research literature, whether they are factors that lead to expenditures, such as prison populations or school enrollment, or elements of forecasting practice, such as with personnel forecasting. Williams and Calabrese have shown that forecast bias arises in expenditure forecasting and can be related to who controls the expenditures. This domain requires substantial additional study.

Beyond these, there are topics that are not well represented here. The generally accepted view of capital budgeting is that strategic underforecasting of costs and overforecasting of revenue lead to project approval (Flyvbjerg 2007). However, this leaves much that is unknown. Is this practice specifically related to megaprojects (large ambitious projects that cost billions), or is it also found with more mundane projects? How is it related to other public finance issues such as Tax Increment Financing or economic development projects that promise jobs and revenue over the long run? Are overruns and underperformance correlated with project size? Turning to more special topics, there are many facets of public finance that rely on forecasts that are not yet well understood. For example, when fiscal years end, some programs must forecast their accruals because they are guarantors of expenditures outside their control. How do they do this and how well do their forecasts perform? And we know virtually nothing about forecasting practices in not-for-profit organizations. These are just a few of the topics that remain to be studied.

Recommendations for Forecasting

The most common forecasting recommendation found in these chapters is that forecasting depends on data, so data should be properly collected and curated; to this we add that data across jurisdictions should follow a common format. This is a problem that the editors have also experienced first hand and find that the lack of standardized data practices in budgeting is a substantial hindrance to the meaningful study of budgeting as well. In fact, the lack of standardized data practices is a substantial concern for budgeting because it prevents the public from comparing their various budgets with those of other jurisdictions.

We also find that there are a great variety of forecasting methods, many of which are tailored to particular forecasting problems. Forecasters should be cautious of believing that the most sophisticated techniques will serve their particular forecasting problem the best. Likely with larger jurisdictions this involves macroeconomic modeling. However, for other jurisdictions and more specific problems, other methods can be appropriate.

While other methods can be appropriate, there is limited research into their effectiveness. Forecasters using these methods should have a heightened awareness of their uncertainty and take special care to communicate it. In addition, forecasters who rely entirely on judgmental forecasts likely should consider supplementing their forecasts with more quantitative approaches. Nevertheless, governments should avoid techniques that require skills they do not have.

Uncertainty arises with even the most sophisticated techniques, especially as the forecast horizon lengthens. Consequently, forecasters should be cautious about the assertions and recommendations made relying on forecasts. While decision-makers may prefer clear unequivocal information, forecasters should avoid claiming more than they actually know.

References

Flyvbjerg, B. (2007). How Optimism Bias and Strategic Misrepresentation in Early Project Development Undermine Implementation. *Concept, 41*, 90–110.

Levine, C. H., Rubin, I. S., & Wolohojian, G. G. (1981). Resource scarcity and the reform model: The management of retrenchment in Cincinnati and Oakland. *Public Administration Review, 41*(6), 619–628.

Index[1]

A

Absolute error, 147–149
Africa, 92, 92n11, 98, 99n15, 103, 105, 106n25
Alabama, 159, 166, 168
Alaska, 164, 167
Analysis of the President's Budget, 3
Arizona, 165, 350
Arkansas, 167
Asia, 99n15, 103
Autoregression, 4, 5, 178, 181, 183, 189, 192–194, 196, 197, 229, 348, 432
Autoregressive integrated moving average, 180, 348, 349, 416

B

Balanced budget constraint, 156
Bangladesh, 103
Basic law, 85
Basic Rules for the Budget, 84–86, 84n16
Bayesian model averaging, 418, 420
Bayesian vector autoregression, 4, 5, 177, 178, 180–183, 186–187, 186n9, 189–190, 193–197, 197n12, 430–432
Best practices, 7, 156, 397
Bhutan, 101
Budget forecasting, 2, 373
Budgeting process, 243
Budget stabilization fund, 159, 160
Bundestag, 76, 77, 84
Burkina Faso, 103

C

California, 6, 182, 182n5, 189, 244, 246, 247, 251, 252, 277, 285, 288, 288n3, 288n4, 290, 295, 307, 350, 380, 391
Capital improvement plan, 309
Charter schools, 309, 326–331, 334–337, 340–343, 433
Cobb-Douglas production function, 14, 31
Cognitive biases, 247, 248

[1] Note: Page numbers followed by 'n' refer to notes.

D. Williams, T. Calabrese (eds.), *The Palgrave Handbook of Government Budget Forecasting*, Palgrave Studies in Public Debt, Spending, and Revenue,
https://doi.org/10.1007/978-3-030-18195-6

Cohort-survival ratio, 306
Collaboration, 90, 90n2, 90n4
Colorado, 352, 367
Combining forecasts, 424
Congressional Budget Office, 2–4, 11, 12, 12n1, 14, 18n9, 23, 26, 27, 30, 31, 31n26, 116–119, 117n5, 121–123, 125, 127–129, 133–141, 134n1, 135n2, 136n4, 143–147, 149, 150, 259, 398, 430, 432
Connecticut, 246, 352
Consensus forecast, 157, 158, 397, 398, 405, 410
Conservative revenue forecasting, 247
Consumer Price Index, 24–26, 24n18, 124, 130
Control account, 79
Criminal justice system, 347–348

D

Debt brake, 71
Debt-to-GDP ratio, 115–122, 117n3, 125, 127–130
Deflator, 24
Delaware, 159
Department of Corrections, 354
Distributed, 209, 210

E

Econometric models, 242, 244–246, 383
Enrollment projections, 303, 321
Ensemble forecast, 415
Enterprise resource planning, 251, 362, 365, 367, 369, 372, 374
Euro, 74, 129
Europe, 93, 106n25, 107, 122, 127, 129, 136n5, 392
European Central Bank, 74
European Monetary Union, 74
European Union, 72–78, 73n2, 75n4, 83, 85, 86, 93, 95, 260, 392
Eurozone, 74, 136n5
Executive forecast, 156
Expenditure forecast, 202
Experts, 82, 83, 398, 406
Exponentially weighted moving average, 419
Extrapolation, 242

F

Federal Budget Code, 85, 86
Federal government, 76
Federalism Reform I, 75
Federalism Reform II, 72, 75, 76
Federal Reserve, 25, 27, 27n22, 29, 127, 135, 403, 419
Federal state, 72, 75, 79
Finance Ministry, 83
Financial planning, 85
Financial trend monitoring system, 278–281, 283, 284, 286, 294
Fiscal health, 278
Fiscal illusion, 218
Florida, 161, 168, 244–247, 283, 287, 306, 309, 350, 366, 380, 398, 401
Forecast accuracy, 133, 310
Forecast bias, 201, 379–382
Forecast horizon, 261n6
Forecasting error, 158, 163, 164, 326

G

General Accountability Office, 116–119, 253
General Accounting Office, 348
Generally accepted accounting principles (GAAP), 282–284, 287
Georgia, 164–167, 165n4

Germany, 2, 3, 71–73, 75, 75n3, 76, 77n6, 78, 80–86, 181, 259, 429
Global South, 93, 99n15, 108
Governmental Accounting Standards Board, 203n3, 244, 278, 282, 287, 294, 380
Governmental Accounting Standards Board Statement 34, 282
Government Finance Officers Association, 159, 203n3, 242, 248, 253, 284, 307, 309, 320, 378, 380, 382, 384, 390, 393, 433
Gray model projections, 306
Great Recession, 4, 6, 19, 22, 26, 71, 115, 117, 120, 129, 144, 145, 178, 179, 182, 188, 234, 250, 252, 288, 293, 304, 367, 381, 391
Gross domestic product, 3, 4, 11–15, 12n2, 15n5, 23, 24n18, 27, 30–32, 71, 73–79, 73n1, 89, 92, 95, 102, 102n17, 102n18, 105, 107, 115–125, 116n2, 117n3, 127–130, 136, 138, 140, 141, 143, 144, 146–149, 159, 183, 259, 420n5, 430

H

Heavily Indebted Poor Countries, 92, 92n11
Holt-Winters, 349
Hours, 15–16, 15n5, 32

I

Illinois, 27, 27n21, 246, 247, 350, 379, 418
Immigration, 15, 127
Independent fiscal authorities, 106–108
Independent fiscal councils, 106–108, 106n25, 106n26, 106n28
Indiana, 158, 162, 401
International City/County Management Association, 203n3, 244, 245, 278
International Monetary Fund, 90n3, 90n4, 91n9, 92n12, 93, 95, 98, 99, 103n20, 104n21, 106, 106n25, 106n27, 106n28, 107, 107n29, 108n30, 159
Iowa, 401, 402

J

Judgmental forecasts, 242–246, 248, 250, 251

K

Kansas, 401
Kentucky, 6, 7, 161, 303, 304, 308, 314–317, 314n1, 377–380, 382, 383, 390, 391, 401, 430
Kenya, 107, 108

L

Labor force participation rate, 15, 16, 16n7, 32
Labor productivity, 17
Labor quality, 32
Länder, 71, 72, 75–86, 75n3, 86n17
Law of Stability and Growth, 84
  StabG, 79, 80, 84
Less Developed Countries, 104n21, 106, 106n25, 107
Louisiana, 401

M

Maastricht Criterion, 78
Maastricht Treaty, 72–75, 77, 129
Maine, 401

Maryland, 27, 27n21, 161, 287, 401, 402
Massachusetts, 166, 350
M-Competition, 262, 264
Mean absolute error, 136, 136n6, 138, 143, 146, 191, 194, 310–315
Mean absolute percent error, 100, 102, 163, 163n2, 164, 167, 168, 191, 194, 196, 259, 260, 260n5, 262, 264, 266, 269, 313–315, 421–423
Mean percent error, 100, 101, 163, 163n2, 312–315, 317
Mean squared error, 311–315
Michigan, 6, 25, 179, 277, 283, 285, 287, 290, 292–295, 401
Microsoft Excel, 243, 249, 251, 309, 365, 367, 371, 372, 374, 420, 421n6
Minnesota, 167, 181, 189, 190
Mississippi, 161, 401
Missouri, 162, 163, 166, 401
Multifactor productivity, 13, 17, 18n9, 19–23, 21n14, 21n15, 23n16, 28

N

Nebraska, 401
Neural networks, 305
New Jersey, 306, 307
New Mexico, 353, 401
New York, 5, 90n2, 204, 204n5, 206, 206n8, 208–210, 217, 219–227, 220n2, 220n3, 221n4, 223n6, 226n8, 232, 236, 238, 307, 308, 328, 373, 378, 380–382, 391, 401, 430
North Carolina, 161, 204, 283, 285, 287, 350, 354, 366, 367, 401, 402
North Dakota, 167

O

Office of Management and Budget, 3, 12n1, 26, 116–118, 118n6, 134, 135n2, 219, 220, 226–238, 226n8, 226n9, 228n11, 232n12, 259
Ohio, 6, 276, 277, 283, 285, 287, 290, 293–295, 365, 430
Oklahoma, 164, 167
Oregon, 167, 351, 354
Organization for Economic Cooperation and Development, 363
Overestimate expenditures, 307

P

Pennsylvania, 287, 307, 309, 350
Percent error, 163n2, 311–312
Personal Consumption Expenditures Chain-Price Index, 24, 24n18, 26
Personnel, 362–370
Personnel forecasting, 362–369
Phillips Curve, 25, 26, 26n20
Productivity, 15n5, 17–18, 20–24, 30–32, 128
Projection, 136n6, 305
Property tax, 224
Public Expenditure and Financial Accountability, 3, 89, 91, 91n9, 99, 99n15, 110

R

Revenue and expenditure forecasts, 321
Revenue estimates, 162
Revenue forecast, 90, 155–161, 166–169, 178
Revenues, 72, 124, 140–144, 187–191, 319
Rhode Island, 159, 401
Risk, 26
Root mean squared error, 136, 136n6, 138, 183, 190, 191, 194, 260

S

School, 6, 304, 306–309, 317–321, 326, 332, 334–337, 342, 380
School district, 304, 306, 308, 309, 319, 321
Semi-autonomous revenue authorities, 3, 89, 92, 104–106, 105n24, 108, 109
Separate forecast, 156
Simulation, 246
Slack, 379–382, 432
Small government revenue forecasting, 242
Solow Growth Model, 13, 14
South Carolina, 165, 165n5, 401
South Dakota, 351
Squared error, 147–149
Stability, 72, 76, 77, 79–81, 81n10, 84, 85
Stability and Growth, 76, 77, 79
State budget, 157, 398, 402
Strategic human resource management, 362, 370, 373
Strategic planning, 243
Structural balance, 243
Symmetrical mean absolute percent error, 260, 262, 264, 266, 269

T

Tanzania, 103
Tennessee, 159, 165, 165n6
Texas, 167, 350, 351, 368
Theil inequality coefficient, 260, 260n5, 268–270, 270n10, 270n12
Togo, 103
Transparency, 106n27, 107, 159–160, 167–168, 406–407
Troika, 3, 11, 12, 12n1, 26, 27, 30, 31n26

U

Uganda, 106n25, 107, 108n30
Uncertainty, 122, 123, 129–130, 435
Underestimate revenues, 307
United Nations, 90n4
United States, 2, 4, 5, 7, 14–16, 19, 22, 27, 72, 75, 86, 93, 117, 122, 123, 127, 133, 134, 261, 268, 305, 306, 345, 347, 392, 398, 430, 432
Utah, 165, 350

V

Vector autoregression, 4, 5, 178, 180–190, 180n4, 192–194, 196, 197, 420n5, 432
Vermont, 166, 401, 402
Virginia, 4, 161, 165, 165n7, 166, 166n8, 168, 177–180, 178n1, 178n2, 178n3, 182, 182n5, 183, 185, 187, 189, 197, 204, 430

W

Washington, 401
West Africa Economic and Monetary Union, 104n21
West Virginia, 164, 167
Workforce Planning, 362, 365, 370
World Bank, 90n4, 91n9, 93, 99, 103n19
Wyoming, 401

The manufacturer's authorised representative in the EU is Springer Nature Customer Service Centre GmbH, Europaplatz 3, 69115 Heidelberg, Germany. If you have any concerns regarding our products, please contact ProductSafety@springernature.com

Printed and bound by CPI Group (UK) Ltd, Croydon, CR0 4YY
05/10/2026
02228422-0003